THE AMERICAN PEOPLE

Creating a Nation and a Society

VOLUME TWO · SINCE 1865

GENERAL EDITORS

GARY B. NASH
University of California, Los Angeles

JULIE ROY JEFFREY
Goucher College

JOHN R. HOWE
University of Minnesota

PETER J. FREDERICK
Wabash College

ALLEN F. DAVIS
Temple University

ALLAN M. WINKLER
University of Oregon

Allen Yarnell, *Administrative Editor*
University of California, Los Angeles

HARPER & ROW, PUBLISHERS, New York
Cambridge, Philadelphia, San Francisco,
London, Mexico City, São Paulo, Singapore, Sydney

Sponsoring Editor: Marianne J. Russell
Development Editor: Johnna G. Barto
Project Editor: Jo-Ann Goldfarb
Text and Cover Design: Robert Bull/Design
Text Art: Vantage Art, Inc.
Cartographer: David Lindroth
Photo Research: Elsa Peterson
Production: Willie Lane
Compositor: Black Dot, Inc.
Printer and Binder: Arcata Graphics/Kingsport

Cover Illustration: John Sloan, *Sixth Avenue Elevated at Third Street*, 1928.
Whitney Museum of American Art, New York.

THE AMERICAN PEOPLE: Creating a Nation and a Society, Volume Two, Since 1865

Library of Congress Cataloging-in-Publication Data

Main entry under title:

The American People.

    Also issued as one-volume ed.
    Includes bibliographies and index.
    Contents: v. 1. To 1877—v. 2. Since 1865.
    1. United States—History. I. Nash, Gary B.
II. Jeffrey, Julie Roy. III.—
E178.1.A49355 1986b   973   85-24898
ISBN 0-06-047335-5 (pbk. : v. 1)
ISBN 0-06-047336-3 (pbk. : v. 2)

85 86 87 88 9 8 7 6 5 4 3 2 1

CONTENTS IN BRIEF

CONTENTS

CHAPTER 20
POLITICS AND PROTEST
626

CHAPTER 21
THE UNITED STATES BECOMES A WORLD POWER
658

PART FIVE
A MODERNIZING PEOPLE
1900–1945

CHAPTER 22
THE PROGRESSIVES CONFRONT INDUSTRIAL AMERICA
690

CHAPTER 23
AMERICA IN THE GREAT WAR
724

CHAPTER 24
AFFLUENCE AND ANXIETY
754

CHAPTER 25
THE GREAT DEPRESSION AND THE NEW DEAL
786

PART SIX
AN ENDURING PEOPLE
1945–1985

APPENDIX

RECOVERING THE PAST

MAPS

CHARTS

PREFACE

The Teton Sioux have a saying that "a people without history is like wind upon the buffalo grass." The Sioux mean by this that the wind will always blow and the grass always grow, but people cannot understand who they are and where they are going without an understanding of the past—where they have been. That is why the Sioux storytellers hand down the history of the tribe from generation to generation.

When we speak of the "people" of American history, we are immediately confronting an extraordinarily complex mixture of human beings. This country's written history began with a convergence of Native Americans, Europeans, and Africans. The United States has always been a nation of immigrants—a magnificent mosaic of cultural backgrounds, religions, and skin shades. This book explores how American society, as it exists today, came to assume its present shape and develop its present forms of government; how as a nation we conduct our foreign affairs and manage our economy; how as a society we live, work, love, marry, raise families, sing, read, study, vote, argue, protest, and struggle—individually and collectively—for fulfillment.

Several special emphases distinguish this book from most textbooks written in the last 20 years. The coverage of presidential elections, diplomatic treaties, and economic legislation is integrated with the human story that underlays these more public aspects of American history. Within a strong chronological framework we have woven together our history as a nation and our history as a people and a society. When a national political event is discussed, for example, we analyze its impact on social and economic life, on life at the state and local level. Wars are described on the battlefield and in the salons of diplomats; but, as history's greatest motors of social change, wars are also discussed on the home front. The interaction of ordinary Americans with extraordinary events runs as a theme throughout the book.

Throughout, we have tried to illuminate the humanness of our history. The authors have often used the words of ordinary Americans and presented their participation in and responses to epic events such as war, industrialization, and reform movements. We have portrayed their material circumstances and woven the experiences of some of them through several chapters. At certain points we have focused on particular communities, describing not only their political, economic, and social contours but also their physical appearances and the rhythm of their everyday life.

GOALS AND THEMES OF THE BOOK

One of our major goals is to provide students with a rich, balanced, and thought-provoking treatment of the American past. By rich and balanced we mean a history that treats the lives and experiences of Americans of all national origins and cultural backgrounds, at all levels of society, and in all regions of the country. By thought-provoking we mean a history that seeks connections between the multiple factors—political, economic, social, religious, intellectual, and biological—that have operated to mold and remold American society over a period of four centuries. By thought-provoking, we mean also a history that encourages students to consider how we are all legatees of a complicated, achievement-filled, and problem-strewn past. The only history befitting a democratic society and nation is one that inspires students to initiate a frank and searching dialogue with their past. We hope to stimulate such a dialogue here.

We also hope to promote discussion about the major themes we identify running through our history:

- ★ the struggle for national unity and identity amidst cultural diversity and conflict;
- ★ the powerful reform impulse in American society, present from the beginning, that for the last two centuries has worked to fulfill the democratic creed in racial, gender, and social relations;
- ★ the competing claims of liberty and authority—in the family, the school, the workplace, the community, and the nation.

STRUCTURE OF THE BOOK

Part Organization The chapters of this book are grouped into six parts to reflect major periods in the development of the nation and society. Each part begins with an *introductory essay* that outlines the significant themes and problems explored in the subsequent chapters. Following this introduction is a two-page display of *parallel events* that occurred during that particular period in history. Not only do these chronologies serve as a preview of the section, but they show what was happening simultaneously, in the political, the social and economic, as well as the cultural and technological spheres. They also help give the reader an integrated picture of how these various events converged to make American history.

Chapter Structure Every chapter begins with a *vignette* recalling the experience of an ordinary American. Chapter 1, for example, is introduced with the tragic story of Opechancanough, a Powhatan tribesman whose entire life of nearly 90 years was consumed by a struggle against the land hunger and alien values brought by Spanish and English newcomers. This brief anecdote serves several purposes. First, it introduces the overarching themes and major concepts of the chapter: the clash of three worlds—red, white, and black—in the North American wilderness, each with different cultural values, life styles, and aspirations. Second, the anecdote launches the chapter in a way which facilitates learning—beginning with the student's engagement with a human story. Lastly, the anecdote suggests that history was shaped by and affected ordinary as well as extraordinary Americans. At the end of the vignette, an *overview* relates the particular facts and ideas to the period under review and spells out the major themes of the chapter.

We aim to facilitate the learning process for the students. Every chapter ends with pedagogical features to reinforce and expand the presentation. A *conclusion* briefly summarizes the main concepts of the chapter and serves as a bridge to the following chapter. An annotated list of *recommended readings* provides supplementary sources for further study or research;

novels contemporary to the period are often included. A *time line* reviews the major events and developments covered in the chapter.

SPECIAL FEATURES

A distinctive feature of this book is the two-page *Recovering the Past* presentation in each chapter. These RTPs, as the authors affectionately call them, introduce students to the fascinating variety of evidence—ranging from tax lists, folk tales, and diaries to tombstones, advertising, and house designs—historians have learned to employ in reconstructing the past. Each RTP gives basic information about the source, its use by historians, and then raises questions for students to consider as they study the example reproduced for their inspection.

In addition to the RTPs we have provided other elements that will enable the instructor to use the text as a basis for class discussion or assignments. The program of *color illustrations* —paintings, cartoons, photographs, maps, and charts—amplifies important themes while presenting visual evidence for student reflection and analysis. Each major part of the text includes a *portfolio* on American cultural life. They begin with an essay discussing trends and themes in the art and artifacts of the period and elaborating on the color illustrations displayed.

SUPPLEMENTAL TEACHING AND LEARNING AIDS

Several companion volumes for both teachers and students have been prepared to enhance this comprehensive presentation of American history.

★ Gary B. Nash has selected and edited a two-volume set of readings, entitled ***Retracing the Past,*** to complement the text. Each reader contains around 25 selections covering political, social, and economic aspects of American history; Volume One focuses on the period until 1877, and Volume Two covers 1865 to the present.

Authors Julie Roy Jeffrey and Peter J. Frederick, both experienced instructional trainers, have written the *Study Guide* and *Instructor's Manual* to accompany the text. Tied closely to the text, both supplements provide a useful basis for reflection and discussion.

* The **Study Guide** (in two volumes) includes chapter outlines, significant themes and highlights, learning goals, list of important dates and names to know, glossary of important terms, learning enrichment ideas, and sample test questions. In addition, the authors provide helpful study hints such as how to underline a chapter.

* For those students who have access to personal computers, the study guide is available on diskettes. **Study-Aid,** a computer program for the Apple II series and the IBM-PC, is keyed directly to the text for learning ease.

* **Teaching the American People** is not merely a file of exam questions for the instructor. It is intended to serve as a resource book for new teachers *and* for busy and tired veterans as well. This manual contains ideas on ways to use the text to enliven the classroom; suggestions for generating class discussion and involving students in an active learning experience; and a list of resources such as films, slides, and photo collections, records and audiocassettes.

* A separate **Test Bank** of approximately 1500 items has been prepared by Carol Brown of Houston Community College. Multiple choice, true-false, and essay questions are included to test students' recall and understanding of the text presentation. The *Test Bank* is also available in computerized form *(Microtest)* for both Apple II and IBM-PC.

* To help you improve your students' geographical and analytical skills, we have also produced a set of color **Transparencies.** For maps showing detailed areas of the country, we have included an inset of the present-day United States with the area under study shaded in. The transparencies also include key charts from the text.

Our aim has been to write a balanced and vivid history of the development of the American nation and its society. We have also tried to provide the support materials to make the teaching and the learning experience enjoyable and rewarding. The reader will be the judge of our success. The authors and Harper & Row welcome your comments.

GBN
JRJ

ACKNOWLEDGMENTS

During the years that this text was being developed, many of our academic colleagues read and criticized the various drafts of the manuscript. For their thoughtful evaluation and constructive suggestions, the authors wish to extend their gratitude to the following reviewers:

Terry Alford, *Northern Virginia Community College*
Paul Bowers, *Ohio State University*
R. J. Bromert, *Southwestern Oklahoma State University*
Robin Brooks, *San Jose State University*
Carol Brown, *Houston Community College*
Jon Butler, *University of Illinois at Chicago*
Clayborne Carson, *Stanford University*
Lester Cohen, *Purdue University*
Kathleen Neils Conzen, *University of Chicago*
Lewis H. Croce, *Mankato State University*
William Ezzell, *DeKalb Community College*
William Freehling, *Johns Hopkins University*

William Geise, *San Antonio College*
Herbert Gutman, *City University of New York*
Carole Haber, *University of North Carolina at Charlotte*
Mitchell Hall, *University of Kentucky*
Susan Hartmann, *University of Missouri, St. Louis*
Richard J. Hopkins, *Ohio State University*
Richard A. Hunt, *Nassau Community College*
Joseph Illick III, *San Francisco State University*
Frederic Jaher, *University of Illinois, Urbana*
George Juergens, *Indiana University*
Richard Liebermann, *LaGuardia Community College*

Paul R. Lucas, *Indiana University*

Archie P. McDonald, *Stephen F. Austin State University*

Howard Miller, *University of Texas at Austin*

Herbert Parmet, *Queensborough Community College*

Mary Rothschild, *Arizona State University*

Richard T. Ruetten, *San Diego State University*

Ronald E. Shaw, *Miami University*

Richard Sorrell, *Brookdale Community College*

C. James Taylor, *University of South Carolina*

Martin Towey, *St. Louis University*

John Trickel, *Richland College*

Eldon Turner, *University of Florida*

Ronald Walters, *Johns Hopkins University*

Allen Yarnell, *University of California, Los Angeles*

Don Zelman, *Tarleton State University*

ABOUT THE AUTHORS

GARY B. NASH is a graduate of Princeton University (B.A., 1955; Ph.D., 1964), where he taught for three years. In 1966 he moved to the University of California, Los Angeles, where he teaches colonial and revolutionary American history. Among the books Nash has authored are: *Quakers and Politics: Pennsylvania, 1681–1726* (1968); *Class and Society in Early America* (1970); *Red, White, and Black: The Peoples of Early America* (1974, 1982); *The Urban Crucible: Social Change, Political Consciousness, and the Origins of the American Revolution* (1979); *Race, Class, and Politics: Essays on Colonial and Revolutionary Society* (1985); and *Forging Freedom: The Black Urban Experience in Philadelphia, 1720–1820* (forthcoming). Nash is a recipient of Guggenheim and American Council of Learned Societies fellowships. His scholarship is especially concerned with the role of common people in the making of history. He served as a general editor of this book.

JULIE ROY JEFFREY received her B.A. degree in history and literature from Radcliffe College in 1962 and taught secondary school for several years. She earned her Ph.D. in history from Rice University in 1972, receiving the award for the best American history dissertation. Since 1972 she has taught at Goucher College, offering the American history survey and historic preservation courses. Jeffrey's major publications include: *Education for Children of the Poor: A Study of the Origins and Implementation of the Elementary and Secondary Education Act of 1965* (1978); *Frontier Women: The Trans-Mississippi West, 1840–1880* (1979); and many articles and papers on the lives and perceptions of nineteenth-century women. She is the recipient of fellowships from the NDEA, Rice, Southwest Center for Urban Research, and the Newberry Library. Honored as an outstanding teacher, Jeffrey has been involved in faculty development activities and curriculum evaluation. Her research interest has focused on the relationship of domestic space and family life and the use of buildings as primary sources. She acted as a general editor of this book.

JOHN R. HOWE received his B.A. (1957) from Otterbein College, and his M.A. (1959) and Ph.D. (1962) degrees from Yale University. From 1961 to 1965 he taught at Princeton University; since then he has been on the faculty of the University of Minnesota. His major publications include *The Changing Political Thought of John Adams* (1966), *The Role of Ideology in the American Revolution* (1970), and *From the Revolution Through the Age of Jackson* (1973). Howe has held a Woodrow Wilson fellowship, a faculty research fellowship from the Charles Warren Center at Harvard University, a Guggenheim fellowship, and a Bush Foundation fellowship. His major research currently involves a manuscript entitled "The Transformation of Public Life in Revolutionary America." His special teaching interests include early American politics up to the Civil War, and Indian-white relations in early America.

PETER J. FREDERICK received his B.A. in history from Harvard in 1959, his M.A. in American culture from the University of Michigan in 1960, and his Ph.D. in history from the University of California at Berkeley in 1966. A committed teacher, he began his career as a teaching assistant at Berkeley in 1960; he has taught at San Francisco State and California State College at Hayward, and since 1970 at Wabash College. Frederick's book, *Knights of the Golden Rule: The Intellectual as Christian Social Reformer in the 1890s*, was a runner-up in the Frederick Jackson Turner Award competition in 1974; other writing includes articles on social activism of intellectuals and educational reform. The recipient of several National Endowment for the Humanities fellowships, he held a Fulbright Lectureship in American culture at the University of Vienna in 1982–1983. Frederick has been recognized with several distinguished teaching awards and has conducted teaching workshops around the country. Areas of special research interest include nineteenth-century American social and intellectual history, black history, and biographies. He coordinated and edited all the *Recovering the Past* sections in this book.

ALLEN F. DAVIS is a professor at Temple University where he is the co-director of the Center for Public History and a specialist in American cultural history. He studied at Dartmouth College (A.B., 1953) and the University of Rochester (M.A., 1954) before earning a Ph. D. at the University of Wisconsin (1959). He has also taught at Wayne State University, at the University of Missouri, and as a visiting professor at the University of Texas at Austin. Davis is the author, co-author, or editor of ten books, including *Spearheads for Reform: The Social Settlements and the Progressive Movement; American Heroine: The Life and Legend of Jane Addams; Conflict and Consensus in American History;* and *Generations: Your Family in Mod-*

ern American History. Formerly the Executive Director of the American Studies Association, he has lectured widely in the United States and Europe. He has received fellowships from the American Council of Learned Societies, the National Endowment for the Humanities, and the American Philosophical Society. Davis has been honored for his writing by the Friends of Literature, The Society of American Historians, and The Christopher Society. He compiled the six art portfolios and acted as an illustration coordinator for this book.

ALLAN M. WINKLER holds a B.A. degree from Harvard (1966), an M.A. from Columbia (1967), and a Ph.D. from Yale (1974). He was a history faculty member at Yale from 1973 to 1978. He served as Bicentennial Professor of American Studies at Helsinki University before joining the faculty of the University of Oregon in 1979. Winkler was the first recipient of the John Adams Chair in American Civilization at the University of Amsterdam in 1984–1985. He is the author of *The Politics of Propaganda: The Office of War Information, 1942–1945* (1978) and *Modern America: The United States from the Second World War to the Present* (1985). Winkler has received grants from the National Endowment for the Humanities, the Fulbright Commission, the American Council for Learned Societies, and the American Philosophical Society; he has been a Mellon Fellow at the Aspen Institute for Humanistic Studies. Formerly a Peace Corps Volunteer, he is most interested in the connections between public policy and popular mood in the recent past. He is currently studying American atomic energy policy.

CHAPTER 17
RECONSTRUCTING AMERICA

In April 1864, one year before Lincoln's assassination, Robert Allston died of pneumonia. His daughter, Elizabeth, was left with a "sense of terrible desolation and sorrow" as the Civil War raged around her, and she and her mother took over the affairs of their many rice plantations. With Yankee troops moving through coastal South Carolina in the late winter of 1864–1865, Elizabeth's sorrow turned to "terror" as Union soldiers arrived in search of liquor, firearms, and hidden valuables. The Allston women survived an insulting search and then fled. In a later raid, Yankee troops encouraged the somewhat reluctant Allston slaves to take furniture and other household goods from the Big Houses, some of which the blacks returned when the Yankees were gone. But before they left, the Union soldiers, in their role as liberators, gave the key to the crop barns to the semifree slaves.

When the war was over, Adele Allston took an oath of allegiance to the United States and secured a written order commanding the blacks to relinquish the keys to the barns. She and Elizabeth made plans to return in the early summer of 1865 to resume control of the family plantations, thereby reestablishing white authority. She was assured that although the blacks had guns and were determined to have the means to a livelihood, "no outrage has been committed against the whites except in the matter of property." Possession of the keys to the barns, Elizabeth wrote, would be the "test case" of whose rights were most important and who was in control.

Not without some fear, Adele and Elizabeth Allston rode up in a carriage to their former home, Nightingale Hall, to confront their former slaves. To their surprise, a pleasant reunion took place. The Allston women greeted the blacks by name, inquired after their children, and caught up on the affairs of those with whom they had lived closely for many years. A trusted black foreman handed over the keys to the barns. This harmonious scene was repeated elsewhere.

But at Guendalos, a plantation owned by an Allston son absent during most of the war fighting with the Confederate army, the women met a very different situation. As their carriage arrived and moved slowly toward the barn, a defiant group of armed ex-slaves lined both sides of the road, following the carriage after it passed by. The tension grew as the carriage stopped by the barn. There the former black driver, Uncle Jacob, was unsure whether to yield the keys to the barns full of rice and corn, put there by black labor. But Mrs. Allston insisted. As Uncle Jacob hesitantly began to hand the keys to her, an angry young man shouted out: "Ef yu gie up de key, blood'll flow." Uncle Jacob slowly slipped the keys back into his pocket.

The tension increased as the blacks sang freedom songs and brandished hoes, pitchforks, and guns in an effort to discourage anyone from going to town for help. Two blacks, however, left the plantation to find some Union military officers to come settle the issue of the keys, most likely on the side of the Allstons. As Adele and Elizabeth waited, word finally arrived that the Union officers, who were difficult to locate, would no doubt be found the next day and would come to Guendalos. The Allstons spent the night restlessly but safely in their house. Early the next morning, they were awakened by a knock at the unlocked front door. Adele slowly opened the door, and there stood Uncle Jacob. Without a word, he handed over the keys to Guendalos.

Most of the essential human ingredients of the Reconstruction era are found in this story. Despite defeat on the battlefields and surrender at Appomattox, southern whites were determined to resume control of both land and labor. Rebellion aside, the law, property titles, and federal enforcement were all on the side of the original owners of the land. The Allston women were friendly to the blacks in a genuine but maternal way and insisted on the restoration of the deferential relationships that existed before the war. Adele and Elizabeth, in short, both feared and cared for their former slaves.

The black freedmen likewise revealed mixed feelings toward their former owners. At different plantations they demonstrated a variety of emotions: anger, loyalty, love, resentment, and pride. Respect was paid to the person of the Allstons but not to their property and crops. The action of the blacks indicated that what they wanted was not revenge but economic independence and freedom.

In this encounter between former slaves and their mistresses, the role of the northern federal officials is most revealing. The Union soldiers, literally and symbolically, gave the keys of freedom to the blacks but did not remain long enough to guarantee that freedom. Although encouraging the freedmen to plunder the master's house and take possession of the crops, when the crucial encounter occurred, the northern officials had disappeared. It is clear that had they been found they would have upheld the land titles of the Allstons. Knowing that, Uncle Jacob handed the keys to land and liberty back to his former owner. The blacks at Guendalos knew that if they wanted to ensure their freedom, they had to do it themselves. Northern help was limited and short-lived.

The goals of each group at the Allston plantations were in conflict with each other. What happened to various human dreams and needs as people sought to form new relationships during Reconstruction is the theme of this chapter. Amid the devastating destruction and countless casualties at the end of a bloody civil war, the survivors sought to put their lives back together again. Victorious but variously motivated northern officials, defeated but defiant southern planters, and impoverished but hopeful freed blacks—all had needs and dreams. In no way could each group fulfill its conflicting goals, yet each had to try. This guaranteed that the Reconstruction era would be a deeply divided one.

THE BITTERSWEET AFTERMATH OF WAR

"There are sad changes in store for both races," the daughter of a Georgia planter wrote in her diary early in the summer of 1865, adding, "I wonder the Yankees do not shudder to behold their work." In order to understand the bittersweet nature of Reconstruction, one must look at the state of the nation in the spring of 1865, shortly after the assassination of President Lincoln.

The United States in 1865

The "Union" was in a state of constitutional crisis in April 1865. The status of the 11 states of the former Confederate States of America was unclear. They had claimed the right to secede, were successful for a time, but finally had failed. The North had denied the South's constitutional right to secede but needed four years of Civil

Conflicting Goals During Reconstruction

VICTORIOUS NORTHERN ("RADICAL") REPUBLICANS	NORTHERN MODERATES —REPUBLICANS AND DEMOCRATS	OLD SOUTHERN PLANTER ARISTOCRACY (EX-CONFEDERATES)	NEW "OTHER SOUTH" —YEOMAN FARMERS AND EX-WHIGS (UNIONISTS)	BLACK FREEDMEN
• Justify the costs of war by remaking southern society in the image of the North • Political but not physical or economic punishment of Confederate leaders • Continue programs of economic progress begun during the war: high tariffs, railroad subsidies, national banking • Maintain the Republican party in power in the nation • Help the freedmen make the transition to full freedom by providing them with the tools of citizenship (suffrage) and equal economic opportunity • Governmental role in achieving these idealistic commitments to justice, equality, and morality	• Speedy establishment of peace and order, reconciliation between North and South • Leniency, amnesty, and merciful readmission of southern states to the Union • Perpetuate the primacy of land ownership, free labor, market competition, and other capitalist values of nineteenth-century American life • Local self-determination of economic and social issues, limited interference by the national government • Limited support for black suffrage • Restraint on efforts to remake social and racial relationships; skeptical of crusades	• Celebrate the noble "lost cause" by defiantly asserting the old ways • Protection from possibilities of northern or black uprising and revenge • Amnesty, pardon, and restoration of confiscated lands • Restore traditional plantation-based market-crop economy with blacks as cheap labor force • Restore traditional political leaders in the states • Restore traditional paternalistic race relations as basis of social order	• Speedy establishment of peace and order, reconciliation between North and South • Recognition of loyal role and economic value of upcountry small yeoman farmers • Create greater diversity in southern economy: capital investments in railroads, factories, and the diversification of agriculture • Displace the planter aristocracy with new political leaders drawn from loyal Unionists and new economic interests • Limited rights and powers to freedmen; suffrage granted only to the educated few	• Physical protection from abuse and terror by local whites • Economic independence through land of one's own (40 acres and a mule) and equal access to trades • Political participation through the right to vote • Equal civil rights and protection under the laws, especially rights of mobility and testimony in court • Educational opportunity and the development of family and cultural bonds

War and over 600,000 deaths to win the point. Were the 11 states part of the Union or not? Lincoln's official position had been that the southern states had never left the Union, which was "constitutionally indestructible." As a result of their rebellion, they were only "out of their proper relation" with the United States. The president, therefore, as commander in chief, had the authority to decide on the basis for setting relations right and proper again.

Congressional opponents of Lincoln argued that by declaring war on the Union, the Confederate states had broken their constitutional ties and had reverted to a kind of prestatehood status like territories or "conquered provinces." Congress, therefore, which decided on the admission of new states, should resolve the constitutional issues and assert its authority over the reconstruction process. Hidden in this conflict between Congress and the president was a powerful struggle between two branches of the national government. As has happened during nearly every war, the executive branch took on broad powers necessary for rapid mobilization of resources and domestic security. Many people believed, however, that Lincoln went far beyond his constitutional authority. As soon as the war was over, Congress sought to reassert its authority, as it would do after every subsequent war.

In April 1865, the Republican party ruled victorious, and virtually alone. Although less than a dozen years old, the Republicans had made immense achievements in the eyes of the northern public. They had won the war, preserved the Union, and freed the slaves. Moreover, they had enacted most of the old Federalist-Whig economic programs on behalf of free labor and free enterprise: a high protective tariff, a national banking system, broad use of the power to tax and to borrow and print money, generous federal appropriations for internal improvements, the Homestead Act for western farmers, and an act to establish land-grant colleges to teach agricultural and mechanical skills. Alexander Hamilton, John Quincy Adams, and Henry Clay might all have applauded. Despite these achievements, the Republican party was still an uneasy grouping of former Whigs, Know-Nothings, Democrats, and antislavery forces.

The Democratic party, by contrast, was in shambles. Republicans depicted southern Democrats as rebels, murderers, and traitors, northern Democrats as weak-willed, disloyal, and opposed to economic growth and progress. Nevertheless, it had been politically important in 1864 for the Republicans to show that the war was a bipartisan effort. A Jacksonian Democrat and Unionist from Tennessee, Andrew Johnson, had therefore been nominated as Lincoln's vice-president. In April 1865, he sat at the head of the government.

The United States in the spring of 1865 was a picture of stark economic contrasts. Northern cities hummed with productive activity while southern cities lay in ruins. Northern factory chimneys poured forth flames and smoke that gave evidence of the production of railroad tracks and engines, steel, textiles, farm implements, and building materials. Southern chimneys were often all that stood, puncturing the skyline in stony silence above the rubble of devastation. Northern railroad tracks laced the land, while in the South railroads and roads lay in ruins. Southern financial institutions were bankrupt, while in the North they flourished. Northern farms, under increasing mechanization, were more productive than ever before, and free farmers took pride that they had amply fed the Union army and urban workers throughout the war. They saw the Union victory as evidence of the superiority of free over slave labor. By contrast, southern farms and plantations, especially those that had lain in the path of Sherman's march, were like a "howling waste." As one observer described it, the countryside " looked for many miles like a broad black streak of ruin and desolation." Said one resident, "The Yankees came through . . . and just tore up everything."

Although there were pockets of relative wealth in some areas, the South was largely devastated as the soldiers demobilized and returned home in April 1865. There was scarcely a family, North as well as South, that had not suffered a serious casualty in the war. Crippled by amputated limbs and suffering from hunger (a half million southern whites faced starvation), the ragtag remains of the Confederate army suffered widespread sickness, destruction, and social disorder as they traveled home. Yet, as a later southern writer, Wilbur Cash, explained, "If this war had smashed the Southern world, it had left the essential Southern mind and will . . . entirely unshaken." Many southerners wanted nothing less than to resist Reconstruction and restore their old world. Others, the minority who had remained quietly loyal to the Union throughout the war, dreamed of a postwar period not of defiance and restoration of the old order but of reconciliation and development of a new one.

Whatever the extremes of southern white attitudes, the dominant social reality in the spring of 1865 was that nearly 4 million former slaves were on their own, facing the challenges of freedom. After an initial reaction of joy and celebration, expressed in jubilee songs, the freedmen quickly became aware of their continuing dependence on former owners. A Mississippi woman stated the uncertainty of her new status this way: "I used to think if I could be free I should be the happiest of anybody in the world. But when my master come to me, and says—Lizzie, you is free! it seems like I was in a kind of daze. And when I would wake up in the morning I would think to myself, Is I free? Hasn't I got to get up before day light and go into the field of work?" For Lizzie and 4 million other blacks, everything—and nothing—had changed.

Hopes Among Freedmen

Throughout the South in the summer of 1865, there were optimistic expectations in the old slave quarters. As Union soldiers marched through Richmond, prisoners in slave-trade jails were heard to chant: "Slavery chain done broke at last! Gonna praise God till I die!" The slavery chain, however, was not broken all at once, but link by link. After Union soldiers swept through an area, Confederate troops might follow, or master and overseer would return, and the slaves learned not to rejoice too quickly or openly. Often the return of the master meant severe whippings, worse treatment, and even death for helping Yankee soldiers loot the house.

The United States in 1865: Crisis at the End of the Civil War

Military casualties
  350,000 Union soldiers dead
  275,000 Confederate soldiers dead

  625,000 Total dead

  275,000 seriously wounded and maimed
  900,000 casualties nationwide in a total male population of 15 million (nearly 1 in 15)
Physical/Economic crisis
  The South devastated, its railroads, industry, and some major cities in ruins; its fields and livestock wasted
Constitutional crisis
  Eleven ex-Confederate states not a part of the Union, their status unclear and uncertain
Political crisis
  Republican party (entirely of the North) dominant in Congress; a former Democratic slaveholder from Tennessee, Andrew Johnson, in the presidency
Social crisis
  Nearly 4 million black freedmen throughout the South face challenges of survival and freedom, along with thousands of hungry demobilized white southern soldiers and displaced white families
Psychological crisis
  Incalculable resentment, bitterness, anger, and despair throughout North and South

Both white southerners and their former slaves suffered in the immediate aftermath of the Civil War, as illustrated by this engraving from **Frank Leslie's Illustrated Newspaper.**

"Every time a bunch of No'thern sojers would come through," recalled one slave, "they would tell us we was free and we'd begin celebratin'. Before we would get through somebody else would tell us to go back to work, and we would go." Another slave recalled celebrating emancipation "about twelve times" in one North Carolina county. So former slaves became cautious about what freedom meant.

Gradually, the freedmen began to express a vision of what life beyond bondage and the plantation might be like. The first thing they did to test the reality of freedom was to leave the plantation, if only for a few hours or days. "If I stay here I'll never know I am free," a South Carolina woman said, and off she went to work as a cook in a nearby town. Some former slaves cut their ties entirely, leaving cruel and kindly masters alike. Some returned to an earlier master, but large numbers of them went to towns and cities for work and to find schools, churches, and association with other blacks, where they would be safe from whippings and retaliation.

Many freedmen left the plantation in search of members of their families. The quest for a missing spouse, parent, or child, sold away years before, was a powerful force in the first few months of emancipation. Black newspapers were filled with advertisements detailing these sorrowful searches. For those who found a spouse or who had been living together in slave marriages, freedom meant getting married legally. Mass wedding ceremonies, sometimes involving many couples, were common sights in the first months of emancipation. Legal marriage was important morally, but it also served such practical purposes as establishing the legitimacy of children and gaining access to land titles and other economic opportunities. Marriage also meant special burdens for black women, who almost immediately assumed a double role as keeper of the house, with all the usual domestic duties performed by women, white or black, and as a producer of income by work outside her home.

Another way in which freedmen demonstrated their new status was by choosing surnames: Lincoln, Grant, and Washington were common. As an indication of the mixed feelings the freedmen had toward their former masters, some would adopt their master's name, while others would pick "any big name 'ceptin' their master's." Often as a symbol of historical identity and family pride, the former slaves selected the name of a first master, "the one my daddy and mammy had."

Emancipation changed black manners around whites as well. Many blacks, even if they were still working on the same plantation, simply behaved differently in order to express what freedom meant. The masks were dropped and the old expressions of humility—tipping a hat, stepping aside, feigning happiness, addressing whites with titles of deference—were discarded. For the blacks, these were necessary symbolic expressions of selfhood; they proved that things were now different. To whites, these behaviors were seen as acts of "insolence," "insubordination," and "puttin' on airs."

However important were choosing names, dropping masks, moving around, getting married, and testing new rights, the primary goal for most freedmen was the acquisition of their own land. "All I want is to git to own fo' or five acres ob land, dat I can build me a little house on and call my home," a Mississippi black said. Only through economic independence, a traditional American goal, could former slaves prove to themselves that emancipation was real.

Many freed blacks, like these young people photographed in Richmond, Virginia, gravitated to urban centers.

During the war, some Union generals had placed liberated slaves in charge of confiscated and abandoned lands. In the Sea Islands off the coast of South Carolina and Georgia, blacks had been working 40-acre plots of land and harvesting their own crops for several years. Some had even been given titles of possession to these lands, while others had been organized by northern philanthropists into growing cotton for the Treasury Department in order to prove the superiority of free labor over slavery. In the Davis Bend section of Mississippi, thousands of ex-slaves worked 40-acre tracts on leased lands formerly owned by Jefferson Davis. In this highly successful experiment, they made profits sufficient to repay the government for initial costs, then lost the land to Davis's brother. A more typical situation, however, was one like the Allston plantations, where in the absence of former owners the blacks simply continued familiar agricultural work.

Many freedmen expected a new economic order as fair payment for their years of involuntary work on the land. "It's de white man's turn ter labor now," a black preacher in Florida told a group of fieldhands. Whites would no longer own all the land, he went on, "fur de Guverment is gwine ter gie ter ev'ry Nigger forty acres of lan' an' a mule." Other freedmen were willing to settle for less: One in Virginia offered to take only one acre of land—"Ef you make it de acre dat Marsa's house sets on." Another was more guarded, aware of how easy the power could shift back to white planters: "Gib us our own land and we take care ourselves; but widout land, de ole massas can hire us or starve us, as dey please." However cautiously expressed, the freedmen had every expectation, fed by the intensity of their dreams, that the promised "forty acres and a mule" was forthcoming. Once land, family unity, and education were achieved, they looked forward to civil rights and the vote.

The White South's Fearful Response

White southerners had equally mixed goals and high expectations at the end of the Civil War. Yeoman farmers and poor whites stood side by side with rich planters in bread lines as together they looked forward to the restoration of their land and livelihood. Suffering from "extreme want and destitution," as a Cherokee County, Georgia, resident put it, white southerners responded with feelings of outrage, loss, and injustice. "I tell you it is mighty hard," said one man, "for my pa paid his own money for our niggers; and that's not all they've robbed us of. They have taken our horses and cattle and sheep *and everything.*" Others felt the loss more personally, as former slaves they thought were faithful or for whom they felt great affection suddenly left. "Something dreadful has happened dear Diary," a Florida woman wrote in May 1865. "My dear black mammy has left us . . . I feel lost, I feel as if someone is dead in the house. Whatever will I do without my Mammy?"

A more dominant emotion than sorrow, however, was fear. The entire structure of southern society was shaken, and the semblance of racial peace and order that slavery had provided was shattered. Many white southerners could hardly imagine a society without blacks in bondage. It was the basis not only of social order but of a life style the larger slaveholders, at least, had long regarded as the perfect model of gentility and civilization. Having lost control of all that was familiar and revered, large planters and small farmers alike feared all kinds of inconveniences and horrors.

The mildest of their fears was having to do various jobs and chores they had rarely done

---

The Promise of Land: 40 Acres

To All Whom It May Concern

Edisto Island, August 15th, 1865

George Owens, having selected for settlement forty acres of Land, on Theodore Belab's Place, pursuant to Special Field Orders, No. 15, Headquarters Military Division of the Mississippi, Savannah, Ga., Jan. 16, 1865; he has permission to hold and occupy the said Tract, subject to such regulations as may be established by proper authority; and all persons are prohibited from interfering with him in his possession of the same.

By command of
R. SAXTON
    Brev't Maj. Gen.,
    Ass't. Comm.
    S. C., Ga., and Fla.

before, like housework. A Georgia woman, Eliza Andrews, complained that it seemed to her "a waste of time for people who are capable of doing something better to spend their time sweeping and dusting while scores of lazy negroes that are fit for nothing else are lying around idle." Worse yet was the "impudent and presumin'" new manners of former slaves, as a North Carolinian put it. Many worried that the rude behavior meant that blacks wanted social equality. Some distressing signs of equality were already apparent. As the freedmen moved about the cities and countryside looking for relatives and work, they rode on streetcars, railroad trains, and steamboats, thus putting whites into the embarrassing position of boarding a train to find that they must sit down next to a former slave.

The worst fears of southern whites were rape and revenge. Impudence and pretensions of social equality, some thought, would lead to intermarriage, which in turn would produce mulattoes, "Africanization," and the destruction of the purity of the white race. Fears of violence were touched off by the presence of black soldiers. Although demobilization occurred rapidly after Appomattox, a few black militia units remained in uniform, parading with guns in southern cities. This stirred fears of black revenge in the hearts of southern whites. Acts of violence by black soldiers against whites in the early years of Reconstruction, however, were very rare.

Believing that their world was turned upside down, the former planter aristocracy tried to set it right again. Their goal was to restore the old plantation order and appropriate racial relationships. The key to reestablishing white dominance were the "black codes" passed by state legislatures in the first year after the end of the war. Many of the codes granted freedmen the right to marry, sue and be sued, testify in court, and hold property. But these rights were qualified. Complicated passages in the codes explained under exactly what circumstances blacks could testify against whites or own property (mostly they could not) or exercise other rights of free persons. Some rights were denied. Racial intermarriage headed the list, but it also included the right to bear arms, possess alcohol-

ic beverages, sit on trains and other public conveyances except in baggage compartments, enter city limits or be on the streets at night, or congregate in large groups.

Many of the alleged rights guaranteed by the black codes—testimony in court, for example—were passed in order to induce the federal government to withdraw its remaining troops from the South. This was a crucial issue, for freedmen were being assaulted, beaten, and terrorized by marauding groups of whites in the aftermath of Appomattox and needed protection. Countless reported and unreported cases of savage and brutal violence were committed against virtually defenseless blacks in the early years of Reconstruction. In one small district of Kentucky, for example, a government agent reported in 1865:

> Twenty-three cases of severe and inhuman beating and whipping of men; four of beating and shooting; two of robbing and shooting; three of robbing; five men shot and killed; two shot and wounded; four beaten to death; one beaten and roasted; three women assaulted and ravished; four women beaten; two women tied up and whipped until insensible; two men and their families beaten and driven from their homes, and their property destroyed; two instances of burning of dwellings, and one of the inmates shot.

No wonder blacks and their white sympathizers wanted protection and the right to testify in court against whites.

For white planters, the violence was another sign of social disorder that could be eased only by restoring a plantation-based society. Moreover, they needed the freedmen's labor. The crucial provisions of the black codes were thus intended to regulate the freedmen's economic status. "Vagrancy" laws provided that any blacks not lawfully employed, which usually meant by a white employer, could be arrested, jailed, fined, or hired out to a man who would assume responsibility for their debts and future behavior. These arrangements struck some as indistinguishable from slavery. The codes regulated the work contracts by which black laborers worked in the fields for white landowners, including severe penalties for leaving before the yearly contract was fulfilled and rules for behavior, attitude, and manners. Thus southern leaders sought to reestablish their dominance. In a scene often repeated, the slaves on a Louisiana plantation listened to a departing Union officer inform them that they were now free, only to be told by the wife of their former master, "Ten years from today I'll have you all back 'gain."

NATIONAL RECONSTRUCTION

The intention of this Louisiana plantation mistress and other planters to control the lives of freedmen was thoroughly supported by the black codes passed by southern legislatures. But what kinds of actions would be taken by the government in Washington? The first statements of the new president were far from reassuring to worried southerners. Johnson took a stern stand against the defeated Confederates, telling congressional Republicans he believed that "treason is a crime and crime must be punished." The freedmen might be free of their former owners after all.

Promised Land Restored to Whites

Richard H. Jenkins, an applicant for the restoration of his plantation on Wadmalaw Island, S. C., called "Rackett Hall," the same having been unoccupied during the past year and up to the 1st of Jan. 1866, except by one freedman who planted no crop, and being held by the Bureau of Refugees, Freedmen and Abandoned Lands, having conformed to the requirements of Circular No. 15 of said Bureau, dated Washington, D. C., Sept. 12, 1865, the aforesaid property is hereby restored to his possession.

. . . The Undersigned, Richard H. Jenkins, does hereby solemnly promise and engage, that he will secure to the Refugees and Freedmen now resident on his Wadmalaw Island Estate, the crops of the past year, harvested or unharvested; also, that the said Refugees and Freedmen shall be allowed to remain at their present houses or other homes on the island, so long as the responsible Refugees and Freedmen (embracing parents, guardians, and other natural protectors) shall enter into contracts, by leases or for wages, in terms satisfactory to the Supervising Board.

Also, that the undersigned will take the proper steps to enter into contracts with the above described responsible Refugees and Freedmen, the latter being required on their part to enter into said contracts on or before the 15th day of February, 1866, or surrender their right to remain on the said estate, it being understood that if they are unwilling to contract after the expiration of said period, the Supervising Board is to aid in getting them homes and employment elsewhere.

The Presidential Plan

President Johnson's initial toughness, however, soon gave way to leniency. On May 29, 1865, he issued two proclamations setting forth his reconstruction program. Like Lincoln, he maintained that the southern states had never left the Union. His first proclamation continued Lincoln's policies by offering "amnesty and pardon, with restoration of all rights of property" to all former Confederates who would take an oath of allegiance to the Constitution and the Union of the United States. There were exceptions: ex-Confederate government leaders and rich rebels whose taxable property was valued at over $20,000. In this latter exception Johnson revealed his old Jacksonian hostility to wealthy aristocratic planters and his preference for leadership by self-made yeoman farmers like himself. Any southerners not covered by the amnesty proclamation could, however, apply for special individual pardons, which Johnson granted to nearly all who applied. By the fall of 1865, only a handful remained unpardoned.

Johnson's second proclamation accepted the reconstructed government of North Carolina and laid out the steps by which other southern states could reestablish state governments. First, the president would appoint a provisional governor, who would call a state convention representing "that portion of the people of said State who are loyal to the United States." This included those who took the oath of allegiance or were otherwise pardoned. The convention should ratify the Thirteenth Amendment, which abolished slavery, void secession, repudiate all Confederate debts, and then elect new state officials and members of Congress.

Under this lenient plan, each of the southern states successfully completed reconstruction and sent newly elected members to the Congress that convened in December 1865. Southern voters indicated their defiant attitude by electing dozens of former officers and legislators of the Confederacy, including a few not yet pardoned. Some state conventions refused to ratify the Thirteenth Amendment, and those that did asserted their right to compensation for the loss of slave property. No state convention provided for black suffrage, and most did nothing to guarantee civil rights, schooling, or economic protection for the freedmen.

By the end of 1865, many questions had presumably been answered. The southern states had formed new governments and had elected new representatives to Congress. The freedmen were going back to work for their former masters under annual contracts. The new president seemed firmly in charge. The reconstruction of the southern states, less than eight months earlier engaged in bloody battle against the Union, seemed to be over. But northern Republicans were far from satisfied when they looked at President Johnson's efforts. Georges Clemenceau, a young French newspaper reporter covering the war, wondered if the North, having paid so many "painful sacrifices," would "let itself be tricked out of what it had spent so much trouble and perseverance to win."

The Congressional Plan

As they looked at the situation late in 1865, northern leaders painfully saw that almost none of their postwar goals—moral, political, or psychological—were being fulfilled. The South seemed far from reconstructed and was taking advantage of the president's program to restore the power of the prewar planter aristocracy. The freedmen were receiving neither equal citizenship nor economic independence. And the Republicans were not likely to maintain their political power and stay in office. Would the Democratic party and the South gain by postwar elections what they had been unable to achieve by civil war?

A song popular in the North in 1866 posed the question: "Who shall rule this American Nation?" Would those who had betrayed their country and "murder the innocent freedmen" rule, or those "loyal millions" who had shed their "blood in battle"? The answer was obvious. Congressional Republicans, led by Congressman Thaddeus Stevens of Pennsylvania and Senator Charles Sumner of Massachusetts, thus asserted their own policies for reconstructing the nation. Many southerners believed that the

Widespread violence against blacks in the wake of emancipation, especially following President Johnson's veto of the Civil Rights Bill, gave rise to the sardonic question, "Slavery is Dead?"

Republican Congress wanted to transform the South in the North's image and to punish it by providing numerous political and economic rights for the freedmen. Although some congressional leaders did indeed have strong punitive and political motivations, as well as a strong sense of responsibility to set the freedmen on their feet, the vast majority of Republicans were moderates. Although branded as "radicals," only for a brief period in 1866 and 1867 did a restrained "radical" rule prevail.

Rejecting Johnson's notion that the South had already been reconstructed, Congress asserted its constitutional authority to decide on its own membership and refused seats to the newly elected senators and representatives from the old Confederate states. Congress then established the Joint Committee on Reconstruction to investigate conditions in the South. Its report documented disorder and resistance and the appalling treatment and conditions of the freedmen. Even before the report was made final in 1866, Congress passed a civil rights bill to protect the fragile rights of the blacks and extended for two more years the Freedmen's Bureau, an agen-

A white mob burned this freedmen's school during the Memphis riot of May 1866.

cy providing emergency assistance at the end of the war. President Johnson vetoed both bills, arguing that they were unconstitutional and calling his congressional opponents "traitors."

Johnson's growing anger forced moderates into the radical camp, and Congress passed both bills over his veto. Both, however, were watered down by weakening the power of enforcement. Southern civil courts, therefore, regularly disallowed black testimony against whites, acquitted whites charged with violence against blacks, sentenced blacks to compulsory labor, and generally made discriminatory sentences for the same crimes. In this judicial climate, racial violence erupted with discouraging frequency.

In Memphis, for example, a race riot occurred in May 1866 that typified race relations during the Reconstruction period and followed the pattern of most urban race riots in America from the colonial era to the 1960s. In the months prior to the riot, there were many cases of unprovoked brutality by local Irish policemen against black Union soldiers stationed at nearby Fort Pickering. A Memphis newspaper suggested that "the negro can do the country more good in the cotton field than in the camp" and criticized what it called "the dirty, fanatical, nigger-loving Radicals of this city" who thought otherwise.

In this inflamed atmosphere, the riot began in a street brawl between the police and some recently discharged but armed black soldiers who forcibly interfered with the arrest of a friend charged with disorderly conduct. After some fighting and an exchange of gunfire, the soldiers went back to their fort. That night, white mobs, led by prominent local officials (one of whom urged the mob to "go ahead and kill the last damned one of the nigger race"), invaded the black section of the city. With the encouragement of the Memphis police, the mobs engaged in over 40 hours of terror, killing, beating, robbing, and raping virtually helpless residents and burning houses, schools, and churches. When it was over, 48 persons, all but two of them black, had died in the riot. The local Union army commander took his time intervening to restore order, arguing that his troops had "a large amount of public property to guard [and] hated Negroes too." A congressional inquiry found that in Memphis, blacks had "no protection from the law whatever."

A month later, Congress proposed to the states the ratification of the Fourteenth Amendment, the single most significant act of the Reconstruction era. The first section of the amendment sought to provide permanent constitutional protection of the civil rights of the freedmen by defining them as citizens. States were prohibited from depriving "any person of life, liberty, or property, without due process of law," and all persons were guaranteed "the equal protection of the laws." In section 2, Congress granted black male suffrage in the South by making blacks whole persons eligible to vote (thus canceling the Constitution's "three-fifths" clause). States that denied this right would have their "basis of representation reduced" proportionally. Other sections of the amendment denied leaders of the Confederacy the right to hold national or state political office (except by act of Congress), repudiated the Confederate debt, and denied claims of compensation by former slave owners for their lost property.

President Johnson urged the southern states not to ratify the Fourteenth Amendment, and ten states immediately rejected it. Johnson then went on the campaign trail in the midterm election of 1866 to ask voters to throw out the radical Republicans. This first campaign since the end of the war was marked by vicious displays of name calling and other low forms of electioneering. The president exchanged insults with hecklers and lashed out against his political opponents. Democrats in both the South and the North appealed openly to racial prejudice in calling for the defeat of those who had passed the Fourteenth Amendment. The nation would be "Africanized," they charged, with black equality threatening both the marketplace and the bedroom.

Republican campaigners, in turn, called Johnson a drunkard and a traitor. Bitter Civil War memories were revived as Republicans "waved the bloody shirt" in telling voters that Democrats were traitorous rebels or draft dodgers, while Republicans were patriotic saviors of the Union and courageous soldiers. Governor Oliver P. Morton of Indiana described the Democratic party as "a common sewer and loathsome receptacle, into which is emptied every element of treason . . . inhumanity and barbar-

ism which has dishonored the age." Although the electorate was moved more by self-interest on other issues than by the persuasive power of these speeches, the result of the election was an overwhelming victory for the Republicans. The mandate was clear that the presidential plan of reconstruction in the seceded states had not worked and that Congress must suggest another.

Therefore, early in 1867, three Reconstruction Acts were passed. The first divided the southern states into five military districts in which military commanders had broad powers to maintain order and protect the rights of property and persons. Congress also defined a new process by which a state could be readmitted to the Union. Qualified voters, which included blacks and excluded unreconstructed rebels, would elect delegates to state constitutional conventions, which then would write new constitutions guaranteeing black suffrage. After the constitutions were ratified by the new voters of the states, elections would be held to choose governors and state legislatures. When a state ratified the Fourteenth Amendment, its representatives to Congress would be accepted, thus completing readmission to the Union.

At the same time as it passed the Reconstruction Acts, Congress also approved a series of bills to restrict the powers of the president and to establish the dominance of the legislative branch over the executive. The Tenure of Office Act, designed to protect the outspoken secretary of war, Edwin Stanton, from removal by Johnson, limited the president's appointment powers. Other measures restricted his power as commander in chief. Johnson behaved exactly as congressional Republicans thought he would, vetoing the Reconstruction Acts, issuing orders to limit the military commanders in the South, and removing cabinet and other government officials sympathetic to Congress's program. The House Judiciary Committee investigated, charging the president with "usurpations of power" and of acting in the "interests of the great criminals" who had led the southern rebellion. It was evident, however, that Johnson was guilty only of holding principles, policies, and prejudices different from congressional leaders, and the House, led by moderate Republicans, rejected the impeachment resolutions.

In August 1867, Johnson finally dismissed Stanton and asked for Senate consent. When this was not forthcoming, the president ordered Stanton to surrender his office, which he refused, barricading himself inside. This time the House rushed impeachment resolutions to a vote, charging the president with "a high misdemeanor" while in office. As constitutionally provided, a trial was held in the Senate, presided over by Chief Justice Salmon P. Chase of the Supreme Court. The evidence seemed clear that Johnson had questionable judgment but had committed no crime that would justify his removal. Yet the passions of the hour made the vote close. With seven Republicans joining Democrats against conviction, the vote was 35 for conviction and 19 against. The effort to find the president guilty as charged fell short of the two-thirds majority required by a single vote. Not for another 100 years would a president, Richard Nixon, again face removal from office through impeachment.

Congressional Moderation

The impeachment crisis revealed that most Republicans were more interested in protecting themselves than the freedmen and in punishing Johnson rather than the South. Congress's political battle against the president was not matched by an idealistic resolve on behalf of the rights and welfare of the freedmen. As early as the state and local elections of 1867, it was clear that voters preferred moderate reconstruction policies. It is important to look not only at what Congress did during Reconstruction but also at what it did not do.

With the exception of Jefferson Davis, Congress did not put leaders of the Confederacy in prison, and only one person, the commander of the infamous Andersonville prison camp, was put to death. Congress did not insist on a long-term probationary period for the southern states before they could be readmitted to the Union. It did not reorganize southern local governments. It did not mandate a national program of education for the 4 million ex-slaves. It did not confiscate and redistribute land to the freedmen, nor did it prevent President Johnson from taking land away from freedmen who had gained possessory titles during the war. It did not, except indirectly, provide economic help to black citizens.

What Congress did do, and that only reluctantly, was grant citizenship and suffrage to the freedmen. At the end of the Civil War, northerners were no more prepared than southerners to make blacks equal citizens. The Fourteenth Amendment required black suffrage in southern states but not in the North. Senate Republicans rejected a general suffrage amendment in 1866, as did a party convention two years later. Between 1865 and 1869, several states in the North and West held referendums proposing black suffrage. Voters in Kansas, Ohio, Michigan, Missouri, Wisconsin, Connecticut, New York, and the District of Columbia (by a vote of 6,521 to 35!) all turned the proposals down. Only in Iowa and Minnesota (on the third try, and then only by devious wording) did northern whites grant the vote to blacks.

Black suffrage gained support, however, after the election of 1868, when General Grant, a military hero regarded as invincible, barely won the popular vote in several states. Congressional Republicans, therefore, took a second look at the importance of a suffrage amendment as a way of adding grateful black votes to party totals. After a bitterly contested fight, repeated in several state ratification contests, the Fifteenth Amendment, forbidding all states to deny the vote to anyone "on account of race, color, or previous condition of servitude," became part of the Constitution in 1870. A black preacher from Pittsburgh observed that "the Republican party had done the Negro good, but they were doing themselves good at the same time."

For political reasons, therefore, Congress gave blacks the vote but not the land, the opposite priority of what the freedmen wanted. Almost alone, Thaddeus Stevens argued that "forty acres . . . and a hut would be more valuable . . . than the . . . right to vote." He had a plan to confiscate the land of the "chief rebels" and to give a small portion of it, divided into 40-acre plots, to the freedmen. But Congress never considered the measure seriously, for it went against deeply held beliefs of the Republican party and the American people in the sacredness of private property. Moreover, northern business interests concerned with the development of southern industry and with investing in southern land were attracted by the idea of a large propertyless class of cheap black laborers.

Although most Americans, in the North as well as the South, opposed confiscation and did not want blacks to become independent landowners, Congress passed an alternative measure. Proposed by George Julian of Indiana, the Southern Homestead Act of 1866 made public lands available to blacks and loyal whites in five southern states. But the land was of poor quality and inaccessible. No transportation, tools, or seed were provided, and most blacks who might have wanted to take advantage of the offer had only until January 1, 1867, to claim their land. But that was nearly impossible for most because they were under contract with white employers until that date. Only about 4,000 black families even applied for the Homestead Act lands, and less than 20 percent of those saw their claims completed. The record of white claimants was not much better. Congressional moderation, therefore, left the freedmen economically weak as they faced the challenges of freedom.

Women and the Reconstruction Amendments

One casualty of the Fourteenth and Fifteenth amendments was the goodwill of the women who had been petitioning and campaigning for suffrage for two decades. They had hoped that their support for the Union effort during the war and the suspension of their own demands in the interests of the more immediate concerns of preserving the Union, nursing the wounded, and emancipating the slaves would be recognized by grateful male legislators. During the war, for example, the Woman's Loyal League, headed by Elizabeth Cady Stanton and Susan B. Anthony, gathered nearly 400,000 signatures on petitions asking Congress to pass the Thirteenth Amendment. They were therefore shocked to see the wording of the Fourteenth Amendment, which for the first time inserted the word *male* in the Constitution in referring to a citizen's right to vote.

Stanton and Anthony campaigned actively against the Fourteenth Amendment, despite the pleas of those who, like Frederick Douglass, had long supported woman suffrage, and who also declared that this was "the Negro's hour." When the Fifteenth Amendment was proposed, they wondered why the word *sex* could not have been added to the "conditions" no longer a basis for denial of the vote. Largely abandoned by radical reconstructionists and abolitionist activists, they had few champions in Congress, however, and that battle was lost too.

Disappointment over the suffrage issue was one of several reasons that led to a split in the

Reconstruction Amendments

AMENDMENT	SUBSTANCE	DATE OF CONGRESSIONAL PASSAGE	OUTCOME OF RATIFICATION PROCESS
Thirteenth	Prohibited slavery in the United States	January 1865	Ratified by 27 states, including 8 southern states, by December 1865
Fourteenth	I. Defined equal national citizenship II. Reduced state representation in Congress proportional to number of disfranchised voters III. Denied former Confederates the right to hold office	June 1866	Rejected by 12 southern and border states by February 1867; radicals made readmission depend on ratification; ratified in July 1868
Fifteenth	Prohibited denial of vote because of race, color, or previous servitude	February 1869	Ratification by Virginia, Texas, Mississippi, and Georgia required for readmission; ratified in March 1870

women's movement in 1869. Anthony and Stanton continued their fight for a national amendment for woman suffrage and other gains, but other women abandoned hope for this and concentrated on securing their rights on a state-by-state basis.

LIFE AFTER SLAVERY

Union army major George Reynolds boasted to a friend late in 1865 that in the area of Mississippi under his command he had "kept the negroes at work, and in a good state of discipline." Clinton Fisk, a well-meaning white who helped to found a black college in Tennessee, told freedmen in 1866 that they could be "as free and as happy" working again for their "old master . . . as any where else in the world." For many blacks such pronouncements sounded familiar, reminding them of white preachers' exhortations during slavery to work hard and obey their masters. Ironically, though, both Fisk and Reynolds were agents of the Freedmen's Bureau, the crucial agency intended to ease the transition from slavery to freedom for the 4 million ex-slaves.

The Freedmen's Bureau

Never in American history has one small agency—underfinanced, understaffed, and undersupported—been given a harder task than was the Bureau of Freedmen, Refugees and Abandoned Lands. Its purposes and mixed successes symbolize, as well as those of any other institution, the tortuous course of Reconstruction.

The purposes of the Freedmen's Bureau included issuing emergency rations of food and providing clothing and shelter to the homeless, hungry victims of the war; establishing medical care and hospital facilities; providing funds for transportation for the thousands of freedmen and white refugees dislocated by the war; helping blacks search for and put their families back together; and arranging for legal marriage ceremonies. The bureau also served as a friend in local civil courts to ensure that the freedmen got fair trials. Although not initially empowered to do so, the agency was responsible for the education of the ex-slaves. To bureau schools came many idealistic teachers from various northern Freedmen's Aid societies.

In addition to these many purposes, the largest task of the Freedmen's Bureau was to serve as an employment agency, tending to the economic well-being of the blacks. This included settling them on abandoned lands and getting them started with tools, seed, and draft animals, as well as arranging work contracts with white landowners. It was in the area of work contracts, as we shall see, that the Freedmen's Bureau served more to "reenslave" the freedmen as impoverished fieldworkers rather than to set them on their way as independent farmers.

Although some agents were idealistic young New Englanders eager to help slaves make the difficult adjustment to freedom, others were Union army officers more concerned with social order than social transformation. Working in the midst of a postwar climate of resentment and violence, Freedmen's Bureau agents were constantly accused of partisan Republican politics,

The Freedmen's Bureau had fewer resources in relation to its purpose than any agency in the nation's history. **Harper's Weekly** *published this engraving of freedmen lining up for aid in Memphis in 1866.*

corruption, and partiality to blacks by local white residents. But even the best-intentioned agents would have agreed with General O. O. Howard, commissioner of the bureau, in a belief in the traditional nineteenth-century American values of self-help, minimal government interference in the marketplace, the sanctity of private property, contractual obligations, and white superiority. The bureau's work served to uphold these values.

On a typical day, these overworked and underpaid agents would visit courts and schools in their district, supervise the signing of work contracts, and handle numerous complaints, most involving contract violations between whites and blacks or property and domestic disputes among blacks. One agent sent a man, who had complained of a severe beating, back to work with the advice, "Don't be sassy [and] don't be lazy when you've got work to do." Another, reflecting his growing frustrations, complained that the freedmen were "disrespectful and greatly in need of instruction." Although helpful in finding work for the freedmen, more often than not the agents found themselves defending white landowners by telling the blacks to obey orders, to trust their employers, and to sign and live by disadvantageous contracts.

Despite mounting pressures to support white landowners, personal frustrations, and even threats on their lives, the agents accomplished a great deal. In little more than two years, the Freedmen's Bureau issued 20 million rations (nearly one-third to poor whites), reunited families and resettled some 30,000 displaced war refugees, treated some 450,000 cases of illness and injury, built 40 hospitals and hundreds of schools, provided books, tools, and furnishings —and even some land—to the freedmen, and occasionally protected their economic and civil rights. Black historian W. E. B. Du Bois wrote an epitaph for the bureau that might stand for the whole of Reconstruction: "In a time of perfect calm, amid willing neighbors and streaming wealth," he wrote, it "would have been a herculean task" for the bureau to fulfill its many purposes. But in the midst of hunger, sorrow, spite, suspicion, hate, and cruelty, "the work of any instrument of social regeneration was . . . foredoomed to failure."

New Economic Dependency

The economic failures of the Freedmen's Bureau, symbolic of the entire congressional program, forced the freedmen into a new economic dependency on their former masters. Although the planter class did not lose its economic and social power in the postwar years, the character of southern agriculture went through some major changes. First, a land-intensive system replaced the labor intensity of slavery. Land ownership was concentrated into fewer and even larger holdings than before the Civil War. From South Carolina to Louisiana, the wealthiest tenth of the population owned about 60 percent of the real estate in the 1870s. Second, these large planters increasingly concentrated on one crop, usually cotton and were tied into the international market. This resulted in a steady drop in food production (both grains and livestock) in the postwar period. And third, reliance on one-crop farming meant that a new credit system emerged in which most farmers, black and white, were dependent on local merchants (often in competition with large landowners) for renting seed, farm implements and animals, provisions, housing, and land itself. These changes affected race relations and class tensions among whites.

This new system, however, took a few years to develop after emancipation. At first, most freedmen signed contracts with white landowners and worked in gangs in the fields as farm laborers very much like during slavery. Watched over by superintendents, who still used the lash to enforce hard toil, they worked from sunrise to sunset. They were paid a meager wage and were issued a monthly allotment of bacon and meal. All members of the family had to work to receive their rations. The freedmen resented this new form of semiservitude, preferring small plots of land of their own to grow vegetables and grains. Moreover, they wanted to be able to send their children to school and insisted on "no more outdoor work" for women.

What the freedmen wanted, a Georgia planter correctly observed, was "to get away from all overseers, to hire or purchase land, and work for themselves." Many blacks, therefore, broke contracts, ran away, engaged in work slowdowns or outright strikes, and otherwise expressed their displeasure with the contract labor system. The former slaves of Adele Allston refused to sign their contracts, even when offered livestock and other favors, and she eventually had to sell much of her land. Another white landowner expressed his frustration over having "to bargain and haggle with our servants about wages." The insistence of blacks on a degree of autonomy and land of their own was the major impetus for the change from the contract system to tenancy and sharecropping. As a South Carolina freedmen put it, "If a man got to go crost de riber, and he can't git a boat, he take a log. If I can't own de land, I'll hire or lease land, but I won't contract."

And so the freedmen became sharecroppers, hiring or leasing small plots of land to work. Families would hitch a team of mules to their old slave cabin to drag it to their assigned plot, as far away from the Big House as possible. The sharecroppers were given seed, fertilizer, farm implements, and all necessary food and clothing to take care of their families. In return, the landlord (or a local merchant) told them what to grow and how much and took a share—usually half—of the harvest. The half retained by the cropper, however, was usually needed to pay for goods bought on credit (at huge interest rates) at the landlord's store. Thus the sharecroppers

A Freedmen's Work Contract

STATE OF SOUTH CAROLINA
Darlington District

ARTICLES OF AGREEMENT

This Agreement entered into between Mrs. Adele Allston Exect of the one part, and the Freedmen and Women of The Upper Quarters plantation of the other part *Witnesseth:*

That the latter agree, for the remainder of the present year, to reside upon and devote their labor to the cultivation of the Plantation of the former. And they further agree, that they will in all respects, conform to such reasonable and necessary plantation rules and regulations as Mrs. Allston's Agent may prescribe; that they will not keep any gun, pistol, or other offensive weapon, or leave the plantation without permission from their employer; that in all things connected with their duties as laborers on said plantation, they will yield prompt obedience to all orders from Mrs. Allston or his [*sic*] agent; that they will be orderly and quiet in their conduct, avoiding drunkenness and other gross vices; that they will not misuse any of the Plantation Tools, or Agricultural Implements, or any Animals entrusted to their care, or any Boats, Flats, Carts or Wagons; that they will give up at the expiration of this Contract, all Tools & c., belonging to the Plantation, and in case any property, of any description belonging to the Plantation shall be willfully or through negligence destroyed or injured, the value of the Articles so destroyed, shall be deducted from the portion of the Crops which the person or persons, so offending, shall be entitled to receive under this Contract.

Any deviations from the condition of the foregoing Contract may, upon sufficient proof, be punished with dismissal from the Plantation, or in such other manner as may be determined by the Provost Court; and the person or persons so dismissed, shall forfeit the whole, or a part of his, her or their portion of the crop, as the Court may decide.

In consideration of the foregoing Services duly performed, Mrs. Allston agrees, after deducting Seventy five bushels of Corn for each work Animal, exclusively used in cultivating the Crops for the present year; to turn over to the said Freedmen and Women, one half of the remaining Corn, Peas, Potatoes, made this season. He [*sic*] further agrees to furnish the usual rations until the Contract is performed.

All Cotton Seed Produced on the Plantation is to be reserved for the use of the Plantation. The Freedmen, Women and Children are to be treated in a manner consistent with their freedom. Necessary medical attention will be furnished as heretofore.

Any deviation from the conditions of this Contract upon the part of the said Mrs. Allston or her Agent or Agents shall be punished in such manner as may be determined by a Provost Court, or a Military Commission. This agreement to continue till the first day of January 1866.

Witness our hand at The Upper Quarters this 28th day of July 1865.

Sharecroppers and tenant farmers, though more autonomous than contract laborers, remained dependent on the landlord for their survival.

were semiautonomous but remained tied to the landlord's will for economic survival.

Under the tenant system, farmers had only slightly more independence. In advance of the harvest, a tenant farmer promised to sell his crop to a local merchant in return for renting land, tools, and other necessities. He also was obligated to purchase goods on credit against the harvest from the merchant's store. At "settling up" time, the income from the sale of the crop was matched with debts accumulated at the store. It was possible, especially after an unusually bountiful season, to come out ahead and eventually to own one's own land. In fact, however, tenants seemed rarely to do so; they remained in debt at the end of each year and were

Changes on the Barrow Plantation, 1860–1881

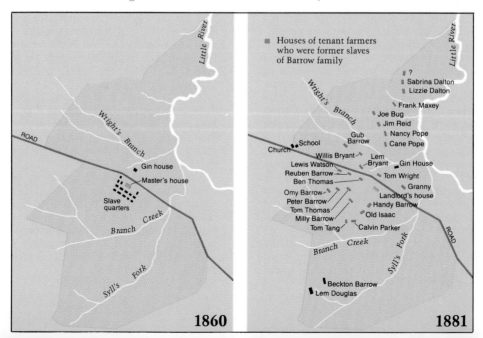

then compelled to pledge the next year's crop. Thus a system of debt peonage replaced slavery, ensuring a continuing cheap labor supply to grow cotton and other staples in the South. Only a very few blacks were able to become independent landowners—about 2 to 5 percent by 1880, but closer to 20 percent in some states by 1900.

These changes in southern agriculture affected yeoman and poor white farmers as well as the freedmen. This raised the threat, always troubling to the planter class, of a coalition between poor black and pro-Unionist white farmers. As a yeoman farmer in Georgia said in 1865, "We should tuk the land, as we did the niggers, and split it, and giv part to the niggers and part to me and t'other Union fellers." But confiscation and redistribution of land was no more likely for white farmers than for the freedmen. Whites, too, were forced to concentrate on growing staples, to pledge their crops against high-interest credit from local merchants, and to face the inevitability of perpetual indebtedness. In the upcountry piedmont area of Georgia, for example, the number of whites who worked their own land dropped from nine in ten before the Civil War to seven in ten by 1880. During the same period, the production of cotton doubled. Reliance on cotton by larger planters meant fewer food crops, which necessitated greater dependence on local merchants for provisions. In 1884, Jephta Dickson of Jackson County, Georgia, purchased over $50 worth of flour, meal, meat, syrup, and peas and corn from a local store, an almost unthinkable situation 25 years earlier, when he would have needed to buy almost no food to supplement his homegrown fare.

In the worn-out flatlands and barren mountainous regions of the South, poor whites found little hope in the era of Reconstruction. Their antebellum heritage of poverty, ill health, and isolation worsened in the years after the war. A Freedmen's Bureau agent in South Carolina described the poor whites in his area as "gaunt and ragged, ungainly, stooping and clumsy in build." They lived a marginal existence, hunting, fishing, and growing corn and potato crops that, as a North Carolinian put it, "come up *puny*, grow *puny*, and mature *puny*." Many poor white farmers, in fact, were even less productive than black sharecroppers. Some became farmhands, earning $6 a month (with board) from other farmers. Other fled to low-paying jobs in urban cotton mills, where they would not have to compete against blacks.

Sharecropping in the South, 1880

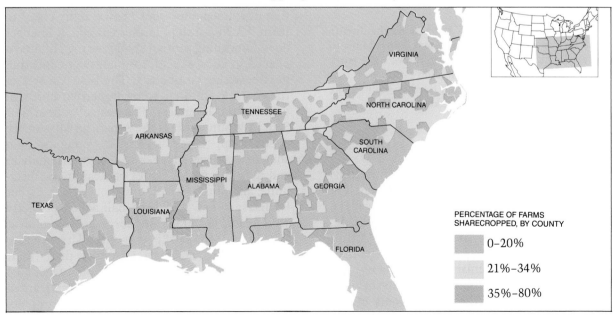

PERCENTAGE OF FARMS
SHARECROPPED, BY COUNTY

0–20%

21%–34%

35%–80%

The cultural life of poor southern whites reflected both their lowly position and their pride. Their religion was emotional and revivalistic, centering on the camp meeting. Music and folklore often focused on debt and chain gangs, as well as on deeds of drinking prowess. In backwoods clearings and bleak pine barrens, men and women told tall tales of superhuman feats and exchanged folk remedies for bad health. In Alabama, there were over 90 superstitious sayings for calling rain. Aesthetic expression, in quilt making and house construction, for example, reflected a marginal culture in which everything was saved and put to use.

In part because their lives were so hard, poor whites persisted in their belief in white superiority. As a federal officer reported in 1866, "The poorer classes of white people . . . have a most intense hatred of the Negro, and swear he shall never be reckoned as part of the population." Many poor whites, therefore, joined the Ku Klux Klan and other southern white terror groups that emerged between 1866 and 1868. But however hard life was for poor whites, blacks were far more often sentenced to chain gangs for the slightest crimes and were bound to a life of debt, degradation, and dependency. The high hopes with which the freedmen had greeted emancipation turned slowly to resignation and disillusionment. Felix Haywood, a former Texas slave, recalled:

> We thought we was goin' to be richer than white folks, 'cause we was stronger and knowed how to work, and the whites . . . didn't have us to work for them anymore. But it didn't turn out that way. We soon found out that freedom could make folks proud but it didn't make 'em rich.

Black Self-Help Institutions

Felix Haywood understood the limitations of government programs and efforts on behalf of the freedmen. It was clear to many black leaders, therefore, that self-help was more reliable. If white institutions were unable to fulfill the promises of emancipation, black freedmen would have to do it themselves. Fortunately, the tradition of black community self-help survived in the organized churches and schools of the antebellum free Negro communities and in the "invisible" cultural institutions of the slave quarters. Religion, as usual, was vital. Emancipation brought an explosion in the growth of membership in black churches. The Negro Baptist church grew from 150,000 members in 1850 to 500,000 in 1870. The various branches of the African Methodist Episcopal church increased fourfold in the decade after the Civil War, from 100,000 to over 400,000 members.

Black ministers continued their tradition as community leaders. Many led efforts to oppose discrimination, some by entering politics. Over one-fifth of the black officeholders in South Carolina were ministers. Most preachers, however, focused on traditional religious themes of sin, conversion, and salvation. An English visitor to the South in 1867 and 1868, after observing a revivalist preacher in Savannah arouse nearly 1,000 people to "sway, and cry, and groan," noted the intensity of black "devoutness." Despite some efforts to restrain the emotionalism characteristic of black worship, most congregations preferred to stay with traditional forms of religious expression. One black woman, when urged to pray more quietly, complained: "We make noise 'bout ebery ting else . . . I want ter go ter Heaben in de good ole way."

The freedmen's desire for education was as strong as for religion. A school official in Virginia echoed the observation of many when he said that the freedmen were "down right crazy to learn." A Mississippi farmer vowed, "If I nebber does do nothing more, I shall give my children a chance to go to school, for I consider education next best ting to liberty." The first teachers of these black children were unmarried northern women, the legendary "Yankee schoolmarms." Sent by groups such as the American Missionary Association, these idealistic young women sought to convert blacks to Congregationalism and to white moral values of cleanliness, discipline, and dutiful work. In October 1865, Esther Douglass found "120 dirty, half naked, perfectly wild black children" in her schoolroom near Savannah, Georgia. Eight months later, she reported to her northern superiors that "their progress was wonderful." They could read, sing hymns, and repeat Bible verses and had learned "about right conduct which they tried to practice."

Glowing reports like this one changed as white teachers grew frustrated with crowded facilities, limited resources, local opposition, and the absenteeism that resulted from the demands of work in the fields. In Georgia, for example, only 5 percent of black children went to school for part of any one year between 1865 and 1870; this contrasted with 20 percent of white children. Furthermore, blacks increasingly preferred their own teachers, who could better understand former slaves. To ensure the training of black preachers and teachers, northern philanthropists founded Howard, Atlanta, Fisk, Morehouse, and other black universities in the South between 1865 and 1867.

Black schools, like churches, became community centers. They published newspapers, provided training in trades and farming, and promoted political participation and land ownership. A black farmer in Mississippi founded both a school and a society to facilitate land acquisition and better agricultural methods. These efforts made black schools objects of local white hostility. A Virginia freedman told a congressional committee that in his county, anyone starting a school would be killed and that blacks were "afraid to be caught with a book." In 1869, in Tennessee alone, 37 black schools were burned to the ground.

White opposition to black education and land ownership stimulated the rise of black nationalism and separatism. In the late 1860s,

Benjamin "Pap" Singleton, a former Tennessee slave who had escaped to Canada, returned home. Observing that "whites had the lands and . . . blacks had nothing but their freedom," Singleton urged them to abandon politics and migrate westward. He organized a land company in 1869, purchased public property in Kansas, and in the early 1870s took several groups from Tennessee and Kentucky to that prairie state to establish separate black towns. In following years, thousands of "exodusters" from the Lower South bought some 10,000 acres of unfertile land in Kansas. There they faced both natural and human obstacles to their efforts to develop self-sufficient communities. Most were forced eventually by climate and hostile neighbors to disband and seek relief.

Despairing of ever finding economic independence in the United States, Singleton and other nationalists urged emigration to Canada and Liberia in the 1880s. One of the leaders of the late-nineteenth-century back-to-Africa movement was the Reverend Henry M. Turner. Like Singleton, Turner believed that the only hope for self-respect and freedom for blacks was in Africa. He too condemned politics, calling the Constitution a "dirty . . . lie" that should be "spit upon by every Negro in the land." Other black leaders, most notably Frederick Douglass, disagreed, asserting that suffrage would eventually lead to full citizenship rights within the United States.

Enthusiasm for education clashed with limited facilities and white values in the early freedmen's schools.

RECONSTRUCTION IN THE STATES

Douglass's confidence in the power of the ballot seemed warranted in the enthusiastic early months under the Reconstruction Acts of 1867. With President Johnson neutralized, national Republican leaders were finally in a position to accomplish their political goals. Local Republicans, taking advantage of the inability or refusal of many southern whites to vote, overwhelmingly elected their delegates to state constitutional conventions in the fall of 1867. With guarded optimism and a sense of the "sacred importance" of their work, black and white Republicans turned to the business of setting up the new state governments.

Republican Rule

Many misconceptions grew about the southern state governments under Republican rule. They were not dominated by illiterate black majorities intent on "Africanizing" the South by passing compulsory racial intermarriage laws, as many whites feared. Nor were these governments unusually corrupt and financially extravagant. Nor did they use massive numbers of federal troops to uphold their will. By 1869, only 1,100 federal soldiers remained in Virginia, and most federal troops in Texas guarded the frontier against Mexico and hostile Indians. Without the support of a strong military presence, then, these new state governments tried to do their

work in a climate of economic distress and increasingly violent harassment.

The new governments elected under congressional Reconstruction were made up of a diverse combination of political groups. Labeled the "black and tan" governments by their opponents to suggest that they were dominated by former slaves and mulattoes, they were actually predominantly white, with the one exception of the lower house of the South Carolina legislature. One part of the new leadership consisted of an old Whiggish elite class of bankers, industrialists, and others interested far more in economic growth and sectional reconciliation than in radical social reforms. A second group consisted of northern Republicans who headed south out of motives similar to those that prompt the migration southward in our own time. These included capitalists seeking economic investment in land, railroads, and new industries; retired Union veterans seeking a warmer climate for health purposes; and missionaries and teachers pursuing an outlet for their idealism in the Freedmen's Bureau schools. Such people were unfairly stuck with the label "carpetbaggers."

A third group participating in the Republican state governments was the blacks. A large percentage of black officeholders were mulattoes, many of them well-educated free blacks who came down from the North as preachers,

Despite threats of white reprisals, black freedmen proudly voted in Republican state governments under the Congressional Reconstruction Plan of 1867.

teachers, and soldiers. Others, such as John Lynch of Mississippi, were self-educated tradesmen or representatives of the small landed class of southern blacks. In South Carolina, for example, of some 255 black state and federal officials elected between 1868 and 1876, two-thirds were literate and one-third owned real estate. Only 15 percent owned no property at all.

This elite class of black leaders was surprisingly moderate, fashioning its political goals squarely in the American republican tradition. Black leaders reminded whites that they, too, were southerners and Americans, attached both to the land of the South and to the white families they had lived with for generations: "The dust of our fathers mingle with yours in the same grave yards. . . . This is your country, but it is ours too." Because of these intermingled pasts, blacks sought no revenge or reversal of power, only respect and equal opportunity as Americans. As the eloquent petition of a black convention in 1865 explained:

> We simply ask that we shall be recognized as *men; . . .* that the same laws which govern *white men* shall govern *black men;* that we have a right of trial by a jury of our peers; that schools be established for the education of *colored children* as well as *white,* and that the advantages of both colors shall, in this respect, be *equal;* that no impediments be put in the way of our acquiring homesteads for ourselves and our people; that, in short, we be dealt with as others are—in equity and justice.

The primary accomplishments of Republican rule in the South consisted of attempts to bring equity and justice to political, economic, and social opportunity, thus elminating the undemocratic features of earlier state constitutions. All states provided universal manhood suffrage and loosened requirements for holding office. The basis of state representation was made fairer by apportioning more legislative seats to the interior regions of southern states. Social legislation included the abolition of automatic imprisonment for debt and laws for the relief of poverty and care of the handicapped. The first divorce laws in many southern states were passed, as were laws granting property rights to married women. Penal laws were mod-

ernized by reducing the list of crimes punishable by death, in one state from 26 to 5.

Under these governments, the task of financially and physically reconstructing the South was undertaken. Tax systems were overhauled, and generous railroad and other capital investment bonds were approved. Harbors, roads, and bridges were rebuilt. Hospitals, asylums, and other state institutions were established. Most important, the Republican governments provided for a state-supported system of public schools, absent before in most of the South. As in the North, these schools were largely segregated, but for the first time education was made available to rich and poor, black and white alike. As a result, black school attendance increased from 5 to over 40 percent and white from 20 to over 60 percent by the 1880s. All of this cost money, and the Republicans did indeed greatly increase tax rates and state debts. All in all, the Republican governments "dragged the South, screaming and crying, into the modern world."

These considerable accomplishments were achieved in the midst of opposition like that expressed in a convention of Louisiana planters, which labeled the Republican leaders "the lowest and most corrupt body of men ever assembled in the South." There was some corruption, to be sure, but mostly in land sales, fraudulent railway bonds, and construction contracts, the kind of graft that had become a way of life in American politics, South and North, in the aftermath of the Civil War. Given their lack of experience with politics, the black role was remarkable. As Du Bois put it, "There was one thing that the white South feared more than negro dishonesty, ignorance, and incompetence, and that was negro honesty, knowledge, and efficiency."

Despite its effectiveness in modernizing southern state governments, the Republican coalition did not last very long. In fact, as the map indicates, Republican rule lasted for different periods of time in different states. In some states, Virginia, for example, the Republicans ruled hardly at all. Situated in the shadow of Washington, conservatives in Virginia professed their agreement with Congress's Reconstruction guidelines while doing as they pleased. As one of the states most devastated by the war, Virginia looked almost immediately to northern investors to rebuild its cities and to develop industry. Blacks and whites alike flocked to the cities for work. The blacks, however, were denied any but low-paying menial jobs and were herded into overcrowded, disease-ridden ghettos called "Little Africas."

Republican rule lasted the longest in the black-belt states of the Deep South, where the black population was equal to or greater than the white. In Louisiana, Reconstruction began with General Ben Butler's occupation of New Orleans in 1862. Although he insisted on granting civil rights to blacks, he was quickly replaced by a succession of Republican governors in the late 1860s more interested in graft, election laws, and staying in office than in the rights and welfare of black Louisianans. Alabama received a flood of northern capital to develop the rich coal, iron-ore, and timber resources of the northern third of the state. Republican rule in Alabama, as in other states, involved a greater role for towns and merchants, the endorsement of generous railroad bonds, and struggles between the old planter aristocracy and a new industrial one.

The return of Democrats to power did not alter either the tensions caused by the emergent new class structure or traditional race relations. In fact, racial violence, intimidation, and coercion played a major role in replacing Republican governments with a restoration of white Democratic rule. As one southern editor put it, "We must render this either a white man's government, or convert the land into a Negro man's cemetery." The Ku Klux Klan was only one of several secret organizations that used force and violence against black and white Republicans to drive them from power. The cases of North Carolina and Mississippi are representative in showing how conservative Democrats were able to regain control.

After losing a close election in North Carolina in 1868, conservatives waged a concentrated campaign of terror in several counties in the piedmont area of the state. If the Democrats could win these counties in 1870, they would most likely win statewide. In the year prior to the election, several prominent Republicans were killed, including a white state senator, whose throat was cut, and a leading black Union League organizer, who was hanged in the courthouse square with a sign pinned to his breast: "Bewar, ye guilty, both white and black." Scores of citizens were flogged, tortured, fired from their jobs, or forced to flee in the middle of the night from burning homes and barns. The courts consistently refused to prosecute anyone for these crimes. Local papers, in fact, charged that they had been committed "by disgusting ne-

Return to the Union During Reconstruction

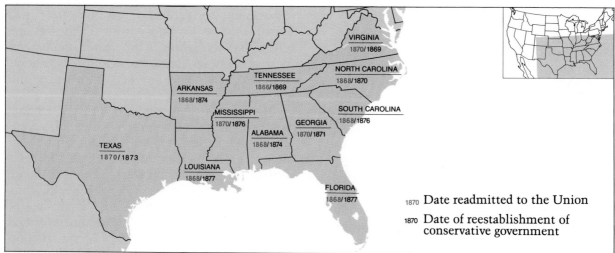

TEXAS
1870/1873

ARKANSAS
1868/1874

LOUISIANA
1868/1877

MISSISSIPPI
1870/1876

ALABAMA
1868/1874

TENNESSEE
1866/1869

GEORGIA
1870/1871

FLORIDA
1868/1877

VIRGINIA
1870/1869

NORTH CAROLINA
1868/1870

SOUTH CAROLINA
1868/1876

1870 Date readmitted to the Union

1870 Date of reestablishment of conservative government

groes and white Radicals." The conservative campaign worked. In the election of 1870, some 12,000 fewer Republicans voted in the two crucial counties than had voted two years earlier, and the Democrats swept back into power.

In the state election in Mississippi in 1875, Democrats used similar tactics, openly announcing that "the thieves . . . , robbers, and scoundrels, white and black," who were in power "deserve death and ought to be killed." In what was called the Mississippi Plan, local Democratic clubs organized themselves into armed militias, marching defiantly through black areas, breaking up Republican meetings, and provoking riots to justify the killing of hundreds of blacks. Armed men were posted during voter registration to intimidate Republicans. At the election itself, anyone still bold enough to attempt to vote was either helped by gun-toting whites to cast a Democratic ballot or driven away from the polls with cannon and clubs. Counties that had earlier given Republican candidates majorities in the thousands, in 1875 managed a total of less than a dozen votes!

Democrats called their victory "redemption." As conservative Democratic administrations resumed control of each state government, Reconstruction came to an end. Redemption

This lithograph, highlighting the Ku Klux Klan's intimidation through violence, was probably produced for popular sale.

was the result of a combination of the persistence of white southern resistance, including violence and other coercive measures, and a loss of will to persist in the North. Albion Tourgée summed up the Reconstruction era in his novel *A Fool's Errand* (1879): "The spirit of the dead Confederacy was stronger than the mandate of the nation to which it had succumbed in battle."

Reconstruction, Northern Style

Congress and President Grant did not totally ignore the violence in the South. Three Force Acts were passed in 1870 and 1871, giving the president strong powers to use federal supervisors to make sure that citizens were not prevented by force or fraud from voting. The third act, known as the Ku Klux Klan Act, declared secret organizations that used disguise and coercion to deprive others of equal protection of the laws illegal. Congress created a joint committee to investigate Klan violence, which reported in 1872 in 13 huge volumes of horrifying testimony. Grant who had supported these measures, delivered special messages to Congress proclaiming the importance of the right to vote, issued proclamations condemning lawlessness, and sent some additional troops to South Carolina. But he refused to send troops to Mississippi to guarantee a safe election in 1875, declaring instead that he and the nation were "tired of these annual autumnal outbreaks."

The success of the Mississippi Plan in 1875, imitated a year later in South Carolina and Louisiana, indicated that congressional reports and presidential proclamations did little to stop the reign of terror against black and white Republicans throughout the South. The Force Acts were wholly inadequate and were themselves weakly enforced. Although there were hundreds of arrests, all-white juries were reluctant to find their fellow citizens guilty of crimes against blacks. They were backed by the United States Supreme Court. In two decisions in 1874, the Court threw out cases against whites found guilty of preventing blacks from voting and held key parts of the Force Acts unconstitutional. In Hamburg, South Carolina, in 1876, several blacks were killed in a riot started in a courtroom when a white mob came to provide its own

We usually read novels, short stories, and other forms of fiction for pleasure, for the enjoyment of plot, style, symbolism, and character development. "Classic" novels such as *Moby Dick, Huckleberry Finn, The Great Gatsby,* and *The Invisible Man,* to name a few American examples, are not only written well but also explore timeless questions of good and evil, of innocence and knowledge, or of noble dreams fulfilled and shattered. Often we enjoy novels because we find ourselves identifying with one of the major characters. Through that person's problems, joys, relationships, and search for identity we gain insights about our own.

We can also read novels as historical sources, for they reveal much about the attitudes, dreams, fears, life styles, and ordinary everyday experiences of human beings in a particular historical period. They also show how people reacted to and felt about the major events of that era. We must be careful, however, to note the date when a novel was written, especially if different from the period written about. The novelist, like the historian, is a product of time and place and has an interpretive point of view.

Consider, for example, the two novels about Reconstruction quoted here. Neither is considered to have great literary merit, yet each reveals much about different interpretations and diversely impassioned attitudes Americans have always had about the post–Civil War era. The novels are *A Fool's Errand* by Albion Tourgée, a northerner, and *The Clansman* by Thomas Dixon, Jr., a southerner.

Tourgée was a young northern teacher and lawyer who fought with the Union army at several major battles during the Civil War. After the war, he moved to North Carolina, partly for health reasons and partly to begin a legal career. He became a judge and was an active Republican, supporting black suffrage and helping to shape the new state constitution and the codification of North Carolina laws in 1868. With jurisdiction over eight counties, Tourgée earned a reputation as one of the fairest judges in the state. Because he boldly criticized the Ku Klux Klan for its campaign of terror against blacks, his life was threatened many times. When the fearless judge finally left North Carolina in 1879, he published an autobiographical novel about his experiences.

The "fool's errand" in the novel is that of the northern veteran, Comfort Servosse, who like Tourgée seeks to fulfill humane goals on behalf of both blacks and whites in post–Civil War North Carolina.

A FOOL'S ERRAND

Albion Tourgee (1879)

When the second Christmas came, Metta wrote again to her sister:

"The feeling is terribly bitter against Comfort on account of his course towards the colored people. There is quite a village of them on the lower end of the plantation. They have a church, a sabbath school, and are to have next year a school. You can not imagine how kind they have been to us, and how much they are attached to Comfort. . . . I got Comfort to go with me to one of their prayer-meetings a few nights ago. I had heard a great deal about them, but had never attended one before. It was strangely weird. There were, perhaps, fifty present, mostly middle-aged men and women. They were singing in a soft, low monotone, interspersed with prolonged exclamatory notes, a sort of rude hymn, which I was surprised to know was one of their old songs in slave times. How the chorus came to be endured in those days I can not imagine. It was—

'Free! free! free, my Lord, free!
An' we walks de hebben-ly way!'

"A few looked around as we came in and seated ourselves; and Uncle Jerry, the saint of the settlement, came forward on his staves, and said, in his soft voice,

"'Ev'nin', Kunnel! Sarvant, Missus! Will you walk up, an' hev seats in front?'

"We told him we had just looked in, and might go in a short time; so we would stay in the back part of the audience.

"Uncle Jerry can not read nor write; but he is a man of strange intelligence and power. Unable to do work of any account, he is the faithful friend, monitor, and director of others. He has a house and piece of land, all paid for, a good horse and cow, and, with the aid of his wife and two boys, made a fine crop this season. He is one of the most promising colored men in the settlement: so Comfort says, at least. Everybody seems to have great respect for his character. I don't know how many people I have heard speak of his religion. Mr. Savage used to say he had rather hear him pray than any other man on earth. He was much prized by his master, even after he was disabled, on account of his faithfulness and character."

His efforts are thwarted, however, by threats, intimidation, a campaign of violent "outrages" against Republican leaders in the county, and a lack of support from the so-called wise men in Congress. Historians have verified the accuracy, down to the smallest

THE CLANSMAN

Thomas Dixon, Jr. (1905)

At noon Ben and Phil strolled to the polling-place to watch the progress of the first election under Negro rule. The Square was jammed with shouting, jostling, perspiring negroes, men, women, and children. The day was warm, and the African odour was supreme even in the open air. . . .

Phil and Ben passed on nearer the polling-place, around which stood a cordon of soldiers with a line of negro voters two hundred yards in length extending back into the crowd.

The negro Leagues came in armed battalions and voted in droves, carrying their muskets in their hands. Less than a dozen white men were to be seen about the place.

The negroes, under the drill of the League and the Freedman's Bureau, protected by the bayonet, were voting to enfranchise themselves, disfranchise their former masters, ratify a new constitution, and elect a legislature to do their will. Old Aleck was a candidate for the House, chief poll-holder, and seemed to be in charge of the movements of the voters outside the booth as well as inside. He appeared to be omnipresent, and his self-importance was a sight Phil had never dreamed. He could not keep his eyes off him. . . .

[Aleck] was a born African orator, undoubtedly descended from a long line of savage spell-binders, whose eloquence in the palaver houses of the jungle had made them native leaders. His thin spindle-shanks supported an oblong, protruding stomach, resembling an elderly monkey's, which seemed so heavy it swayed his back to carry it.

The animal vivacity of his small eyes and the flexibility of his eyebrows, which he worked up and down rapidly with every change of countenance, expressed his eager desires.

He had laid aside his new shoes, which hurt him, and went barefooted to facilitate his movements on the great occasion. His heels projected and his foot was so flat that what should have been the hollow of it made a hole in the dirt where he left his track.

He was already mellow with liquor, and was dressed in an old army uniform and cap, with two horse-pistols buckled around his waist. On a strap hanging from his shoulder were strung a half-dozen tin canteens filled with whiskey.

tims. In the end, his analysis of the ultimate failure of Reconstruction blames the shortsightedness and incompleteness of the northern congressional program even more than southern violent resistance.

In the year of Tourgée's death, 1905, another North Carolinian published a novel, yet with a very different analysis of Reconstruction and its fate. Thomas Dixon was born during the Civil War. He was a lawyer, North Carolina state legislator, Baptist minister, lecturer, and novelist. *The Clansman*, subtitled "A Historical Romance of the Ku Klux Klan," reflects turn-of-the-century attitudes most white southerners still had about Republican rule during Reconstruction. According to Dixon, once the "Great Heart" Lincoln was gone, a power-crazed, vindictive radical Congress, led by scheming Austin Stoneman (Thaddeus Stevens), sought to impose corrupt carpetbagger and brutal black rule by bayonet on a helpless South. Only through the inspired leadership and redemptive role of the Ku Klux Klan was the South saved from the horrors of rape and revenge.

Dixon dedicated *The Clansman* to his uncle, a Grand Titan of the Klan in North Carolina during the time when two crucial counties were being transformed from Republican to Democratic majorities through intimidation and terror. No such violence shows up in Dixon's novel. Although *The Clansman* clearly twisted the truth of many historical events, it is an accurate and faithful representation of a dominant attitude southerners—and northerners as well—had about those events. When the novel was made the basis of D. W. Griffith's film classic, *Birth of a Nation*, in 1915, these attitudes were firmly imprinted on the twentieth-century American mind.

Both novels convey the events and attitudes of the era by creating clearly defined heroes and villains. Both include exciting chase scenes, narrow escapes, daring rescues, and tragic, heart-throbbing deaths. Both include romantic subplots in which a young white southern man falls in love with a young white northern woman. In each novel, however, the author's primary purpose was to convey his views of the politics of Reconstruction. The romantic elements were added, like sugarcoating around a pill, to make readers enjoy the medicine the novelist wanted them to take. The following are two brief excerpts from each novel, a poor substitute for reading them in their entirety. Notice the obvious differences of style and attitude in the descriptions of Uncle Jerry and Old Aleck.

details, of the events in Tourgée's novel. While exposing the brutality of the Klan, Tourgée includes loyal southern Unionists, respectable planters ashamed of Klan violence, and even guilt-ridden poor white klansmen who try to protect or warn intended vic-

form of "justice" to some black militiamen who had been arrested for parading on Independence Day. Although the Ku Klux Klan's power was officially ended, the attitudes (and tactics) of Klansmen were not.

The American people, like their leaders, were tired of the battles over the freedmen and were shifting their attention to other matters than fulfilling idealistic principles. Frustrated with the difficulties of trying to transform an unwilling South and seemingly ungrateful blacks, the easiest course was to give blacks their citizenship and the vote and move on to something else. After the interruptions of civil war and its aftermath, most Americans were primarily interested in starting families, finding work, and making money. This meant firing furnaces in the new steel plant in Wheeling, West Virginia, pounding in railroad ties for the Central Pacific in the Nevada desert, struggling to teach in a one-room schoolhouse in Vermont for $23 a month, or battling heat, locusts, and railroad rates on a family homestead in Kansas.

There was "reconstruction" going on in the North as well as the South—an accelerating economic revolution of enormous proportions. As Klansmen met in dark forests to plan their next raid in North Carolina in 1869, the Central Pacific and Union Pacific railroads met at Promontory Point, Utah, completing the transcontinental railroad. As black farmers were "haggling" over work contracts with white landowners in Georgia, the National Labor Union and Knights of Labor were being organized by white workers in Pennsylvania. As southern white tenant farmers found themselves more alienated from rich landowners and merchants, midwestern farmers were organizing the National Grange of the Patrons of Husbandry. And as economic relationships changed, so did the Republican party.

Heralded by the tone of moderation in the state election of 1867 and the national election of Grant in 1868, the Republicans had changed from the party of moral reform to one of material interest. In the continuing struggle in American politics between "virtue and commerce," commerce was again winning. No longer willing to support an agency like the Freedmen's Bureau, Republican politicians had no difficulty supporting huge grants of money and land to the

To most northerners, the Civil War's end meant renewing family ties and resuming the routine of life at home, as shown in this 1868 Currier & Ives print.

railroads. As blacks were told to go to work and help themselves, the Union Pacific was being given subsidies of between $16,000 and $48,000 for each mile of track laid across western plains and mountains. As Susan B. Anthony and others were tramping through the snows of upstate New York with petitions for rights of suffrage and citizenship, Boss Tweed and others were defrauding the citizen-taxpayers of New York of millions of dollars by construction and other boondoggles. The fraudulent railroad bonds in southern states were minor crimes compared to the extent of official graft in northern cities and state governments, as well as at the federal level.

A sordid grasping for wealth and power emerged in the nation around 1869, the year financier Jay Gould almost succeeded in cornering the gold market. Henry Adams, the descendant of two presidents, was a young man living in Washington, D.C., during this era. As he wrote later in his autobiography, *The Education of Henry Adams* (1907), he had high expectations in 1869 that Grant, like another "great soldier" and president, George Washington, would restore the moral order and peace that the nation needed. But when Grant announced the members of his cabinet, a group of Army cronies and rich friends to whom he owed favors, Adams felt betrayed, complaining that "a great soldier might be a baby politician."

Ulysses Grant himself was an honest man,

but his judgment of integrity in others was flawed. During his administration occurred a series of scandals that touched several cabinet officers and relatives and even two vice-presidents. Under Grant's appointments, outright graft, as well as loose prosecution and generally negligent administration, flourished in a half dozen departments. Most scandals involved large sums of public money. The Whiskey Ring affair, for example, cost the public millions of dollars in lost tax revenues siphoned off to government officials. Gould's gold scam received the unwitting aid of Grant's Treasury Department and the knowing help of his brother-in-law.

Nor was Congress pure in these various schemes. The Crédit Mobilier was the largest of several scandals in which construction companies for transcontinental railroads (in this case a dummy company) received generous bonds and work contracts in exchange for giving congressmen gifts of money, stocks, and railroad lands. An Ohio congressmen described the House of Representatives in 1873 as "an auction room where more valuable considerations were disposed of under the speaker's hammer than any place on earth." Henry Adams spoke for many Americans when he said that Grant's administration "outraged every rule of decency."

In a novel written about Washington life during this period called *Democracy* (1880), Adams's main character, Mrs. Madeleine Lee, sought to uncover "the heart of the great American mystery of democracy and government." What she found were corrupt legislators and lobbyists in an unprincipled pursuit of power and wealth. "Surely something can be done to check corruption?" Mrs. Lee asked her friend one evening. "Are we forever to be at the mercy of thieves and ruffians? Is a respectable government impossible in a democracy?" The answer she heard was hardly reassuring: "No responsible government can long be much better or much worse than the society it represents."

Was the whole postwar society at fault, then, for this decline in public morality? What had become of the ideals and humanitarian efforts of an earlier generation of Americans? For the time being, at least, they were replaced by attention to the further development of industry, the making of inventions, the building of transcontinental railroads, and the settlement of the western agricultural, cattle, and mining frontiers. Throughout the land, it was an age of materialistic "go-getters" (see Chapters 18 and 19).

The election of 1872 marked the decline of public interest in moral issues. A "liberal" faction of the Republican party, unable to dislodge Grant, broke off and nominated Horace Greeley, editor of the New York *Tribune*, for president. The liberal Republicans advocated free trade, which meant lower tariffs and fewer grants to railroads, and honest, limited government, which meant civil service reform and noninterference in southern race relations. Democrats, lacking notable presidential candidates, also nominated Greeley, even though he had spent much of his earlier career assailing Democrats as "rascals." Despite his wretched record, Grant easily won a second term. Greeley was beaten so badly, he said, that "I hardly knew whether I was running for the Presidency or the Penitentiary." He died three weeks later.

The End of Reconstruction

Soon after Grant's second inauguration, a financial panic, caused by overconstruction of railroads and the collapse of some crucial eastern banks, created a terrible depression that lasted throughout the mid-1870s. In times of economic hardship, economic issues dominated politics, further pulling attention away from the plight of the freedmen. As Democrats took control of the House of Representatives in 1874 and looked toward winning the White House in 1876, politicians talked about such issues as new scandals in the Grant administration, General Custer's shocking defeat in the Big Horn Mountains of Montana, unemployment and various proposals for public works expenditures for relief, the availability of silver and greenback dollars, and high tariffs.

No one, it seemed, talked much about the rights and conditions of southern freedmen. Senator Charles Sumner's civil rights bill, intended to put teeth into the Fourteenth Amendment, was passed in 1875 by a guilty Congress largely out of respect for Sumner's death during the debates. But the act was not enforced and was declared unconstitutional by the Supreme Court eight years later. Congressional Reconstruction, long dormant, had ended. The election of 1876 sealed the conclusion.

As their nominee for president in 1876, the Republicans turned to a former governor of Ohio, Rutherford B. Hayes, partly because of his reputation for honesty, partly because he had been an officer in the Union army (a necessity for post–Civil War candidates), and partly because, as Henry Adams put it, he was "obnoxious to no one." The Democrats chose Governor Samuel J. Tilden of New York, who achieved national recognition as a civil service reformer in breaking up the corrupt Tweed Ring.

Tilden won a majority of the popular vote and appeared to have enough electoral votes for victory. Twenty more electoral votes were disputed, all but one in the Deep South states of Louisiana, South Carolina, and Florida, where some federal troops still remained on duty and where Republicans still controlled the voting apparatus. Democrats, however, had applied various versions of the Mississippi Plan to intimidate voters. As one astute reporter put it, the Republican party in the South was "dead as a doornail." How to resolve the disputed electoral votes? Congress created a special electoral commission consisting of five senators, five representatives, and five Supreme Court justices, seven of whom were Democrats and eight Republicans. The vote in each disputed case was 8 to 7 along party lines. Hayes was given all 20 votes, enough to win, 185 to 184.

The Democrats were furious and threatened to stop the Senate from officially counting the electoral votes and thus prevent Hayes's inauguration. The country was in a state of crisis, and some wondered if civil war might start again. But unlike the 1850s, when passions over slavery were aroused, this time compromise was possible on a basis of mutual interests between northerners and southerners interested in modernization of the southern economy through capital investments. They focused on a Pacific railroad linking New Orleans with the West Coast. Southerners wanted northern dollars but not northern political influence. This meant no social agencies, no federal enforcement of the Fourteenth and Fifteenth amendments, and no military occupation, not even the small symbolic presence left in 1876.

As the inauguration date approached, and as newspapers echoed outgoing President Grant's call for "peace at any price," the forces of mutual self-interest concluded "the compromise of 1877." The Democrats agreed to suspend their resistance to the counting of the electoral votes, and on March 2, Rutherford B. Hayes was declared president. In exchange for the presidency, Hayes ordered the last remaining troops out of the South, appointed a former Confederate general to his cabinet, supported federal aid to bolster economic and railroad development in the South, and announced his intentions to let southerners handle race relations themselves. He then went on a goodwill trip to the South, where he told blacks in an Atlanta speech that "your rights and interests would be safer if this great mass of intelligent white men were let alone by the general government." The message was clear: Hayes would not enforce the Fourteenth and Fifteenth amendments, thus initiating a pattern of executive inaction not broken until the middle of the twentieth century. But the immediate crisis was averted, officially ending the era of Reconstruction.

CONCLUSION: The Price of Peace

The compromise of 1877 cemented the reunion of South and North. In blustery speeches, American statesmen boasted about the opportunities for economic development based on the reconciliation between the formerly estranged sections. Republican party dominance in the White House, though not in Congress, was preserved, with three exceptions, until 1932. In the 12 years between Appomattox and Hayes's inauguration, the diverse dreams of victorious northern Republicans, defeated white southerners, and hopeful black freedmen had conflicted with each other. There was little chance that all could be fulfilled. The peace of 1877 was preserved "at any price," and the price was paid by the freedmen.

In 1880, Frederick Douglass summarized the tragedy of Reconstruction for the freedmen:

> Our Reconstruction measures were radically defective. . . . To the freedmen was given the machinery of liberty, but here was denied to them the steam to put it in motion. They were given the uniform of soldiers, but no arms; they were called citizens, but left subjects; they were called free, but left almost slaves. The old master class . . . retained the power to starve them to death, and wherever this power is held there is the power of slavery.

Douglass went on to say, however, that as he examined the great strides blacks had made in economic survival and education, it was a wonder to him "not that freedmen have made so little progress, but, rather, that they have made so much; not that they have been standing still, but that they have been able to stand at all."

A few years later, W. E. B. Du Bois wrote a short story about two boyhood playmates, one black and one white, from the fictional town of Altamaha, Georgia. Both young men were named John and both were sent north to school to prepare for leadership of their respective communities, the black John as a teacher and the white John as a judge and possible governor of the state. While they were away, the black and white people of Altamaha, each race thinking of its own John and not of the other, except with "a vague unrest," waited for "the coming of two young men, and dreamed . . . of new things that would be done and new thoughts that all would think."

After several years, both Johns returned to Altamaha, but the hopes and dreams of a new era of racial justice and harmony were shattered by a series of tragic events. Neither John understood the people of the town, and each was in turn misunderstood. Black John's school was closed because he was teaching ideals of liberty. Heartbroken and discouraged as he walked through the forest near town, he surprised the white John in an attempted rape of his sister. Without a word, black John picked up a fallen limb and with "all the pent-up hatred of his great black arm" smashed his boyhood playmate to death. Within hours he was lynched.

Du Bois's story capsulizes the human cost of the Reconstruction era. The black scholar's hope for reconciliation by "a union of intelligence and sympathy across the color-line" was smashed in the tragic encounter between the two Johns. Both young men, each once filled with glorious dreams, lay dead under the pines of the Georgia forest. Dying with them were hopes that interracial harmony, intersectional trust, and humane, just, equal opportunities and rights for the freedmen might be the legacies of Reconstruction. Conspicuously absent in the forest scene was the influence of the victorious northerners. They had turned their attention to other, less noble causes.

Recommended Reading

The two best brief overviews of the Reconstruction era are John Hope Franklin, *Reconstruction After the Civil War* (1961) and Kenneth Stampp, *The Era of Reconstruction, 1865–1877* (1965). A recent collection of essays on the issues of the era can be found in Morgan Kousser and James M. McPherson, eds., *Region, Race, and Reconstruction: Essays in Honor of C. Vann Woodward* (1982). For a controversial but brilliantly insightful analysis of Reconstruction from a black perspective, see W. E. B. Du Bois, *Black Reconstruction* (1935) and *The Souls of Black Folk* (1903).

The fullest, most moving account of the black experience in the transition from slavery to freedom is Leon Litwack's massive and sensitive work, *Been in the Storm So Long: The Aftermath of Slavery* (1980). See also Willie Lee Rose, *Rehearsal for Reconstruction* (1964), an account of the earliest adjustments to freedom in the Sea Islands. The southern white response to emancipation is described in James Roark, *Masters Without Slaves: Southern Planters in the Civil War and Reconstruction* (1977).

The economy of the South and the freedmen's experience with land are described in Roger Ransom and Richard Sutch, *One Kind of Freedom: The Economic Consequencs of Emancipation* (1977). A more optimistic view is in Robert Higgs, *Competition and Coercion: Blacks in the American Economy, 1865–1914* (1977). An excellent new work showing the white experience with tenancy in the changing economy of the South is Stephen Hahn, *The Roots of Southern Populism* (1983). For an excellent view of the New South, see C. Vann Woodward, *Origins of the New South, 1877–1913* (1951). The Freedmen's Bureau has been the subject of several studies, the best of which are Peter Kolchin, *First Freedom* (1972); Claude

Oubré, *Forty Acres and a Mule: The Freedmen's Bureau and Black Land Ownership* (1978); and Donald Nieman, *To Set the Law in Motion: The Freedmen's Bureau and the Legal Rights of Blacks, 1865–1868* (1979). Continuing racial prejudice in the South and North is the subject of C. Vann Woodward, *The Strange Career of Jim Crow*, 3d rev. ed. (1974) and Rayford Logan, *The Betrayal of the Negro*, rev. ed (1965).

Northern politics during Reconstruction have been widely discussed. See LaWanda Cox and John Cox, *Politics, Principles, and Prejudice, 1865–1866* (1963); Eric McKitrick, *Andrew Johnson and Reconstruction* (1960); David Donald, *The Politics of Reconstruction* (1965); and Michael Les Benedict, *A Compromise of Principle: Congressional Republicans and Reconstruction, 1863–1869* (1974). Grant's presidency and the abandonment of the freedmen by northern Republicans can be traced in William McFeeley, *Grant: A Biography* (1981) and William Gillette, *Retreat from Reconstruction, 1869–1879* (1979). The campaign of violence that ended the Republican governments in the South is told with gripping horror in Allen Trelease, *White Terror: The Ku Klux Klan Conspiracy and Southern Reconstruction* (1971). The end of Reconstruction is the subject of C. Vann Woodward's classic little book *Reunion and Reaction* (1956).

Five novels written at different times and representing different interpretations of the story of Reconstruction are Albion Tourgée, *A Fool's Errand* (1879); Thomas Dixon, *The Clansman* (1905); W. E. B. Du Bois, *The Quest of the Silver Fleece* (1911); Howard Fast, *Freedom Road* (1944); and Ernest Gaines, *The Autobiography of Miss Jane Pittman* (1971).

TIME LINE

1865	Civil War ends
	Lincoln assassinated; Andrew Johnson becomes president
	Johnson proposes general amnesty and reconstruction plan
	Racial confusion, widespread hunger, and demobilization
	Thirteenth Amendment ratified
	Freedmen's Bureau established
1865–1866	
	Black codes
	Repossession of land by whites and freedmen's contracts
1866	Freedmen's Bureau renewed and Civil Rights Act passed over Johnson's veto
	Southern Homestead Act
	Ku Klux Klan formed
	Tennessee readmitted to Union
1867	Reconstruction Acts passed over Johnson's veto
	Impeachment controversy
	Freedmen's Bureau ends
1868	Fourteenth Amendment ratified
	Impeachment of Johnson fails
	Ulysses Grant elected president
1868–1870	Ten states readmitted under congressional plan
1869	Georgia and Virginia reestablish Democratic party control

1870	Fifteenth Amendment ratified
1870s–1880s	Black "exodusters" migrate to Kansas
1870–1871	Force Acts
	North Carolina and Georgia reestablish Democratic control
1872	General Amnesty Act
	Grant reelected president
1873	Crédit Mobilier scandal
	Panic causes depression
1874	Alabama and Arkansas reestablish Democratic control
1875	Civil Rights Act
	Mississippi reestablishes Democratic control
1876	Hayes-Tilden election
1876–1877	South Carolina, Louisiana, and Florida reestablish Democratic control
1877	Compromise of 1877; Rutherford B. Hayes assumes presidency and ends Reconstruction
1880s	Tenancy and sharecropping prevail in the South
	Disfranchisement and segregation of southern blacks begins

PART FOUR
AN INDUSTRIALIZING PEOPLE

1865–1900

In the last half of the nineteenth century, Americans rapidly left the problems of the Civil War era behind and turned their energies toward transforming their society from one based on agriculture to one based on heavy industry. This economic and social transition was neither smooth nor steady. But by 1900, the United States had emerged as one of the world's great industrial powers.

Chapters 18, 19, and 20 form a unit. Chapter 18, "The Farmer's World," examines the ways in which American farmers modernized and vastly expanded production after the Civil War. Even though agriculture provided the basis for urban industrial development, many farmers did not win the rewards they had anticipated. The South remained backward despite efforts to modernize. Rural protest publicized farmers' complaints and contributed to the formation of a powerful third party. While the postwar period was difficult for some farmers, it was disastrous for Native Americans. By 1900, the power of the Plains Indians had been broken and the reservation system finally set in place.

Chapter 19, "The Rise of Smokestack America," focuses on the character of industrial progress and urban expansion. We explore the growing diversity of the American work force and its various experiences in and responses to the new world of industry. The labor conflicts of the period indicate the difficulty of these years for most working-class Americans.

In Chapter 20, "Politics and Protest," we turn to middle-class Americans, the first to benefit from industrial progress. Despite their many comforts and opportunities, however, middle-class Americans had concerns that led them to play an increasing role in urban, state, and national politics. Usually they worked for moderate reform, which they hoped would bring about human betterment and social harmony.

Chapter 21, "The United States Becomes a World Power," demonstrates the international consequences of the country's successful industrialization. Like other world powers, the United States nourished imperial ambitions in the 1890s and acquired its own colonies. But expansionism brought difficult dilemmas in America's relationship with the rest of the world. After 1900, the United States continued to play a more active role in international affairs but stood aside from the race for colonies.

CULTURAL and TECHNOLOGICAL

1860s Bessemer and open-hearth steel processes introduced

1865 Vassar College founded
1866 Atlantic Cable laid
1867 First Horatio Alger novels published
First elevated railway in New York City
1869 First transcontinental railroad link completed

1870 Thomas Edison invents stock ticker
1870s Expansion of public schools and higher education begins

1873 Mark Twain and Charles Dudley Warner coin the expression "Gilded Age"
1874 Barbed wire patented
First electric streetcar runs in New York City

1875 Wellesley College founded
First running of the Kentucky Derby
1876 Centennial Exposition in Philadelphia
Alexander Graham Bell invents telephone
First major baseball league formed
1877 Mark Twain, *Adventures of Tom Sawyer*
C. H. Hines begins making root beer

1879 Henry George, *Progress and Poverty*
Light bulb perfected

1880s Social Darwinism and Social Gospel
1881 Tuskegee Institute founded

1883 Brooklyn Bridge
1884 W. D. Howells, *The Rise of Silas Lapham*

SOCIAL and ECONOMIC

1866 National Labor Union founded
1867 National Grange founded
1868 Eight-hour day for federal employees
1869 Prohibition party formed
Knights of Labor formed

1870 Wyoming Territory grants suffrage to women
J. D. Rockefeller forms Standard Oil of Ohio
1870s Tweed Ring exposed
1872 Chicago fire
Yellowstone National Park established
Montgomery Ward, first mail-order house, opens
1873 Bethlehem Steel begins production
1873–1879 Depression
1874 Women's Christian Temperance Union founded
Greenback party formed

1875–1876 Indian Wars in Black Hills

1877 Nez Percé Indian uprisings
Black exodusters to Kansas
Railroad strikes

1880s "New South"

1882 Standard Oil Trust established
1883–1885 Depression
1884 Southern Farmers' Alliance founded

POLITICAL

1867 Alaska purchased
1868–1874 "Granger" Laws

1871 Indian Appropriation Act
Army suppresses Apache

1875 Specie Resumption Act
United States–Hawaii commercial treaty

1877 Rutherford B. Hayes becomes president
Munn v. Illinois
1878 Bland-Allison Act

1880 James A. Garfield elected
1880s Bossism and urban reform
1881 Garfield assassinated; Chester A. Arthur becomes president
1882 Chinese Exclusion Act
1883 Pendleton Civil Service Act
1884 Grover Cleveland elected

1865–1900

CULTURAL and TECHNOLOGICAL

1888   Edward Bellamy, *Looking Backward*
1889   Andrew Carnegie, "The Gospel of Wealth"

1890s   Electric trolleys
1890   Alfred Thayer Mahan, *Influence of Sea Power upon History*
1891   Hamlin Garland, *Main-Travelled Roads*

1893   Stephen Crane, *Maggie: A Girl of the Streets*
World's Exposition in Chicago
City Beautiful movement

1895   Elizabeth Cady Stanton, *Woman's Bible*
1896   Charles Sheldon, *In His Steps*
1898   Charlotte Perkin Gilman, *Women and Economics*

1899   John Dewey, *School and Society*

1900   Theodore Dreiser, *Sister Carrie*

SOCIAL and ECONOMIC

1885   "New Immigration"
1886   AFL founded
Haymarket Riot
1887   College Settlement House Association founded
1888   Colored Farmers' Alliance established
1889   Hull House founded
1889–1890   Ghost Dance
Battle of Wounded Knee

1890   General Federation of Women's Clubs founded
National American Women Suffrage Association formed
1892   Homestead strike
1893   Anti-Saloon League founded
1893–1897   Depression
1894   Pullman strike
Coxey's march

1895   Atlanta Compromise speech

POLITICAL

1887   Dawes Act
Interstate Commerce Act
1888   Benjamin Harrison elected

1890   Sherman Anti-Trust Act
Sherman Silver Purchase Act
McKinley Tariff
1890s   Jim Crow laws and disfranchisement attempts in the South
1892   Populist Party formed
Cleveland elected to second term
1893   Hawaiian coup by American sugar growers

1895   Cuban Revolution
United States v. E. C. Knight
1896   William McKinley elected
Plessy v. Ferguson
1898   Sinking of the *Maine*
Spanish-American War
Treaty of Paris
Annexation of Hawaii and the Philippines
1899–1900   Open Door notes
1899–1902   Philippine-American War

1900   Boxer Rebellion in China
1901   McKinley assassinated; Theodore Roosevelt becomes president
1902   Platt Amendment
1904   Roosevelt Corollary

CHAPTER 18
THE FARMER'S WORLD

In 1873, Milton Leeper, his wife Hattie, and their baby Anna climbed into a wagon piled high with their possessions and set out to homestead in Boone County, Nebraska. Once on the claim, the Leepers confidently dreamed of their future. Wrote Hattie to her sister in Iowa, "I like our place the best of any around here." "When we get a fine house and 100 acres under cultivation," she added, "I wouldn't trade with any one." But Milton had broken in only 13 acres when disaster struck. Hordes of grasshoppers appeared, and the Leepers fled their claim and took refuge in the nearby town of Fremont.

There they stayed for two years. Milton worked first at a store, then hired out to other farmers. Hattie sewed, kept a boarder, and cared for chickens and a milk cow. The family lived on the brink of poverty but never gave up hope. "Times are hard and we have had bad luck," Hattie acknowledged, but "I am going to hold that claim . . . there will [be] one gal that won't be out of a home." In 1876, the Leepers triumphantly returned to their claim with a modest sum of $27 to help them start over.

The grasshoppers were gone, there was enough rain, and preaching was only half a mile away. The Leepers, like others, began to prosper. Two more daughters were born and cared for in the comfortable sod house, "homely" on the outside but plastered and cozy within. As Hattie explained, the homesteaders lived "just as civilized as they would in Chicago."

Their luck did not last. Hattie, pregnant again, fell ill and died in childbirth along with her infant son. Heartbroken, Milton buried his wife and child and left the claim. The last frontier had momentarily defeated him, although he would try farming in at least four other locations before his death in 1905.

The Leepers' failure to establish a successful homestead reflected some of the constraints of rural life in the late nineteenth century. Another farmer described the paradoxical rewards of bountiful crops. "We were told two years ago to go to work and raise a big crop; that was all we needed. We went to work and plowed and planted; the rains fell, the sun shone, nature smiled, and we raised the big crop they told us to; and what came of it? Eight cent corn, ten cent oats, two cent beef and no price at all for butter and eggs—that's what came of it." Still a third perspective on the agricultural frontier comes from Red Cloud, a Sioux, who told railroad surveyors in Wyoming, "We do not want you here. You are scaring away the buffalo."

This chapter focuses on the experiences of red, white, and black rural Americans in the late nineteenth century. During these years, farmers joined the modern industrial world. With the help of machinery, they enormously expanded land under cultivation, produced bumper crops, and shipped them by railroad to markets. They hoped to profit from the country's economic transformation at the same time that they contributed to it by providing cheap food for industrial workers. Yet all too frequently, farmers felt cheated by the unpredictable and often meager rewards they received. Their anguish did not match that of the Native Americans, who were robbed of their land, nor of American black farmers mired in debt peonage. But their pain was sharp enough to turn some into critics of American life and to push others into politics.

THE MODERNIZATION OF AGRICULTURE

Between 1865 and 1900, the nation's farms more than doubled in number as Americans pushed into the vast areas west of the Mississippi and broke virgin land. In both newly settled and older areas, farmers raised specialized crops with the aid of modern machinery and relied on the expanding railroad system to send them to market (see Chapter 19). The character of agriculture became increasingly capitalistic. Farmers, as one New Englander pointed out, "must understand farming as a business; if they do not it will go hard with them."

Rural Myth and Reality

The number of Americans who still farmed the land testified to the continuing vitality of the rural tradition. In the late eighteenth century, Benjamin Franklin praised "industrious frugal farmers," who populated the country's interior, while Thomas Jefferson viewed them as the "deposit for substantial and genuine virtue" and fundamental to the health of the republic.

The notion that the farmer and farm life symbolized the essence of America persisted as the United States industrialized. The popularity of inexpensive Currier and Ives prints, depicting idyllic rural scenes, suggests how captivated Americans were by the idealized view of country life. Healthy, well-dressed, vigorous farmers are the sturdy yeomen of Jefferson's imagination. Farm wives appear robust and attractive, apparently satisfied with the rhythms of country life. Rural children amuse themselves in pleasant diversions—skating, fishing, riding on wagons, gathering fruit. They live in solid, cozy houses. All is well in the countryside.

Another set of Currier and Ives prints implied that there need be no conflict between the new technological industrial world and rural America. Trains, representing the new, chug peacefully through farmlands, while cheering children and trusting adults look on. Railroads bring progress but not the destruction of the land or the livelihood of those on it.

The prints were nostalgic wishful thinking. However much Americans wanted to believe that no tension existed between technological

Average Farm Acreage, 1860–1900

REGION	1860	1870	1880	1890	1900
Land in Farms (1,000 acres)					
United States	407,213	407,735	536,082	623,219	841,202
North Central	107,900	139,215	206,982	256,587	317,349
South	225,514	189,556	234,920	256,606	362,036
West	12,718	16,219	26,194	47,282	96,407
Northeast	61,082	62,744	67,986	62,744	65,409
Average Acreage per Farm (acres)					
United States	199	153	134	137	147
North Central	140	124	122	133	145
South	335	214	153	140	138
West	367	336	313	324	393
Northeast	108	104	98	95	97

Source: U.S. Bureau of the Census.

Agriculture in the 1880s

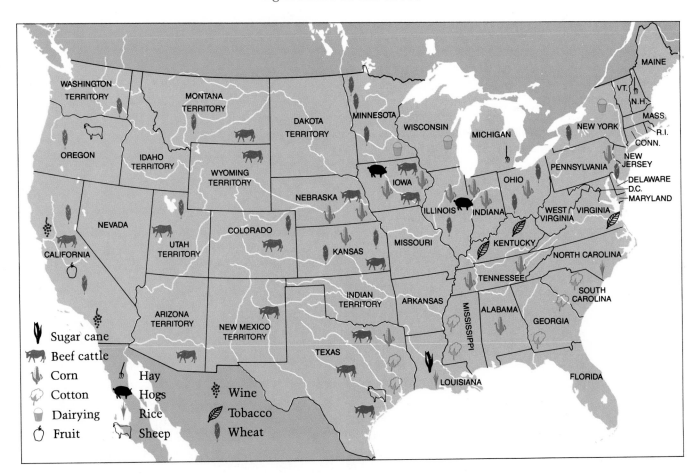

Sugar cane
Beef cattle
Corn   Hay
Cotton   Hogs   Wine
Dairying   Rice   Tobacco
Fruit   Sheep   Wheat

progress and agriculture, it did. Farmers were no longer the backbone of the work force. In 1860, they represented almost 60 percent of the labor force; by 1900, less than 37 percent of employed Americans were farmers. At the same time, farmers' contribution to the nation's wealth declined from a third to a quarter.

Nor were farmers the independent yeomen of the rural myth. They were increasingly entangled with the industrial and urban world. Reliable, cheap transportation allowed them to specialize in the market crop most suited to their location. Farmers on the Great Plains now grew most of the country's wheat, while those in the Midwest replaced that crop with corn, which they used as feed for their hogs and cattle. Eastern farmers turned to vegetable, fruit, and dairy farming. Some, like Milachi Dodge from New Hampshire, gave up farming altogether. As he explained, when his "boys came home" from the Civil War, "they did not want to work on a farm, and I sold my farm out." Cotton continued to dominate the economy of the South, although tobacco, wheat, and rice were also cultivated there. In the Far West, grain, fruits, and vegetables predominated.

As farmers specialized in cash crops for national and international markets, their success depended increasingly on outside forces and demands. Bankers and loan companies provided the necessary capital to expand farm operations, middlemen stored and sometimes sold produce, railroads carried farm goods to market. A prosperous American economy put money into laborers' pockets for food purchases. Even international conditions affected the American farmer. After 1870, exports of wheat, flour, and animal products rose, with wheat becoming the country's chief cash crop. Thus the cultivation of wheat in Russia and Argentina meant fewer foreign buyers for American grain. The decision of several European countries between 1879 and 1883 to ban American pork imports, which they feared were infected with trichinosis, translated into losses for American stock raisers.

Farming had become a modern business.

The appeal of an idealized view of life helps to explain the popularity of Currier & Ives prints in mid-nineteenth century America.

"Watch and study the markets and the ways of marketmen . . . learn the art of 'selling well,'" one rural editor advised his readers in 1887. "The work of farming is only half done when the crop is out of the ground." Like other businesses of the post–Civil War era, farming depended more and more on machinery. "It is no longer necessary for the farmer to cut his wheat with sickle or cradle, nor to rake it and bind it by hand; to cut his cornstalks with a knife and shock the stalks by hand; to thresh his grain with a flail," reported one observer. Harvesters, binders, and other new machines, pulled by work animals, performed these tasks for him.

These machines diminished much of the drudgery of farming life and made the production of crops easier, more efficient, and cheaper. Moreover, they allowed a farmer to cultivate far more land than he had been able to do with hand tools, so that by 1900 more than twice as much land was in cultivation as there had been in 1860. But machinery was expensive, and many American farmers had to borrow to buy it. In the decade of the 1880s, mortgage indebtedness grew 2½ times faster than agricultural wealth.

New Farmers, New Farms

As farmers became dependent on machinery, brought new land into cultivation, raised specialized crops, and sent them to faraway markets, they operated much like other nineteenth-century businessmen. Some even became large-scale entrepreneurs. Small family farms still typified American agriculture, but vast mechanized operations, devoted to the cultivation of one crop, appeared, especially west of the Mississippi River. These farms had a few huge barns for storage of machinery and a handful of other farm buildings but few gardens, trees, or outbuildings. No churches or villages interrupted the monotony of the landscape.

The bonanza farms, established in the late 1870s on the northern plains, symbolized the trend to large-scale agriculture. Thousands of acres in size, these wheat farms required large capital investments (many were, in fact, owned by corporations) and depended on machinery, a hired work force, and efficient managers. The farm that Oliver Dalrymple operated for two Northern Pacific Railroad directors used 200 pairs of harrows and 125 seeders for planting. Harvesting the grain required 155 binders and 26 steam threshers. At peak times, the farm's work force numbered 600 men. The result was a harvest of 600,000 bushels of wheat in 1882. Although bonanza farms were not typical, they highlighted the dramatic agricultural changes that were occurring everywhere on a smaller scale.

Bonanza farms, a development of the 1870s, foreshadowed the agribusiness concerns of the twentieth century.

Agricultural Productivity, 1800–1900

CROP AND PRODUCTIVITY INDICATOR	1800	1840	1880	1900
Wheat				
Worker-hours/acre	56	35	20	15
Yield/acre (bushels)	15	15	13	14
Worker-hours/100 bushels	373	233	152	108
Corn				
Worker-hours/acre	86	69	46	38
Yield/acre (bushels)	25	25	26	26
Worker-hours/100 bushels	344	276	180	147
Cotton				
Worker-hours/acre	185	135	119	112
Yield/acre (pounds of lint)	147	147	179	191
Worker-hours/bale	601	439	318	280

Source: U.S. Bureau of the Census.

Overproduction and Falling Prices

Farmers so fervently subscribed to the rural myth captured by Currier and Ives that they did not initially realize that the technology they embraced might backfire. Gradually they began to discover unanticipated problems as they cultivated more land with the assistance of machinery. Productivity rose 40 percent between 1869 and 1899. Almost every crop showed impressive statistical gains. The yields for some crops like wheat were so large, however, that the domestic market could not absorb them.

The prices farm products commanded steadily declined. In 1867, corn sold for 78 cents a bushel. By 1873, it had fallen to 31 cents, and by 1889 to 23 cents. Wheat similarly plummeted from about $2 a bushel in 1867 to only 70 cents a bushel in 1889. Cotton profits also spiraled downward, the value of a bale depreciating from $43.60 in 1866 to $30.00 in the 1890s.

This pattern of falling prices did not automatically hurt farmers. The late nineteenth century was a deflationary period. Because paper money was withdrawn gradually after the Civil War and not much silver was coined, the supply of money rose more slowly than productivity. As a result, prices fell by more than half between the end of the Civil War and 1900. Farmers were getting less for their crops but were also paying less for their purchases.

Deflation may have encouraged overproduction, however. To make the same amount of money, it seemed to many farmers that they had to raise larger and larger crops. As they did, prices fell even lower. Furthermore, deflation increased the real value of debts. In 1888, it took 174 bushels of wheat to pay the interest on a $2,000 mortgage at 8 percent. By 1895, it took 320 bushels.

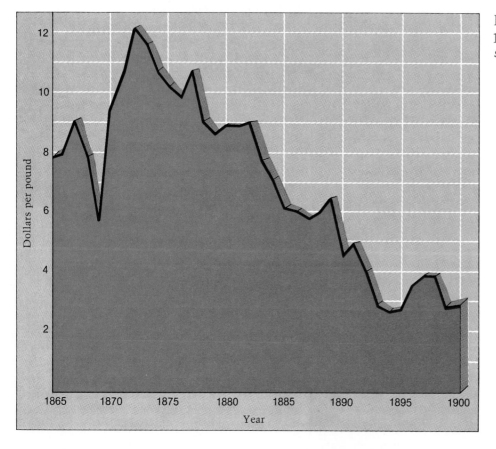

Price of Wheat Flour, 1865–1900

Source: U.S. Bureau of the Census.

Farming on the Great Plains

Between 1870 and 1900, the acreage devoted to farming tripled west of the Mississippi. The rapid expansion of land under cultivation was closely linked to the opening of the Great Plains (North and South Dakota, Kansas, Nebraska, Oklahoma, and Texas) to agricultural settlement.

In the mid-nineteenth century, farmers had passed over the Plains, regarding them as unsuitable for farming, and continued on to the Far West. Views of the farming potential of the Plains changed after the Civil War, however. Railroads eager for business as they laid down new lines, town boosters eager for inhabitants, and land speculators eager to sell their holdings all undertook major promotional efforts to persuade farmers to settle the Plains. "This is the sole remaining section of paradise in the western world; all the wild romances of the gorgeous orient dwindle into nothing when compared to the everyday realities of Dakota's progress," one newspaper exclaimed. "All that is needed is to plow, plant and attend to the crops properly; the rains are abundant." The rainfall, which was above average for the region in the 1880s, seemed to substantiate the argument regarding adequate moisture.

Industrial innovations of the late nineteenth century also facilitated the expansion of agriculture. At approximately the 98th meridian, the prairies with their tall grasses merged into the short grasses of the Plains. Few trees grew there, and this was one reason why emigrants chose not to stop. Only with a cheap fencing material to replace wood could the Great Plains states be settled and cultivated. The breakthrough occurred in the 1870s, when Joseph Glidden, a visitor to a county fair, noticed an exhibit that featured a strip of wood with protruding points. The device was to hang on fences to keep animals out. Why not, thought Glidden, make fencing wire with protruding barbs? Before long, he and a partner were mass-producing hundreds of miles of barbed wire fencing, as were their eager competitors. The region's unpredictable weather posed another kind of problem, especially at harvest time. Twine binders, which speeded up the grain harvesting, minimized the possibility of crop loss. Water shortages were relieved by the 1890s, when mail-order steel windmills for pumping water from deep underground wells became available.

In the first boom period of settlement, lasting from 1879 to the early 1890s, tens of thousands of eager families like the Leepers moved onto the Great Plains and began farming. Some made claims under the Homestead Act, which granted 160 acres to any family head or adult who lived on the claim for five years or who paid $1.25 an acre after six months of residence. Because homestead land was frequently less desirable than land held by railroads and speculators, however, most settlers bought land outright rather than taking up claims.

The costs of getting started were thus more substantial than the Homestead Act would suggest. Western land was cheap compared to farmland in the East, but an individual farmer was fortunate if he could buy a good quarter section for under $500. The costs of machinery would ultimately reach about $700. Although some farmers thought it made better economic sense to lease rather than to buy land, many had to rent because they lacked the capital to purchase land and set up operations. In 1880, some 20 percent of the Plains farmers were tenants, and this percentage rose over time.

Many of the new settlers were immigrants, making the Great Plains the second most important destination for them. The most numerous arrived from Germany, the British Isles, and Canada. Many Scandinavians, Czechs, and Poles also moved to the new frontier. Unlike the single male immigrants flocking to American cities for work, these newcomers came with their families. From the beginning, they intended to put down roots in the new country and stay.

Life on the Plains frontier often proved to be difficult. Wrote Miriam Peckham, a Kansas homesteader:

> I tell you Auntie no one can depend on farming for a living in this country. Henry is very industrious and this year had in over thirty acres of small grain, 8 acres of corn and about an acre of potatoes. We have sold our small grain . . . and it come to $100; now deduct $27.00 for cutting,

$16.00 for threshing, $19.00 for hired help, say nothing of boarding our help, none of the trouble of drawing 25 miles to market and 25 cts on each head for ferriage over the river and where is your profit. I sometimes think this a God forsaken country, the [grass]hopper hurt our corn and we have 1/2 a crop and utterly destroyed our garden. If one wants trials, let them come to Kansas.

Peckham's letter highlights the uncertainties of frontier life: the costs of machinery, the vagaries of crops and markets, the threat of pests and natural disasters. Her letter also points to the shortage of cash. Unlike earlier emigrants to the Far West, who had to have the means to finance the six-month trip, many Plains pioneers took up their homesteads with only a few dollars in their pockets. Frontier diaries often noted the marginality of early frontier operations, describing loans from family in the East and debts. The phrase "did not pay for it" occurs repeatedly. Survival often depended on how well the family managed to do during the crucial first years. If they succeeded in raising and selling their crops, they might accumulate the capital needed to continue. But if nature was harsh or their luck bad, or if they were unable to adjust to new conditions, the chances of failure were great.

Many settlers found the vast treeless plains depressing and even frightening. One New England visitor explained, "It has been terrible on settlers, on the women especially, for there is no society and they get doleful and feel almost like committing suicide for want of society." This was the point many authors chose to emphasize. O. E. Rolvaag's novel *Giants in the Earth* (1927) shows the wife of a Norwegian immigrant farmer driven to madness and death. Hamlin Garland's *Main-Travelled Roads* (1891) pictures overworked, hopeless women whom the frontier defeats. As Garland explained, he had written his stories in a "mood of resentment" after visiting "my mother on a treeless farm."

Life on the Plains was not always so discouraging as these authors suggest. Willa Cather, who spent her childhood in Nebraska, showed both the harshness and the lure of prairie life in her novels. Alexandra Bergson, the main character of *O Pioneers!* (1913), loves the land: "It

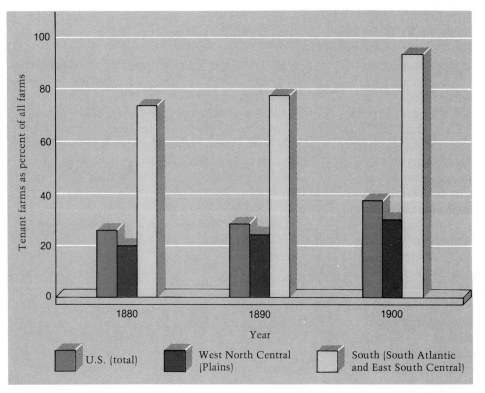

Percentage of Farms Operated by Tenants, 1880–1900

Source: U.S. Bureau of the Census.

seemed beautiful to her, rich and strong and glorious." The thousands of letters and diaries that survive from the period also provide a more positive picture of farming life. Elam Bartholemew's diary contains news of visitors, trips, and social events. In 1880, only six years after he had settled in northern Kansas, Elam's journal reveals that 1,081 people stopped at his home. His wife served 783 meals to visitors. Trips to church, parties, sings, and neighborhood get-togethers brightened family life. There were many occasions when the Bartholemews "enjoyed ourselves very much."

The Plains frontier required many adjustments, however. Scarce water and violent changes in temperature called for new modes of behavior and resourcefulness. Without firewood, farmers learned to burn corncobs and twisted wheat for warmth. The log cabin, long the symbol of frontier life, disappeared as inventive settlers discovered how to build houses of sod "bricks." Although from a distance such houses often looked like mounds of earth, "homely old things," as Hattie Leeper described them, they frequently had glass windows, wooden shingles, and even plastered interiors. Dark and gloomy to our eyes, they were comfortable, cozy, and practical for the settlers. Walls, 2 to 3

Unlike their counterparts farther east, Plains settlers were forced to abandon traditional modes of shelter. The Rawding family lived in a house with a sod roof in Nebraska in 1886.

feet thick, kept out the scorching summer heat and fierce cold of winter, the moaning winds, and the prairie fires. The solidity of the sod house provided a welcome contrast to the impersonal power and scale of nature.

The first boom on the Great Plains halted abruptly in the late 1880s and early 1890s. Falling agricultural prices reduced profits. Then, the unusual rainfall that had lured farmers to settle semiarid regions disappeared. A devastating drought followed. One farmer reported in 1890 that he had earned $41.48 from his wheat crop, yet his expenses for seed and threshing amounted to $56.00. Many were destitute and survived on boiled weeds, a few potatoes, and a little bread and butter. Although cash was scarce on the frontier, credit had not been. Many farmers had accumulated debts they now could not repay. Thousands lost their farms to creditors. Some stayed on as tenants. Homesteaders like the Leepers gave up. By 1900, two-thirds of homesteaded farms had failed. Many homesteaders fled east. In western Kansas, the population declined by half between 1888 and 1892. The wagons of those who retreated bore the epitaph of their experience: "In God We Trusted: In Kansas We Busted."

The Early Cattle Frontier

In the mid-1870s, two Plains settlers became embroiled in a conflict that symbolized the meeting of the farming and cattle frontiers. John Duncan was a cattleman and Peter Schmidt a German farmer. Duncan allowed his cattle to roam over the Plains and feed on its grasses. Some wandered onto Schmidt's property, devoured his corn, and destroyed his garden. Schmidt managed to run the cattle off but was outraged at the damage. For many years, such incidents had been rare, for few farmers were living on the Plains. As settlement increased in the 1880s and 1890s, they became more common.

The early cattle frontier was a post–Civil War phenomenon, rooted in Union military strategy. During the war, the North had split the South in two and cut Texas off from Confederate markets. At the end of the war, Texas had 5 million longhorns roaming the range. The postwar burst of railroad construction provided a way of turning cattle into dollars. If the cattle were driven north from Texas to railroad connections where they could then be shipped to slaughtering and packing houses in cities like Chicago and Kansas City, their value would soar. Thus started the first cattle drives, so well known through stories, movies, and television. In the late 1860s, cowboys herded thousands of longhorns north to towns like Abilene, Wichita, and Dodge City.

Some of the cattle were sold to ranchers on the Great Plains, where grasses were ripe for grazing. In the late 1870s and early 1880s, huge ranches appeared in eastern Colorado, Wyoming, and Montana and in western Kansas, Nebraska, and the Dakotas. These ventures, many owned by outside investors, paid off handsomely. Because the cattle could roam at will over the public domain, they cost owners little

The romantic figure of the cowboy sprang into the popular imagination from books of fiction illustrated by artists such as Frederick Remington.

as they fattened up. A Texas steer, bought for $7 or $8, could be set out to graze and then sold for $60 or $70. The cowboys (a third of them Mexican and black) who herded the steers, however, earned only meager wages of $25 and $40 a month, just enough to pay for a fling in the saloons, dance halls, and gambling palaces in Dodge City or Abilene when taking the cattle to market.

By the mid-1880s, the first phase of the cattle frontier was coming to an end. As the clash between Peter Schmidt and John Duncan indicated, farmers were moving onto the Plains, buying up public lands once used for grazing, and fencing them in. But the struggle between cattle ranchers and farmers was not the only reason for the cattle frontier's collapse. Eager to make as large a profit as possible, ranchers overstocked their herds in the mid-1880s. Hungry cattle ate everything in sight, then grew weak as grass became scarce. As was so often the case on the Plains, the weather had a part to play. A winter of memorable blizzards followed the very hot summer of 1885. Cattle, usually able to forage for themselves during the winter months, could not dig through the deep snow to the grass and died from starvation. By spring, 90 percent of the cattle were dead. As one cattleman's journal observed, "An overstocked range must bleed when the blizzards sit in judgment." Frantic owners dumped their remaining cattle on the market, getting $8 or even less for each animal.

In the aftermath, those ranchers who remained stock raisers adopted new techniques. Experimenting with new breeds, they began to replace their longhorns, to fence their herds in, and to feed them grain during the winter months. Consumers were hungering for tender beef rather than the tough flesh of animals who roamed the Plains in any case, and these new methods satisfied the market. Ranching, like farming, was becoming more a modern business and less the colorful adventure portrayed in popular culture.

Cornucopia on the Pacific

When gold was discovered in California, Americans rushed west to find it. But as one father told his eager son, "Plant your lands; these be your best gold fields." He was right; farming eventually proved to be California's greatest asset. But farming in California hardly resembled the rural life Currier and Ives depicted. Nor did it embody the hopes of the framers of the Homestead Act.

Although federal and state land policies supposedly promoted "homes for the homeless," little of California's land was actually homesteaded or developed as small family farms. When California entered the Union, Mexican ranchers held vast tracts of land, which never became part of the public domain. Neither Mexican-Americans nor small farmers profited from the 20 years of confusion over the legitimacy of Mexican land titles. Speculators did, and acquired much of the Californios' land. Consequently, small farmers faced steep prices when they wished to buy land. The costs of starting out in California were substantial. As Charles Reed observed in 1869, "Land which but two years ago could have been bought . . . for from $1 to $1.25 per acre cannot now be bought for less than $10 to $15 per acre."

Generous grants from the public domain (16 percent by 1880) were awarded to the railroads. Railroads encouraged settlers to put down roots, then sold the improved land to the highest bidder. In 1871, reformer Henry George described California as "not a country of farms but a country of plantations and estates. Agriculture is speculation. . . . There is no state in the Union in which settlers have been more persecuted, so robbed as in California."

George accurately observed the large size of California's farms. In 1870, the average California farm was 482 acres, while in the United States at large the average farm was only 153 acres and in the North Central region 124 acres. By 1900, farms of 1,000 acres or more made up two-thirds of the state's farmland.

California's landscape reflected the reality of large-scale farming. As one California visitor reported to the New York *Times* in 1887, "You go through miles and miles of wheat fields, you see the fertility of the land and the beauty of the scenery, but where are the hundreds of farm houses . . . that you would see in Ohio or Iowa?"

Small farmers and ranchers did exist, of course, but they found it difficult to compete with large, mechanized operators using cheap migrant laborers (usually Mexican or Chinese). One wheat farm in the San Joaquin Valley was so vast that workers started plowing in the morning at one end of the 17-mile field, ate lunch at its halfway point, and camped at its end that night before returning the next day.

The value of much of California's agricultural land, especially the southern half of the Central Valley, depended on water. Many gold rush immigrants were stunned by the appearance of the summer landscape. The grasses were brown and yellow; the earth was parched, and in places the temperature rose above 100 degrees Fahrenheit. By the 1870s, however, water, land, and railroad companies were taking on the huge costs of building dams, headgates, and canals and then selling hitherto barren lands along with water rights, passing along the costs to settlers in the form of high prices. By 1890, over a quarter of California's farms benefited from irrigation.

Although grain was initially California's most valuable crop, it faced stiff competition from farmers on the Plains and in other parts of the world. Some argued that "land capable of raising Adriatic figs, Zante currants, French prunes, Malaga raisins, Batavia oranges, Sicily lemons, citrons, limes, dates and olives, and our own incomparable peaches, apricots, nectarines, pears, quinces, plums, pomegranates, apples, English and native walnuts, chestnuts, pecans and almonds, in a climate surpassing that of Italy, is too valuable for the cultivation of simple cereals." But high railroad rates and primitive shipping conditions limited the volume of fresh fruit and vegetables sent to market. When the first shipment of 300 boxes of California oranges went east in 1877, they took a whole month to reach St. Louis. As growers around Los Angeles turned to the cultivation of navel oranges in the late 1870s, however, the Southern Pacific Railroad recognized the profits the fruit might bring to the railroad. In 1881, it halved its rates and entered into a rate war with the newly constructed Santa Fe Railroad. By 1890, benefiting from the lower rates, 4,000 carloads of oranges headed east.

The introduction of refrigerated railroad cars

By 1900, efficient railroads and refrigerated freight cars made fresh fruit and other products accessible to most of the nation. Note the bananas and other nonlocal products in this Vermont country store.

in the 1880s also boosted fruit and vegetable production. In June 1888, fresh apricots and cherries successfully survived the trip from California to New York. A few years later, California fruit was being sold in London. Some travelers even began to grumble that the railroads treated produce better than people. Per-

haps the complaint was true. The daily eastern express contained "two sleeping cars, two or three passenger cars, and twenty cars loaded with green fruit." The comments highlighted the fact that successful agriculture in California depended on the railroad system, irrigation, and the use of machinery.

THE SECOND GREAT REMOVAL

Black Elk, an Ogalala Sioux, recalled an ominous dream:

> A long time ago my father told me what his father told him, that there was once a Lakota [Sioux] holy man, called Drinks Water, who dreamed what was to be; and this was long before the coming of the Wasichus [white men]. He dreamed . . . that a strange race had woven a spider's web all around the Lakotas. And he said: "When this happens, you shall live in square gray houses, in a barren land, and beside those square gray houses you shall starve."

So great was the wise man's sorrow that he died soon thereafter. During Black Elk's lifetime, the nightmarish prophecy came true.

As farmers settled the western frontier and became entangled in a national economy, they clashed with the Indian tribes who lived on the land. In California, disease and violence killed off 90 percent of the Native American population in the 30 years following the gold rush. Elsewhere, the struggle between Native Americans and whites was both prolonged and bitter.

Background to Hostilities

As pointed out in Chapter 14, the Plains Indians' way of life centered around hunting the buffalo. Increased emigration to California and Oregon in the 1840s and 1850s interrupted tribal pursuits and animal migration patterns. The federal government tried to persuade the Plains tribes to stay far away from white wagon trains and white settlers. Yet this policy was meaningless to Native Americans. As Lone Horn, a Miniconjon chief, explained when American commissioners at the 1851 Fort Laramie Council asked him if he would be satisfied to live on the Missouri River, "When the buffalo comes close to the river, we come close to it. When the buffaloes go off, we go off after them." The concept of land ownership and settled life made little sense to the Plains Indians, just as nomadic life seemed barbarous to whites.

During the Civil War, tribes that President Andrew Jackson had earlier resettled in Oklahoma divided in their support of the Union and the Confederacy. Some of the tribes kept slaves. Most feared that northerners could not be trusted. Thus some of the tribes sided with the Confederacy, while others remained loyal to the Union. After the war, however, all "were treated as traitors." The federal govenment nullified earlier pledges and treaties, leaving Indians defenseless against further incursions on "their" lands. As settlers pushed into Kansas, Indians living in Kansas were shunted into Oklahoma.

The White Perspective

At the end of the Civil War, a state of war existed between red and white men on the Plains. The shameful massacre of friendly Cheyenne at Sand Creek, Colorado, by the Colorado Volunteers in 1864 sparked widespread hostilities. Although not all whites condoned the slaughter, the deliberations of the congressional commission authorized to make peace on the Plains illustrated the limits of their point of view. The commission, which included the commander of the Army in the West, Civil War hero General William T. Sherman, accepted as fact that "an industrious, thrifty, and enlightened population" of whites would occupy most of the West. All Native Americans, the commission believed, should relocate in one of two areas: the western half of present-day South Dakota, and Oklahoma. There they would learn the ways of white society and receive instruction in agricultural and mechanical arts. The offer of annuities, food, and clothes, it was

thought, would help placate the Indians and ease their transition from a "savage" to a "civilized" life.

At two major conferences in 1867 and 1868, Native American chiefs listened to these proposals. Some agreed with the terms; others did not. As Santanta, a Kiowa chief, explained, "I don't want to settle. I love to roam over the prairies." In any case, the agreements extracted were not binding since none of the chiefs had authority to speak for their tribes. The U.S. Senate dragged its feet in approving the treaties. The Cheyenne, Kiowa, and Comanche took to the warpath. Supplies promised to Indians who settled in the reserved areas failed to materialize, and wildlife proved too sparse to support them. These Indians soon drifted back to their former hunting grounds.

As General Sherman had warned, however, "All who cling to their old hunting ground are hostile and will remain so till killed off." To his brother he had written, "The more we can kill

Comanche leader Asa-to-yet, photographed c. 1870, demonstrates by his dress the clash between cultures that Native Americans continued to face.

this year, the less will have to be killed the next war." Sherman entrusted General Philip Sheridan with the duty of dealing with the Indians in 1867. Sheridan introduced a new tactic of winter campaigning. The intent was to seek out the Indians who divided into small groups during the winter and to exterminate them.

The completion of the transcontinental railroad in 1869 added yet another pressure for "solving" the Indian question. Transcontinental railroads wanted rights-of-way through Indian lands and needed white settlers to make their operations profitable. Not only did they carry thousands of hopeful settlers to the West, but miners and hunters as well.

In his 1872 annual report, the commissioner for Indian affairs, Francis Amasa Walker, addressed the two fundamental questions troubling whites: how to prevent Indians from blocking movement and settlement throughout the Great Plains and what to do with them once they had been controlled. Walker wanted to buy the "savages" off since they could, after all, mount 8,000 warriors in the field. With promises of food and gifts, he hoped to lure them onto reservations, where they would be subjected to "a rigid reformatory discipline."

Coercion would be necessary since Indians, according to Walker, were "unused to manual labor, and physically unqualified for it by the habits of the chase . . . without forethought and without self control . . . with strong animal appetites and no intellectual tastes or aspirations to hold those appetites in check." The reservations he described in his proposal for their betterment sounded more like prisons than schools. Indians could not leave the reservation without permission and could be arrested if they tried to do so. Though Walker considered himself to be a "friend of humanity" and wished to save the Indians from destruction, he also thought that their only choice was to "yield or perish."

The Tribal View

Native Americans did not yield passively to such attacks on their ancient way of life and to the violation of treaties. Black Elk remembered that in 1863, when he was only 3, his father had his leg broken in a fierce battle against the white men. "When I was older," he recalled,

I learned what the fighting was about. . . . Up on the Madison Fork the Wasichus had found much of the yellow metal that they worship and that makes them crazy, and they wanted to have a road up through our country to the place where the yellow metal was; but my people did not want the road. It would scare the bison and make them go away, and also it would let the other Wasichus come in like a river. They told us that they

The spectacular Native American victory over General Custer's army in 1876 had little effect on the onslaught of white civilization.

wanted only to use a little land, as much as a wagon would take between the wheels; but our people knew better.

Black Elk's father and many others soon decided that fighting was their only recourse. "There was no other way to keep our country." But "wherever we went, the soldiers came to kill us, and it was all our country."

Broken promises fed Indian resistance. In 1875, the federal govenment allowed gold prospectors to stream into the Black Hills, part of the Sioux reservation and considered a holy place by them. The Sioux, led by Chiefs Sitting Bull, Crazy Horse, and Rain-in-the-Face, took to the warpath. Despite their victory over General George Custer at the Battle of Little Big Horn in 1876, the well-supplied and well-armed U.S. Army finally overwhelmed them. Crazy Horse was murdered. Elsewhere, General Sherman defeated Native American tribes in Texas, while in the Pacific Northwest, Nez Percé Chief Joseph surrendered.

An important ingredient of white victory was the wholesale destruction of the buffalo. The animals were central to the Indian way of life, culture, and religion. As one Pawnee chief explained, "Am afraid when we have no meat to offer, Great Spirit . . . will be angry & punish us." But the herds of buffalo gradually died out as railroads crossed the Plains with settlers, miners, and hunters. Eager sportsmen shot the beasts from train windows. Railroad crews ate the meat. Cattle competed for grass. The demand for buffalo bones for fertilizer and hides for robes and shoes encouraged the destruction.

The slaughter, which had claimed 13 million animals by 1883, is one that many modern wildlife enthusiasts find disgraceful. The Indians considered white men demented. "They just killed and killed because they liked to do that," said one, while when "we hunted the bison . . . [we] killed only what we needed." But the slaughter fitted the plans of those determined to curb the movements of Native Americans. As Secretary of the Interior Columbus Delano explained in 1872, "I cannot regard the rapid disappearance of the game from its former haunts as a matter prejudicial to our management of the Indians." Rather, he said, "as they

become convinced that they can no longer rely upon the supply of game for their support, they will return to the more reliable source of subsistence furnished at their agencies."

The Dawes Act

Changes in federal policy also contributed to the disintegration of Native American culture and life. In 1870, Congress ended the practice, in effect since the 1790s, of treating the tribes as sovereign nations. This attempt to undermine tribal integrity and the prestige of tribal leaders (who would no longer be recognized as speaking for their tribes) was accompanied by other measures. The government urged tribes to establish court systems in place of tribal justice and extended federal jurisdiction to the reservations. Tribes were also warned not to gather for religious ceremonies.

The Dawes Severalty Act of 1887 pulled together the strands of federal Indian policy that emerged after the Civil War and set its course for the rest of the century. The legislation ended the traditional policy of treating individual Indians as members of their tribes. Believing that tribal bonds kept Indians in savagery, reformers intended to destroy them. As Theodore Roosevelt noted approvingly, the bill was "a mighty pulverizing engine to break up the tribal mass." Rather than allotting reservation lands to tribal groups, the legislation declared that each individual family head was eligible for a homestead grant of 160 acres. By holding out this lure, the framers of the bill hoped to encourage Indians to settle in one place and to farm as white men did. Those who accepted allotments would become citizens and presumably forget their tribal identity. Although Indian agents explained that Native Americans opposed the Dawes Act, Congress did not hesitate to legislate on their behalf.

Another motive was also at work. Even if each Indian male claimed 160 acres, millions of "surplus" acres would remain for sale and for white settlement. Within 20 years of the Dawes Act, Native Americans had lost 60 percent of their lands. The federal govenment held the profits from land sales "in trust" and used them for the "civilizing" mission.

Weekly and monthly magazines constitute a rich primary source for the historian, offering a vivid picture of the issues of the day and useful insights into popular tastes and values. With advances in the publishing industry and an increasingly literate population, the number of these journals soared in the years following the Civil War. In 1865, only 700 periodicals were published. Twenty years later there were 3,300. As the *National Magazine* grumbled, "Magazines, magazines, magazines! The news-stands are already groaning under the heavy load, and there are still more coming."

Some of these magazines were aimed at the mass market. *Frank Leslie's Illustrated Newspaper*, established in 1855, was one of the most successful. At its height, circulation reached 100,000. Making skillful use of pictures (sometimes as large as 2 by 3 feet and folded into the magazine), the weekly magazine covered important news of the day as well as music, drama, sports, and books. Although Leslie relied more heavily on graphics and sensationalism than modern news weeklies, his publication was a forerunner of *Newsweek* and *Time*.

Another kind of weekly magazine was aimed primarily at middle- and upper-class readers. Editors like the oft-quoted Edwin Lawrence Godkin of *The Nation*, with a circulation of about 30,000, hoped to influence those in positions of authority and power by providing a forum for the discussion of reform issues. In contrast, *Scribner's* revealed a more conservative, middle-of-the-road point of view. Both magazines, however, exuded a confident, progressive tone characteristic of middle-class Americans.

Harper's Weekly was one of the most important magazines designed primarily for middle- and upper-class readers. Established in 1857, this publication continued in print until 1916. The success of *Harper's Weekly*, which called itself a "family newspaper," rested on a combination of its moderate point of view and an exciting use of illustrations and cartoons touching on contemporary events. In this magazine, for example, are found the cartoons of Thomas Nast. In large part because of the use of graphics, in 1872 the circulation of *Harper's Weekly* reached a peak of 160,000.

Illustrated here is a page from the January 16, 1869, issue of *Harper's Weekly*. The layout immediately suggests the importance of graphics. Most of the page is taken up with the three pictures. The top and bottom pictures are wood engravings based on drawings by Theodore R. Davis, one of *Harper's* best known illustrator-reporters. The center picture was derived from a photograph.

The story featured on this page concerns a victory of General George Custer in the war against the Cheyenne tribe. Davis had been a correspondent in the West covering Custer's actions in 1867. But when news of Custer's victory arrived, Davis was back in New York. He thus drew upon his imagination for the two scenes reproduced on this page. What kind of characterization of Native Americans does Davis give in the picture at the top of the page? What view of American soldiers does he suggest? At the bottom of the page, you can see soldiers slaughtering "worthless" horses while Cheyenne tepees burn in the background. Would the average viewer have any sympathy for the plight of the Cheyennes by looking at this picture? This "victory," in fact, involved not only the slaughter of horses but also of all males over age 8.

The editors' decision to insert a picture that had nothing to do with the incident being reported was obviously significant. As you can see, the subject is a white hunter who had been killed and scalped by Indians. What kind of special relationship were the editors suggesting by placing the picture of one dead white hunter in the center of a page that primarily covered a specific conflict between the Indians and the U.S. Army? How might the reader respond to the group of pictures as a whole? How do you? How does the text contribute to the overall view of the Indian–white relationship that the pictures suggest? By considering the choice of graphics and text, you can begin to discover how magazines provide insight, not only into the events of the day but also into the ways magazines shaped the values and perspectives of nineteenth-century men and women.

Harper's Weekly, *January 16, 1869*

CUSTER'S INDIAN SCOUTS CELEBRATING THE VICTORY OVER BLACK KETTLE.—[SKETCHED BY THEO. R. DAVIS.]

THE INDIAN WAR.

THE Indian Peace Commission of 1867 accomplished greater harm than benefit. Treaties were entered into with the Cheyennes, Arrapahoes, Kiowas, Comanches, and at the recommendation of the Commission the Powder River country was abandoned. This latter action was construed as the result of timidity on the part of the Government, and immediately the Sioux extended their depredations to the Pacific Railroad, on the Platte, while the Indians south of the Arkansas attempted to drive the whites out of the Smoky Hill country.

Last August the Cheyennes took the war-path, and the valleys of the Saline and Solomon rivers became the theatre of a relentless savage war. It was at first supposed that the Cheyennes were about to attack a hostile tribe, but soon the mask was laid aside, and in less than a month one hundred whites fell victims to the tomahawk and scalping-knife. The chiefs of the Arrapahoes had promised to

THE SCALPED HUNTER.—[PHOTOGRAPHED BY WM. S. SOULE.]

proceed to Fort Cobb and get their annuities, and thence withdraw to their reservation. Instead of fulfilling their promises, they began a series of depredations on the line between Fort Wallace and Denver, in Colorado Territory. The Kiowas and Comanches about the same time entered into an agreement at Fort Zarah to remain at peace, and left with that impression fixed on the minds of those who represented the Government. The next information was that the Kiowas and Comanches had joined the Cheyennes and Arrapahoes. General SHERIDAN, taking the practical view of the condition of affairs within the limits of his department, at once transferred his head-quarters to the field, and commenced preparations for a determined war. General SULLY's fight near this point, FORSYTH's gallant fight on the Arrikaree fork of the Republican, CARPENTER's and GRAHAM's fight on the Beaver branch of the Republican, General CARR's decisive fight in the same vicinity, and General CUS-

CUSTER'S COMMAND SHOOTING DOWN WORTHLESS HORSES.—[SKETCHED BY THEO. R. DAVIS.]

Ghost Dance

By the 1890s, Native Americans were curbed but not entirely broken. The Ghost Dance movement, which envisioned help from the Great Spirit rather than the Indians themselves, indicated tribal weakness. Based on the promises of the Paiute prophet Wovoka, who told believers that natural disasters would strike down whites while Indians, dancing as ghosts, avoided destruction, the movement spread from tribe to tribe. Believers expressed their faith and hope by rituals of dancing and meditation. The more frequently they danced, the quicker the whites were to vanish.

Although Wovoka prophesied that whites would disappear without the assistance of Indians, American settlers were not so sure. Indian agents tried to prevent the dancing. When the Indians refused, attempts were made to arrest a Sioux medicine man, Sitting Bear. In the confusion of arrest, Sitting Bear was killed. Bands of Sioux left the reservation. The army followed in swift pursuit. Using the most up-to-date machine guns, the army massacred 200 men, women, and children, in the snow at Wounded Knee in 1890.

Thus arose the lament of Black Elk, who saw his people diminished, starving, despairing:

> Once we were happy in our own country and we were seldom hungry, for then the two-leggeds and the four-leggeds lived together like relatives, and there was plenty for them and for us. But then the Wasichus came, and they have made little islands for us and other islands for the four-leggeds, and always these islands are becoming smaller, for around them surges the gnawing flood of the Washichus; and it is dirty with lies and greed.

THE NEW SOUTH

Of all the nation's agricultural regions, the South was the poorest. In 1880, southerners' yearly earnings were only half the national average. But despite poverty and backwardness, some southerners during the late nineteenth century dreamed of making the agricultural South the rival of the industrial North.

The vision of a modern, progressive, and self-sufficient South had roots in the troubled decade of the 1850s. At that time, southern intellectuals and writers had argued that the South must throw off its dependence on the North and on cotton. "The smoke of the steam engine should begin to float over the cotton fields, and the hum of spindles and the click of looms make music on all our mountain streams," the editor of the New Orleans *Picayune* insisted.

Southerners Face the Future

But not enough southerners had listened. Now, after the disastrous experience of war and reconstruction, the cry for regional self-sufficiency grew sharper. Publicists of the movement for a "New South" argued that southern backwardness did not stem from the war itself, as so many southerners wished to believe, but from basic conditions in southern life, a rural economy based on cotton foremost among them. The defeat only made clearer the reality of the nineteenth century. Power and wealth came not from cotton but from factories, machines, and cities.

Henry Grady, editor of the Atlanta *Constitution* and the New South's most famous spokesman, dramatized the need for change with his story of a southerner's funeral:

> They buried him in the midst of a marble quarry; they cut through solid marble to make his grave; and yet a little tombstone they put above him was from Vermont. They buried him in the heart of a pine forest, and yet the pine coffin was imported from Cincinnati. They buried him within touch of an iron mine, and yet the nails in his coffin and the iron in the shovel that dug his grave were imported from Pittsburgh. . . . They put him away . . . in a New York coat and a Boston pair of shoes and a pair of breeches from Chicago and a shirt from Cincinnati, leaving him

nothing to carry into the next world with him to remind him of the country in which he lived and for which he fought for four years, but the chill of blood in his veins and the marrow in his bones.

Regional pride and self-interest clearly dictated a new course. As Grady told a Boston audience in 1886, industrial advances would allow the South to match the North in another, more peaceful contest. "We are going to take a noble revenge," he said, "by invading every inch of your territory with iron, as you invaded ours twenty-nine years ago."

In hundreds of speeches, editorials, pamphlets, articles, and books, spokesmen for the New South tried to persuade fellow southerners of the need for change. Southerners must abandon prewar ideals that glorified leisure and gentility and adopt the ethic of hard work. To lure northern bankers and capitalists, New South advocates held out attractive investment possibilities. Since the South was short of capital, northern assistance was as critical to realizing the dream as was southern cooperation. Thus, said one New South advocate persuasively, "the profits to be reaped from investments in the South . . . appear to be fabulous." He confidently predicted that the South would become the "El Dorado of the next half century."

These arguments did not fall on deaf ears. In a bid to attract manufacturers, several southern state governments offered tax exemptions and cheap labor based on leasing state prison convicts. Texas and Florida awarded the railroads land grants, and cities like Atlanta and Louisville mounted huge industrial exhibitions as incentives to industrial progress. Middle-class southerners were impressed and increasingly accepted new entrepreneurial values in place of prewar ideals of leisure and gentility. The most startling example of commitment to the vision of a New South may have come in 1886 when southern railroad companies decided to bring their tracks into line with the "standard" northern gauges. On a Sunday in May, 8,000 men equipped with sledgehammers and crowbars attacked the 2,000 miles of track belonging to the Louisville and Nashville Railroad Company and moved the western rail 3 inches to the east. On that same day, they also adjusted the iron wheels of 300 locomotives and 10,000 pieces of rolling stock to fit the new gauge.

During the late nineteenth century, northern money flowed south as dollars replaced the moral fervor and political involvement of the Civil War and Reconstruction years. In the 1880s, northerners increased their investment in the cotton industry sevenfold and financed the expansion of the southern railroad system. In turn, northern investments stimulated southern cities to embark on an extended period of expansion. By 1900, some 15 percent of all southerners lived in cities, whereas only 7 percent had in 1860. (The national averages for these years were 40 percent and 20 percent, respectively.)

The city of Birmingham, Alabama, became one of the symbols of the New South. In 1870, the site of the future city was a peaceful cornfield. The next year, two northern real estate speculators arrived on the scene, encouraged in their booster schemes by the area's rich iron deposits. Despite a siege of cholera and the depression of the 1870s, Birmingham became within a 30-year period the center of the southern iron and steel industry. By 1890, a total of 38,414 people lived in the city. Coke ovens, blast furnaces, rolling mills, iron foundries, and machine shops belched smoke where once there had only been fields. Millions of dollars of finished goods poured forth from the city's mills and factories and were carried away over eight railroad lines.

Other southern cities flourished as well. Memphis prospered from its lumber industry and the manufacturing of cottonseed products, while Richmond became the country's tobacco capital even as its flour mills and iron and steel foundries continued to produce wealth. Augusta, Georgia, became the "Lowell of the South," a leader in the emerging textile industry that blossomed in Georgia, North and South Carolina, and Alabama. Augusta's eight cotton mills employed about 2,800 workers, many of them women and children.

The Other Side of Progress

New South leaders, a small group of merchants, industrialists, and planters, bragged about the growth of the iron and textile industries and paraded statistics to prove the success of efforts to modernize. The South, one writer boasted, was "throbbing with industrial and railroad activity." But despite such optimism about matching or even surpassing the North's economic performance, the South made slow progress.

Older values persisted. Indeed, New South spokesmen paradoxically kept older chivalric values alive by romanticizing the recent past. "In the eyes of Southern people," one publication asserted, "all Confederate veterans are heroes." Loyalty to the past impeded full acceptance of a new economic order. It was significant that despite the interest in modernization, the southern school system lagged far behind that of the North.

Although new industries and signs of progress abounded, the South did not better its position relative to the North. Whereas in 1860 the South had 17 percent of the country's manufacturing concerns, by 1904 it had only 15 percent. During the same period, the value of its manufactures grew from 10.3 percent of the total value of manufactures in the United States to only 10.5 percent. Commerce and government work still were responsible for urban growth, as they had been before the Civil War. The South's achievements were not insignificant during a period in which northern industry and cities rapidly expanded, but they were not enough to make the South the equal of the North.

Moreover, the South failed to reap many of the benefits of industrialization. Southern businessmen like Richmond banker and railroad president John Skelton Williams hoped "to see in the South in the not distant future many railroads and business institutions as great as the Pennsylvania Railroad, the Mutual Life Insurance Company, the Carnegie Steel Company or the Standard Oil Company." This was not to happen. As in the antebellum period, the South was an economic vassal of the North.

Southern industrialism did not change that status. There were more and more southern businessmen, but with the exception of the American Tobacco Company, no great southern corporations arose. Instead, southerners worked for northern companies and corporations, which absorbed southern businesses or dominated them financially. By 1900, for example, five corporations directed three-quarters of the railroad mileage in the South (excluding Texas), and northern bankers controlled all five. Northerners also took over the southern steel industry.

As this happened, profits flowed north. "Our capitalists are going into your country," the Lowell *Manufacturers' Record* accurately noted, "because they see a chance to make money there, but you must not think that they will give your people the benefit of the money they make. That will come North and enrich their heirs, or set up public libraries in our country towns." As dollars fled north, so too went the power to make critical decisions. In many cases, northern directors determined that southern mills and factories could handle only the early stages of processing, while northern factories finished the goods. Thus southern cotton mills sent yarn and coarse cloth north for completion. Southern manufacturers who did finish their products, hoping to compete in the marketplace, found that railroad rate discrimination robbed their goods of any competitive edge.

Individual workers in the new industries may have found factory life preferable to sharecropping, but their rewards were meager. The thousands of women and children in factories were silent testimony to the fact their husbands and fathers could not earn sufficient wages to support them at home. As usual, women and children earned lower wages than men. Managers justified these policies toward women and children. The employment of children, claimed one Augusta factory president, was "a matter of charity with us; some of them would starve if they were not given employment. . . . Ours are not overworked. The work we give children is very light." Actually, many children at his factory were doing the same work as adults, for children's pay.

In general, all workers earned lower wages and worked longer hours in the South than elsewhere. Per capita income was the same in 1900 as it had been in 1860—and only half the national average. In North Carolina in the 1890s, workers were paid an average of 50 cents a day and toiled 70 hours a week. Black workers, who made up 6 percent of the southern manufacturing force in 1890 (but who were excluded from textile mills), usually had the worst jobs and lowest wages.

Cotton Still King

Although New South advocates envisioned the South's transformation from a rural to an industrial society, they always recognized that agriculture had to be transformed as well. "It's time for an agricultural revolution," Grady proclaimed. "When we once decide that southern lands are fit for something else besides cotton, and then go to work in earnest to multiply and diversify our products and industries, independence and wealth will be the certain reward of our intelligent and industrious farmers."

The overdependence on "King Cotton" hobbled southern agriculture by making farmers the victims of faraway market forces and an oppressive credit system. Old cotton plantations must be subdivided into small diversified farms, Grady advised. He was especially impressed by the possibilities of truck farming, which could produce "simply wonderful profits." A good truck farm, he argued, "would give employment throughout the entire season, and at the end of it

the fortunate farmer would have before him the assurance that diversified crops and a never-failing market alone afford, with no [fertilizer] . . . bills to settle, and no liens past or to come to disturb his mind."

A new agricultural South with new class and economic arrangements did emerge, but it was not the one Grady and others envisioned. Despite the breakup of some plantations following the Civil War, large landowners proved resourceful in holding on to their property and in dealing with postwar conditions, as Chapter 17 showed. As they adopted new agricultural arrangements, former slaves sank into debt peonage.

White farmers on small and medium-size holdings fared only slightly better in the New South than black tenants and sharecroppers. Immediately after the war, high cotton prices had tempted them to raise as much cotton as they could. Then prices began a disastrous decline (from 11 cents a pound in 1875 to less than 5 cents in 1894). "At the close of the war a 500 lb. bale of cotton would bring $100," a Cherokee County, Georgia, tenant complained in 1891, "and today it will bring $32.50." Yeoman farmers became entangled in debt. Each year, farmers found themselves buying supplies on credit from merchants so that they could plant the

The predominance of cotton in southern agriculture remained unchallenged in the decades after the Civil War.

next year's crop and support their families until harvest time. In return, merchants demanded their exclusive business and acquired a lien (or claim) on their crops. But when harvest time came and crops were sold (at declining prices), farmers usually discovered they had not earned enough to settle with the merchant, who had charged dearly for store goods and whose annual interest rates might exceed 100 percent. Each year, thousands of farmers fell further and further behind.

Such was the case of S. R. Simonton, a South Carolina farmer. Between 1887 and 1895, he spent $2,681 at T. G. Patrick's furnishing house. Because he could manage to pay back only $687, he lost his land and became a tenant farmer. Others shared the same fate. The number of tenants slowly crept upward, while the number of small independent farmers fell. By 1900, over half the South's white farmers and three-quarters of its black farmers were tenants. Although tenancy was increasingly all over rural America, nowhere did it rise more rapidly than in the Deep South.

These patterns had baneful results for individual southerners and for the South as a whole. Caught in a cycle of debt and poverty, few farmers could think of improving agricultural techniques or diversifying crops. In their desperate attempt to pay off debts, they concentrated on cotton, despite falling prices. "Cotton brings money, and money pays debt," was the small farmer's slogan. Landowners also pressured tenants to raise a market crop. Far from diversifying, as Grady had hoped, farmers increasingly limited the number of crops they raised. By 1880, the South was not growing enough food to feed its people adequately. Poor nutrition contributed to chronic bad health and sickness.

The Nadir of Black Life

Grady and other New South advocates painted a picture of a strong, prosperous, and industrialized South, a region that could deal with the troublesome race issue without the interference of any "outside power." Grady had few regrets over the end of slavery, which he thought had contributed to southern economic backwardness. Moreover, since he realized that black labor would be crucial to the transformation he sought, he advocated racial cooperation.

But racial cooperation did not mean equality. Grady assumed that blacks were racially inferior and supported an informal system of segregation. "The negro is entitled to his freedom, his franchise, to full and equal legal rights," Grady wrote in 1883. But "social equality he can never have. He does not have it in the north, or in the east, or in the west. On one pretext or another, he is kept out of hotels, theatres, schools and restaurants."

By the time of Grady's death in 1889, a much harsher perspective on southern race relations was replacing his view. In 1891, at a national assembly of women's clubs in Washington, D.C., a black woman, Frances Ellen Watkins Harper, anticipated efforts to strip the vote from blacks and appealed to the white women at the meeting not to abandon black suffrage. "I deem it a privilege to present the negro," she said, "not as a mere dependent asking for Northern sympathy or Southern compassion, but as a member of the body politic who has a claim upon the nation for justice, simple justice." This claim, she continued, was for "protection to human life," for "the rights of life and liberty," and for relief from charges of ignorance and poverty. These were "conditions which men outgrow." Women, of all people, should understand this and not seek to achieve their own right to vote at the expense of the vote for black men. "Instead of taking the ballot from his hands, teach him how to use it, and add his quota to the progress, strength, and durability of the nation."

The decision by congressional leaders in 1890 to shelve a proposed act for protecting black civil rights and the defeat of the Blair bill providing federal assistance for educational institutions left black Americans vulnerable, as Frances Harper realized. The traditional sponsor of the rights of freedmen, the Republican party, left blacks to fend for themselves as a minority in the white South. The courts also abandoned blacks. In 1878, the Supreme Court declared unconstitutional a Louisiana statute banning discrimination in transportation. In 1882, the Court voided the Ku Klux Klan Act of 1871, deciding that the civil rights protections of the

Fourteenth Amendment applied to states rather than to individuals. In 1883, the provisions of the Civil Rights Act of 1875, which assured blacks of equal rights in public places, were declared unconstitutional.

Neither political nor media leaders in the North opposed these actions. In fact, northerners increasingly resorted to negative stereotypes in discussing blacks. They were pictured as either ignorant, lazy, loyal, childlike fools or as lying, stealing, raping degenerates. Obviously, they could not be left to themselves nor given the same rights and freedoms whites enjoyed. Instead, blacks needed the paternal protection of the superior white race. These stereotypes filled the magazines and newspapers and were perpetuated in cartoons, advertisements, "coon songs," serious art and theater, and the minstrel shows that dominated northern entertainment.

The *Atlantic Monthly* in 1890 anticipated a strong current in the magazine literature when it expressed doubts that this "lowly variety of man" could ever be brought up to the intellectual and moral standards of whites. Other magazines openly opposed suffrage as wasted on those too "ignorant, weak, lazy and incompetent" to make good use of it. *Forum* magazine suggested that "American Negroes" had "too much liberty." When this freedom was combined with natural "race traits" of stealing and hankering after white women, the *Forum* advised in 1893,

Stereotypes of blacks in the popular media ranged from patronizing to defamatory.

black crime increased. Only lynching and burning would work to deter the "barbarous" rapist and other "sadly degenerated" Negroes corrupted since the Civil War by independence and too much education. The author concluded that the Negro question was "more vital" than gold, silver, or the tariff. Unrestrained by northern public opinion, and with the blessing of Congress and the Supreme Court, southern citizens and legislatures sought to make blacks permanently second-class members of southern society.

In the political sphere, white southerners amended state constitutions to disenfranchise black voters. By various legal devices—the poll tax, literacy tests, "good character" and "understanding" clauses administered by white voter registrars, and all-white primary elections— blacks lost the right to vote. The most ingenious method was the "grandfather clause," which specified that only citizens whose grandfathers were registered to vote on January 1, 1867, could cast their ballots. This virtually excluded blacks. Beginning with Mississippi in 1890, all 11 former Confederate states changed their constitutions by 1910 to exclude the black vote. The results were dramatic. Louisiana, for example, contained 130,334 registered black voters in 1896. Eight years later, there were only 1,342.

A second tactic in the 1890s was the passage of state and local laws that legalized informal segregation in public facilities. Beginning with railroads and schools, "Jim Crow" laws were extended to libraries, hotels, restaurants, hospitals, asylums, prisons, theaters, parks and playgrounds, cemeteries, toilets, morgues, sidewalks, drinking fountains, and nearly every possible place where blacks and whites might intermingle. The Supreme Court upheld these laws in 1896 in *Plessy* v. *Ferguson* by declaring that "separate but equal" facilities did not violate the equal protection clause of the Fourteenth Amendment. The Court's decision opened the way for as many forms of legal segregation as the imaginations of southern lawmakers could devise.

Political and social discrimination made it ever more possible to keep blacks permanently confined to agricultural and unskilled labor and dependent on whites for their material welfare.

In 1900, nearly 84 percent of black workers nationwide engaged in some form of agricultural labor as farmhands, overseers, sharecroppers, or tenant or independent farmers or in service jobs, primarily domestic service and laundry work. These had been the primary slave occupations. The remaining 16 percent worked in forests, sawmills, mines, and, with northward migration, in northern cities. Gone were the skilled black tradesmen of slavery days. At the end of the Civil War, at least half of all skilled craftsmen in the South had been black. But by the 1890s, the percentage had decreased to less than 10 percent, as whites systematically excluded blacks from the trades. Such factory work as blacks had been doing was also reduced, largely in order to drive a wedge between poor blacks and whites to prevent unionization. In Greensboro, North Carolina, for example, where in 1870 some 30 percent of all blacks worked in skilled trades or factory occupations, by 1910 blacks in the skilled trades had been reduced to 8 percent, and not a single black worked in a Greensboro factory. The exclusion of blacks from industry prevented them from acquiring the skills and habits that would enable them to rise into the middle class as would many European immigrants and their children by the mid-twentieth century.

Blacks did not accept their declining position passively. In the mid-1880s, they enthusiastically joined the mass worker organization, the Knights of Labor (discussed in Chapter 19), first in cities such as Richmond and Atlanta, then in rural areas. As one South Carolina black explained, "We are bo[u]nd to join something what will lead to better rights than we have." Probably blacks made up between half and a third of the Knights' membership in the South. But southern whites grated at the Knights' policies of racial cooperation, fearing that economic cooperation might lead to social equality. "The forcing of a colored man among the white people here had knocked me out of the order," reported one. The Charleston *News and Courier* warned of the dangers of "miscegenation" and claimed that the South would be left "in the possession of . . . mongrels and hybrids." As blacks continued to join it, whites abandoned the order in growing numbers. The flight of whites weak-

ened the organization in the South, and a backlash of white violence finally smashed it.

Against this backdrop, incidents of lawless lynchings and other forms of violence against blacks increased. On February 21, 1891, the New York *Times* reported that in Texarkana, Arkansas, a mob apprehended a 32-year-old black man, Ed Coy, charged with the rape of a white woman, tied him to a stake, and burned him alive. As Coy proclaimed his innocence to a large crowd, his alleged victim herself somewhat hesitatingly put the torch to his oil-soaked body. The *Times* report concluded that only by the "terrible death such as fire . . . can inflict" could other blacks "be deterred from the commission of like crimes." Ed Coy was one of over 1,400 black men lynched or burned alive during the 1890s. About a third were charged with sex crimes. The rest were accused of a variety of "crimes" related to not knowing their place: marrying or insulting a white woman, testifying in court against whites, having "a bad reputation."

Diverging Black Responses

White discrimination and exploitation nourished new protest tactics and ideologies among blacks. For years, Frederick Douglass had been proclaiming that blacks should remain loyal Americans and count on the promises of the Republican party. But on his deathbed in 1895, his last words were allegedly "Agitate! Agitate! Agitate!"

Among black expressions of protest, one was a woman's. In Memphis, Tennessee, Ida B. Wells, the first woman to become editor of an important newspaper, launched a campaign against lynching in 1892. So hostile was the response from the white community that Wells carried a gun to protect herself. When white citizens finally destroyed the press and threatened her partner, Wells left Memphis to pursue her activism elsewhere.

Other voices called for black separatism within white America. T. Thomas Fortune wrote in the black New York *Freeman* in 1887 that "there will one day be an African Empire." Three years later, he organized the Afro-American League (a precursor of the NAACP), insisting that blacks must join together to fight the rising tide of discrimination. "Let us stand up," he urged, "in our own organization where color will not be a brand of odium." The league encouraged independent voting, opposed segregation and lynching, and urged the establishment of black institutions like banks to support black businesses. As a sympathetic journalist explained, "The solution of the problem is in our own hands. . . . The Negro must preserve his identity."

While some promoted black nationalism, most blacks worked patiently but persistently within white society for equality and social justice. In 1887, J. C. Price formed the Citizens Equal Rights Association, which supported the continuation of various petitions and direct-action campaigns to protest segregation. The Association also called for state laws to guarantee equal rights in the aftermath of the Supreme Court's 1883 ruling. Other blacks boycotted streetcars in southern cities, and Daniel Payne, a Methodist bishop, got off the Jim Crow car on a Florida train and with great ceremony walked to a church conference. Other blacks petitioned Congress, demanding reparations for unpaid labor as slaves.

Effort to escape oppression in the South, like "Pap" Singleton's movement to found black towns in Tennessee and Kansas, continued. In the 1890s, black leaders lobbied to make the Oklahoma Territory, recently opened to white settlement, an all-black state. Blacks founded 25 towns there, as well as in other states and even Mexico. But these attempts, like earlier ones, were short-lived, crippled by limited funds and the hostility of white neighbors. Singleton eventually recommended migration to Canada or Liberia as a final solution, and later black nationalist leaders also looked increasingly to Africa. Bishop Henry McNeal Turner, a former Union soldier and prominent black leader, despaired of ever securing equal rights for blacks in the United States. He described the Constitution as "a dirty rag, a cheat, a libel" and said that it ought to be "spit upon by every Negro in the land." In 1894, he organized the International Migration Society to return blacks to Africa, arguing that "this country owes us forty billions of dollars" to help. He succeeded in sending two boatloads of emigrants to Liberia, but this colonization effort worked no more successfully than those earlier in the century.

As Douglass had long argued, no matter how important African roots might be, blacks had been in the Americas for generations and would have to win justice and equal rights here. W. E. B. Du Bois, the first black to receive a Ph.D. from Harvard, agreed. Yet in 1900, he attended the first Pan-African Conference in London, where he argued that blacks must lead the struggle for liberation both in Africa and in the United States. It was at this conference that Du Bois first made his prophetic comment that "the problem of the Twentieth Century" would be "the problem of the color line."

Despite these vigorous voices of militant anger and nationalistic fervor, most black Americans continued to follow the slow, moderate self-help program of Booker T. Washington, the best-known black leader in America. Born a slave, Washington had risen through hard and obedient work to become the founder (in 1881) and principal of Tuskegee Institute in Alabama, which he personally and dramatically built into the largest and best-known industrial training school in the country. At Tuskegee, young blacks received a highly disciplined education in scientific agricultural techniques and vocational skilled trades. Washington believed that economic self-help and the familiar Puritan virtues of hard work, frugality, cleanliness, and moderation were the way to success. He spent much of his time traveling the North to secure generous gifts to support Tuskegee from northern philanthropists. In time, he became a favorite of the American entrepreneurial elite.

In 1895, Washington was asked to deliver a speech at the Cotton States and International Exposition in Atlanta, celebrating three decades of industrial and agricultural progress since the Civil War. He took advantage of that invitation, a rare honor for the former slave, to make a significant statement about the position of blacks in the South. Without a hint of protest, Washington decided "to say something that would cement the friendship of the races." He therefore proclaimed black loyalty to the economic development of the South while accepting the lowly status of southern blacks. "It is at the bottom of life we must begin, and not at the top," he declared. "In all things that are purely social we can be as separate as the fingers, yet one as the hand in all things essential to mutual progress." Washington also effectively renounced black interest in either the vote or civil rights as well as social equality with whites. Whites throughout the country enthusiastically acclaimed Washington's address, but many blacks called his "Atlanta Compromise" a serious setback in the struggle for black rights.

Washington has often been charged with conceding too quickly that political rights should follow rather than precede economic well-being. In 1903, Du Bois confronted Washington directly in *The Souls of Black Folk*, arguing instead for the "manly assertion" of a program of equal civil rights, suffrage, and high-

er education in the ideals of liberal learning. A trip through the black belt of Dougherty County, Georgia, showed Du Bois the "forlorn and forsaken" condition of southern blacks. The young sociologist saw that most blacks were confined to various forms of dependent agricultural labor, "fighting a hard battle with debt" year after year. Although "here and there a man has raised his head above these murky waters . . . a pall of debt hangs over the beautiful land." Beneath all others was the cotton picker, who, with the help of his wife and children, would have to work from sunup to sundown to pick the 100 pounds of cotton to make 50 cents. The lives of most blacks were still tied to the land of the South. If they were to improve their lives, rural blacks would have to organize.

PROTESTING FARMERS

During the post–Civil War period, many farmers both black and white, began to realize that only by organizing could they hope to ameliorate the conditions of rural life. Not all were dissatisfied with their lot, however. Midwestern farmers and farmers near city markets successfully adjusted to new economic conditions and had little reason for discontent. As this chapter has pointed out, however, farmers in both the South and the West faced new problems and difficulties. Many of them were ready to join farm organizations.

The Grange

The earliest effort to organize white farmers came in 1867 when Oliver Kelley founded the National Grange of the Patrons of Husbandry. At first the organization emphasized social and cultural goals. The Grange hoped to encourage "a cordial and social fraternity of the farmers all over the country," Kelly explained. Farmers needed to become progressive—"to read and think, to plant fruit and flowers, [and] beautify their homes."

The social and fraternal goals were shortly joined by other more aggressive ones. Dudley Adams, speaking to an Iowa Grange in 1870,

pointed to the powerlessness of "the immense helpless mob" of farmers who were the victims of "human vampires." Their salvation lay in organization, Adams maintained.

More and more farmers, especially those in the Midwest and the South, agreed with Adams. The depression of the 1870s (discussed in Chapter 19) sharpened discontent. By 1875, an estimated 800,000 had joined the Grange. The "Farmers' Declaration of Independence," read before local granges on July 4, 1873, captured the new activist spirit. The time had come, the declaration announced, for farmers suffering from "oppression and abuse" to rouse themselves and, by "all lawful and peaceful means," to cast off "the tyranny of monopoly." While the declaration clearly expressed rural discontent, it gave few indications that Grangers recognized the complex reasons for their problems.

Grangers were looking for culprits close to home. Middlemen seemed to be obvious examples of the oppressors. They gouged the American farmer by raising the prices of finished goods farmers needed to buy and by lowering the prices they received for their products. Some of the Granger "reforms" attempted to bypass middlemen by establishing buying and selling cooperatives. Although many of the cooperatives failed, they indicated that farmers realized that they could not respond to new conditions on an individual basis but needed to act collectively.

Operators of grain elevators also drew fire. Midwestern farmers claimed that these merchants often misgraded their wheat and corn and paid less than its worth. But the railroads, America's first big business, were the greatest offenders. As the next chapter will show, cutthroat competition among railroad companies generally brought lower rates. But even though rates dropped nationwide, the railroads often set high rates in rural areas. Moreover, railroads awarded discriminatory rebates to large shippers and put small operators at a disadvantage.

Although the Grange was originally nonpolitical, farmers recognized that they had to take political action if they were to confront the mighty railroads. Other groups also wished to see some controls imposed on the railroads.

Originally a social organization, the Grange soon adopted a political agenda to represent agrarian interests.

Many western businessmen were victimized by railroad policies that favored large Chicago grain terminals and long-distance shippers over local concerns. Between 1869 and 1874, both businessmen and farmers in Illinois, Iowa, Wisconsin, and Minnesota lobbied for state railroad laws. The resulting Granger Laws (an inaccurate name because the Grangers should not be given complete credit for them) established the maximum rates railroads and grain elevators could charge. Other states passed legislation setting up railroad commissions with power to regulate railroad rates. In some states, railroad pools were declared illegal, as were rebates, passes, and other practices that seemed to represent "unjust discrimination and distortion."

Railroad companies and grain elevators quickly challenged the legality of the new laws. In 1877, the Supreme Court upheld the legislation in *Munn* v. *Illinois*. Even so, it soon became apparent that although state commissions had authority over local rates and fares, they could not control long-haul rates. To make up for the money they lost on local hauls, railroads often raised long-haul charges, thus frustrating the intent of the laws. Other complicated issues involved determining what was a fair rate, who was competent to decide that rate, and what was a justifiable return for the railroad. The tangle of questions that state regulation raised proved difficult to resolve at the local level.

Although the Granger Laws failed to solve the questions involved in attempts to control the railroads, they established an important principle. As the Supreme Court decision made clear, state legislatures had the power to regulate businesses of a public nature like the railroads. But the failure of the Granger Laws led to greater pressure on Congress to continue the struggle against big business.

Interstate Commerce Act

In 1887, Congress responded to farmers, railroad managers who wished to regulate the fierce competition that threatened to bankrupt their companies, and shippers who objected to transportation rates by passing the Interstate Commerce Act. That legislation required that railroad rates be "reasonable and just" and that rate schedules be made public and declared practices such as rebates illegal. The act also set up the first federal regulatory agency, the Interstate Commerce Commission (ICC). The ICC had the power to investigate and prosecute lawbreakers, but the legislation limited its authority to control over commerce conducted between states.

Like state railroad commissions, the ICC found it difficult to define a reasonable rate. Moreover, thousands of cases overwhelmed the tiny staff in the early months of operation. In the long run, the lack of enforcement power was most serious. The ICC's only recourse was to bring offenders into the federal courts and engage in lengthy legal proceedings. Few railroads worried about defying ICC directions on rates. When they appeared in court four or five years later, they often won their cases from judges suspicious of new federal authority. Between 1887 and 1906, a total of 16 cases made their way to the Supreme Court; 15 of them were decided in the railroads' favor. As one railroad executive candidly admitted, "There is not a road in the country that can be accused of living up to the rules of the Interstate Commerce Law."

The Southern Farmers' Alliance

The Grange declined in the late 1870s as the nation recovered from depression. But neither farm organizations nor farm protest died. Depression struck farmers once again in the late 1880s and worsened as the 1890s began. Official statistics told the familiar, dismal story of falling prices for cereal crops grown on the plains and prairies. A bushel of wheat that had sold for $1 in 1870 was worth 60 cents in the 1890s. Kansas farmers, in 1889, were selling their corn for a mere 10 cents a bushel. The national currency shortage, which usually reached critical proportions at harvest time, helped to push agricultural prices ever lower. And while prices declined, the load of debt climbed. Mortgage rates ranged between 18 and 36 percent, and shipping rates were high. It sometimes cost a farmer as much as one bushel of corn to send another one to market.

A Kansas farmer's letter reveals some of the human consequences of such statistics:

> At the age of 52 years, after a long life of toil, economy and self-denial, I find myself and family virtually paupers. With hundreds of cattle, hundreds of hogs, scores of good horses, and a farm that rewarded the toil of our hands with 16,000 bushels of golden corn, we are poorer by many dollars than we were years ago. What once seemed a neat little fortune and a house of refuge for our declining years . . . has been rendered valueless.

Under these pressures, farmers turned again to organization, education, and cooperation. The Southern Farmers' Alliance was one of the most important reform organizations. Its roots stretched back to the late 1870s on the Texas frontier. A decade later, the Alliance launched an ambitious organizational drive, sending lecturers throughout the South and onto the western plains. Eventually, Alliance lecturers reached 43 states and territories, bringing their message to 2 million farming families.

Traveling lecturers explained the nature and goals of the Alliance, whipped up enthusiasm, and helped to establish state alliances. In turn, county alliances and local farmers' clubs, each with their own lecturers, were organized to complete a far-reaching agrarian network. Alliance newspapers like the *Progressive Farmer* in North Carolina and the *National Economist*, published in Washington, D.C., reinforced the message Alliance members heard at local, county, and state meetings.

An article in the *National Economist* pointed out some of the Alliance's fundamental beliefs. "The agricultural population of to-day is becoming rapidly aroused to the fact that agriculture, as a class, can only be rendered prosperous by radical changes in the laws governing money, transportation, and land." The economic and social position of farmers had slipped, even though as producers the farming class was critical to national well-being. The farmer's condition was, in the words of an Alliance song, "a sin," the result of the farmer's forgetting that "he's the man that feeds them all." Alliance lecturers proposed various programs that would help realize their slogan: "Equal rights to all, special privileges to none."

On the one hand, the Alliance experimented with buying and selling cooperatives in order to free farmers from the clutches of supply merchants, banks, and other credit agencies. Although these efforts often failed in the long run, they taught the value of cooperation to achieve common goals. On the other hand, the Alliance supported legislative efforts to regulate powerful monopolies and corporations, which they believed gouged the farmer. Many Alliance members also felt that increasing the money supply was critical to improving the position of farmers and supported a national banking system empowered to issue paper money.

The Alliance also called for a variety of measures to improve the quality of rural life: better public schools for rural children, state agricultural colleges, and an improvement in the status of women. "This order has the good sense, magnanimity and moral courage," declared Hattie Huntingdon of Louisiana, "to lay aside deeply-rooted prejudices handed down from the barbaric past and admit women into its fold and proclaim to the world that it believes in equal rights to all."

By 1890, discontent swept over America's farmlands. In the Midwest, where farmers were prospering by raising hogs and cattle on cheap grain, and in the East, where farmers were growing fruit and vegetables for urban markets, discontent was muted. But that summer in Kansas, hundreds of farmers packed their families into wagons to set off for Alliance meetings or to parade in long lines through the streets of nearby towns and villages. Floats garnished with evergreens proclaimed that the farmers' new organization focused on live issues, not the dead ones Congress debated.

Similar scenes occurred throught the West and the South. A farmer's wife, Zenobia Wheeless, captured the hopeful spirit of the protest in her letter to North Carolina Alliance leader Leonidas Polk. "We rode sixteen miles . . . to hear Brother Tracy [an organizer from Texas]— started about sun-up and trotted all the way . . . . Brother Tracy's lecture was very interesting . . . it seemed that all eyes were riveted upon him." Zenobia's enthusiasm led her to write, "Brother Polk, if you will come to some of our appointments in reach of us, I will ride the same distance to hear a lecture from you, if I knew there would not be a single sister to accompany me." Never had there been such a wave of organizational activity in rural America. In 1890, more than a million farmers counted themselves as Alliance members.

The Alliance network also included black farmers. In 1888, black and white organizers established the Colored Farmers' Alliance, headed by a white Baptist minister, R. M. Humphrey. The Colored Farmers' Alliance recognized that black and white farmers faced common economic problems and must cooperate to ameliorate their shared plight. The fact that many southern cotton farmers depended on black labor and had a different perspective from blacks was not immediately recognized as a barrier. In 1891, however, cotton pickers working on plantations near Memphis, Tennessee, went on strike. White posses chased the strikers, lynched 15 of them, and demonstrated that racial tensions simmered just below the surface.

The Ocala Platform

In December 1890, the National Alliance gathered in Ocala, Florida, to develop an official platform. As delegates deliberated, it became clear that most of them thought the federal government had failed to address the farmers' problems. "Congress must come nearer the people or the people will come nearer the Congress," warned the Alliance's president. Both parties were far too subservient to the "will of corporation and money power." Thus the platform called for the direct election of U.S. senators. Alliance members supported lowering the tariff, a much debated topic in Congress, but their justification, emphasizing the need to reduce prices for "the poor of our land," had a radical ring. Their money plank went far beyond what any national legislator was likely to consider. Rejecting the notion that only gold had value or, indeed, that precious metals had to be the basis for currency, Alliance leaders boldly envisioned a new banking system controlled by the federal govenment. They demanded that the government take an active economic role by increasing the amount of money in circulation in the form of Treasury notes and silver. More money would lead to inflation, higher prices, and a reduction in debt, they believed.

The platform also called for the creation of subtreasuries (federal warehouses) in agricultural regions where farmers could store their produce at low interest rates until market prices favored selling. To tide farmers over until that time, the federal government would loan farmers up to 80 percent of the current local price for their products. Thus the platform plan would free farmers from the twin evils of the credit merchant and depressed prices at harvest time. Other demands included a graduated income tax and support for the regulation of transportation and communication networks. If regulation failed, the government was called upon to take over both networks and run them for the public's benefit.

In the context of late nineteenth-century political life, almost all of these planks were radical. They demanded that the government take aggressive action to assist the country's farmers at a time when the government favored big business (see Chapter 20). Even though a majority of farmers did not belong to the Alliance, many Americans feared that the organization was capable of upsetting political arrangements. The New York *Sun* reported that the Alliance had caused a "panic" in the two major parties. The Alliance's warning that the people would replace their representatives unless they were better represented was already coming true. Although the Alliance was not formally in politics, it had supported sympathetic candidates in the fall elections of 1890. A surprising number of these local and state candidates had won. Alliance victories in the West harmed the Republican party enough to cause President Harrison to refer to "our election disaster."

Having entered politics indirectly, dissatisfied Alliance members pressed for an independent political party. For a short time they hoped that the Democratic party might respond to their concerns, but it soon appeared that legislators who courted Alliance votes conveniently forgot their pledges once elected. Alliance sup-

port did not necessarily bring action on issues of interest to farmers, nor even respect. One Texas farmer reported that the chairman of the state Democratic executive committee "calls us all skunks" and observed that "anything that has the scent of the plowhandle smells like a polecat" to the Democrats. On the national level, no one seemed much interested in the Ocala platform. As one North Carolinian observed, "I am not able to perceive any very great difference between the two parties."

Among the first to realize the necessity of forming an independent third party was Georgia's Tom Watson. "We are in the midst of a great crisis," he argued. "We have before us three or four platforms . . . [and] the Ocala platform is the best of all three. It is the only one that breathes the breath of life. . . . Let the Democratic party take warning." Watson also realized that electoral success in the South would depend on unity between white and black farmers.

The People's Party

In February 1892, the People's, or Populist, party was established, with almost 100 black delegates in attendance. Leonidas Polk, president of the Alliance and promoter of a political coalition between the South and the West, emerged as the natural choice as the party's presidential candidate that fall. "The time has arrived," he thundered, "for the great West, the great South, and the great Northwest, to link their hands and hearts together and march to the ballot box and take possession of the government, restore it to the principles of our fathers, and run it in the interest of the people." But by the time the party met at its convention in July in Omaha, Nebraska, Polk had died. The party nominated James B. Weaver, a Civil War veteran from Iowa, as its presidential candidate, and James G. Field, a former Confederate soldier, for vice-president.

The platform preamble, written by Ignatius Donnelly, a Minnesota farmer, author, and politician, caught much of the urgent spirit of the agrarian protest movement in the 1890s:

> We meet in the midst of a nation brought to the verge of moral, political and material ruin. Cor-

ruption dominates the ballot box, the legislatures, the Congress, and touches even the ermine of the bench. The people are demoralized. . . . The fruits of the toil of millions are boldly stolen to build up colossal fortunes . . . we breed two great classes—paupers and millionaires.

The charge was clear: "The controlling influences dominating the old political parties have allowed the existing dreadful conditions to develop without serious effort to restrain or prevent them."

The Omaha platform demands, drawn from the Ocala platform of 1890, were greatly expanded. They included more means of direct democracy (direct election of senators, direct primaries, the initiative, referendum, and the secret ballot) and several planks intended to enlist the support of urban labor (eight-hour day, immigration restriction, and condemnation of the use of Pinkerton agents as an "army of mercenaries . . . a menace to our liberties"). The People's party also endorsed a graduated income tax, the free and unlimited coinage of silver at a ratio of 16 to 1 (meaning that the U.S. Mint would have to buy silver for coinage at 1/16 the current official price of the equivalent amount of gold), and, rather than regulation, government ownership of railroads, telephone, and telegraph. "The time has come," the platform said, "when the railroad corporations will either own the people or the people must own the railroads."

The Populist party attempted to widen the nature of the American political debate to promote a new vision of the government's role, and to address the farmers' problems. But the tasks facing the party in its attempt to win power were monumental. Success at the polls meant weaning the South away from the Democratic party, encouraging southern whites to work with blacks, and persuading voters of both parties to abandon familiar political ties. Nor were all Alliance members eager to follow their leaders into the third party. At the most basic level, the Populists had to create the political machinery necessary to function in the 1892 electoral campaign.

Despite these obstacles, the new party pressed forward. Unlike the candidates of the major parties in 1892, Benjamin Harrison and

Grover Cleveland, Weaver actively campaigned. In the South, he faced rowdy audiences, rotten eggs, and rocks from hostile Democrats, who disapproved of attempts to form a biracial political coalition. The results of the campaign were mixed. Although Weaver won over a million popular votes (the first third-party candidate to do so), he carried only four states (Kansas, Colorado, Idaho, and Nevada) and parts of two others (Oregon and North Dakota) for a total of 22 electoral votes. The attempt to break the stranglehold of the Democratic party on the South had failed. Democrats raised the cry of "nigger rule" and fanned racial fears. Those white farmers who viewed the alliance with blacks as one of necessity voted Democratic. Intimidation tactics and violence frightened off others. Just as important, Weaver failed to appeal to city workers, who were suspicious of the party's anti-urban tone and its desire for higher agricultural prices (which meant higher food prices); to people living east of the Mississippi; and even to relatively prosperous midwestern farmers, who saw little of value in the Omaha platform.

Although the People's party failed to appeal to a cross section of American voters in 1892, it gained substantial support. Miners and mine owners in states like Montana, Colorado, and New Mexico favored the demand for coinage of silver. Most populists, however, were rural Americans in the South and West who for one reason or another were out of the mainstream of American life. Economic grievances sharpened political discontent. But Populists were often no poorer or more debt-ridden than other farmers. They did tend to lead more isolated lives, however; often their farms were far from towns, villages, and railroads. They felt powerless to affect the workings of their political, social, and economic world. Thus they responded to a party offering to act as their advocate.

Farmers who were better integrated into their world tended to believe they could work through existing political parties. In 1892, when thousands of farmers and others were politically and economically discontented, they voted for Cleveland and the Democrats, not the Populists.

Yet the Populists did not lose heart in 1892, as Chapter 20 will show. Populist governors were elected in Kansas and North Dakota. The party swept Colorado. It was obvious that the showing of the party in the South, where even Tom Watson lost his bid for a congressional seat, stemmed from violent opposition and fraud on the part of the Democrats. Georgia Democrats manipulated black votes to defeat Populists. Returns in Richmond County revealed a Democratic majority of 80 percent in a total vote twice the size of the actual number of legal voters.

CONCLUSION: The Reality of Agricultural America

The late nineteenth century was a turbulent time in rural America. The Indian "problem," which had plagued Americans for 200 years, was tragically solved for a while, but not without resistance and bloodshed. Few whites were troubled by these events. Most were caught up in the challenge of responding to a fast-changing world. Believing themselves to be the backbone of the nation, white farmers brought the Indian lands into cultivation, modernized their farms, and raised bumper crops. But success and a comfortable competency eluded many of them. Some, like Milton Leeper, never gave up hope or farming. Many were caught in a cycle of poverty and debt. Others fled to the cities, where they joined the industrial work force described in the next chapter. Many turned to collective action and politics. Their actions demonstrate that they did not merely react to events but attempted to shape them.

Recommended Reading

Gilbert C. Fite provides a detailed study of the last agricultural frontier in *The Farmer's Frontier, 1865–1900* (1966). Henry Nash Smith discusses changing views of the Plains in *Virgin Land: The American West as Symbol and Myth* (1950). J. B. Jackson deals with the transformation of landscape in *American Space: The Centennial Years, 1865–1976* (1972). Annette Kolodny deals with women's perceptions of the West in *The Land Before Her: Fantasy and Experience of the American Frontiers, 1630–1860* (1984). Land policy is the subject of Paul W. Gates, *History of Public Land Law Development* (1978), while Alan G. Bogue discusses farm indebtedness in *Money at Interest: The Farm Mortgage on the Middle Border* (1955). Fred C. Luebke has edited a collection of essays dealing with immigrants on the Plains frontier, *Ethnicity on the Great Plains* (1980). Howard R. Lamar provides a history of the Southwest in *The Far Southwest, 1846–1880* (1963), and Earl Pomeroy covers the Far West in *The Pacific Slope: A History of California, Oregon, Washington, Idaho, Utah, and Nevada* (1965).

R. W. Paul writes of the mining frontier in *Mining Frontiers of the Far West, 1848–1880* (1963). Robert R. Dykstra explores urban development and social ten-sions on the cattle frontier in *The Cattle Towns: A Social History of the Kansas Cattle Trading Centers* (1970). Joseph B. Frantz and Julian E. Choate focus on the cowboy in *The American Cowboy: The Myth and the Reality* (1968).

On relations between whites and Native Americans, see William T. Hagan, *American Indians* (1979 ed.) and Wilcomb E. Washburn, *The Indian in America* (1975). Also useful are Ronald T. Takaki, *Iron Cages: Race and Culture in Nineteenth-Century America* (1979); Francis P. Prucha, *American Indian Policy in Crisis: Christian Reformers and the Indians* (1976); and Ralph K. Andrist, *The Long Death: The Last Days of the Plains Indians* (1964). John G. Neihardt, *Black Elk Speaks* (1932) is the account of a holy man of the Ogalala Sioux.

For the New South, see C. Vann Woodward, *The Origins of the New South, 1877–1913* (1951) and Paul M. Gaston, *The New South Creed: A Study in Southern Mythmaking* (1970). Also helpful are Robert C. McMath and Orville V. Burton, eds., *Toward a New South: Studies in Post-Civil War Southern Communities* and Blaine A. Brownell and David R. Goldfield, eds., *The City in Southern History* (1977). On race relations, see H. N. Rabinowitz, *Race Relations in the*

Urban South (1978) and Morgan Kousser, *The Shaping of Southern Politics: Suffrage Restriction and the Establishment of the One-Party South* (1974).

Lawrence Goodwyn provides a provocative study of populism in *The Populist Moment: A Short History of the Agrarian Revolt in America* (1978). Other studies include Sheldon Hackney, *Populism to Progressivism in Alabama* (1969); Bruce Palmer, *"Men Over Money": The Southern Populist Critique of American Capitalism* (1980); and Peter H. Argersinger, *Populism and Politics: William Alfred Peffer and the People's Party* (1974). An analysis of the organization that gave birth to populism is to be found in Robert C. McMath, *Populist Vanguard: A History of the Southern Farmers' Alliance* (1975).

Good novels include Willa Cather, *My Ántonia* (1918) and O. E. Rolvaag, *Giants in the Earth* (1927).

TIME LINE

1860s	Cattle drives from Texas begin
1865–1867	Sioux Wars on the Great Plains
1867	National Grange founded
1869	Transcontinental railroad completed
1869–1874	Granger Laws
1873	Financial panic triggers economic depression
1874	Barbed wire patented
1875	Black Hills gold rush incites Sioux War
1876	Custer's last stand at Little Big Horn
1877	*Munn* v. *Illinois* Bonanza farms in the Great Plains
1880s	"New South"
1881	Tuskegee Institute founded
1883–1885	Depression
1884	Southern Farmers' Alliance founded
1886	Severe winter ends cattle boom
1887	Dawes Severalty Act Interstate Commerce Act Farm prices plummet
1888	Colored Farmers' Alliance founded
1890	Afro-American League founded Sioux Ghost Dance movement Massacre at Wounded Knee Ocala platform
1890s	Black disenfranchisement in South Jim Crow laws passed in South Declining farm prices
1892	Populist party formed
1895	Booker T. Washington's "Atlanta Compromise" address
1896	*Plessy* v. *Ferguson*

CHAPTER 19
THE RISE OF SMOKESTACK AMERICA

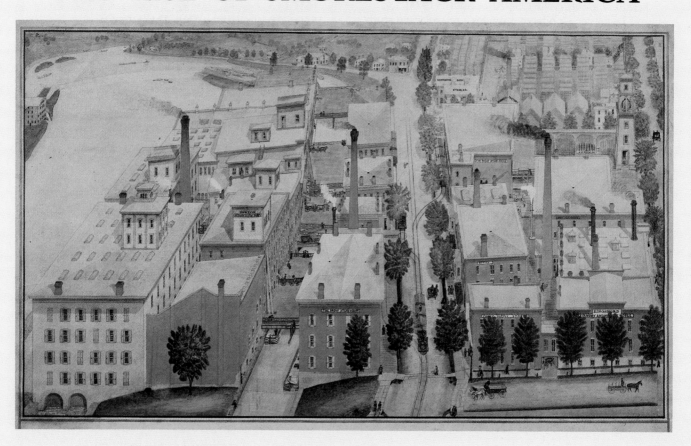

By 1883, Thomas O'Donnell had lived in the United States for over a decade. He was 30 years old, married, with two young children. His third child had died in 1882, and O'Donnell was still in debt over the funeral. Money was scarce, for O'Donnell was a textile worker in Fall River, Massachusetts, and not very well educated. "I went to work when I was young," he explained, "and have been working ever since." However, O'Donnell worked only sporadically at the mill. New machines needed "a good deal of small help," and the mill owners preferred to hire man-and-boy teams. Since O'Donnell's children were only 1 and 3, he often saw others preferred for day work. Once, when he was passed over, he recalled, "I said to the boss . . . what am I to do; I have got two little boys at home . . . how am I to get something for them to eat; I can't get a turn when I come here. . . . I says, 'Have I got to starve; ain't I to have any work?' "

O'Donnell and his family were barely getting by even though he worked with pick and shovel when he could. He estimated that he had earned only $133 over the course of the previous year. Rent came to $72. The family spent $2 for a little coal but depended for heat on driftwood that O'Donnell picked up on the beach. Clams were a major part of the family diet, but there were days when there was nothing to eat at all.

The children "got along very nicely all summer," but it was now November, and they were beginning to "feel quite sickly." It was hardly surprising. "One has one shoe on, a very poor one, and a slipper, that was picked up somewhere. The other has two odd shoes on, with the heel out." His wife was healthy but not ready for winter. She had two dresses, one saved for church, and "an undershirt that she got given to her, and . . . an old wrapper, which is about a mile too big for her; somebody gave it to her."

O'Donnell was describing his family's marginal existence to a Senate committee that was gathering testimony in Boston in 1883 on the relations between labor and capital. As the senators heard the tale, they asked him why he did not go west. "It would not cost you over $1,500," said one senator. The gap between senator and worker could not have been more dramatic. O'Donnell replied, "Well, I never saw over a $20 bill . . . if some one would give me $1,500 I will go." Asked by the senator if O'Donnell had friends who could provide him with the funds, O'Donnell sadly replied no.

The senators, of course, were far better acquainted with the world of comfort and leisure than they were with the poverty of families like the O'Donnells. From their vantage point, they could clearly see the fruits of industrial progress. As the United States became a world industrial leader in the years after the Civil War, its factories poured forth an abundance of ever-cheaper goods ranging from steel rails and farm reapers to mass-produced parlor sets. These were years of tremendous growth and significant economic and social change. Manufacturing replaced agriculture as the leading source of economic growth between 1860 and 1900. By 1890, a majority of the American work force held nonagricultural jobs; over a third lived in cities. A rural nation of farmers was becoming a nation of industrial workers and city dwellers.

As O'Donnell's testimony illustrates, however, change and progress were not synonymous for everyone. Although no nationwide studies of poverty existed, estimates suggest that perhaps half of the American population was too poor to take advantage of the new goods of the age.

This chapter examines America's transformation between 1865 and 1900. During these years, the industrial system expanded and became immensely productive. Big business became the common form of organization, the city the preferred location for manufacturing. New labor needs were met by a growing industrial work force, much of it foreign-born. The chapter's central theme grows out of O'Donnell's story: as the United States built up its railroads, cities, and factories, its production and profit orientation resulted in the maldistribution of wealth and power. Although many were too exhausted by life's daily struggles to protest new inequalities, strikes and other forms of working-class resistance punctuated the period. The social problems that accompanied the country's industrial development would capture the attention of reformers and politicians for decades to come.

THE CHARACTER OF INDUSTRIAL PROGRESS

When Americans went to war in 1861, agriculture was the country's leading source of economic growth. Forty years later, manufacturing had taken its place. During these years, the production of manufactured goods outpaced the growth of population. By 1900, three times as many goods per person existed as in 1860. Per capita income increased by over 2 percent a year. But these aggregate figures disguise the fact that many people did not win any gains at all.

As the character of American manufacturing shifted, new regions grew to industrial importance. From New England to the Midwest lay the country's industrial heartland. New England was still a center of light industry, and the Midwest continued to process natural resources. Now, however, the production of iron, steel, and transportation equipment joined the older manufacturing operations there. In the Far West, manufacturers concentrated on processing the region's natural resources, but heavy industry made strides as well. In the South, the textile industry put down roots by the 1890s, although the South as a whole was far less industrialized than either the North or the Midwest.

Rise of Heavy Industry

Although many factors contributed to the dramatic rise in industrial productivity, the changing nature of the industrial sector itself explains many of the gains. Manufacturers before the Civil War had concentrated either on producing textiles, clothing, and leather products or on processing agricultural and natural resources like grain, hogs, or lumber. While these industries continued to be important, heavy industry, which produced goods like steel, iron, petroleum, and machinery, grew rapidly. The manufacturing of "producer's goods" (goods intended for other producers rather than consumers) provided the basis for economic growth.

Population and Economic Growth, 1855–1919

	1855–1890	1889–1919
Population	2.5%	1.8%
Real gross product	4.0	3.9
Real product per capita	1.5	2.1
Total factor input	3.7	2.2
Labor	3.0	1.8
Nonlabor	4.6	3.1
Total factor productivity	0.3	1.7
Real product per unit of		
Labor input	1.0	2.0
Nonlabor input	−0.6	0.7

Source: Porter, *Encyclopedia of Economic History,* 1980.

Farmers, who bought machinery for their farms; manufacturers, who installed new equipment in their factories; and railroads, which bought steel rails for their tracks, all contributed to rising productivity figures.

Technological innovations that revolutionized production lay behind the rise of heavy industry. The evolution of the steel industry shows the transforming power of new technology. Before the Civil War, the production of iron was a slow and expensive process. Skilled and highly paid workers provided the backbone of the work force. The introduction of the Bessemer and open-hearth processes in the 1870s made it possible to convert iron ore cheaply and more easily into hard steel. The need for skilled workers declined. Dramatic changes in the steel industry resulted. The industry as a whole expanded, production soared, and prices fell. When Andrew Carnegie introduced the Bessemer process into his plant in the mid-1870s, the price of steel plummeted from $100 a ton to $50. In another two years the price dropped to $40; by 1890, steel cost only $12 a ton.

In turn, the production of a cheaper, stronger, and more durable material than iron created new goods, new demands, and new markets. The railroads had relied on iron rails, which flattened

New developments in industry and engineering spawned marvels such as the Brooklyn Bridge, hailed as a triumph of our time.

and split in a few years. Now they consumed 1.5 million tons of hard steel rails a year as they built new lines across the country. Bridge builders soon realized the possibilities of steel-cable suspension designs, and architects such as Louis Sullivan began to use steel for the nation's first high-rise buildings. Countless Americans bought steel in more humble forms: wire, nails, bolts, needles, screws.

New sources of power facilitated the conversion of American industry to mass production. Because steam engines and coal were so expensive, early manufacturers had depended on water power provided by streams and rivers. With the opening of new anthracite coal deposits, however, the cost of this fuel dropped, and American industry rapidly shifted to steam. In 1869, about half of the industrial power used came from water; by 1900, steam engines accounted for 80 percent of the nation's industrial energy supply. Steam freed industry to relocate from riversides, mostly in rural areas, to the cities and thus played a critical role in the growth of factory-filled cities in the late nineteenth century.

The completion of the transportation and communications network after the Civil War was fundamental to economic growth. In 1860, most railroads were located in the East and Midwest. From 1862 on, both national and state governments vigorously promoted railroad construction with land grants from the public domain. Eventually the railroads received over 180 million acres, an area about 1½ times the size of Texas. Similarly, counties and cities donated land for stations and terminals, bought railroad stock, made loans and grants, and gave tax breaks to railroads.

With such incentives, the first transcontinental railroad was completed in 1869. A burst of railroad construction followed. Four additional transcontinental lines and miles of feeder and branch roads were laid down in the 1870s and 1880s. By 1890, trains rumbled across 165,000 miles of tracks. As railroads crisscrossed the country, Western Union lines arose alongside them. Mass production and distribution depended on fast, efficient, and regular transportation. The completion of the national system both encouraged and supported the adoption of mass production and mass marketing.

Meeting Capital Needs

All these changes demanded huge amounts of capital. The creation of the railroad system alone cost over a billion dollars by 1859, in contrast to the canal system's modest price tag of under $2 million. The completion of the national railroad network required another $10 billion. Reduced opportunities for investments abroad encouraged British, French, and German investors to pour funds into American enterprise. Foreigners contributed a third of the sum needed to complete the railroad system. Americans were also eager to support new ventures, and began to devote an increasing percentage of the national income to investment purposes rather than consumption.

Although savings and commercial banks continued to invest the capital of their depositors, investment banking houses like Morgan & Co. played a new and significant role in matching resources with economic enterprises. Investment bankers marketed investment opportunities. They bought up blocks of corporate bonds (which offered set interest rates and eventually the repayment of principal) at a discount for interested investors and also sold stocks (which paid dividends only if the company made a profit). Because stocks were riskier investments than bonds, buyers were at first cautious. But when John Pierpont Morgan, a respected investment banker, began to market stocks, they became more popular. The market for industrial securities rapidly expanded in the 1880s and 1890s. Although some Americans feared the power of investment bankers, they were integral to the economic expansion of the late nineteenth century.

Railroads: The First Big Business

As the nature of the American economy changed, big businesses became the characteristic form of economic organization. Big businesses, with large amounts of capital, could afford to build huge factories, buy and install the latest, most efficient machinery, hire hundreds of workers, and use the most up-to-date methods. The result was more goods at lower prices. Machines costing thousands of dollars mass-produced goods costing pennies.

The railroads were the pioneers of big business and a great modernizing force in America. After the Civil War, railroad companies expanded rapidly. In 1865, the typical railroad was only 100 miles long. Twenty years later, it was 1,000. In 1888, a medium-size Boston railroad company had three times as many employees and received six times as much income as the Massachusetts state government.

The size of railroads, the huge costs of construction, maintenance, and repair, and the complexity of operations required unprecedented amounts of capital and new management techniques. No single person could finance a railroad or hope to supervise its operations involving hundreds of miles of track and hundreds of employees. Nor could any one person resolve the thorny issues raised by such a large enterprise. How should the operations and employees be organized? What were the long-term and short-term needs of the railroad? What were proper rates? What should be company policy toward unions? What share of the profits did workers deserve? The creation of large businesses posed these questions and many more.

Unlike small businesses with modest overhead costs, railroads faced high constant costs. Maintaining equipment and roads was expensive. In addition, railroads carried a high burden of debt, incurred to pay for construction and expansion. The necessity of meeting regular interest payments and expenses forced railroads to do as much business and to use their equipment as intensively as possible. If 20 cars were almost as expensive to pull as 25, why not haul 25?

High costs and the need to use equipment intensively encouraged aggressive and competitive business techniques. To attract freight, railroads wooed customers with low rates. Railroad freight charges dropped steadily during the last quarter of the century. When two lines or more competed for the same traffic, railroads often offered lower rates than their rivals or secret rebates (cheaper fares in exchange for all of a company's business). Rate wars helped customers, but they could end in a railroad's bankruptcy. Instability plagued the railroad industry even as it expanded.

In the 1870s, railroad leaders attempted to stabilize conditions by eliminating ruinous and ruthless competition. As George Perkins of the

Chicago, Burlington, and Quincy Railroad explained, "The struggle for existence and the survival of the fittest is a pretty theory, but it is also a law of nature that even the fittest must live as they go along." Railroad leaders established "pools," informal agreements to set uniform rates or to divide up the traffic. Yet pools never completely succeeded in ending competition. Too often, individual companies disregarded their agreements, especially when the business cycle took a downturn.

Railroad leaders were also tempted to control costs and counter the late-nineteenth-century pattern of falling prices by slashing their

Conveniences such as the dining car meant more complex management problems for railroad administrators.

workers' wages. Owners justified their strategy by reasoning that they had taken all the business risks. As a result, railroads were plagued by worker unrest, some of which will be described later in this chapter.

The huge scale and complexity of the railroads required new management techniques. In 1854, the directors of the Erie Railroad hired engineer and inventor Daniel McCallum to devise a system to make railroad managers and their employees more accountable. In his report the following year, McCallum highlighted the differences between large and small organizations. In a small organization, one could pay personal attention to all the details of operation. But McCallum argued that, "any system that might be applicable to the business and extent of a short road would be found entirely inadequate to the wants of a long one."

McCallum's system, emphasizing the division of responsibilities and a regular flow of information, attracted widespread interest, and railroads became the pioneers in rationalized administrative practices and management techniques. Their procedures became models for other businesses in decision making, scheduling, and engineering. The behavior the railroads exhibited—their competitiveness, their attempt to underprice one another, their eventual interest in merger, their tendency to cut workers' wages—were also followed by other big businesses in the late nineteenth century as they faced similar economic conditions.

Growth in Other Industries

By the last quarter of the century, the textile, metal, and machinery industries equaled the railroads in size. In 1870, the typical iron and steel firm employed under 100 workers. Thirty years later, the average work force was four times as large. By 1900, more than 1,000 American factories had giant labor forces ranging between 500 and 1,000. Almost 450 others employed more than 1,000 workers. Big business had come of age.

Business expansion was accomplished in one of two ways (or a combination of both). Some owners like Andrew Carnegie integrated their businesses vertically. Vertical integration meant adding operations either before or after the production process. Even though he had introduced the most up-to-date innovations in his steel mills, Carnegie realized he needed his own sources of pig iron, coal, and coke. This was "backward" integration, away from the consumer, in order to avoid dependence on suppliers. When Carnegie acquired steamships and railroads to transport his finished products, he was integrating "forward," toward the consumer. Companies that integrated vertically frequently achieved economies of scale through more efficient management techniques.

Other companies copied the railroads and integrated horizontally by combining similar businesses. The objective was not to control the various stages of production, as was the case with vertical integration, but rather to gain a monopoly of the market in order to eliminate competition and to stabilize prices. Horizontal integration sometimes resulted in some economies and thus greater profits, but not always. But the control over prices that monopoly provided did boost earnings.

John D. Rockefeller's company, Standard Oil of New Jersey, used the strategy of horizontal integration. By a combination of astute and ruthless techniques, Rockefeller bought or drove out his competitors. Although Standard Oil never achieved a complete monopoly of the market, by 1898 it was refining almost 84 percent of the nation's oil. As Rockefeller concluded, "The day of individual competition [in the oil business] . . . is past and gone."

Rockefeller's remarks accurately characterized new economic conditions. As giant businesses competed intensely, often cutting wages and prices, smaller and weaker producers were driven under or absorbed. Business ownership became increasingly concentrated. In 1870, some 808 American iron and steel firms competed in the marketplace. By 1900, the number had dwindled to less than 70.

Like the railroads, many big businesses chose to incorporate. Although corporations were not new, most manufacturing firms were unincorporated in 1860. By 1900, corporations turned out two-thirds of the country's industrial goods.

Business gained many advantages by incorporating. The sale of stock made it possible to raise sums for large-scale operations. The principle of limited liability protected investors, while the corporation's legal identity ensured its survival after the death of original and subsequent shareholders. Longevity suggested a measure of stability that heightened the attractiveness of the corporation as an investment.

Increase in Size of Industries, 1860–1900

INDUSTRY	Average Establishment Size (Workers) 1860	1900
Agricultural implements	8	65
Carpets and rugs	31	214
Cotton goods	112	287
Glass	81	149
Hosiery and knit goods	46	91
Iron and steel	65	333
Leather	5	40
Malt liquors	5	26
Paper and wood pulp	15	65
Shipbuilding	15	42
Silk and silk goods	39	135
Slaughtering and meatpacking	20	61
Tobacco	30	67
Woolen goods	33	67

Source: U.S. Bureau of the Census.

The Unpredictable Economic Cycle

The transformation of the economy was neither smooth nor steady. Rockefeller described his years in the oil business as "hazardous" and confessed that he did not know "how we came through them."

Two depressions, one from 1873 to 1879 and the other from 1893 to 1897, were far more severe than economic downturns before the Civil War. Prewar depressions stemmed from collapsing land values, unsound banking practices, and changes in the supply of money. The depressions of the late nineteenth century, when the economy was larger and more interdependent, were industrial in character and far-ranging in impact. Large-scale unemployment, a new phenomenon in American life, accompanied them.

During expansionary years, manufacturers flooded markets with their goods. The pattern of falling prices that characterized the postwar period and the fierce competition between producers may well have combined to encourage overproduction. When the market was finally saturated, sales and profits declined, and the economy spiraled downward. Owners cut back on production and laid workers off. Industrial workers, now an increasing percentage of the American work force, depended solely on wages for their livelihood. As they economized and bought less food, farm prices also plummeted. Farmers, like wage workers, cut back on purchases. Business and trade stagnated, and the railroads were finally affected. Eventually, the cycle bottomed out, but in the meantime, millions had been unemployed, thousands of businesses had gone bankrupt, and many Americans had suffered deprivation and hardship.

URBAN EXPANSION IN THE INDUSTRIAL AGE

The new industrial age was one of rapid urban expansion. Before the Civil War, manufacturers had relied on water power and chosen rural sites for their factories. Now as they shifted to steam power, they selected urban locations that offered them workers, specialized services, and local markets. Although technological innovations like electric lights (invented in 1879) and telephones (1876) were still not widespread, they further increased the desirability of urban sites. The railroad network provided manufacturers with the necessary links to distant materials and markets. Industry, rather than commerce or finance, was the force behind urban expansion between 1870 and 1900.

Cities of all sizes grew. The population of New York and Philadelphia doubled and tripled. Smaller cities, especially those in the industrial Midwest like Omaha, Duluth, and Minneapolis, boasted impressive growth rates. Southern cities, as we saw in Chapter 18, also shared in the dramatic growth. In the Far West during the 1880s, Spokane exploded from 350 to 20,000 and Tacoma from 1,100 to 36,000. In 1870, some 25 percent of Americans lived in cities; by 1900, fully 40 percent of them did.

A Growing Population

The American population, as a whole, was growing at a rate of about 2 percent a year, but cities were expanding far more rapidly. What accounted for the dramatic increase in urban population?

Certainly not a high birthrate. Although more people were born than died in American cities, births made only a modest contribution to the urban population explosion. The general pattern of declining family size that had emerged before the Civil War continued. By 1900, the average woman bore only 3.6 children, in contrast to 5.2 in 1860. In cities, moreover, families tended to have fewer children than their rural counterparts. And urban children faced a host of health hazards like tuberculosis, diarrhea, and diphtheria. All city residents were vulnerable, but children especially so. The death rate for infants was twice as high in cities as in the countryside. In the 1880s, half the children born in Chicago would not live to celebrate their fifth birthday.

Migration from Farms and Towns

The swelling population of late nineteenth-century cities came from the nation's small towns and farms and from abroad. For both

Ten Largest Cities in the United States, 1850 and 1890

1850	1890
1. New York	1. New York
2. Philadelphia	2. Chicago
3. Baltimore	3. Philadelphia
4. Boston	4. St. Louis
5. New Orleans	5. Boston
6. Cincinnati	6. Baltimore
7. Brooklyn	7. Pittsburgh
8. St. Louis	8. San Francisco
9. Albany	9. Cincinnati
10. Pittsburgh	10. Cleveland

Source: U.S. Bureau of the Census.

foreigners and Americans alike, the decision to relocate resulted from a combination of pressures, some encouraging them to abandon their original homes, others attracting them to the urban environment.

For rural Americans, the "push" came from the modernization of agricultural life. Factories poured out farm machines that replaced human hands. By 1896, one man with machinery could harvest 18 times as much wheat as a farmer working with hand tools in 1830. Then, too, rural life was often monotonous and drab.

Work in the industrial city was the prime attraction. Although urban jobs were often dirty, dangerous, and exhausting, so too, was farmwork. Moreover, by 1890, manufacturing workers were earning hundreds of dollars more a year than farm laborers. Some industrial workers, like the miners in the Far West, earned even more. Part of the difference between rural and urban wages was eaten up by the higher cost of living in the city, but not all.

An intangible but important lure was the glitter of city life. The young man who found Kansas City to be a "gilded metropolis" filled with "marvels," a veritable "round of joy," was dazzled by the excitement of urban life, its culture and amusements. Shops, theaters, restaurants, churches, department stores, newspapers, ball games, and the urban throng all amazed young men and women who had grown up on farms and in small towns. Although these pleasures were often out of reach, the fascination remained.

Novelists like Theodore Dreiser and Stephen Crane captured both the glamor and dangers of city life. Writing in a style termed literary realism, they examined social problems and cast their characters in carefully depicted local settings. Dreiser's novel *Sister Carrie* (1900) follows a typical country girl as she comes to Chicago. Carrie dreams of sharing Chicago's amusements and fantasizes a life of wealth, excitement, and ease. She finds, however, that the city's luxuries and pleasures are far from the reach of a mere factory employee. She discovers that by using her sex she can enjoy the city's pleasures. Many readers were shocked to discover that Carrie's "sin" was never punished. The novel ends with a contemplative but not repentant Carrie.

In *Maggie: A Girl of the Streets* (1893), Stephen Crane's heroine meets punishment at the story's end. As a young girl, Maggie retains her purity in the heart of New York's most appalling slums. Eventually, the city's pleasures lead to a loss of innocence. Maggie turns in despair to prostitution, and the reader is left at the novel's conclusion to guess whether Maggie has been murdered or commits suicide. Crane, and others, were as fascinated as they were repelled by the urban environment. Whether Eden or Sodom, the industrial city cast a powerful spell over American writers and American culture.

Southern blacks, often single and young, also fed the migratory stream into the cities. In the West and North, blacks comprised only a tiny part of the population: 3 percent in Denver in the 1880s and 1890s, 2 percent in Boston. In southern cities, however, they were more numerous. About 44 percent of Atlanta's residents in the late nineteenth century were black, and in Nashville, blacks made up about 38 percent of the population. No matter where they were,

Cities like Chicago offered a variety of sights, sounds, and activities which attracted those raised in rural isolation.

however, the city offered them few rewards, no glamor, and many dangers.

Newcomers from Overseas

During the 40 years before the Civil War, 5 million immigrants poured into the United States to seek their fortune. From 1860 to 1900, almost 14 million arrived. Although three-quarters of them stayed in the Northeast, they also could be found in most cities across the nation except in the South. In many of these cities, they outnumbered native-born whites.

As the flow of immigration increased, the national origin of immigrants shifted. Until 1880, three-quarters of the immigrants, often called the "old immigrants," hailed from the British Isles, Germany, and Scandinavia. Irish and Germans were the largest groups. Then the pattern slowly began to change. By 1890, Irish, English, Germans, and Scandinavians made up only 60 percent of all immigrants, while "new immigrants" from southern and eastern Europe

(Italy, Poland, Russia, Austria, Hungary, Greece, Turkey, and Syria) comprised most of the rest. Italian Catholics and eastern European Jews were the most numerous, followed by Slavs. The changing pattern is captured by one comparison. In 1870, probably 90 percent of the country's European immigrants came from Britain, Ireland, or western Europe. In 1900, less than half did.

Cheaper and better transportation made the great tide of migration possible, but dissatisfaction with conditions at home sparked the decision to leave. Overpopulation diminished opportunities. "The first thing I remember is that we lived in a little cabin in the greatest poverty," recalled one new American. Sometimes famine was a driving force, as it was when the Irish potato crop failed in the 1840s. Disease and epidemics forced others from their homelands. "We would have eaten each other had we stayed," claimed one Italian immigrant.

Efforts to modernize European economies also encouraged immigration. New agricultural

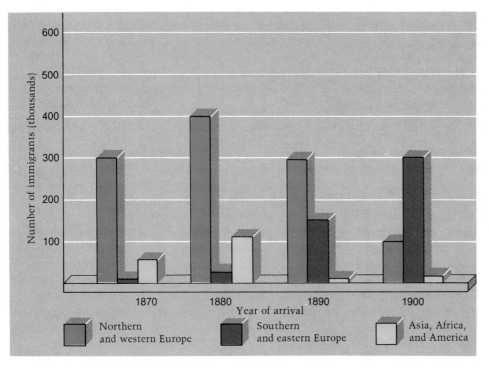

Immigration: Source and Volume, 1870–1900

Source: U.S. Bureau of the Census.

techniques led landlords to consolidate their land, thereby evicting longtime tenants. Artisans and craftsmen whose skills were obsolete with the introduction of machinery pulled up stakes and headed for the United States. Government policies pushed others to leave. In eastern Europe, especially in Russia, the official persecution of minorities and the expansion of the draft for the czar's army led millions of Jewish families and others to emigrate.

Opportunity in the "golden land" of America also detached thousands of immigrants from their homelands. State commissioners of immigration and American railroad and steamship companies, eager for workers and customers, wooed potential immigrants. Friends and relatives in America encouraged others to follow. Their letters described favorable living and working conditions and contained promises of helping newcomers find work. Often passage money was slipped between the pages as well. The ways in which people already in this country helped to facilitate the emigration of those still at home has led to the description of this movement of people as a "chain migration."

Like rural and small-town Americans, Europeans came primarily to work. When times were good in the United States, migration was heavy. When times were bad, numbers fell off. Most immigrants were young single men, who, in contrast to immigrants before the Civil War, had few skills. (Jews, however, came most often in family groups, and women predominated among the Irish.) They hoped to earn enough money in America to realize their ambitions at home. A surprising number, perhaps as many as a third, eventually returned home.

Asian immigrants, the majority of them from southern China, also came to the United States in the late nineteenth century. They too fled overpopulation, depressed conditions, unemployment, and crop failures and hoped for work in the "Land of the Golden Mountains." "We were very very much in debt because of the local warfare," explained one immigrant. "We planted each year, but we were robbed. We had to borrow. When news about the Gold Rush in California was spread by the shippers, my father decided to take the big chance."

Although only 264,000 Chinese came to the

Possibly coming to join a male family member, these women were photographed as they landed at the Battery in New York City.

United States between 1860 and 1900, they constituted a significant minority on the West Coast. Most of them were unskilled male contract laborers who had promised to work for a number of years and then return to their homeland. They performed some of the hardest and dirtiest jobs in the West, including railroad and levee construction and mining and factory work. They also often performed work that American men shunned, and they started hundreds of laundries in western communities.

The Industrial City

This growing and variegated population, the increasing concentration of manufacturing in urban areas, and improvements in transportation led to new physical and social arrangements in American cities. The private sector and the profit motive determined the way cities developed, and the results depressed many observers. James Bryce, a Scottish visitor, discovered that in American cities "monotony haunts one like a nightmare." Slums, which were not new, seemed disturbing because so many people lived in them. Yet these same cities also boasted of grand mansions, handsome business and industrial buildings, grandiose civic monuments, and acres of substantial middle-class homes.

By the last quarter of the nineteenth century, the jumbled arrangements of the antebellum walking city, whose size and configuration had been limited by the necessity of walking to work, disappeared. Where once substantial houses, businesses, and small artisan dwellings had stood side by side, central business districts emerged. Here were banks, shops, theaters, professional firms, and businesses. Few people lived downtown, although many worked or shopped there. Surrounding the business center were areas of light manufacturing and wholesale activity with housing for workers. Beyond these working-class neighborhoods stretched middle-class residential areas. Then came the suburbs, with "pure air, peacefulness, quietude, and natural scenery." Scattered throughout the city were pockets of industrial activity surrounded by crowded working-class housing.

This new pattern, with the poorest city residents clustered near the center, is familiar today. However, it was a reversal of the early-nineteenth-century urban form when at least some of the most desirable housing was to be found in the heart of the city. New living arrangements were also more segregated by race and class than those in the preindustrial walking city. Homogeneous social and economic neighborhoods emerged, and it became more unusual

Commuting to work from the suburbs became a common pattern as trains and streetcars became larger and faster.

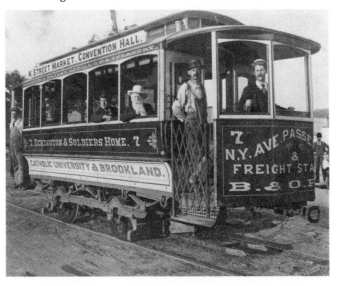

than before for a poor, working-class family to live near a middle- or upper-class family.

The changing urban geography was closely connected to the dense development of the central business district, the rise of heavy industry, and improvements in transportation. Better transportation increasingly allowed middle- and upper-class residents to live away from their work and from grimy industrial districts.

The urban transportation revolution started modestly in the 1820s and 1830s with the horse-drawn omnibus. This slow-moving vehicle accommodated only 10 to 12 passengers. Its expensive fares obliged most people to seek housing within walking distance of their work. In the 1850s, many cities introduced horse railways. Pulling cars over rails with as many as 25 passengers, horses could cover 5 to 6 miles an hour. The horse railways, which radiated from city centers like the spokes of a wheel, allowed the city to expand outward about 4 miles. The cost of a fare limited ridership to the middle and upper classes. The introduction of cable cars, trolley cars, and subways after 1880 further extended city boundaries and broadened residential choices for the middle class.

Neighborhoods and Neighborhood Life

Working-class neighborhoods clustered near the center of most industrial cities. Here lived newcomers from the American countryside, and since most immigrants settled in cities, crowds of foreigners as well.

Ethnic groups frequently chose to concentrate in particular neighborhoods, often located near industries requiring their labor. In Detroit in 1880, for example, 37 percent of the city's native-born families lived in one area while 40 percent of the Irish inhabited the "Irish West Side." Over half the Germans and almost three-quarters of the Poles lived on the city's east side. Although such neighborhoods often had an ethnic flavor, with small specialty shops and foreign-language signs, they were not ethnic ghettos. Immigrants and native-born Americans often lived in the same neighborhoods, on the same streets, and even in the same houses. Toward the end of the century, when ethnic enclaves emerged, they were just that—enclaves within a neighborhood. Italians might live in one block but Jews on the next.

Working-class neighborhoods were often what would be called slums today. They were crowded, unsanitary, and inadequately provided with public services. Many workers lived in houses once occupied by middle- and upper-class residents, now divided and subdivided to accommodate more people than the original builders had intended. Others lived in tenements, specially constructed to house as many families as possible, or in cheaply built housing for one or more families. Facilities were woefully inadequate. Outdoor privies, often shared by several families, were the rule. Water came from outdoor hydrants and had to be carried inside for cooking, washing, and cleaning. When there were indoor fixtures, they frequently emptied waste directly into unpaved alleys and courts. Adequate sewage systems did not exist. Piles of garbage and waste material stank in the summer and froze in the winter. Even when people kept their own living quarters clean, their outside environment was unsanitary and unhealthy. It was no surprise that urban death rates were so high. Only at the turn of the century did the public health movement begin to make a dent in these living conditions.

Not every working-class family lived in abject circumstances. Skilled workers might rent comfortable quarters, and a few might even own their own houses. A study of 397 working-class families in Massachusetts found the family of one skilled worker living "in a tenement of five rooms in a pleasant and healthy locality, with good surroundings. The apartments are well furnished and parlor carpeted." The family even had a sewing machine. But the unskilled and semiskilled workers were not so fortunate. The Massachusetts survey described the family of an unskilled ironworker crammed into a tenement of four rooms,

> in an overcrowded block, to which belong only two privies for about fifty people. When this place was visited the vault had overflowed in the yard and the sink-water was also running in the same place, and created a stench that was really frightful. . . . The house inside, was badly furnished and dirty, and a disgrace to Worcester.

Drab as many working-class neighborhoods were, working families created a community life that helped to alleviate some of the dreariness of their physical surroundings. The expense of moving around the city helped encourage a neighborhood and family focus. So too, paradoxically, did the long hours spent at work. What free time and energy one had were apt to be spent close to home.

A wide range of institutions and associations came to life in urban neighborhoods. Frequently they were based on ethnic ties. They made residents feel at home in the city yet at the same time often separated them from native-born Americans and other ethnic groups. Irish associational life, for example, focused around the Roman Catholic parish church, its Irish priest, and its many clubs and group activities, Irish nationalist organizations, and ward politics. Irish saloons were convivial places for men to meet, socialize, drink, and talk politics. Jews, on the other hand, gathered in their synagogues, Hebrew schools, and Hebrew- and Yiddish-speaking literary groups. Germans had their family saloons and educational and singing societies. While such activities may have slowed assimilation into American society and discouraged intergroup contact, they provided companionship, social life, and a bridge between life in "the old country" and life in America. Working-class men and women were far from being mere victims of their environment. They found the energy, squeezed out the time, and even saved the money to support a network of social ties and associations.

Black Americans faced the most wretched living conditions of any group in the city. In the North, they often lived in segregated black neighborhoods. In southern cities, they could be found scattered in back alleys and small streets. Many could only afford to rent rooms.

Some of the suffering that accompanied life in squalid neighborhoods was tempered by the rich associational life that emerged wherever former slaves gathered in the late nineteenth century. Black churches enjoyed phenomenal growth. The Afro-American Methodist Episcopal Church, with a membership of 20,000 in 1856, established churches in every city and sizable town and by 1900 claimed more than

400,000 members. Often associated with churches were mutual aid societies. By 1880, some 193 had been established in Savannah, Georgia, alone.

Some urban blacks in the late nineteenth century also rose into the middle class and, in spite of the heavy odds against them, created the nucleus of professional and artistic life. Henry Ossawa Tanner gained international recognition as a painter by 1900, black educators such as George Washington Williams wrote some of the first Afro-American histories, and novelists such as Charles W. Chesnutt, William Wells Brown, and Paul Laurence Dunbar produced noteworthy novels and short stories.

Beyond working-class neighborhoods and pockets of black housing lay streets of middle-class houses. Here lived the urban lower middle class: clerks, shopkeepers, bookkeepers, salesmen, and small tradesmen. Their salaries allowed them to buy or rent houses that offered some privacy and comfort. Separate spaces for cooking and laundry work kept hot and often odorous housekeeping tasks away from other living areas. The houses boasted up-to-date features like gas lighting and bathrooms. Outside, the neighborhoods were cleaner and more attractive than those in the inner city. Residents could pay for garbage collection, gaslights, and other improvements.

Streetcar Suburbs

On the fringes of the city were houses for the substantial middle class and the rich, who either made their money in business, commerce, and the professions or inherited family fortunes. Public transportation sped them downtown to their offices and then back to their families. For example, Robert Work, a modestly successful cap and hat merchant, moved his family to a $5,500 house in West Philadelphia in 1865 and commuted more than 4 miles to work. The 1880 census revealed his family's comfortable life style. The household contained two servants, two boarders, his wife, and their eldest son, who was still in school. The Works' house had running hot and cold water, indoor bathrooms, and other modern conveniences of the age like central heating. Elaborately carved furniture, rugs,

draperies, and lace curtains probably graced the downstairs, where the family entertained and gathered for meals. Upstairs, comfortable bedrooms provided a maximum of privacy for family members. The live-in servants, who did most of the housework, shared little of this space or privacy, however. They were restricted to the kitchen and pantry and to bedrooms in the attic.

The Social Geography of the Cities

Industrial cities of this era were places where people were sorted out according to class, occupation, and race. The physical distances between upper- and middle-class neighborhoods and working-class neighborhoods meant that city dwellers often had little firsthand knowledge of people who were different from themselves. Ignorance led to distorted views and social disapproval. Middle-class newspapers unsympathetically described laboring men as "loafing in the sunshine" and criticized the "crowds of idlers, who, day and night, infect Main Street." Yet those "crowds of idlers" were often men who could not find work. The comments of a working-class woman to her temperance visitors in 1874 suggest the sharp view from the bottom of society up: "When the rich stopped drinking, it would be time to speak to the poor about it."

Wealthy citizens, living in luxurious homes in prosperous neighborhoods, had little understanding of the daily lives of the poor.

INDUSTRIAL WORK

The presence of so many foreigners affected the character and composition of the urban working class. Immigrants made up a seventh of the population in the late nineteenth century. But because most were young men of working age, they composed a fifth of the labor force and over 40 percent of laborers in the manufacturing and extractive industries. In cities, where they tended to settle, they comprised more than half of the population in general and of the working class in particular. As a Protestant clergyman observed, "Not every foreigner is a working man, but in the cities, at least, it may be said that every working man is a foreigner."

The Importance of Ethnic Diversity

The fact that more than half of the urban industrial class was foreign, unskilled, and often had only a limited command of English had a tremendous impact on industrial work, urban life, labor protest, and local politics. Eager for the unskilled positions rapidly being created as mechanization and mass production took hold, immigrants often had little in common with native-born workers or even with one another. American working-class society was thus a mosaic of nationalities, cultures, religions, and interests, a patchwork where colors clashed as often as they complemented one another.

The ethnic diversity of the industrial work force helps explain its occupational patterns. Although every city offered somewhat different employment opportunities, generally occupation was related to ethnic background and experience.

At the top of the working-class hierarchy, native-born Protestant whites held a disproportionate share of well-paying skilled jobs. They were the aristocrats of the working class. Their jobs demanded expertise and training, as had been true of skilled industrial workers in the pre–Civil War period. But their occupations bore the mark of late nineteenth-century industrialism. They were machinists, iron puddlers and rollers, engineers, foremen, conductors, carpenters, plumbers, mechanics, and printers.

Beneath native-born whites, skilled northern European immigrants filled most of the positions in the middle ranks of the occupational structure. The Germans, who arrived with training as tailors, bakers, brewers, and shoemakers, moved into similar jobs in this country, while Cornish and Irish miners secured skilled jobs in western mines. The Jews, who had tailoring experience in their homelands, became the backbone of the garment industry (where they faced little competition from American male workers, who considered it unmanly to work on women's clothes).

But Irish peasants and newly arrived Italians, Slavs, and others had no urban-industrial experience. They labored in most of the unskilled, dirty jobs near the bottom of the occupational ladder. They relined blast furnaces in steel mills, carried raw materials or finished products from place to place, or cleaned up after skilled workers. Often they were carmen or day laborers on the docks, ditchdiggers, or construction workers. Hiring was often on a daily basis. Unskilled work provided little in the way of either job stability or income.

At the very bottom, blacks occupied the

Opportunities for advancement rarely existed for black workers. On this Philadelphia project the hod-carriers were black but the bricklayers were white.

most marginal positions as janitors, servants, porters, and laborers. Racial discrimination generally excluded them from industrial jobs, even though their occupational background differed little from that of rural white immigrants. Since there were always plenty of whites eager to work, it was not necessary to hire blacks except occasionally as scabs during a labor strike. "It is an exceptional case where you find any colored labor in the factories," observed one white, "except as porters. Neither colored female . . . nor male laborer is engaged in the mechanical arts."

The Changing Nature of Work

The rise of big business, which relied on mechanization for the mass production of goods,

Labor Force Distribution, 1870–1900

Source: U.S. Bureau of the Census.

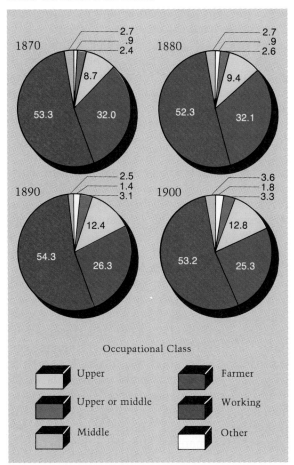

changed the size and shape of the work force and the nature of work itself. More and more Americans were becoming wage earners rather than independent artisans. The number of manufacturing workers doubled between 1880 and 1900, with the fastest expansion in the unskilled and semiskilled ranks.

But the need for skilled workers remained. New positions, as in steam fitting and structural ironwork, appeared as industries expanded and changed. Older skills became increasingly obsolete, however. Moreover, all skilled workers faced the possibility that technical advances would eliminate their favored status or that employers would eat away at their jobs by having unskilled helpers take over parts of them. In industries as different as shoemaking, cigar making, and iron puddling, new methods of production and organization undermined the position of skilled workers.

Work Settings and Experience

The workplace could be a dock or cluttered factory yard, a multistoried textile mill, a huge barnlike steel mill with all the latest machinery, or a mine tunnel thousands of feet underground. A majority of American manufacturing workers now labored in factories (rather than the shops of an earlier age), and the numbers of those working in large plants dominated by the unceasing rhythms of machinery increased steadily.

Some Americans, however, still toiled in small shops and sweatshops tucked away in basements, lofts, or immigrant apartments. Even in these smaller settings, the pressure to produce was almost as relentless as in the factory, for volume, not hours, determined pay. When contractors cut wages, workers had to speed up to earn the same pay.

The organization of work divided workers from one another. Those paid by the piece were competing against the speed, agility, and output of other workers. It was hard to feel any bonds with these unknown and unseen competitors. In large factories, workers separated into small work groups and mingled only rarely with the rest of the work force. The clustering of ethnic groups in certain types of work also undermined worker solidarity.

All workers had one thing in common: a very long working day. Although the hours of work had fallen from the 12 hours per day expected in factories before the Civil War, people still spent over half their waking hours on the job—usually ten hours a day, six days a week. Different occupations had specific demands. Bakers worked a 65-hour week, canners toiled for 77. Sweatshop workers might labor far into the night long after factory workers had gone home.

Work was usually unhealthy, dangerous, inconvenient, and comfortless. Although a few states passed laws to regulate work conditions, enforcement was spotty. Few owners paid much attention to the location of toilets, drinking facilities, or washing areas. Nor did they concern themselves with the health or safety of their employees. Women bent over sewing machines developed digestive illnesses and curved spines. New drilling machinery introduced in western mines filled the shafts with tiny stone particles that caused lung disease. Accident rates in the United States far exceeded those of Europe's industrial nations. Each year, 35,000 died from industrial mishaps. Iron and steel mills were the big killers, although railroad casualties alone mounted to 6,000 fatalities a year during the 1890s. Nationwide, nearly one-quarter of the men reaching the age of 20 in 1880 would not reach their forty-fourth birthday (compared to 7 percent today). American business owners had little legal responsibility—and some felt none—for employees' safety or health. The law placed the burden of avoiding accidents on workers, who were expected to quit if they thought conditions were unsafe.

Industrial workers labored at jobs that were also increasingly specialized and monotonous. The size of many firms allowed a kind of specialization that was impossible in a small enterprise. Even skilled workers did not produce a complete product, and the range of their skills was narrowing. "A man never learns the machinist's trade now," one New Yorker grumbled. "The different branches of the trade are divided and subdivided so that one man may make just a particular part of a machine and may not know anything whatever about another part of the same machine." Cabinetmakers found themselves not crafting cabinets but putting together and finishing pieces made by others. It was not surprising that many skilled workers complained that they were being reduced to the status of drudges and wage slaves.

Still, industrial work provided some personal benefits. Large, complex operations with high fixed costs could usually not afford to shut down and wait out hard times. Workers in these firms congratulated themselves for securing jobs in an apparently more stable environment. "The mass of workingmen," said one, "like to feel that their situations are as permanent as possible, and this they cannot do when employed in a small shop."

Other aspects of the new arrangements helped humanize the workplace. Workers who obtained their jobs through family and friends found themselves in the same departments with them. In most industries, the foreman controlled day-to-day activities. It was the foreman who selected workers from the crowds at the gate, fired those who proved unsatisfactory, selected appropriate materials and equipment, and determined the order and pace of production. Since the foreman was himself a member of the working class who had climbed his way up, he

Factory work was unusually uncomfortable and hazardous. Here workers in the Stetson hat factory cut fur for hats to be sewn together by hand.

might understand and sympathize with subordinates. Yet the foreman could also be authoritarian and harsh, especially if the workers he supervised were unskilled or belonged to another ethnic group.

The Worker's Share in Industrial Progress

Industrialists like Andrew Carnegie and John D. Rockefeller made huge fortunes during the late nineteenth century. They symbolized the continuing pattern of wealth concentration that had begun in the early period of industrialization. In 1890, the top one percent of American families possessed over a quarter of the wealth, while the share held by the top 10 percent was about 73 percent. Economic growth still benefited those who tried to direct its path, and they claimed the lion's share of the rewards.

But what of the workers who tended the machines that lay at the base of industrial wealth? Working-class Americans made up the largest segment of the labor force (probably around 60 percent), so their experience reveals important facets of the American social and economic system and American values.

Statistics of increasing production, of ever more goods, tell part of the story. Figures on real wages also reveal something important. Industry still needed skilled workers and paid them well. Average real wages rose over 50 percent between 1860 and 1900. Skilled manufacturing workers, who made up about a tenth of the nonagricultural working class in the late nineteenth century, saw their wages rise by about 74 percent. But unskilled wages increased by only 31 percent. The differential was substantial and widened as the century drew to a close.

Taken as a whole, the working class accrued substantial benefits in the late nineteenth century, even if its share of the total wealth did not increase. American workers had more material comforts than their European counterparts. But the general picture conceals the realities of working-class economic life. A U.S. Bureau of Labor study of working-class families in 1889 revealed great disparities of income: a laborer earned $384 a year, while a carpenter took home $686. The carpenter's family lived comfortably

in a four-room house. Their breakfast usually included meat or eggs, hotcakes, butter, cake, and coffee. Such hearty fare was out of the question for the laborer's family, however; they ate bread and butter as the main portion of two of their three daily meals.

For workers who could not secure steady employment, rising real wages were meaningless. Workers, especially those who were unskilled, often found work only sporadically. When times were slow or conditions depressed, as they were between 1873 and 1879 and 1893 and 1897, employers, especially those in small firms, laid off both skilled and unskilled workers and reduced wages. Even in a good year like 1890, one out of every five men outside of agriculture had been unemployed at least a month. One-quarter lost four months or more.

Since unemployment insurance did not exist, workers had no cushion against losing their jobs. One woman grimly recalled, "If the factory shuts down without warning, as it did last year for six weeks, we have a growing expense with nothing to counterbalance." Older workers who had no social security or those who had had accidents on the job but no accident insurance had severely reduced incomes. Occasionally, kindhearted employers offered assistance in hard times, but it was rarely enough. The Lawrence Manufacturing Company compensated one of its workers $50 for the loss of a hand and awarded another $66.71 for a severed arm.

Although nineteenth-century ideology pictured men as breadwinners, many working-class married men could not earn enough to support their families alone. A working-class family's standard of living thus often depended on its number of workers. Today, two-income families are common. But in the nineteenth century,

Unemployment Rates, 1870–1899

PERIOD	AVERAGE PERCENT UNEMPLOYED	PEAK YEAR	PERCENT UNEMPLOYED IN PEAK YEAR
1870–1879	10%	1876	12–14%
1880–1889	4	1885	6–8
1890–1899	10	1894	15+

married women did not usually take outside employment, although they contributed to family income by taking in sewing, laundry, and boarders. In 1890, only 3.3 percent of married women were to be found in the paid labor force.

The Family Economy

If married women did not work for pay outside their homes, their children did. The laborer whose annual earnings amounted to only $384 depended on his 13-year-old son, not his wife, to go out and earn the $196 that was so critical to the family's welfare. Sending children into the labor market was an essential survival strategy for many working-class Americans. In 1880, one-fifth of the nation's children between the ages of 10 and 14 held jobs.

Child labor was closely linked to a father's income, which in turn depended on skill, ethnic background, and occupation. Immigrant families more frequently sent their young children out to work (and also had more children) than native-born families. Middle-class reformers who had sentimental views of childhood and who thought all children should be under the care of mothers and teachers were disapproving. As one investigator of working-class life reported, "Father never attended school, and thinks his children will have sufficient schooling before they reach their tenth year, thinks no advantage will be gained from longer attendance at school, so children will be put to work as soon as able." Reformers believed that such fathers condemned their children to future poverty by taking them out of school, whereas sending children to work was actually a means of coping with the immediate threat of poverty.

Women at Work

By age 14, many more young people were working for wages. Half of all Philadelphia's students had quit school by that age. Daughters as well as sons were expected to take positions, although young women from immigrant families were more likely to be working than young American women. As *Arthur's Home Magazine* for women pointed out, a girl's earnings would help "to relieve her hard-working father of the burden of her support, to supply home with comforts and refinements, to educate a younger brother."

Employed women earned far less than men. An experienced female factory worker might be paid between $5 and $6 a week, while an unskilled male laborer could make about $8. Discrimination, present from women's earliest days in the work force, persisted. Still, factory jobs were desirable because they paid better than other kinds of work open to women.

Employment opportunities for women were narrow, and ethnic taboos and cultural traditions helped to shape choices. About a quarter of working women secured factory jobs. Italian and Jewish women (whose background ruled out domestic work) clustered in the garment industry, while Poles and Slavs went into textiles, food processing, and meatpacking. In some industries, like textiles, women composed an important segment of the work force. But about 40 percent of them, especially those from Irish, Scandinavian, or black families, took jobs as maids, cooks, laundresses, and nurses.

Domestic service meant low wages, unpleasant working conditions, and little free time, usually one evening a week and part of Sunday. A Minneapolis housemaid described her ex-

Status of Young People (12–20) by Ethnicity in Detroit in 1900

ETHNIC GROUP	SCHOOL	WORK	HOME
Native white American*	54.7%	40.4%	4.9%
	56.1	16.9	27.0
Black	50.0	50.0	0.0
	45.5	40.9	13.6
Irish	43.2	48.6	8.1
	43.2	39.8	17.0
German	30.5	59.5	10.0
	29.2	45.1	25.8
Polish	26.4	63.5	10.1
	26.1	56.2	17.6
Russian	53.3	30.0	16.7
	17.4	60.9	21.7

Note: Percentage of boys are indicated in blue; percentage of girls are indicated in red.
*Born in the United States of two American-born parents.
Source: Zunz, *The Changing Face of Inequality*, 1982.

hausting routine. "I used to get up at four o'clock every morning and work till ten P.M. every day of the week. Mondays and Tuesdays, when the washing and ironing was to be done, I used to get up at two o'clock and wash or iron until breakfast time." Nor could domestics count on much sympathy from their employers. "Do not think it necessary to give a hired girl as good a room as that used by members of the family," said one lady of the house. "She should sleep near the kitchen and not go up the front stairs or through the front hall to reach her room."

Although a servant received room and board, the pay hovered between $2 and $5 a week. The fact that so many women took domestic work despite the job's disadvantages speaks clearly of their limited opportunities.

The dismal situation facing working women drove some, like Rose Haggerty, into prostitution. Burdened with a widowed and sickly mother and four younger brothers and sisters, Rose went to work at age 14 in a New York paper-bag factory. She earned $10 a month, but $6 went for rent. Her fortunes improved when a friend helped her buy a sewing machine. Rose then sewed shirts at home, often working as long as 14 hours a day. Her earnings supported her family until the piecework rate for shirts was suddenly slashed in half. In desperation, Rose contemplated suicide. But when a sailor offered her money for spending the night with him, she realized she had an alternative. Prostitution meant food, rent, and heat for her family. "Let God Almighty judge who's to blame most," the 20-year-old Rose reflected, "I that was driven, or them that drove me to the pass I'm in."

Prostitution appears to have increased in the late nineteenth century, although there is no way of knowing the actual numbers of women involved. Probably most single women accepted the respectable jobs open to them. They tolerated discrimination and low wages because their families depended on their contributions. They also knew that when they married, they would probably leave the paid work force behind forever.

Marriage hardly ended women's work, however. Like colonial families, late nineteenth-century working-class families operated as economic units. The unpaid domestic labor of working-class wives was critical to family survival. With husbands away for 10 to 11 hours a day, women bore the burden and loneliness of caring for children. They did all the domestic chores. Since working-class families could hard-

Domestic work was exhausting and underpaid, but for women of some cultures it was the only respectable form of employment.

ly afford labor-saving conveniences, housework was time-consuming and arduous. Without a refrigerator, a working-class woman spent part of each day shopping for food (more expensive in small quantities). The washing machine, advertised to do the "ordinary washing of a family in only one or two hours," was out of the question with a price tag of $15. Instead, women carried water from outside pumps, heated it up on the stove, washed clothes, rinsed them with fresh water, and hung them up to dry. Ironing was a hot and unpleasant job in small and stuffy quarters. Keeping an apartment or house clean when the atmosphere was grimy and roads unpaved and littered with refuse and horse dung was a challenge.

As managers of family resources, married women had important responsibilities. What American families had once produced for themselves now had to be bought. It was up to the working-class wife to scour secondhand shops to find cheap clothes for her family. She was the one to make all the small domestic economies that were vital to survival. One woman trying to make ends meet said, "In summer and winter alike I must try to buy the food that will sustain us the greatest number of meals at the lowest price."

Women also supplemented family income by taking in work. Jewish and Italian women frequently did piecework and sewing at home. In the Northeast and Midwest, between 10 and 40 percent of all working-class families kept boarders. Immigrant families, in particular, often chose to make ends meet by taking single young countrymen into their homes. The cost was the added burden of work (providing meals and clean laundry), the need to juggle different work schedules, and the sacrifice of privacy. But the advantages of extra income far outweighed the disadvantages for many working-class families.

Black women's working lives again indi-

Popular with those who could afford it, the washing machine appeared after the Civil War but remained out of reach for working-class families.

cate the great obstacles blacks faced in late nineteenth-century cities. Although few married white women worked outside the home, black women did so both before and after marriage. In southern cities in 1880, about three-quarters of single black women and one-third of married women worked outside the home. This contrasted to percentages for white women of 24 percent and 7 percent. Since industrial employers would not hire black women, most of them had to work as domestics or laundresses. The high percentage of married black women in the labor force reflected the marginal wages their husbands earned. But it also may be explained partially by the lessons black women had derived from slavery, where they had learned that children could thrive without the constant attention of their mothers.

CONFLICT BETWEEN CAPITAL AND LABOR

Industrial workers did not passively accept their lot in the new industrial America. Although they welcomed the progress the factory made possible, they rejected their employers' claim to

most of the profits. Bad pay, poor working conditions, and long hours, they argued, reduced workers to the status of wage slaves. Fashioning their arguments from their republican legacy, workers claimed that the Republic itself was in danger of being undermined as citizen workers were degraded.

On-the-Job Protests

Many workers staunchly resisted unsatisfactory working conditions such as those described by a Detroit tinner, who complained that bosses treated employees "like any other piece of machinery, to be made to do the maximum amount of work with the minimum expenditure of fuel." Skilled workers, like iron puddlers and window-glass blowers, had indispensable knowledge about the production process and practical experience and were in a key position to direct on-the-job actions. Sometimes their goal was to retain control over critical work decisions. Detroit printers, for example, struggled to hold on to the privilege of distributing headlines and white space (the "fat") rather than letting their bosses hand out the "fat" as a special reward and means of increasing competition among workers. Others hoped to humanize work. Cigar makers clung to their custom of having one worker read to others as they performed their tedious chores. Often workers sought to control the pace of production.

While unlimited production might furnish the owner with large profits, it was likely to harm workers. A glutted market meant massive layoffs, a reduction in the prices paid for piecework, and worsening work conditions. Thus workers established informal production quotas on the job. An experienced worker might whisper to a new hand, "See here, young fellow, you're working too fast. You'll spoil our job for us if you don't go slower."

A newspaper account of a glassblowers' strike in 1884 illustrates the clashing perspectives of capital and labor. With an eye toward increasing profits, the boss tried to speed up production. "He knew if the limit was taken off, the men could work ten or twelve hours every day in the week; that in their thirst for the mighty dollar they would kill themselves with labor; they would 'black sheep' their fellows by doing the labor of two men." But his employees resisted his proposal, refusing to drive themselves to exhaustion for a few dollars more.

Their goal was not riches but a decent pace of work and a respectable reward. Thus, "they thundered out no. They even offered to take a reduction that would average ten percent all around, but they said, 'We will keep the forty-eight box limit.' Threats and curses would not move them."

In attempting to protect themselves and preserve the dignity of their labor, workers devised ways of combating employer attempts to speed up the production process. They denounced fellow workers who refused to honor production codes as "hogs," "runners," "chasers," and "job wreckers"; they ostracized and even injured them. As the banner of the Detroit Coopers' Union proudly proclaimed at a parade in 1880: "Each for himself is the bosses' plea/ [but] Union for all will make you free."

Absenteeism, drunkenness at work, and general inefficiency were other widespread worker practices that contained elements of protest. In three industrial firms in the late nineteenth century, one-quarter of the workers stayed home at least one day a week. Some of these lost days were due to layoffs, but not all. The efforts of employers to impose stiff fines on absent workers were measures of their frustration at workers who refused to cooperate.

To a surprising extent, workers made the final protest by quitting their jobs altogether. Most employers responded by penalizing workers who left without giving sufficient notice—to little avail. A Massachusetts labor study in 1878 found that although two-thirds of them had been in the same occupation for more than ten years, only 15 percent of the workers surveyed were in the same job. A similar rate of turnover occurred in the industrial work force in the early twentieth century. Workers unmistakably and clearly voted with their feet.

Strike Activity

The most direct and strenuous attempts to change conditions in the workplace came in the form of thousands of strikes punctuating the late nineteenth century. In 1877, railroad workers staged the first nationwide industrial strike. This was the first time the military was called out in force to break a strike; violent clashes

Students of history can discover fascinating materials on nineteenth-century life by exploring the published records of the American political system. The *Congressional Globe*, the proceedings of the Senate and the House, privately published from 1833 to 1873, reveals the nature of congressional deliberations in an era when debate, such as that over the Compromise of 1850 in the Senate, was the focus of the national political process. After 1873, the government published these proceedings in the *Congressional Record*. The *Record* is not a literal transcription of debate, for members can edit their remarks, insert speeches, and add supporting materials. Still, it gives a good sense of the proceedings of both the Senate and the House.

Much of the serious work of government, past and present, takes place in congressional committees. One foreign observer called Congress "not so much a legislative assembly as a huge panel from which committees are selected." The committee system is almost as old as the constitutional system itself and is rooted in the Constitution's granting of the lawmaking power to Congress. From the start, Congress divided into assorted committees to gather information, enabling members to evaluate legislative proposals intelligently.

Two kinds of committees existed in the House and Senate. Standing committees had permanent responsibility for reviewing legislative proposals on a host of financial, judicial, foreign, and other affairs. By 1892, the Senate had 44 standing committees, and the House had 50. Select committees were temporary, often charged with investigating specific problems. In the late nineteenth century, congressional committees investigated such problems as Ku Klux Klan terrorism, the sweatshop system, tenement house conditions, and relations between labor and capital. In each case, extensive hearings were held.

Congressional hearings have become increasingly important sources of historical evidence in recent years. Hearings show the Senate and the House of Representatives in action as they seek to translate popular sentiment into law. But they also reveal public attitudes themselves as they record the voices of Americans testifying in committee halls. Because one function of legislative hearings is to enable diverse groups to express their frustrations and desires, they often contain the testimony of witnesses drawn from many different social and economic backgrounds. Included here is the partial testimony of a Boston laborer, Thomas O'Donnell, who appeared before the Senate Committee on Education and Labor in 1883. Because working-class witnesses like O'Donnell usually left no other record of their experiences or thoughts, committee reports and hearings provide an invaluable insight into the lives and attitudes of ordinary people.

Hearings also reveal the attitudes and social values of committee members. Hence, caution is needed in the use of hearings. Witnesses often have vested interests and are frequently coached and cautious in what they communicate on the stand. Committee members often speak and explore questions for other reasons, usually political, than to illuminate issues.

Despite these limitations, committee hearings are rich sources of information. In this excerpt, what can you learn about the life of the witness testifying before the committee? In what way are the values of the committee members in conflict with those of the witness? Why is the chairman so harsh toward the witness? Is he entirely unsympathetic? Why do you think the questioner overemphasizes the relationship between moral beliefs and economic realities? What kinds of social tensions does the passage reveal?

Have you observed any recent hearings of congressional investigating committees on television? Are moral behavior and hunger still topics of concern for Americans? How is the interaction between modern haves and have-nots similar to and different from those between O'Donnell and the committee members in 1883? Do ethical beliefs and economic realities still separate social classes?

HEARINGS ON THE RELATIONS BETWEEN LABOR AND CAPITAL

Q. You get a dollar a day, wages?—**A.** That is the average pay that men receive. The rents, especially in Somerville, are so high that it is almost impossible for the working men to live in a house.

Q. What rent do you pay?—**A.** For the last year I have been paying $10 a month, and most of the men out there have to pay about that amount for a house—$10 a month for rooms.

Q. For a full house, or for rooms only?—**A.** For rooms in a house.

Q. How many rooms?—**A.** Four or five.

Q. How much of your time have you been out of work, or idle, for the last full year, say?—**A.** I have not been out of work more than three weeks altogether, because I have been making a dollar or two peddling or doing something, when I was out of work, in the currying line.

Q. Making about the same that you made at your trade?—**A.** Well, I have made at my trade a little more than that, but that is the average.

Q. Are you a common drunkard?—**A.** No, sir.

Q. Do you smoke a great deal?—**A** Well, yes, sir; I smoke as much as any man.

The **CHAIRMAN.** I want to know how much you have got together in the course of a year, and what you have spent your money for, so that folks can see whether you have had pay enough to get rich on.

The **WITNESS.** A good idea.

The **CHAIRMAN.** That is precisely the sort of idea that people ought to know. How much money do you think you have earned during this last year; has it averaged a dollar a day for three hundred days?

The **WITNESS.** I have averaged more than that; I have averaged $350 or $400, I will say, for the year.

Q. You pay $10 a month rent; that makes $120 a year?—**A.** Yes, sir.

The **CHAIRMAN.** I have asked you these questions in this abrupt way because I want to find out whether you have spent much for practices that might have been dispensed with. You say you smoke?

The **WITNESS.** Yes, sir.

Q. How much a week do you spend for that?—**A.** I get 20 cents worth of tobacco a week.

Q. That is $10.40 a year?—**A.** Yes, sir.

Q. And you say you are not a common drunkard?—**A.** No, sir.

Q. Do you imagine that you have spent as much more for any form of beer, or ale, or anything of that kind, that you could have got along without?—**A.** No, sir.

Q. How much do you think has gone in that way?—**A.** About $1 or $2.

Q. During the whole year?—**A.** Yes, sir.

Q. That would make $11.40 or $12.40—we will call it $12—gone for wickedness. Now, what else, besides your living, besides the support of your wife and children?—**A.** Well, I don't know as there is anything else.

Q. Can you not think of anything else that was wrong?—**A.** No, sir.

Q. Twelve dollars have gone for sin and iniquity; and

$120 for rent; that makes $132?—**A.** Yes.

Q. How many children have you?—**A.** Two.

Q. Your family consists of yourself, your wife, and two children?—**A.** Yes.

Q. One hundred and thirty-two dollars from $400 leaves you $268, does it not?—**A.** Yes, sir.

Q. And with that amount you have furnished your family?—**A.** Yes, sir.

Q. You have been as economical as you could, I suppose?—**A.** Yes.

Q. How much money have you left?—**A.** Sixty dollars in debt.

Q. How did you do that?—**A.** I don't know, sir.

Q. Can you not think of something more that you have wasted?—**A.** No, sir.

Q. Have you been as careful as you could?—**A.** Yes, sir.

Q. And you have come out at the end of the year $60 in debt?—**A.** Yes, sir.

Q. Have you been extravagant in your family expenses?—**A.** No, sir; a man can't be very extravagant on that much money. . . .

Q. And there are four of you in the family?—**A.** Yes, sir.

Q. How many pounds of beefsteak have you had in your family, that you bought for your own home consumption within this year that we have been speaking of?—**A.** I don't think there has been five pounds of beefsteak.

Q. You have had a little pork steak?—**A.** We had a half a pound of pork steak yesterday; I don't know when we had any before.

Q. What other kinds of meat have you had within a year?—**A.** Well, we have had corn beef twice I think that I can remember this year—on Sunday, for dinner.

Q. Twice is all that you can remember within a year?—**A.** Yes—and some cabbage.

Q. What have you eaten?—**A.** Well, bread mostly, when we could get it; we sometimes couldn't make out to get that, and have had to go without a meal.

Q. Has there been any day in the year that you have had to go without anything to eat?—**A.** Yes, sir, several days.

Q. More than one day at a time?—**A.** No.

Q. How about the children and your wife—did they go without anything to eat too?—**A.** My wife went out this morning and went to a neighbor's and got a loaf of bread and fetched it home, and when she got home the children were crying for something to eat.

Q. Have the children had anything to eat to-day except that, do you think?—**A.** They had that loaf of bread—I don't know what they have had since then, if they have had anything.

Q. Did you leave any money at home?—**A.** No, sir.

Q. If that loaf is gone, is there anything in the house?—**A.** No, sir; unless my wife goes out and gets something; and I don't know who would mind the children while she goes out.

between strikers, the police, and the military ensued. A wave of confrontations occurred thereafter. Between 1881 and 1905, an unbelievable 36,757 strikes involving over 6 million workers erupted, three times the strike activity in France.

These numbers suggest that far more than the "poorest part" of the workers were involved. Many investigations of this era found evidence of widespread working-class discontent. When Samuel M. Hotchkiss, commissioner of the Connecticut Bureau of Labor Statistics, informally surveyed the state's workers in 1887, he was shocked by the "feeling of bitterness," the "distrust of employers," the "discontent and unrest." These sentiments exploded into strikes, sabotage, and violence, most often linked to demands for higher wages and shorter hours.

Nineteenth-century strike activity underwent important changes, however, as the consciousness of American workers expanded. In the period of early industrialization, discontented laborers rioted in their neighborhoods rather than at their workplaces. The Lowell protests of the 1830s (Chapter 11) were not typical. Between 1845 and the Civil War, however, strikes at the workplace began to replace neighborhood riots. Although workers showed their anger against their employers by turning out and often called for higher wages, they had only a murky sense that they might use the strike as a weapon to force employers to improve working conditions.

As industrialization transformed work and an increasing percentage of the work force entered factories, collective actions at the workplace proliferated. Local and national unions played a more important role in organizing protest, conducting 60 percent of the strikes between 1881 and 1905. As working-class leaders realized more clearly the importance of collective action in dealing with their opponents and perceived how transportation had tightly knit the nation together, they also tried to coordinate local and national efforts. By 1891, more than one-tenth of the strikes called by unionized workers were sympathetic strikes. Coordination between strikers employed by different companies improved as workers tried to order capitalism by making the same wage demands. Finally,

wages among the most highly unionized workers became less of an issue. Workers tried to create more humane conditions. Some tried to end subcontracting and the degradation of skills. Others, like the glassblowers, struggled to enforce work rules. Indeed, by the early 1890s, over one-fifth of strikes involved the rules governing the workplace.

Labor Organizing

The Civil War experience colored labor organizing in the postwar years. As one working-class song pointed out, workers had borne the brunt of that struggle. "You gave your son to the war / The rich man loaned his gold / And the rich man's son is happy to-day, / And yours is under the mold." Now workers who had fought to save the Union argued that wartime sacrifices justified efforts to gain justice and equality in the workplace.

Labor leaders quickly realized the need for national as well as local organizations to protect the laboring class against "despotic employers." In 1866, several craft unions and reform groups joined in a national federation, the National Labor Union. Claiming 300,000 members by the early 1870s, the organization supported a range of causes including temperance, women's rights, and the establishment of cooperatives to bring the "wealth of the land" into "the hands of those who produce it," thus ending "wage slavery."

The call for an eight-hour day reveals some of the basic assumptions of the organized labor movement. Few workers thought of employers as a hostile class or of the economic system as so flawed that it must be eliminated. But they did believe bosses were often dangerous tyrants. The long hours employers demanded threatened to turn citizens into slaves. But the eight-hour day would curb the power of owners and allow workers the time to cultivate the qualities necessary for republican citizenship.

Many of the NLU's specific goals survived, although the organization did not. An unsuccessful attempt to create a political party and the depression of 1873 decimated the NLU and many local unions as well. Survival and the search for a job took precedence over union causes.

The Knights of Labor and the AFL

As the depression wound down, a new mass organization, the Noble Order of the Knights of Labor, rose to national importance. Founded as a secret society in 1869, the order became public and national when Terence V. Powderly was elected Grand Master Workman in 1879. The Knights of Labor sought "to secure to the workers the full enjoyment of the wealth they create." Since the industrial system denied workers their fair share as producers, the Knights of Labor proposed to mount a cooperative system of production alongside the existing system. "There is no reason," Powderly believed, "why labor cannot, through cooperation, own and operate mines, factories and railroads." Cooperative efforts would give workers the economic independence necessary for citizenship, while an eight-hour day would provide them with the leisure for moral, intellectual, and political pursuits.

The Knights of Labor opened its ranks to all American producers. By producers the Knights of Labor meant all contributing members of society—skilled and unskilled, black and white, men and women. Only the idle and corrupt (bankers, speculators, lawyers, saloonkeepers, and gamblers) were to be excluded. Membership was even open to sympathetic merchants and manufacturers. In fact, many shopkeepers joined the order and advertised their loyalty as "friend of the workingman."

This inclusive membership policy meant that the Knights potentially had the power of great numbers. They grew in spurts, attracting miners between 1874 and 1879 and skilled urban tradesmen between 1879 and 1885. The great masses of unskilled workers poured in thereafter.

Although Powderly frowned upon using the strike as a labor weapon, the organization reaped the benefits of grass-roots strike activity. Local struggles proliferated after 1883. In 1884, unorganized workers of the Union Pacific Railroad walked off the job when management announced a wage cut. Within two days, the company caved in, and the men joined the Knights of Labor. The next year, a successful strike against the Missouri Pacific Railroad brought in another wave of members. Then, in 1886, the Haymarket Riot in Chicago led to such a growth in labor militancy that in that single year the membership of the Knights of Labor ballooned from 100,000 to 700,000.

The "riot" at Haymarket was, in fact, a peaceful protest meeting connected with a lockout at the McCormick Reaper Works. When the Chicago police arrived to disperse the crowd, a bomb exploded. Seven policemen were killed. Although no one knows who planted the bomb, eight anarchists were tried and convicted. Overheated newspaper accounts put the blame on "long-haired, wild-eyed, bad-smelling, atheistic, reckless foreign wretches, who never did an honest hour's work in their lives."

Labor agitation and turbulence spilled over into politics. In 1884 and 1885, the Knights of Labor lobbied to secure a national contract labor law and state anticonvict labor laws. The organization also pressed successfully for the creation of a federal Department of Labor. As new members poured in, however, direct political action became increasingly attractive. Between 1885 and 1888, the Knights of Labor sponsored candidates in 200 towns and cities in 34 states and 4 territories. They achieved many electoral victories. In Waterloo, Iowa, a bank janitor ousted a successful attorney to become the town's mayor. Despite local successes, no national labor party emerged. But in the 1890s, the Knights cooperated with the Populists in their attempt to reshape American politics and society.

Despite the dramatic surge in membership, the Knights of Labor could not sustain their momentum as the voice for the American laboring people. A strike against Jay Gould's southwestern railroad system in 1886 failed, tarnishing the Knights' reputation. Consumer and producer cooperatives fizzled; the policy of accepting both black and white workers led to strife and discord in the South. The two major parties proved adept at coopting labor politicians. As labor politicians became respectable, they left the rank and file to fend for themselves.

The failure of local leaders was paralleled by the failure of national leadership. Powderly was never able to unify or direct his diverse following. His concern with general reform issues and political action dissatisfied those pressing for better wages and work conditions. Nor could Powderly control the militant elements who opposed him. Local, unauthorized strike actions were often ill-considered and violent. Lawlessness helped neither the organization as a whole nor its members. By 1890, the membership had dropped to 100,000, although the Knights of Labor continued to play a role well into the 1890s.

In the 1890s, the American Federation of Labor, founded in 1886, replaced the Knights of Labor as the nation's dominant union. The history of the Knights indicated the problems of a national union that admitted all who worked for wages but officially rejected strike action in favor of methods like politics and arbitration. The leader of the AFL, Samuel Gompers, had a different notion of effective worker organization. Gompers's experience as head of the Cigarmakers' Union in the 1870s and as a founder of the Federation of Organized Trades and Labor Unions in 1881 convinced him that skilled workers should put their specific occupational interests before the interests of workers as a whole. By so doing, they could control the supply of skilled labor and keep wages up.

Gompers organized his union as a federation of skilled trades—cigar makers, iron molders, ironworkers, carpenters, and others—each one autonomous yet linked through an executive council to work together for prolabor national legislation and mutual support during boycott and strike actions. Gompers was a practical man who believed in "pure and simple unionism." He repudiated the notion of a cooperative commonwealth and dreams of ending the wage system, accepting the fact that workers "are a distinct and practically permanent class of modern society." Thus he focused on immediate, realizable "bread and butter" issues, particularly higher wages, shorter hours, industrial safety, and the right to organize.

Although Gompers rejected direct political action as a means of obtaining labor's goals, he did believe in the value of the strike. He told a congressional hearing in 1899 that unless working people had "the power to enter upon a strike, the improvements will all go to the employer and all the injuries to the employees." He was a shrewd organizer and knew from bitter experi-

ence the importance of dues high enough to sustain a strike fund through a long, tough fight.

Under Gompers's leadership, the AFL grew from 140,000 in 1886 to nearly one million by 1900. Although his notion of a labor organization was elitist, he succeeded in steering his union through a series of crises, fending off challenges from socialists to his left and corporate opposition to strikes from his right. But there was no room in his organization for the unskilled or for blacks, who were judged to be of an "abandoned and reckless disposition."

The AFL made a brief and halfhearted attempt to unionize women in 1892. Hostile male attitudes constituted a major barrier against organizing women. Men resented women as co-workers and preferred them to stay in the home. The AFL stood firmly for the principle that "the man is the provider" and that women who work in factories "bring forth weak children." The Boston Central Labor Union declared in 1897 that "the demand for female labor [is] an insidious assault upon the home . . . it is the knife of the assassin, aimed at the family circle." Change was slow in coming. In 1900, the International Ladies Garment Workers Union (ILGWU) was established. Although women were the backbone of the organization, men dominated the leadership.

Working-Class Setbacks

Despite the growth of working-class organizations, workers lost many of their battles with management. Some of the more spectacular clashes reveal why working-class activism often ended in defeat and why so many workers lived precariously on the edge of poverty.

In 1892, silver miners in Coeur d'Alene, Idaho, went on strike when their employers installed machine drills in the mines, reduced skilled workers to shovelmen, and announced a wage cut of a dollar a day. The owners, supported by state militiamen and the federal government, successfully broke the strike by using scabs, but not without armed fighting. Several hundred union men were arrested, herded into huge bull pens, and eventually tried and found guilty of a wide variety of charges. Out of the defeat emerged the Western Federation of Miners, founded by "Big Bill" Haywood, whose chief political goal was an eight-hour law for miners. The pattern of struggle in Coeur d'Alene was followed in many subsequent strikes, most notably in the Cripple Creek mining area of Colorado in 1894.

Determined mine owners characteristically met strikes by shutting off credit to unionmen, hiring strikebreakers and armed guards to break the union, and paying spies to infiltrate unions. Violence was frequent, and each confrontation usually ended with the arrival of state militia, the erection of bull pens, incarceration or intimidation of strikers and their local sympathizers, legal action, and elaborate blacklisting systems. In spite of this, the WFM won as many strikes as it lost.

The Homestead and Pullman Strikes

The most serious setback to labor occurred in 1892 at the Homestead steel mills near Pittsburgh, Pennsylvania. The Homestead plant had been recently purchased by Andrew Carnegie,

Pinkerton detectives as pictured in **Harper's Weekly,** *1892, leaving the scene of the Homestead steel strike.*

who put Henry Clay Frick in charge. Together they wanted to eliminate the Amalgamated Association of Iron, Steel, and Tin Workers, which threatened to increase its organization of the steel industry. After three months of stalemated negotiations over a new wage contract, Frick issued an ultimatum. Unless the union accepted wage decreases, he would lock them out and replace them with others. As the deadline passed, Frick erected a formidable wood and barbed wire fence around the entire plant, with searchlight and guard stands on it, and hired 300 armed Pinkerton agents to guard the factory. As they arrived on July 6, they engaged armed steelworkers in a daylong gun battle. Several men on both sides were killed, and the Pinkertons were driven off.

Frick telegraphed Pennsylvania's governor, who sent 8,000 troops to crush both the strike and the union. Two and a half weeks later, Alexander Berkman, a New York anarchist who sympathized with the plight of the oppressed Homestead workers, broke into Frick's office and attempted to assassinate him. The events at Homestead dramatized the lengths to which both labor and capital would go to achieve their ends.

Observing these events, Eugene Victor Debs of Terre Haute, Indiana, for many years an ardent organizer of railroad workers, wrote that "if the year 1892 taught the workingmen any lesson worthy of heed, it was that the capitalist class, like a devilfish, had grasped them with its tentacles and was dragging them down to fathomless depths of degradation." Debs saw 1893 as the year in which organized labor would "escape the prehensile clutch of these monsters." But 1893 brought a new depression and even worse challenges and setbacks for labor. Undaunted, Debs succeeded in combining several of the separate railroad brotherhoods into a united American Railway Union (ARU). Within a year, over 150,000 railroadmen were in the ARU, and Debs won a strike against the Great Northern Railroad, which had attempted to slash workers' wages.

Debs faced his toughest crisis at the Pullman Palace Car Company in Chicago. Pullman was planned as a model company town with management controlling all aspects of workers' lives. "We are born in a Pullman house, fed from the Pullman shop, taught in the Pullman school, catechized in the Pullman church, and when we die we shall be buried in the Pullman cemetery and go to the Pullman hell," said one worker wryly.

Late in 1893, as the depression worsened, Pullman cut wages by one-third and laid off many workers but made no reductions in rents or prices in the town stores. Forced to pay in rent what they could not recover in wages, working families struggled to survive the winter. In some cases parents kept their children home from school because they had no shoes or coats and could keep warm only in bed. Those still at work suffered speedups, intimidations, and further wage cuts. Desperate and "without hope," the Pullman workers joined the ARU in the spring of 1894 and went out on strike.

In late June, after Pullman refused to submit the dispute to arbitration, Debs led the ARU into a sympathetic strike in support of the striking Pullman workers. Carefully advising his lieutenants to "use no violence" and "stop no trains," Debs sought to boycott trains handling Pullman cars throughout the West. As the boycott spread, the General Managers Association, which ran the 24 railroads centered in Chicago, came to the support of George Pullman, convinced that "we have got to wipe him [Debs] out." After hiring some 2,500 strikebreakers, they appealed to the state and federal governments for military and judicial support in stopping the strike.

Governor Altgeld of Illinois, sympathizing with the workers and believing that local law enforcement was sufficient, opposed the use of federal troops. But Richard Olney, a former railroad lawyer and President Cleveland's attorney general, persuaded the president that only federal troops could restore law and order. On July 2, Olney obtained a court injunction to end the strike as a "conspiracy in restraint of trade." Two days later, Cleveland ordered federal troops in to support the injunction and crush the strikers.

Violence now escalated rapidly. Local and federal officials hired armed guards, and the railroads paid them to help the troops. Within two days, strikers and guards were engaged in bitter fighting, freight cars were burned, and

over $340,000 worth of railroad property was destroyed. The press described "Unparalleled Scenes of Riot, Terror and Pillage" and "Frenzied Mobs Still Bent on Death and Destruction." As troops continued to pour into Chicago, the violence worsened, leaving scores of workers dead.

Debs's resources were near an end unless he could enlist wider labor support. "Capital has combined to enslave labor," he warned other labor groups. "We must all stand together or go down in hopeless defeat." When Samuel Gompers refused his support, the strike ended. Debs and several other leaders were arrested for contempt of the court injunction of July 2 and found guilty. A lifelong Democrat, Debs soon became a confirmed socialist. His arrest and the defeat of the Pullman strike provided a deathblow to the American Railway Union. In 1895, the Supreme Court upheld the legality of using an injunction to stop a strike and provided management with a powerful weapon to use against unions in subsequent years. The labor movement emerged from the 1890s with a distinct disadvantage in its conflicts with organized capital.

Although in smaller communities strikes against outside owners might receive support from the local middle class, these labor conflicts illustrate the widespread conviction among the American middle and upper class that unions and their demands were un-American. Many claimed to accept the idea of a worker organization. But they would not concede that unions should participate in making economic or work decisions. Most employers violently resisted union demands as infringements of their rights to hire and fire, to lock workers out, to hire scabs, or to reduce wages in times of depression. However, the sharp competition of the late nineteenth century combined with a pattern of falling prices stiffened employers' resistance to workers' demands. State and local governments and the courts frequently supported them in their battles to curb worker activism.

The severe depressions of the 1870s and 1890s also undermined working-class activism. Workers could not focus on union issues when survival itself was in question. They could not afford union dues nor turn down offers of work, even at wages below union standards. Many unions collapsed during hard times. Of the 30 national unions in 1873, fewer than 10 managed to survive the depression.

A far more serious problem was the reluctance of most workers to organize even in favorable times. In 1870, less than one-tenth of the industrial work force belonged to unions, about the same as on the eve of the Civil War. Thirty years later, despite the expansion of the work force, only 8.4 percent (mostly skilled workers) were union members.

Why were workers so slow to join unions? Certainly, diverse work settings made it difficult for workers to recognize common bonds. Moreover, many unskilled workers sensed that labor aristocrats did not have their interest at heart. Said one Cleveland Pole, "The [union] committee gets the money, 'Bricky' Flannigan [a prominent Irish striker] gets the whiskey, and the Polack gets nothing."

Moreover, many native-born Americans still clung to the tradition of individualism. "The sooner working-people get rid of the idea that somebody or something is going to help them," one Massachusetts shoemaker declared, "the better it will be for them." Others continued to nourish dreams of escaping from the working class and entering the ranks of the middle class. The number of workers who started their own small businesses attests to the power of that ideal, which prevented an identification with working-class causes.

The ethnic and religious diversity of the work force also made it difficult to forge a common front. No other industrial country depended so heavily on immigrants for its manufacturing labor force. The lack of common cultural traditions and goals created friction and misunderstandings. In addition, immigrants clustered in certain jobs and were insulated from other workers, both foreign-born and American. Ethnic and related skill differences also clouded common class concerns.

The perspective of immigrant workers contributed to their indifference to unions and to tension with native-born Americans. Many foreigners planned to return to their homeland and had limited interest in changing conditions in the United States. Moreover, since their goal was to work, they took jobs as scabs. Much of

the violence that accompanied working-class actions erupted when owners brought in strikebreakers. To some Americans, immigrants were to blame for both low wages and failed worker actions. Divisions among workers were often as bitter as those between strikers and employers. When workers divided, employers benefited.

The tension within laboring ranks was most dramatically displayed in the anti-Chinese campaign of the 1870s. In that decade, white workers in the West began to blame the Chinese for the economic hardships whites suffered. A meeting of San Francisco workers in 1877 in favor of the eight-hour day exploded into a rampage against the Chinese. The destruction of 25 laundries marked the beginning of months of anti-Chinese activities in the West. Angry mobs killed Chinese workers in Tacoma, Seattle, Denver, and Rock Springs, Wyoming. "The Chinese must go! They are stealing our jobs!" became a rallying cry for American workers.

Hostility was expressed at the national level with the Chinese Exclusion Act of 1882. The law prohibited the immigration of both skilled and unskilled Chinese workers for a ten-year period. It was extended in 1892 and made permanent in 1902. While both middle- and working-class Americans supported sporadic efforts to cut off immigration, working-class interest illuminated the deep divisions that undermined worker unity.

At the same time, many immigrants, especially those who were skilled, did support unions and cooperate with native-born Americans. In 1886, immigrants made up two-thirds of Illinois's union membership. Moreover, ethnic bonds could serve labor causes by tying members to one another and to the community at large. For example, in the 1860s and 1870s, as the Molders' Union in Troy, New York, battled with manufacturers, its Irish membership won sympathy and support from the Irish-dominated police force, the Roman Catholic church, fraternal orders, and public officials.

The importance of workers' organizations and of their informal actions on the job lies not so much in their successful outcomes as in the implicit criticism they offered of American society. Using the language of republicanism, many workers lashed out at an economic order that robbed them of their dignity and humanity. As producers of wealth, they protested that so little of it was theirs. As members of the working class, they rejected the middle-class belief in individualism and social mobility.

The Balance Sheet

Except for skilled workers, most laboring people found it impossible to earn much of a share in the material bounty created by industrialization. Newly arrived immigrants especially suffered from low pay and economic uncertainty. Long hours on the job and the necessity of walking to and from work left workers little free time. Family budgets could include, at best, only small amounts for reading material and recreation. Even a baseball game ticket was a luxury.

Yet this view of the harshness of working-class life is partly determined by our own standards of what is acceptable today. Since so few working-class men or women recorded their thoughts and reactions, it is hard to know just what they expected or how they viewed their experiences. But their perspectives were influenced by their cultural heritages and backgrounds. The family tenement, one Polish immigrant remarked, "seemed quite advanced when compared with our home in Khelm [Chelm]." American poverty was preferable to

Russian pogroms. A ten-hour factory job might be an improvement over farmwork that started at dawn and ended at dusk.

Studies of several cities show that nineteenth-century workers achieved limited but very real occupational mobility. A few, one in five in Los Angeles and Atlanta during the 1890s, for example, managed to climb into the middle class. Most immigrant workers were stuck in ill-paid, insecure jobs, but their children ended up doing somewhat better. The son of an unskilled laborer might move on to become a semiskilled or skilled worker as new immigrants took the jobs at the bottom.

Mobility, like occupation, was related to background. Native-born whites, Jews, and Germans rose more swiftly and fell less often than Irish, Italians, or Poles. Cultural attitudes, family size, education, and group leadership all contributed to different ethnic mobility patterns. Jews, for example, valued education and sacrificed to keep children in school. By 1915, Jews represented 85 percent of the free City College student body in New York City, 20 percent of New York University's student body, and one-sixth of those studying at Columbia University. With an education, they moved upward. The Slavs, however, who valued a steady income over mobility and education, took their children out of school and sent them to work at an early

Two Nineteenth-Century Budgets

Monthly budget of a laborer, his wife, and child in 1891; his income is $23.67.

Food	$6.51
Rent	9.02
Furniture	3.61
Taxes and insurance	3.32
Utilities	2.94
Sundries	1.09
Tobacco	.66
Medicine	.29
Clothes	.21
Dry goods	.16
Postage	.10
Transportation	.08
	$28.01

Monthly budget of a married bank accountant with no children in 1892; his income about $66.50.

Food	$13.22
Rent	9.88
Taxes and insurance	7.11
Utilities	4.99
Dry goods	2.45
Sundries	2.10
Transportation	1.71
Reading material	.53
Liquor and tobacco	.42
Furniture	.30
Medicine	.27
Clothes	.19
	$43.17

Source: Zunz, *The Changing Face of Inequality,* 1982.

age. This course of action, they believed, not only helped out the family but gave the child a head start in securing reliable, stable employment. Italians valued family above individual success and heeded the southern Italian proverb, "Do not make your child better than you are." Differing attitudes and values led to different aspirations and career patterns.

The one group that enjoyed no mobility at all was Afro-Americans. They were largely excluded from the industrial occupational structure and restricted to unskilled jobs. Unlike immigrant industrial workers, they did not have the opportunity to move to better jobs as new unskilled workers took the positions at the bottom.

Although occupational mobility was limited for immigrants, there were often other kinds of rewards that compensated for the lack of success at the workplace. The Irish, for example, did not move as rapidly into better occupations as some other groups, but they did manage to buy their own houses. Coming from a country where home ownership had been all but impossible, the acquisition of a house may well have loomed as a great achievement. Home ownership allowed a family to earn extra income by taking in boarders; in addition, it provided some protection against the uncertainties of industrial life and the coming of old age. The Irish also proved adept politicians and came to dominate big-city government in the late nineteenth century.

Their political success opened up city jobs, particularly in the police force, to the Irish. In 1886, one-third of Chicago's police force was Irish-born; many more were second-generation Irish-Americans. Moreover, the Irish dominated the hierarchy of the Catholic church. Members of the group who did not share in this mobility could benefit from ethnic connections and take pride in their group's achievements.

Likewise, participation in social clubs and fraternal orders partially compensated for lack of advancement at work. Ethnic associations, parades, and holidays provided a sense of identity and security that offset the limitations of the job world.

Moreover, a few rags-to-riches stories always encouraged the masses who struggled. The family of John Kearney, in Poughkeepsie, New York, for example, achieved modest success. After 20 years as a laborer, John managed to start his own business as a junk dealer. He became his own boss and even bought a simple house. His sons started off in better jobs than their father. One became a grocery-store clerk, later a baker, a policeman, and finally, at the age of 40, an inspector at the waterworks. Another was an iron molder, while the third son was a post-office clerk and eventually the superintendent of city streets. This was success, even if not on the scale of the industrial giants like Andrew Carnegie and John D. Rockefeller. It was enough to keep the American dream alive.

CONCLUSION: The Complexity of Industrial Capitalism

The late nineteenth century was a period of rapid growth as the United States became one of the world's industrial giants. Many factors contributed to the "wonderful accomplishments" of the age. They ranged from sympathetic government policies to the rise of big business and the emergence of a cheap industrial work force. But it was also a turbulent period. Many Americans benefited only marginally from the new wealth. Some of them protested by joining unions, by walking out on strike, or by on-the-job actions. Most lived their lives more quietly and never had the opportunity that Thomas O'Donnell did of telling their story to others. But as the next chapter shows, middle-class Americans began to wonder about the O'Donnells of the country. It is to their concerns, worries, and aspirations that we now turn.

Recommended Reading

The late nineteenth-century industrial world has been the subject of lively historical investigation. A helpful overview of economic change is provided by Stuart Bruchey, *Growth of the Modern American Economy* (1975); Alfred W. Niemi, *U.S. Economic History: A Survey of the Major Issues* (1975); and Robert L. Heilbroner, *The Economic Transformation of America* (1977). Samuel P. Hays gives a useful analysis in *The Response to Industrialism, 1885–1914* (1957), while Robert Weibe investigates one preoccupation of the age in *The Search for Order, 1877–1920* (1967).

On big business, see Glenn Porter, *The Rise of Big Business, 1860–1910* (1973) and Alfred D. Chandler, Jr., *The Visible Hand: The Managerial Revolution in American Business* (1977). Edward C. Kirkland illuminates the business mind in *Dream and Thought in the Business Community, 1860–1900* (1964), while his *Industry Comes of Age: Business, Labor, and Public Policy, 1860–1900* (1961) gives a general survey of business in the late nineteenth century.

Zane Miller's *The Urbanization of America* (1973) is one of several good introductions to city growth in the late nineteenth century; see also Sam Bass Warner, Jr., *Streetcar Suburbs: The Process of Growth in Boston, 1870–1900* (1962). Gunther Barth examines urban culture in *The Rise of Modern City Culture in Nineteenth-Century America* (1980). James Borchert explores black life in *Alley Life in Washington: Family, Community, Religion, and Folklife in the City, 1850–1970* (1980).

For the immigrant experience, begin with Thomas J. Archdeacon, *Becoming American: An Ethnic History* (1983) and consult Stephan Thernstrom, ed., *The Harvard Encyclopedia of American Ethnic Groups* (1980). Alan M. Kraut brings together varied material on immigrants in *The Huddled Masses: The Immigrant in American Society, 1880–1921* (1982), while *Ethnic Chicago* (1981), edited by Peter Jones and Melvin G. Holli, deals with different immigrant groups in that city.

Studies of working-class life and work include Herbert G. Gutman, *Work, Culture, and Society in Industrializing America* (1976); David M. Gordon, Richard Edwards, and Michael Reich, *Segmented Work, Divided Workers: The Historical Transforma-*

tion of Labor in the United States (1982); Daniel Nelson, *Managers and Workers: Origins of the New Factory System in the United States, 1880–1920* (1975); Daniel T. Rodgers, *The Work Ethic in Industrial America* (1978); David Montgomery, *Workers' Control in America: Studies in the History of Work, Technology, and Labor Struggles* (1970); Daniel J. Walkowitz, *Worker City, Company Town: Iron and Cotton-Worker Protest in Troy and Cohoes, New York, 1855–84* (1978); and Theodore Hershberg, ed., *Philadelphia: Work, Space, Family, and Group Experience in the Nineteenth Century* (1981).

Labor conflicts are the focus of Robert V. Bruce's *1877: Year of Violence* (1959). Leon Fink explores the Knights of Labor in several communities in *Workingmen's Democracy: The Knights of Labor and American Politics* (1983).

Women and work are the subject of Alice Kessler-Harris, *Out to Work: A History of Wage-Earning Women in the United States* (1982); Julie Matthaei, *An Economic History of Women in America: Women's Work, the Sexual Division of Labor, and the Development of Capitalism* (1982); and David M. Katzman, *Seven Days a Week: Women and Domestic Service in Industrializing America* (1978).

Irvin G. Wyllie investigates the idea that hard work would result in upward mobility in *The Self-Made Man in America: The Myth of Rags to Riches* (1954). The realities of mobility and assimilation are studied by Stephan Thernstrom in *Poverty and Progress: Social Mobility in a 19th Century City* (1964) and in *The Other Bostonians: Poverty and Progress in the American Metropolis, 1880–1970* (1973). Similar works include Clyde and Sally Griffen, *Natives and Newcomers: The Ordering of Opportunity in Mid-Nineteenth-Century Poughkeepsie* (1978); Michael P. Weber, *Social Change in an Industrial Town: Patterns of Progress in Warren, Pennsylvania, from Civil War to World War I* (1976); and Thomas Kessner, *The Golden Door: Italian and Jewish Immigrant Mobility in New York City, 1880–1915* (1977).

Novels of the period include Theodore Dreiser, *Sister Carrie* (1900); Stephen Crane, *Maggie: A Girl of the Streets* (1893); Abraham Cahan, *The Rise of David Levinsky* (1917); and Thomas Bell, *Out of This Furnace* (1976 edition).

TIME LINE

1843–1884	"Old immigration"
1844	Telegraph invented
1850s	Steam power widely used in manufacturing
1859	Value of U.S. industrial production exceeds value of agricultural production
1866	National Labor Union founded
1869	Transcontinental railroad completed Knights of Labor organized
1870	Standard Oil of Ohio formed
1870s–1880s	Consolidation of continental railroad network
1873	Bethlehem Steel begins using Bessemer process
1873–1879	Depression
1876	Alexander G. Bell invents telephone
1877	Railroad workers hold first nationwide industrial strike
1879	Thomas Edison invents incandescent light
1882	Chinese Exclusion Act
1885–1914	"New immigration"
1886	American Federation of Labor founded Haymarket Riot in Chicago
1887	Interstate Commerce Act
1890	Sherman Anti-Trust Act
1892	Standard Oil of New Jersey formed Coeur d'Alene strike Homestead steelworkers strike
1893	Chicago World's Fair
1893–1897	Depression
1894	Pullman railroad workers strike
1900	International Ladies' Garment Workers Union founded Corporations responsible for two-thirds of U.S. manufacturing

CHAPTER 20
POLITICS AND PROTEST

In his best-selling utopian novel *Looking Backward* (1888), Edward Bellamy likened the American society of his day to a huge stagecoach. Dragging the coach along sandy roads and over steep hills were "the masses of humanity." While they strained desperately "under the pitiless lashing of hunger" to pull the coach, at the top sat the favored few, riding well out of the dust in breezy comfort. The fortunate few, however, were constantly fearful that they might lose their seats from a sudden jolt, fall to the ground, and have to pull the coach themselves.

Bellamy's famous coach allegory introduced a utopian novel in which the class divisions and pitiless competition of the nineteenth century were replaced by a classless, caring, cooperative new world. Economic anxieties and hardships were supplanted by satisfying labor and leisure. In place of the coach, all citizens in the year 2000 walked together in equal comfort and security under a huge umbrella over the sidewalks of the city. Bellamy's outlook on American life was a middle-class reformist one. His book had an enormous appeal not only because of his humane economic analysis but also because he clothed it in the form of a novel, complete with futuristic technological wonders, a double-dream trick ending, and a romantic love story.

As the novel opens, it is 1887. The hero, Julian West, a wealthy Bostonian, falls asleep worrying about the effect local labor struggles might have on his upcoming wedding. When he wakes up, it is the year 2000. The new society he discovers through his genial guide, Dr. Leete, is one in which all citizens live in material comfort and happiness. The utopia had come about peacefully through the development of one gigantic trust, owned and operated by the national government. All citizens between 21 and 45 work in an industrial army with equalized pay and work difficulty. Retirement after age 45 is devoted to hobbies, reading, culture, and such minimal political and judicial leadership as is needed in a society without crime, poverty, graft, vice, or war.

Bellamy's treatment of the role of women in the world of 2000 reflected his own era's struggle with changing relationships. On the one hand, new labor-saving gadgets relieved women of housework, and they served, like men, in the industrial army. Women married not for dependence but for love and could even initiate romantic relationships. On the other hand, the women Bellamy portrayed were still primarily responsible for shopping, supervision of domestic and aesthetic matters, and nurturing the young. In a special women's division of the industrial army, they worked shorter hours in "lighter occupations." The purpose of equality of the sexes and more leisure, the novel made clear, was to enable women to cultivate their "beauty and grace." Moreover, "their power of giving happiness to men," Dr. Leete said, "has been of course increased."

Bellamy's book was immensely popular. Educated middle-class Americans were attracted by his vision of a society in which humans were both morally good and materially well off. Readers were intrigued not only by all that was new but also by how much of the old society was preserved. The traditional male view of woman's place and purpose was one example. But Bellamy also retained such familiar values as individual taste and incentive, private property, and rags-to-riches presidents. Like most middle-class Americans of his day, he disapproved of European socialism. Although the collectivist features of Bellamy's utopia were socialistic, he and his admirers called his system "nationalism" and looked to conventional politics to implement it. In the early 1890s, with Americans buying nearly 10,000 copies of *Looking Backward* every week, over 160 Nationalist clubs were formed to crusade for the adoption of Bellamy's ideas.

In the transformation of industrial, urban, and agrarian life in the United States in the late nineteenth century, the dreams and aspirations of many Americans went unfulfilled, as we have seen. The wealthiest 10 percent, who rode high on the social coach, dominated politics. Except for token expressions of support, they ignored the cries of factory workers, immigrants, farmers, blacks, and other victims of change. But as the century drew to a close, the call for political reform was heard more often, not just from these victims but also from middle-class Americans like Bellamy. They were motivated both by fears of a general disruption and by a genuine humane commitment to help the less fortunate.

This chapter describes, first, conventional American politics at the national and local level from Reconstruction to the early 1890s, and second, the world of the comfortable classes, including the dilemmas and burdens of middle-class women and men and their protests against the corrosive problems of urban industrial life. The chapter concludes with an account of the Populist revolt in the 1890s, culminating in the election of 1896.

POLITICS IN THE GILDED AGE

American government in the 1870s and 1880s supported the interests of those who rode at the top of the coach. Although some modern observers think the national government should have tackled problems like poverty, unemployment, and trusts, few nineteenth-century Americans would have agreed. They mistrusted organized power and believed in laissez-faire, a doctrine by which government largely kept its hands off economic problems. After the traumas of the Civil War era, when a strong, centralized state pursued high moral causes, late nineteenth-century political leaders favored a period of governmental passivity. This would permit the continuing pursuit of industrial expansion and wealth. As Republican leader Roscoe Conkling explained, the primary role of government was "to clear the way of impediments and dangers, and leave every class and every individual free and safe in the exertions and pursuits of life."

What followed, Henry Adams observed, was the most "thoroughly ordinary" period in American politics since Columbus. Ordinary politics, however, did not necessarily mean honest politics, as he knew well: "One might search the whole list of Congress, Judiciary, and Executive during the twenty-five years 1870–95 and find little but damaged reputation." Few eras of American government were as corrupt as this one, and Adams was especially sensitive to this

Starry-eyed Edward Bellamy captured the imagination of millions with his futuristic Looking Backward.

decline in the quality of democratic politics. His autobiography, *The Education of Henry Adams* (1907), contrasted the low political tone of his own age with the exalted political morality of the days of grandfather John Quincy Adams and great-grandfather John Adams.

Politicians, Parties, and Presidents

In a satirical book in 1873, Mark Twain, with Charles Dudley Warner, coined the expression "Gilded Age" as a synonym for political corruption during Grant's presidency. The expression, with its suggestion of shallow glitter, has come to characterize social and political life in the last quarter of the nineteenth century. In these years, the dominant branch of government was Congress, and the moral quality of legislative leadership was typified by men such as James G. Blaine and Roscoe Conkling. Despite a scandal in which he was paid for supporting favors to railroads and then lied about it afterwards, Blaine was probably the most popular Republican politician of the era. A man of enormous charm, intelligence, wit, and ability, he served his country as senator from Maine, twice as secretary of state, and was a serious contender for the presidency in every election from 1876 to 1892.

Blaine's intraparty foe, Roscoe Conkling, was even more typical. The New York *Times* described him as "a man by whose career and character the future will judge of the political standards of the present." A stalwart Republican who controlled the rich patronage jobs of the New York customhouse, Conkling spent most of his career in patronage conflicts with fellow Republicans. He quarreled even more with civil service reformers, who believed government jobs should be dispensed for merit rather than party loyalty. Conkling could imagine no other purpose of politics and accused them of wanting the jobs for themselves. "Their real object is office and plunder." Fittingly, his career ended when he resigned from the Senate in a patronage dispute with President Garfield. Though he served in Congress for over two decades, Conkling never drafted a bill. This did not hurt his career, for in the Gilded Age, legislation was not Congress's primary purpose.

In 1879, a student of legislative politics, Woodrow Wilson, expressed his disgust with the degradation of politics in the Gilded Age in eight words: "No leaders, no principles; no principles, no parties." There was little to distinguish the two major parties from each other. They differed not over principles but patronage, not over issues but the spoils of office. At stake in elections were not laws but the thousands of government jobs at the disposal of the winning candidate and his party. In a shrewd analysis of the American political system in the late nineteenth century, an English observer, Lord James Bryce, concluded that the most cohesive force in American politics was "the desire for office and for office as a means of gain." The two parties, like two bottles of liquor, Bryce said, bore different labels, yet "each was empty."

The clear ideological party positions taken during the Civil War and Reconstruction had all but disappeared. The Republican party frequently reminded voters of its role in winning the Civil War and preserving the Union. Republican votes still came from northeastern Yankee industrial interests and from New England migrants across the Upper Midwest. The main support for Democrats still came primarily from southern whites, northern workers, and Irish Catholic and other urban immigrants. For a few years, Civil War and Reconstruction issues generated party differences. But after 1876, on national issues at least, party labels did indeed mark "empty" bottles.

The two parties were evenly matched. In three of the five presidential elections between 1876 and 1892, one percent of the vote separated the two major candidates. In 1880, for example, James Garfield defeated his Democratic opponent by only 7,018 votes. In 1884, Grover Cleveland squeaked by James G. Blaine by a popular vote margin of 48.5 to 48.2 percent. In two elections (1876 and 1888), the electoral vote winner had fewer popular votes. Further evidence of political stalemate was that neither party was able to control the White House and both houses of Congress for long. Although all the presidents in the era except Cleveland were Republicans, the Democrats controlled the House of Representatives in eight of the ten sessions of Congress between 1875 and 1895.

Presidential Elections, 1872–1892

YEAR	CANDIDATES	PARTY	POPULAR VOTE	ELECTORAL VOTE
1872	U. S. GRANT	Republican	3,596,745 (56%)	286
	H. Greeley	Democrat	2,843,446 (44%)	66
1876	S. Tilden	Democrat	4,284,020 (51%)	184
	R. B. HAYES	Republican	4,036,572 (49%)	185
1880	J. GARFIELD	Republican	4,449,053 (48%)	214
	W. S. Hancock	Democrat	4,442,035 (48%)	155
	J. B. Weaver	Greenback-Labor	308,578 (3%)	0
1884	G. CLEVELAND	Democrat	4,911,017 (48.5%)	219
	J. Blaine	Republican	4,848,334 (48.2%)	182
		Minor parties	325,739 (3.3%)	0
1888	G. Cleveland	Democrat	5,540,050 (48.6%)	168
	B. HARRISON	Republican	5,444,337 (47.9%)	233
		Minor parties	396,441 (3.5%)	0
1892	G. CLEVELAND	Democrat	5,554,414 (46%)	277
	B. Harrison	Republican	5,190,802 (43%)	145
	J. B. Weaver	Populist	1,027,329 (9%)	22

Note: Winner's name is in capital letters.

Lord Bryce titled one of the chapters of his book on American politics "Why Great Men Are Not Chosen Presidents." Gilded Age presidents were an undistinguished group. They played only a minor role in national life, especially when compared to industrial entrepreneurs like Carnegie, Rockefeller, Swift, and Armour. None of them—Rutherford B. Hayes (1877–1881), James Garfield (1881), Chester A. Arthur (1881–1885), Grover Cleveland (1885–1889 and 1893–1897), and Benjamin Harrison (1889–1893)—served two consecutive terms. None was strongly identified with any particular issue. None has been highly regarded by historians.

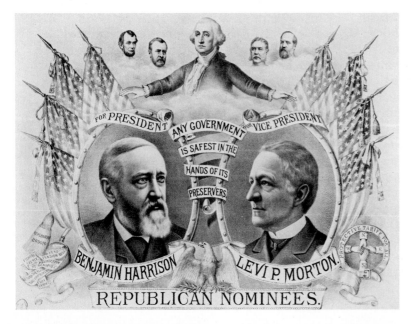

Although the tariff protectionist Harrison defeated Cleveland in 1888 (reversed in 1892), all Gilded Age presidents were essentially "preservers" rather than innovators.

Although Cleveland was the only Democrat in the group, his positions differed little from those of the Republicans. Upon his election in 1884, financier Jay Gould sent him a telegram stating his confidence that "the vast business interests of the country will be entirely safe in your hands." When Cleveland violated the expectation that presidents should not initiate ideas by devoting his entire annual message in 1887 to a call for a lower tariff, Congress listened politely and did nothing. Voters turned him out of office a year later.

Most Americans expected their presidents to take care of party business by rewarding faithfuls with government positions. The scale of patronage was enormous. Garfield complained of having to dispense thousands of jobs as he took office in 1881, worrying, he said, "whether A or B should be appointed to this or that office." Garfield is remembered primarily for being shot early in his administration by a disappointed office seeker. He achieved heroic stature only by hanging on for 2½ months before he died. His successor, Chester Arthur, was so closely identified with Conkling's patronage operation that when Garfield's shooting was announced, a friend said with shocked disbelief, "My God! Chet Arthur in the White House!"

National Issues

Arthur surprised his doubters by proving himself a capable and dignified president, responsive to the growing demands for civil service reform. Four issues were important at the national level in the Gilded Age: the tariff, currency, civil service, and government regulation of railroads (see Chapter 18). In confronting these issues, legislators tried to serve both their own self-interest and the national interest of an efficient, productive economy.

The tariff was one issue where party, as well as regional attitudes toward the use of government power, made some difference. Republicans believed in using the state to support business interests and stood for a high protective tariff. A nation demonstrated its "intelligence," one orator said, by using law to promote a "dynamic and progressive" society. The tariff would protect American businessmen as well as wage earners and farmers from the competition and products of foreign labor. By contrast, Democrats stressed that a low tariff exemplified the "economic axiom . . . that the government is best which governs least." High tariffs falsely substituted the aims and actions of the state for those that should come from "individual initiative."

Although Democrats were identified with a low tariff position and Republicans with a high one, in reality there was little consistency in either party's stand. In practice, politicians accommodated local interests each time the tariff was adjusted. Democratic senator Daniel Vorhees of Indiana explained, "I am a protectionist for every interest which I am sent here by my constituents to protect." Other legislators acted similarly on behalf of their states. Those supporting a high protective tariff to shield them from foreign competition represented Pennsylvania iron and steel manufacturers, West Virginia coal miners, and Louisiana beet growers. But New York importers, southern cotton growers, and western farmers and cattle ranchers, who depended on foreign markets, wanted lower tariffs.

Tariff revisions were bewilderingly complex in their accommodation to these many special interests. As one senator knowingly said, "The contest over a revision of the tariff brings to light a selfish strife which is not far from disgusting." Usually, a tariff included a mixture of higher and lower rates that defied understanding. Since the federal government depended on tariffs and excise taxes (primarily on tobacco and liquor) for most of its revenue, there was little chance that the tariff would be abolished or substantially lowered. Moreover, the surpluses produced by the tariff during the Gilded Age helped the parties finance patronage jobs as well as government programs.

The question of money was also complicated. During the Civil War, the federal government had circulated paper money (greenbacks) that could not be exchanged for gold or silver. In the late 1860s and 1870s, politicians debated whether the United States should return to a metallic standard, which would allow paper money to be exchanged for specie. Proponents of a hard-money policy supported either withdrawing all paper money from circulation or making it convertible to specie. They opposed increasing the volume of money because they thought it would lead to higher prices. Greenbackers, who advocated soft money, argued that there was not enough currency in circulation for an expanding economy and urged increasing the supply of paper money. An indequate money supply, they believed, led to falling prices and an increase in interest rates, which harmed farmers, industrial workers, and all those in debt.

Hard-money interests had more power and influence. In 1873, Congress demonetized silver. In 1875, it passed the Specie Resumption Act, gradually retiring greenbacks from circulation and putting the nation firmly on the gold standard. But as large supplies of silver were discovered and mined in the West, pressure was resumed for increasing the money supply by coining silver. Soft-money advocates pushed for the unlimited coinage of silver in addition to gold. A compromise of sorts was reached in 1878 with passage of the Bland-Allison Act requiring the Treasury to buy between $2 million and $4 million of silver each month and to coin it as silver dollars. Despite the increase in money supply, the period was not an inflationary one but a time of falling prices, disappointing the supporters of soft money. Their response was to push for more silver, which continued the controversy into the 1890s.

The third issue of the Gilded Age was civil service reform, "a subject" Henry Adams observed, "almost as dangerous in political conversation in Washington as slavery itself in the old days before the war." The worst feature of the spoils system was that parties financed themselves by assessing holders of patronage jobs, often as much as one percent of their annual salaries. Reformers, most of whom were upper- and middle-class white American-born Protestants, pressed for competitive examinations, allegedly to ensure the creation of a professional, honest, nonpartisan permanent civil service. But what some wanted was to deny the spoils of office to immigrants and their urban political machine bosses.

Civil service reform had first been raised during the Grant administration, but little was accomplished. The assassination of Garfield, however, created enough public support to force

Congress to take action. The Pendleton Act of 1883 established a system of merit examinations covering about one-tenth of federal offices. A mighty reform, the Pendleton Act failed to transform American political life. Gradually, more bureaucrats fell under its coverage, but parties became no more honest. As campaign contributions from government employees dried up, parties turned to other financial sources. In 1888, record corporate contributions helped to elect Harrison.

The Lure of Local Politics

The fact that the major parties did not disagree substantially on issues like money and civil service does not mean that nineteenth-century Americans found politics dull or uninteresting. In fact, far more eligible voters turned out in the late nineteenth century than at any time since. Between 1876 and 1896, some 78.5 percent of those eligible to vote for president did so. By contrast, in the 1984 election, less than 55 percent of eligible Americans voted for president.

What explains such an amazing nineteenth-century turnout? Americans went to the polls in large numbers for many reasons, but the most compelling ones were local. Iowa corn farmers voted for state representatives who favored curbing the power of the railroads to set high grain-shipping rates. While Irish Catholics in New York sought political support for their parochial schools, third-generation middle-class American Protestants from Illinois or Connecticut voted for laws that would compel attendance at public schools. Nashville, Tennessee, whites supported laws that established segregated railroad cars and other public facilities. Milwaukee German brewery workers voted against local temperance laws because they valued both their jobs and their beer. Ohio and Indiana Protestant farmers, on the other hand, believing they were protecting social order and morality against hard-drinking Catholic immigrants, pushed for temperance laws.

The influx of the new immigrants, especially in the mushrooming cities, played a large role in stimulating political participation. As traditional ruling groups, usually native-born, left local government for business, where they found more money and status, urban bosses stepped in. Their power to control city government rested on an ability to deliver the votes of poor, uneducated immigrants. In countless ways, the bosses helped these constituents in return for votes. Bosses like "Big Tim" Sullivan of New York and "Hinky Dink" Kenna of Chicago operated informal welfare systems. They handed out jobs and money for rent, fuel, and bail. Sullivan gave new shoes as birthday presents to all poor children in his district, as well as turkeys to poor families at Thanksgiving. Above all, party bosses provided a personal touch in a strange and forbidding environment. As one boss explained, "I think that there's got to be in every ward somebody that any bloke can come to—no matter what he's done—and get help."

New York City's Tammany Hall boss, George Washington Plunkitt, perfected the relationship of mutual self-interest with his constituents, as the accompanying account shows. The favors he provided in return for votes ranged from attending weddings and funerals to influencing police and the courts. His clients included not only Jewish brides, Italian mourners, and burned-out tenants but also job seekers, store owners, saloonkeepers, and madams, all of whom needed favors. State party leaders were no less effective than urban bosses in mobilizing voters. In 1900, for example, Pennsylvania Republican party leaders were said to have lists of over 800,000 voters, each one annotated with his usual voting behavior. An Indiana Republican state chairman appointed 10,000 district workers in 1884 responsible for discovering the "social and political affiliation" of every single voter.

Party leaders also won votes by making political participation exciting. Nineteenth-century campaigns were punctuated by parades, rallies, and oratory. Campaign buttons, handkerchiefs, songs, and other paraphernalia generated color and excitement in political races where substantive issues were not at stake. In the election of 1884, for example, emotions ran high over the moral lapses of the opposition candidate. The Democrats made much of Blaine's record of dishonesty, chanting in election eve parades and rallies: "Blaine! Blaine! James G.

Blaine! / Continental liar from the state of Maine!" Republicans, in turn, learning of an illegitimate child fathered by Grover Cleveland, answered with their own chant: "Ma! Ma! Where's my pa? / Gone to the White House, Ha! Ha! Ha!" Cleveland won, in part because a Republican clergyman unwisely called the Democrats the party of "Rum, Romanism, and Rebellion" on election eve in New York. The remark backfired, and the Republicans lost both New York, which should have been a safe state, and the election.

The response of voters in New York in 1884 demonstrated that local and ethnocultural issues rather than national and economic questions explained party affiliation and political behavior. If voters were cool toward the tariff and civil service, they expressed strong interest in temperance, anti-Catholicism, compulsory school attendance and Sunday laws, aid to parochial schools, racial issues, restriction of immigration, and "bloody shirt" reminders of the Civil War.

Party membership reflected voter interest in these important cultural, religious, and ethnic questions. Midwestern Scandinavians and Lutherans, for example, tended to be Republicans, as were northerners who belonged to Protestant denominations. These groups believed in positive government action. Since the Republican party had proved its willingness in the past to mobilize the power of the state to reshape society, people who wished to regulate moral and economic life were attracted to it. Catholics and various immigrant groups found the Democratic party more to their liking because it opposed government efforts to regulate morals. Said one Chicago Democrat, "A Republican is a man who wants you t' go t' church every Sunday. A Democrat says if a man wants t' have a glass of beer on Sunday he can have it."

These differences caused spirited local contests, particularly over prohibition. Many Americans considered drinking a serious social problem. By 1880, the annual consumption of brewery beer had risen in 30 years from 2.7 to 17.9 gallons per capita. Although this increase could have been the result of changes in drinking habits, many feared that alcoholism was on the increase. Certainly the number of saloons ballooned. In one city, saloons outnumbered churches 31 to 1. This shocked those who believed that drinking would destroy the American character, corrupt politics, and lead to brutality, crime, and unrestrained sexuality. Women especially supported temperance because they were often the targets of drunken male violence. Rather than trying to persuade individuals to give up drink, as the temperance movement had done earlier in the century, many now sought to make drinking a crime.

The battle in San Jose, California, illustrates the strong passions such efforts aroused. In the 1870s, temperance reformers put on the ballot a local option referendum to ban the sale of liquor in San Jose. Women, using their influence as guardians of morality, erected a temperance tent where they held conspicuous daily meetings. Despite denunciations from some clergymen and heckling from some of the town's drinkers, the women refused to retreat to their homes. On election eve, a large crowd appeared at the temperance tent, but a larger one turned up at a proliquor rally. In the morning, women roamed the streets, urging men to adopt the referendum. Children were marched around to the polls and saloons, singing, "Father, dear father, come home with me now." By afternoon the mood grew ugly, and the women were harassed and threatened by drunken men. The prohibition proposal lost by a vote of 1,430 to 918.

Similarly emotional conflicts occurred in the 1880s at the state level over other issues, especially education. In Iowa, Illinois, and Wisconsin, Republicans sponsored laws mandating that children attend "some public or private day school," defined as schools that provided instruction in English. The intent of these laws was to undermine parochial schools, which taught in the language of the immigrants. In Iowa, where a state prohibition law was passed as well, the Republican slogan was "A schoolhouse on every hill, and no saloon in the valley." Confident in their cause, Protestant Iowa Republicans proclaimed that "Iowa will go Democratic when hell goes Methodist." It went Republican. But in Wisconsin, the Bennett law for compulsory school attendance was so strongly anti-Catholic that it backfired. Many voters, disillusioned with Republican moralism, shifted to the Democratic party. Campaigns like these,

which both reflected and nourished ethnic tension, continued into the 1890s.

Republican Legislation in the Early 1890s

For many years, the decade of the 1890s was mistakenly called the "gay nineties." The decade is best understood, however, as a time dominated by a terrible depression and by worsening economic and social conflict. The rise in agrarian discontent, lynchings, and violent and repressive labor strikes all testify to this. But even before the onset of depression, Congress began to shift away from laissez-faire toward activism in order to confront national problems.

In the first six months of 1890, Republicans in Congress moved forward with legislation in five areas: pensions for Civil War veterans and their dependents, trusts, the tariff, the money question, and rights for blacks. The Dependent Pensions Act, providing generous support of $160 million a year to Union veterans and their dependents, sailed through Congress and was quickly signed into law by President Harrison.

The Sherman Anti-Trust Act also passed easily, with only one nay vote. The bill declared illegal "every contract, combination . . . or conspiracy in restraint of trade or commerce." Although the bill was vague and not really

Women, often targets of drunken male violence, campaigned for temperance as well as for equal rights. Here Victoria Claflin Woodhull reads a suffrage proposal to the House Judiciary Committee in 1871.

intended to break up large corporations, it addressed anxieties many Americans felt about the effect of business combinations on equal opportunity. Five years later, the Supreme Court showed that the Sherman Act would not hurt trusts. In *United States* v. *E. C. Knight,* the Court ruled that the American Sugar Refining Company, which controlled more than 90 percent of the nation's sugar refining capacity, was not in violation of the Sherman Act.

A tariff bill introduced in 1890 by Ohio Republican William McKinley generated more controversy. McKinley's bill, which he said was "made for the American people and American interests," attempted to make good the Republican stance on protection by raising certain tariff rates. Despite heated opposition from agrarian interests, whose products were generally not protected, the bill passed the House. In the Senate, however, nearly 500 amendments extended debates and stimulated rumors of large defections to the Democrats. "The charge against the protective policy which has injured it most," Blaine reflected, "is that its benefits go wholly to the manufacturer and the capitalist, and not at all to the farmer." Republican leaders succeeded in modifying the bill to please some farmers, and the McKinley Tariff scraped by, 33 to 27.

Silver was even trickier. Recognizing the appeal of free silver to agrarian debtors, Republican leaders feared the party might be destroyed by the issue. Senator Sherman proposed a compromise measure that momentarily satisfied almost everyone. The Sherman Silver Purchase Act ordered the Treasury to buy 4.5 million ounces of silver monthly (nearly all the silver produced) and to issue Treasury notes for it. Silverites were pleased by the proposed increase in the money supply. Opponents felt they had averted the worst, free coinage of silver. The gold standard remained secure.

As the party of action, the Republicans were prepared to confront violations of the voting rights of southern blacks in 1890. President Harrison told the editor of the New York *Tribune,* "I feel very strong upon the question of a free ballot." Political considerations paralleled moral ones. Since 1877, the South had become a Democratic stronghold, where party victories could be traced to fraud and intimidation of black Republican voters. "To be a Republican . . . in the South," one Georgian noted, "is to be a foolish martyr." Republican legislation, then, would honor old commitments to the freedmen and improve party fortunes in the South. An elections bill, proposed by Massachusetts senator Henry Cabot Lodge, would protect voter registration and ensure fair elections by setting up mechanisms for investigating charges of bribery and fraud and dealing with contested elections. A storm of disapproval from Democrats greeted the measure, which they labeled the "Force Bill." Cleveland called it "a dark blow at the freedom of the ballot," while the Mobile *Daily Register* claimed that it "would deluge the South in blood." Although House Speaker Reed steered the bill through the House, Senate Democrats delayed action with a filibuster.

Meanwhile, Republicans worried that they could not pass both the elections bill and the McKinley Tariff, which was languishing in the Senate. Pennsylvania senator Matt Quay, who had skillfully directed Harrison's election in 1888, proposed that if the Democrats ceased their delaying tactics so that the tariff could come to a vote, the Republicans would agree to put off consideration of the elections bill. The ploy worked, marking the end of major party efforts to protect black voting rights in the South until the 1960s. In a second setback for black southerners, the Senate defeated a bill to provide federal aid to schools in the South, mostly black, that did not receive their fair share of local and state funds. These two failed measures were the last gasp of the Republican party's commitment to the idealistic principles of Reconstruction. As we saw in Chapter 19, the decade that followed these defeats was one of growing violent oppression of southern blacks and a steady loss of their rights. "The plain truth is," said the New York *Herald,* "the North has got tired of the negro."

The legislative efforts of the summer of 1890, impressive by nineteenth-century standards, fell far short of solving the nation's problems. Trusts grew more rapidly after the Sherman Act than before. Union veterans were pleased by their pensions, but southerners were incensed that Confederate veterans were not covered. Others regarded the pension measure as extravagant and labeled the 51st Congress the "billion-dollar Congress." Despite efforts to please farmers, many still viewed tariff protection as a benefit primarily for eastern manufacturers. Farm prices continued to decline, and gold and silver advocates were only momentarily silenced. Black rights were put off to another time. Nor did Republican legislative activism lead the Republicans to a "permanent tenure of power," as party leaders had hoped. Voters abandoned the GOP in droves in the 1890 congressional elections, dropping the number of Republicans in the House from 168 to 88.

Two years later, Cleveland won a presidential rematch with Harrison. His inaugural address underlined the lesson he drew from the legislative activism of the Republicans in 1890. "The lessons of paternalism ought to be unlearned," he said, "and the better lesson taught that while the people should . . . support their government, its functions do not include the support of the people."

The Depression of 1893

Cleveland's philosophy of government soon faced a difficult test. No sooner had he taken office than began one of the worst depressions ever to grip the American economy, lasting from 1893 to 1897. As had been true in 1873, the severity of the depression was heightened by the growth of a national economy and economic interdependence.

The depression started in Europe and spread to the United States as overseas buyers cut back on their purchases of American products. Shrinking markets abroad soon crippled American manufacturing. Moreover, many foreign investors, worried about the stability of American currency after passage of the Sherman Silver Purchase Act, dumped some $300 million of their securities in the United States. As gold left the country to pay for these securities, the nation's supply of money declined. At the same time, falling prices hurt farmers, many of whom discovered that it cost more to raise their crops and livestock than they could recover in the market. Workers fared no better, as wages fell faster than the price of food and rent.

The collapse in 1893 was caused not only by overseas economic developments but also by serious overextensions of the economy at home, especially in railroad construction. Farmers,

moreover, troubled by falling prices, planted more and more crops, hoping somehow that the market would pick up. As the realization of overextension spread, confidence faltered, then gave way to financial panic. When the stock market crashed early in 1893, investors frantically sold their shares, companies plunged into bankruptcy, and the cycle of disaster spread. People rushed to exchange paper notes for gold, reducing gold reserves and confidence in the economy even further. Banks called in their loans, which by the end of the year led to 16,000 business bankruptcies and 500 bank failures.

The decrease in available capital and diminished buying power of rural and small-town Americans (still half the population) forced massive factory closings. Within a year, an estimated 3 million Americans, 20 percent of the work force, were unemployed. Suddenly people began to look fearfully at the presence of tramps wandering from city to city looking for work. "There are thousands of homeless and starving men in the streets," one young man reported from Chicago, indicating that he had seen "more misery in this last week than I ever saw in my life before."

As in Bellamy's coach allegory, the misery of the many was not shared by the few, which only increased discontent. While unemployed men groveled in garbage dumps for food, the wealthy gave lavish parties sometimes costing $100,000. At one such affair, diners ate their meal mounted on horses; at another, many guests proudly proclaimed that they had spent over $10,000 on their dresses. While poor families shivered in poorly heated tenements, the very rich built million-dollar summer resorts at Newport, Rhode Island, or grand mansions on New York's Fifth Avenue and Chicago's Gold Coast. While Lithuanian immigrants walked or rode streetcars to Buffalo steel factories to work, wealthy men skimmed across lakes and oceans in huge pleasure yachts. J. P. Morgan owned three, one with a crew of 85 sailors. Amid such inequalities of wealth Supreme Court Justice John Harlan noticed "a deep feeling of unrest" in the nation; agrarian activist "Sockless" Jerry Simpson more bluntly described "a struggle between the robbers and the robbed."

Nowhere were these inequalities more apparent than in Chicago during the World's Columbian Exposition, which opened on May 1, 1893, five days before plummeting prices on the stock market began the depression. The Chicago World's Fair was designed, as President Cleveland said in an opening-day speech, to show off the "stupendous results of American enterprise." When he pushed an ivory telegraph key, he started electric current that unfurled flags, spouted water through gigantic fountains, lit 10,000 electric lights, and powered huge steam

Major Legislative Activity of the Gilded Age

*National**

1871	Civil Service Commission created
1873	Coinage Act demonitizes silver
	"Salary Grab" Act (increased salaries of Congress and top federal officials) partly repealed
1875	Specie Resumption Act retires greenback dollars
1878	Bland-Allison Act permits partial coining of silver
1882	Chinese Exclusion Act
	Federal Immigration Law restricts certain categories of immigrants and requires head tax of all immigrants
1883	Standard time (four time zones) established for the entire country
	Pendleton (Civil Service) Act
1887	Interstate Commerce Act sets up Interstate Commerce Commission
	Dawes Act divides Indian tribal lands into individual allotments
1890	Dependent Pension Act grants pensions to Union army veterans
	Sherman Anti-Trust Act
	Sherman Silver Purchase Act has goverment buy more silver
	McKinley Tariff sets high protective rates
	Federal Elections Bill to protect black voting rights in South fails in Senate
	Blair bill to provide support for equal education defeated
1891	Immigration law gives federal government control of overseas immigration
1893	Sherman Silver Purchase Act repealed
1894	Wilson-Gorman Tariff lowers duties slightly
1900	Currency Act puts United States on gold standard

*State and Local**

1850s–1880s	State and local laws intended to restrict or prohibit consumption of alcoholic beverages
1871	Illinois Railroad Act sets up railroad commission to fix rates and prohibit discrimination
1874	Railroad regulatory laws in Wisconsin and Iowa
1881	Kansas adopts statewide prohibition
1882	Iowa passes state prohibition amendment
1880s	Massachusetts, Connecticut, Rhode Island, Montana, Michigan, Ohio, and Missouri all pass local laws prohibiting consumption of alcohol
1889	New Jersey repeals a county-option prohibition law of 1888
	Bennett Law in Wisconsin and Edwards Law in Illinois mandate compulsory attendance of children at schools in which instruction is in English
	Kansas, Maine, Michigan and Tennessee pass antitrust laws
1889–1890	Massachusetts debates compulsory-schooling-in-English bill
1889–1902	Eleven ex-Confederate states amend state constitutions and pass statutes restricting the voting rights of blacks
1890–1910	Eleven ex-Confederate states pass segregation laws
1891	Nebraska passes eight-hour workday law
1893	Colorado adopts woman suffrage
1894–1896	Woman suffrage referendums defeated in Kansas and California

*Note the kinds of laws in question at the different levels.

engines, 37 in one building alone. For six months, some 27 million visitors strolled around the White City designed by Daniel H. Burnham and admired its wide lagoons, white plaster buildings modeled on classical styles, and exhibit halls filled with inventions. Built at a cost of $31 million, the fair celebrated the marvelous mechanical accomplishments of American enterprise. Its elegant design stimulated a "City Beautiful" movement that made many cities more attractive and enjoyable for their residents.

But as well-to-do fairgoers sipped pink champagne, men, women, and children in the immigrant wards of Chicago less than a mile away drank contaminated water, crowded into packed tenements, and looked in vain for jobs. The area around Jane Addams's Hull House was especially disreputable, with saloons, gambling halls, brothels, and pawnshops dotting the neighborhood. "If Christ came to Chicago," a British journalist, W. T. Stead, wrote in a book of that title in 1894, this would be "one of the last precincts into which we should care to take Him." Stead's book showed readers the "ugly sight" of corruption, poverty, and wasted lives

in a city with 200 millionaires and 200,000 unemployed men.

Despite the magnitude of despair during the depression, national politicians and leaders were reluctant to respond. Only mass demonstrations forced city authorities to provide soup kitchens and places for the homeless to sleep. When an army of unemployed led by Jacob Coxey marched into Washington in the spring of 1894 to press for some form of public work relief, its leaders were arrested for stepping on the grass of the Capitol. Cleveland's reputation for callous disregard for citizens suffering from the depression worsened later that summer when he sent federal troops to Chicago to crush the Pullman strike. The president focused his efforts on tariff reform and repeal of the Silver Purchase Act, which he blamed for the depression. Few leaders in either major party, however, thought the federal government was responsible for alleviating the sufferings of the people.

Others, however, came forward with ideas and programs to deal not only with the problems spawned by the depression but also with those stemming from the country's dramatic urban and industrial transformation since the Civil

Consciousness of the depression-worsened disparity between rich and poor was especially heightened during the World's Columbian Exposition in Chicago in 1893.

War. Unskilled Slavic workers tending blast furnaces in Steelton, Pennsylvania, railway firemen in Terre Haute, Indiana, and pregnant Italian immigrant women in New Haven, Connecticut, tenements did not need an economic collapse to make them aware of these problems. But for many middle-class Americans, the depression, coming near the end of a century of triumphant progress symbolized by the Chicago exposition, served as a catalyst for the reexamination of the society America had become.

THE LIFE OF THE MIDDLE CLASS

Americans with middling incomes had reason to be sensitive to the economic polarization and social conflict around them. Middle-class Americans neither dragged the coach in ceaseless toil nor sat at the very top. But this steadily growing group of educated professionals, white-collar clerks and salesmen, corporation managers, and public employees was determined to enjoy a smooth ride. With a relatively comfortable position on the coach, they had much to lose. By the 1890s, the average income for middle-class Americans had risen by about 30 percent since the Civil War. Although the general cost of living rose even faster than income, the difference was met by more members of the family holding jobs and by taking in lodgers in middle-class homes. By 1900, 36 percent of urban families owned their own homes, many of which were made more comfortable by the addition of indoor private bathrooms, iceboxes, and other conveniences.

The progress of American industry had raised the living standard for increasing numbers of Americans, who were better able to purchase consumer products manufactured, packaged, and promoted in an explosion of technological inventions and shrewd marketing techniques. The following familiar products and brands were invented or mass-produced for the first time in the 1890s: Del Monte canned fruits and vegetables, National Biscuit Company (Nabisco) crackers, Van Camp's pork and beans, Wesson oil, Lipton tea, Wrigley's Juicy Fruit chewing gum, Cracker Jacks, Tootsie Rolls, the

A comfortable well-furnished home represented years of hard work and careful, planning for middle-class Americans from New Mexico to Virginia, as reflected here.

RECOVERING THE PAST

Historians recover the past, as we have seen, not only through the printed words in books, diaries, magazines, tax lists, and government documents but also through such visual records as paintings, photographs, and buildings. All material objects recovered from the past, in fact, help historians understand how people lived and what they valued and thought. The products of the human experience include everything from tools to toys, farm implements to furniture, and cooking pots to clothes. Historians have learned from anthropologists that every object, no matter how trivial, tells them something about people's lives. We call such objects material culture.

Consider, for example, the mail-order catalog, according to one historian a "characteristically American kind of book." The origins of buying products through the mail can be traced back to Benjamin Franklin's promotion of his stove, the Pennsylvania fireplace, in 1744. But the significance of the mail-order catalog emerged with the spectacular success of the Montgomery Ward and Sears, Roebuck catalogs in the 1880s and 1890s. The tremendous growth of the

Two pages from the Sears, Roebuck & Co. catalog, 1897

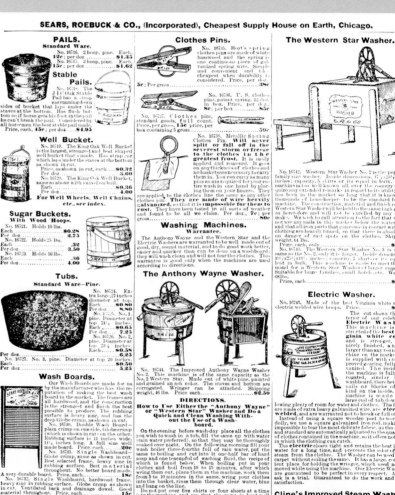

639a

Sears, Roebuck catalog, the "Farmer's Bible," from a circulation of 318,000 in 1897 to over 3 million by 1907, is not our focus here, nor is the way in which it brought city goods to rural Americans. But for historians seeking to discover how middle-class Americans lived in the late nineteenth century, the mail-order catalog is a gold mine of information. It provides insight into the economics of pricing policies, the aesthetics of advertising, and social aspects of style and taste; and it is also a "paperback museum" of the objects the American people bought and used daily.

Shown here are two pages from the Sears, Roebuck fall catalog of 1897 depicting women's clothing and washing machines. What do these pages reveal about fashions and prices in 1897, the state of technology, and the image and role of women? How do these pages compare with the equivalent items from a contemporary Sears catalog? What changes have occurred and what has not changed since the turn of the century? What other items of material culture do you think would be especially revealing of middle-class life?

Hershey bar, shredded wheat, Aunt Jemima pancake mix, Jello-O, Campbell's soup, Fig Newtons, Canada Dry ginger ale, Coca-Cola, Pepsi-Cola, and Michelob beer. Cooked chopped meat put between two pieces of bread was first sold (for 7 cents) and called a "hamburger" in 1899.

Numerous other familiar items were developed during the last decade of the century: bottle caps, aluminum saucepans, book matches, zippers, Gillette razors, Kodak cameras, the motion picture camera, phonographs and, of course, the gasoline-engine motorcar. The first major amusement park in America, Coney Island, and the first public golf course both opened in the 1890s. Bicycling became a popular middle-class activity, basketball was invented, and professional baseball emerged as America's favorite spectator sport during the decade. In 1897, the first Cheyenne rodeo and the first Boston marathon took place.

More time for recreation and greater access to consumer goods signaled the power of industrialism to transform the lives of middle-class Americans. Once favored with greater buying power, middle-class Americans sought to organize efficient ways of producing, purchasing, and consuming the newfound wealth. American women were both agents of the rise in consumer spending and were themselves often on display as stylish objects of leisure and ostentatious wealth.

Shopping for home furnishings, clothes, and other items became an integral part of many middle-class women's lives. William Dean Howells, an author who believed that literature should realistically reflect life, described the newly rich middle classes in his novel *The Rise of Silas Lapham* (1884). Howells depicted one of Lapham's two daughters, Irene, who spent her abundant leisure in shopping and on her appearance every day. Many of these goods that Irene and others bought so eagerly were to be found in the new department stores that began to appear in the central business districts in the 1870s. These stores fed women's desire for material possessions at the same time as they revolutionized retailing.

Shopping was just one example of middle-class women's new leisure. A plentiful supply of immigrant servant girls relieved urban middle-class wives of many housekeeping chores, and smaller families lessened the burdens of motherhood.

New Freedoms for Middle-Class Women

At the same time that many middle-class women enjoyed more leisure time and enhanced purchasing power, they won new freedoms. Several states granted women more property rights in marriage, adding to their growing sense of independence. Women, moreover, had finally cast off confining crinolines and bustles. The new dress, a shirtwaist blouse and ankle-length skirt, was more comfortable for working, school, and sports. The *Ladies' Home Journal* recommended bicycling, tennis, golf, gymnastics—even having fewer babies—to women in the early 1890s. This "new woman" was celebrated as *Life* magazine's attractively active, slightly rebellious "Gibson girl."

Women used their new freedom to join organizations of all kinds. Literary societies, charity groups, and reform clubs like the Women's Christian Temperance Union gave women organizational experience, awareness of their talents, and contact with people and problems away from their traditional family roles. The General Federation of Women's Clubs, founded

Increased leisure time and changing styles of dress led to new freedoms and the popularity of sports for the middle class in the 1890s, as seen in this picture of women bicyclists in Crawfordsville, Indiana.

in 1890, had one million members by 1920. The depression of 1893 stimulated many women to become socially active investigating slum and factory conditions, but some began this work even earlier. Jane Addams told her graduating classmates at the Rockford, Illinois, Female Seminary in 1881 to lead lives "filled with good works and honest toil," then went off herself to found Hull House, a social settlement that did more than its share of good works.

Job opportunities for these educated middle-class women were generally limited to social service and teaching school. Still regarded as a suitable female occupation, teaching was a highly demanding job as urban schools expanded under the pressure of a burgeoning population. Women teachers, many of them hired only because they accepted lower pay, often faced classes of 40 to 50 children in poorly equipped rooms. In Poughkeepsie, New York, teachers earned the same salaries as school janitors. By the 1890s, the willingness of middle-class women to work for low pay opened up other jobs as office workers, department store clerks, nurses, and service personnel. In San Francisco, for example, the number of clerical jobs doubled between 1852 and 1880. By 1900, nearly 20

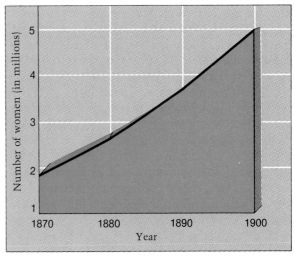

Growth of Women in the Labor Force, 1870–1900
Source: U.S. Bureau of the Census.

percent of American women were in the labor force, although most were immigrant women in low-paying jobs. Moving up to status jobs was difficult, even for middle-class women.

In the years after the Civil War, educational opportunities for women expanded. New wom-

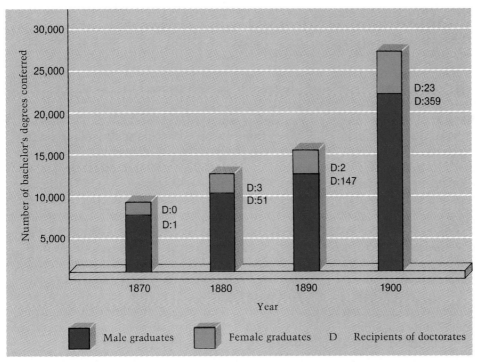

Increase in Higher Education, 1870–1900

Source: U.S. Department of Commerce.

en's colleges such as Smith, Mount Holyoke, Vassar, Bryn Mawr, and Goucher offered students programs similar to those at competitive men's colleges, while state schools in the Midwest and West dropped prohibitions against women. The numbers of women attending college rose. In 1890, 13 percent of all college graduates were women, a figure that increased to nearly 20 percent by 1900.

Higher education prepared women for conventional female roles as well as for work and public service. A few courageous graduates succeeded in joining the professions, but they had to overcome numerous barriers. Many medical schools refused to accept women students. As a Harvard doctor explained in 1875, a woman's monthly period "unfits her from taking those responsibilities which are to control questions often of life and death." Despite the obstacles, 2,500 women had managed to become physicians and surgeons by 1880 (comprising 2.8 percent of the total). Women were less successful at breaking into the legal world. In 1880, there were fewer than 50 female lawyers in the entire country, and as late as 1920, only 1.4 percent of the nation's lawyers and judges were women. George Washington University did not admit women to law school because mixed classes would be an "injurious diversion of attention of the students." Despite such resistance, by the first years of the twentieth century the number of women professionals (including teachers) was increasing at three times the rate of men.

One reason for the greater independence of American women was that they were having fewer babies (an average of 3.56 in 1900, half as many as in 1800). This was especially true of educated women. In 1900, nearly one in five married women was childless. Decreasing family size and an increase in the divorce rate (one of 12 marriages in 1905) added to men's fears that the family, traditional sex roles, and social order were threatened by the new woman. Theodore Roosevelt called this "race suicide" and argued that the falling white birthrate endangered national self-interest.

Arguments against the new woman intensified as many men reaffirmed Victorian stereotypes of "woman's sphere." Magazine editors and ministers borrowed from biology, sociology, and theology to support the notion that a woman's place was in the home. One male orator in 1896 attacked the new woman's public role because "a woman's brain involves emotions rather than intellect." This fact, he cautioned, "painfully disqualifies her for the sterner duties to be performed by the intellectual faculties. The best wife and mother and sister would make the worse legislator, judge and police."

Many men worried about female independence because it threatened their own masculinity. Male campaigns against prostitution and for sex hygiene, as well as efforts to reinforce traditional sex roles, reflected their deeper fears that female passions might weaken male vigor. The intensity of men's opposition to the new woman put limits on her emerging freedom.

Struggle for Suffrage

Many women understandably felt pulled between their public and private lives, between their obligations to self, family, and society. This tension was not usually openly expressed. A few women writers, however, began to express the frustrations and dilemmas of middle-class women. Kate Chopin's novel *The Awakening* (1899) portrayed a young woman who, in awakening to her own sexuality and life's possibilities beyond being a "mother-woman," defied conventional expectations of woman's role. Her sexual affair and eventual suicide prompted a St. Louis newspaper to say of the novel that it was "too strong drink for moral babes and should be labeled 'poison.'"

Some middle-class women, Jane Addams, for example, avoided marriage altogether, preferring the supportive, integrative relationships found in the female settlement house community. "Married life looks to me . . . terribly impoverished for women," a Smith College graduate observed, declaring that "most of my deeper friendships have been with women." A few women boldly advocated free love or, less openly, formed lesbian relationships. Although most preferred traditional marriages and chose not to work outside the home, the generation of women that came of age in the 1890s married less—and later—than any other in American history.

One way women reconciled the conflicting pressures between their private and public lives, as well as deflected male criticism, was to see their work as maternal. Addams called Hull House "the great mother breast of our common humanity." The women's clubs took as their motto the intention to "show a more glorious womanhood . . . the mother-women working with all as well as for all." One of the leading female organizers of coal workers was "Mother" Jones, and the fiery feminist anarchist Emma Goldman titled her monthly journal *Mother Earth.* By using maternal, nurturant language to describe their work, women furthered the very arguments used against them. Many, of course, remained economically dependent on men, and all women still lacked the essential rights of citizenship to effect basic change. The struggle to achieve those rights demanded not social but political activism.

In the years after the Seneca Falls Convention in 1848, women's civil and political rights advanced very slowly. Although in several western states they received the right to vote in municipal and school-board elections, only the territory of Wyoming, in 1869, had granted full political equality before 1890. Colorado, Utah, and Idaho enfranchised women in the 1890s, but no other states granted suffrage until 1910. This slow pace was in part the result of an antisuffrage movement led by an odd combination of ministers, saloon interests, and those men who felt threatened in various ways by women's voting rights. "Equal suffrage," said a Texas senator, "is a repudiation of manhood."

In the 1890s, leading suffragists reappraised the situation. The two wings of the women's rights movement, split since 1869, combined in 1890 as the National American Woman Suffrage Association (NAWSA). Although Elizabeth Cady Stanton and Susan B. Anthony continued to head the association, they were both in their seventies, and effective leadership soon passed to younger, more moderate women. The new leaders concentrated on the single issue of the vote rather than dividing their energies among

Woman's new role as a professional, such as this Red Cross nurse in the Spanish-American War, was often defended and praised in terms of its similarity to the role of a mother in the home.

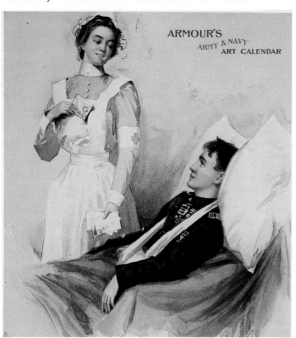

The young Jane Addams was one of the college-educated women who chose to remain unmarried and pursue a career of social reform serving immigrant families in her Hull House, Chicago neighborhood.

the many causes Stanton and Anthony had espoused. Moderate leaders were also embarrassed by Stanton's *Woman's Bible* (1895), a devastating attack on the religious argument against women's suffrage. At the NAWSA convention in 1896, despite the pleas of Anthony not to "sit in judgment" on her good friend, a resolution renouncing any connection with Stanton's book passed by a vote of 53 to 41.

Changing leadership meant a shift from principled to expedient arguments for the suffrage. Since 1848, suffragists had made their argument primarily from principle, citing, as Stanton argued at a congressional hearing in 1892, "the individuality of each human soul; our Protestant idea, the right of individual conscience and judgment; our republican idea, individual citizenship." But Stanton's leadership was on the wane, and the younger generation shifted to three expedient arguments. The first was that women needed the vote to pass self-protection laws that would guard them against the hazards peculiar to women presented by rapists, state age-of-consent laws, and industrial work. As Florence Kelley argued, "No disfranchised class of workers can . . . hold its own in competition with enfranchised rivals." The second argument insisted that modern urban life would benefit from women's maternal concern for improved health, living conditions, and morals. Addams called women "urban housekeepers" who would clean up tenements, saloons, factories, and corrupt politics.

The third expedient argument also reflected urban middle-class reformers' prejudice against non-Protestant newcomers to the city. As immigrant men arrived in America, they were almost immediately permitted to vote, a vote often bought by the local machine boss. Suffragists argued that educated, native-born American women should be given the vote to counteract the undesirable influence of ignorant, illiterate, and immoral male immigrants. In a speech in Iowa in 1894, Carrie Chapman Catt, who would succeed Anthony as president of NAWSA in 1900, argued that the "Government is menaced with great danger . . . in the votes possessed by the males in the slums of the cities," a danger that could be averted only by cutting off that vote and giving it instead to women. In the new

century it would be under the leadership of women like Catt that suffrage would finally be secured.

Male Mobility and the Success Ethic

As women's lives were changing, so also were men's. "What a tremendous question it is—what shall I be?" 20-year-old Charles William Eliot wrote to a friend just before the Civil War. As the postwar economy expanded, many new job opportunities opened up for middle-class men. The growing complexity of census classifications attests to some of them. Where once the census taker had noted only the occupation of "clerk," now were listed "accountant," "salesman," and "shipping clerk." As the lower ranks of the white-collar world became more specialized, the number of middle-class jobs increased.

To prepare for these new careers, Americans required more education. The number of public high schools in the United States increased from 160 in 1870 to 6,000 in 1900. By 1900, 31 states and territories had compulsory school attendance laws.

Higher education also expanded in this period. The number of students in colleges and universities nearly doubled, from 53,000 in 1870 to 101,000 in 1900. Charles Eliot went on to become an outstanding educator, serving as president of Harvard from 1869 to 1909. He led Harvard through a period of dynamic growth, introducing several reforms such as higher faculty salaries and sabbatical leaves as well as the "elective" system of course selection for students. Harvard's growth reflected the rise of the university to a new stature in American life. As the land-grant state universities (made possible by the Morrill Act of 1862) continued to expand, generous gifts from wealthy businessmen helped to found leading research universities such as Stanford, Johns Hopkins, and the University of Chicago.

These developments led to greater specialization and professionalism, opening up still more careers in various fields of education, medicine, law, and business. Before the Civil War, a Swedish pioneer in Wisconsin described a young man he knew, who after "working as a mason . . .

laid aside the trowel, got himself some medical books, and assumed the title of doctor." But by the 1890s, with government licensing and the rise of professional schools, no longer were tradesman likely to read up on medicine and become doctors. In fact, the word *career* did not take on its modern meaning until 1893. In this period, organizations like the American Medical Association and the American Bar Association were regulating and professionalizing membership. The number of law schools doubled in the last quarter of the century, and 86 new medical schools were founded in the same period. Dental schools increased from 9 to 56 between 1875 and 1900.

The need for lawyers, bankers, architects, and insurance agents to serve business and industry expanded career opportunities. Between 1870 and 1900, the number of engineers, chemists, metallurgists, and architects grew rapidly. As large companies formed, many more managerial positions were required. As the public sector expanded, new careers in social service and government opened up as well. Many of these positions were filled by young professional experts emerging from graduate training in the social sciences. The professional disciplines of history, economics, sociology, psychology, and political science all date from the last 20 years of the nineteenth century.

The social ethic of the age stressed that economic rewards were available to anyone who fervently sought them. Many people argued that unlike Europe, where family background and social class determined social rank, in America few barriers held back those of good character and diligent work habits. Those who doubted that this opportunity existed needed only to be reminded of the examples of Benjamin Franklin and Abraham Lincoln. The Great Emancipator himself had said that "if any continue in the condition of a hired laborer for life it is because of a dependent nature which prefers it, or singular folly or improvidence or misfortune." Writers, lecturers, clergymen, and politicians zealously propagated the rags-to-riches tradition of upward mobility. Self-help manuals that outlined the steps to success for self-made men became widely available.

The best-known popularizer of the rags-to-riches myth was Horatio Alger, Jr. His 119 novels, with titles like *Luck and Pluck*, *Strive and Succeed*, and *Bound to Rise*, were read by millions of American boys. In a typical Alger novel, the story opens with the hero leading the low life of a shoeshine boy in the streets. Dressed in rags, he sleeps in packing crates and unwisely spends what little money he has on tobacco, liquor, gambling, and the theater. A chance opportunity occurs, like diving into the icy waters of the harbor to save the life of the daughter of a local banker, and changes the Alger hero's life. He gives up his slovenly ways to work hard, save his money, and study. Eventually he rises to a prominent position, like vice-president of the bank owned by the rescued girl's father. Although moralists pointed to virtuous habits as crucial in Alger's heroes, success often depended as much on luck as on pluck.

Unlimited and equal opportunity for upward advancement in America has never been as easy as the "bootstraps" ethic maintains. But the persistence of the success myth owes something to the fact that many Americans, particularly those who began well, did rise rapidly. Native-born, middle-class whites tended to have the skills, resources, and connections that opened up the most desirable jobs. Financier Jay Gould overstated the case in maintaining that most of the nation's business and financial leaders were self-made men. "Nearly every one that occupies a prominent position has come up from the ranks," he said. In fact, the typical big businessman was a white, Anglo-Saxon Protestant from a middle- or upper-class family whose father was most likely in business, banking, or commerce.

The Gospel of Wealth

Ideology supported the importance of winning the race to the top. Ministers preached countless sermons and wrote treatises emphasizing the moral superiority of the wealthy and justifying social class arrangements. Episcopal bishop William Lawrence wrote that it was "God's will that some men should attain great wealth." Philadelphia Baptist preacher Russell Conwell's famous sermon, "Acres of Diamonds," delivered 6,000 times to an estimated audience of 13 million, praised riches as a sure sign of "godliness" and stressed the power of money to "do good."

Industrialist Andrew Carnegie expressed the ethic most clearly. In his article "The Gospel of Wealth" (1889), Carnegie celebrated the benefits of better goods and lower prices that resulted from competition, arguing that "our wonderful material development" outweighed the harsh costs of competition. The concentration of wealth in the hands of a few leading industrialists, he concluded, was "not only beneficial but essential to the future of the race." Those most fit would bring order and efficiency out of the chaos of rapid industrialization. Carnegie's defense of the new economic order in his article and in a book, *Triumphant Democracy* (1886), found as many supporters as Bellamy's *Looking Backward*. Partly this was because Carnegie insisted that the rich were obligated to spend some of their wealth to benefit their "poorer brethren." Carnegie built hundreds of libraries, most still operating in large and small towns throughout the United States. In later years, the philanthropist turned his attentions to other projects, including world peace.

Carnegie's ideas about wealth were drawn from an ideology known as social Darwinism, based on the work of Charles Darwin, whose famous *Origin of Species* was published in 1859. Darwin had concluded that plant and animal species had evolved through a process of natural selection. In the struggle for existence, some species managed to adapt to their environment and survived. Others failed to adapt and perished. Herbert Spencer, an English social philosopher, adopted these notions of the "survival of the fittest" and applied them (as Darwin had not) to human society. Progress, he said, resulted from relentless competition in which the weak failed and were eliminated while the strong climbed to the top. He believed that "the whole effort of nature is to get rid of such as are unfit, to clear the world of them, and make room for better."

When Spencer visited the United States in 1882, leading men of business, science, religion, and politics thronged to honor him with a lavish banquet at Delmonico's restaurant in New York City. Here was the man whose theories justified their amassed fortunes because they were men of "superior ability, foresight, and adaptability." Spencer warned against any interference in the economic world by tampering with the natural laws of selection. The select at the dinner heaped their praise on Spencer as founder of not only a new sociology but also a new religion.

The luxury of a fashionable home full of ornate fine art was accessible to anyone who worked hard, according to advocates of the Gospel of Wealth and social Darwinism. Successful families like the Vanderbilts, they said, represented humanity's "fittest" element. Contrast this scene with that of the middle- and lower-class families pictured earlier in this chapter.

Spencer's American followers, like Carnegie and William Graham Sumner, a professor of political economy at Yale, familiarized the American public with the basic ideas of social Darwinism. They emphasized that poverty was the inevitable consequence of the struggle for existence and that attempts to end it were pointless, if not immoral. Although Sumner's emotional hero was the middle-class "forgotten man" like his father, his writings defended the material accumulations of the wealthy. To take power or money away from millionaires, Sumner scoffed, was "like killing off our generals in war." It was "absurd," he wrote, to pass laws permitting society's "worst members" to survive or to "sit down with a slate and pencil to plan out a new social world." Sumner was so consistent in his opposition to government intervention that he also opposed protective tariffs, which led some irritated rich Yale alumni to seek his dismissal.

The scientific vocabulary of social Darwinism, with its insistence on natural law, seemingly injected scientific rationality into what often seemed a baffling economic order. Underlying laws of political economy, like the laws governing the natural world, dictated all economic affairs. Social Darwinists also believed in the superiority of the Anglo-Saxon race, which they argued had reached the highest stage of evolution. Their theories were used to justify race supremacy and imperialism as well as the monopolistic efforts of American businessmen. Railroad magnate James J. Hill said that the absorption of smaller railroads by larger ones was the industrial analogy of the victory in nature of the fit over the unfit. John D. Rockefeller, Jr., told a YMCA class in Cleveland that "the growth of a large business is merely a survival of the fittest." Like the growth of a beauty rose, "the early buds which grow up around it" must be sacrificed. This was, he said, "merely the working out of a law of nature and a law of God."

Others took a less rosy outlook. Brooks Adams, brother of Henry, wrote that social philosophers like Spencer and Sumner were "hired by the comfortable classes to prove that everything was all right." Fading aristocratic families like the Adamses, who were being displaced by a new industrial elite, may have felt a touch of envy and loss of status. They succeeded, however, in suggesting that social change was not as closed as the social Darwinists claimed.

MIDDLE-CLASS REFORM

In the late 1870s, Henry George observed that wherever the highest degree of "material progress" had been realized, "we find the deepest poverty." George's book, *Progress and Poverty* (1879), was an early statement of the contradictions of American life. With Bellamy's *Looking Backward*, it was one of the most influential books of the age, selling 2 million copies by 1905. Although George admitted that economic growth had produced wonders, he pointed out the social costs and rejected the gloomy social Darwinian notion that nothing could be done about them. His solution was to break up landholding monopolists who profited from the increasing value of their land and rents they collected from those who actually did the work. He proposed, therefore, a "single tax" on the unearned increases in land value received by landlords. His solution may seem overly simple, but George's optimistic faith in the capacity of humans to effect change made him appealing to middle-class intellectual reformers.

Pragmatism: Underpinning for Reform

The pragmatists, led by two philosophers, John Dewey (see Chapter 22) and William James, established a far more complex foundation for reform efforts than did Henry George. James, a professor at Harvard, argued that while environment was important, so too was human will. What a person wanted or thought could influence the course of human events. "What is the 'cash value' of a thought, idea, or belief?" James asked. What was its result? "The ultimate test for us of what a truth means," he suggested, was in the consequences of a particular idea, in "the conduct it dictates."

In an early study, "Great Men and Their Environment" (1880), James emphasized the role of extraordinary individuals in fostering change. James and other intellectuals, especially many of the young social scientists gathering statistics about American society, rejected the social determinism of Herbert Spencer. They argued that the application of intelligence and human will could change the "survival of the fittest" into the "fitting of as many as possible to survive." Their position encouraged educators, economists, and reformers of every stripe, giving them an intellectual justification to struggle against the misery and inequalities of wealth found in many sectors of their society.

Settlements and Social Gospel

Jane Addams understood the gap between progress and poverty. She saw it in the misery in the streets of Chicago in the winter of 1893. For some time she had been aware that life in big cities for working-class families was bitter and hard. "The stream of laboring people goes past you," she wrote, and as "you see hard working-men lifting great burdens . . . your heart sinks with a sudden sense of futility." Born in a small rural community in Illinois, Addams found herself attracted on a visit to Europe in the mid-1880s not to art galleries and cathedrals but to urban factories and slums. Such conditions, she knew, existed in the United States as well, and she developed a plan "to aid in the solution of the social and industrial problems which are engendered by the modern conditions of life in a great city."

Vida Scudder, too, "felt the agitating and painful vibrations" of the depression. Like Addams, this young professor of literature at Wellesley College had been influenced by English settlement house models. When she returned from study at Oxford "kindled with the flame of social passion," Scudder was resolved to do something to alleviate the suffering of the poor. She and six other Smith College graduates formed the College Settlements Association, an organization of college women who founded and worked in settlement houses.

Like Addams and Scudder, other middle-class activists worried about social conditions, particularly the degradation of life and labor in America's cities, factories, and farms. They were mostly professionals—lawyers, ministers, teachers, journalists, and academic social scientists. Influenced by European social prophets like Karl Marx, Leo Tolstoy, and Victor Hugo and by Americans such as Emerson, Whitman, and Bellamy, most turned to the ethical teachings of Jesus for inspiration in solving social problems.

The message they began to preach in the 1890s was highly idealistic, ethical, and Christian. They preferred a society marked by cooperation rather than competition, where self-sacrifice rather than self-interest held sway and, as they liked to say, where people were guided by the "golden rule rather than the rule of gold." They meant, in short, to apply the ethics of Jesus to industrial and urban life in order to bring about the kingdom of heaven on earth. Some preferred to put their goals in more secular terms; they spoke of radically transforming American society. Most, however, worked within existing institutions. As middle-class intellectuals, they tended to stress an educational approach to problems. But they were also practi-

"Your heart sinks with a sudden sense of futility," wrote Jane Addams when she viewed the living conditions of America's urban poor.

cal, involving themselves in an effort to make immediate, tangible improvements by running for public office, crusading for legislation, mediating labor disputes, and living in poor neighborhoods.

The settlement house movement typified the blend of idealism and practicality characteristic of middle-class reformers in the 1890s. In the fall of 1889, Addams opened Hull House in Chicago and Scudder started Denison House in Boston. A short time later, on New York's Lower East Side, Lillian Wald opened her "house on Henry Street." The primary purpose of the settlement houses was to help immigrant families, especially women, adapt Old World rural styles of childbearing and child care, housekeeping, cooking, and health care to the realities of urban living in America. This meant launching day nurseries, kindergartens, boarding rooms for working women, and classes in sewing, cooking, nutrition, health care, and speaking English. The settlements also frequently organized young people's sports clubs and coffeehouses as a way of keeping them out of the saloons.

A second purpose of the settlement house movement was to provide college-educated

Many of the settlement houses included public health clinics, like this one at Vida Scudder's Denison House in Boston.

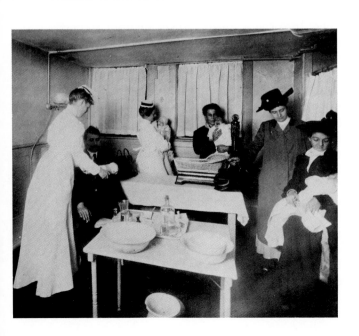

women with meaningful work at a time when they faced professional barriers and to allow them to preserve the strong feelings of sisterhood they had experienced in college. Settlement houseworkers, Scudder wrote, were like the "early Christians" in their renunciation of worldly goods and dedication to a life of service. Living in a settlement was in many ways an extension of woman's traditional role as nurturer of the weak. A third goal was to gather data exposing social misery in order to spur legislative action, such as developing city building codes for tenements, abolishing child labor, and improving safety in factories. Hull House, Addams said, was intended in part "to investigate and improve the conditions in the industrial districts of Chicago."

The settlement house movement, with its dual emphasis on the scientific gathering of facts and spiritual commitment, nourished the new academic study of sociology, first taught in divinity schools. Many organizations were founded to blend Christian belief and academic study in an attempt to change society. One was the American Institute of Christian Sociology, founded in 1893 by Josiah Strong, a Congregational minister, and Richard T. Ely, a University of Wisconsin economist. Similar organizations were the Christian Social Union, the Church Association for the Advancement of the Interests of Labor, and the Society of Christian Socialists.

These organizations viewed the purpose of religion as collective redemption rather than individual salvation. The latter was the prevailing view as presented in the wave of urban revivals led by the portly Dwight Moody in the 1870s. The revivals appealed to lower-class rural folk who were either drawn to the city by expectant opportunities or pushed there by economic ruin. They were supported by businessmen, who felt that religion would make workers and immigrants more docile. Revivalists emphasized the battle against sin through individual conversion. These revivals helped nearly to double Protestant church membership in the last two decades of the century. Although some urban workers drifted into secular faiths like socialism, most remained conventionally religious.

In the 1890s many Protestant ministers immersed themselves in the Social Gospel movement, which tied salvation to social betterment. Like the settlement house workers, these religious leaders sought to make Christianity relevant to industrial and urban problems. In Columbus, Ohio, Congregational minister Washington Gladden advocated collective bargaining and various forms of corporate profit sharing in books such as *Working Men and Their Employers, Social Salvation,* and *Applied Christianity.* A young Baptist minister in the notorious Hell's Kitchen area of New York City, Walter Rauschenbusch, raised an even louder voice. Often called upon to conduct funeral services for children killed by the airless, diseased tenements and sweatshops, Rauschenbusch was fired to unleash scathing attacks on the selfishness of capitalism and the irrelevance of a church that preached individual salvation rather than "social redemption." His progressive ideas for social justice and a welfare state were later published in two landmark Social Gospel books, *Christianity and the Social Crisis* (1907) and *Christianizing the Social Order* (1912).

Perhaps the most influential book promoting social Christianity was a best-selling novel, *In His Steps,* published in 1897 by Charles Sheldon. *In His Steps* portrayed the dramatic transformations in business relations, tenement life, and urban politics made possible by the work of a few community leaders who resolved to base all their actions on the single question, What would Jesus do? For a minister, this meant seeking to "bridge the chasm between the church and labor." For the idle rich, it meant settlement house work and reforming prostitutes. For landlords and factory owners, it meant taking action to improve living and working conditions for tenants and laborers. Although streaked with naive sentimentality characteristic of much of the Social Gospel, Sheldon's novel prepared thousands of influential middle-class Americans for progressive civic leadership after the turn of the century.

Reforming the City

The crucial event in *In His Steps* was a city election pitting moral middle-class reformers against seedy saloon interests and corrupt urban political machines. No late nineteenth-century institution needed reforming as much as urban government. The president of Cornell University described American city governments as "the worst in Christendom—the most expensive, the most inefficient, and the most corrupt." A Philadelphia committee found "inefficiency, waste, badly paved and filthy streets, unwholesome and offensive water, and slovenly and costly management" to have been the rule for years. New York and Chicago were even worse.

Rapid urban growth taxed the abilities of city leaders. Population increase and industrial expansion created new demands for service. Flush toilets, thirsty horses pulling street railways, and industrial users of water, for example, all exhausted the capacity of municipal waterworks built for an earlier age. As city governments struggled to respond to new needs, they raised taxes and incurred vast debts. This combination of rapid growth, indebtedness, and poor services, coupled with the influx of new immigrants, prepared fertile ground for graft and "bossism."

The rise of the boss was intimately connected to the growth of the city. As cities mushroomed, new voters appeared, many of them immigrants. Traditional ruling groups, native-born in most cases, left government for business, where more money and status beckoned. Into the resulting power vacuum stepped the boss. In an age of urban expansion, bosses dispensed patronage jobs in return for votes and contributions to the party machine. They awarded street railway, gas line, and other utility franchises and construction contracts to local businesses in return for kickbacks and other favors. They also passed on tips to friendly real estate men about the location of projected city improvements. Worse yet, the bosses received favors from the owners of saloons, brothels, and gambling clubs in return for their help with police protection, bail, and influence with the courts. These institutions, however unsavory we might think them today, were vital to the urban economy and played an important role in easing the immigrants' way into American life. For many young women, the brothel was a means of economic survival. For men, the saloon was the center of social life, as well as a place for cheap meals and information about work and aid to his family.

"Bossism" deeply offended middle-class urban reformers, who were unkindly dubbed "goo-goos" for their insistence on purity and good government. They opposed not only graft and vice but also the perversion of democracy by the exploitation of ignorant immigrants. As one explained, the immigrants "follow blindly leaders of their own race, are not moved by discussion, and exercise no judgment of their own." Indeed, he concluded, they were "not fit for the suffrage."

The programs of urban reformers were similar in most cities. They not only worked for the "Americanization" of immigrants in public schools (and opposed parochial schooling) but also formed clubs or voters' leagues to discuss the failings of municipal government. They delighted in making spectacular exposures of electoral irregularities and large-scale graft. These discoveries led to strident calls for ousting the mayor, often an Irish Catholic, and replacing

William Tweed, most famous of the city bosses, is represented as a continuing force long after his death in this cartoon by Thomas Nast.

him with an honest reform candidate, usually an Anglo-Saxon Protestant.

Clearly implied in the reformers' agenda to strip power from the bosses was a preference for urban political leadership by people like themselves. Most urban reformers could barely hide their distaste for the "city proletariat mob," as one put it. They proposed to replace the bosses with expert city managers, who would bring honest professionalism to city government. They hoped to make government less costly and thereby lower taxes. One effect of their emphasis on cost efficiency was to cut services to the poor. Another was to disenfranchise working-class and ethnic groups, whose political participation depended on the old ward boss system.

Not all urban reformers were elitist, managerial types. Samuel Jones, for example, both opposed the boss system and had a passionate commitment to democratic political participation by the urban immigrant masses. An immigrant himself, Jones was a self-made man in the rags-to-riches mold. Beginning in poverty in the oil fields of Pennsylvania, he worked his way up to the ownership of several oil fields and a factory in Toledo, Ohio. Once successful, however, Jones espoused a different ethic than Carnegie's "Gospel of Wealth." He was, he said, "a Golden Rule man," converted by a combination of firsthand contact with the "piteous appeals" of people put out of work by the depression and by his reading of Emerson, Whitman, Tolstoy, and the New Testament.

In 1894, Jones resolved "to apply the Golden Rule as a rule of conduct" in his factory. He instituted an eight-hour day for his employees, a $2 minimum wage per day (50 to 75 cents higher than the Toledo average for ten hours), a cooperative insurance program, and an annual 5 percent Christmas dividend. He hired ex-criminals and outcasts that no one else would employ and plastered the Golden Rule all over his factory walls. Anticipating various twentieth-century industrial reforms, Jones created a company cafeteria, where he offered a hot lunch for 15 cents, a Golden Rule park for workers and their families, employee music groups, and a Golden Rule Hall, where he regularly invited prominent visionaries, many of them socialists, to speak.

In 1897, declaring that "after three years of a

test I am pleased to say the Golden Rule works," Jones decided to extend his notions of cooperation and brotherhood to city government, much like Hazen Pingree had been doing in nearby Detroit. Running as a maverick Republican, Jones was elected to an unprecedented four terms as mayor of Toledo. Installed by the voters, he advocated municipal ownership of natural gas, street railways, and other utilities; public works jobs and housing for the unemployed; more civic parks and playgrounds; and free municipal baths, pools, skating rinks, sleigh rides, vocational education, and kindergartens.

Few of these reforms were implemented, yet Jones's unorthodox ideas and behavior incurred the wrath of nearly every prominent citizen in Toledo. As a pacifist, he did not believe in violence or coercion of any kind. Therefore, he took away policemen's side arms and heavy clubs. When he sat as judge in police court, he regularly dismissed most cases of petty theft and drunkenness brought before him, charging that the accused were victims of an unjust social order and that only the poor went to jail for such crimes. He refused to advocate closing the saloons or brothels, and when prostitutes were brought before him, he usually dismissed them only after fining every man in the room 10 cents—and himself a dollar—for permitting prostitution to exist. The crime rate in Toledo, a notoriously sinful city, decreased during his tenure, and Jones was adored by the plain people. When he died in 1904, nearly 55,000 persons, "tears streaming down their faces," filed past his coffin.

THE ELECTION OF 1896

"Golden Rule" Jones was ahead of his time, anticipating many urban reforms of the twentieth century. National politicians, too, struggling to find appropriate measures to end the depression and impress voters in the mid-1890s, initiated some modern political ideas and changed the composition of the two major parties—but not without being pushed by a strong third party, the Populists. The election of 1896 was one of the most critical in American history, for it upset the party equilibrium that had characterized politics since the Civil War.

A Crucial Election Campaign

Although the People's party had lost its bid to gain control of the national government in 1892 (see Chapter 18), the crisis of the depression of 1893 created new political opportunities. Democratic president Grover Cleveland responded to the depression by repealing the Sherman Silver Purchase Act in an effort to stabilize currency. Wealthy silver mine owners were infuriated. Cleveland's handling of Coxey's march and the Pullman strike also alienated workers. In 1894, large numbers of voters abandoned the Democrats, giving both the Populist and Republican parties high hopes for electoral success in 1896.

As the election approached, Populist leaders focused on the issues of fusion and silver. Populist successes in 1894 had come through the tactic of fusing with one of the major parties by agreeing on a joint ticket. But fusion always required abandoning much of the Populist platform, thus weakening the party's distinctive character. Under the influence of silver mine owners, many Populists became convinced that the hope of the party lay in a single-issue commitment to the free and unlimited coinage of silver. Weaver expected both parties to nominate gold candidates, which would send disappointed silverites to the Populist standard.

The Republicans, holding their convention first, nominated William McKinley on the first ballot. A congressman from 1877 to 1891 and twice governor of Ohio, McKinley was happily identified with the high protective tariff that bore his name. Republicans were quick to cite the familiar argument that prosperity depended on the gold standard and protection and blamed the depression on Cleveland's attempt to lower the tariff. The excitement of the Democratic convention in July contrasted with the staid, smoothly organized Republican one. Cleveland had already been repudiated by his party as state after state elected convention delegates pledged to silver. Gold Democrats, however, had enough power left to wage a close battle for the platform plank on money.

The surprise nominee of the convention was an ardent young silverite, William Jennings Bryan, a 36-year-old congressman from Nebraska. Few saw him as presidential material, but as a member of the Resolutions Committee, Bryan arranged to give the closing argument for a silver plank himself. His dramatic speech swept the convention for silver and ensured his own nomination. "I come to speak to you," Bryan cried out, "in defense of a cause as holy as the cause of liberty—the cause of humanity." At the conclusion of what was to become one of the most famous political speeches in American history, Bryan attacked the goldbugs and promised, "Having behind us the producing masses of this nation . . . and toilers everywhere, we will answer their demand for a gold standard by saying to them: 'You shall not press down upon the brow of labor this crown of thorns, you shall not crucify mankind upon a cross of gold.'" As he spoke, Bryan stretched out his arms as if on a cross, and the convention exploded with applause.

Populist strategy lay in shambles with the

William Jennings Bryan, surprise nominee at the 1896 Democratic Convention, was a vigorous proponent of "the cause of humanity."

nomination of a Democratic silver candidate. Some party leaders favored fusion with the entire Democratic ticket. Antifusionists were outraged, in part because the Democratic vice-presidential candidate, Arthur Sewall, was an East Coast banker and hard-money man. An unwise compromise was achieved when the Populist convention nominated Bryan but instead of Sewall chose Populist Tom Watson of Georgia as his running mate. The existence of two silverite slates damaged Bryan's electoral hopes.

During the campaign, McKinley stayed at his home in Canton, Ohio, where some 750,000 admirers came to visit him, helped by low excursion rates offered by the railroads. Republican strategy featured an unprecedented effort to reach voters through a highly sophisticated mass-media campaign, heavily financed by such major corporations as Standard Oil and the railroads. Party leaders hired thousands of speakers to support McKinley and distributed over 200 million pamphlets to a voting population of 15 million. The literature, distributed in 14 languages, was designed to appeal to particular national, ethnic, regional, and occupational groups. To all these people, McKinley was advertised as "the advance agent of prosperity."

From his front porch in Canton, McKinley responded to Bryan's challenge by aiming his appeal not only at the business classes but also at unemployed workers, to whom he promised "a full dinner pail." He also spoke about the money issue, declaring that "our currency today is . . . as good as gold." Free silver, he maintained, would lead to inflation and more economic disaster. Recovery depended not on money but on tariff reform, which would stimulate American industry and provide jobs—"not open mints for the unlimited coinage of the silver of the world," he said, "but open mills for the full and unrestricted labor of American workingmen."

In sharp contrast to the Republican stay-at-home policy, Bryan took his case to the people. Three million people in 27 states heard him speak as he traveled over 18,000 miles, giving as many as 30 speeches a day. Bryan's message was simple. Prosperity would return, with free coinage of silver. Government policies should attend to the needs of the producing classes rather than the vested interests that believed in the gold standard. "That policy is best for this country," Bryan proclaimed, "which brings prosperity first to those who toil." But his rhetoric favored rural toilers. "The great cities rest upon our broad and fertile prairies," he had said in the "Cross of Gold" speech. "Burn down your cities and leave our farms, and your cities will spring up again as if by magic; but destroy our farms and the grass will grow in the streets of every city in the country." Urban workers were little inspired by this rhetoric, nor were immigrants impressed by Bryan's prairie moralizing.

To many people, Bryan's nomination represented a threat to social harmony. Influential East Coast opinion molders overwhelmingly opposed the brash young Nebraskan. Theodore Roosevelt wrote that "this silver craze surpasses belief. Bryan's election would be a great calamity." A Brooklyn minister declared that the Democratic platform was "made in Hell." One newspaper editor said of Bryan that he was just like Nebraska's Platte River: "six inches deep and six miles wide at the mouth." Others branded him a "madman" and an "anarchist." The New York *Mail* wrote that "no wild-eyed and rattle-brained horde of the red flag ever proclaimed a fiercer defiance of law, precedent, order, and government."

With such intense interest in the election, it was predictable that voters would turn out in record numbers. In key states like Illinois, Indiana, and Ohio, 95 percent of those eligible to vote went to the polls. When the voting was over, McKinley had won 271 electoral votes to Bryan's 176. Over 7 million Americans from all segments of society voted for the "advance agent of prosperity." Millionaire Mark Hanna jubilantly wired McKinley: "God's in his heaven, all's right with the world." Bryan had been defeated by the largest majority since Grant trounced Greeley in 1872.

Although Bryan won over 6 million votes (46 percent of the total), more than any previous Democratic winner, he failed to carry the Midwest and lost parts of the South and Far West. Nor could he make large inroads into the votes of the urban middle-classes and industrial masses, who had little confidence that the Democrats could stimulate economic growth or cope with the problems of industrialism. McKinley's promise of a "full dinner pail" was more convincing than the untested formula for free silver. But chance also played a part in Bryan's defeat. Bad wheat harvests in India, Australia, and Ar-

Election of 1896

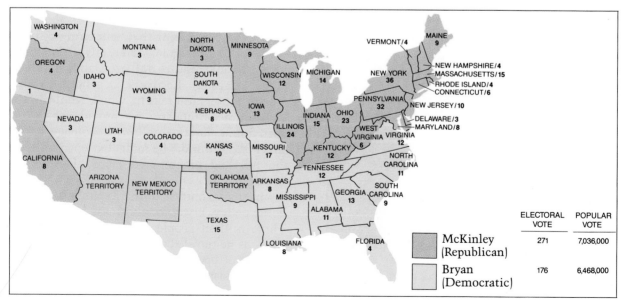

	ELECTORAL VOTE	POPULAR VOTE
McKinley (Republican)	271	7,036,000
Bryan (Democratic)	176	6,468,000

gentina drove up grain prices in the world market. Many of the complaints of American farmers evaporated amid rising farm prices.

The New Shape of American Politics

The landslide Republican victory marked the end of the political equilibrium and party identifications that had characterized American politics since the end of the Civil War. Republicans assumed a new image as the party of prosperity and lost their identification with the politics of piety. The Democratic party, which would remain under Bryan's leadership until 1912, took on the mantle of reform and moralism. Populists, demoralized by fusion with a losing campaign, fell apart and disappeared. Asked a despondent Populist, Ignatius Donnelly, "Will the sun of triumph never rise? I fear not." His pessimism was premature, for within the next 20 years most Populist issues were taken over and adopted by politicians of the major parties.

Another result of the election of 1896 was a change in the pattern of political participation. After 1896, the Republicans were the dominant party in America for 16 years. They held sway in the North and West, while the Democrats, their rolls diminished by those who abandoned the party in 1896, especially from cities, could dominate political life only in the South. Few states had hotly contested two-party political battles. There seemed less and less reason to continue party activities aimed at bringing out large numbers of voters. Likewise, the individual voter had less and less motivation to cast a ballot, especially since election results were so often a foregone conclusion. Many black voters in the South, moreover, were disfranchised. Thus the high rate of political participation that had characterized the nineteenth century since the Jackson era gradually declined. In the twentieth century, political involvement among poorer Americans lessened considerably, a phenomenon unique among western industrial countries.

McKinley had promised that Republican rule meant prosperity, and no sooner did he take office than the economy recovered. Discoveries of gold in the Yukon and Alaskan Klondike increased the money supply, thus killing the silver mania until the early 1930s. Industrial production returned to full capacity. In a tour of the Midwest in 1898, McKinley spoke to cheering crowds about the hopeful economic picture. "We have gone from industrial depression to industrial activity," he told citizens of Clinton, Iowa. "We have gone from labor seeking employment to employment seeking labor." His audience burst into enthusiastic applause.

McKinley's election marked not only the return of an era of economic health but also the emergence of the executive as the preeminent focus of the American political system. Just as McKinley's campaign set the pattern for the extravagant efforts to win office that have dominated modern times, his conduct as president foreshadowed the nature of the twentieth-century presidency. McKinley rejected traditional views of the president as the passive executor of laws, instead playing an active role in dealing with Congress and the press. His frequent trips away from Washington testified to his respect for public opinion. Some historians regard McKinley as the first of the modern presidents. As we shall see in the next chapter, he transformed the presidency into a potent force not only in domestic life but in world affairs as well.

CONCLUSION: Looking Forward

The chapter began with Edward Bellamy's imaginary look backward from the year 2000 at the grim economic realities and unresponsive politics of American life in the late nineteenth century. Through the efforts of middle-class reformers like Jane Addams, Walter Rauschenbusch, and "Golden Rule" Jones, as well as through the promise of a new national politics represented by the influence of populism on the major parties, many Americans began to look forward to the kind of cooperative, caring, and cleaner world envisioned in Bellamy's utopian novel.

As the year 1900 approached, people took a predictably intense interest in what the new century would be like. Henry Adams, still the pessimist, saw an ominous future, predicting the explosive and ultimately destructive energy of unrestrained industrial development, symbolized by the "dynamo" and other engines of American power. Such forces, he warned, would overwhelm the gentler, moral forces represented by art, woman, and religious symbols like the Virgin. But others were more optimistic, preferring to place their confidence in America's historic role as an exemplary nation, demonstrating to the world the moral superiority of its economic system, democratic institutions, and middle-class Protestant values. Surely the new century, most thought, would see not only the continued perfection of these values and institutions but also the spread of American influence throughout the world. Such confidence resulted in an outward thrust by the American people even before the old century had ended. We turn to that in the next chapter.

Recommended Reading

The politics of the Gilded Age is treated usefully in the context of other developments of late nineteenth-century life in H. Wayne Morgan, *From Hayes to McKinley: National Party Politics, 1877–1896* (1969); John A. Garraty, *The New Commonwealth, 1877–1890* (1968); Robert Wiebe, *The Search for Order, 1877–1920* (1967); Samuel P. Hays, *The Response to Industrialism, 1885–1914* (1957); and Morton Keller, *Affairs of State: Public Life in Late Nineteenth Century America* (1977). A recent analysis of politics in the 1890s (and a good example of the "new political history") is R. Hal Williams, *Years of Decision: American Politics in the 1890s* (1978). The new social and political history is well represented by Richard Jensen, *The Winning of the Midwest: Social and Political Conflict, 1888–1896* (1971) and Paul Kleppner, *The Third Electoral System, 1853–1892: Parties, Voters, and Political Cultures* (1979).

The lives of middle-class men and women are understood best by a variety of different approaches. See Peter Filene, *Him/Her/Self: Sex Roles in Modern America* (1974) and the relevant chapters in Mary Ryan's excellent survey, *Womanhood in America*, 3d ed. (1983). An astute study of the battle for the vote is Aileen Kraditor, *The Ideas of the Woman's Suffrage Movement, 1890–1920* (1965). Social Darwinism and the success ethic are covered in Richard Hofstadter, *Social Darwinism in American Thought*, rev. ed. (1955); Irvin G. Wyllie, *The Self-Made Man in America* (1954); and John Cawelti, *Apostles of the Self-Made Man: Changing Concepts of Success in America* (1965).

Novels that capture the flavor of middle-class life in the late nineteenth century include Mark Twain and Charles Dudley Warner, *The Gilded Age* (1873); William Dean Howells, *The Rise of Silas Lapham* (1885) and *A Hazard of New Fortunes* (1889); Kate Chopin, *The Awakening* (1899); and Charles Sheldon, *In His Steps* (1896). Stephen Crane, *Maggie: A Girl of the Streets* (1895); Theodore Dreiser, *Sister Carrie* (1900); and Frank Norris, *The Octopus* (1901) depict a middle-class view of both middle- and lower-class life.

Two classic works on late nineteenth-century reform are Richard Hofstadter, *Age of Reform: From Bryan to F.D.R.* (1955) and John Sproat, *"The Best Men" Liberal Reformers in the Gilded Age* (1968). The best studies of middle-class urban reformers and the bossism they opposed are John Allswang, *Bosses, Machines, and Urban Voters* (1977); Arthur Mann, *Yankee Reformers in an Urban Age: Social Reform in Boston, 1880–1900* (1954); and Allen F. Davis, *Spearheads for Reform: The Social Settlements and the Progressive Movement, 1890–1914* (1967). See also William Riordon's delightful recovery of the words of a typical boss, *Plunkitt of Tammany Hall* (1963, originally published in 1905). One can understand the personal views and feelings of the urban reformers by reading about their lives, either through a biographical study of ten reformers, Peter

Frederick, *Knights of the Golden Rule: The Intellectual as Christian Social Reformer in the 1890s* (1976), or through two revealing autobiographies, Jane Addams, *Twenty Years at Hull House* (1910) and Vida Scudder, *On Journey* (1937).

The profound impact of the depression of 1893 is seen in Charles Hoffman, *The Depression of the Nineties: An Economic History* (1970) and David P. Thelen, *The New Citizenship: Origins of Progressivism in Wisconsin, 1885–1900* (1972). Populism and the election of 1896 are covered in a straightforward account by Paul Glad, *McKinley, Bryan and the People* (1964) and the titles listed in Chapter 18.

TIME LINE

1873	Congress demonetizes silver
1875	Specie Resumption Act
1877	Rutherford B. Hayes becomes president
1878	Bland-Allison Act
1879	Henry George, *Progress and Poverty*
1880	James A. Garfield elected president
1881	Garfield assassinated; Chester A. Arthur succeeds to presidency
1883	Pendleton Civil Service Act
1884	Grover Cleveland elected president W. D. Howells, *The Rise of Silas Lapham*
1887	College Settlement House Association founded
1888	Edward Bellamy, *Looking Backward* Benjamin Harrison elected president
1889	Jane Addams establishes Hull House Andrew Carnegie promulgates "The Gospel of Wealth"
1890	General Federation of Women's Clubs founded Sherman Anti-Trust Act Sherman Silver Purchase Act McKinley Tariff Elections bill defeated
1890s	Wyoming, Colorado, Utah, and Idaho grant woman suffrage
1892	Cleveland elected president for the second time; Populist party wins over a million votes Homestead steel strike
1893	World's Columbian Exposition, Chicago
1893–1897	Financial panic and depression
1894	Pullman strike Coxey's march on Washington
1895	*United States* v. *E. C. Knight*
1896	Charles Sheldon publishes *In His Steps* Populist party fuses with Democrats William McKinley elected president
1897	"Golden Rule" Jones elected mayor of Toledo, Ohio Economic recovery begins

CHAPTER 21
THE UNITED STATES BECOMES
A WORLD POWER

In January 1899, as the United States Senate was locked in a dramatic debate over whether to ratify the Treaty of Paris concluding the recent war with Spain over Cuban independence, American soldiers uneasily faced Filipino rebels across a neutral zone around the outskirts of Manila, capital city of the Philippines. Until recently, the Americans and Filipinos had been allies, together defeating the Spanish to accomplish the liberation of the Philippines. The American fleet under Commodore George Dewey had destroyed the Spanish naval squadron in Manila Bay on May 1, 1898. Three weeks later, an American ship personally delivered from exile the native Filipino insurrectionary leader, Emilio Aguinaldo, to lead rebel forces on land while the Americans patrolled the seas and waited for reinforcements.

At first the Filipinos looked on the Americans as liberators. Although the United States' intentions were never clear, Aguinaldo believed that as in Cuba, the Americans had no territorial ambitions. They would simply drive the Spanish out and then leave themselves. In June, therefore, Aguinaldo declared the independence of the Philippines and began setting up a constitutional form of government. American officials pointedly ignored the independence ceremonies. When the armistice ended the war in August, American troops denied Filipino soldiers the right to liberate and occupy Manila and shunted them off to the suburbs. The armistice agreement recognized American rights to "the harbor, city, and bay of Manila." Later that fall, the Treaty of Paris gave the United States the entire Philippine Island archipelago.

Consequently, tension mounted in the streets of Manila and along 14 miles of trenches separating American and Filipino soldiers. Taunts, obscenities, and racial epithets were shouted across the neutral zone. Barroom skirmishes and knifings punctuated the city at night; American soldiers searched houses without warrants and took goods from stores without paying for them. Their behavior was not unlike that of English soldiers in Boston in 1775.

On the night of February 4, 1899, Private William Grayson and Private Miller of Company B, 1st Nebraska Volunteers, were on patrol by their regimental outpost in Santa Mesa, a Manila suburb surrounded on three sides by insurgent trenches. The Americans had orders to shoot any Filipino soldiers found in the neutral area. As the two Americans cautiously worked their way to an advanced point near a bridge over the San Juan River, they heard a Filipino signal-whistle up ahead, answered by another. Then a red lantern flashed from a nearby blockhouse. The two froze as four Filipinos emerged from the darkness on the road ahead. "Halt!" Grayson shouted. The native lieutenant in charge answered, "Halto!" either mockingly or because he had similar orders. Standing less than 15 feet apart, the two men repeated their commands. After a moment's hesitation, Grayson fired, killing his opponent with one bullet. As the other Filipinos jumped out at them, Grayson and Miller killed two more. Then they turned and ran back to their own lines, shouting warnings of attack. A full-scale battle followed.

The next day, Commodore Dewey cabled Washington that the "insurgents have inaugurated general engagement" and promised a hasty suppression of the insurrection. The outbreak of hostilities marked the end of the Senate debates. On February 6, the Senate ratified the Treaty of Paris, thus formally annexing the Philippines.

The Filipino-American War lasted two years longer than the Spanish-American War that caused it and involved several times more troops and casualties. In what came to be a guerrilla war with some similarities to those fought later in the twentieth century in Asia and Central America, native nationalists tried to undermine the American will to fight by hit-and-run attacks. American soldiers, meanwhile, remained in heavily garrisoned cities, foraying out on search-and-destroy missions intended to root out rebels and pacify the countryside.

Costs to both sides were high. In all, nearly 200,000 American troops were sent to that distant Asian land; 4,234 were buried there, and 2,800 more were wounded. The cost was $400 million. Filipino casualties were much greater. In addition to the 18,000 killed in combat, an estimated 200,000 Filipinos (20 percent of the population) died of famine and disease because U.S. soldiers burned villages and destroyed crops and livestock to disrupt the economy and deny rebel fighters their food supply. Atrocities on both sides increased with the frustrations of a lengthening war. Although Aguinaldo was captured in 1901, the war did not end until July 1902.

Clustered in trenches against Filipino nationalists, the presence of American soldiers in the faraway Philippine Islands in 1899 was a harbinger of twentieth-century wars to come.

How did all this happen? What brought Private Grayson to "shoot my first nigger," as he put it, halfway around the world in distant Asia? For the first time in history, regular American soldiers found themselves fighting outside North America. The "champion of oppressed nations," as Aguinaldo said, had turned into an oppressor nation itself, actively expanding the American way of life and American institutions to faraway peoples against their will.

The war in the Philippines marked a critical transformation in America's role in the world. Within a few years at the turn of the century, the United States acquired an empire, however small by European standards, and established itself as a world power. This chapter will review the historical dilemmas of America's role in the world, especially those of the expansionist nineteenth century. Then we will examine the motivations for the intensified expansionism of the 1890s and how they were manifested in Cuba, the Philippines, and elsewhere. Finally, we will look at how the fundamental patterns of modern American foreign policy were established for Latin America, Asia, and Europe in the early twentieth century.

STEPS TOWARD EMPIRE

The forces that brought Privates Grayson and Miller far from home in Nebraska to the Philippines lay deep in American history. As early as the Puritan migration from England to Massachusetts Bay in the seventeenth century, Americans faced a dilemma of how to do good in a world that does wrong. John Winthrop sought to set up a "city on a hill" in the New World, a model community of righteous living for others in the world to behold and imitate. "Let the eyes of the world be upon us," Winthrop said, and that wish, reaffirmed during the American Revolution, became a permanent goal of American policy toward the outside world.

America as a Model Society

Americans in the nineteenth century continued to believe in the idea of the nation's special mission. The Monroe Doctrine in 1823 pointed out moral differences between the monarchical, arbitrary governments of Europe and the free republican institutions of the New World. As the American Revolutionary model was followed in the Spanish colonies in South and Central America, Monroe warned Europe to stay out. In succeeding decades, a number of distinguished European visitors (discussed in Chapter 13) came to study "democracy in America" to see for themselves "the great social revolution" at work. They found widespread democracy, representative and responsive political and legal institutions, a religious commitment to the notion of human perfectibility, unlimited energy, and the ability to utilize unregulated economic activity and inventive genius to produce more things for more people.

Who could resist such a model? In a world that was evil, the American people believed that they stood as a transforming force for good. Many others agreed. The problem was how a nation committed to isolationism was to do the transforming. One way was to encourage other nations to observe and imitate the good example set by the United States. But often other nations preferred their own society or were attracted to other models of modernization, as has frequently happened in the twentieth century. This implied a more aggressive foreign policy.

Indeed, assertive self-interest and internationalism as well as selfless idealism and isolationism have guided the American rise to power in the world. Americans have rarely simply focused on perfecting the good example at home, waiting for others to copy it. This requires patience and passivity, two traits not prevalent in Americans. Rather, throughout history, the American people have actively and sometimes

United States Territorial Expansion

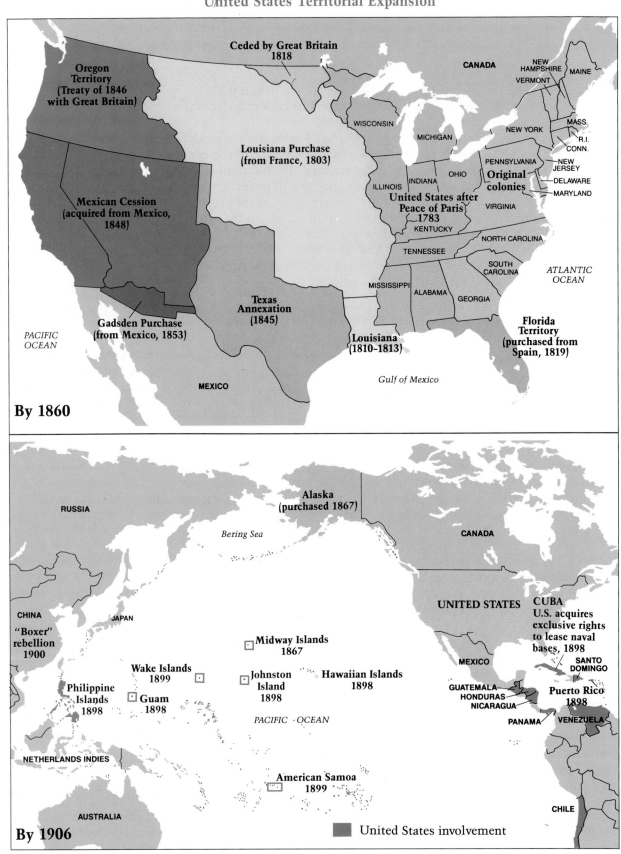

By 1860

Oregon Territory (Treaty of 1846 with Great Britain)

Ceded by Great Britain 1818

CANADA

Louisiana Purchase (from France, 1803)

WISCONSIN
MICHIGAN
ILLINOIS INDIANA OHIO
KENTUCKY
TENNESSEE
MISSISSIPPI ALABAMA GEORGIA

NEW HAMPSHIRE MAINE
VERMONT
NEW YORK MASS.
R.I. CONN.
PENNSYLVANIA NEW JERSEY
Original colonies DELAWARE
MARYLAND
United States after Peace of Paris 1783 VIRGINIA
NORTH CAROLINA
SOUTH CAROLINA

ATLANTIC OCEAN

Mexican Cession (acquired from Mexico, 1848)

PACIFIC OCEAN

Gadsden Purchase (from Mexico, 1853)

Texas Annexation (1845)

Louisiana (1810–1813)

Florida Territory (purchased from Spain, 1819)

MEXICO

Gulf of Mexico

By 1906

RUSSIA

Alaska (purchased 1867)

Bering Sea

CANADA

CHINA
JAPAN
"Boxer" rebellion 1900

UNITED STATES CUBA
U.S. acquires exclusive rights to lease naval bases, 1898

MEXICO
SANTO DOMINGO

Midway Islands 1867

Wake Islands 1899

Johnston Island 1898
Hawaiian Islands 1898

Philippine Islands 1898
Guam 1898

GUATEMALA
HONDURAS
NICARAGUA
Puerto Rico 1898

PANAMA VENEZUELA

PACIFIC OCEAN

NETHERLANDS INDIES

American Samoa 1899

AUSTRALIA

CHILE

United States involvement

forcefully imposed their ideas and institutions on others. The international crusades of the United States, well intentioned if not always well received, have usually been motivated by a mixture of idealism and self-interest. Hence the effort to spread the exemplary American model to an imperfect world has been both a blessing and a burden, both for others and for the American people themselves.

The first century of American independence was marked by a continuous and consistent expression of continental expansionism. Jefferson's purchase of the Louisiana Territory in 1803 and the grasping for Florida and Canada by War Hawks in 1812 signaled an intense American interest in territorial growth. Although the United States remained "unentangled" in European affairs for most of the century, as both Washington and Jefferson had advised, the American government and people were very much entangled elsewhere. To the Cherokee, Seminole, Sioux, Nez Percé, Navajo, and other Native American nations, the United States was far from isolationist. Nor did the Canadians, the Spanish in Florida, or the Mexicans in Texas and California consider the Americans nonexpansionist. Until midcentury, the United States pursued its "Manifest Destiny" (see Chapter 14) by expanding across the North American continent. But in the 1850s, Americans began to look outward beyond their own continent. This trend was marked most significantly by Commodore Perry's visit to Japan, the expansion of the China trade, and the various expeditions into the Caribbean in search of more cotton lands and a canal connecting the two oceans.

Expansion After Seward

These outward thrusts were accelerated under the influence of Lincoln's secretary of state, William Seward. During the Civil War, Seward was preoccupied with preventing the Confederacy from receiving foreign aid and diplomatic recognition. But once the war ended, he revived his vision of an America that would hold a "commanding sway in the world." Although restrained in his territorial ambitions, Seward believed that the United States was destined to exert commercial domination "on the Pacific ocean, and its islands and continents." His goal was that from markets, raw materials, and trade would come the "regeneration of . . . the East."

Toward this end, Seward purchased Alaska from Russia in 1867 for $7.2 million. He also acquired a coaling station in the Midway Islands in the mid-Pacific and paved the way for American commercial expansion in Korea, Japan, and China. Moreover, he advocated the annexation of Cuba and other islands of the West Indies and tried to negotiate a treaty securing an American-built canal through the isthmus of Panama. Seward dreamed of "possession" of the whole North and Central American continent and ultimately of "control of the world." Although his larger dreams went unrealized, his interest in expansion into the Caribbean persisted among business interests and politicians after Cuba's attempted revolt against Spain in 1868.

Urged on by friends two years later, President Grant tried to force the Senate to annex Santo Domingo (Hispaniola), an island near Cuba. Supporters cited the strategic importance of the Caribbean and made forceful arguments for the economic value of raw materials and markets that the addition of Santo Domingo would bring. Senatorial opponents argued that expansionism violated the American principle of self-determination and government by the consent of the governed. They pointed out, moreover, that the native peoples of the Caribbean were brown-skinned, culturally inferior, non-English-speaking, and therefore unassimilable. Finally, they argued that expansionism would be likely to involve foreign entanglements, necessitating a large, expensive navy, growth in the size of government, and higher taxes. The Senate rejected the treaty to annex Santo Domingo.

Although reluctant to add territory outright, American interests in Latin America and Asia, fed by Seward's hunger for commercial dominance, continued. A number of statesmen asserted the United States' unmistakable influence in these areas. President Hayes said in 1880 that despite a treaty with England pledging joint construction and control of a canal across either Panama or Nicaragua, he was certain that if such a canal were built, it would be "under American control" and would be considered "virtually a part of the coast line of the United States." But nothing came of diplomatic efforts with Nicaragua to smooth the way for an American-built canal except Nicaraguan suspicions of U.S. intentions.

In 1881, Secretary of State James G. Blaine sought to convene a conference of American nations to promote hemispheric peace and trade. Although motivated mostly by his presidential ambitions, his effort nevertheless led to the first Pan-American Conference eight years later. The Latin Americans may have wondered what Blaine intended, for in 1881 he intervened in three separate border disputes in Central and South America, in each case at the cost of goodwill and trust, especially from Chile and Mexico.

Ten years later, relations with Chile were harmed again when several American sailors on shore leave were involved in a barroom brawl in Valparaiso. Two Americans were killed and several others injured. American pride was also injured, and President Benjamin Harrison sent an ultimatum calling for a "prompt and full reparation." After threats of war, Chile complied.

Similar incidents occurred as American expansionists pursued Seward's goals in the Pacific. In the mid-1870s, American sugar-growing interests in the Hawaiian Islands were strong enough to place whites in positions of influence over the native monarchy. In 1875, they succeeded in obtaining a reciprocity treaty admitting Hawaiian sugar duty free to the United States. When the treaty was renewed two years later, the United States also gained rights to a naval base at Pearl Harbor on the island of Oahu.

Native Hawaiians resented the growing influence of American sugar interests, especially as they contracted to bring in large numbers of Japanese immigrant workers. In 1891, the strongly nationalist Queen Liliuokalani assumed the throne in Hawaii and promptly abolished the constitution, seeking to establish control over whites in the name of "Hawaii for the Hawaiians." In 1893, with the help of U.S.

Iolani Palace, former home of Queen Liliuokalani, was the scene of annexation ceremonies in 1898, when Hawaii became a U.S. territory.

gunboats and marines, the whites staged a palace coup (a revolution later called one "of sugar, by sugar, for sugar") and sought formal annexation by the friendly Harrison administration. But before final Senate ratification could be achieved, Grover Cleveland, who opposed imperial expansion, returned to the presidency for his second term and stopped the move. He was, however, unable to remove the white sugar growers from power in Hawaii. They waited patiently for a more desirable time for annexation, which came in the midst of the war in 1898.

Moving ever-closer toward the fabled markets of the Far East, the United States acquired a naval station at Pago Pago in the Samoan Islands in 1878. However, it had to share the port with Great Britain and Germany. In an incident in 1889, American and German naval forces almost engaged each other, but a typhoon wiped out both navies and ended the crisis. Troubles in the Pacific also occurred in the late 1880s over the American seizure of several Canadian ships in fur seal–fishing disputes in the Bering Sea. This issue was settled only by the British threat of naval action and with the ruling of an international arbitration commission, which ordered the United States to pay damages.

The United States confronted the English closer to home as it sought to replace Britain as the most influential nation in Central American affairs. In 1895, a boundary dispute between Venezuela and British Guiana threatened to bring British intervention against the Venezuelans. President Cleveland, in need of a popular political issue because of the depression, discovered the political value of a tough foreign policy by defending a weak sister American republic against the British bully. He asked Secretary of

State Richard Olney to send a message to Great Britain. Olney's note, which was stronger than Cleveland had intended, invoked the Monroe Doctrine, declared the United States as "practically sovereign on this continent" and demanded British acceptance of international arbitration to settle the dispute. The British ignored the note, and war threatened. Although England was the chief rival of the United States for economic influence in the Caribbean, both sides eventually realized that war between them would be "an absurdity." The dispute was settled by agreeing to an impartial American commission to settle the boundary.

These increasing conflicts in the Caribbean and Pacific signaled the rise of an American presence beyond the borders of the United States. Yet as of 1895, the nation had neither the means nor a consistent policy for enlarging its role in the world. The diplomatic service was small, inexperienced, and unprofessional. Around the world, American emissaries kept sloppy records, issued illegal passports, involved themselves in petty local issues and frauds, and exhibited insensitive behavior toward native cultures. It was not until the 1930s that a high embassy official in Peking spoke Chinese. The U.S. Army, numbering about 28,000 men in the mid-1890s, ranked thirteenth in the world, behind that of Bulgaria. The navy, which had been dismantled after the Civil War and partially rebuilt under President Arthur, ranked no higher than tenth and included too many ships powered by dangerously outdated boilers. These limited and backward instruments of foreign policy were inadequate to support the aspirations of an emerging world power, especially one whose rise to power had come so quickly.

EXPANSIONIST MOTIVES IN THE 1890s

In 1893, the historian Frederick Jackson Turner wrote that for three centuries "the dominant fact in American life has been expansion." Turner observed that the "extension of American influence to outlying islands and adjoining countries" indicated that expansionism would

continue. Although not himself an imperialist, Turner's observations struck a responsive chord in a country that had always been restless, mobile, and optimistic. With the western American frontier closed, Americans would surely look for new frontiers, for mobility and markets as well as for morality and missionary activity. The motivations for the expansionist impulse of the late 1890s were similar to those that had prompted people to settle the New World in the first place: greed, glory, and God. We will examine these impulses under the categories of profits, patriotism, piety (defined broadly as moral mission), and politics.

Searching for Overseas Markets

Albert Beveridge of Indiana bragged in 1898 that "American factories are making more than the American people can use; American soil is producing more than they can consume. Fate has written our policy for us; the trade of the world must and shall be ours." Americans like Beveridge believed in the dream of Seward, Blaine, and others to establish a commercial empire in the islands and adjoining countries of the Caribbean Sea and the Pacific Ocean. With a strong belief in free enterprise and open markets for investing capital and selling products, American businessmen saw potentially huge profits in the heavily populated areas of Latin America and Asia. They also viewed it as essential to get their share of these markets in order to stay competitive with European countries. The attraction was enhanced by the availability in those lands of abundant raw materials such as sugar, coffee, fruits, oil, rubber, and minerals.

An increase in commerce necessitated the support of a stronger navy and the existence of coaling stations and colonies. Business interests, which were supplanting agricultural interests in the political arena, began to shape diplomatic and military strategy. As Senator Orville Platt of Connecticut said in 1893, "A policy of isolation did well enough when we were an embryo nation, but today things are different. . . . We are sixty-five million of people, the most advanced and powerful on earth, and regard to our future welfare demands an abandonment of the doctrines of isolation." By 1901, the economic adviser for the State Department described overseas commercial expansion as "a natural law of economic and race development."

Not all businessmen in the 1890s agreed that commercial expansion backed by a vigorous foreign policy was an unmixed good. Some saw

it as dangerous and costly, preferring traditional trade with Canada and Europe rather than risky new ventures in Asia and Latin America. Securing colonies and developing markets and investment opportunities far from the American mainland not only would require initially high expenses but also might involve the United States in wars with commercial rivals or native peoples in distant places. Some businessmen, furthermore, thought it more important in 1897 to secure the recovery from the depression than to secure little islands in Asia.

But the decrease in domestic consumption during the depression also encouraged businessmen to expand into new markets to sell surplus goods. The tremendous growth of American industrial and agricultural production in the post–Civil War years made expansionism an attractive alternative to drowning in overproduction. For many businessmen, new markets were preferable to cutting prices, which would redistribute wealth by allowing the lower classes to buy excess goods, or laying off workers, which would increase social unrest. Thus many reasons, not least the fear of overproduction and a desire to remain competitive in international markets, convinced hesitant businessmen to expand. They were led by the newly formed National Association of Manufacturers, which emphasized foreign trade in 8 of 14 purposes outlined in 1896: "The trade centres of Central and South America are natural markets for American products."

Despite the depression of the 1890s, these products appeared at a staggering rate. The United States moved from fourth in the world in manufacturing in 1870 to first in 1900, doubling the number of factories and tripling the value of farm output, mainly cotton, corn, and wheat. The United States led the world not only in railroad construction (206,631 miles of tracks in 1900, four times more than in 1870) but also in agricultural machinery and mass-produced technological products such as sewing machines, electrical implements, telephones, cash registers, elevators, and cameras. Manufactured goods grew nearly fivefold between 1895 and 1914.

Not surprisingly, the total value of American exports tripled, jumping from $434 million in 1866 to nearly $1.5 billion in 1900. By 1914, exports had risen to $2.5 billion, a 67 percent increase over 1900. The increased trade continued to go mainly to Europe rather than Asia. In 1900, for example, only 3 to 4 percent of U.S. exports went to China and Japan. Nevertheless, interest in Asian markets grew, especially as agricultural production continued to increase and prices remained low. Farmers dreamed of selling their surplus wheat to China. They were supported in this case by James J. Hill of the Great Northern Railroad, who printed wheat cookbooks in various Asian languages and distributed them in the Far East, hoping to fill his westward-bound boxcars and merchant ships with wheat and other grains.

Investment interest and activity followed a similar pattern. American direct investments abroad increased from an estimated $634 million to $2.6 billion between 1897 and 1914. Although investments were largest in Britain, Canada, and Mexico, the potential of Asia and Central America received the most attention. Central American investment increased from $21 million in 1897 to $93 million by the eve of World War I, mainly in mines, railroads, and banana and coffee plantations. At the turn of the century came the formation and growth of America's biggest multinational corporations—the United Fruit Company, Alcoa Aluminum,

Amalgamated Copper, Du Pont, American Tobacco, and others. Although slow to respond to investment and market opportunities abroad, these companies soon supported an aggressive foreign policy and the expansion of America's role in the world.

Patriotism and the Foreign Policy Elite

American interest in investments, markets, and raw materials abroad reflected a determination not to be left out of the international competition among European powers and Japan for commercial spheres of influence and colonies in Asia, Africa, and Latin America. England, France, and Germany were frequently on the verge of war with one another as they scrambled for colonies as a measure of economic worth and national glory. In 1898, a State Department memorandum stated that the "enlargement of foreign consumption of the products of our mills and workshops has . . . become a serious problem of statesmanship as well as commerce." The memo went on to note that "we can no longer afford to disregard international rivalries now that we ourselves have become a competitor in the world-wide struggle for trade." The national state, then, recognized its role in supporting commercial interests, and politicians were eager to be of service.

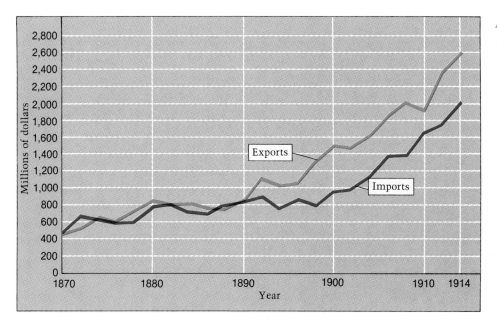

American Foreign Trade, 1870–1914

Some people, however, saw national glory and greatness itself as a legitimate motivation for expansionism. In the late 1890s, a small group of men centered around Assistant Secretary of the Navy Theodore Roosevelt and Senator Henry Cabot Lodge of Massachusetts emerged as highly influential leaders of a changing American foreign policy. These vigorous and intensely nationalistic young men wanted a shift in official policy from "continentalism" to what Lodge called the "large policy." They were successful. By 1899, Assistant Secretary of State John Bassett Moore wrote that the United States had finally moved "into the position of what is commonly called a world power. . . . Where formerly we had only commercial interests, we now have territorial and political interests as well." Roosevelt agreed that economic interests should take second place to questions of what he called "national honor."

The new foreign policy elite was much influenced by the writings of Alfred Thayer Mahan, a naval strategist and author of several books on the importance of sea power to national greatness. Mahan had captained a warship sent to protect American property in Central America in 1885. His study of history argued that in a world of Darwinian struggle for survival, national power depended on naval supremacy, control of sea lanes, and vigorous development of domestic resources and foreign markets. He advocated colonies in both the Caribbean and the Pacific, linked by a canal built and controlled by the United States. Strong nations, Mahan wrote, had a special responsibility to dominate weak ones. In a world of constant "strife," where "everywhere nation is arrayed against nation," it was imperative that Americans begin "to look outward." National pride and glory would surely follow.

The Missionary Impulse

As Mahan's and Roosevelt's statements suggest, a strong sense of duty and the missionary ideal of doing good for others also motivated expansionism. A statesman once boasted that "with God's help, we will lift Shanghai up and up, ever up, until it is just like Kansas City." Richard Olney agreed, saying in 1898 that "the mission of this country is . . . to forego no fitting opportunity to further the progress of civilization." Motivated by America's sense of itself as a model nation, such statements sometimes rationalized the exploitation and oppression of weaker peoples. Although the European countries had their own justifications for imperialism, Americans such as Roosevelt, Lodge, and Mahan all would have agreed with the following paraphrase of popular expansionist beliefs:

Advocates of expansionism urged enlarging the size of the U.S. Navy, part of which is pictured here in 1892. The armored warship Maine, soon to figure in the outbreak of the Spanish-American War, is shown in the middle foreground.

Certain nations are more civilized than others. These nations are peopled by those who are white, Anglo-Saxon, Protestant, and English-speaking. They enjoy free enterprise and republican political institutions, meaning representative government, shared power, and the rule of law. Further evidence of the civilized nature of such nations includes their advanced technological and industrial development, large middle classes, and high degree of education and literacy. The prime examples in the world are England, Germany, and the United States.

In the natural struggle for existence, the races and nations that survive and prosper, such as these, prove their fitness and superiority over others. The United States, as a matter of history, geographic location, and political genius, is so favored and fit that God has chosen it to take care of and uplift less favored peoples. This responsibility cannot be avoided. It is a national duty, or burden—the "white man's burden"—that civilized nations undertake to bring peace, progressive values, and ordered liberty to the world.

These ideas, widespread in popular thought, described America's providential sense of itself. As a missionary put it in 1885, "The Christian nations are subduing the world in order to make mankind free." Josiah Strong, a Congregational minister, was one of the most ardent advocates of American missionary expansionism. Although his book *Our Country* (1885) was concerned primarily with internal threats to American social order, in a long chapter titled "The Future of the Anglo-Saxon Race" Strong made his case for an outward thrust. He argued that in the struggle for survival among nations, the United States had emerged as the center of Anglo-Saxonism and was "divinely commissioned" to spread the blessings of political liberty, Protestant Christianity, and civilized values over the earth. "This powerful race," he wrote, "will move down upon Mexico, down upon Central and South America, out upon the islands of the sea, over upon Africa and beyond." In a cruder statement of the same idea, Albert Beveridge said in 1899 that God had prepared English-speaking Anglo-Saxons to become "the master organizers of the world to establish and administer governments among savages and senile peoples."

If not so crudely, missionaries carried similar Western values to non-Christian lands around the world. China was a favorite target. The number of American Protestant missionaries in China increased from only 436 in 1874 to 5,462 in 1914. The largest increase came in the 1890s. Although the missionaries were not as effective as they had hoped to be, the estimated number of Christian converts in China jumped from 5,000 in 1870 to nearly 100,000 in 1900. This number, a small fraction of the Chinese population, included many young reformist intellectuals who absorbed Western ideas in Christian mission colleges and went on to lead the Revolution of 1912 that brought an end to the Manchu dynasty. Economic relations between China and the United States increased at approximately the same rate as missionary activity. The number of American firms in China grew from 50 to 550 between 1870 and 1930, while trade increased 15-fold.

Politics and Public Opinion

These figures suggest how economic, religious, moral, and nationalistic motivations became interwoven in American expansionism in the late 1890s. Although less significant than the other motives, politics also played a role. For the first time in American history, public opinion over international issues loomed large in presidential politics. The psychological tensions and economic hardships of the depression of the 1890s jarred national self-confidence. Foreign adventures and the glories of expansionism provided an emotional release from domestic turmoil and promised to restore patriotic pride—and maybe even win votes.

This process was helped by the rise of a highly competitive popular press, the penny daily newspaper, which brought international issues before ordinary citizens. When several newspapers in New York City, most notably William Randolph Hearst's *Journal* and Joseph Pulitzer's *World*, competed to see which could stir up more public support for the Cuban rebels in their struggle for independence from Spain, politicians ignored the public outcry at their peril. The daily reports of Spanish atrocities in 1896 and 1897 kept public moral outrage constantly before President McKinley as he considered his course of action. His Democratic opponent, William Jennings Bryan, entered the fray. Although in principle a pacifist, he too advocated United States intervention in Cuba on moral grounds of a holy war to help the oppressed. Bryan even raised a regiment of Nebraska volunteers to go off to the war, but the Republican administration kept him far from battle and therefore far from the headlines.

Politics, then, in addition to profits, patriotism, and piety, was a motivating factor in the expansionist impulse of the 1890s. These four motivations interacted to influence the Spanish-American War, the annexation of the Philippine Islands, and the foreign policy of President Theodore Roosevelt.

Support for the military became fashionable with the help of the popular press. Here officers of the Massachusetts State Militia pose with their wives who have come to visit them at summer encampment.

CUBA AND THE PHILIPPINES

Lying 90 miles off the southern tip of Florida, Cuba had been the object of intense American interest for a half century. Although successful in thwarting American adventurism in Cuba in the 1850s, Spain was unable to halt the continuing struggle of the Cuban people for relief from exploitive slave labor in the sugar plantations and for independence.

The Road to War

When the Cuban revolt flared up anew in 1895, the Madrid government again failed to implement reforms but instead sent General "Butcher" Weyler with 50,000 troops to quell the disturbance. When Weyler began herding rural Cuban citizens into "reconcentration" camps, Americans were outraged. An outpouring of sympathy swept the nation, especially as reports came back of the miserable conditions and horrible suffering in the camps. Sensational-

ist newspapers in the United States, competing for readers, stirred up sentiment with pages of bloody stories of atrocities. "The old, the young, the weak, the crippled—all are butchered without mercy," wrote the New York *World*.

The Cuban struggle appealed to a country convinced of its role as protector of the weak and defender of the right of self-determination. One editorial deplored Spanish "injustice, oppression, extortion, and demoralization" while describing the Cubans as heroic freedom fighters "largely inspired by our glorious example of beneficent free institutions and successful self-government." Motivated by genuine humanitarian concern and a sense of duty, many Americans held Cuba rallies to raise money and food for famine relief. They called for land reforms, and some advocated armed intervention, but neither President Cleveland nor President McKinley wanted a war over Cuba.

Self-interested motives also played a role.

For many years, Americans had looked with great interest on the profitable resources and strategic location of the island. American companies had invested extensively in Cuban sugar plantations. By 1897, trade with Cuba had reached $27 million per year. Appeals for reform had much to do with ensuring a stable environment for further investments, as well as for the protection of sugar fields against the ravages of civil war.

The election of 1896 diverted attention from Cuba to the issues of free silver and jobs, but only temporarily. A new government in Madrid recalled Weyler and seemed ready to bring about some reforms, even promising a degree of self-government to the Cubans. But these concessions were halfhearted. Conditions worsened in the reconcentration camps, and the American press kept the plight of the Cuban people before the public. McKinley, anxious not to take any action that might upset business recovery from the depression, skillfully resisted the pressure for war. But his skill could not control Spanish misrule or Cuban aspirations for freedom. The fundamental causes of the war—Spanish intransigence in the face of persistent Cuban rebellion and American sugar interests and sympathies for the underdog—were seemingly unstoppable.

Events early in 1898 sparked the outbreak of war. Rioting in Havana intensified both Spanish repression and American outrage. As pressures for war increased, a letter from the Spanish minister to the United States, Depuy de Lôme, calling McKinley a "weak" hypocritical politician, was intercepted by spies and made public. The American populace was inflamed as Hearst's New York *Journal* called De Lôme's letter "the worst insult to the United States in its history."

A second event was more serious. When the rioting broke out, the U.S. battleship *Maine* was sent to Havana harbor to protect American citizens. Early in the evening on February 15, a tremendous explosion blew up the *Maine*, killing 262 men. American advocates of war, who assumed Spanish responsibility, called immediately for intervention. Newspaper publishers offered rewards for discovery of the perpetrators of the crime and broadcast slogans like "Remember the *Maine!* To hell with *Spain!*"

Assistant Secretary of State Theodore Roosevelt, who had been preparing for war for some time, said that he believed the *Maine* had been sunk "by an act of dirty treachery on the part of the Spaniards" and that he would "give anything if President McKinley would order the fleet to Havana tomorrow." When the president did not, Roosevelt privately declared that McKinley had "no more backbone than a chocolate éclair" and continued to ready the navy for action. Although an official board of inquiry concluded that an external submarine mine caused the explosion, to this day no one is certain of the source. Probably a faulty boiler or some other internal problem set off the explosion, a possibility even Roosevelt later conceded.

After the sinking of the *Maine*, Roosevelt took advantage of Secretary of the Navy John D. Long's absence from the office one day to send a cable to Commodore George Dewey, commander of the United States Pacific fleet at Hong Kong. Roosevelt's message ordered Dewey to fill his ships with coal and, "in the event" of a declaration of war with Spain, to sail to the

Remembering the Maine, *citizens decorated its mast in observance of the second anniversary of its sinking in Havana Harbor.*

Philippines and make sure "the Spanish squadron does not leave the Asiatic coast." Roosevelt wrote in his diary that night that "the Secretary is away and I am having immense fun running the Navy." When Long returned to work and discovered his assistant's action, he wrote that "Roosevelt has come very near causing more of an explosion than happened to the *Maine.*"

Roosevelt's act was not impetuous, as Long thought, but consistent with naval policies he had been urging upon his more cautious superior for more than a year. As early as 1895, the navy had formulated plans for attacking the Philippines. Influenced by Mahan and Lodge, Roosevelt advocated the continuing creation of a large, modern navy, which had been suspended in the mid-1890s. He also believed that the United States should construct an interoceanic canal, acquire the Danish West Indies (the Virgin Islands), annex Hawaii outright, and oust Spain from Cuba. As Roosevelt told McKinley late in 1897, he was putting the navy in "the best possible shape" for "when war began." His order to Dewey, then, reflected a well-thought-out strategy to implement the "large policy" necessary for the advance of civilization.

The public outcry over the *Maine* drowned out McKinley's efforts to calm the populace and avoid war. The issues had become highly political, especially with midterm elections in the fall and a presidential race only two years away. Fellow Republican Senator Lodge warned McKinley that "if war in Cuba drags on through the summer with nothing done we shall go down to the greatest defeat ever known." McKinley hoped that the Madrid government would make the necessary concessions in Cuba and sent some tough demands in March. But the Spanish response was delayed and inadequate, refusing to grant full independence to the Cubans.

On April 11, 1898, President McKinley sent an ambiguous message to Congress that seemed to call for war. Two weeks later, Congress authorized the use of troops against Spain and passed a resolution recognizing Cuban independence, actions amounting to a declaration of war. In a significant additional resolution, the Teller Amendment, Congress stated that the United States had no intentions of annexing Cuba, guaranteeing the Cubans the right to

determine their own destiny. Senator George F. Hoar of Massachusetts, who later assailed the United States for its war against the Filipinos, declared that the intervention in Cuba would be "the most honorable single war in all history," undertaken without "the slightest thought or desire of foreign conquest or of national gain or advantage."

"A Splendid Little War"

As soon as war was declared, Theodore Roosevelt resigned his post in the Navy Department and cabled Brooks Brothers to rush a "lieutenant-colonel's uniform" to him. Black regiments as well as white headed to Tampa, Florida, with Roosevelt to be shipped to Cuba. One black soldier, noting the stark differences in the southern reception of the segregated regiments, commented, "I am sorry that we were

Although accused of weakness, McKinley was a wise, vigorous, and far-seeing president in an expansionist era.

not treated with much courtesy while coming through the South." Blacks were especially sympathetic to the Cuban people's independence because of a common heritage. As one soldier wrote in his journal, "Oh, God! at last we have taken up the sword to enforce the divine rights of a people who have been unjustly treated." As the four-month war neared its end in August, John Hay wrote Roosevelt that "it has been a splendid little war; begun with the highest motives, carried on with magnificent intelligence and spirit." It was a good feeling, a very American one, selflessly rescuing the oppressed and helping them achieve self-rule. As one soldier wrote home, describing his arrival in Puerto Rico: "It's a wonderful sight how the natives respect us. They take off their hats and say Viva Americana."

It was a "splendid" war also because compared to the long, bloody Civil War or even the British fight with the Boers in South Africa going on at the same time, the war with Spain was short and relatively easy. Naval battles were won almost without return fire. At both major naval engagements, Manila Bay and Santiago Bay, only two Americans died, one of them from heat prostration while stoking coal. The islands of Guam and Puerto Rico were taken virtually without a shot. Only 385 men died from Spanish bullets, but over 5,000 succumbed to tropical diseases.

The Spanish-American War was splendid in other ways, as letters from American soldiers suggest. One young man wrote that his comrades were all "in good spirits" because oranges and coconuts were so plentiful and "every trooper has his canteen full of lemonade all the time." Another wrote his mother that he found Cuba not only cooler but better than Texas in many ways: "Our money is worth twice as much as Spanish money. We do not want for anything." And another wrote his brother that he was having "a lot of fun chasing Spaniards."

But for many men, the war was anything but splendid. One soldier wrote that "words are inadequate to express the feeling of pain and sickness when one has the fever. For about a week every bone in my body ached and I did not care much whether I lived or not." Another wrote, "One of the worst things I saw was a man shot while loading his gun. The Spanish Mauser bullet struck the magazine of his carbine, and . . . the bullet was split, a part of it going through his scalp and a part through his neck. . . . He was a mass of blood."

The "power of joy in battle" that Teddy Roosevelt felt "when the wolf rises in the heart" was not a feeling shared by all American sol-

The Spanish-American War

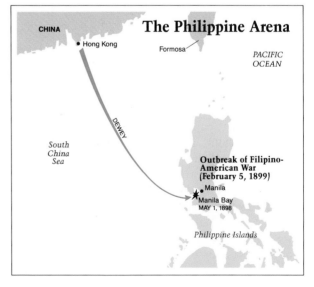

The celebrated charge of "Teddy's Rough Riders" up San Juan Hill, which so greatly helped Roosevelt's political career, was protected by black troops like these from the Ninth U.S. Calvary (on right).

diers. Roosevelt's brush with death at Las Guásimas and his celebrated charge up San Juan Hill near Santiago, his flank protected by black troops, made 3-inch headlines and propelled him toward the New York governor's mansion in Albany. "I would rather have led that charge," he said later, "than served three terms in the U.S. Senate." Nonetheless, no one did as much during the war as Roosevelt to advance not only his political career but also the cause of expansion and national glory.

The Philippines Debates

Roosevelt's act of ordering Dewey to Manila initiated the chain of events that led to the annexation of the Philippines. The most crucial battle of the Spanish-American War took place on May 1, 1898, when Dewey totally destroyed the Spanish fleet in Manila Bay and cabled McKinley for additional troops. The president said later that upon receiving Dewey's cable he was not even sure "within two thousand miles" where "those darned islands were." Actually, McKinley had approved Roosevelt's policies and knew what course of action to pursue. He sent twice as many troops as Dewey had asked for and began the process of shaping American

public opinion to accept the "political, commercial [and] humanitarian" reasons for annexing all 7,000 Philippine islands. The Treaty of Paris gave the United States all of them in exchange for a $20 million payment to Spain.

The treaty was sent to the Senate for ratification during the winter of 1898–1899. Senators for and against annexation hurled arguments at each other across the floor of the Senate as American soldiers hurled oaths and taunts across the neutral zone at Aguinaldo's insurgents near Manila. Private Grayson's encounter in February, marked the passage of the treaty in the Senate and began the Filipino-American War. The treaty barely received the necessary two-thirds majority, primarily because the Republicans made an effective case and because they had Democratic support.

The debates over the Philippines took place in a wider arena than the Senate. The entire nation joined in, as the issues loomed much larger than the islands in question. At stake were two very different views of foreign policy and of America's vision of itself. Although he spent several months quietly seeking advice, listening to public opinion, and acting as if he were unsure what to do, McKinley finally recommended annexation.

Many Democrats supported the president out of fear of being labeled disloyal, as had happened in the 1860s. Fellow Republicans confirmed McKinley's arguments for annexation, adding even more racist ones. Filipinos were described as childlike, savage, stunted in size, dirty, and backward. Comparisons were made with blacks and Native Americans, and policies were proposed befitting the inferior condition in which white Americans saw the Filipinos. Roosevelt called Aguinaldo "a renegade Pawnee" and said that the Filipinos had no right "to administer the country which they happen to be occupying." The attitudes favoring annexation, therefore, asserted Filipino inferiority and incapacity for self-rule while also reflecting America's proud sense of itself in 1900 as a nation of civilized order and progress.

McKinley's Annexation Argument

In a speech to a group of expansionist Methodist ministers and missionaries in 1900, President McKinley explained his reasons for recommending annexation of the Philippines. His statement summarizes most of the reasons for expansionism. It also offers a fascinating glimpse into the inner process of presidential decision making (or at least of how a President later sought to justify a decision).

The truth is I didn't want the Philippines and when they came to us as a gift from the gods, I did not know what to do about them. . . . And one night it came to me this way—(1) that we could not give them back to Spain—that would be cowardly and dishonorable; (2) that we could not turn them over to France or Germany—our commercial rivals in the Orient—that would be bad business and discreditable; (3) that we could not leave them to themselves—they were unfit for self-government—and they would soon have anarchy and misrule over there worse than Spain's was; and (4) that there was nothing left for us to do but to take them all, and to educate the Filipinos, and uplift and civilize and Christianize them, and by God's grace do the very best we could by them, as our fellowmen for whom Christ also died. And then I went to bed, and went to sleep, and slept soundly, and the next morning I sent for the chief engineer of the War Department (our map-maker), and I told him to put the Philippines on the map of the United States, and there they are, and there they will stay while I am President!

Other Americans were not so positive about such "progress." A small but vocal group organized in the Anti-Imperialist League vigorously opposed both the war and annexation. Many of them represented a fading elite, feeling displaced by the younger generation of modern expansionists. By attacking imperialism, the anti-imperialists struck out against the forces of modernism that they felt threatened their social position. They included a cross section of American dignitaries: ex-presidents Harrison and Cleveland, Samuel Gompers and Andrew Carnegie, William James, Jane Addams, Mark Twain, and many others.

The major anti-imperialist arguments pointed out how imperialism in general and annexation in particular contradicted American ideals. First, the annexation of territory without immediate or planned steps toward statehood was unprecedented and unconstitutional. Second, to occupy and govern a foreign people without their consent was a violation of the ideals of the Declaration of Independence. In one of the strongest anti-imperialist statements, Senator Hoar, who had called the war in Cuba "honorable," described the war in the Philippines in the following way:

> We changed the Monroe Doctrine from a doctrine of eternal righteousness and justice, resting on the consent of the governed, to a doctrine of brutal selfishness looking only to our own advantage. We crushed the only republic in Asia. We made war on the only Christian people in the East. We converted a war of glory to a war of shame. We vulgarized the American flag. We introduced perfidy into the practice of war. We inflicted torture on unarmed men to extort confession. We put children to death. We devastated provinces. We baffled the aspirations of a people for liberty.

A third argument was that social reforms needed at home demanded American energies and money before foreign expansionism. "Before we attempt to teach house-keeping to the world," one writer put it, we needed "to set our own house in order."

Not all anti-imperialist arguments were so noble. Some were practical or downright racist. One position alleged that since the Filipinos were nonwhite, Catholic, and inferior in size and intelligence, they were unassimilable. Annexation would lead to miscegenation and contamination of Anglo-Saxon blood. Senator Ben Tillman of South Carolina argued that although it was permissible to "walk on the necks of every colored race" whites came into contact with, he still opposed "incorporating any more colored men into the body politic." The practical argument suggested that once in possession of the Philippines, the United States would have to defend them, possibly even acquiring more territories. This would require higher taxes and bigger government in order to build and support the navy that holding such possessions demanded. Some saw the Philippines as a burden that would require American troops to fight distant Asian wars.

The last argument became fact when Private Grayson's encounter started the Filipino-American War. As U.S. treatment of the Filipinos during the war became more and more like Spanish mistreatment of the Cubans, the hypocrisy of American behavior became even more evident. This was especially true for black American soldiers who fought in the Philippines. They identified with the dark-skinned insurgents, whom they saw as tied to the land, burdened by debt, and pressed by poverty like themselves. They were also called "nigger" from morning to night. "I feel sorry for these people," a sergeant in the 24th Infantry wrote. "You have no idea the way these people are treated by the Americans here."

The war starkly exposed the hypocrisies of shouldering the white man's burden. Upon reading a report that 8,000 Filipinos had been killed in the first year of the war, Carnegie wrote a letter, dripping with sarcasm, congratulating McKinley for "civilizing the Filipinos. . . . About 8000 of them have been completely civilized and sent to Heaven. I hope you like it." Another writer penned a devastating one-liner: "Dewey took Manila with the loss of one man— and all our institutions." One of the most active anti-imperialists, Ernest Howard Crosby, wrote a parody of Rudyard Kipling's "White Man's Burden," which he titled "The Real 'White Man's Burden'":

Take up the White Man's burden.
  Send forth your sturdy kin,
And load them down with Bibles
  And cannon-balls and gin.
Throw in a few diseases
  To spread the tropic climes,
For there the healthy niggers
  Are quite behind the times.

They need our labor question, too,
  And politics and fraud—
We've made a pretty mess at home,
  Let's make a mess abroad.

The efforts of Crosby and other anti-imperialists were unsuccessful, failing either to prevent annexation or to interfere with the war effort. However prestigious and sincere, they had little or no political power. They were seen as an older, conservative, elite group of Americans opposed to the kind of dynamic progress represented by Teddy Roosevelt and other expansionists. They were out of tune with the period of exuberant national pride, prosperity, and promise.

Expansionism Triumphant

By 1900, Americans had ample reason to be patriotic. Within a year, the United States had

Bringing "civilization" to the Filipinos, American soldiers stand guard over captured guerrillas in 1899.

acquired several island territories, thereby joining the other great powers of the world. But several questions arose over what to do with the new territories. What was their status? Were they colonies? Would they be granted statehood or would they develop gradually from colonies to constitutional parts of the United States? Moreover, did the native peoples of Hawaii, Puerto Rico, Guam, and the Philippines have the same rights as American citizens on the mainland? Were they protected by the U.S. Constitution? The answers to these difficult questions emerged in a series of Supreme Court cases, congressional acts, and presidential decisions.

Although slightly different governing systems were worked out for each new territory, the solution in each was to define its status somewhere between subject colony and candidate for statehood. Territorial status came closest. The native people were usually allowed to elect their own legislature for internal lawmaking but had governors and other judicial and administrative officials appointed by the American president. William Howard Taft, for example, was McKinley's appointee as the first civilian governor in the Philippines, where he was effective in moving the Filipinos toward self-government. Final independence did not come until 1946, however, and elsewhere the process was equally slow. The question of constitutional rights was resolved by deciding that Hawaiians and Puerto Ricans, for example, would be treated differently from Texans and Oregonians. In the "insular cases" of 1901, the Supreme Court ruled that these people would achieve citizenship and constitutional rights only when Congress said they were ready. To the question, Does the Constitution follow the flag?, the answer, as Secretary of State Elihu Root put it, was, "Ye-es, as near as I can make out the Constitution follows the flag—but doesn't quite catch up with it."

The optimistic, nationalistic spirit of the American people was revealed most clearly in the election of 1900, when McKinley defeated Bryan more resoundingly than in 1896. Bryan's intentions to make imperialism the "paramount issue" of the campaign failed, in part because the debates on the Philippines question had ended long before the campaign began, the issue settled in favor of annexation. The Philippine-American War was actually popular, and it was politically unwise to risk being branded a traitor by opposing it. In the closing weeks of the campaign, Bryan and the Democrats shied away from imperialism and the war as a "paramount issue" and focused more on economic issues—trusts, labor question, and (again) free silver.

But Bryan fared no better on those issues. The discovery of gold in Alaska had returned prosperity to American workers. Cries for reform fell on deaf ears. The McKinley forces rightly claimed that under four years of Republican rule more money, jobs, thriving factories, and manufactured goods had been created. Moreoever, McKinley pointed to the tremendous growth in American prestige abroad. Spain had been kicked out of Cuba, and the American flag flew in many places around the globe. It had been a triumphant four years. As a disappointed Tom Watson put it, noting the end of the Populist revolt with the war fervor over Cuba, "The Spanish war finished us. The blare of the bugle drowned out the voice of the reformer."

He was more right than he knew. Within one year, the active expansionist, Theodore Roosevelt, went from assistant secretary of the navy

Presidential Elections, 1896–1900

YEAR	CANDIDATES	PARTY	POPULAR VOTE	ELECTORAL VOTE
1896	W. McKINLEY	Republican	7,035,638 (51%)	271
	W. J. Bryan	Democrat/Populist	6,467,946 (47%)	176
1900	W. McKINLEY	Republican	7,219,530 (52%)	292
	W. J. Bryan	Democrat	6,358,071 (46%)	155

Note: Winner's name is in capital letters.

to colonel of the Rough Riders to governor of New York. For some Republican politicos, who thought he was too vigorous, unorthodox, and independent, this quick rise to prominence as a potential rival to McKinley came too fast. One way to eliminate Roosevelt politically, or at least slow him down, they thought, was to make him vice-president, which they did at the Republican convention in 1900. But six months into McKinley's second term, while attending an exposition in Buffalo, McKinley was shot and killed by an anarchist, the third presidential assassination in less than 40 years. "Now look," exclaimed party boss Mark Hanna, who had opposed putting Roosevelt on the ticket; "that damned cowboy is President of the United States!"

ROOSEVELT'S ENERGETIC DIPLOMACY

At a White House dinner party in 1905, a guest told a story about his visit to the Roosevelt home when Teddy had been a baby. "You were in your bassinet, making a good deal of fuss and noise," the guest reported, "and your father lifted you out and asked me to hold you." Secretary of State Elihu Root looked up from his plate and asked, "Was he hard to hold?" Whether true or not, the story reveals much about President Roosevelt's principles and policies on foreign affairs. As president from 1901 to 1909, and as the most dominating American personality for the 15 years between 1897 and 1912, Roosevelt made much fuss and noise about the activist role he thought the United States should play in the world. As he implemented his policies, it often seemed as if he was "hard to hold." Roosevelt's energetic foreign policy in Latin America, Asia, and Europe paved the way for the vital role of the United States as a world power.

Foreign Policy as Darwinian Struggle

Roosevelt's personal principles and presidential policies went together. He was an advocate of both individual physical fitness and collective national strength. As an undersized, weak young boy who suffered humiliating drubbings by schoolmates, he undertook a rigorous program of strengthening his body through boxing and other exercise. During summers spent on his ranch in the North Dakota Badlands, Roosevelt learned to value "the strenuous life" of the cowboy. He read Darwin and understood that life among humans, as in nature, was a constant struggle for survival.

Roosevelt extended his beliefs about strenuous struggle from individuals to nations. His ideal was "a nation of men, not weaklings." To be militarily prepared and to fight well were, for Roosevelt, the tests of racial superiority and national greatness. "All the great masterful races," he said, "have been fighting races." Although he believed in Anglo-Saxon superiority, he admired—and feared—the military prowess of the Japanese. Powerful nations, like individuals, Roosevelt believed, had a duty to cultivate qualities of vigor, strength, courage, and moral commitment to civilized values. In practical terms this meant developing natural resources, building large navies, and being constantly prepared to fight. "I never take a step in foreign policy," he wrote, "unless I am assured that I shall be able eventually to carry out my will by force."

Although known for his advice to "speak softly and carry a big stick," Roosevelt often not only wielded a large stick but spoke loudly as well. In one speech in 1897 he used the word *war* 62 times, saying that "no triumph of peace is quite so great as the supreme triumphs of war." But despite his bluster, Roosevelt was usually restrained in the exercise of force. For helping to end the Russo-Japanese War, he was awarded the Nobel Peace Prize in 1906. The purpose of the big stick and the loud talk was to preserve order and peace in the world. "To be prepared for war," he said, "is the most effectual means to promote peace."

Roosevelt divided the world into civilized and uncivilized nations, the former usually defined as Anglo-Saxon and English-speaking. The civilized nations had a responsibility to "police" the uncivilized, not only maintaining order but also spreading superior values and institutions. This "international police power," as Roosevelt called it, was the "white man's burden." As part of this burden, civilized nations sometimes had to fight wars against the uncivilized, as the British did against the Boers in South Africa and the Americans did in the Philippines. These wars were justified because the blessings of culture and racial superiority were passed on to the vanquished by the victors.

A war between two civilized nations, however, such as between Germany and England, was wasteful and foolish, upsetting order in the world. Above all, Roosevelt believed in the balance of power. Strong, advanced nations had a duty to use their power to preserve order and peace. This included the United States after 1898, especially after the annexation of the Philippines. The United States had "no choice," Roosevelt said, but to "play a great part in the world." Americans could no longer "avoid responsibilities" that followed from "the fact that on the east and west we look across the waters at Europe and Asia."

As Roosevelt looked across the oceans, he developed a highly personal style of diplomacy. Rather than relying on the Department of State, he preferred face-to-face contact and personal exchange of letters with foreign ambassadors, ministers, and heads of state. Under Roosevelt, foreign policy was made while horseback-riding with the German ambassador or while discussing history with the ambassador from France. A British emissary observed that Roosevelt had a "powerful personality" and a commanding knowledge of the world. As a result, ministries from London to Tokyo respected both the president and the power of the United States.

When threat of force was inadequate to accomplish his goals, Roosevelt used direct personal intervention as a third-party mediator. "In a crisis the duty of a leader is to lead," he said. Congress was too slow and deliberate to play a significant role in foreign affairs. When he wanted Panama, Roosevelt bragged later, "I took the Canal Zone" rather than submitting a long "dignified State Paper" for congressional debate on an appropriate policy. And while Congress debated the appropriateness of his actions, he was fond of pointing out, the building of the canal across Panama began. Roosevelt's energetic executive activism in foreign policy set a pattern followed by nearly every twentieth-century American president.

The "big stick" came to be a memorable image in American diplomacy as Teddy Roosevelt sought to make the United States a policeman not only of the Caribbean basin, but also of the whole world.

One of the most enjoyable ways of recovering the values and attitudes of the past is through political cartoons. Ralph Waldo Emerson once said, "Caricatures are often the truest history of the times." A deft drawing of a popular or unpopular politician can freeze ideas and events in time, conveying more effectively than columns of type the central issues of the day and creating an immediate response in the viewer. It is this freshness that makes caricatures such a valuable source when attempting to recover the past. Cartoonists are often at their best when they are critical, exaggerating a physical feature of a political figure or capsuling public sentiment against the government.

The history of political cartoons in the United States goes back to Benjamin Franklin's "Join or Die" cartoon calling for colonial cooperation against the French in 1754. But political cartoons were rare until Andrew Jackson's presidency. Even after such cartoons as "King Andrew the First" in the 1830s, they did not gain notoriety until the advent of Thomas

Nast's cartoons in *Harper's Weekly* in the 1870s. Nast drew scathing cartoons exposing the corruption of William "Boss" Tweed's Tammany Hall, depicting Tweed and his men as vultures and smiling deceivers. "Stop them damn pictures," Tweed ordered. "I don't care so much what the papers write about me. My constitutents can't read. But, damn it, they can see pictures." Tweed sent some of his men to Nast with an offer of $100,000 to "study art" in Europe. The $5,000-a-year artist negotiated up to a half million dollars before refusing Tweed's offer. "I made up my mind not long ago to put some of those fellows behind bars," Nast said, "and I'm going to put them there." His cartoons helped drive Tweed out of office.

The emergence of the United States as a world power and the rise of Theodore Roosevelt gave cartoonists plenty to draw about. An impetus to political cartoons was given by the rise of cheap newspapers such as William Randolph Hearst's *Journal* and Joseph Pulitzer's *World*. When the Spanish-American War broke out, newspapers whipped up public sentiment

"The Spanish Brute Adds Mutilation to Murder,"
by Grant Hamilton, in Judge, *July 9, 1898*

"Liberty Halts American Butchery
in the Philippines," from Life, *1899*

by having artists draw fake pictures of Spaniards stripping American women at sea and encouraging cartoonists to depict the "Spanish brute." Hearst used these tactics to increase his paper's daily circulation to one million copies. But by the time of the Philippines debates, many cartoonists took an anti-imperialist stance, pointing out American hypocrisy. Within a year cartoonists shifted from depicting "The Spanish Brute Adds Mutilation to Murder" (1898) to "Liberty Halts American Butchery in the Philippines" (1899). The cartoons are very similar in condemning "butchery" of native populations, but the target has of course changed. Although Uncle Sam as a killer is not nearly as menacing as the figure of Spain as an ugly gorilla, in both cartoons there is a similarity of stance, the blood-soaked swords, and a trail of bodies behind.

When Theodore Roosevelt rose to the presidency, cartoonists rejoiced. His physical appearance and personality made him instantly recognizable, a key factor in the success of a political cartoon. His broad grin, eyeglasses, and walrus mustache were the kind of features that fueled the cartoonist's imagination. A man of great energy, Roosevelt's style was as distinctive as his look. Other factors, such as the "Rough Rider" nickname, the symbol of the "big stick," and policies like "gunboat diplomacy" made Teddy the perfect target for political cartoons.

To understand and appreciate the meaning of any cartoon, certain facts must be ascertained, such as the date, artist, and source of the cartoon, the particular historical characters, events, and context depicted in it, the significance of the caption, and the master symbols employed by the cartoonist. The two remaining cartoons, "Panama or Bust" (1903) and "For President!" (1904), were both printed in American daily newspapers. Aside from the context and meaning of each cartoon, which should be obvious, note how the cartoonists use familiar symbols from Roosevelt's life and American history to underline the ironic power of their point. How many can you identify, and how are they used?

"Panama or Bust," from The New York Times, *1903*

FOR PRESIDENT!

"For President," by L. C. Gregg,
in the Atlanta Constitution, *1904*

Policeman of the Caribbean

As late as 1901, the Monroe Doctrine was still regarded, according to Roosevelt, as the "equivalent to an open door in South America." To the United States this meant that although no nation had a right "to get territorial possessions," all nations had equal commercial rights in the Western Hemisphere south of the Rio Grande. But as American investments poured into Central America and Caribbean islands, that policy changed to one of the primary right of the United States to dominant influence in the lands of the Caribbean basin. Order was indispensable for profitable economic activity.

This change was demonstrated in 1902, when Germany and Great Britain seized several Venezuelan gunboats and blockaded its ports in order to force the Venezuelan government to pay defaulted debts. Roosevelt was especially worried that German influence would replace the British. He insisted that the European powers accept arbitration of the disputed financial claims and threatened to "move Dewey's ships" to the Venezuelan coast to enforce his intentions. The crisis passed, largely for other reasons, but Roosevelt's threat of force made the paramount presence and self-interest of the United States in the Caribbean very clear.

After the Spanish were expelled from Cuba, the United States supervised the island under Military Governor General Leonard Wood until 1902, when the Cubans elected their own congress and president. The United States honored Cuban independence, as it had promised to do in the Teller Amendment. But through the Platt Amendment, which Cubans reluctantly attached to their constitution in 1901, the United States obtained many economic rights in Cuba, a naval base at Guantanamo Bay, and the right of intervention if Cuban sovereignty were ever threatened. Newspapers in Havana assailed this violation of their newfound independence. One cartoon, titled "The Cuban Calvary," showed a figure representing "the Cuban people" crucified between two thieves, represented as Wood and McKinley.

American policy intended to make Cuba a model of how a newly independent nation could achieve orderly self-government with only minimal guidance. Cuban self-government, however, was shaky. By 1906, an internal political crisis between rival factions threatened to plunge the infant nation into civil war. Roosevelt was disappointed, if not downright furious, with "that infernal little Cuban republic." At Cuba's request, he sent warships to patrol the coastline and special commissioners and troops "to restore order and peace and public confidence." As he left office in 1909, Roosevelt proudly proclaimed that "we have done our best to put Cuba on the road to stable and orderly government." The road was paved with sugar. U.S. trade with Cuba increased from $27 million in the year before 1898 to an average of $43 million per year during the following decade. Along with economic development, American political and even military involvement in Cuban affairs continued throughout the century.

The pattern repeated itself on other Caribbean islands. The Dominican Republic, for example, suffered from unstable governments and economic ill health. In 1904, as a revolt erupted, European creditors pressured the Dominican government for payment of $40 million in defaulted bonds. With the presence of U.S. warships to discourage European intervention, the United States took over the collection of customs in the republic. Two years later, the United States intervened to settle a disruptive conflict between two Central American strongmen in Guatemala and Nicaragua, where American bankers controlled nearly 50 percent of all trade.

Roosevelt's policy that civilized nations should "insist on the proper policing of the world" was clarified in 1904 in his annual message. The goal of the United States, he said, was to have "stable, orderly and prosperous neighbors." A country that paid its debts and kept order "need fear no interference from the United States." A country that did not, but rather committed "chronic wrong-doing" and loosened the "ties of civilized society," would require the United States to intervene as "an international police power." This doctrine became known as the Roosevelt Corollary to the Monroe Doctrine. Whereas Monroe's doctrine had warned European nations not to intervene in the Western Hemisphere, Roosevelt's corollary justified American intervention. Starting with a desire to protect property, loans, and investments, the United States often interceded in these countries to maintain order. This meant supporting the brutal regimes of small elites who owned most of the land, suppressed social unrest, and acted as surrogates of American policy. As the St. Louis *Post-Dispatch* commented, the Monroe Doctrine now could be understood to mean "you mind your business and we'll mind yours."

After 1904, the Roosevelt Corollary was invoked in several Caribbean countries. Intervention usually required the landing of U.S. Marines to counter the threat posed by political instability and bankruptcy to American economic interests: railroads, mines, and the production of sugar, bananas, and coffee. Occupying the capital and major seaports, American marines, bankers, and customs officials usually remained for several years, until they were satisfied that stability had been reestablished. Roosevelt's successors, William Howard Taft and Woodrow Wilson, pursued the same interventionist policy. Later presidents, most recently Ronald Reagan, would do likewise.

Taking the Panama Canal

In justifying the intervention of 2,600 American troops in Honduras and Nicaragua, Philander Knox, secretary of state from 1909 to 1913, said that "we are in the eyes of the world, and because of the Monroe Doctrine, held responsible for the order of Central America, and its proximity to the Canal makes the preservation of peace in that neighborhood particularly necessary." The building of the Panama Canal was not yet finished when Knox spoke, but it had already become a vital cornerstone of United States policy in the region. Three problems had to be surmounted in order to fulfill the long-sought goal of an interoceanic connection. First, an 1850 treaty bound the United States to build a canal jointly with Great Britain. But in 1901, John Hay, secretary of state between 1901 and 1905, convinced the British to cancel the treaty in exchange for an American guarantee that the canal, once built, would be "free and open to the vessels of commerce and of war of all nations." A second problem was where to build the canal. After considering a lengthy but technically easy route through Nicaragua, American engineers settled on the shorter but more rugged path across the isthmus of Panama, where a French firm, the New Panama Company, had already begun work.

The third problem was that Panama was a province of Colombia and thus could not negotiate with the United States. The Colombian government was unimpressed with the share of a likely settlement the Americans would provide in buying up the New Panama Canal Company's $40 million in assets. Indeed, in 1903, the

Despite protests from the Panamanian government, in 1903 the United States acquired the right to build and operate a canal across the isthmus. An enormous engineering undertaking, the Panama Canal was completed in 1914.

Colombian senate rejected a treaty negotiated by Hay, but mostly on nationalistic, not financial, grounds. Roosevelt, angered by this rebuff, called the Colombians "Dagoes" and "foolish and homicidal corruptionists" who, like highway robbers, he thought, tried to "hold us up."

Aware of Roosevelt's fury, encouraged by hints of American support, and eager for the economic benefits the building of a canal would bring, Panamanian nationalists in 1903 staged a revolution led by several rich families and a Frenchman, Philippe Bunau-Varilla of the New Panama Canal Company. The Colombian army, dispatched to quell the revolt, was deterred by the presence of an American warship; local troops were separated from their officers, who were bought off. The bloodless revolution occurred on November 3; the next day, Panama declared its independence. On November 6, the United States officially recognized the new government in Panama. Although Roosevelt did not formally encourage the revolution, it would not have occurred without American money and support.

On November 18, Hay and Bunau-Varilla signed a treaty establishing the American right to build and operate a canal through Panama and to exercise "titular sovereignty" over the 10-mile-wide Canal Zone for 99 years. The Panamanian government protested the treaty, to no avail, and a later government called it "the treaty that no Panamanian signed." Roosevelt, boasting later that he "took the canal," claimed that his diplomatic and engineering achievement, completed in 1914, would "rank . . . with the Louisiana Purchase and the acquisition of Texas."

Opening the Door to China

Throughout the nineteenth century, American relations with China were restricted to a small but profitable trade. The British, in competition with France, Germany, and Russia, took advantage of the weak, crumbling Manchu dynasty by making trade treaties with China. These gave access to treaty ports and most-favored-nation trading privileges in various spheres of influence throughout the country. After 1898, Americans with dreams of exploit-

ing the seemingly unlimited markets of China wanted to join the competition and enlarge their share. The United States, too, wanted favorable commercial rights and a place to sell surplus goods. Moral interests, however, including many missionaries, reminded Americans of their revolutionary tradition against European imperialism. They made clear their opposition to crass U.S. commercial exploitation of a weak nation and supported the preservation of China's political integrity against continuing interference by the European powers.

American attitudes toward the Chinese people reflected this confusion of motives. Some Americans held an idealized view of China as the center of Eastern wisdom and saw a "special relationship" between the two nations. But the dominant American attitude viewed the Chinese as heathen, exotic, backward, and immoral. This negative stereotype was reflected in the

European and American forces cooperated in quelling China's Boxer Rebellion in 1900. Here a European count makes his entrance at Peking's Sacred Gate, escorted by Bengal Lancers subject to the British crown.

Exclusion Act of 1882 and the riots in western states against Chinese workers in the 1870s and 1880s. The Chinese, in turn, regarded the United States with a mixture of curiosity, resentment, suspicion, and disdain, as well as with admiration for a potential, if arrogant, guardian.

The annexation of Hawaii, Samoa, and the Philippines in 1898 and 1899 convinced Secretary of State Hay that the United States should announce its own policy for China. The result was the Open Door notes of 1899–1900, which became the cornerstone of U.S. policy in Asia for much of the twentieth century. The first note, focusing on customs-collection issues, opened a door for American trade by declaring the principle of equal access to commercial rights in China by all nations. The second note, addressing Russian movement into Manchuria, called upon all countries to respect the "territorial and administrative integrity" of China. This second principle opened the way for a larger American role in Asia, offering China protection from foreign invasions and preserving a balance of power in the Far East.

An early test of this new role came during the Boxer Rebellion in 1900. The Boxers were a society of young traditionalist Chinese in revolt against both the Manchu dynasty and the growing Western presence and influence in China. During the summer of 1900, fanatical Boxers killed some 242 missionaries and other foreigners and besieged the western quarter of Peking. Eventually, an international military force of 19,000 troops, including some 3,000 Americans sent from the Philippines, marched on Peking to end the siege.

The American relationship with China was plagued by the exclusionist immigration policy. Despite the barriers and riots, Chinese workers kept coming to the United States, entering illegally from Mexico and British Columbia. In 1905, Chinese nationalists at home boycotted American goods and called for a change in immigration policy. Roosevelt, who had a low opinion of the Chinese as a "backward" people, bristled with resentment and sent troops to the Philippines as a threat. Halfheartedly, he also asked Congress for a modified immigration bill, but nothing came of it.

A year later, he faced a similar crisis with Japan. The San Francisco school board, claiming that Japanese children were "crowding the whites out of the schools," segregated them into separate schools and asked Roosevelt to persuade Japan to stop the emigration of its people. Though the Japanese were insulted, they agreed to limit the migration of unskilled workers to the United States in a gentleman's agreement signed in 1907. In return, the segregation law was repealed, but not without disturbing the harmonious relations between the two nations.

Despite exclusion and insults, the idea that the United States had a unique guardian relationship with China persisted into the twentieth century. Since Japan had ambitions in China, this created a rivalry between Japan and the United States, testing the American commitment to preserve the Open Door in China and the balance of power in Asia. Economic motives in Asia, however, proved to be less significant. Investments there developed very slowly, as did the dream of the "great China market" for American grains and textiles. Although textile exports to China increased from $7 million to nearly $24 million in a decade, the China trade always remained larger in imagination than in reality.

Japan and the Balance of Power

Roosevelt relied on the skillful use of diplomacy and negotiation rather than American military intervention to balance one Asian power against another. The Boxer Rebellion of 1900 left Russia, with 50,000 troops in Manchuria, the strongest nation in eastern Asia. Roosevelt's admiration for the Japanese as a "fighting" people and a valuable factor in "the civilization of the future" contrasted with his low respect for the Russians, whom he described as "corrupt," "treacherous," and "incompetent." As Japan moved into Korea and Russia into Manchuria, Roosevelt hoped that each would check the growing power of the other.

Because of increasing Russian strength, Roosevelt welcomed news in 1904 that Japan had launched a successful surprise attack on Port Arthur in Manchuria, beginning the Russo-Japanese War. He was "well pleased with the

Japanese victory," he told his son, "for Japan is playing our game." But when Japanese victories continued, on sea and on land, many Americans worried that Japan might play the game too well, shutting the United States out of Far Eastern markets. Roosevelt shifted his support toward Russia. When the Japanese expressed interest in an end to the war, the American president was pleased to exert his influence.

Roosevelt's role in bringing the two foes to the conference table won him the Nobel Peace Prize. His goal was to achieve peace and leave a balanced situation. "It is best," he wrote, that Russia be left "face to face with Japan so that each may have a moderative action on the other." The negotiations and resulting treaty were carried out in the summer of 1905 near Portsmouth, New Hampshire. No single act better symbolizes the new posture of American power and presence in the world than the signing of a peace treaty ending a war in Manchuria between Russia and Japan halfway around the globe in New Hampshire!

The Treaty of Portsmouth actually left Japan dominant in Manchuria and established the United States as the major balance to Japan's power. Almost immediately, the Japanese developed a naval base at Port Arthur, built railroads, and sought exclusive rights of investment and control in the Chinese province. In part because of his lack of respect for the Chinese, Roosevelt willingly recognized Japan's "dominance in Manchuria," as well as its control in Korea. But in return, in the Root-Takahira Agreement of 1908, he received Japan's promise to honor U.S. control in the Philippines and to make no further encroachments into China.

These agreements over territorial divisions barely covered up the tensions in Japanese-American relations. Some Japanese were angry that they had not received in the Portsmouth Treaty the indemnities they had wanted from Russia, and they blamed Roosevelt. American insensitivity to the immigration issue also left bad feelings. In Manchuria, U.S. Consul General Willard Straight aggressively pushed an anti-Japanese program of financing capital investment projects in banking and railroads. This policy, later known as "dollar diplomacy" under

Roosevelt's successor, William Howard Taft, like the pursuit of markets, was larger in prospect than results. Nevertheless, the United States was in Japan's way, and rumors of war circulated in the world press.

It was clearly time for Roosevelt's version of the "big stick." In 1907, he told Secretary of State Root that he was "more concerned over the Japanese situation than almost any other. Thank Heaven we have the navy in good shape." Although the naval buildup had begun over a decade earlier, under Roosevelt the U.S. Navy had developed into a formidable force. From 1900 to 1905, outlays to the navy more than doubled, from $56 million to $117 million. Such a naval spending binge was without peacetime precedent. In 1907, to make it clear that "the Pacific was as much our home waters as the Atlantic," Roosevelt sent his new, modernized "Great White Fleet" on a goodwill tour around the world. The first stop was the Japanese port of Yokohama. Although American sailors were greeted warmly, the act may have stimulated navalism in Japan, which came back to haunt the United States in 1941. But for the time being, the balance of power in Asia was preserved.

Preventing War in Europe

The United States was willing to stretch the meaning of the Monroe Doctrine to justify sending marines and engineers to Latin America and the navy and dollars to Asia. Treaties, agreements, and the protection of territories and interests entangled the United States with foreign nations from Panama and the Dominican Republic to the Philippines and Manchuria. Toward Europe, however, the traditional policies of neutrality and nonentanglement continued. Neither the moral civilizing of unregenerate natives nor American self-interest seemed appropriate in Europe. Still, there was an American role to be played even there, and Roosevelt was anxious to play it.

The most powerful nations of the world were European. Roosevelt therefore believed that the most serious threats to world peace and civilized order lay in relationships among Germany, Great Britain, and France. He established two fundamental policies toward Europe that with only minor variations would define the U.S. role throughout the century. The first was to make friendship with Great Britain the cornerstone of U.S. policy. As Roosevelt told King Edward VII in 1905, "In the long run the English people are more apt to be friendly to us than any other." Second, the crucial goal of a neutral power like the United States was to prevent the outbreak of a general war in Europe among strong nations. Toward this end Roosevelt depended on his personal negotiating skills and began the practice of summit diplomacy.

It is difficult now to think of England as anything other than the most loyal friend of the United States outside of North America. Yet throughout most of the nineteenth century, England was America's chief enemy and commercial rival. From the War of 1812 to the Venezuelan border crisis of 1895, conflict with Great Britain developed in squabbles over old debts and trade barriers, disputes over Canadian borders and fishing jurisdictions, and British interference in the American Civil War.

The Venezuelan crisis and a number of other events at the turn of the century shocked the United States and England into an awareness of their mutual interests. Both nations appreciated the neutrality of the other in their respective wars shouldering the "white man's burden" against the Filipinos and the Boers. Roosevelt

United States Involvement in Asia, 1898–1909

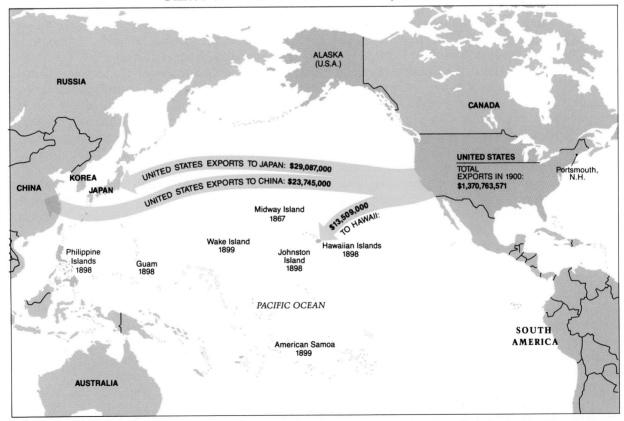

Japanese-American	**1904–1905**	Russo-Japanese War; Peace Treaty signed in Portsmouth, N.H.	**1906**	San Francisco School Affair
relations:			**1907**	Gentlemen's Agreement
			1908	Root-Takahira Agreement
	1905	Taft-Katsura Agreement	**1907–1909**	Great White Fleet

supported British imperialism because he favored the dominance of "the English-speaking race" and because he believed that England was "fighting the battle of civilization." Furthermore, both nations were concerned about the growth of German power in Europe, Africa, and the Far East. As German naval power increased, England had to bring its fleet closer to home. Friendly allies were needed to police parts of the world formerly patrolled by the British navy. England therefore concluded a mutual-protection treaty with Japan in 1902 and willingly let the Americans police Central America and the Caribbean Sea.

Similarities of language and cultural traditions, as well as strategic self-interest, drew the two countries together. Roosevelt's personal style furthered the connection. He was clearly and unashamedly pro-British, and his most intimate circle of friends included many Englishmen. Although Roosevelt sometimes made blustery speeches critical of English policies, his British bias was never in doubt. He knew, as he wrote Lodge in 1901, that the United States had "not the least particle of danger to fear" from England and that the major menace to peace in Europe would come from German ambitions and militarism. As Roosevelt left the presidency in 1909, one of his final acts was to proclaim the special American friendship with Great Britain.

German Kaiser Wilhelm II often underestimated the solidity of the Anglo-American friendship and thought that Roosevelt was really pro-German, an error the American president skillfully used. He cultivated the kaiser to make him think they were friends sharing mutual interests. Wilhelm therefore sought Roosevelt's support on several diplomatic issues between 1905 and 1909. In each case Roosevelt was able to flatter the kaiser while politely rejecting his overtures. The relationship gave Roosevelt a unique advantage in influencing affairs in Europe in order to prevent an outbreak of war.

The Moroccan crisis in 1905 and 1906 is illustrative. European powers competed for colonies and spheres of influence in Africa as well as in Asia. Germany in particular resented French dominance along the North African coast in Morocco and feared the recent Anglo-French entente. The kaiser precipitated a crisis in the summer of 1905 by delivering a bellicose speech in Casablanca, Morocco, intended to split the British and French and to force an opening of commercial doors in Morocco. In this endeavor he sought help from Roosevelt. The French were outraged at Wilhelm's boldness, and war threatened.

Roosevelt intervened, arranging a conference in Algeciras, Spain, to prevent war and settle the issues of commerce and police administration in Morocco. Although he sent an experienced diplomat and close friend to represent the United States at Algeciras, the critical negotiations occurred in the correspondence between Wilhelm and Roosevelt. In the spring of 1906 a treaty was signed that displeased the kaiser. The French secured "exclusive" administration of Morocco, and the Germans suffered a humiliating defeat. As Roosevelt explained his own role, "I was most suave and pleasant with the Kaiser, yet when it became necessary . . . I stood him on his head with great decision."

Roosevelt's successful countering of meddlesome German policies continued, as did his efforts in preventing war. At the Hague conference on disarmament in 1907, the kaiser sought an agreement to reduce British naval supremacy, a superiority Roosevelt thought "quite proper." The German emperor also tried to promote a German-Chinese-American entente to balance the Anglo-Japanese Treaty in Asia. Roosevelt rebuffed all these efforts. While on a European tour in 1910, the retired American president was warmly entertained and celebrated by Wilhelm, who continued to misunderstand him. Roosevelt, meanwhile, kept on urging his English friends to counter the German naval buildup in order to maintain peace in Europe.

In 1911, Roosevelt wrote that there would be nothing worse than that "Germany should ever overthrow England and establish the supremacy in Europe she aims at." German interest "to try her hand in America," he thought, would surely follow. To avert such horrors, Roosevelt's policy for Europe included cementing friendship with England and, while maintaining official neutrality, using diplomacy to prevent hostilities among European powers. The relationship between Great Britain and Germany continued to deteriorate, however, and by 1914 a new American president, Woodrow Wilson, would face the terrible reality that Roosevelt had so skillfully helped to prevent. When World War I finally broke out, no American was more eager to fight on the British side against the Germans than the hero of San Juan Hill.

CONCLUSION: The Responsibilities of Power

Since the earliest settlements in Massachusetts Bay, Americans had struggled with the dilemma of how to do good in a world that did wrong. The realities of power in the 1890s brought increasing international responsibilities. Roosevelt said in 1910 that because of "strength and geographical situation" the United States had itself become "more and more the balance of power of the whole world." This ominous responsibility was also an opportunity to extend American economic, political, and moral influence around the globe.

As president in the first decade of the twentieth century, Roosevelt established the basic policies of the United States toward the rest of the world. Americans dominated and policed Central America and the Caribbean Sea to maintain order, protect investments and other economic interests, and keep European influence out. In the Far East, Americans marched through Hay's Open Door with treaties, troops, navies, and dollars to protect the newly annexed Philippine Islands, to develop markets and investments, and to preserve the balance of power in Asia. In Europe, the United States sought both to remain neutral and uninvolved in European affairs and at the same time to cement Anglo-American friendship and prevent "civilized" nations from going to war with one another.

How well these policies worked would be seen later in the twentieth century. Whatever the particular judgment, the fundamental ambivalence of America's sense of itself as a model "city on a hill," an example to others, remained. As widening involvements around the world—the Philippine-American War, for example—painfully demonstrated, it was difficult for the United States to be both responsible and good, both powerful and loved. The American people thus learned to experience both the satisfactions and burdens of the missionary role.

Recommended Reading

The best overviews of the emergence of America as a world power in the late nineteenth century, each emphasizing different motives for expansion, are Walter La Feber, *The New Empire: An Interpretation of American Expansion, 1860–1898* (1963); Milton Plesur, *America's Outward Thrust, 1865–1890* (1971); Robert Beisner, *From the Old Diplomacy to the New, 1865–1900* (1975); and Charles Campbell, *The Transformation of American Foreign Relations, 1865–1900* (1976).

On the immediate causes of expansionism in the 1890s and the war with Spain, see Ernest May, *Imperial Democracy: The Emergence of America as a Great Power* (1961); H. Wayne Morgan, *America's Road to Empire: The War with Spain and Overseas Expansion* (1965); and David Healy, *U.S. Expansion: Imperialist Urge in the 1890s* (1970). Particular aspects of American expansion are discussed in Rubin Weston, *Racism in U.S. Imperialism: The Influence of Racial Assumptions on American Foreign Policy,*

1893–1946 (1972); William Widenor, *Henry Cabot Lodge and the Search for an American Foreign Policy* (1980); and Emily Rosenberg, *Spreading the American Dream: American Economic and Cultural Expansion, 1890–1945* (1982). McKinley's leadership is covered in Lewis Gould, *The Presidency of William McKinley* (1980).

On the Spanish-American War see Frank Freidel, *The Splendid Little War* (1958). More recent works are David Trask, *The War with Spain in 1898* (1981), and a fascinating account of the war experiences of black soldiers, Willard Gatewood, Jr., *"Smoked Yankees" and the Struggle for Empire: Letters from Negro Soldiers, 1898–1902* (1971). The brutal suppression of the Philippine rebels is described in Leon Wolff, *Little Brown Brother: How the United States Purchased and Pacified the Philippine Islands at the Century's Turn* (1961) and Richard Welch, *Response to Imperialism: The United States and the Philippine-American War, 1899–1902* (1979). Some anti-imperialists are treated in Robert Beisner, *Twelve Against Empire: The Anti-Imperialists, 1898–1900* (1975). Gerald Linderman discusses the war at home in *The Mirror of War: American Society and the Spanish-American War* (1974).

The standard work on Roosevelt's foreign policy is Howard Beale, *Theodore Roosevelt and the Rise of America to World Power* (1956). Newer interpretations can be found in Raymond Esthus, *Theodore Roosevelt and the International Rivalries* (1970) and Frederick Marks II, *Velvet on Iron: The Diplomacy of Theodore Roosevelt* (1979). Charles E. Neu, *An Uncertain Friendship: Theodore Roosevelt and Japan, 1906–1909* (1967) traces that relationship, and Dana Munro, *Intervention and Dollar Diplomacy in the Caribbean, 1900–1920* (1964) discusses the Roosevelt Corollary. A lengthy but readable story of the Panama Canal is David McCollough, *The Path Between the Seas: The Creation of the Panama Canal, 1870–1914* (1977). Walter La Feber has documented how thoroughly American interests have dominated Central America in *The Panama Canal* (1978) and *Inevitable Revolutions: The United States in Central America* (1983).

TIME LINE

1823	Monroe Doctrine
1857	Trade opens with Japan
1867	Alaska purchased from Russia
1870	Failure to annex Santo Domingo (Hispaniola)
1875	Sugar reciprocity treaty with Hawaii
1877	United States acquires naval base at Pearl Harbor
1878	United States acquires naval station in Samoa
1882	Chinese Exclusion Act
1889	First Pan-American conference
1890	Alfred Mahan publishes *Influence of Sea Power upon History*
1893	Hawaiian coup by American sugar growers
1895	Renewed outbreak of Cuban revolt against Spanish / Venezuelan boundary dispute
1896	Weyler's reconcentration policy in Cuba / McKinley-Bryan presidential campaign
1897	Theodore Roosevelt's speech at Naval War College

1898
	January	De Lôme letter
	February	Sinking of the battleship *Maine*
	April	Spanish-American War; Teller Amendment
	May	Dewey takes Manila Bay
	July	Annexation of Hawaiian Islands
	August	Americans liberate Manila; war ends
	December	Treaty of Paris; annexation of the Philippines

1899	Senate ratifies Treaty of Paris / Philippine-American War begins / American Samoa acquired
1899–1900	Open Door notes
1900	Boxer rebellion in China / William McKinley reelected president
1901	Supreme Court insular cases / McKinley assassinated; Theodore Roosevelt becomes president
1902	Philippine-American War ends / U.S. military occupation of Cuba ends / Platt Amendment / Venezuela debt crisis
1903	Panamanian revolt and independence / Hay–Bunau-Varilla Treaty
1904	Roosevelt Corollary
1904–1905	Russo-Japanese War ended by treaty signed at Portsmouth, New Hampshire
1904–1906	United States intervenes in Nicaragua, Guatemala, Cuba
1905–1906	Moroccan crisis
1906	Roosevelt receives Nobel Peace Prize
1907	Gentleman's agreement with Japan
1908	Root-Takahira Agreement
1909	U.S. Navy ("Great White Fleet") sails around the world
1911	U.S. intervenes in Nicaragua
1914	Opening of the Panama Canal / World War I begins
1916	Partial home rule granted to the Philippines

PORTFOLIO FOUR

THE ART OF
AN INDUSTRIALIZING PEOPLE

1 8 6 5 – 1 9 0 0

The time from the Civil War to the turn of the century has been called the Gilded Age. But the period is also referred to as the American Renaissance because so many neoclassical public and private buildings were constructed during these years and so many artists, collectors, and architects identified with the period of the Renaissance in Europe. It was also an age of opulence, when great fortunes were made and the very wealthy could afford to build summer "cottages" that looked like European palaces in Newport, Rhode Island; the Berkshires; and elsewhere. But usually when they filled their houses with art, it was to Europe that they looked, for American painting had little prestige next to the great masters. Many American artists, at least those who could afford it, trained in Europe, and many remained there. Europe seemed more supportive of artists than did the United States, where the machine was rapidly replacing the craftsman and the emphasis seemed to be on business success rather than artistic excellence.

Yet all was not bleak. The years from 1865 to 1900 witnessed a great burst of creative energy in America. It was during this period that many American cities built museums and libraries. Stimulated in part by the Centennial Exposition in Philadelphia in 1876, but even more by the World Columbian Exposition in Chicago in 1893, many American cities founded new cultural institutions. These new museums contained little American art in the beginning, and they were always closed on Sundays, making it impossible for the working class to visit them. Eventually, however, they would help to create a cultural renaissance in America.

Architects contributed to the new era by designing impressive new urban structures. Henry Hobson Richardson (1838–1886) popularized buildings patterned after the Romanesque style, while others experimented with a more utilitarian approach. Louis Sullivan (1856–1924), the most prominent architect of the Chicago school, argued that "form follows function." His business buildings and skyscrapers, even with their organic decorations, seemed revolutionary in much of the country, where architects continued to adapt European styles for their clients.

American artists also experimented with new forms during this time of industrial expansion and ostentatious display. Despite the heavy hand of European tradition, American artists such as Winslow Homer and Thomas Eakins established their own style. Eakins used the camera and new scientific studies of light and anatomy to create an authentic American realistic style. He also helped to train a new generation of American artists in Philadelphia, Chicago, New York, and other cities.

Another kind of American art flourished in this period as well. Far removed from and untouched by the formal study of art on either continent, thousands of American folk artists, untrained but talented, created enduring symbols for a growing nation. Whether the result was a carefully designed quilt, painted furniture, a wall mural, or a weather vane crafted by a farmer in his spare time, the art of the people sometimes seemed to have more vitality than the art of the museums.

Mary Cassatt, *Baby Reaching for an Apple*, 1893.
Virginia Museum, Richmond. Anonymous gift.

Mary Cassatt (1844–1926) was one of the outstanding artists of her generation and the most important American impressionist. She was the only American to exhibit her work alongside that of Degas, Renoir, and Monet. Although her father opposed her becoming an artist, she studied at the Pennsylvania Academy of Fine Arts in Philadelphia before going to Europe, where she spent most of her life. Even though she was already well known in Europe when she **returned to Philadelphia for a visit in 1898, the Philadelphia *Ledger* reported: "Mary Cassatt, sister of Mr. Cassatt, President of the Pennsylvania Railroad, returned from Europe yesterday. She has been studying painting in France and owns the smallest Pekingese dog in the world." One French critic had called her one of the two most important living American artists, but in America she was important for owning a small dog.**

Winslow Homer, *Snap the Whip*, 1872.
Butler Institute of American Art, Youngstown, Ohio.

Winslow Homer (1836–1910) is best known for his paintings of life near the sea, but here he depicts a rural scene of boys playing a favorite game. Like many nineteenth-century painters, Homer made his living for years by doing engravings to illustrate magazine articles. He documented American life in the last decades of the nineteenth century, but he was always more than an illustrator. He was concerned with light, order, and organization. Some of his later paintings, in fact, move toward an abstract design.

Thomas Eakins, *Max Schmitt in a Single Scull*, 1871.
Metropolitan Museum of Art, New York. Alfred N. Punnett Fund and gift of George D. Pratt.

Thomas Eakins (1844–1916) spent most of his life in Philadelphia, though he studied for a time in Europe. As a painter, he depended on science as a means of understanding reality. He studied anatomy in order to understand the human body. He also studied engineering and photography and was one of the first artists to use stop-motion photographs to perfect his paintings. In *Max Schmitt* it is possible to tell exactly the time of day and the season of the year. The iron bridge in the background reminds us that Eakins painted in an age being transformed by industrialism. Sometimes his attempts to be faithful to the real world got him into trouble. The art jury at the Centennial Exposition rejected his picture *The Gross Clinic* as "distasteful and not art." In 1886, he resigned from his position at the Pennsylvania Academy of Fine Arts because the directors censured him for allowing young women to paint a nude male model.

Thomas Pollock Anshutz, *Cabbages*, 1879.
Metropolitan Museum of Art, New York. Morris K. Jesup Fund.

Among Eakins's many students were Henry O. Tanner (1859–1937), the nineteenth century's most distinguished Afro-American artist, and Thomas Pollock Anshutz (1851–1912), born in Kentucky and trained in New York and Paris. Upon Eakins's resignation from the Academy, Anshutz assumed his post and perpetuated his style. Glimpses of lower-class life such as *Ironworkers Noontime* characterize Anshutz's work. In *Cabbages*, he forthrightly depicts the poverty of this black family, yet portays them with grace and dignity.

The quilt was made by Harriet Powers, a black woman born a slave in Atlanta, Georgia, in 1837. An example of the beauty and usefulness of folk art created by women of all backgrounds, the quilt interprets biblical history in a sincere yet imaginative manner. The upper left panel depicts Eve being tempted by a tiger-striped (and footed) serpent, while at center left we see the bloody murder of Abel by his brother Cain. The far right panel in the bottom row depicts Joseph, Mary, and the baby Jesus accompanied by symbolic crosses and the star of Bethlehem.

Harriet Powers,
Bible Quilt, c. 1885.
National Museum of American History, Smithsonian Institution, Washington.

C. Graham, *The Ferris Wheel*,
World's Columbian Exposition, 1893.
Chicago Historical Society.

William Morris Hunt (1827–1895) was one of the most popular architects of his day. He specialized in designing homes patterned after European mansions for the very rich. The ornate and elaborate decoration of this dining room contrasts with the spare and simple steel Ferris wheel designed by George Washington Gales for the Chicago World's Columbian Exposition in 1893. Made of the same steel that made skyscrapers possible, the Ferris wheel was 250 feet in diameter and fascinated a generation just getting accustomed to the beauty and power of the machine.

Dining room, William Vanderbilt's Marble House,
completed 1892.
Preservation Society of Newport County, Rhode Island.
Photo Richard Cheek.

PART FIVE
A
MODERNIZING
PEOPLE

1900–1945

In the first half of the twentieth century, the powerful and populous society that Americans had built was faced with repeated challenges. Two costly world wars and the greatest economic depression the modern world has known occurred within the lifetime of most Americans born in the late nineteenth century. But the United States emerged in 1945, at the end of World War II, with its political and economic system intact and indeed strengthened, though American society was considerably altered in the process.

Chapter 22, "The Progressives Confront Industrial America," explores the greatest outburst of reformist thought and activity since the antebellum period. It explains how the progressives, while accepting the basic structure of the capitalist system, attempted to bring moral vision and scientific expertise to bear on the problems created by rapid industrialization, urbanization, and immigration after the Civil War. Chapter 23, "America in the Great War," addresses the transforming power of extended military conflict on business, government, labor, race relations, the role of women, and American foreign policy.

The era between World War I and World War II is the subject of Chapters 24 and 25. In Chapter 24, "Affluence and Anxiety," the so-called Roaring Twenties are revealed as an era of paradox, filled with prosperity mixed with poverty, optimism alongside disillusionment, inventiveness combined with intolerance, and flamboyant heroism countered by fallen idols. Chapter 25, "The Great Depression and the New Deal," probes the causes and effects of the Great Depression of 1929–1939 and analyzes the attempts of Franklin Roosevelt's New Deal to repair the economic and social damage it caused.

Although the New Deal introduced key elements of the modern capitalist welfare state and greatly increased the regulatory power of the federal government, it never proved able to lift the country from economic depression. That, ironically, came about only with American involvement in World War II. Chapter 26, "The American People and World War II," presents this devastating conflict as both a momentous military struggle between Allied and Axis powers and as a powerful engine of social change within American society. It also shows how the war spawned a complex diplomatic contest between the Eastern and Western blocs of the Allied Powers, led by the United States and the Soviet Union, for ascendancy in the postwar age.

PARALLEL EVENTS

| | 1900 | 1905 | 1910 | 1915 | 1920 |

CULTURAL and TECHNOLOGICAL

- 1901 Frank Norris, *The Octopus*
- 1903 Wright brothers make first heavier-than-air flight
- 1906 Upton Sinclair, *The Jungle*
- 1908 Frank Lloyd Wright designs Robie House in Chicago
- 1909 First Model T Ford produced
- 1910 Jane Addams, *Twenty Years at Hull House*
- 1911 Frederick Winslow Taylor, *The Principles of Scientific Management*
- 1913 First assembly line at Ford Motor Company; Armory Show, New York
- 1914 Panama Canal completed
- 1915 D. W. Griffith produces *The Birth of a Nation*
- 1916 Margaret Sanger organizes New York Birth Control League
- 1920 First commercial radio broadcast, WWJ Detroit
- 1922 Sinclair Lewis, *Babbitt*

SOCIAL and ECONOMIC

- 1901 United States Steel Corporation organized
- 1902 Anthracite coal strike
- 1903–1910 Muckrakers attack social evils and corruption
- 1905 Industrial Workers of the World (IWW) organized
- 1907 Panic caused by business failures; Gentleman's agreement stops emigration of Japanese laborers to United States
- 1908 *Muller v. Oregon* upholds Oregon law limiting hours of work for women
- 1909 National Association for the Advancement of Colored People (NAACP) organized
- 1910 Triangle fire in New York kills 146 textile workers
- 1913 Federal Reserve System organized; Department of Labor organized
- 1914 Clayton Act strengthens antitrust legislation
- 1917 Literacy test for new immigrants established
- 1917–1918 Espionage Act and Sedition Act passed
- 1918–1919 Influenza epidemic kills 500,000 people in United States
- 1919 United States becomes creditor nation for the first time.
- 1921 Immigration limited to 3 percent of each nationality in country in 1910

POLITICAL

- 1900 William McKinley reelected president
- 1901 McKinley assassinated; Theodore Roosevelt becomes president; Socialist Party of America formed
- 1904 Roosevelt reelected
- 1906 Hepburn Act; Pure Food and Drug Act; Meat Inspection Act
- 1908 William Howard Taft elected president
- 1910 Mann-Elkins Act
- 1912 Woodrow Wilson elected president
- 1913 Sixteenth Amendment provides for an income tax; Seventeenth Amendment provides for direct election of senators
- 1914 World War I begins in Europe
- 1915 *Lusitania* sunk
- 1916 Wilson reelected
- 1917 United States declares war on Germany and Austria-Hungary
- 1918 War ends in Europe
- 1919 Senate defeats League of Nations treaty; Eighteenth Amendment establishes prohibition; National Prohibition Enforcement Act
- 1920 Warren G. Harding elected president; Nineteenth Amendment provides for woman suffrage
- 1921–1922 Washington conference to limit naval armaments

| 1900 | 1905 | 1910 | 1915 | 1920 |

1900–1945

CULTURAL and TECHNOLOGICAL

1925 John Scopes convicted of illegally teaching theory of evolution in Tennessee
1926 Langston Hughes, *Weary Blues*
1927 Charles Lindbergh flies alone to Paris
      Sacco and Vanzetti executed
      The Jazz Singer, first feature-length talking movie
1929 William Faulkner, *The Sound and the Fury*

1934–1938 Radar developed by Army Signal Corps and U.S. Navy

1935 Walt Disney releases *Flowers and Trees*, first movie in color
1935–1943 WPA artists' and writers' projects

1938 Nylon and fiberglass developed
1939 John Steinbeck, *The Grapes of Wrath*
      New York World's Fair
      First scheduled television broadcast

1941 Penicillin, one of the first "miracle drugs," developed

1942 Jet plane first tested in United States

1943 Wendell Willkie, *One World*
1944 First electronic calculator developed
      Serviceman's Readjustment Act ("GI Bill")

1945 First atomic bomb exploded in New Mexico

SOCIAL and ECONOMIC

1924 Immigration limited to 2 percent of nationality in country in 1890

1925 A & W Root Beer becomes first fast-food franchise

1929 Stock market crash

1934 Indian Reorganization Act

1935 Committee for Industrial Organization (CIO) formed

1936 United Auto Workers hold sit-down strike at General Motors plant in Flint, Michigan

1938 Fair Labor Standards Act

1941 President Roosevelt issues Executive Order 8802 outlawing discrimination in defense industries

1942 Congress of Racial Equality (CORE) founded

1944 Bretton Woods Conference sets up World Bank and International Monetary Fund

POLITICAL

1923 Harding dies; Calvin Coolidge becomes president
      Teapot Dome scandal
1924 Coolidge reelected

1928 Herbert Hoover elected president

1932 Franklin Roosevelt elected president
1933 TVA, CCC, NIRA, AAA, and other New Deal acts passed

1935 Social Security, WPA, and other New Deal legislation passed
1936 Roosevelt reelected
1937 National Housing Act passed

1939 World War II begins in Europe

1940 Roosevelt reelected for third term
1941 Japanese attack Pearl Harbor; Japan and Germany declare war on United States
1942 United States defeats Japanese in Battle of Midway
      Allies invade North Africa
1944 Invasion of Normandy
      Roosevelt reelected for fourth term

1945 United States drops atomic bomb on Hiroshima and Nagasaki
      World War II ends
      Roosevelt dies; Harry S. Truman becomes president

CHAPTER 22
THE PROGRESSIVES CONFRONT INDUSTRIAL AMERICA

Frances Kellor, a young woman who grew up in Ohio and Michigan, received her law degree in 1897 from Cornell University and became one of the small but growing group of professionally trained women. Deciding that she was more interested in solving the nation's social problems than in practicing law, she moved to Chicago, studied sociology, and trained herself as a social reformer. Kellor believed passionately that poverty and inequality could be eliminated in America. She also had the progressive faith that if Americans could only hear the truth about the millions of people living in urban slums, they would rise up and make changes. She was one of the experts who provided the evidence to document what was wrong in industrial America.

Like many progressives, Kellor believed that environment was more important than heredity in determining ability, prosperity, and happiness. Better schools and better housing, she thought, would produce better citizens. Even criminals, she argued, were simply victims of environment. Kellor demonstrated that poor health and deprived childhoods explained the only differences between the criminals and the college students. If it were impossible to define a criminal type, then it must be possible to reduce crime by improving the environment.

Kellor was an efficient professional. Like the majority of the professional women of her generation, she never married but devoted her life to social research and social reform. She lived for a time at Hull House in Chicago and at the College Settlement in New York, centers not only of social research and reform but also of lively community. For many young people, the settlement, with its sense of commitment and its exciting conversation around the dinner table, provided an alternative to the nuclear family or the single apartment.

While staying at the College Settlement, Kellor researched and wrote a muckraking study of employment agencies, published in 1904 as *Out of Work*. She revealed how employment agencies exploited immigrants, blacks, and other recent arrivals in the city. Kellor's book, like the writing of most progressives, spilled over with moral outrage. But Kellor went beyond the moralism to suggest corrective legislation at the state and national levels.

Kellor became one of the leaders of the movement to Americanize the immigrants pouring into the country in unprecedented numbers. Between 1899 and 1910, over 8 million immigrants came to the United States, most from southern and eastern Europe. Many people feared that this flood of immigrants threatened the very basis of American democracy. Kellor and her co-workers represented the side of progressivism that sought state and federal laws to protect the new arrivals from exploitation and to establish agencies and facilities to educate and Americanize them. Another group of progressives, often allied with organized labor, tried to pass laws to restrict immigration. Kellor did not entirely escape the racism that was a part of her generation's world view, but she did maintain that all immigrants could be made into useful citizens.

Convinced of the need for a national movement to push for reform legislation, Kellor helped to found the National Committee for Immigrants in America, which tried to promote a national policy "to make all these people Americans," and a federal bureau to organize the campaign. Eventually she helped establish the Division of Immigrant Education within the Department of Education. But it was a political movement led by Theodore Roosevelt that excited her most.

Kellor, more than almost any other single person, had been responsible for alerting Roosevelt to the problems the immigrants faced in American cities. When Roosevelt formed the new Progressive party in 1912, she was one of the many social workers and social researchers who joined him. She campaigned for Roosevelt and directed the Progressive Service Organization, to educate voters in all areas of social justice and welfare after the election. After Roosevelt's defeat and the collapse of the Progressive party in 1914, Kellor continued to work for Americanization. She spent the rest of her life promoting justice, order, and efficiency and trying to find ways for resolving industrial and international disputes.

Frances Kellor personified the two most important aspects of progressivism, the first nationwide reform movement of the modern era: one, commitment to social justice under industrial capitalism, and two, a search for order and efficiency in a world made more complex by rapid industrialization, immigration, and spectacular urban growth. This chapter traces some of the most important aspects of progressivism, a broad but sometimes internally divided movement that influenced almost all aspects of American life. It will look at the social justice movement that sought to promote reform among the poor and to improve life for the victims of an industrial civilization. It surveys life among the workers in the progressive era, a group that reformers sometimes helped but often misunderstood. Then it traces the reform movements in the cities and the states. Finally, it examines progressivism at the national level during the administrations of Theodore Roosevelt and Woodrow Wilson.

THE SOCIAL JUSTICE MOVEMENT

The social justice movement in its broadest sense tried to humanize the industrial city. The leaders, many of them women, were most often middle-class social workers, ministers, intellectuals, and writers. Many had been shocked by reading books like Henry George's *Progress and Poverty* (1879) and Edward Bellamy's *Looking Backward* (1888) and by the 1893 depression (see Chapter 20). They hoped to improve housing, build better schools, abolish child labor, and limit the hours of work for both men and women. They wanted parks and playgrounds and a better life for the poor and the recent immigrants. Sometimes, however, they seemed more interested in controlling the threat of the poor and foreign-born than in promoting reform, and they quite consciously tried to teach middle-class values. But like all progressives, they believed that by altering the environment they could reconstruct society and eliminate poverty. Combining optimism with moral idealism, they had no intention of abandoning corporate capitalism or dramatically altering the American system of government. They did not always agree among themselves over tactics or even about the reform agenda, but all knew that change was necessary if American democracy was to survive in an urban industrial age.

The Muckrakers

The publicists of the progressives' concerns were a group of writers, labeled the muckrakers, who exposed corruption and other evils in American society. Theodore Roosevelt gave the muckrakers their name when, in a speech in 1906, he compared some of the writers to the man with the muckrake in John Bunyan's *Pilgrim's Progress*. He was so busy raking the dirt that he never looked up or tried to do anything about it.

In part the muckrakers were a product of a revolution in journalism that had begun in the 1890s. Nineteenth-century magazines, like *Atlantic, Century,* and *Scribner's,* had small circulations and appealed only to a highly educated audience. The new magazines, like *American, McClure's,* and *Cosmopolitan,* had slick formats, carried more advertising, and sold more widely. Several had circulations of more than a half million in 1910. Competing with each other for readers, editors eagerly published the articles of a new generation of investigative reporters who wanted to let the public know about what was wrong in American society.

Lincoln Steffens, a young California journalist, wrote a series of articles for *McClure's* exposing the connections between respectable urban businessmen and corrupt politicians. When published in 1904 as *The Shame of the Cities,* Steffens's account became a battle cry for people determined to clean up the graft in city government. Ida Tarbell, a teacher turned journalist, had grown up near Titusville in western Pennsylvania, almost next door to the first oil well in the United States. She published several successful books, including biographies of Napoleon and Lincoln, before turning her attention to the Standard Oil Company and John D. Rockefeller. Her exposé, based on years of research, did not try to hide her outrage at Rockefeller's ruthless ways and unfair business practices.

After Steffens and Tarbell achieved popular success with their articles and books, many others followed. Ray Stannard Baker exposed the railroads; David Graham Phillips showed how politics and business were allied at the highest level in *The Treason of the Senate* (1906). Robert Hunter, a young settlement worker, shocked the American people in 1904 with his book *Poverty*. Setting the minimum annual income at $460 for a family of five, he found 10 million people living below that level. Realistic fiction also mirrored such concerns. Upton Sinclair's novel *The Jungle* (1906) described the horrors of the Chicago meatpacking industry, while Frank Norris in *The Octopus* (1901) dramatized the railroad's stranglehold on the farmers.

Working Women and Children

Nothing disturbed the social justice progressives more than the sight of children, sometimes

Child labor was one of the first evils the progressives sought to abolish. These boys, employees in a Pennsylvania mine, were photographed in 1911 by Lewis Hine for the Child Labor Committee.

as young as 8 or 10, working long hours in dangerous and depressing factories. Young people had worked in factories since the beginning of the industrial revolution, but that did not make the practice any less horrible to the reformers. "Children are put into industry very much as we put in raw material," Jane Addams objected, "and the product we look for is not better men and women, but better manufactured goods."

The social justice reformers documented horrible tales about bootblacks, newspaper boys, and the army of young factory workers of both sexes who risked their health and ruined their lives for a few pennies. "Annie Chihlar, a delicate-looking little girl, was found working at 144 West Taylor Street," one report from Chicago began. Annie, it turned out, was only 12 and underweight with a bad curvature of the spine. But her employer produced a doctor's certificate saying she was in perfect health, and her mother insisted that she needed her daughter's income to help support the family's younger children. The reformers sometimes appeared to have little sympathy for the families like Annie's who depended on the wages of their children. Instead they focused on the human resources being wasted and tried to pass laws to protect the child in industrial America.

Florence Kelley was one of the most important leaders in the crusade against child labor. Kelley had grown up in an upper-class Philadelphia family and graduated from Cornell in 1882. Like Addams and Kellor, she was a member of the first generation of college women. When the University of Pennsylvania refused her admission as a graduate student because she was a woman, she went to the University of Zurich in Switzerland. There she married a Polish physician and was converted to socialism. But the marriage failed. Some years later, Kelley moved to Chicago with her three children, became a Hull House resident, and poured her energies into the campaign against child labor. Energetic and outgoing, she was called by one of her friends "explosive, hot-tempered, determined . . . a smoking volcano that at any moment would burst into flames." When she could find no attorney in Chicago who would argue a child labor case against some of the prominent corporations, she went to law school, passed the bar exam, and argued the cases herself.

Although Kelley and the other child labor reformers won a few cases, they quickly realized that they needed state laws if they were going to have any real influence. Marshaling their evidence about the tragic effects on growing children of long working hours in dark and damp factories, they successfully pressured the Illinois state legislature to pass an anti–child labor law. A few years later, however, the state supreme court declared the law unconstitutional.

Child labor was an emotional issue, not only because many businesses made large profits by employing children but also because many legislators and government officials, remembering their own rural childhoods, argued that it was good for the children's character to work hard and take responsibility.

In the first decade of the twentieth century, the reformers moved to the national level. Florence Kelley again led the charge. In 1899, she had become secretary of the National Consumers League, an organization that enlisted consumers in a campaign to pressure elected officials and corporations to ensure that products were produced under safe and sanitary conditions. It was not Kelley, however, but Edgar Gardner Murphy, an Alabama clergyman, who suggested the formation of the National Child Labor Committee. Like many other Social Gospel ministers, Murphy believed that the church had a responsibility to reform society as well as to save souls. He was appalled by the number of young children who worked in the textile mills in the South, where they were exposed to great danger and condemned to "compulsory ignorance."

The National Child Labor Committee, with headquarters in New York, drew up a model state child labor law, encouraged state and city campaigns, and coordinated the movement around the country. Two-thirds of the states passed some form of child labor law between 1905 and 1907, but many laws had loopholes and exempted a large number of children, including newsboys and youngsters who worked in the theater. The committee also supported a national bill introduced in Congress by Indiana senator Albert Beveridge in 1906 "to prevent the employment of children in factories and mines." The bill went down to defeat. However, the child labor reformers convinced Congress in 1912 to establish a children's bureau in the Department of Labor. Despite these efforts, compulsory school attendance laws did more to reduce the number of children who worked than federal and state laws, which proved difficult to pass and even more difficult to enforce.

The crusade against child labor was a typical social justice reform effort. Its origins lay in the moral indignation middle-class reformers felt at the sight of little children and adolescents ruining their lives in factories. But the reform effort did not stop at moral outrage. The reformers gathered statistics, took photographs documenting the abuse of children, and marshaled their evidence to lobby for legislation first on the local level, then in the states, and eventually in Washington. Like other progressive reform efforts, the battle against child labor was only partly successful.

The reformers were especially concerned for the young people who got into trouble with the law, often for pranks that in rural areas would have seemed harmless. They feared for young people tried by adult courts and thrown into jail with hardened criminals. Almost simultaneously in Denver and Chicago, reformers organized juvenile courts. The judges in these courts had the authority to put the delinquent youths on probation, take them from their families and make them wards of the state, or assign them to an institution. The juvenile court did work in many cases and often helped prevent young delinquents from adopting a life of crime. Yet the juvenile offender was frequently deprived of all rights of due process, a fact that the Supreme Court finally recognized in 1967, when it ruled that children were entitled to procedural rights when accused of a crime.

Closely connected with the anti–child labor movement was the effort to limit the hours of work for women. It seemed inconsistent at best to protect a girl until she was 16 and then give her the "right to work from 8 A.M. to 10 P.M., thirteen hours a day, seventy-eight hours a week for $6." Florence Kelley and the National Consumers League led the campaign. It was foolish and unpatriotic, they argued, to allow "the mothers of future generations" to work long hours in dangerous industries. As a Pennsylvania superior court stated, "Adult females are a class as distinct as minors separated by natural conditions from all other laborers, and are so constituted as to be unable to endure physical exertion and exposure. . . ."

The most important court case, however, came before the Supreme Court in 1908. Josephine Goldmark, a friend and co-worker of Kelley's at the Consumers League, wrote the brief for *Muller* v. *Oregon* that her brother-in-law, Louis Brandeis, used when he argued the case. The Court upheld the Oregon ten-hour law largely because of Goldmark's sociological argument, which detailed the danger and disease that factory women faced. After the Supreme Court decision, most states fell into line and passed protective legislation for women, though many companies found ways to circumvent the laws. Even the work permitted by the law seemed too long to some women. "I think ten hours is too much for a woman," one factory worker stated. "I have four children and have to work hard at home. Make me awful tired. I would like nine hours. I get up at 5:30. When I wash, I have to stay up till one or two o'clock."

By contending that "women are fundamentally weaker than men in all that makes for endurance: in muscular strength, in nervous energy, in the powers of persistent attention and application," the reformers won some protection for women workers. But their arguments that women were weaker than men would eventually be turned around and used to reinforce gender segregation of the work force for the next half century.

In addition to working for protective legislation for working women, the social justice progressives also campaigned for woman suffrage. Unlike some supporters who argued that middle-class women would offset the ignorant and corrupt votes of immigrant men, these social reformers supported votes for all women. Addams argued that urban women not only could vote intelligently but also needed the vote to protect, clothe, and feed their families. Women in an urban age, she suggested, needed to be municipal housekeepers. Through the suffrage they would ensure that elected officials provided adequate services—pure water, uncontaminated food, proper sanitation, and police protection. The progressive insistence that all women needed the vote helped to push woman suffrage toward the victory that would come during World War I.

Home and School

The social justice progressives, who had imbibed much of the philosophy of pragmatism, believed that if they could only provide better housing and education, they would alter the lives of the poor and create a better world. Books such as Jacob Riis's *How the Other Half Lives* (1890) horrified them. With vivid language and haunting photographs, Riis, a Danish immigrant turned reformer, documented the overcrowded tenements, the damp, dark alleys, and the sickness and despair that affected people who lived in New York's slums. Reformers had been trying to improve housing for the poor for years. They had constructed model tenements and other housing projects, often called "philanthropy plus 5 percent" because investors promised to take only a limited return on their money. They sent "friendly visitors" into these projects to collect the rent and to teach the immigrants how to live like the middle class. Riis led a movement in New York to replace the worst slums with parks and playgrounds. In the first decade of the twentieth century, the progressives took a new approach toward the housing problems. They collected statistics, conducted surveys, organized committees, and constructed exhibits to demonstrate the effect of urban overcrowding. Then they set out to pass tenement house laws.

New York City, which had some of the worst tenement housing, took the lead. Lawrence Veiller, a short, stocky, bearded graduate of City College of New York, realized the need for reform during the depression of 1893. An expert on all aspects of housing, Veiller organized an exhibition with photographs, maps, and statistical studies to demonstrate the need for change and then drafted a model tenement house bill. It passed the New York legislature in 1901 and was soon copied by other states. The New York law required fire escapes, a window for each room, and a water closet for each apartment. But the new laws were often evaded or modified. They did not solve the problems of slum housing, but the progressives kept up the fight. In 1910, they organized the National Housing Association, and some of them looked ahead to federal laws and even to government-subsidized housing.

The housing reformers combined a moral sense of what needed to be done to create a more just society with practical ability to organize public opinion and get laws passed. They also had a paternalistic view toward the poor. Many reformers were depressed by the clutter and lack of privacy in immigrant tenements. One reformer's guide, *How to Furnish and Keep House in a Tenement Flat*, recommended "wood-stained and uncluttered furniture surfaces, iron beds with mattresses, and un-upholstered chairs. . . . Walls must be painted not papered . . . screens provide privacy in the bedrooms; a few good pictures should grace the walls. . . ." But often immigrant family ideals and values differed from those of the middle-class reformers. The immigrants actually preferred clutter and did not mind the lack of privacy. Despite the reformers' efforts to separate life's functions into separate rooms, most immigrants still crowded into the kitchen and hung religious objects rather than "good pictures" on the walls.

Ironically, many middle-class women reformers who tried to teach the working-class families how to live in their tenement flats had never organized their own homes. Often they lived in settlement houses, where they ate in a dining hall and never had to worry about cleaning, cooking, or doing laundry. Some of them, however, began to realize that the domestic tasks expected of women of all classes kept many of them from taking their full place in society. Charlotte Perkins Gilman, author of *Women and Economics* (1898), dismantled the traditional view of "woman's sphere" and sketched an alternative. Suggesting that entrepreneurs ought to build apartment houses designed to allow women to combine motherhood with careers, she advocated shared kitchen facilities and a common dining room, a laundry run by efficient workers, and a roof-garden day nursery run by a professional teacher.

Gilman, who criticized private homes as "bloated buildings, filled with a thousand superfluities," was joined by a few radicals in promoting new living arrangements. Most Americans, however, of all political persuasions continued to view the home as sacred space where the mother ruled supreme and created an atmosphere of domestic tranquility for the husband and children.

Next to better housing, the progressives stressed better schools as a way to produce better citizens. As they existed, public school systems were often rigid and corrupt. Far from producing citizens who would help to transform society, the schools seemed to reinforce the conservative habits that blocked change. A reporter who traveled around the country in 1892 discovered mindless teachers who drilled pupils through repetitious and rote learning. A Chicago teacher advised her students, "Don't stop to think, tell me what you know." When asked why the students were not allowed to move their heads, a New York teacher replied, "Why should they look behind when the teacher is in front of them?"

Progressive education, like many other aspects of progressivism, revolted against the rigid and the formal in favor of flexibility and change.

New York's tenement house bill of 1901 sent inspectors into the slums to cite violations. Yet landlords often found ways to avoid complying with the new standards.

Progressive education had many roots. One was the kindergarten movement imported from Germany in the mid-nineteenth century. The kindergarten sought to help children learn through creative play. If the very young could learn through joyous and experimental participation in art and music, why could not that spirit be used for students at other levels of education? The social settlements provided another source for progressive education. At Hull House in Chicago, the Henry Street Settlement in New York, and other centers, social workers discovered that they needed new methods to interest immigrant adults. Trying to teach grown men and women how to read English by using children's books with poems like "I am a yellow bird, I can sing. I can fly, I can sing to you" seemed not only ridiculous but also impractical. Other sources of progressive education were the vocational schools in the city and the agricultural schools in the country, both of which tried to teach practical skills and relate education to the real world.

John Dewey, a practitioner of the pragmatic approach to social change, was the key philosopher of progressive education. Growing up in Burlington, Vermont, he tried throughout his life to create a sense of the small rural community in the city. In his laboratory school at the University of Chicago, he experimented with new educational methods. He replaced the school desks, which were bolted down and always faced the front, with seats that could be moved into circles and arranged in small groups. The movable seat, in fact, became one of the symbols of the progressive education movement.

Dewey insisted that the schools be child-centered, not subject-oriented. Teachers should teach children rather than teach history or mathematics. Dewey did not mean that history and math should not be taught but that those subjects should be related to the students' experience. Students should learn by doing. They should actually build a house, not just study how others constructed houses. Students should not just learn about democracy; the school itself should operate like a democracy. Dewey also maintained, somewhat controversially, that the schools should become instruments for social reform. But like most progressives, Dewey was never quite clear whether he wanted the schools to help the students adjust to the existing world or whether he wanted the schools to turn out graduates who would change the world. Although he wavered on that point, the spirit of progressive education, like the spirit of progressivism in general, was optimistic. The schools could create more flexible, better-educated, more understanding adults who would go out to improve society.

Crusades Against Saloons, Brothels, and Movie Houses

Given their faith in the reforming potential of healthy and educated citizens, it was logical that most social justice progressives opposed the sale of alcohol. Some came from Protestant homes where the consumption of any liquor was considered a sin, but most favored prohibition for the same reasons they opposed child labor and favored housing reform. They saw eliminating the sale of alcohol as part of the process of reforming the city and conserving human resources.

Americans did drink great quantities of beer, wine, and hard liquor, and the amount they consumed rose rapidly after 1900, peaking between 1911 and 1915. An earlier temperance movement had achieved some success in the 1840s and 1850s (see Chapter 12), but only three states still had prohibition laws in force. The modern antiliquor movement began in the 1890s with a concerted effort on the part of the Women's Christian Temperance Union, the Anti-Saloon League, and a coalition of religious leaders and social reformers. During the progressive era, temperance forces had considerable success in influencing legislation. Seven states passed temperance laws between 1906 and 1912.

The reformers were appalled to see young children going into saloons to bring home a pail of beer for the family. They were horrified by tales of alcoholic fathers beating wives and children. But most often progressives focused on the saloon and its social life. Drug traffic, prostitution, and political corruption all seemed somehow related to the saloon. "Why should the community have any more sympathy for the

RECOVERING THE PAST

As we saw in Chapter 16, photographs are a revealing way of recovering the past visually. But when looking at a photograph, especially an old one, it is easy to assume that it is an accurate representation of the past. Photographers, however, like novelists and historians, have a point of view. They take their pictures for a reason, and often to prove a point. As one photographer remarked, "Photographs don't lie, but liars take photographs."

To document the need for reform in the cities, progressives collected statistics, made surveys, described settlement house life, and even wrote novels. But they discovered that the photograph was often more effective than words. Jacob Riis, the Danish-born author of *How the Other Half Lives* (1890), a devastating exposure of conditions in New York City tenement house slums, was also a pioneer in urban photography. Others had taken pictures of dank alleys and street urchins before, but Riis was the first to photograph slum conditions with the express purpose

of promoting reform. At first he hired photographers, but then he bought a camera and taught himself how to use it. He even tried a new German flash powder to illuminate dark alleys and tenement rooms in order to record the horror of slum life.

Riis made many of his photographs into lantern slides and used them to illustrate his lectures on the need for housing reform. Although he was a creative and innovative photographer, his pictures were often far from objective. His equipment was awkward, his film slow. He had to set up and prepare carefully before snapping the shutter. His views of tenement ghetto streets, and poor children now seem almost like clichés, but they were designed to make Americans angry, thus arousing them to reform.

Another important progressive photographer was Lewis Hine. Trained as a sociologist, like Riis he taught himself photography. Hine used his camera to illustrate his lectures at the Ethical Culture School in New York. In 1908, he was hired as a full-time

International Museum of Photography at George Eastman House, Rochester, New York

Lewis Hine, Carolina Cotton Mill, *1908*

investigator by the National Child Labor Committee. His haunting photographs of children in factories helped to convince many Americans of the need to abolish child labor. Hine's children were appealing human beings. He showed them eating, running, working, and staring wistfully out factory windows. His photographs avoided the pathos that Riis was so fond of recording, but just as surely they documented the need for reform.

Another technique that the reform photographer used was the before-and-after shot. The two photographs shown here of a one-room apartment in Philadelphia early in the century illustrate how progressive reformers tried to teach immigrants to imitate middle-class manners. The "before" photograph shows a room cluttered with washtubs, laundry, cooking utensils, clothes, tools, even an old Christmas decoration. In the "after" picture, much of the clutter has been cleaned up. A window has been installed to let in light and fresh air. The wallpaper, presumably a haven for hidden bugs and germs, has been torn off. The cooking utensils and laundry have been put away. The woodwork has been stained, and some ceremonial objects have been gathered on a shelf.

What else can you find that has been changed? How well do you think the message of photographic combinations like this one worked? Would the immigrant family be happy with the new look and condition of their room? Could anyone live in one room and keep it so neat?

As you look at these, or any photographs, ask yourself, What is the photographer's purpose and point of view? Why did he take the picture at this particular angle? Why does he center on these people or these objects? What does the photographer reveal about his or her purpose? What does the photograph reveal unintentionally? How have fast film and new camera styles changed photography? What subjects do reform-minded photographers train their cameras on today?

Anonymous before and after photographs of an immigrant family in Philadelphia

saloon . . . than . . . for a typhoid-breeding pool of filthy water . . . a swarm of deadly mosquitoes, or . . . a nest of rats infected with bubonic plague?'' an irate reformer asked.

Although they never quite understood the role alcohol played in the social life of many ethnic groups, Jane Addams and other settlement workers appreciated the role of the saloon as a neighborhood social center. Addams started a coffeehouse at Hull House in an attempt to lure the neighbors away from the evils of the saloon. In his study *Substitutes for the Saloon*, Raymond Caulkins, a young social worker, suggested parks, playgrounds, municipal theaters, and temperance bars as replacements for the saloons, where so many men gathered after work.

The progressives never found an adequate replacement for the saloon, but they set to work to pass local and state prohibition laws. As in many other progressive efforts, they joined forces with diverse groups to push for change. Their combined efforts led to victory on December 22, 1917, when Congress sent to the states for ratification a constitutional amendment prohibiting the sale, manufacturing, or importing of intoxicating liquor within the United States. The spirit of sacrifice for the war effort facilitated its rapid ratification.

In addition to the saloon, the progressives saw the urban dance hall and the movie theater as threats to the morals and well-being of young people, especially young women. The motion picture, which had been invented in 1889, developed as an important form of entertainment only during the first decade of the twentieth century. At first, the ''nickelodeons,'' as the early movie theaters were called, appealed mainly to a lower-class and largely ethnic audience. In 1902, New York City had 50 theaters; by 1908, there were over 400 showing 30-minute dramas and romances.

It was not until just before World War I, when D. W. Griffith produced long epics such as *The Birth of a Nation*, that the movies began to attract a middle-class audience. Many early films were imported from France, Italy, and Germany; because they were silent, it was easy to use subtitles in any language. But one did not need to know the language, or even be able to

read, to enjoy the action. That was part of the attraction of the early films. Many had plots that depicted premarital sex, adultery, and violence, and, unlike later films, many attacked authority and had tragic endings. The *Candidate* (1907) showed an upper-class reform candidate who gets dirt thrown at him for his efforts to clean up the town. The film *Down With Women* (1907) showed well-dressed men denouncing woman suffrage and the incompetence of the weaker sex, but throughout the film only strong women are depicted. In the end, when the hero is arrested, a woman lawyer defends him.

Some of the films stressed slapstick humor or romance and adventure; others bordered on pornography. The reformers objected not only to the plots and content of the films but also to the location of the theaters, near saloons and burlesque houses, and to their dark interiors. ''In the dim auditorium which seems to float on the world of dreams . . . an American woman may spend her afternoon alone,'' one critic wrote. ''She can let her fantasies slip through the darkened atmosphere to the screen where they drift in rhapsodic amours with handsome stars.'' It was these fantasies, in addition to the other things they imagined were going on in the dark, that disturbed the reformers. But for young immigrant women, who made up the bulk of the

Reformers objected to films such as Tess of the Storm Country, *which dealt with the subject of unwed motherhood. Nevertheless, some immigrant women found these films appealing.*

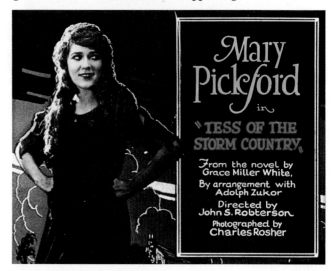

audience at most of the early movie theaters, the films provided some of the few exciting moments in their lives. One daughter of strict Italian parents remarked, "The one place I was allowed to go by myself was the movies. I went to the movies for fun. My parents wouldn't let me go anywhere else, even when I was twenty-four."

The saloons, dance halls, and movie theaters all seemed dangerous to progressives interested in improving life in the city because they all appeared to be somehow connected with the worst evil of all, prostitution. Campaigns against prostitution had been waged since the early nineteenth century, but they were nothing compared with the progressives' crusade to wipe out what they called "the social evil." All major cities and many smaller ones appointed vice commissions and made elaborate studies of prostitution. The reports, which often ran to several thick volumes, were typical progressive documents. Compiled by experts, they were filled with elaborate statistical studies and laced with moral outrage.

The progressive antivice crusade attracted many kinds of people, for often contradictory reasons. There were racists and immigration restrictionists who maintained that it was always the inferior people, blacks and recent immigrants, especially those from southern and eastern Europe, who became prostitutes and pimps. There were some connected with the social hygiene movement who denounced prostitution as part of their campaign to fight ignorance and prudity about sex. A number of women reformers joined the campaign and ar-

gued for a single sexual standard. They wanted men to be as chaste and as pure as women. Others worried about prostitutes spreading venereal disease to unfaithful husbands, who would pass it on to unsuspecting wives and unborn babies, leading eventually to race suicide. Most progressives, however, stressed the environmental causes of vice. They viewed prostitution, along with child labor and poor housing, as evils that could be eliminated through education and reform.

Most of the progressive antivice reformers stressed the economic causes of prostitution. "Is it any wonder," the Chicago Vice Commission asked, "that a tempted girl who receives only six dollars per week working with her hands sells her body for twenty-five dollars per week when she learns there is a demand for it and men are willing to pay the price?" "Do you suppose I am going back to earn five or six dollars a week in a factory," one prostitute asked an investigator, "when I can earn that amount any night and often much more?"

Despite all their reports and all the publicity, the progressives failed to end prostitution and did virtually nothing to address its roots in poverty. They wiped out a few red-light districts, closed a number of brothels, and managed to push a bill through Congress (the Mann-Elkins Act of 1910) that prohibited the interstate traffic of women for immoral purposes. Perhaps more important, in several states they got the age of consent for women raised, and in 20 states they made the Wassermann test for venereal disease mandatory for both men and women before a marriage license could be issued.

THE WORKER IN THE PROGRESSIVE ERA

The progressive reformers sympathized with industrial workers who struggled to earn a living for themselves and their families. But often they had little understanding of what it was like to sell one's strength by the hour. Middle-class reformers and working-class leaders occasionally cooperated during the progressive era, but often their goals were as divergent as their experiences.

Adjusting to Industrial Labor

John Mekras arrived in New York from Greece in 1912 and traveled immediately to Manchester, New Hampshire, where he found a job in the giant Amoskeag textile mill. He did not speak a word of English. "So they took me to the employment office," he later remembered, "and I went there, and the man who hands out the jobs sent me to the spinning room. There I don't know anything about the spinning. I'm a farmer. I don't know anybody when I get in there. Just like a lost sheep I feel there. Everybody, especially the women, they talk to me nice but I don't know what the boss is talking about." Mekras didn't last long at the mill. He was one of the many industrial workers who had difficulty adjusting to factory work in the early twentieth century.

Many workers, whether they were from Greece, from eastern Europe, from rural Vermont, or from Michigan, confronted a bewildering world based on order and routine. Like the young women who went to the textile factories in Lowell in the 1820s and 1830s, they faced difficult adjustments (see Chapter 11). On the farm, in small towns, or in craft shops, workers had engaged in task-oriented work. They decided when and how the job was to be done. They organized their own time. Often on a festival day, a nice day in summer, or a bad day in the winter, they did not work. But in the factory, the clock, the bell tower, and the boss

Immigrants accustomed to rural life found American cities bewildering. These Jews, immigrating to Texas from St. Petersburg, experienced the same difficulty in reverse.

dominated life. They were ordered to work at 6 A.M., told when to break for lunch and when to quit at night. Often the boss stood over them to make sure they did their job right. As had been true earlier, many workers resented the pressure and routine of factory work. They resisted the routine by staying home on a festival day or taking unauthorized breaks. Often they got fired or quit. In the woolen industry, the annual turnover of workers between 1907 and 1910 was more than 100 percent. In New York needle shops in 1912 and 1913, the turnover rate was over 250 percent. Overall in American industry, one-third of the workers stayed at their jobs less than a year.

This industrial work force, still composed largely of immigrants, had a fluid character. Many migrants, especially those from southern and eastern Europe, expected to stay only for a short time and then return to their homeland. "Italians come to America with the sole intention of accumulating money," one Italian-American writer complained in 1905. "Their dreams, their only care is the bundle of money . . . which will give them, after 20 years of deprivation, the possibility of having a mediocre standard of living in their native country." Many men came alone—70 percent in some years. They saved money by living in a boarding-house. In 1910, two-thirds of the workers in Pittsburgh made less than $12 a week, but by lodging in boarding houses and paying $2.50 a month for a bed, they could save perhaps one-third of their pay. "Here in America one must work for three horses," one immigrant wrote home. "The work is very heavy, but I don't mind it," another wrote; "let it be heavy, but may it last without interruption."

About 40 percent of those who immigrated to America in the first decade of the twentieth century returned home, according to one estimate. In the years of economic downturn, such as 1908, more Italians and Austro-Hungarians left the United States than entered it. For many immigrants, the American dream never materialized. But these reluctant immigrants provided the mass of unskilled labor that American industry exploited and sometimes consumed much the way other Americans exploited the land and the forests. The great pool of immigrant workers meant profits for American industry.

The nature of work continued to change in the early twentieth century as industrialists extended late-nineteenth-century efforts to make their factories and their work forces more efficient and productive. In some industries, the invention of new machines revolutionized work and eliminated skilled jobs. Glassblowing machines invented about 1900, for example, replaced thousands of glassblowers or reduced them from craftsmen to workers. Power-driven machines, better-organized operations, and, finally, the moving assembly line, first perfected by Henry Ford, transformed the nature of work and turned most laborers into unskilled tenders of machines.

John Brophy, a coal miner and labor official, remembered how much pride his father had in his work as a miner. "The skill with which you undercut the vein, the judgment in drilling the coal after it has been undercut and placing the exact amount of explosive so that it would do an effective job of breaking the coal from the solid . . . indicated the quality of his work." But by the beginning of the twentieth century, undercutting machines and the mechanization of most mining operations robbed the miners of any pride in their work.

It was more than machines, however, that changed the nature of industrial work. The principles of scientific management, which set out new rules for organizing work, were just as important. The key figure was Frederick Taylor, the son of a prominent Philadelphia family. Taylor had a nervous breakdown while at a private school. When his physicians prescribed manual labor as a cure, he went to work as a laborer at the Midvale Steel Company in Philadelphia. Working his way up rapidly while studying engineering at night, he became chief engineer at the factory in 1880s. Later he used this experience to rethink the organization of industry.

Taylor was obsessed with efficiency. He proved that a worker with a short-handled shovel could do more work than one with a long-handled shovel. Most of all he studied all kinds of workers and timed the various components of their jobs with a stopwatch. "The work of every workman is fully planned out by the management at least one day in advance," Taylor wrote in 1898, "and each man receives in most cases complete written instructions, describing in detail the task which he is to accomplish, as well as the means to be used in doing the work."

Many owners enthusiastically adopted Taylor's concepts of scientific management, seeing an opportunity to make their factories more profitable. But in most cases the workers resented the drive for efficiency. Foremen disliked taking orders from college men who had never run a machine. The workers hated the stopwatch, the demand for more speed in each operation, and the tighter managerial control. "We don't want to work as fast as we are able to," one machinist remarked. "We want to work as fast as we think it comfortable for us to work."

Union Organizing

Samuel Gompers, the ex-cigar maker and head of the American Federation of Labor, attacked Taylorism, realizing that it would reduce workers to "mere machines." "The heart of the workingman is sound," Gompers claimed as he defended the American labor union member against Taylor's charge that he loafed and worked inefficiently. Gompers never found an effective way to counter Taylor's charges, but the AFL prospered during the progressive era. Between 1897 and 1904, union membership grew from 447,000 to over 2 million, with three out of every four union members claimed by the AFL. By 1914, the AFL alone had over 2 million members. The "pure and simple unionism" preached by Gompers was most successful among coal miners, railroad workers, and the building trades. Gompers, as we saw in Chapter 19, ignored the growing army of unskilled and immigrant workers and concentrated on a strategy of raising the wages and improving the working conditions of the skilled craftsmen who were members of unions affiliated with the AFL.

For a time Gompers's strategy seemed to work. Several industries negotiated with the AFL as a way of avoiding disruptive strikes. The National Civic Federation, formed in 1905, was made up of business leaders, labor organizers, and representatives of the community. It supported conservative unionism and condemned the twin evils of socialism on the one hand and antiunion employers on the other. But the cooperation was short-lived. Labor unions were defeated in a number of disastrous strikes, and the National Association of Manufacturers launched an aggressive counterattack. "Organized labor . . . does not place its reliance upon reason and justice," the NAM president charged. "It is in all essential features a mob knowing no master except its own will. Its history is stained with blood and ruin." The tactics used were familiar ones. The NAM and other employer associations provided strikebreakers, used industrial spies, and blacklisted union members to prevent them from obtaining other jobs.

The Supreme Court came down squarely on management's side, ruling in the *Danbury Hatters* case in 1908 that trade unions were subject to the Sherman Anti-Trust Act. Thus union members themselves could be held personally liable for money lost by a business during a strike. The courts at all levels usually sided with employers. They often declared strikes illegal and were quick to issue restraining orders, making it impossible for workers to interfere with the operation of a business.

Many of the social justice progressives sym-

Union Membership, 1900–1920

Source: U.S. Bureau of the Census.

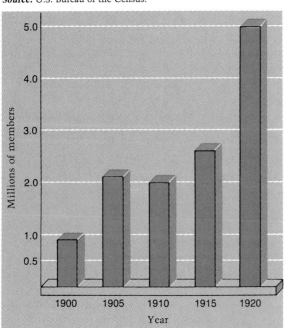

pathized with the working class but spent more time promoting protective legislation than in strengthening organized labor. They also found themselves cast in the role of mediators during industrial disputes. Often it was difficult for the upper- and middle-class reformers to comprehend what life was really like for those who had to work six days a week.

Working women and their problems aroused more sympathy among progressive reformers than did the plight of working men. The number of women working outside the home increased steadily during the progressive era, from over 5 million in 1900 to nearly 8.5 million in 1920. But few belonged to unions, only a little over 3 percent in 1900, and the percentage declined by half by 1910 before increasing a little after that date with aggressive organizing in the textile industry and the clothing trades.

Although the AFL had hired Mary Kenney as an organizer in the 1890s and accepted a few women's unions into affiliation, as a general rule the policy of Gompers and the other leaders was to oppose organizing women workers (see Chapter 19). "The demand for female labor," one labor leader announced, "is an insidious assault upon the home . . . it is the knife of the assassin, aimed at the family circle."

Yet of necessity women continued to work to support themselves and their families. Many upper-class women reformers tried to help these working women in a variety of ways. The settlement houses organized day-care centers, clubs, and classes, and many reformers tried to pass protective legislation. Tension and misunderstanding often cropped up between the reformers and the working women, but one organization in which there was genuine cooperation was the Women's Trade Union League. Founded in 1903, the League was organized by Mary Kenney and William English Walling, a socialist and reformer, but it also drew local leaders from the working class, such as Rose Schneiderman, a Jewish immigrant cap maker, and Leonora O'Reilly, a collar maker. The league established branches in most of the large eastern and midwestern cities and served for more than a decade as an important force in helping to organize women into unions. The league forced the AFL to pay more attention to women, helped out in time of strikes, put up bail money for those arrested, and publicized the plight of working women.

Garment Workers and the Triangle Fire

Thousands of young women, most of them Jewish and Italian, were employed in the garment industry in New York City. Most were between 16 and 25; some lived with their families, and others lived alone or with a roommate. They worked a 56-hour, six-day week and made about $6 for their efforts. New York was the center of the garment industry, with over 600 shirtwaist (blouse) and dress factories employing more than 30,000 workers. Like other industries, garment manufacturing had changed in the first decade of the twentieth century. Once conducted in thousands of dark and dingy tenement rooms, now all the operations were centralized in large loft buildings in lower Manhattan. These buildings were an improvement over the sweating labor of the tenements, but many were overcrowded, and they had few fire escapes or safety features. In addition, the owners applied scientific management techniques in order to increase their profits, and that made life miserable for the workers. Most of the

The fire at the Triangle Shirtwaist Company in 1910 killed scores of women workers and launched a statewide investigation of working conditions.

women had to rent their own sewing machines and even had to pay for the electricity they used. They were penalized for mistakes or for talking too loudly. They were usually supervised by a male contractor who badgered them and sometimes even asked for sexual favors.

In 1909, some of the women went out on strike to protest the working conditions. The International Ladies' Garment Workers Union (ILGWU) and the Women's Trade Union League supported them. But strikers were beaten and sometimes arrested by unsympathetic policemen and by strikebreakers on the picket lines. At a mass meeting held at Cooper Union in New York on November 22, 1909, Clara Lemlich, a young shirtwaist worker who had been injured on the picket line and was angered by the long speeches and lack of action, rose and in an emotional speech in Yiddish demanded a general strike. The entire audience pledged its agreement. The next day all over the city, the shirtwaist workers went out on strike. "The uprising of the twenty thousand," as the strike was called, startled the nation. One young worker wrote in her diary, "It is a good thing, that strike is. It makes you feel like a grown-up person." The Jews learned a little Italian and the Italians a little Yiddish so that they could communicate. Many social reformers, ministers, priests, and rabbis urged the strikers on. Mary Dreier, an upper-class reformer and president of the New York branch of the Womens' Trade Union League, was arrested for marching with the strikers. A young state legislator, Fiorello La Guardia, later to become a congressman and mayor of New York, was one of many public officials to aid the strikers.

The shirtwaist strikers won, but the victory was limited. Over 300 companies accepted the union's terms, but others refused to go along. The young women went back to work amid still oppressive and unsafe conditions. That became dramatically obvious on Saturday, March 25, 1910, when, near closing time, a fire broke out on the eighth floor of the ten-story loft building housing the Triangle Shirtwaist Company near Washington Square in New York. There had been several small fires in the factory in previous weeks, so no one thought much about another one. But this one was different. Within minutes, the top three floors of the factory were a raging inferno. Many exit doors were locked. The elevators broke down. There were no fire escapes. Forty-six women jumped to their deaths, some of them in groups of three and four holding hands. Over 100 died in the flames.

Shocked by the Triangle fire, the state legislature appointed a commission to investigate working conditions in the state. One investigator for the commission was a young social worker, Frances Perkins, who in the 1930s would become secretary of labor. She led the politicians through the dark lofts, filthy tenements, and unsafe factories around the state to show them the conditions under which young women worked. The result was the passage of bills in the state legislature limiting the work of women to 54 hours, abolishing labor by children under 14, and improving safety regulations in factories. One of those who helped pass the legislation in Albany was a young state senator named Franklin Delano Roosevelt.

The investigative commission was a favorite progressive tactic. When there was a problem, reformers often got a city council, a state legislature, or the federal government to appoint a commission. If they could not find a government body to give them a mandate, they made their own studies. They brought in experts, compiled statistics, and published reports.

The federal Industrial Relations Commission, created in 1912 to study the causes of industrial unrest and violence, conducted one of the most important investigations. As it turned out, the commission spent most of its time investigating a dramatic and tragic incident of labor-management conflict in Colorado, known as the Ludlow Massacre. A strike broke out in the fall of 1913 in the vast mineral-rich area of southern Colorado, much of it controlled by the Colorado Fuel and Iron Industry, a company largely owned by the Rockefeller family. It was a paternalistic empire where workers lived in company towns and sometimes in tent colonies. They were paid in company scrip and forced to shop at the company store. When the workers, supported by the United Mine Workers, went on strike demanding an eight-hour day, better safety precautions, and the removal of armed guards, the company refused to negotiate. The strike

turned violent, and in the spring of 1914, strikebreakers and national guardsmen fired on the workers. Eleven children and two women were killed in an attack on a tent city near Ludlow, Colorado.

The Industrial Relations Commission called John D. Rockefeller, Jr., to testify and implied that he was personally guilty of the murders. The commission decided in its report that violent class conflict could be avoided only by limiting the use of armed guards and detectives, by restricting monopoly, by protecting the right of the workers to organize, and, most dramatically, by redistributing wealth through taxation. The commission's report, not surprisingly, fell on deaf ears. Most progressives denied the commission's conclusion that class conflict was inevitable.

Radical Labor

Not everyone accepted the progressives' faith in investigations and protective labor legislation. Nor did everyone approve of Samuel Gompers's conservative tactics or his emphasis on getting better pay for skilled workers. A group of about 200 radicals met in Chicago in 1905 to form a new union as an alternative to the AFL. They called it the Industrial Workers of the World and talked of one big union. Like the Knights of Labor in the 1880s, the IWW would welcome all workers: the unskilled and even the unemployed, women, blacks, Asians, and all other ethnic groups. Daniel De Leon of the Socialist Labor party attended the organizational meeting, and so did Eugene Debs. Debs, who had been converted to socialism after the Pullman strike of 1894, had already emerged by 1905 as one of the outstanding radical leaders in the country. Also attending, was Mary Harris Jones, who dressed like a society matron but attacked labor leaders "who sit on velvet chairs in conferences with labor's oppressors." In her sixties at the time, everyone called her "Mother" Jones. She had been a dressmaker, a Populist, and a member of the Knights of Labor. During the 1890s, she had marched with miners' wives on the picket line in western Pennsylvania. She was imprisoned and denounced, but by 1905 she was already a legend.

Presiding at the Chicago meeting was "Big Bill" Haywood. He had been a cowboy, a miner, and a prospector. Somewhere along the way he had lost an eye and mangled a hand, but he had a booming voice and a passionate commitment to the American working class. "We are here to confederate the workers of this country into a working-class movement that shall have for its purpose the emancipation of the working class from the slave bondage of capitalism." Denouncing Gompers and the AFL, he talked of class conflict. "The purpose of the IWW," he proclaimed, "is to bring the workers of this country into the possession of the full value of the product of their toil."

The IWW remained a small organization, troubled by internal squabbles and disagreements. Debs and De Leon left after a few years. Haywood remained the dominant figure in the movement, which played an important role in organizing the militant strike of textile workers in Lawrence, Massachusetts, in 1912 and the following year in Paterson, New Jersey, and Akron, Ohio. But the IWW had its greatest success organizing itinerant lumbermen and migratory workers in the Northwest.

Many American workers still did not feel, as did European workers, that they were engaged in a perpetual class struggle with their capitalist employers. Some immigrant workers, intent on earning enough money to go back home, had no time to join the conflict. Most of those who stayed in the United States were consoled by the promises of the American dream. Thinking they might secure a better job or move up into the middle class, they avoided labor militancy. They knew that even if they failed, their sons and daughters would profit from the American way. The AFL, not the IWW, became the dominant American labor movement. But for a few the IWW represented a dream of what might have been. For others its presence, even though it was small and largely ineffective, meant that perhaps someday a European-style working-class movement might develop in America.

REFORM IN THE CITIES AND STATES

The reform movements of the progressive era usually started at the local level, then moved to the state level and finally to the nation's capital. Progressivism in the cities and states had roots in the depression and discontent of the 1890s. The reform banners called for more democracy, more power for the people, and for legislation regulating railroads and other businesses. Yet the professional and business classes were the movement's leaders. They intended to bring order out of chaos and to modernize the city and the state during a time of rapid growth.

Municipal Reformers

Americans have always seen their cities as places of sin, avarice, and corruption rather than as centers of civilization. William Jennings Bryan expressed some of this antiurban feeling in his famous "Cross ot Gold" speech, when he stressed the superiority of the farms over the cities. There seemed something almost un-American about the American city: "If a man stayed in the city long enough he would almost inevitably lose those qualities that made him an American," David Graham Phillips, a muckraking journalist and novelist, had one of his characters in *The Golden Fleece* announce.

American cities grew rapidly in the last part of the nineteenth and the first part of the twentieth centuries. New York, which had a population of 1.2 million in 1880, grew to 3.4 million by 1900 and to 5.6 million in 1920. Chicago expanded even more dramatically, from 500,000 in 1880 to 1.7 million in 1900 and to 2.7 million in 1920. Cleveland's population doubled between 1880 and 1900 and doubled again before 1920. Even in the South, where urbanization was slower, Birmingham increased from 38,000 in 1900 to 178,000 in 1920. In California, Los Angeles was a town of 11,000 in 1880 but multiplied ten times by 1900, and then increased by five times, to more than a half million, by 1920.

The spectacular and continuing growth of the cities caused massive problems and created a

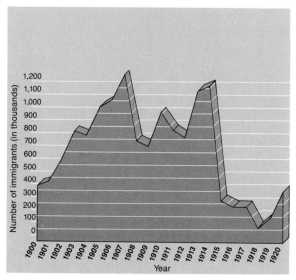

Immigration to the United States, 1900–1920

Source: U.S. Bureau of the Census.

need for housing, transportation, and municipal services. But it was the kind of people who were moving into the cities that worried many observers. Americans from the small towns and farms continued to be attracted to the urban centers, as they had throughout the nineteenth century. But the greatest surge in population was caused by immigration. Fully 40 percent of New York's population and 36 percent of Chicago's was foreign-born in 1910, and if one added the children of the immigrants, the percentage approached 80 percent in some cities. Huge sections of the cities in the Northeast and the Midwest were filled with sights, sounds, and smells that seemed strange and threatening to the native-born Americans who ventured there. They might as well have been in Naples or Warsaw. These new immigrants from eastern and western Europe, according to Francis Walker, the president of MIT, were "beaten men from beaten races, representing the worst failures in the struggle for existence." They seemed to threaten the American way of life and the very tenets of democracy.

The municipal reform movements of the progressive era were motivated in part by a fear of the city and its new inhabitants. But they also were an extension of the many efforts to clean

up the cities in the late nineteenth century. They built on the reform campaigns of "Golden Rule" Jones and Hazen Pingree (see Chapter 20). But there was a greater sense of urgency, perhaps because urban problems seemed to have reached a crisis stage.

The twentieth-century reformers, mostly middle-class citizens like those in the nineteenth, wanted to regulate and control the sprawling metropolis, restore democracy, reduce corruption, and limit the power of the political bosses and their immigrant allies. They formed committees and appointed commissions. There were committees of 15 and committees of 100; there were bureaus of municipal research, civic clubs, voters' leagues, and good government associations. Usually these organizations were composed of businessmen and professionals, often allied with settlement workers, ministers, and experts from the universities.

When these reformers talked of restoring power to the people, they usually meant their

This famous photograph by Alfred Stieglitz captures the spirit of those who crowded into steerage to emigrate to America.

Cities grew so rapidly that they became not only unmanageable, but so crowded as to make movement difficult. This 1909 photograph shows Dearborn Street, looking south from Randolph Street, in Chicago.

kind of people. One Rhode Island reformer put it bluntly:

> It stands to reason that a man paying $5,000 taxes in a town is more interested in the well-being and development of his town than the man who pays no taxes. . . . It equally stands to reason that the man of the $5,000 tax should be assured a representation in the committee which lays the tax and spends the money which he contributes. . . . Shall we be truly democratic and give the property owners a fair share or shall we develop a tyranny of ignorance which shall crush him?

Not all reformers were so candid, and the municipal reform movements in most cities did try to make the urban scene more livable for all kinds of people. But the chief aim of municipal reform was to make the city more organized and efficient for the business and professional classes.

Municipal reform movements varied from city to city. In Boston, the reformers tried to strengthen the power of the mayor, to break the hold of the city council, and to eliminate the corruption associated with the council. The reformers succeeded in removing all party designations from city election ballots, and they extended the term of the mayor from two to four years. But to their chagrin, in the election of

1910 the reform candidate was defeated by a foe of reform, the Irish Politician John Fitzgerald (the grandfather of John F. Kennedy), who was elected for the longer term. In other cities, the reformers used different tactics, but they almost always did elaborate studies and carried on campaigns to reduce corruption.

The most dramatic innovation was the commission form of government that replaced both mayor and council with nonpartisan administrators. This innovation began quite accidentally when a hurricane devastated Galveston, Texas, in September 1900. In one of the worst natural disasters in the nation's history, over 6,000 people were killed and more than half the city wiped out. The existing government was helpless to deal with the crisis, so the state legislature appointed five commissioners to run the city during the emergency. The idea spread to Houston, Dallas, and Austin and to many other cities in other states. It proved most popular in small to medium-sized cities in the Midwest and Pacific Northwest. By the time of World War I, more than 400 cities had adopted the commission form. Dayton, Ohio, went one step further: After a disastrous flood in 1913, the city hired a city manager to run the city and to report to the elected council. Government by experts was the perfect symbol of what most progressive municipal reformers had in mind.

The commission and the expert manager did not replace the mayor in most large cities. One of the most flamboyant and successful of the progressive mayors was Tom Johnson of Cleveland. Johnson had made a fortune by investing in utility and railroad franchises before he was 40. But he read Henry George's *Progress and Poverty* and was so influenced by it that he began a second career as a reformer. After serving in Congress, he was elected mayor of Cleveland in 1901. During his two terms in city hall he managed to reduce transit fares and to build parks and municipal bath houses throughout the city. Johnson also broke the connection between the police and prostitution in the city by promising the madams and the brothel owners that he would not bother them if they would be orderly and not steal from their customers or pay off the police. His most controversial move, however, was to push for city ownership of the street railroads and utilities (sometimes called municipal socialism). "Only through municipal ownership," he argued, "can the gulf which divides the community into a small dominant class on one side and the unorganized people on the other be bridged." Johnson was defeated in 1909 in part because he alienated so many powerful business interests, but one of his lieutenants, Newton D. Baker, was elected mayor in 1911 and carried on many of his programs.

The City Beautiful

In Cleveland, both Tom Johnson and Newton Baker promoted the arts, music, and adult education. They also supervised the construction of a civic center, a library, and a museum. Most other American cities during the progressive era set out to beautify and to bring culture to the metropolitan centers. They were influenced at least in part by the great, classical white city constructed for the Chicago World's Fair of 1893 and by the grand European boulevards such as the Champs Élysées in Paris. The architects of the "city beautiful movement" preferred the impressive and ceremonial architecture of Rome or of the Renaissance for libraries, museums, railroad stations, and other public buildings. The huge Pennsylvania Station in New York was modeled after the imperial Roman baths of Caracalla, while the Free Library in Philadelphia was an almost exact copy of a building in Paris. The city beautiful leaders tried to make the city more attractive and meaningful for the middle and upper classes. The museums and the libraries were closed on Sundays, the only day the working class could possibly visit them.

Another group of progressives, especially those connected with the social settlements, were more concerned with neighborhood parks and playgrounds than with the ceremonial boulevards and grand buildings. Hull House established the first public playground in Chicago. Jacob Riis, the housing reformer, and Lillian Wald of the Henry Street Settlement campaigned in New York for small parks and for the opening of schoolyards on weekends. Some progressives, including many settlement workers, looked back nostalgically to their rural childhoods and desperately tried to get urban children out of the city in the summertime to rural camps. But they also tried to make the city more livable as well as more beautiful.

Most progressives had an ambivalent attitude toward the city. They feared it, and they loved it. Some saw the great urban areas filled with immigrants as a threat to American democracy, but one of Tom Johnson's young assistants, Frederic C. Howe, wrote a book called *The City: The Hope of Democracy* (1905). Hope or threat, the progressives realized that the United States had become an urban nation and that the problems of the city had to be faced one way or another.

Reform in the States

The progressive movements in the states had many roots and took many forms. In some states, especially in the West, progressive attempts to regulate railroads and utilities were simply an extension of populism. In other states, the reform drive bubbled up from reform efforts in the cities. Most states passed laws during the progressive era designed to extend democracy and give more authority to the people. Initiative and referendum laws allowed citizens to originate legislation and to overturn laws passed by the legislature, while recall laws gave the people a way to remove elected officials. Most of these "democratic" laws worked better in theory than in practice, but the passage of the laws in many states did represent a genuine effort to remove special privilege from government.

Much of the state legislation was concerned with the aspect of progressivism that sought order and efficiency, but many states passed social justice measures as well. Maryland enacted the first workmen's compensation law in 1902, giving employees pay for days missed because of job-related injuries. Illinois approved a law giving aid to mothers with dependent children. Several states passed anti-child labor bills, and Oregon's ten-hour law restricting women's labor became a model for other states.

The states with the most successful reform movements elected strong and aggressive governors: Charles Evans Hughes in New York, Hoke Smith in Georgia, Hiram Johnson in California,

Woodrow Wilson in New Jersey, and Robert La Follette in Wisconsin. Next to Wilson, La Follette was the most famous and in many ways the model progressive governor. Born in a small town in Wisconsin, he graduated from the University of Wisconsin in 1879 and was admitted to the bar. Practicing law during the 1890s in Madison, the state capital, he received a large retainer from the Milwaukee Railroad, and he defended the railroad against both riders and laborers who sued the company.

But Wisconsin, like most of the rest of the country, was hard hit by the depression of 1893. More than a third of the citizens in the state were out of work; farmers lost their farms, and many small businesses went bankrupt. At the same time, the rich seemed to be getting richer. "Men are rightly feeling that a social order like the present, with its enormous wealth side by side with appalling poverty . . . cannot be the final form of human society," a Milwaukee minister announced. As grass-roots discontent spread across the state, a group of municipal reformers in Milwaukee attacked the giant corporations and the street railways. Several newspapers joined the battle and denounced special privilege and corruption wherever they found it. Everyone could agree on the need for tax reform, for railroad regulation, and for more participation of the people in government.

La Follette, who had been little interested in reform in his early career, took advantage of the general mood of discontent to win the governorship in 1901. "Now his face was calm—now a thundercloud—now full of sorrow," one newspaper reported. It seemed ironic that La Follette, who had once taken a retainer from a railroad, now was elected governor by attacking the railroads, but La Follette was a shrewd politician. He used professors from the University of Wisconsin, just across town from the capital building, to prepare reports and do statistical studies. Then he worked with the legislature to pass a state primary law and an act regulating the railroads. "Go back to the first principles of democracy, go back to the people" was his battle cry. The "Wisconsin idea" attracted the attention of journalists like Lincoln Steffens and Ray Stannard Baker, and they helped to popularize the "laboratory of democracy" around the country. La Follette became a national figure and was elected to the Senate in 1906.

The progressive movement did improve government and make it more responsible to the people in states like Wisconsin. For example, the railroads were brought under the control of a railroad commission. But by 1910, the railroads no longer complained about the new taxes and restrictions. They had discovered that it was to their advantage to make their operations more efficient, and often they were able to convince the commission that they should raise rates or abandon the operation of unprofitable lines. Progressivism in the states, like progressivism everywhere, had mixed results. But the spirit of reform that swept through the country was real, and progressive movements on the local level did eventually have an impact on Washington, especially during the administrations of Theodore Roosevelt and Woodrow Wilson.

THEODORE ROOSEVELT AND THE SQUARE DEAL

President William McKinley was shot in Buffalo, New York, on September 6, 1901, by Leon Czolgosz, an anarchist. He died eight days later, making Theodore Roosevelt, at 42, the youngest man ever to become president. The nation mourned its fallen leader, while in many cities anarchists and other radicals were rounded up for questioning. McKinley had not been a great president, but he had looked dignified and was respected by the American people.

No one knew what to expect from Roosevelt. Mark Hanna, a senator from Ohio and a conservative Republican leader, protested when Roosevelt had been nominated for vice-president, "Don't you realize that there's only one life between that madman and the White House?" But some of the social justice progressives remembered that Roosevelt had suggested that the soldiers ought to fire on the strikers during the Pullman strike in 1894. Roosevelt was controversial when he took office, and he remained controversial when he left the White

House 7½ years later. But even his enemies could agree that he was a dominant force in American life.

A Strong and Controversial President

Roosevelt, though young, came to the presidency with considerable experience. He had run unsuccessfully for mayor of New York, served a term in the New York state assembly, spent four years as a United States civil service commissioner, and served two years as the police commissioner of New York City. His exploits in the Spanish-American War brought him to the public's attention, but he had also been an effective assistant secretary of the navy and a reform governor of New York. While police commissioner and governor, he had been influenced by a number of progressives. Jacob Riis, the housing reformer, became one of his friends and led him on nighttime explorations of the slums of New York City. He had also impressed a group of New York settlement workers with his genuine concern for human misery, his ability to talk to all kinds of people, and his willingness to learn about social problems. But no one was sure how Roosevelt would act as president. He came from an upper-class family and had associated with the important and the powerful all over the world. He had published a number of books and was one of the most intellectual presidents since

Young and energetic, Theodore Roosevelt was a dynamic though controversial president.

Thomas Jefferson. But none of these things assured that he would be a progressive in office.

Roosevelt loved being president. He called the office a "bully pulpit," and he enjoyed talking to the people and the press. His high-pitched voice might have been a handicap, but he made up for it with great enthusiasm and exuberance. With an appealing personality and a sense of humor, he made a good subject for the new mass-market newspapers and magazines. The American people quickly adopted him as their favorite. They called him "Teddy" and named a stuffed bear after him. According to one Englishman, he was second only to Niagara Falls as an American phenomenon. Sometimes his exuberance got a little out of hand. On one occasion he took a foreign diplomat on a nude swim in the Potomac River. You have to understand, another observer remarked, that "the president is really only six years old."

Roosevelt was much more than an exuberant 6-year-old. He was the strongest president since Lincoln. By reorganizing and revitalizing the executive branch, reorganizing the army command structure, and modernizing the consular service, he made many aspects of the federal government more efficient. He established the Bureau of Corporations, appointed independent commissions staffed with experts, and enlisted talented and well-trained men to work for the government. "TR," as he became known, called a White House conference on the care of dependent children, and in 1905 he even summoned college presidents and football coaches to the White House to discuss ways to limit violence in football. He angered many social justice progressives by not going far enough. In fact, on one occasion Florence Kelley was so furious with him that she walked out of the oval office and slammed the door. But he was the first president to listen to the pleas of the progressives and to invite them to the White House. Learning from experts like Frances Kellor, he became more concerned with social justice as time went on.

Dealing with the Trusts

One of Roosevelt's first actions as president was to attempt to control the large industrial corporations. He took office in the middle of an unprecedented movement of business consolidation. Between 1897 and 1904, some 4,227 companies combined to form 257 large corporations. U.S. Steel, the first billion-dollar corporation, was formed in 1901 by joining Carnegie Steel with its eight principal competitors. In one stroke the new company controlled two-thirds of the market, and J. P. Morgan made $7 million for supervising the operation. The Sherman Anti-Trust Act of 1890 had been virtually useless in controlling the trusts, but a new outcry from muckrakers and progressives called for regulation. Some even demanded the return to the age of small business. Roosevelt was not opposed to bigness, nor to the right of businessmen to make money. "Our aim is not to do away with corporations," he remarked in 1902; "on the contrary, these big aggregations are the inevitable development of modern industrialism." But he thought some businessmen were arrogant, greedy, and irresponsible. "We draw the line against misconduct, not against wealth," he said.

To the shock of much of the business community, he directed his attorney general to file suit to dissolve the Northern Securities Company, a giant railroad monopoly put together by James J. Hill and financier J. P. Morgan. Morgan came to the White House to tell Roosevelt, "If we have done anything wrong, send your man to my man and they can fix it up." Roosevelt was furious, and he was determined to let Morgan and other businessmen know that they could not deal with the president of the United States as just another tycoon.

The government won its case and proceeded to prosecute some of the largest corporations, including Standard Oil of New Jersey and the American Tobacco Company. However, Roosevelt's antitrust policy did not end the power of the giant corporations or even alter their methods of doing business. More disturbing to consumers, it did not force down the price of kerosene, cigars, or railroad tickets. But it did breathe some life into the Sherman Anti-Trust Act, and it increased the role of the federal government as regulator.

Roosevelt sought to strengthen the regulatory powers of the federal government in other ways. He steered the Elkins Act through Congress in 1903 and the Hepburn Act in 1906, which together strengthened the power of the Interstate Commerce Commission (ICC). The first act eliminated the use of rebates by railroads, a way that many large corporations had used to get favored treatment. The second act broadened the power of the ICC and gave it the right to investigate and enforce rates. Both bills,

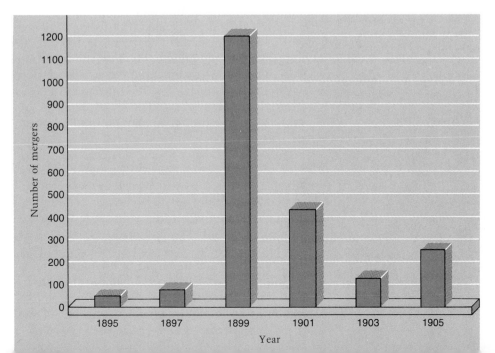

Business Mergers, 1895–1905

Source: U.S. Bureau of the Census.

however, were watered down by congressional opposition, and they did not end the abuses or satisfy the farmers and small businessmen who had always been the railroads' chief critics.

Roosevelt was a firm believer in corporate capitalism. He detested socialism and felt much more comfortable around business executives than labor leaders. Yet he saw his role as mediator and regulator. His view of the power of the presidency was illustrated in 1902 during the anthracite coal strike. Led by John Mitchell of the United Mine Workers, the coal miners went on strike to protest low wages, long hours, and unsafe working conditions. In 1901, a total of 513 coal miners had been killed. The mine owners, who often were also railroad owners, refused to talk to the miners. They hired strikebreakers and used private security forces to threaten and intimidate the miners. The employer's position in its extreme form was articulated by George F. Baer of the Reading Railroad.

Before the Pure Food and Drug Act of 1906, patent medicines routinely contained addictive and dangerous drugs. By 1912, though the problem persisted, public awareness had increased dramatically.

He argued that workingmen had no right to strike or to say anything about working conditions: "The rights and interests of the laboring man will be protected and cared for, not by the labor agitators, but by the Christian man to whom God in His infinite wisdom has given the control of the property interests of the country, and upon the successful management of which so much depends."

Although Roosevelt had no particular sympathy for labor, he certainly would not have gone as far as Baer. In the fall of 1902, however, schools began closing for lack of coal, and it looked like many citizens would suffer through the winter. Coal that usually sold for $5 a ton rose to $14. Roosevelt called the owners and representatives of the union to the White House even though the businessmen protested that they would not deal with "outlaws." Finally, the president appointed a commission that included representatives of the union as well as the community. Within weeks, the miners went back to work with a 10 percent raise.

Meat Inspection and Pure Food and Drugs

Roosevelt's first major legislative reform began almost accidently in 1904 when Upton Sinclair, a 26-year-old muckraking journalist, started to collect information and to do research on the conditions in the Chicago stockyards. Born in Baltimore, Sinclair had grown up in New York, where he wrote dime novels to pay his tuition at City College. He was converted to socialism by his reading and by his association with a group of idealistic young writers in New York. Though he knew little about Chicago, he was driven by a desire to expose the exploitation of the poor and oppressed in America. He was impressed with the data the settlement workers had collected on all aspects of urban problems. Sinclair boarded at the University of Chicago settlement while he did research, conducted interviews, and wrote the story that would be published in 1906 as *The Jungle*.

Sinclair's novel told the story of the Rudkus family, who emigrated from Lithuania to Chicago filled with ambition and hope. But the American dream failed for them. Sinclair documented exploitation in his fictional account, but it was his description of contaminated meat that received most of the attention. He described spoiled hams treated with formaldehyde and sausages made from rotten meat scraps, rats, and other refuse. Hoping to convert his readers to socialism, what Sinclair did instead was to turn their stomachs and cause a public outcry for better regulation of the meatpacking industry.

Selling 25,000 copies in its first six weeks, *The Jungle* disturbed many people including Roosevelt, who, it was reported, could no longer enjoy his breakfast sausage. Roosevelt ordered a study of conditions in the meatpacking industry and then used the report to pressure Congress and the meatpackers to accept a bill introduced by Albert Beveridge, the progressive senator from Indiana.

In the end, the Meat Inspection Act of 1906 was a compromise. It enforced some federal inspection and mandated sanitary conditions in all companies selling meat in interstate commerce. The meatpackers defeated a provision that would have required the dating of all meat. Some of the large meatpackers supported the compromise bill because it gave them an advantage in their battle with the smaller firms. Yet the bill was a beginning. It illustrates how muckrakers, social justice progressives, and public outcry eventually led to reform legislation. It also shows how Roosevelt used the public mood and manipulated the political process to get a bill through Congress. Many of the progressive reformers were disappointed with the final result, but Roosevelt was always willing to settle for half a loaf rather than none at all. Ironically, the Meat Inspection Act helped restore the public's confidence in the meat industry and aided the industry increase its profits.

Taking advantage of the publicity that circulated around *The Jungle,* a group of reformers, writers, and government officials pushed for legislation to regulate the sale of food and drugs. Americans consumed an enormous quantity of patent medicines, which they purchased through the mail, from traveling salesmen, and from local stores. One article pointed out in 1905:

> Gullible Americans will spend this year some seventy-five million dollars in the purchase of patent medicines. In consideration of this sum it will swallow huge quantities of alcohol, an appalling amount of opiates and narcotics, a wide assortment of varied drugs ranging from powerful and dangerous heart depressants to insidious liver stimulants; and, far in excess of all other ingredients, undiluted fraud. For fraud exploited by the skillfulest of advertising bunco men is the basis of the trade.

Many packaged and canned foods contained dangerous chemicals and impurities. One popular remedy, Hosteter's Stomach Bitters, was revealed on analysis to contain 44 percent alcohol. Coca-Cola, a popular soft drink, actually contained cocaine for a few years, and many medicines were laced with opium. Many people, including women and children, became alcoholics or drug addicts in their search to feel better. The Pure Food and Drug Act that passed Congress on the same day in 1906 as the Meat Inspection Act was not a perfect bill by any means, but it was a beginning. It prevented some of the worst abuses, including eliminating the cocaine from Coca-Cola.

Conservation

Although Roosevelt was pleased with the new legislation for regulating the food and drug industries, he always considered his conservation program his most important domestic achievement. An outdoorsman, hunter, and amateur naturalist since his youth, he was also a close friend of Gifford Pinchot, who had been educated in France and Germany in the scientific management of forests. For more than a century it appeared that American natural resources were inexhaustible, but by 1900 it became obvious to Pinchot and Roosevelt that much of the forests had been destroyed, the rivers polluted and filled with silt, the land eroded, and other resources exploited for private gain. Roosevelt called a conservation conference in 1908. The conservation pioneers, who were usually scientists and experts from the East, talked of planned uses of natural resources. But lumbermen, ranchers, miners, and all who thought they could make a profit out of the land opposed any attempt to turn land over to federal control. Another group, however, led by men like John Muir, a naturalist, thought the land should be preserved in its wild state. Muir helped organize the Sierra Club in 1892 and also led the successful campaign to create Yosemite National Park in California.

As usual, Roosevelt took a middle course, siding with Pinchot and his followers. But during his administration, over 150 million acres were set aside as public land, three times the area of federal lands when he took office.

Progressivism for Whites Only

Like most of his generation, Roosevelt thought in stereotyped racial terms. He believed that blacks and Asians were inferior, and he feared that the Anglo-Saxon race was being threatened in America by massive migrations from southern and eastern Europe. Yet Roosevelt was a politician, and he made gestures of goodwill to most groups. He even invited Booker T. Washington to the White House in 1901, though he was viciously attacked by many in the South for this break in etiquette. He also appointed several qualified blacks to minor federal posts, most notably Dr. William D. Crum to head the Charleston, South Carolina, customs house in 1905. But at other times he seemed insensitive to the needs and feelings of black Americans. This was especially true in his handling of the Brownsville, Texas, riot of 1906. Members of a black army unit stationed there, angered by discrimination against them, rioted one hot August night. Exactly what happened no one was sure, but one white man was killed and several wounded. Waiting until after the midterm elections of 1906, Roosevelt ordered all 167 members of three companies dishonorably discharged. It was an unjust punishment for an unproved crime, and 66 years later the secretary of the army granted honorable discharges to the men, most of them by that time dead.

The progressive era coincided with the years of greatest segregation in the South, but even the most advanced progressives seldom included blacks in their reform schemes. Hull House, like most social settlements, was segregated, although Jane Addams more than most progressives struggled to overcome the racist attitudes of her day. She helped found a settlement that served a black neighborhood in Chicago, and she spoke out repeatedly against lynching. Addams also supported the founding of the National Association for the Advancement of Colored People in 1909, the most important progressive-era organization aimed at promoting equality and justice for black people. Actually it was the work of three other settlement workers and the cooperation of W. E. B. Du Bois that led to the formation of the NAACP.

William English Walling and his wife Anna Strunsky were lecturing in the Midwest in 1908 on the plight of the Russian peasant when they heard of a race riot in Springfield, Illinois. Suddenly the problems of blacks in Abraham Lincoln's hometown seemed more pressing than the difficulties of Russian peasants. Walling wrote an angry article on the black problem, which was read by Mary White Ovington, a New York settlement worker whose book, *Half a Man* (1911), was, next to Du Bois's study, *The Philadelphia Negro* (1899), the best study of the way blacks lived in northern cities. Ovington and Walling involved Henry Moskowitz, another settlement worker and reformer, and together they gained the support of a number of prominent citizens, including Oswald Garrison Villard, grandson of abolitionist William Lloyd Garrison.

The white social reformers enlisted the help of Du Bois, who had moved further away from

Tuskegee Institute followed Booker T. Washington's philosophy of black advancement through accommodation to the white status quo.

the conservative and accommodationist policies of Booker T. Washington. Incensed by the increase in lynching, the disenfranchisement of blacks in most southern states, and the race riots in Springfield, Atlanta, and other cities, Du Bois had called a conference of young and militant blacks in 1905. They met in Canada, not far from Niagara Falls, and issued an angry statement. The Niagara Movement, as it came to be called, was small but distinctly different from Washington's approach. "We want to *pull down* nothing but we don't propose to be pulled down . . . ," the platform announced. "We believe in *taking what we can get* but we don't believe in being satisfied with it and in permitting anybody for a moment to imagine we're satisfied." When the Niagara movement combined with the NAACP, Du Bois became editor of its journal, *The Crisis.* He toned down his rhetoric, but he tried to promote equality for all blacks. The NAACP was a typical progressive organization, seeking to work within the American system to promote reform. But to Roosevelt and to many others who called themselves progressives, the NAACP seemed dangerously radical.

William Howard Taft

After two terms as president, Roosevelt decided to step down. "I believe in a strong executive," he remarked in 1908. "I believe in power, but I believe that responsibility should go with power, and that it is not well that the strong executive should be a perpetual executive." But he apparently regretted his decision even before he left the presidency. He was only 50 years old and at the peak of his popularity and power. Since the United States system of government provides little creative function for former presidents, Roosevelt decided to travel and to go big-game hunting in Africa. But before he left he handpicked his successor.

William Howard Taft, Roosevelt's personal choice for the Republican nomination in 1908, was a distinguished lawyer, federal judge, and public servant. Born in Cincinnati, he had been the first civil governor of the Philippines and secretary of war under Roosevelt. After defeating William Jennings Bryan for the presidency in

1908, he quickly ran into difficulties. In some ways he seemed more progressive than Roosevelt. His administration instituted more suits against monopolies in one term than Roosevelt had in two. He supported the eight-hour day and legislation to make mining safer and urged the passage of the Mann-Elkins Act in 1910, which strengthened the ICC by giving it more power to set railroad rates and extending its jurisdiction over telephone and telegraph companies. Taft also encouraged the process that eventually led to the passage of the federal income tax, which was authorized under the Sixteenth Amendment, ratified in 1913. It probably did more to transform the relationship of the government to the people than all other progressive measures combined.

Taft's biggest problem was his style and personality. He was a huge man, weighing over 300 pounds. Rumors circulated that he found it necessary to have a special oversized bathtub installed in the White House. Easily made fun of, the president had a ponderous prose and a dull speaking style that failed to inspire the public. He also lacked Roosevelt's political skills and angered many of the progressives in the Republican party, especially the midwestern insurgents led by Senator Robert La Follette of Wisconsin. Many progressives were annoyed when he signed the Payne-Aldrich Tariff, which midwesterners thought left rates on cotton and wool cloth and other items too high and played into the hands of the eastern industrial interests. Even Roosevelt was infuriated when his successor reversed many of his conservation policies and fired Chief Forester Gifford Pinchot, who had attacked Secretary of the Interior Richard A. Ballinger for giving away rich coal lands in Alaska to mining interests. Roosevelt broke with Taft, letting it be known that he was willing to run again for president. This set up one of the most exciting and significant elections in American history.

The Election of 1912

Woodrow Wilson won the Democratic nomination for president in 1912. Born two years before Roosevelt, Wilson came from a very different background and would be cast in opposition to the former president during most of his political career. Yet the two had much in common. Both made important contributions to progressivism and to the development of liberalism in America.

Wilson was the son and grandson of Presbyterian ministers. Growing up in a comfortable and intellectual household, he very early seemed more interested in politics than in religion. After graduating from Princeton University in 1879, he studied law at the University of Virginia and practiced law briefly in Atlanta before entering graduate school at The Johns Hopkins University in Baltimore. Soon after receiving his Ph.D. he published a book, *Congressional Government* (1885), that established his reputation as a shrewd analyst of American politics. He taught history briefly at Bryn Mawr College near Philadelphia and at Wesleyan in Connecticut before moving to Princeton. Less flamboyant than Roosevelt, he was an excellent public speaker with the power to convince people with his words.

In 1902, Wilson was elected president of Princeton University, and during the next few years he established a national reputation as an educational leader. His greatest success was the preceptorial system, which brought undergraduates together with young instructors in small groups. A few years later, however, he failed in his attempt to eliminate the elite eating clubs and to make the graduate school the center of the university. Wilson had never lost interest in politics, however, so when offered a chance by the Democratic machine to run for governor of New Jersey, he took it eagerly. In his two years as governor he showed courage as he quickly alienated some of the conservatives who had helped to elect him. Building a coalition of reformers, he worked with them to pass a direct primary law and a workmen's compensation law. He also created a commission to regulate transportation and public utility companies. By 1912, Wilson was not only an expert on government and politics but had also acquired the reputation of a progressive.

Roosevelt, who had been speaking out on a variety of issues since 1910, competed with Taft for the Republican nomination, but Taft, as the incumbent president and party leader, was able to win it. Roosevelt, however, startled the nation by walking out of the convention and forming a new political party, the Progressive party. The new party would not have been formed without Roosevelt, but the party was always more than Roosevelt. It appealed to progressives from all over the country who had become frustrated with the conservative leadership in both parties.

Many social workers and social justice progressives supported the Progressive party because of its platform, which contained provisions they had been advocating for years. The Progressives supported an eight-hour day, a six-day week, the abolition of child labor under age 16, and a federal system of accident, old age, and unemployment insurance. Unlike the Democrats, the Progressives also endorsed woman suffrage. "Just think of having all the world listen to our story of social and industrial injustice and have them told that it can be righted," one social worker exclaimed.

Most of those who supported the Progressives in 1912 did not realistically think they could win, but they were convinced that they could organize a new political movement that would replace the Republican party, just as the Republicans had replaced the Whigs after 1856. To this end, Progressive leaders, led by Kellor, set up the Progressive Service, designed to apply the principles of social research to educating voters between elections.

The Progressive convention in Chicago seemed to many observers more like a religious revival meeting than a political gathering; others thought it seemed like a social work conference. The delegates sang "Onward Christian Soldiers," "The Battle Hymn of the Republic," and "Roosevelt, Oh Roosevelt" (to the tune of "Maryland, My Maryland"). They waved their bandannas, and when Jane Addams rose to second Roosevelt's nomination, a large group of women marched around the auditorium with a banner that read "Votes for Women." The Progressive cause "is based on the eternal principles of righteousness," Roosevelt announced. "In the end the cause itself shall triumph."

The enthusiasm for Roosevelt and the Progressive party was misleading, for behind the unified facade there were many disagreements.

Roosevelt had become more progressive on many issues since leaving the presidency. He even attacked the financiers "to whom the acquisition of untold millions is the supreme goal of life, and who are too often utterly indifferent as to how these millions are obtained." But he was not as committed to social reform in many areas as were some of the delegates. Perhaps the most divisive issue was the controversy over seating black delegates from several southern states. A number of social justice progressives fought hard to include a plank in the platform supporting equality for blacks and for seating the black delegation. Roosevelt, however, thought he had a realistic chance to carry several southern states, and he was not convinced that black equality was an important progressive issue. In the end, no blacks sat with the southern delegates, and the platform made no mention of black equality.

The political campaign in 1912 became a contest primarily between Roosevelt and Wilson, with Taft, the Republican candidate, ignored by most reporters who covered the campaign. On one level the campaign became a debate over political philosophy, concerning the proper relationship of government to society in a modern industrial age. Roosevelt borrowed some of his ideas from a book, *The Promise of American Life* (1909), written by Herbert Croly, a young journalist. But he had also been working out his own philosophy of government. He spoke of the "new nationalism." In a modern industrial society, he argued, large corporations were "inevitable and necessary." What was needed was not the breakup of the trusts but increased power in the hands of the federal government to regulate business and industry and to ensure the rights of labor, women and children, and other groups. He argued for using Hamiltonian means to assure Jeffersonian ends, for using strong central government to guarantee the rights of the people.

Wilson responded with a slogan and program of his own. Using the writings of Louis Brandeis, Wilson talked of the "new freedom." He sought to restore the old forms of economic competition and equality of opportunity and argued against too much federal power. "Free men need no guardians," he argued and suggested that big government would inevitably lead to benefits for big business. "What I fear . . . is a government of experts," Wilson declared, as he attacked Roosevelt's programs as simply "regulated monopoly."

The level of debate during the campaign was

Major Parties in the Presidential Election of 1912

	ELECTORAL VOTE	POPULAR VOTE
Wilson (Democratic)	435	6,296,547
Roosevelt (Progressive / Bull Moose)	88	4,118,571
Taft (Republican)	8	3,486,720

impressive, making this one of the few elections in American history when important ideas were actually discussed. But it is easy to exaggerate the differences between Roosevelt and Wilson. There was some truth in the charge of William Allen White, the editor of the Emporia *Gazette* in Kansas, when he remarked, "Between the New Nationalism and the New Freedom was that fantastic imaginary gulf that always had existed between Tweedle-dum and Tweedle-dee." Certainly in the end the things that Roosevelt and Wilson could agree on were more important than the issues that divided them. Both Roosevelt and Wilson urged reform within the American system. Both defended corporate capitalism and both opposed socialism and radical labor organizations such as the IWW. Both wanted to promote more democracy and strengthen conservative labor unions. Both were very different in style and substance from the fourth candidate, Eugene Debs, who ran on the Socialist party ticket in 1912.

Debs, in 1912, was the most important socialist leader in the country. The socialists, unlike the progressives, argued for fundamental change in the American system. Socialism was always a minority movement in the United States, but it had its greatest success in the first decade of the twentieth century. Thirty-three cities including Milwaukee, Wisconsin; Reading, Pennsylvania; Butte, Montana; Jackson,

Michigan; and Berkeley, California, chose socialist mayors. Socialists Victor Berger from Wisconsin and Meyer London from New York were elected to Congress. The most important socialist periodical, *Appeal to Reason*, published in Girard, Kansas, increased its circulation from about 30,000 in 1900 to nearly 300,000 in 1906. Socialism appealed to a diverse group. Some reformers, such as Florence Kelley and William English Walling, joined the party because of their frustration with the slow progress of reform, but the party also attracted many recent immigrants.

A tremendously appealing figure and a great orator, Debs had run for president in 1900, 1904, and 1908, but in 1912 he reached much wider audiences in many parts of the country. His message differed radically from that of Wilson or Roosevelt. The Socialist party is "organized and financed by the workers themselves," he announced, "as a means of wresting control of government and industry from the capitalists and making the working class the ruling class of the nation and the world." Debs polled almost 900,000 votes in 1912 (6 percent of the popular vote), the greatest vote ever achieved by a socialist in the United States. Wilson received 6.3 million votes, Roosevelt a little more than 4 million, and Taft 3.5 million. But Wilson garnered 435 electoral votes, Roosevelt 88, and Taft only 8.

WOODROW WILSON AND THE NEW FREEDOM

Wilson was elected largely because Roosevelt and the Progressive party split the Republican vote. But once elected, Wilson became a vigorous and aggressive chief executive who set out to translate his ideas about progressive government into legislation. Wilson was the first southerner elected president since Zachary Taylor in 1848 and only the second Democrat since the Civil War. Wilson, like Roosevelt, had to work with his party, and that restricted how progressive he could be. But he was also constrained by his own background and inclinations. Still, like Roosevelt, Wilson became more progressive during his presidency.

Tariff and Banking Reform

Wilson was not as charismatic as Roosevelt. No one called him "Woody." He had a more difficult time relating to people in small groups, but he was an excellent public speaker who dominated through the force of his intellect. He probably had an exaggerated belief in his ability to persuade and a tendency to trust his own intuition too much. Ironically, his early success in getting his legislative agenda through Congress probably contributed to the overconfidence that would get him into difficulty later in foreign affairs. But his ability to push his legislative program through Congress during his first two years in office was matched only by Franklin Roosevelt during the first months of the New Deal and by Lyndon Johnson in 1965.

Within a month of his inauguration, Wilson went before a joint session of Congress to outline his legislative program. He recommended reducing the tariff to eliminate favoritism, freeing the banking system from Wall Street control, and restoring competition in industry. By appearing in person before Congress, he broke a precedent established by Thomas Jefferson. First on his agenda was tariff reform. The Underwood Tariff passed in 1913 was not a free-trade bill, but it did reduce the schedule for the first time in many years.

Attached to the Underwood Tariff bill was a provision for a small and slightly graduated income tax, which had been made possible by the passage of the Sixteenth Amendment. It imposed a modest rate of 1 percent on income over $4,000 (thus exempting a large proportion of the population), with a surtax rising to 6 percent on high incomes. The income tax was enacted to replace the money lost from lowering the tariff. Wilson seemed to have no interest in using it to redistribute wealth in America.

The next item on Wilson's agenda was re-

Many progressives were disappointed in Wilson for his refusal to support a constitutional amendment granting women the right to vote.

form of the banking system. The financial panic of 1907 had revealed the need for a central bank, but few people could agree on the exact nature of the reforms. The progressive faction of the Democratic party, armed with the findings of the Pujo Committee's investigation of the money trust, argued for a banking system and a currency controlled by the federal government. The congressional committee, led by Arsène Pujo of Louisiana, had revealed a massive consolidation of banks and trust companies and a system of interlocking directorates and informal arrangements that concentrated resources and power in the hands of a few firms such as the J. P. Morgan company. But talk of banking reform raised the specter among conservative Democrats and the business community of socialism, populism, and the monetary ideas of William Jennings Bryan.

The bill that passed Congress was a compromise. In creating the Federal Reserve System, it was the first reorganization of the banking system since the Civil War. The bill provided for 12 Federal Reserve Banks and a Federal Reserve Board appointed by the president. The bill also created a flexible currency, based on the federal reserve notes, that could be expanded or contracted as the situation required. The Federal Reserve System was not without its flaws, as later developments would show, and it did not end the power of the large eastern banks; but it was an improvement, and it appealed to the part of the progressive movement that sought order and control.

Despite these reform measures, Wilson was not very progressive in some of his actions during his first two years in office. In the spring of 1914, he failed to support a bill that would have provided long–term rural credit financed by the federal government. He refused to support a woman suffrage amendment, arguing that the states should decide who could vote. He also failed to support an anti–child labor bill after it had passed the House. But most distressing to some progressives, he permitted the segregation of blacks in several federal departments.

Booker T. Washington had remarked on Wilson's election, "Mr. Wilson is in favor of the things which tend toward the uplift, improvement, and advancement of my people, and at his hands we have nothing to fear." But when southern Democrats, suddenly in control in many departments, began dismissing black federal officeholders, especially those "who boss white girls," Wilson did nothing. When the NAACP complained that the shops, offices, rest rooms, and lunchrooms of the Post Office and Treasury Departments and the Bureau of Engraving were segregated, Wilson replied, "I sincerely believe it to be in their [the blacks'] best interest."

Moving Closer to a New Nationalism

How to control the great corporations in America was a question much debated by Wilson and Roosevelt during the campaign. Wilson's solution was the Clayton Act, submitted to Congress in 1914. The bill prohibited a number of unfair trading practices, outlawed the interlocking directorate, and made it illegal for corporations to purchase stock in other corporations if this tended to reduce competition. It was not clear how the government would enforce these provisions and ensure the competition that Wilson's New Freedom doctrine called for, but the bill became controversial for another reason. Labor leaders protested that the bill had no provision exempting labor organizations

from prosecution under the Sherman Anti-Trust Act. When a section was added exempting both labor and agricultural organizations, Samuel Gompers hailed it as labor's Magna Charta. It was hardly that because the courts interpreted the provision so that labor unions remained subject to court injunctions during strikes despite the Clayton Act.

More important than the Clayton Act, which both supporters and opponents realized was too vague to be enforced, was the creation of the Federal Trade Commission (FTC), modeled after the ICC, with enough power to move directly against corporations accused of restricting competition. The FTC was the idea of Louis Brandeis, but it was accepted by Wilson even though it seemed to move him more toward the philosophy of New Nationalism.

The Federal Trade Commission and the Clayton Act did not end monopoly, and the courts in the next two decades did not increase the government's power to regulate business. Yet during Wilson's first two years, more power had been centered in the federal government and in the executive branch. Like Roosevelt, Wilson had not satisfied the advanced progressives, but the outbreak of war in Europe and the need to win the election of 1916 would influence him in becoming more progressive in the next years.

Presidential Elections of the Progressive Era

YEAR	CANDIDATES	PARTY	POPULAR VOTE	ELECTORAL VOTE
1904	THEODORE ROOSEVELT	Republican	7,628,834 (56.4%)	336
	Alton B. Parker	Democratic	5,084,401 (37.6%)	140
	Eugene V. Debs	Socialist	402,460 (3.0%)	0
1908	WILLIAM H. TAFT	Republican	7,679,006 (51.6%)	321
	William J. Bryan	Democratic	6,409,106 (43.1%)	162
	Eugene V. Debs	Socialist	420,820 (2.8%)	0
1912	WOODROW WILSON	Democratic	6,286,820 (41.8%)	435
	Theodore Roosevelt	Progressive	4,126,020 (27.4%)	88
	William H. Taft	Republican	3,483,922 (23.2%)	8
	Eugene V. Debs	Socialist	897,011 (6.0%)	0
1916	WOODROW WILSON	Democratic	9,129,606 (49.3%)	277
	Charles E. Hughes	Republican	8,538,221 (46.1%)	254

Note: Winners' names appear in capital letters.

CONCLUSION: The Limits of Progressivism

The progressive era was a time when many Americans set out to promote reform because they saw poverty, despair, and disorder in the country transformed by immigration, urbanism, and industrialism. The progressives, unlike the socialists, however, saw nothing fundamentally wrong with the American system. Progressivism was largely a middle-class movement that sought to help the poor, the immigrants, and the working class. Yet the poor were rarely consulted about policy, and many groups, especially blacks, were almost entirely left out of reform plans. Progressives had an optimistic view of human nature and an exaggerated faith in statistics, commissions, and committees. They talked of the need for more democracy, but they often succeeded in promoting a government run by experts. They believed there was a need to regulate business, promote efficiency, and spread social justice, but these were often contradictory goals. In the end, their regulatory laws tended to aid business and to strengthen corporate capitalism, while social justice and equal opportunity remained difficult to achieve.

Progressivism was a broad, diverse, and sometimes contradictory movement that had its roots in the 1890s and came to a climax in the early twentieth century. It began with many local movements and moved to the

Key Progressive Era Legislation

YEAR	LEGISLATION	PROVISIONS
1901	New York State Tenement House Law	Prohibited the worst tenement houses; required fire escapes, lights in dark hallways, a window for each room, etc. (Soon copied by other states.)
1902	Maryland Workmen's Compensation Law	Paid workers benefits for injuries on the job.
1902	Wisconsin Direct Primary Law	Allowed voters rather than politicians to select candidates.
1902	Oregon initiative and referendum laws	Gave voters power to initiate legislation and vote on important issues.
1902	National Reclamation Act (Newlands Act)	Set aside proceeds from sale of public lands to promote irrigation projects in the West.
1903	Oregon women's labor law	Limited work for women in industry to ten hours a day.
1903	Elkins Act	Strengthened Interstate Commerce Act by eliminating rebates.
1906	Hepburn Act	Authorized ICC to fix maximum railroad rates.
1906	Pure Food and Drug Act	Prohibited sale and transportation of adulterated or fraudulently labeled foods and drugs.
1906	Meat Inspection Act	Enforced sanitary conditions in meatpacking plants.
1910	Mann Act	Prohibited interstate transportation of women for immoral purposes.
1913	Sixteenth Amendment	Authorized federal income tax.
1915	La Follette Seaman's Act	Regulated conditions of employment of maritime workers.
1916	Federal Farm Loan Act	Provided farmers with low-interest long-term loans.
1916	Federal Child Labor Law	Barred products produced by children from interstate commerce. (Declared unconstitutional in 1918.)
1919	Eighteenth Amendment	Prohibited sale and production of intoxicating liquors.
1920	Nineteenth Amendment	Gave women the right to vote.

state and finally to the national level. Neither Theodore Roosevelt nor Woodrow Wilson was an advanced progressive, but during both administrations, progressivism achieved some success. Both presidents strengthened the power of the presidency, and both promoted the idea that the federal government had the responsibility to regulate and control and to promote social justice. Progressivism would be altered by World War I, but it survived, with its strengths and weaknesses, to have an impact on American society through most of the twentieth century.

Recommended Reading

A good starting point for an exploration of the progressive movement is Arthur S. Link and Richard L. McCormick, *Progressivism* (1983). Robert H. Wiebe, *The Search for Order* (1967) emphasizes the middle-class nature of the movement as well as the drive for efficiency and professionalization. Gabriel Kolko, *The Triumph of Conservatism* (1963) sees most of the campaigns for progressive legislation as led by businessmen for their own advantage. Paul Boyer, *Urban Masses and Moral Order in America, 1820–1920* (1978) finds a continuity of the reform impulse across a century and rates fear of immigrants and the city and a desire for social control as the most important ingredients of progressivism.

Allen F. Davis, *Spearheads for Reform* (1967) and Roy Lubove, *The Progressives and the Slums* (1962) emphasize the social justice movement. Lawrence Cremin, *The Transformation of the School* (1951) is the best book on progressive education. Ruth Rosen, *The Lost Sisterhood* (1982) tells the fascinating story of the crusade against prostitution. David P. Thelen,

The New Citizenship (1972) describes the origins of progressivism in Wisconsin, the state where it reached its greatest triumphs, while Dewey W. Grantham, *Southern Progressivism* (1983) details the impact of progressivism on a region often thought to have been little influenced by the movement. David Brody, *Workers in Industrial America* (1980) and Alice Kessler-Harris, *Out to Work* (1982) both have perceptive chapters on the impact of progressivism on industrial workers.

John Morton Blum, *The Progressive Presidents* (1980) and John Milton Cooper, Jr., *The Warrior and the Priest* (1983) give interesting interpretations of Roosevelt and Wilson. Nick Salvatore, *Eugene V. Debs* (1982) is the best biography of America's most important radical.

Novels include Upton Sinclair's *The Jungle* (1906), a classic muckraking novel about the meatpacking industry, and Charlotte Perkins Gilman's *Her Land* (1915), a story of a female utopia.

TIME LINE

1901	McKinley assassinated; Theodore Roosevelt becomes president Robert La Follette elected governor of Wisconsin Tom Johnson elected mayor of Cleveland Model tenement house bill passed in New York Formation of U.S. Steel
1902	Anthracite coal strike
1903	Women's Trade Union League founded Elkins Act
1904	Roosevelt reelected Lincoln Steffens publishes *The Shame of the Cities*
1905	Frederic C. Howe writes *The City: The Hope of Democracy* Industrial Workers of the World formed
1906	Upton Sinclair publishes *The Jungle* Hepburn Act Meat Inspection Act Pure Food and Drug Act
1907	Financial panic
1908	*Muller* v. *Oregon* *Danbury Hatters* case William Howard Taft elected president
1909	Herbert Croly publishes *The Promise of American Life* NAACP founded
1910	Ballinger-Pinchot controversy Triangle Shirtwaist Company fire Mann-Elkins Act
1911	Frederick Taylor publishes *The Principles of Scientific Management*
1912	Progressive party founded by Theodore Roosevelt Woodrow Wilson elected president Children's Bureau established in Department of Labor Industrial Relations Commission founded
1913	Sixteenth Amendment (income tax) ratified Underwood Tariff Federal Reserve System established Seventeenth Amendment (direct election of senators) passed
1914	Clayton Act Federal Trade Commission Act AFL has over 2 million members Ludlow (Colorado) Massacre

CHAPTER 23
AMERICA IN THE GREAT WAR

On April 7, 1917, the day after the United States officially declared war on Germany, Edmund P. Arpin, Jr., a young man of 22 from Grand Rapids, Wisconsin, decided to enlist in the army. The war seemed to provide a solution for his aimless drifting. It was not patriotism that led him to join the army but his craving for adventure and excitement. A month later, he was at Fort Sheridan, Illinois, along with hundreds of other eager young men, preparing to become an army officer. He felt a certain pride and sense of purpose, and especially a feeling of comradeship with the other men, but the war was a long way off.

Arpin finally arrived with his unit in Liverpool on December 23, 1917, aboard the *Leviathan*, a German luxury liner that the United States had interned when war was declared and pressed into service as a troop transport. In England, he discovered that American troops were not greeted as saviors. Hostility against the Americans simmered partly because of the previous unit's drunken brawls. Despite the efforts of the United States government to protect its soldiers from the sins of Europe, drinking seems to have been a preoccupation of the soldiers in Arpin's outfit. Arpin also learned something about French wine and women, but he spent most of the endless waiting time learning to play contract bridge.

Arpin saw some of the horror of war when he went to the front with a French regiment as an observer, but his own unit did not engage in combat until October 1918, when the war was almost over. He took part in the bloody Meuse-Argonne offensive, which helped end the war. But he discovered that war was not the heroic struggle of carefully planned campaigns that newspapers and books described. War was filled with misfired weapons, mixups, and erroneous attacks. Wounded in the leg in an assault on an unnamed hill and awarded a Distinguished Service Cross for his bravery, Arpin later learned that the order to attack had been recalled, but the word had not reached him in time.

When the armistice came, Arpin was recovering in a field hospital. He was disappointed that the war had ended so soon, but he was well enough to go to Paris to take part in the victory celebration and to explore some of the famous Paris restaurants and nightclubs. In many ways the highlight of his war experiences was not a battle or his medal but his adventure after the war was over. With a friend he went absent without leave and set out to explore Germany. They avoided the military police, traveled on a train illegally, and had many narrow escapes, but they made it back to the hospital without being arrested.

Edward Arpin was in the army for two years. He was one of 4,791,172 Americans who served in the army, navy, or marines. He was one of the 2 million who got overseas, and one of the 230,074 who were wounded. Some of his friends were among the 48,909 who were killed. When he was mustered out of the army in March 1919, he felt lost and confused. Being a civilian was not nearly as exciting as being in the army and visiting new and exotic places.

Arpin eventually settled down. He became a successful businessman, married, and raised a family. A member of the American Legion, he periodically went to conventions and reminisced with men from his division about their escapades in France. Although the war changed their lives in many ways, most would never again feel the same sense of common purpose and adventure. "I don't suppose any of us felt, before or since, so necessary to God and man," one veteran recalled.

This chapter will explore some of the ways the Great War (as Arpin's generation called it) altered the lives of ordinary Americans and also how it influenced the larger forces of history. We will look at the twisted path that led the United States into the war and at the wartime experiences of the men who went overseas as well as those who stayed at home. For some, the war was a great adventure; for others, it led to tragedy and despair. For most, the war was a patriotic crusade, and those opposed to the government's policies were often treated as traitors. The United States continued its rise during the war as a major world power, but the Russian Revolution of 1917 abruptly changed the nature of diplomacy and altered the international agenda. In 1919 and 1920, the Senate rejected membership in the League of Nations, yet the United States could not remain isolated from international problems. In some ways, the war years marked the triumph of progressive reform. In other ways, hate and intolerance characterized the period.

THE EARLY YEARS OF THE WAR

Few Americans expected the Great War that erupted in Europe in the summer of 1914 to affect their lives or alter their comfortable world. When a Serbian student terrorist assassinated Archduke Franz Ferdinand of Austria-Hungary in Sarajevo, the capital of Bosnia, a country most Americans had never heard of, it precipitated a series of events leading to the most destructive war the world had ever known.

Despite Theodore Roosevelt's successful peacekeeping attempts in the first decade of the century (see Chapter 21), relationships among the European powers had not improved in any fundamental way. As European nations built up their military forces, they created a complex series of treaties with one another. Austria-Hungary and Germany (the Central Powers) became military allies, while Britain, France, Italy, and Russia (the Allied Powers) agreed to assist one another in case of attack. Americans stood by in disbelief as the assassination ultimately pulled all the major European powers into the vortex of war.

Education, science, social reform, and negotiation had supposedly replaced all-out war as a way of solving international disputes. "It looks as though we are going to be the age of treaties rather than the age of wars, the century of reason rather than the century of force," a leader of the American peace movement had declared only two years before. But as news of the German invasion of Belgium and reports of the first bloody battles began to reach the United States in late summer, it seemed to most Americans that madness had replaced reason. Europeans "have reverted to the condition of savage tribes roaming the forests and falling upon each other in a fury of blood and carnage," the New York *Times* announced.

The American sense that the nation would never succumb to the barbarism of war, combined with the knowledge that the Atlantic Ocean separated Europe from the United States, contributed to a great sense of relief after the first shock of the war began to wear off. The belief that the United States had no major stake in the outcome of the war and would stay uninvolved was reinforced by Woodrow Wilson's official proclamation of neutrality on August 4, 1914. The president was preoccupied with his own personal tragedy. His wife, Ellen Axson Wilson, died of Bright's disease, at the age of 54, the day after his proclamation. Two weeks later, still engulfed by his own grief, he urged all Americans to "be neutral in fact as well as in name . . . impartial in thought as well as in action." The United States, he argued, must preserve itself "fit and free" in order to do what "is honest and disinterested . . . for the peace of the world." But it was obvious that it was going to be difficult to stay uninvolved, at least emotionally, with the battlefields of Europe.

American Reactions

Many social reformers who had devoted their lives to eliminating poverty and suffering despaired when they heard the news from Europe. Even during its first months, the war seemed to deflect energy away from reform. "We are three thousand miles away from the smoke and flames of combat, and have not a single regiment or battleship involved," remarked John Haynes Holmes, a liberal New York minister. "Yet who in the United States is thinking of recreation centers, improved housing or the minimum wage?" Settlement worker Lillian Wald responded to the threat of war by helping to lead a "woman's peace" parade down Fifth Avenue. Fifteen hundred women, all dressed in black, marched to protest the war. Jane Addams of Hull House helped to organize the Woman's Peace party. Drawing upon traditional conceptions of female character, she argued that women had a special responsibility to work for peace and to speak out against the blasphemy of war because women and children suffered most in any war, especially in a modern war where civilians as well as soldiers became targets.

While many people worked to promote an international plan to end the war through mediation, others could hardly wait to take part in the great adventure. Hundreds of young American men, most of them students or recent college graduates, volunteered to join ambulance

European Alignments in 1914

units, to take part in the war effort without actually fighting. Among the most famous of them were Ernest Hemingway, John Dos Passos, and E. E. Cummings, who later turned their wartime adventures into literary masterpieces. Others volunteered for service with the French Foreign Legion or joined the Lafayette Escadrille, a unit of pilots made up of well-to-do American volunteers attached to the French army. Many of these young men were inspired by an older generation who pictured war as a romantic and manly adventure. One college president talked of the chastening and purifying effect of armed conflict, and Theodore Roosevelt preached the virtues of the strenuous life and projected an image of war that was something like a football game where red-blooded American men could test their idealism and manhood.

Alan Seeger, a graduate of Harvard in 1910, was one of those who believed in the romantic and noble purpose of the war. He had been living

The war in Europe appealed to the sense of adventure in many young American men. However, as in all wars, the women they left behind found it hard to say goodbye.

in Paris since 1912, and when the war broke out, he quickly joined the French Foreign Legion. For the next two years, he wrote sentimental poetry, articles, and letters describing his adventures. "You have no idea how beautiful it is to see the troops undulating along the road . . . with the captains and lieutenants on horse back at the head of the companies," he wrote his mother. When Seeger was killed in 1916, he became an instant hero. Some called him "America's Rupert Brooke," after the gallant British poet who died early in the war.

Many Americans visualized war as a romantic struggle for honor and glory because the only conflict they remembered was the "splendid little war" of 1898. For them war meant Theodore Roosevelt charging up San Juan Hill and Commodore Dewey destroying the Spanish fleet in Manila harbor without the loss of an American life. Many older Americans recalled the Civil War, but the horrors of those years had faded, and only the memory of heroic triumphs remained. As Oliver Wendell Holmes, the Supreme Court justice who had been wounded in the Civil War, remarked, "War, when you are at it, is horrible and dull. It is only when time has passed that you see that its message was divine."

The reports from the battlefields, even during the first months of the war, should have indicated that the message was anything but divine, but most Americans ignored that. The fighting soon bogged down to a costly and bloody routine. Soldiers on both sides dug miles of trenches and strung out barbed wire to protect them. Thousands were killed in offenses that gained only a few yards or nothing at all. Jane Addams was troubled by other aspects of the struggle. When she returned from Europe in 1915, she reported the stories she had heard, that the young men were tired of war and that the troops were given alcohol and drugs to get into the spirit of the bayonet charge. But she was denounced as a silly old maid who knew nothing of the military and foolishly diminished the bravery and the honor of the soldiers.

Theodore Roosevelt was one of those who attacked Addams. Along with his friend Leonard Wood, the army chief of staff, he led a movement to prepare American men for war. Wood was determined that upper-class and college-educated men be ready to lead the nation into battle. In 1913, he established a camp for college men at Plattsburg, New York, to give them some experience with military life, with order, discipline, and command. By 1915, thousands had crowded into the Plattsburg Training Camp; even the mayor of New York enrolled. The young men learned to shoot rifles and to endure long marches and field exercises. But most of all, they associated with one another. Gathered around the campfire at night, they heard Wood and other veterans tell of winning glory and honor on the battlefield. In their minds at least, they were already leading a bayonet charge against the enemy, and the enemy was Germany.

Difficulties of Neutrality

Despite Wilson's efforts to promote neutrality, most Americans favored the Allied cause. Some 8 million Austrian- and German-Americans lived in the United States, and some of them naturally supported the cause of the Central Powers. Yet most were so thoroughly Americanized that they had no particular interest in the war. The hatred of some of the Irish against the British led them to take sides not so much for Germany as against England. A few Swedish-Americans distrusted Russia so vehemently that they had difficulty in supporting the Allies. A number of American scholars, physicians, and intellectuals had fond memories of studying in Germany. To them, Germany meant great universities and cathedrals, music and culture. It also represented social planning, health insurance, unemployment compensation, and many of the programs for which the progressives had been fighting.

For most Americans, however, the ties of language and culture tipped the balance toward the Allies. After all, did not the English-speaking people of the world have special bonds and special responsibilities to promote civilization and ensure justice in the world? American connections with the French were not so close, but they were even more sentimental. The French, everyone remembered, had supported the American Revolution, and the French people had given the Statue of Liberty, the very symbol of American opportunity and democracy, to the United States.

Other reasons made real neutrality nearly impossible. Trade, both exports and imports, between the United States and the Allies was much more important than with the Central Powers, and people who controlled trade and ran the great financial institutions favored the Allies. Wilson's advisers, especially Robert Lansing and Edward House, openly supported the French and the British. Most of the newspapers in the country were also owned and edited by people with close ethnic, cultural, and sometimes economic ties to the British and the French. The newspapers were quick to picture the Germans as barbaric Huns and to accept and embellish the atrocity stories that came from the front, some of them planted by British propaganda experts. Gradually for Wilson, and probably for most Americans, the idea that all Europeans were barbaric and decadent was replaced with the perception that England and France were fighting for civilization and culture against the forces of Prussian evil. That did not mean, however, that the American people were willing to go to war to preserve the civilization. They were willing to let France and England do that.

Woodrow Wilson also sympathized with the Allies for practical and idealistic reasons. He wanted to keep the United States out of the war, but he had no objection to using force to promote diplomatic ends. "When men take up arms to set other men free, there is something sacred and holy in the warfare," he had written. Moreover, Wilson believed that by keeping the United States out of the war, he might control the peace. The war, he hoped, would show the futility of imperialism and of empires and would usher in a world where there would be free trade in products and in ideas. The United States had a special role to play in this new world and in leading toward an orderly international society. "We are the mediating nation of the world [and] we are therefore able to understand all nations."

To remain neutral while maintaining trade with the belligerents became increasingly difficult. To remain neutral while having something to say about the peace eventually became impossible. It was the need to trade and the desire to control the peace that finally led the United States into the Great War.

World Trade and Neutrality Rights

The United States was part of an international economic community in 1914 in a way that it had not been a hundred years earlier during the last great world war, the Napoleonic Wars. The outbreak of war in Europe in the summer of 1914 caused an immediate economic panic in the United States. On July 31, 1914, the Wilson administration closed the stock exchange to prevent an unloading of European securities and a panic of selling. It also adopted a policy discouraging loans by American banks to belligerent nations. Most difficult was the matter of neutral trade. Wilson insisted on the rights of Americans to trade with both the Allies and the Central Powers, but Great Britain instituted an effective naval blockade, mined the North Sea, and began seizing American ships, even those carrying food and raw materials to Italy, the Netherlands, and other neutral nations. The first crisis that Wilson faced was whether or not to accept the British blockade, which went far beyond traditional international law. To do so would be to surrender one of the rights he believed in most ardently, the right of free trade.

Wilson eventually backed down and accepted British control of the sea. His conviction that the destinies of the United States and Great Britain were intertwined outweighed his idealistic belief in free trade. Consequently, American trade with the Central Powers declined between 1914 and 1916 from $169 million to just over $1 million and with the Allies increased during the same period from $825 million to over $3 billion. At the same time, the United States government eased the restrictions on private loans to belligerents. In March 1915, the House of Morgan loaned the French government $50 million, and in the fall of 1915, the French and British obtained an unsecured loan of $500 million from American banks. With dollars as well as sentiments, the United States gradually ceased to be neutral.

Germany retaliated against British control of the seas with submarine warfare. The new weapon, the U-boat (*Unterseeboot*), created unprecedented problems. According to nineteenth-century international law, a belligerent warship was obligated to warn a passenger or merchant ship before attacking, but the chief advantage of the submarine was surprise. Rising to the surface to issue a warning would have meant being blown out of the water by an armed merchant ship.

On February 4, 1915, Germany announced a submarine blockade of the British Isles. Until Britain gave up its campaign to starve the German population, the Germans would sink even neutral ships. Wilson warned Germany that it would be held to "strict accountability" for illegal destruction of American ships or lives.

In March 1915, a British liner en route to Africa was sunk, with the loss of 103 lives, one of them an American. How should the United States respond? Wilson's advisers could not agree. Robert Lansing, a legal counsel at the State Department, urged the president to issue a strong protest, charging a breach of international

The sinking of the Lusitania shocked Americans and illustrated the complexity and horror of modern warfare.

law. William Jennings Bryan, the secretary of state, on the other hand argued that an American traveling on a British ship was guilty of "contributory negligence" and urged Wilson to prohibit all Americans from traveling on belligerent ships in the war zone. Wilson never did settle the dispute, for on May 7, 1915, a greater crisis erupted. A German U-boat torpedoed the British luxury liner *Lusitania* off the Irish coast. The liner, which was not armed but was carrying war supplies, sank within 18 minutes. Nearly 1,200 people, including many women and children, drowned. Among the dead were 128 Americans. Suddenly Americans were introduced to the horror of total war fought with modern weapons, a war that killed civilians, including women and children, just as easily as it killed soldiers.

The tragedy horrified most Americans. Newspapers denounced the act as "mass murder." One writer called the Germans "wild beasts." Some even called for a declaration of war. Wilson and most Americans had no idea of going to war in the spring of 1915, but the president refused to take Bryan's advice and prevent further loss of American lives by simply prohibiting all Americans from traveling on belligerent ships. Instead, he sent a series of protest notes demanding reparation for the loss of American lives and a pledge from Germany that it would cease attacking ocean liners without warning. Bryan resigned as secretary of state over the tone of the notes and charged that the United States was not being truly neutral. Some denounced Bryan as a traitor, but others charged that if the United States really wanted to stay out of the war, Bryan's position was more logical, consistent, and humane than Wilson's. The president replaced Bryan with Robert Lansing, who was much more eager than Bryan to oppose Germany, even at the risk of war.

The tense situation was eased late in 1915, when the German ambassador radioed from the battleship *Arabic* his promise (the *Arabic* pledge) that Germany would not attack ocean liners without warning. But the *Lusitania* crisis caused an outpouring of books and articles urging the nation to prepare for war. The National Security League, the most effective of the preparedness groups, called for a bigger army and navy, a system of universal military training, and "patriotic education and national sentiment and service among the people of the United States."

Organizing on the other side were a group of progressive reformers and social workers who formed the American Union Against Militarism. They feared that those urging preparedness were deliberately setting out to destroy liberal social reform at home and to promote imperialism abroad.

But Wilson sympathized with the preparedness groups to the extent of asking Congress on November 4, 1915, for an enlarged and reorganized army. The bill met great opposition, especially from southern and western congressmen, but the Army Reorganization Bill that Wilson signed in June 1916 increased the regular army to just over 200,000 and integrated the National Guard into the defense structure. Few Americans, however, expected those young men to go to war. One of the most popular songs of 1916 was "I Didn't Raise My Boy to Be a Soldier." Even before American soldiers arrived in France, however, Wilson used the army and the marines in Mexico and Central America.

Intervening in Mexico and Central America

Woodrow Wilson came to office in 1913 with a plan to promote liberal and humanitarian ends, not only in domestic policies but also in foreign affairs. Wilson had a vision of a world purged of imperialism, a world of free trade, but a world where American ideas and American products would find their way. Combining the zeal of a Christian missionary with the conviction of a college professor, he spoke of "releasing the intelligence of America for the service of mankind" and of enriching the commerce of the United States and the world "with the products of our mines, our farms, and our factories, with the creations of our thought and the fruits of our character." With his secretary of state, William Jennings Bryan, Wilson denounced the "big stick" and "dollar diplomacy" of the Roosevelt and Taft years. Yet in the end, his administration used force more systematically than those of his predecessors. The rhetoric was different, yet just as much as Roosevelt, Wilson was concerned with maintaining order and stability in the countries to the south in order to promote American economic and strategic interests.

At first Wilson's foreign policy seemed to be reversing some of the most callous aspects of dollar diplomacy in Central America. Bryan signed a treaty with Colombia in 1913 that agreed to pay $5 million for the loss of Panama and virtually apologized for the way the Roosevelt administration had treated Colombia. The Senate, not so willing to admit that the United States had been wrong, refused to ratify the treaty. But a new spirit permeated foreign policy.

The change in spirit proved illusory. After a disastrous civil war in the Dominican Republic, the United States offered in 1915 to take over the country's finances and police force. But when the Dominican leaders rejected a treaty making their country virtually a protectorate of the United States, Wilson ordered in the marines. They took control of the government in May 1916. Although the Americans built roads, schools, and hospitals, many people resented the American presence. In neighboring Haiti, the situation was somewhat different, but the results were similar. The marines landed at Port-au-Prince in the summer of 1915 to prop up a pro-American regime. In Nicaragua, the Wilson administration kept the marines sent by Taft in 1912 to keep the pro-American regime of Aldolfo Díaz in place and acquired the right, through treaty, to intervene at any time to preserve order and protect American property. Except for a brief period in the mid-1920s, the marines remained until 1933.

Wilson's policy of intervention ran into greatest difficulty in Mexico, a country that had been ruled for more than 40 years by Porfirio Díaz, a dictator who kept order and welcomed American investors. Indeed, by 1910, more than 40,000 American citizens lived in Mexico, and more than a billion dollars of American money was invested in the country. Americans controlled 75 percent of the mines, 70 percent of the rubber, and 60 percent of the oil. In 1911, however, Francisco Madero, a reformer who wanted to destroy the privileges of the upper classes, overthrew Díaz. Two years later, he was deposed and murdered by order of Victoriano Huerta, the head of the army. This was the situation when Wilson became president.

To the shock of many diplomats and businessmen, Wilson refused to recognize the Huerta government. Everyone admitted that Huerta was a ruthless dictator, but diplomatic recognition, the exchange of ambassadors, and the regulation of trade and communication had never meant approval. In the world of business and diplomacy, it merely meant that a particular government was in power. But Wilson, to the great concern of American businessmen, set out to remove what he called a "government of butchers." "The United States Government intends not merely to force Huerta from power," he wrote to a British diplomat, "but also to exert every influence it can to secure Mexico a better government under which all contracts and business concessions will be safer than they have ever been."

Although Wilson's intervention in Mexico drew criticism from many, others felt he was not forceful enough with the Huerta government.

At first Wilson applied diplomatic pressure. Then, using a minor incident as an excuse, he asked Congress for power to involve American troops if necessary. Few Mexicans liked Huerta, but they liked even less the idea that a *Norte Americano* was interfering in their affairs. Hence they rallied around the dictator. As they had in 1847, the United States landed troops at Veracruz. Angry Mexican mobs destroyed American property wherever they could find it. Many Europeans and Latin Americans as well as Americans were outraged by Wilson's action.

Wilson's military intervention succeeded in forcing Huerta out of power, but a civil war between forces led by Venustiano Carranza and those led by General Francisco "Pancho" Villa ensued. When Villa made a raid on Columbus, New Mexico, in March 1916, Wilson sent an expedition led by Brigadier General John Pershing to track down Villa and his men. The strange and comic scene developed of an American army charging 300 miles into Mexico unable to catch the retreating villain. Not surprisingly,

given the history of Mexican-American relations, the Mexicans feared that Pershing's army was planning to occupy northern Mexico. Carranza shot off a bitter note to Wilson accusing him of threatening war, but Wilson refused to withdraw the troops. Tensions rose. An American patrol attacked a Mexican garrison, with loss of life on both sides. Just as war seemed inevitable, Wilson agreed to call the troops home and to recognize the Carranza government. But this was in January 1917, and if it had not been for the growing crisis in Europe, it is likely that war would have resulted.

The tragedy was that Wilson, who idealistically wanted the best for the people of Mexico and Central America and who thought he knew exactly what they needed, managed to intervene too often and too blatantly to protect the strategic and economic interests of the United States. In the process, his policy alienated one-time friends of the United States. His policies would contribute to future difficulties in both Latin America and Europe.

United States Involvement in the Caribbean

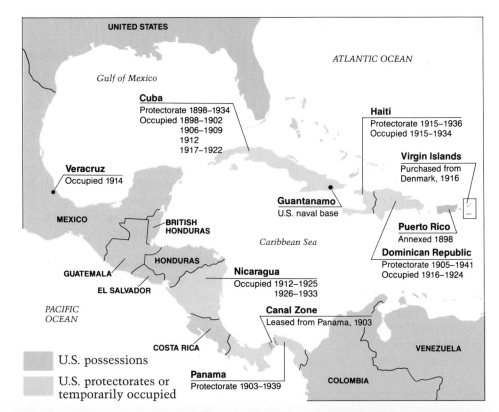

THE UNITED STATES ENTERS THE WAR

America's decision to go to war in 1917 was opposed by a significant minority, and the decision would remain controversial when it was reexamined in the 1930s. But once involved, the government and the American people made the war into a patriotic crusade that touched on all aspects of American life.

The Election of 1916

American political campaigns do not stop even in times of international crisis. As 1915 turned to 1916, Wilson had to think of reelection as well as of preparedness, submarine warfare, and the Mexican campaign. At first glance, the president's chances of reelection seemed poor. He had won in 1912 only because Theodore Roosevelt and the Progressive party had split the Republican vote. If those who had supported the Progressives in 1912 returned to the Republican fold, Wilson's chances were slim indeed. Because the Progressive party had done very badly in the 1914 congressional elections, Roosevelt gave signs that he would seek the Republican nomination rather than be a third-party candidate.

Wilson was aware that he had to win over those who had voted for Roosevelt in 1912. In January 1916, he appointed Louis D. Brandeis to the Supreme Court. The first Jew ever to sit on the highest court, Brandeis was confirmed over the strong opposition of many legal organizations. His appointment pleased the social justice progressives because he had always championed reform causes. They made it clear to Wilson that the real test for them was whether or not he supported the anti-child labor and workmen's compensation bills pending in Congress.

In August, Wilson put heavy pressure on Congress and obtained passage of the Workmen's Compensation Bill, which gave some protection to federal employees, and the Keatings-Owen Child Labor Bill, which prohibited the shipment in interstate commerce of goods produced by children under 14 and in some cases under 16. This bill, which was later declared unconstitutional, was a far-reaching proposal that for the first time used federal control over interstate commerce to dictate the conditions under which businessmen could manufacture products.

To attract farm support, Wilson pushed for passage of the Federal Farm Loan Act, which created 12 Federal Farm Loan Banks to extend long-term credit to farmers. Urged on by organized labor as well as by many progressives, he supported the Adamson Act, which established an eight-hour day for all interstate railway workers. Within a few months, Wilson reversed the New Freedom doctrines he had earlier supported and brought the force of the federal government into play on the side of reform. The flurry of legislation early in 1916 provided one climax to the progressive movement. The strategy seemed to work, for progressives of all kinds enthusiastically endorsed the president.

The election of 1916, however, turned as much on foreign affairs as on domestic policy. The Republicans ignored Theodore Roosevelt and nominated instead the staid and respectable Charles Evans Hughes, a former governor of New York and Supreme Court justice. Their platform called for "straight and honest neutrality" and "adequate preparedness." In a bitter campaign, Hughes attacked Wilson for not more vigorously promoting American rights in Mexico and for giving in to the unreasonable demands of labor. Wilson, on his part, implied that the election of Hughes would mean war with both Mexico and Germany and that his opponents were somehow not "100 percent Americans." As the campaign progressed, the peace issue became more and more important, and the cry "He kept us out of war" echoed through every Democratic rally. It was a slogan that would seem strangely ironic in only a few months.

The election was extremely close. In fact, Wilson went to bed on election night thinking he had lost the presidency. The election was not finally decided until it was learned that California had gone Democratic (by less than 4,000 votes). Wilson won by carrying the West as well as the South.

Deciding for War

Wilson's victory in 1916 was generally interpreted as a mandate for staying out of the European war. But the campaign rhetoric made the president nervous. He had tried to emphasize Americanism, not neutrality. As he told one of his advisers, "I can't keep the country out of war. They talk of me as though I were a god. Any little German lieutenant can put us into war at any time by some calculated outrage."

People who supported Wilson as a peace candidate applauded in January 1917 when he went before the Senate to clarify the American position on a negotiated settlement of the war. The German government had earlier indicated that it might be willing to go to the conference table. Wilson outlined a plan for a negotiated settlement before either side had achieved victory. It would be a peace among equals, "a peace without victory," a peace without indemnities and annexations. The peace settlement Wilson outlined contained his idealistic vision of the postwar world as an open marketplace, and it could have worked only if Germany and the Allies were willing to settle for a draw instead of victory.

The German government refused to accept a peace without victory, probably because early in 1917 the German leaders thought they could win. On January 31, 1917, the Germans announced that they would sink on sight any ship, belligerent or neutral, sailing toward England or France. A few days later, in retaliation, the United States broke diplomatic relations with Germany. But Wilson—and probably most Americans—still hoped to avert war without shutting off American trade. As goods began to pile up in warehouses and American ships stayed idly in port, however, pressure mounted to arm American merchant ships. An intercepted telegram from the German foreign secretary, Arthur Zimmermann, to the German minister in Mexico increased anti-German feeling. If war broke out, the German minister was to offer Mexico the territory it had lost in Texas, New Mexico, and Arizona in 1848. In return, Mexico would join Germany in a war against the United States. When this telegram was released to the press on March 1, 1917, many Americans demanded war against Germany. Wilson still hesitated.

As the country waited on the brink of war, news of revolution in Russia reached Washington. That event would prove as important as the war itself. The March 1917 revolution in Russia was a spontaneous uprising of the workers, housewives, and soldiers against the czarist government because of the intolerable conditions that the war had brought. The army had suffered staggering losses at the front. The civilian population was in desperate condition. Food was scarce, and the railroads and industry had nearly collapsed. The rebels overthrew Czar Nicholas II and established a republic led by Alexander Kerensky. At first Wilson and other Americans were enthusiastic. The overthrow of the feudal aristocracy seemed in the spirit of the American Revolution. Wilson hoped the new regime would fight the war more vigorously against Germany and then join in organizing a world free of imperialism and dictatorship. But within months, the revolution took a more extreme turn. Lenin (whose real name was Vladimir Ilyich Ulyanov) returned from exile in Switzerland and led the radical Bolsheviks to victory over the Kerensky regime in November 1917.

Lenin, a brilliant lawyer and revolutionary tactician, was a follower of Karl Marx (1818–1883). Marx, a German intellectual and radical philosopher, had described the alienation of the working class under capitalism and predicted a growing split between the proletariat (the unpropertied workers) and the capitalists. Lenin extended Marx's ideas and argued that capitalist nations would eventually be forced to go to war over raw materials and markets. Believing that capitalism and imperialism went hand in hand, Lenin, unlike Wilson, argued that the only way to end imperialism was to end capitalism. It was the new Soviet Union, not the United States, that was the model for the rest of the world to follow; communism, Lenin predicted, would eventually dominate the globe. The Russian Revolution posed a threat to Wilson's vision of the world and to his plan to bring the United States into the war "to make the world safe for democracy."

More disturbing than the first news of revolution in Russia, however, was the situation in the North Atlantic, where German U-boats sank five American ships between March 12 and March 21, 1917. Wilson no longer hesitated. On April 2, he urged Congress to declare war. His words conveyed a sense of mission about the United States' entry into the war, but Wilson's voice was low and somber. "It is a fearful thing," he concluded, "to lead this great, peaceful people into war, into the most terrible and disastrous of all wars. . . ." The war resolution swept the Senate 82 to 6 and the House of Representatives 373 to 50.

Once war was declared, most Americans forgot their doubts and joined the glorious cause. Young men rushed to enlist; women volun-

The declaration of war gave Americans a sense of purpose and adventure that was created in part by recruiting posters and government propaganda.

teered to become nurses or to serve in other ways. Towns were united by patriotism.

A Patriotic Crusade

The declaration of war did not unite everyone in the country behind the war effort. Some pacifists and socialists opposed the war, while a black newspaper, *The Messenger*, decried the conflict. "The real enemy is War rather than Imperial Germany," wrote Randolph Bourne, a young New York intellectual. "We are for peace," Morris Hillquit, a socialist leader, announced. "We are unalterably opposed to the killing of our manhood and the draining of our resources in a bewildering pursuit of an incomprehensible 'democracy' . . . a pursuit which begins by suppressing the freedom of speech and press and public assemblage, and by stifling legitimate political criticism." "To whom does war bring prosperity . . . ?" Senator George Norris of Nebraska asked on the Senate floor. "Not to the soldier . . . not to the broken hearted widow . . . not to the mother who weeps at the death of her brave boy. . . . War brings no prosperity to the great mass of common patriotic citizens. We are going into war upon the command of gold. . . . I feel that we are about to put the dollar sign on the American flag."

For most Americans in the spring of 1917, the war seemed remote. A few days after the war was declared, a Senate committee listened to a member of the War Department staff list the vast quantities of materials needed to supply an American army in France. One of the senators, jolted awake, exclaimed, "Good Lord! You're not going to send soldiers over there, are you?"

To convince senators and citizens alike that the war was real and that American participation was just, Wilson appointed a Committee on Public Information, headed by George Creel, a muckraking journalist from Denver. The Creel Committee launched a gigantic propaganda campaign to persuade the American public that the United States had gone to war to promote the cause of freedom and democracy and to prevent the barbarous hordes from overrunning Europe and eventually the Western Hemisphere. The committee organized a national network of "four-minute men," local citizens with the proper political views who could be used to whip up a crowd to a frenzy of patriotic enthusiasm. These local rallies, enlivened by bands and parades, urged people of all ages to support the war effort and to buy war bonds. The Creel Committee also produced literature for the schools, much of it prepared by college professors who volunteered their services. One pamphlet, titled *Why America Fights Germany*, described in lurid detail a possible German invasion of the United States. The committee also prepared short propaganda movies.

The patriotic crusade soon became stridently anti-German and anti-immigrant. Most school districts banned the teaching of German. In the words of the California Board of Education, German was "a language that disseminates the ideals of autocracy, brutality and hatred." Anything German became suspect. Sauerkraut was renamed "liberty cabbage," and German measles became "liberty measles." Music by German composers was often banned from symphony concerts. Many German-Americans lost their jobs and were ostracized by their neighbors. South Dakota prohibited the use of German on the telephone, and in Iowa a state official announced, "If their language is disloyal, they should be imprisoned. If their acts are disloyal, they should be shot." Occasionally the patriotic fever led to violence. The most notorious incident happened in St. Louis, which had a large German population. Robert Prager, a young German-American, was seized by a mob in April 1918, stripped of his clothes, dressed in an American flag, marched through the streets, and lynched. The eventual trial led to the acquittal of the ringleaders on the grounds that the lynching was a "patriotic murder."

The Wilson administration, of course, did not condone violence and murder, but war always leads to extremist behavior. Not only German-Americans were suspect, but also radicals, pacifists, or anyone who raised doubts about the American war efforts or the government's policies. In New York, the black editors of *The Messenger* were given 2½-year jail sentences for the paper's article "Pro-Germanism Among Negroes." In Wisconsin, Senator Robert La Follette, who had voted against the war resolution, was burned in effigy and censored by the faculty of the University of Wisconsin. At a number of universities, professors were dismissed, sometimes for as little as questioning the morality or the necessity of America's participation in the war. James M. Cattell, one of the country's leading psychologists, lost his job at Columbia University for mildly criticizing American policies and for being a nonconformist. Heated patriotism, as it often does, led to fear of subversion and irrational hate.

On June 15, 1917, Congress, at Wilson's behest, passed the Espionage Act, which provided imprisonment of up to 20 years or a fine of up to $10,000 (or both) for persons who incited rebellion, made false reports to help the enemy, or tried to obstruct the recruiting operation or the draft. The act also allowed the postmaster general to prohibit from the mails any matter he thought advocated treason or forcible resistance to United States laws. The act was used to stamp out dissent, even to discipline anyone who questioned the administration's policies. Using the act, Postmaster General Albert S. Burleson banned the magazines *American Socialist* and *The Masses* from the mails.

Congress later added the Trading with the Enemy Act and a Sedition Act. The latter prohibited disloyal, profane, scurrilous, or abusive remarks about the form of government, flag, or uniform of the United States. It even prohibited citizens from opposing the purchase of war bonds. In the most famous case tried under the act, Eugene Debs was sentenced to ten years in prison for opposing the war. In 1919, the Supreme Court upheld the conviction, even though Debs had not explicitly urged the violation of the draft laws. Not all Americans agreed with the decision, for while still in prison Debs polled close to one million votes in the presidential election of 1920. In the end, 2,168 persons were prosecuted and 1,055 were convicted under the Espionage and Sedition acts. But these figures do not include the thousands informally persecuted and deprived of their liberties and their right of free speech by Americans who succumbed to the fear brought on by wartime hysteria.

A group of amateur loyalty enforcers, called the American Protective League, cooperated with the Justice Department. They often reported nonconformists and anyone who did not appear 100 percent loyal. People were arrested for criticizing the Red Cross or a government agency. One woman was sent to prison for writing, "I am for the people and the government is for the profiteers." Ricardo Flores Magon, a leading Mexican-American labor organizer in the Southwest, was sentenced to 20 years in prison for criticizing Wilson's Mexican policy. In Cincinnati, a pacifist minister, Herbert S. Bigelow, was dragged from the stage where he was about to give a speech, taken to a wooded area by a mob, bound and gagged, and whipped. The attorney general of the United States, speaking of those who opposed the government policies, said, "May God have mercy on them for they need expect none from an outraged people and an avenging government."

The Civil Liberties Bureau, an outgrowth of the American Union Against Militarism, protested the blatant abridgment of freedom of speech during the war, but the protests fell on deaf ears at the Justice Department and in the White House. Rights and freedoms have been reduced or suspended during all wars, but the massive disregard for basic rights was greater during World War I than during the Civil War. This was ironic because Wilson had often written and spoken of the need to preserve freedom of speech and civil liberties. During the war, however, he tolerated the vigilante tactics of his own Justice Department, offering no more than feeble protest. Wilson was so convinced his cause was just that he ignored the rights of those who opposed him.

Raising an Army

How should a democracy recruit an army in time of war? The debate over a volunteer army versus the draft had been going on for several years before the United States entered the war. People who favored some form of universal military service argued that college graduates, farmers, and young men from the slums of eastern cities could learn from one another as they trained together. The opponents of a draft pointed out that people making such claims were most often the college graduates, who assumed they would command the boys from the slums. The draft was not democratic, they

argued, but the tool of an imperialist power bent on ending dissent. "Back of the cry that America must have compulsory service or perish," one of the opponents charged, "is a clearly thought out and heavily backed project to mold the United States into an efficient, orderly nation, economically and politically controlled by those who know what is good for the people." Memories of massive draft riots during the Civil War also led some to fear a draft.

Wilson and his secretary of war, Newton Baker, both initially opposed the draft. Baker, formerly a progressive mayor of Cleveland, was rumored to be a pacifist. In the end, both Wilson and Baker concluded that the draft was the most efficient way to organize military manpower. Ironically, it was Theodore Roosevelt who tipped Wilson in favor of the draft. Even though his health was failing and he was blind in one eye, the old Rough Rider was determined to recruit a volunteer division and lead it personally against the Germans. The officers would be Ivy League graduates and men trained at the Plattsburg camp, with some places reserved for the descendants of prominent Civil War generals and a few French officers, in memory of Lafayette. There would be a German-American regiment and a black regiment (led by white officers). Roosevelt pictured himself leading this mixed but brave and virile group to France to restore the morale of the Allied troops and win the war.

The thought of his old enemy Theodore Roosevelt blustering about Europe so frightened Wilson that he gave his support to the Selective Service Act in part, at least, to prevent such volunteer outfits as Roosevelt planned. Yet controversy filled Congress over the bill, and the House finally insisted that the minimum age for draftees should be 21, not 18. On June 5, 1917, some 9.5 million men between the ages of 21 and 31 registered, with little protest. In August 1918, the act was extended to men between the ages of 18 and 45. In all, over 24 million men registered and over 2.8 million were inducted, making up over 75 percent of those who served in the war.

The draft worked well, but it was not quite the perfect system that Wilson claimed. Most Americans took seriously their obligation of "service" during time of war, but there were flaws in the system. Because so much of the control was vested in the local draft boards, favoritism and political influence allowed some to stay at home. Draft protests erupted in a few places, the largest in Oklahoma, where a group of tenant farmers planned a march on Washington to take over the government and end the "rich man's war." The Green Corn Rebellion, as it came to be called, died before it got started. A local posse arrested about 900 rebels and took them off to jail.

Some men escaped the draft. Some were deferred because of war-related jobs, while others resisted by claiming exemption for reasons of conscience. The Selective Service Act did exempt men who belonged to religious groups that forbade members from engaging in war, but religious motivation was often difficult to define, and nonreligious conscientious objection was even more complicated. Thousands of conscientious objectors were inducted. Some served in noncombat positions; others went to prison. Roger Baldwin, a leading pacifist, was jailed for refusing military service. But Norman Thomas, a socialist, urged young men to register for the draft and to express their dissent within the democratic process.

THE MILITARY EXPERIENCE

Family albums in millions of American homes contain photographs of young men in uniform, some of them stiff and formal, some of them candid shots of soldiers on leave in Paris or Washington or Chicago. These photographs testify to the importance of the war to a generation of Americans. For years afterward, the men and women who lived through the war sang "Tipperary," "There's a Long, Long Trail," and "Pack Up Your Troubles" and remembered rather sentimentally what the war had meant to them. For some, the war was a tragic event. But for others it was a liberating experience and the most exciting period in their lives.

The American Doughboy

The typical soldier, according to the Medical Department, stood 5 feet 7½ inches tall, weighed 141½ pounds, and was about 22 years old. He was given a physical exam, an intelligence test, and a psychological test, and he probably watched a movie called *Fit to Fight*, which warned him about the dangers of venereal disease. The majority of the American soldiers had not attended high school. The median amount of education for native whites was 6.9 years and for immigrants 4.7 years but was only 2.6 years for southern blacks. As many as 31 percent of the recruits were declared illiterate, but the tests were so primitive that they probably tested social class more than anything else. More than half the recent immigrants from eastern Europe ranked in the "inferior" category. Fully 29 percent of the recruits were rejected as physically unfit for service, which shocked the health experts.

Most World War I soldiers were ill-educated and unsophisticated young men, quite different from Ernest Hemingway's heroes or even from Edmund Arpin. They came from the farms, small towns, and urban neighborhoods. They came from all social classes and ethnic groups, yet most were transformed into soldiers. In the beginning, however, they didn't look the part because uniforms and equipment were in short supply. Many men had to wear their civilian clothes for months, and they often wore out their shoes before they were issued army boots. "It was about two months or so before I looked really like a soldier," one recruit remembered.

The military experience changed the lives and often the attitudes of many young men. Women also served with the army. Some went overseas as nurses and telephone operators. Others volunteered for a tour of duty with the Red Cross, the Salvation Army, or the YMCA. Yet the military experience in World War I was predominantly male. Even going to training camp was a new and often frightening experience. A leave in Paris or London, or even in New York or New Orleans, was an adventure to

Many American women served overseas as nurses with the Red Cross or Salvation Army. They also worked in field kitchens.

remember for a lifetime. Even those who never got overseas or who never saw a battle would recall their wartime experiences with growing fondness as the years went by. They joined the American Legion, whose purpose was "to preserve the memories and incidents of our associates in the great war . . . to consecrate and sanctify our comradeship." They also experienced more subtle changes. Many soldiers saw their first movie in the army or had their first contact with trucks and cars. Military service changed the shaving habits of a generation because the new safety razor was standard issue. The war also led to the growing popularity of the cigarette rather than the pipe or cigar because a pack of cigarettes fitted comfortably into a shirt pocket and a cigarette could be smoked during a short break. The war experience also caused many men to abandon the pocket watch for the more convenient wristwatch, which had been considered effeminate before the war.

The Black Soldier

Shortly after the United States entered the war, W. E. B. Du Bois, the black leader and editor of *The Crisis,* urged blacks to close ranks and support the war. Although Du Bois did not speak

for all blacks, he and others predicted that the war experience would cause the "walls of prejudice" to crumble gradually before "the onslaught of common sense." The walls did not crumble, and the black soldier was never treated equally or with fairness during the war. But many blacks served with distinction, and many had their own perceptions changed by the army experience. Blacks had served in all American wars, and many fought valiantly in the Civil War and the Spanish-American War. Yet black soldiers had most often been assigned to menial tasks and kept in segregated units. Black leaders hoped it would be different this time.

The Selective Service Act made no mention of race, and blacks in most cases registered without protest. But many whites, especially in the South, feared having too many blacks trained in the use of arms. This fear was increased in August 1917, when racial violence erupted in Houston, Texas, involving soldiers from the regular army's all-black 24th Infantry Division. Harassed by the Jim Crow laws, which had been tightened for their benefit, a group of soldiers went on a rampage, killing 17 white civilians. Over 100 soldiers were court martialed; 13 were condemned to death. Those

Assigned to segregated units, black soldiers were also excluded from white recreation facilities. Here black women in Newark, New Jersey, aided by white social workers, sponsored a club to entertain "their men in the service."

convicted were hanged three days later before any appeals could be filed.

This violence, coming only a month after a race riot in East St. Louis, Illinois, brought on in part by the migration of blacks from the South to the area, caused great concern about the handling of black soldiers. Secretary of War Baker made it clear that the army had no intention of upsetting the status quo, but the appointment of Emmett J. Scott, secretary of Tuskegee Institute, as a special assistant to Baker reassured some blacks. Yet the basic government policy was of complete segregation and careful distribution of black units throughout the country.

Some blacks were trained as junior officers and were assigned to the all-black 92nd Division, where the high-ranking officers remained white. But a staff report decided that "the mass of colored drafted men cannot be used for combatant troops." Most of the black soldiers, including about 80 percent of those sent to France, were used as stevedores and common laborers. Usually they were supervised by white noncommissioned officers. "Everyone who has handled colored labor knows that the gang bosses must be white if any work is to be done," remarked Lieutenant Colonel U. S. Grant, the grandson of the Civil War general. Other black soldiers were used as servants, drivers, and porters for the white officers. It was a demeaning and ironic policy for a government that advertised itself as standing for justice, honor, and democracy.

Over There

The war that Wilson declared the war to make the world safe for democracy was at once a traditional and a revolutionary struggle. It was the last time that cavalry played any important part in battle and the first to dramatize the significance of technology to victory. As the British cavalry charged German lines with sabers aloft, machine guns mowed them down, just as machine guns slaughtered the thousands of soldiers who leaped from their trenches in vain efforts to win a few yards of enemy territory. Airplanes, used early in the war only for observation, by 1918 were creating terror below with their bombs. Tanks made their first appear-

ance in 1916. Chemical warfare in the form of poison gas introduced a whole new dimension to warfare and dramatized that the day of chivalry had ended.

To this ghastly war, in which both attackers and defenders suffered huge numbers of casualties, Americans made important contributions. In fact, without their help, the Allies might have lost. But the American contribution was most significant only in the war's final months. When the United States entered the conflict in the spring of 1917, the fighting had dragged on for nearly three years. After a few rapid advances and retreats, the war in western Europe had settled down to a tactical and bloody stalemate. The human costs of trench warfare were horrifying. In one battle in 1916, a total of 60,000 British soldiers were killed or wounded in a single day, yet the battle lines did not move an inch. By the spring of 1917, the British and French armies were down to their last reserves. Italy's army had nearly collapsed. In the east, the Russians were engaged in a bitter internal struggle, and in November the Bolshevik Revolution would cause them to sue for a separate peace, freeing the German divisions on the eastern front to join in one final assault in the west.

World War I was incredibly costly in lives lost and property destroyed.

Historians have discovered that movies, if carefully studied, reveal dress and hairstyles, customs, social attitudes, and other aspects of life during the period in which they were made. Even more revealing in some ways are films designed explicitly to educate and indoctrinate. Most of the early films were made simply to entertain, but very quickly government officials, businessmen, and others realized the power of the new medium. Thomas Edison made propaganda films about the dangers of tuberculosis as early as 1910, and by the time of World War I, others were making short films to show the public how to prevent everything from typhoid fever to tooth decay.

After the United States entered World War I, the Commission on Training Camp Activities made a film called *Fit to Fight* that was shown to almost all male servicemen. It was an hourlong drama following the careers of five young recruits. Four of them, by associating with the wrong people and through lack of willpower, caught venereal disease. The film interspersed a simplistic plot with grotesque shots of men with various kinds of venereal disease. The film also glorified athletics, especially football and boxing, as a substitute for sex. It emphasized the importance of patriotism and purity for America's fighting force. In one scene, Bill Hale, the only soldier in the film to remain pure, breaks up a peace rally and beats up the speaker. "It serves you right," the pacifist's sister remarks; "I'm glad Billy punched you."

Fit to Fight was so successful that the government commissioned another film, *The End of the Road*, to be shown to women who lived near military bases. The film is the story of Vera and Mary. Although still reflecting progressive attitudes, the film's message is somewhat different from *Fit to Fight*. Vera's strict mother tells her daughter that sex is dirty, leaving Vera to pick up "distorted and obscene" information about sex on the street. She falls victim to the first man who comes along and contracts a venereal disease. Mary, on the other hand, has an enlightened mother who explains where babies come from. When Mary grows up, she rejects marriage and becomes a professional woman, a nurse. In the end, she falls in love with a doctor and gets married. *The End of the Road* has a number of subplots and many frightening shots of syphilitic sores. Several illustrations show the dangers of indiscriminate sex. Among

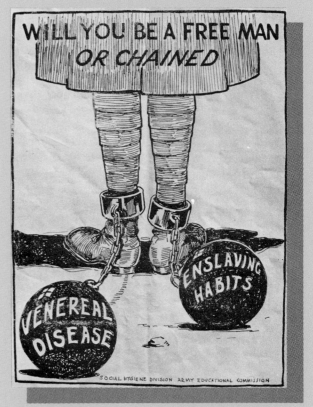

Social hygiene poster issued by the U.S. Commission on Training Camps during World War I

other things, the film preached the importance of science, sex education, and the need for self-control. A quotation from the description of *The End of the Road* provided by the government for those who used the film is reprinted here.

What do the anti-VD films tell us about the attitudes, ideas, and prejudices of the World War I period? What images do they project about men, women, and sex roles? Would you find the same kind of moralism, patriotism, and fear of VD today? Have attitudes toward sex changed? Were you shown sex education films in school? Were they like these? Who sponsored them? What can historians learn from such films? How do other movies—popular feature films as well as documentaries—reflect American culture and American values today?

Scenes from the War Department Commission on Training Camps' film Fit to Fight

THE END OF THE ROAD

This is an extraordinary motion picture prepared by the War Department Commission on Training Camp Activities as a part of the Social Hygiene campaign of the United States Government. It handles certain social and sex problems in their relation to women with a frank treatment which is a direct consequence of a new attitude engendered by the war.

These problems have been made at once more acute and more complex by the war. War conditions have disturbed the emotional equilibrium of the people and have tended to multiply the intricacies of sex reactions, particularly among young girls brought into social contact with the soldier. The film is intended to stimulate and strengthen the efforts being made to teach the womanhood and girlhood of our country the vital need of right social adjustments. . . .

Inasmuch as one of the most terrible and socially vital results of sexual misconduct is venereal infection, this has been advisedly stressed, though not accentuated. Throughout, the effort has been to make disease appear to be, as it actually is in life, the often inevitable price of loose living, ignorance, thoughtlessness, and irresponsibility. Realism of the most striking sort is used in this picture. Some clinical cases shown, for example, were photographed in the women's wards, Blackwell's Island, New York.

The fundamental idea of the film is educational, but, quite inevitably, it contains a definite trend throughout towards the moral inspiration which follows any exposition of fine examples and standards of living contrasted with those of opposite stamp.

The film may with propriety be shown to mixed audiences, whether of boys and girls, or adults, though it was designed primarily for girls and women. It presents a valuable lesson to boys and men, for it tellingly illustrates the tragedies resulting from the so-called double standard. Parents, especially mothers, will find in the film the answer to many of their questions and doubts.

The Allies desperately needed fresh American troops, but those troops had to be trained, equipped, and transported to the front. That took time.

A few token American regiments arrived in France in the summer of 1917 under the command of General John J. "Black Jack" Pershing, a tall, serious, Missouri-born graduate of West Point. He had fought in the Spanish-American War and led the Mexican expedition in 1916. When the first troops marched in a parade in Paris on July 4, 1917, the emotional French crowd shouted, "Vive les Américains," and showered them with flowers, hugs, and kisses. But the American commanders were worried that many of their soldiers were so inexperienced that they did not even know how to march, let alone fight. The first Americans saw action near Verdun in October 1917. By March 1918, over 300,000 American soldiers had

reached France, and by November 1918, more than 2 million.

One reason that the United States forces were slow to see actual combat was Pershing's insistence that they be kept separate from the French and British divisions. An exception was made for four regiments of black soldiers who were assigned to the French army. Despite the American warning to the French that they should not overpraise the black troops or "spoil the Negroes" by allowing them to mix with the French civilian population, these soldiers fought so well that the French later awarded three of the regiments the Croix de Guerre, their highest unit citation.

In the spring of 1918, with Russia out of the war and with the British blockade becoming more and more effective, the Germans launched an all-out, desperate offensive to win the war before full American military and industrial

The Western Front of the Great War in 1918

power became a factor in the contest. By late May, the Germans had pushed to within 50 miles of Paris. American troops were thrown into the line and helped stem the German advance at Château-Thierry, Belleau Wood, and Cantigny, place names that would later be endowed with almost sacred significance by the proud survivors. Americans also took part in the Allied offensive led by General Ferdinand Foch of France in the summer of 1918.

In September, over one-half million American troops were involved in the first distinctly American offensive action near St. Mihiel. One enlisted man remembered how he "saw a sight which I shall never forget. It was zero hour and in one instant the entire front as far as the eye could reach in either direction was a sheet of flame, while the heavy artillery made the earth quake." The Americans suffered over 7,000 casualties, but they captured more than 16,000 German soldiers. The victory, even if it came against exhausted and retreating German troops, seemed to vindicate Pershing's insistence on a separate American army. The British and French commanders were critical of what they considered the disorganized, inexperienced, and ill-equipped American forces. They especially denounced the quality of the American high-ranking officers. One French report in the summer of 1918 suggested that it would take at least a year before the American army could become a "serious fighting force."

In a few months more, the war would be over. Over a million American soldiers took part in the final Allied offensive near the Meuse River and the Argonne forest. It was in this battle that Edmund Arpin was wounded. Many of the men were inexperienced, and some, who had been rushed through training as "90-day wonders," had never handled a rifle before arriving in France. There were many disastrous mistakes and bungled situations. The most famous blunder was the "lost battalion." An American unit advanced beyond its support and was cut off and surrounded. The battalion suffered 70 percent casualties before it could be rescued.

The performance of the all-black 92nd Division was also controversial. The 92nd had been deliberately dispersed around the United States and had never trained as a unit. Its higher officers were white and constantly asked to be transferred. Many of its men were only partly trained and poorly equipped, and they were constantly being called away from their military duties to work as stevedores and common laborers. At the last minute during the Meuse-Argonne offensive, the 92nd was assigned to a particularly difficult position on the line. They had no maps and no wire-cutting equipment. Battalion commanders lost contact with their men, and on several occasions the men broke and ran in the face of enemy fire. The whole division was withdrawn in disgrace, and this incident was used for years to argue that black soldiers would never make good fighting men. Those who made this argument forgot the difficulties under which the 92nd fought and the valor and courage shown by those troops assigned to the French army.

With few exceptions, the Americans fought hard and well. The French and British criticized American inexperience and disarray, but they admired their exuberance, their "pep," and marveled at their extravagance. The ability to move huge numbers of men and equipment efficiently was a major American achievement. One British officer, surveying the abundance of American men and materiel, remarked, "For any particular work they seem to have about five times as much of both as we do." They suffered over 120,000 casualties in the Meuse-Argonne campaign alone. Sometimes it seemed that they simply overwhelmed the enemy with their numbers. One officer estimated that he lost ten soldiers for every German his men killed in the final offensive. Despite the worldwide influenza epidemic of 1918, which eventually killed more American soldiers than did German bullets, the American Expeditionary Force was probably the healthiest army ever assembled. The American army lost 15 of every 1,000 soldiers per year to disease, compared to 65 per 1,000 in the Civil War.

The war produced a few American heroes. Sergeant Alvin York, a former conscientious objector from Tennessee, was probably the most famous. Using only his rifle and pistol, he single-handedly killed or captured 160 Germans. The press made him into a celebrity, but his heroics were not typical. The war was finally won with artillery and the machine gun and, near the end, by the tank, the truck, and the airplane. "To be shelled when you are in the open is one of the most terrible of human experiences," one American soldier wrote. "You hear this rushing, tearing sound as the thing comes toward you, and then the huge explosion as it strikes, and infinitely worse, you see its hideous work as men stagger, fall, struggle, or lie quiet and unrecognizable."

The United States entered the war late but still lost more than 48,000 men and had many more wounded. But the British lost 900,000 men, the French 1.4 million, and the Russians 1.7 million. American units fired French artillery pieces; American soldiers were usually transported in British ships and wore helmets and other equipment modeled after the British. The United States purchased clothing and blankets, even horses, in Europe. American fliers, including heroes like Eddie Rickenbacker, flew French and British planes. The United States contributed huge amounts of men and supplies in the last months of the war, and that finally tipped the balance. But they had entered late and sacrificed little compared to France and England. That would influence the peace settlement.

DOMESTIC IMPACT OF THE WAR

For at least 30 years before the United States entered the Great War, a debate raged over the proper role of the federal government in regulating industry and protecting people who could not protect themselves. Controversy also centered on the question of how much power the federal government should have to tax and control individuals and corporations, and over the proper relation of the federal government to state and local governments. There had been little agreement, even within the Wilson administration, over the proper role of the federal government. In fact, Wilson had only recently moved away from what he defined in 1912 as the New Freedom. But the war and the problems it raised increased the power of the federal government in a variety of ways. The debate did not end, but the United States emerged from the war a more modern nation, with more power residing in Washington.

Financing the War

The war by one calculation cost the United States over $33 billion, though if one adds interest and veterans benefits, the total reaches nearly $112 billion. Early in the war, when an economist suggested that the war might cost the United States $10 billion, everyone laughed. Yet many in the Wilson administration knew the war was going to be expensive, and they set out to raise the money by borrowing and by increasing taxes.

Secretary of the Treasury William McAdoo, who had grown up in Georgia and Tennessee but had built a successful career on Wall Street, shouldered the task of financing the war. He studied the policies that Treasury Secretary Salmon Chase had followed during the Civil War. He decided that Chase had made a mistake in not appealing to the emotions of the people. A war must be "a kind of crusade," he remarked. His campaign to sell war bonds or liberty bonds to ordinary American citizens at a very low interest rate called forth patriotic sentiment. "Lick a Stamp and Lick the Kaiser," one poster urged. Celebrities such as film stars Mary Pickford and Douglas Fairbanks promoted the bonds, and McAdoo employed the Boy Scouts to sell them. "Every Scout to Save a Soldier" was the slogan. He even implied that people who did not buy bonds were traitors. "A man who can't lend his government $1.25 per week at the rate of 4% interest is not entitled to be an American citizen," he announced. A banner flew over the main street in Gary, Indiana, which made the point of the campaign clear: "ARE YOU WORTHY TO BE FOUGHT AND DIED FOR? BUY LIBERTY BONDS."

The public responded enthusiastically, but they discovered after the war that their bonds had dropped to about 80 percent of their face value. Because the interest on the bonds was tax-exempt, well-to-do citizens profited more from buying the bonds than did ordinary men, women, and children who joined the bond drives. But the wealthy were not as pleased with McAdoo's other plan to finance the war by raising taxes. The War Revenue Act of 1917 boosted the tax rate sharply, levied an excess profits tax, and increased estate taxes. Another bill the next year raised the tax on the largest incomes to 77 percent. The wealthy protested, but a number of progressives were just as unhappy with the bill, for they wanted to confiscate all income over $100,000 a year. Despite taxes and liberty bonds, however, World War I, like the Civil War, was financed in large part by inflation. Food prices, for example, nearly doubled between 1917 and 1919.

Increasing Federal Power

At first Wilson tried to work through a variety of state agencies to mobilize the nation's resources. It was quickly apparent, however, that more central control and authority was needed, so he created a series of federal agencies to deal with the war emergency. The first crisis was food. Poor grain crops for two years and an increasing demand for American food in Europe resulted in shortages. To solve the problem, Wilson appointed Herbert Hoover, a young engineer who had won great prestige as head of the Commission for Relief of Belgium, to head the Food Administration. Hoover set out to meet the crisis not so much through government regulation as through an appeal to the patriotism of farmers and consumers alike. He instituted a series of "wheatless" and "meatless" days and urged housewives to cooperate. In Philadelphia, a large sign announced, "FOOD WILL WIN THE WAR; DON'T WASTE IT."

Women emerged during the war as the most important group of consumers. They were urged to save, just as later they would be urged to buy. The *Ladies' Home Journal* announced, "To lose the war because we were unwilling to make the necessary efforts and the required sacrifices in regard to the food supply would be one of the most humiliating spectacles in history."

The Wilson administration used the power of the federal government to organize the re-

Increased taxes and the sale of Liberty Bonds were not enough to finance the war effort; inflation made up the difference.

sources of the country in the war effort. The War Industries Board, led by Bernard Baruch, a shrewd Wall Street broker, used the power of the government to control scarce materials and, on occasion, to set prices and priorities. The government itself went into the shipbuilding business. At the largest shipyard, at Hog Island, near Philadelphia, as many as 35,000 men were employed, but the yard did not launch its first ship until the late summer of 1918. For all the efforts of the Emergency Fleet Corporation, American ships could not be produced quickly enough to affect the outcome of the war.

The government also got into the business of running the railroads. When a severe winter and a lack of coordination brought the rail system to near collapse in December 1917, Wilson put all the nation's railroads under the control of the United Railway Administration. The government spent more than $500 million to improve the rails and equipment, and during the 1918 the railroads did run more efficiently than they had under private control. Some businessmen complained of "war socialism," and they resented the way government agencies forced them to comply with rules and regulations. But most came to agree with Baruch that business had much to gain from a close working relationship with government. They could improve the quality of their products, promote efficiency, and increase profits.

War Workers

The Wilson administration sought to protect and extend the rights of organized labor during the war, while at the same time mobilizing the manpower necessary to keep the factories running. The National War Labor Board insisted on adequate wages and reduced hours, and it tried to prevent the exploitation of women and children working under government contracts. On one occasion, when a munitions plant refused to accept the War Labor Board's decision, the government simply took over the factory. At the same time, when workers threatened to strike, the board often ruled that they could work or be drafted into the army.

The Wilson administration, however, favored the conservative labor movement of Samuel Gompers and the AFL; at the same time, the Justice Department proceeded to put the radical Industrial Workers of the World "out of business." Beginning in September 1917, federal agents conducted massive raids on IWW offices and arrested most of the leaders. The government tolerated the ruthless activity of vigilante groups around the country. In Bisbee, Arizona, the local sheriff, with 2,000 deputies, rounded up 1,200 striking workers and transported them by boxcar to New Mexico. They spent two days in the desert heat without food or water before being rescued. In Butte, Montana, six masked men brutally murdered Frank Little, an IWW organizer. "Had he been arrested and put in jail for his seditious and incendiary talks," Senator H. L. Meyers of Montana suggested, "he would not have been lynched."

Samuel Gompers took advantage of the crisis to strengthen the AFL's position to speak for labor. He lent his approval to administration policies by making clear that he opposed the IWW and the socialists and communists as well. Convincing Wilson that it was important to protect the rights of organized labor during wartime, he announced that "no other policy is compatible with the spirit and methods of democracy." As the AFL won a voice in homefront policy, its membership increased from 2.7 million in 1916 to over 4 million in 1917. Organized labor's wartime gains, however, would prove only temporary.

The war opened up industrial employment opportunities for black men. With 4 million men in the armed forces and the flow of immigrants interrupted by the war, American manufacturers for the first time hired blacks in large numbers. In Chicago before the war, only 3,000 black men held factory jobs. In 1920, more than 15,000 did. Many were doing work that had once been reserved for whites.

The hope of finding an industrial job in a northern city encouraged black families to leave the South, where most blacks had remained after the Civil War. This movement north, often called the Great Migration, continued in the postwar decades. It was the beginning of a significant change in the character of the black community.

The war also created new employment opportunities for women. Posters and patriotic speeches urged women to do their duty for the war effort. "Not Just Hats Off to the Flag, but Sleeves Up for It," one poster announced. Another showed a woman at her typewriter, the shadow of a soldier in the background, with the message: "Stenographers, Washington Needs You."

Women responded to these appeals out of patriotism, as well as out of a need to increase their earnings and to make up for inflation, which diminished real wages. "I used to go to work when my man was sick," one woman reported, "but this is the first time I ever had to go to work to get enough money to feed the kids, when he was working regular." Women went into every kind of industry. They labored in brickyards and in heavy industry, became conductors on the railroad, and turned out shells in munition plants. They even organized the Woman's Land Army to mobilize female labor for the farms. They demonstrated that women could do any kind of job, whatever the physical or intellectual demands. "It was not until our men were called overseas," one woman banking executive reported, "that we made any real onslaught on the realm of finance, and became tellers, managers of departments, and junior and senior officers." One black woman who gave up her position as a live-in servant to work in a paper-box factory declared, "I'll never work in nobody's kitchen but my own any more. No indeed, that's the one thing that makes me stick to this job, but when you're working in anybody's kitchen, well you out of luck. You almost have to eat on the run; you never get any time off." As black women moved out of domestic service, they took jobs in textile mills or even in the stockyards. Racial discrimination, however, even in the North, prevented them from moving too far up the occupational ladder.

Even though women demonstrated that they could take over jobs once thought suitable only for men, their progress during the war proved temporary. Only about 5 percent of the women employed during the war were new to the work force, and almost all of them were unmarried. For most it meant a shift of occupations or a move up to a better-paying position. Moreover,

The absence of able-bodied men brought women into heavy industry and other formerly male occupations. However, the war did not change the idea that women's place was in the home.

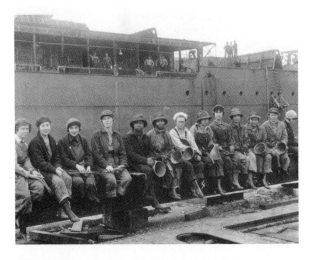

war accelerated trends already under way. It increased the need for telephone operators, sales personnel, secretaries, and other white-collar jobs, and in these occupations women soon became a majority. Telephone operator, for example, became an almost exclusively female job. There were 15,000 operators in 1900 but 80,000 in 1910, and by 1917 women represented 99 percent of all operators as the telephone network spanned the nation. In the end, the war provided limited opportunities for some women, but it did not change the dominant perception that a woman's place was in the home. And after the war was over, the men returned, and the gains made by women almost disappeared. There were 8 million women in the work force in 1910, and only 8.5 million in 1920.

The Climax of Progressivism

Many of the progressives, especially the social justice progressives, opposed the United States' entry into the war until a few months before the United States declared war. But after April 1917, many began to see the "social possibilities of war." They deplored the death and destruction, the abridgment of freedom of speech, and the patriotic spirit that accompanied the war. But they applauded the social planning stimulated by the conflict. They approved the Wilson administration's support of collective bargaining, the eight-hour day, and protection for women and children in industry. They applauded Secretary of War Baker when he announced, "We cannot afford, when we are losing boys in France, to lose children in the United States at the same time." They welcomed the experiments with government-owned housing projects, and they applauded the wartime successes of woman suffrage and prohibition. Many endorsed the government takeover of the railroads and control of business during the war.

For many social justice progressives who had fought hard, long, and frustrating battles trying to humanize the industrial city, the very fact that suddenly people in high places were listening and approving programs was stimulating. "Enthusiasm for social service is epidemic," one social worker wrote in the summer of 1917; "a luxuriant crop of new agencies is springing up.

We scurry back and forth to the national capital; we stock offices with typewriters and new letterheads; we telephone feverishly regardless of expense, and resort to all the devices of efficient 'publicity work.' . . . It is all very exhilarating, stimulating, intoxicating."

One of the best examples of the influence of the progressives on wartime activities was the Commission on Training Camp Activities, set up early in the war to solve the problem of mobilizing, entertaining, and protecting American servicemen at home and abroad. Chairman of the commission was Raymond Fosdick, a former settlement worker and expert on European and American police systems. He appointed a number of experts from the Playground Association, the YMCA, and social work agencies. They set out to organize community singing and baseball, establish post exchanges and theaters, and even provide university extension lectures to educate and protect the servicemen. The overriding assumption was that the military experience would help produce better citizens, people who would be ready to vote for social reform once they returned to civilian life.

The Commission on Training Camp Activities also incorporated the progressive crusades against alcohol and prostitution. The Military Draft Act prohibited the sale of liquor to men in uniform and gave the president power to establish zones around all military bases where prostitution and alcohol would be prohibited. Some military commanders protested, and at least one city official argued that prostitutes were "God-provided means for the prevention of the violation of innocent girls, by men who are exercising their 'God-given passions.'" Yet the commission, with the full cooperation of the Wilson administration, set out to wipe out sin, or at least to put it out of the reach of servicemen. "Fit to fight" became the motto. "Men must live straight if they would shoot straight," one official announced. It was a typical progressive effort combining moral indignation with the use of the latest scientific prophylaxis. The commissioners prided themselves on having eliminated by 1918 all the red-light districts near the training camps and producing what one person called "the cleanest army since Cromwell's day." When the boys go to France, the secretary of war

remarked, "I want them to have invisible armour to take with them. I want them to have armour made up of a set of social habits replacing those of their homes and communities."

France tested the "invisible armour." The government, despite hundreds of letters of protest from American mothers, decided that it could not prevent the soldiers from drinking wine in France, but it could forbid them to buy or accept as gifts anything but light wine and beer. If Arpin's outfit is typical, the soldiers often ignored the rules. Sex was even more difficult to regulate in France than liquor. Both the British and the French armies had tried to solve the problem of venereal disease by licensing and inspecting prostitutes. Clemenceau, the French premier, found it difficult to comprehend the American attitude toward prostitution, and on one occasion he accused the Americans of spreading disease throughout the French civilian population and graciously offered to provide the Americans with licensed prostitutes. General Pershing considered the letter containing the offer "too hot to handle." So he gave it to Fosdick, who showed it to Baker, who remarked, "For God's sake, Raymond, don't show this to the President or he'll stop the war." The Americans never accepted Clemenceau's offer, and he continued to be baffled by the American progressive mentality.

Suffrage for Women

In the fall of 1918, while American soldiers were mobilizing for the final offensive in France and hundreds of thousands of women were working in factories and serving as Red Cross and Salvation Army volunteers near the army bases, Woodrow Wilson spoke before the Senate to ask its support of woman suffrage, which he maintained was "vital to the winning of the war." Wilson had earlier opposed the vote for women. His positive statement at this late date was not important, but his voice was a welcome addition to a rising chorus of support for an amendment to the Constitution that would permit the female half of the population to vote.

Not everyone favored woman suffrage. Many people still argued that the vote would make women less feminine, more worldly, and less able to perform their primary tasks as wives and mothers. The National Association Opposed to Woman Suffrage argued that it was only radicals who wanted the vote and declared that woman suffrage, socialism, and feminism were "three branches of the same Social Revolution."

Carrie Chapman Catt, an efficient administrator and tireless organizer, devised the strategy that finally secured the vote for women. Catt, who grew up in Iowa, joined the Iowa Woman Suffrage Association as a young woman of 28 shortly after her first husband died. Before remarrying, she insisted on a legal agreement giving her four months a year away from her husband to work for the suffrage cause. In 1915, she became president of the National American Woman Suffrage Association (NAWSA), the organization founded by Elizabeth Cady Stanton and Susan B. Anthony in 1869.

Catt coordinated the state campaigns with the work in Washington, directing a growing army of dedicated workers. The Washington headquarters sent precise information to the states on ways to pressure congressmen in local districts. In Washington, they maintained a file on each congressman and senator. "There were facts supplied by our members in the states about his personal, political, business and religious affiliations; there were reports of interviews . . . there was everything that could be discovered about his stand on woman suffrage. . . ."

The careful planning began to produce results, but a group of more militant reformers were impatient with the slow progress and broke off from NAWSA to form the National Women's Party (NWP) in 1916. This group was led by Alice Paul, a Quaker from New Jersey, who had participated in some of the suffrage battles in England. Paul and her group picketed the White House, chained themselves to the fence, and blocked the streets. They carried banners that asked, "MR. PRESIDENT, HOW LONG MUST WOMEN WAIT FOR LIBERTY?" In the summer of 1917, the government arrested over 200 women and charged them with "obstructing the sidewalk." It was just the kind of publicity the militant group sought, and they made the most of it. Wilson, fearing even more embarrassment, began to cooperate with the more moderate reformers.

The careful organizing of the NAWSA and the more militant tactics of the NWP both contributed to the final success of the woman suffrage crusade. The war did not cause the passage of the Nineteenth Amendment, but it did accelerate the process. Fourteen state legislatures petitioned Congress in 1917 and 26 in 1919, urging the enactment of the amendment. Early in 1919, the House of Representatives passed the suffrage amendment 304 to 90, and the Senate approved by a vote of 56 to 25. Fourteen months later, the required 36 states had ratified the amendment, and women at last had the vote. "We are no longer petitioners," Catt announced in celebration. "We are not wards of the nation, but free and equal citizens." "This is the woman's age," declared Margaret Dreier Robins of the Woman's Trade Union League. "At last after centuries of disabilities and discriminations, women are coming into the labor and festival of life on equal terms with men."

PLANNING FOR PEACE

Woodrow Wilson turned the participation of the United States in the war into a religious crusade to change the nature of international relations. It was a war to make the world safe for democracy—and more. On January 8, 1918, in part to counteract the Bolshevik charge that the war was merely a struggle among imperialist powers, he announced his plan to organize the peace. Called the Fourteen Points, it argued for "open covenants of peace openly arrived at," freedom of the seas, equality of trade, the self-determination of all peoples. But his most important point, the fourteenth, called for an international organization, a "league of nations," to preserve peace.

The Paris Peace Conference

Late in 1918, Wilson announced that he would break precedent and become the first president to leave the country while in office in order to head the American delegation in Paris. Wilson was determined to go to Paris, believing that he alone could overcome the forces of greed and imperialism in Europe and bring peace to the world. Wilson and his entourage of college professors, technical experts, and advisers set sail for Paris on the *George Washington* on December 4, 1918. Lansing, House, and a number of other able men were there. Conspicuously missing, however, was Henry Cabot Lodge or any other Republican senator.

This would prove a serious blunder, for the Senate would have to approve any treaty negotiated at Paris. In the congressional elections of 1918, the Republicans had gained control of both houses of Congress. It is difficult to explain Wilson's lack of political shrewdness, except that he disliked Lodge intensely and hated the process of political bargaining and compromise. Preferring to announce great principles, he had supreme confidence in his ability to persuade and to get his way by appealing to the people.

Wilson's self-confidence grew during a triumphant tour through Europe before the conference. The ordinary people greeted him like a savior who had brought the tragic war to an end. The American president had greater difficulty convincing the political leaders at the peace conference of his genius or his special grace. At Paris, he faced the reality of European power politics and the personalities of David Lloyd George of Great Britain, Vittorio Orlando of Italy, and Georges Clemenceau of France. John Maynard Keynes, the young British economist who was an observer at the peace conference, described Wilson as a "blind and deaf Don Quixote" and pictured him as an impractical idealist trapped and manipulated by the shrewd European diplomats.

Wilson was more naive and more idealistic than his European counterparts, but despite being ill part of the time, he was a clever negotiator who won many concessions at the peace table, sometimes by threatening to go home if his counterparts would not compromise. The European leaders were determined to punish Germany and enlarge their empires. Wilson, however, believed that he could create a new kind of international relations based on his Fourteen Points. He achieved limited acceptance of the idea of the self-determination of people, his dream that each national group could have its own country and that the people should decide in what country they wanted to live.

The peacemakers carved the new countries of Austria, Hungary, and Yugoslavia out of what had been the Austro-Hungarian Empire. In addition, they created Poland, Czechoslovakia, Finland, Estonia, Latvia, and Lithuania, in part to help contain the threat of bolshevism in eastern Europe. France was allowed to occupy the industrial Saar region of Germany for only 15 years with a plebiscite at the end of that time to determine whether the people wanted to become a part of Germany or France. Italy gained the port city of Trieste but was denied the neighboring city of Fiume with its largely Italian-speaking population. Dividing up the map of Europe was difficult at best, but perhaps the biggest mistake that Wilson and other major leaders made was to give the small nations little power at the negotiating table to exclude Soviet Russia entirely.

Wilson won some points at the peace negotiations, but he also had to make major concessions. He was forced to agree that Germany should pay reparations (later set at $33 billion), lose much of its oil- and coal-rich territory, and

The "Big Four" in December 1919: Italy's Orlando, Britain's Lloyd George, France's Clemenceau, and the U.S. President Wilson.

admit to its war guilt. He accepted a mandate system, to be supervised by the League of Nations, that allowed France and Britain to take over portions of the Middle East and allowed Japan to occupy Germany's colonies in the Pacific. This was not a "peace without victory," and the sense of betrayal felt by the German people would later have grave repercussions. Wilson also did not win approval for freedom of the seas or the abolition of trade barriers as he wished, but he did gain endorsement for the League of Nations, the organization he hoped would prevent all future wars. The League consisted of a council of the five great powers, elected delegates from the smaller countries, and a World Court to settle disputes. But the key to collective security was contained in Article 10 of the League covenant, which pledged all members "to respect and preserve as against external aggression the territorial integrity" of all other members.

Women for Peace

While the statesmen met at Versailles to sign the peace treaty hammered out in Paris and to divide up Europe, a group of prominent and successful women, lawyers, physicians, administrators, and writers from all over the world, including many from the Central Powers, met in Zurich, Switzerland. The American delegation was led by Jane Addams and included Florence Kelley of the National Consumers League; Alice Hamilton, a professor at Harvard Medical School; and Jeanette Rankin. As congresswoman from Montana (one of the few states where women could vote), Rankin had voted against the war resolution in 1917. Some of the women who gathered at Zurich had met in 1915 at The Hague, in the Netherlands, to propose an end to the war through mediation. Now they met amid the devastation of war to promote a peace that would last. At their conference they formed the Women's International League for Peace and Freedom. Electing Addams president of the new organization, they denounced the harsh peace terms, which called for disarmament of only one side and exacted great economic penalties against the Central Powers. Prophetically, they predicted that the peace treaty would result in the spread of hatred and anarchy and "create all

over Europe discords and animosities which can only lead to future wars."

Hate and intolerance were legacies of the war. They were present at the Versailles peace conference, where Clemenceau especially wanted to humiliate Germany for the destruction of French lives and property. Also hanging over the conference was the Bolshevik success in Russia. Lenin's vision of a communist world order, led by workers, conflicted sharply with Wilson's dream of an anti-imperialist, free trade, capitalist world. The threat of revolution seemed so great that Wilson and the Allies sent American and Japanese troops into Russia in 1919 to attempt to defeat the Bolsheviks and create a moderate republic. But by 1920, the troops had failed in their mission. They withdrew, but Russians never forgot the event, and the threat of bolshevism remained.

Wilson's Failed Dream

Probably most Americans supported the concept of the League of Nations in the summer of 1919. A few, like former senator Albert Beveridge of Indiana, an ardent nationalist, denounced the League as the work of "amiable old male grannies who, over their afternoon tea, are planning to denationalize America and denationalize the nation's manhood." But 33 governors endorsed the plan. Yet in the end, the Senate refused to accept American membership in the League. The League of Nations treaty, one commentator has suggested, was killed by its friends and not by its enemies.

First there was Lodge, who had earlier endorsed the idea of some kind of international peacekeeping organization but who objected to Article 10, claiming that it would force Americans to fight the wars of foreigners. Chairman of the Senate Foreign Relations Committee, Lodge came from a distinguished Massachusetts family. Like Wilson, he was a lawyer and a scholar as well as a politician. But in background and personality, he was very different from Wilson. A Republican senator since 1893, he had great faith in the power and prestige of the Senate. He disliked all Democrats, especially Wilson, whose idealism and missionary zeal infuriated him.

Then there was Wilson, whose only hope of

passage of the treaty in the Senate was a compromise to bring moderate senators to his side. But Wilson refused to compromise or to modify Article 10 to allow Congress the opportunity to decide whether or not the United States would support the League in time of crisis. Angry at his opponents, who were exploiting the disagreement for political advantage, he stumped the country to convince the American people of the rightness of his plan. The people did not need to be convinced. They greeted Wilson much the way the people of France had. Traveling by train, he gave 37 speeches in 29 cities in the space of three weeks. When he described the graves of American soldiers in France and announced that American boys would never again die in a foreign war, the people responded with applause.

After one dramatic speech in Pueblo, Colorado, Wilson collapsed. His health had been failing for some months, and the strain of the trip was too much. He was rushed back to Washington, where a few days later he suffered a massive stroke. For the next year and a half, the president was incapable of running the government. Protected by his wife and his closest advisers, Wilson became irritable and depressed and unable to lead a fight for the League. For a year and a half the country limped along without a president.

After many votes and much maneuvering, the Senate finally killed the League treaty in March 1920. Had the United States joined the League of Nations, it probably would have made little difference in the international events of the 1920s and 1930s. Nor would American participation have prevented World War II. The United States did not resign from the world of diplomacy or trade, nor did the United States with that single act become isolated from the rest of the world. But the rejection of the League treaty was symbolic of the refusal of many Americans to admit that the world and America's place in it had changed dramatically since 1914.

CONCLUSION: The Divided Legacy of the Great War

For Edmund Arpin and many of his friends, who left small towns and urban neighborhoods to join the military forces, the war was a great adventure. For the next decades, at American Legion conventions and Armistice Day parades, they continued to celebrate their days of glory. For others who served, the war's results were more tragic. Many died. Some came home injured, disabled by poison gas, or unable to cope with the complex world that had opened up to them.

In a larger sense, the war was both a triumph and a tragedy for the American people. The war created opportunities for blacks who migrated to the North, for women who found more rewarding jobs, and for farmers who suddenly discovered a demand for their products. But much of the promise and the hope proved temporary.

The war provided a certain climax to the progressive movement. The passage of the woman suffrage amendment and the use of federal power in a variety of ways to promote justice and order pleased reformers, who had been working toward these ends for many decades. But the results were often disappointing. Much federal legislation was dismantled or reduced in effectiveness after the war, and votes for women had little initial impact on social legislation.

The Great War marked the coming of age of the United States as a world power, but the country seemed reluctant to accept the new responsibility. The war stimulated patriotism and pride in the country, but it also increased intolerance. With this mixed legacy from the war, the country entered the new era of the 1920s.

Recommended Reading

Two excellent books featuring different points of view on Woodrow Wilson's foreign policy and the United States' entry into the war are N. Gordon Levin, Jr., *Woodrow Wilson and World Politics* (1968) and Ernest R. May, *The World and American Isolation* (1966). Also see Arthur S. Link, *Woodrow Wilson: Revolution, War, and Peace* (1979). The response of the peace advocates is detailed in C. Roland Marchand, *The American Peace Movement and Social Reform* (1973).

The best general account of the American military involvement in the Great War is Edward M. Coffman, *The War to End All Wars* (1968). Arthur D. Barbeau and Florette Henri, *The Unknown Soldiers: Black American Troops in World War I* (1974) describes the experience of blacks in the military. David M. Kennedy, *Over Here* (1980) is the most comprehensive survey of the impact of the war on American society.

More specialized studies include Donald Johnson, *The Challenge to America's Freedoms* (1963), on civil liberties during the war, and Carol S. Gruber, *Mars and Minerva* (1975), on the impact of the war on higher education. Maurine W. Greenwald, *Women, War, and Work* (1980) describes the influence of the war on women workers. Frederick C. Luebke, *Bonds of Loyalty* (1974) details the experience of German-Americans. Rodolfo Acuna, *Occupied America* (1981) has a section on Mexican-Americans and the war. Christopher Lasch, *The American Liberals and the Russian Revolution* (1962) describes the impact of the Russian Revolution on American policy and attitudes. See also John L. Gaddis, *Russia, the Soviet Union, and the United States* (1978).

Aileen S. Kraditor, *The Ideas of the Women Suffrage Movement* (1965) describes the campaign to win votes for women, which reached a climax during the war. Stanley Cooperman, *World War I and the American Novel* (1970) traces the literary impact of the war. Paul Fussell, *The Great War and Modern Memory* (1975) focuses primarily on the British experience but is indispensable for understanding the importance of the war for the generation that lived through it.

There are many novels focusing on the war. Erich Remarque highlights the horror of war from the European point of view in *All Quiet on the Western Front* (1929). John Dos Passos shows war as a bitter experience in *Three Soldiers* (1921), and Ernest Hemingway portrays its futility in *A Farewell to Arms* (1929).

TIME LINE

1914	Archduke Ferdinand assassinated; World War I begins
	United States declares neutrality
	American troops invade Mexico and occupy Veracruz
1915	Germany announces submarine blockade of Great Britain
	Lusitania sunk
	Arabic pledge
	Marines land in Haiti
1916	Army Reorganization Bill
	Expedition into Mexico
	Wilson reelected
	Workmen's Compensation Bill
	Keatings–Owen Child Labor Bill
	Federal Farm Loan Act
	National Women's Party founded
1917	Germans resume unrestricted submarine warfare
	United States breaks relations with Germany
	Zimmermann telegram
	Russian Revolution
	United States declares war on Germany
	War Revenue Act
	Espionage Act
	Committee on Public Information established
	Trading with the Enemy Act
	Selective Service Act
	War Industries Board formed
1918	Sedition Act
	Flu epidemic sweeps nation
	Wilson's Fourteen Points
	American troops intervene in Russian Revolution
1919	Paris peace conference
	Eighteenth Amendment prohibits alcoholic beverages
	Senate rejects Treaty of Versailles
1920	Nineteenth Amendment grants woman suffrage

CHAPTER 24
AFFLUENCE AND ANXIETY

John and Lizzie Parker were black sharecroppers who lived in a "stubborn, ageless hut squatted on a little hill" in central Alabama. They had two daughters, one age 6, the other already married. The whole family worked hard in the cotton fields, but they had little to show for their labor. One day in 1917, she straightened her shoulders and declared, "I'm through. I've picked my last sack of cotton. I've cleared my last field."

Like many southern blacks, the Parkers sought opportunity and a better life in the North. World War I cut off the flow of immigrants from Europe, and suddenly there was a shortage of workers. Some companies sent special trains into the South to recruit blacks. John Parker signed up with a mining company in West Virginia. The company offered free transportation for his family. "You will be allowed to get your food at the company store and there are houses awaiting for you," the agent promised.

The sound of the train whistle seemed to promise better days ahead for her family as Lizzie gathered her possessions and headed north. But it turned out that the houses in the company town in West Virginia were little better than those they left in Alabama. After deducting for rent and for supplies from the company store, almost nothing was left at the end of the week. John hated the dirty and dangerous work in the mine and realized that he would never get ahead by staying there. Instead of venting his anger on his white boss, he ran away, leaving his family in West Virginia.

John drifted to Detroit, where he got a job with the American Car and Foundry Company. It was 1918, and the pay was good, more than he had ever made before. After a few weeks, he rented an apartment and sent for his family. For the first time Lizzie had a gas stove and an indoor toilet, and Sally, who was now 7, started school. It seemed as if their dream had come true. John had always believed that if he worked hard and treated his fellow man fairly, he would succeed.

Detroit was not quite the dream, however. It was crowded with all kinds of migrants, attracted by the wartime jobs at the Ford Motor Company and other factories. The new arrivals increased the racial tension already present in the city. Sally was beaten up by a gang of white youths at school. Even in their neighborhood, which had been solidly Jewish, the shopkeeper and the old residents made it clear they did not like blacks moving into their community. The Ku Klux Klan, which gained many new members in Detroit, also made life uncomfortable for the blacks who had moved north to seek jobs and opportunity.

Suddenly the war ended, and almost immediately John lost his job. Then the landlord raised the rent, and the Parkers were forced to leave their apartment for housing in a section just outside the city near Eight Mile Road. While the surrounding suburbs had paved streets, wide lawns, and elegant houses, this black ghetto had dirt streets and shacks that reminded the Parkers of the company town where they had lived in West Virginia. Lizzie had to get along without her bathroom. Here there was no indoor plumbing and no electricity, only a pump in the yard and an outhouse.

The recession winter of 1921–1922 was particularly difficult. The auto industry and the other companies laid off most of their workers. John could find only part-time employment, while Lizzie worked as a domestic servant for white families. Because no bus route connected the black community to surrounding suburbs, she often had to trek miles through the snow. The shack they called home was often freezing cold, and it was cramped because their married daughter and her husband had joined them in Detroit.

Lizzie did not give up her dream, however. With strength, determination, and a sense of humor, she kept the family together. In 1924, Sally entered high school. By the end of the decade, Sally had graduated from high school, and the Parkers finally had electricity and indoor plumbing in the house, though the streets were still unpaved. Those unpaved streets stood as a symbol of their unfulfilled dream. The Parkers, like most of the blacks who moved north in the decade after World War I, had improved their lot, but they still lived outside Detroit—and, in many ways, outside America.

Like most Americans in the 1920s, the Parkers, Alabama sharecroppers who moved north, pursued the American dream of success. For them, a comfortable house and a steady job, a new bathroom, and an education for their daughter constituted that dream. For others during the decade, the symbol of success was a new automobile, a new suburban house, or perhaps making a killing on the stock market. The twenties were a time of prosperity when most Americans had a sense of living in an era of technology, an era in which new, modern products made life easier and more exciting. Yet many, like the Parkers, found their dream just out of reach.

This chapter traces some of the conflicting trends of an exciting decade. We will explore the currents of intolerance that influenced almost all the events and social movements of the time. We will also explore some of the developments in technology, especially the automobile, which changed life for almost everyone during the twenties. We will examine a number of groups—women, blacks, industrial workers, and farmers—who had their hopes raised but not always fulfilled during the decade. Finally, we will look at the way business, politics, and foreign policy were intertwined during the age of Harding, Coolidge, and Hoover.

POSTWAR PROBLEMS

The enthusiasm for social progress that marked the war years evaporated in 1919. Public housing, social insurance, government ownership of the railroads, and many other experiments quickly ended. The sense of progress and purpose that the war had fostered withered. The year following the end of the war was marked by strikes and violence, by fear that Bolsheviks, blacks, foreigners, and others were destroying the American way. Some of the fear and intolerance resulted from wartime patriotism, some from the postwar economic and political turmoil that forced Americans to deal with new and immensely troubling situations.

Red Scare

Americans in the past had feared radicals and other groups that seemed to be conspiring to overthrow the American way. Catholics, Mormons, Populists, and immigrants of many political views had all been attacked as dangerous and "un-American." But before 1917, anarchists seemed to pose the worst threat. The Russian Revolution changed that. *Bolshevik* suddenly became the most dangerous and devious radical, while *communist* was transformed from one who was a member of a utopian community to a

dreaded, threatening subversive. For some Americans, Bolshevik and German became somehow mixed together, especially after the Treaty of Brest-Litovsk in 1918 removed the new Soviet state from the war. In the spring of 1919, with the Russian announcement of a policy of worldwide revolution and with Communist uprisings in Hungary and Bavaria, many Americans feared that the Communists planned to take over the United States. There were a few American Communists, but they never posed a real threat to the United States or to the American way of life.

The war had badly splintered the Socialist party. Some Socialists, like Eugene Debs, opposed American participation, while others, like William English Walling and Edward Russell, left the party and supported the American war effort. In some cases the dilemma of how to deal with the war split families. This happened to the Stokes family. J. G. Phelps Stokes, a tall, slender graduate of Yale whose father had made a fortune in Manhattan real estate became a socialist when as a settlement worker he saw the contrast between the way his family lived and the way new immigrants struggled on New York's Lower East Side. In one of the biggest weddings of 1905, Stokes married Rose Pastor, a poet, writer, and native of Russia. When the war came, Stokes resigned from the Socialist party and joined the army, but Rose opposed the war and eventually became one of the first American Communists.

Rose Pastor Stokes, John Reed, and a few other American idealists were inspired by developments in Russia. Reed, the son of a wealthy businessman, was born in Portland, Oregon, and went east to private school and then to Harvard. He was a cheerleader for the football team and dabbled at writing, but he spent most of his time in college having a good time. After graduation he traveled and then drifted to Greenwich Village, where he joined his classmate Walter Lippmann and Max Eastman, Mabel Dodge, and other intellectuals and radicals. Reed was converted to socialism by this group, who made him understand that "my happiness is built on the misery of others." Reed was in Europe shortly after the war began and was horrified by the carnage in what he considered a capitalistic war. The news of the Russian czar's abdication in 1917 brought him to Russia just in time to witness the bloody Bolshevik takeover. His eyewitness account, *Ten Days That Shook the World*, optimistically predicted a worldwide revolution. When he saw how little hope there was for that revolution in postwar America, he returned to the Soviet Union. The authoritarian nature of the new regime, which seemed to contradict some of its idealistic rhetoric, shook Reed's faith before his death from typhus in 1920, however.

Working-Class Protest

Reed was one of the romantic American intellectuals who saw great hope for the future in the Russian Revolution. His mentor Lincoln Steffens, the muckraking journalist, remarked after a visit to the Soviet Union a few years later, "I have been over into the future and it works." But relatively few Americans, even among those who had been socialists, and fewer still among the workers, joined the Communist party. Perhaps in all there were 25,000 to 40,000, and those were split into two groups, the American Communist Party and the Communist Labor Party. The threat to the American system of government was very slight. But in 1919, the Communists seemed to be a threat, particularly

as a series of devastating strikes erupted across the country. Workers in the United States had suffered from wartime inflation, which had almost doubled prices between 1914 and 1919, while most wages remained the same. During 1919, about 4 million workers took part in 4,000 strikes. Few wanted to overthrow the government; they simply wanted higher wages and, in some cases, shorter hours.

On January 21, 1919, some 35,000 shipyard workers went on strike in Seattle, Washington. Within a few days, a general strike paralyzed the city; transportation and business stopped. The mayor of Seattle called for federal troops to put down the strike. Within five days, using strong-arm tactics, the mayor put down the strike and was hailed across the country as a "red-blooded patriot."

Yet the strikes continued elsewhere. In September 1919, all 343,000 employees of U.S. Steel walked out in an attempt to win an eight-hour day and "an American living wage." The average workweek in the steel industry in 1919 was 68.7 hours; the unskilled worker averaged $1,400 per year, while the minimum subsistence for a family of five that the same year was estimated at $1,575. Within days, the strike spread to Bethlehem Steel. From the beginning, the owners blamed the strikes on the Bolsheviks. They put ads in the newspapers urging the workers, "Stand By America, Show Up the Red Agitator." They also imported strikebreakers, provoked riots, broke up union meetings, and finally used police and soldiers to end the strike. Eighteen strikers were killed. Because most people believed the Communists had inspired the strike, the issue of long hours and poor pay got lost, and eventually the union surrendered.

While the steel strike was still in progress, the police in Boston went on strike. Like most other workers, the police were struggling to survive on prewar salaries in inflationary times. The Boston newspapers blamed the strike on Communist influence, but one writer warned that the strike could not succeed because "behind Boston in this skirmish with Bolshevism stands Massachusetts, and behind Massachusetts stands America." College students and army veterans volunteered to replace the police and prevent looting in the city. The president of

Harvard assured the students that their grades would not suffer. The strike was quickly broken, and the striking policemen were dismissed. When Samuel Gompers urged Governor Calvin Coolidge to ask the Boston authorities to reinstate them, Coolidge responded with the laconic statement that made him famous and eventually helped him win the presidency: "There is no right to strike against the public safety by anybody, anywhere, anytime."

Strikes were bad enough, especially strikes that seemed inspired by dangerous radicals, but bombs were even worse. The "bomb-throwing radical" had become almost a cliché, probably stemming from the hysteria over the Haymarket Riot of 1886. On April 28, 1919, a bomb was discovered in a small package delivered to the home of the mayor of Seattle. The next day, the maid of a former senator from Georgia opened a package, and a bomb blew her hands off. In June, other bombings occurred, including one that shattered the front part of the home of Attorney General A. Mitchell Palmer in Washington. The bombings seem to have been the work of misguided radicals who thought they might start a genuine revolution in America. But their effect was to provide substantial evidence that revolution was around the corner, even though most American workingmen wanted only shorter hours, better working conditions, and a chance to realize the American dream.

The strikes and bombs, combined with the general postwar mood of distrust and suspicion, persuaded many people that there was a real and immediate threat to the nation. No one was more convinced than A. Mitchell Palmer. From a Quaker family in a small Pennsylvania town, he had graduated with highest honors from Swarthmore College and had been admitted to the Pennsylvania bar in 1893 at the age of 21. After serving for three terms as a congressman, he helped swing the Pennsylvania delegation to Wilson at the 1912 convention. Wilson offered him the post of secretary of war, but Palmer turned it down because of his Quaker pacifism. He did support the United States' entry into the war, however, and served as alien property custodian, a job created by the Trading with the Enemy Act. It was this position that apparently convinced him of the danger of radical subversive activities in America. The bombing of his home when he was attorney general intensified his fears, and in the summer of 1919, he determined to find and destroy the Red network. He organized a special antiradical division within the Justice Department and put a young man named J. Edgar Hoover in charge of coordinating all information on domestic radical activities.

As he became more and more obsessed with the "Red menace," Palmer instituted a series of raids, beginning in November 1919. Simultaneously, in several cities, his men rounded up 250 members of the Union of Russian Workers, many of whom were beaten and roughed up in the process. In December, 249 aliens, including the famous anarchist Emma Goldman, were deported, although very few were Communists and even fewer had any desire to overthrow the government of the United States. Palmer's men raided private homes, meeting halls, and organization offices. In Detroit, 500 people were arrested on false charges and forced to sleep or stand in a corridor of a building for 25 hours before they were released. In Boston, 800 people were rounded up, marched in chains, then held in an unheated prison on an island in the harbor.

The Palmer raids, which probably constituted the most massive violation of civil liberties in America history to this date, found few dangerous radicals but did fan the flames of fear and intolerance in the country. In Indiana, a jury quickly acquitted a man who had killed an alien for yelling, "To hell with the United States." In Everett, Washington, a member of the IWW was dragged from his jail cell, castrated, and hanged from a railroad bridge. Billy Sunday, the Christian evangelist, suggested that the best solution was to shoot aliens rather than to deport them.

Palmer became a national hero for ferreting out Communists, even though saner minds protested his tactics. Assistant Secretary of State Louis Post insisted that the arrested aliens be given legal rights, and in the end only about 600 were deported, out of the more than 5,000 arrested. The worst of the "Red Scare" was over by the end of 1920, but the fear of radicals and the emotional patriotism survived throughout the decade to color almost every aspect of politics, daily life, and social legislation.

The Red Scare promoted many patriotic organizations and societies, which took as their task the elimination of communism from American life. These organizations made little distinction among socialists, Communists, liberals, and progressives, and they found Bolsheviks everywhere. The best-known organization was the American Legion, but there was also the American Defense Society, the Sentinels of the Republic (whose motto was "Every Citizen a Sentinel, Every Home a Sentry Box"), the National Association for Constitutional Government, the United States Flag Association, and the Daughters of the American Revolution. Such groups provided a sense of purpose and a feeling of belonging in a rapidly changing America. But often what united their efforts was an obsessive fear of Communists and radicals.

Some of the organizations made special targets of women social reformers. One group attacked the "Hot-House, Hull House Variety of Parlor Bolshevists," and during the 1920s circulated a number of "spider-web charts" that purported to connect liberals and progressives, especially progressive women, to Communist organizations. In one such chart, even the Needlework Guild and the Sunshine Society were accused of being influenced by Communists. The connections were made only through the use of half truths, innuendos, and outright lies. To protest their charges did little good, for those who made the charges knew the truth and would not be deflected from their purpose of exterminating dangerous radicals. As late as 1926, *Scabbard and Blade,* the publication of the Reserve Officers Training Corps, denounced Jane Addams as the head of an international conspiracy and the "most dangerous woman in America."

Ku Klux Klan

The superpatriotic societies exploited the fear that the American way of life was being subverted from within by radicals and Bolsheviks. The Ku Klux Klan built on similar fears but added anti-Catholicism, anti-Semitism, and antiblack attitudes to promote its own version of "100 percent Americanism." The Klan was organized in Georgia by William J. Simmons, a lay preacher, salesman, and member of many fraternal organizations. He immediately appointed himself the Imperial Wizard. Simmons took the name of the old antiblack Reconstruc-

tion organization that was glorified in 1915 by an immensely popular feature film called *The Birth of a Nation.* The new Klan adopted the white-sheet uniform from the old Klan and admitted only white gentile Americans.

Unlike the original organization, which took almost anyone who was white, the new Klan was thoroughly Protestant and explicitly anti-foreign, anti-Semitic, and anti-Catholic. The Klan declared that "America is Protestant and so it must remain." It opposed the teaching of evolution; glorified old-time religion; supported immigration restriction; denounced short skirts, petting, and "demon rum"; and upheld patriotism and the purity of women. The Klan grew slowly until after the war. In some places, returning veterans could join the Klan and the American Legion at the same table. The Klan added over 100,000 new members in 1920 alone. It grew rapidly because of some aggressive recruiting but also because of the fear and confusion of the postwar period.

The Klan was strong in many small towns and rural areas in the South, where it set out to keep the returning black soldiers in their proper

Modeled on the Reconstruction anti-black organization, the new Ku Klux Klan opposed Jews, Catholics, and liberals as well as blacks.

place, but the Klan also spread through all sections of the country, and at least half the members came from urban areas. The Klan was especially strong in the working-class neighborhoods of Detroit, Indianapolis, Atlanta, and Chicago, where fear of everything un-American was increased by the migration of blacks and other ethnic groups to the next street or the next block. The Klan opposed Catholic schools, declared that the Bible should be read in every school every day, and opposed the League of Nations and the World Court. At the peak of its power, the Klan had perhaps 2 million members, and in some states, especially Indiana, Oklahoma, Louisiana, and Texas, the Klan influenced politics and determined some elections. The Klan's power declined after 1924, but widespread fear of Catholicism and everything un-American remained.

The Sacco-Vanzetti Case

One result of the Red Scare and of the unreasoned fear of foreigners and radicals, which dragged on through much of the decade, was the conviction and sentencing of two Italian anarchists, Nicola Sacco and Bartolomeo Vanzetti. Arrested May 5, 1920, for allegedly murdering a guard during a robbery of the shoe factory in South Braintree, Massachusetts, the two were convicted and sentenced to die in the summer of 1921 on what many liberals considered circumstantial and flimsy evidence. Indeed, it seemed to many that the two Italians, who spoke in broken English and were admitted anarchists, were punished because of their radicalism and their foreign appearance.

It is not clear, even to this day, whether or not Sacco and Vanzetti were guilty of the crime, but the case took on symbolic significance as many intellectuals in Europe and America rallied to their defense and to the defense of civil liberties. Appeal after appeal failed, but finally the governor of Massachusetts appointed a commission to reexamine the evidence in the case. The commission reaffirmed the verdict, and the two were executed in the electric chair on August 23, 1927. But the case and the cause would not die. On the fiftieth anniversary of their deaths in 1977, the governor of Massachusetts exonerated Sacco and Vanzetti and cleared their names.

Bartolomeo Vanzetti and Nicola Sacco, memorialized in a series of paintings by Ben Shahn, may have been innocent of the murder for which they were executed.

THE BENEFITS OF PROSPERITY

Although the decade after World War I was a time of intolerance and anxiety, it was also a time of industrial expansion and unprecedented prosperity. Fueled by new technology, more efficient manufacturing methods, and innovative advertising, industrial production almost doubled during the decade, while the gross national product rose by an astonishing 40 percent. A construction boom created new suburbs around American cities, and the cities themselves were transformed by a new generation of skyscrapers. Everywhere there were signs of prosperity and expansion. After recovering from a postwar depression in 1921 and 1922, the economy took off. The number of telephones installed nearly doubled between 1915 and 1930. Plastics, rayon, and cellophane altered the habits of millions of Americans, while new products, such as cigarette lighters, reinforced concrete, dry ice, and Pyrex glass, created new demands unheard of a decade before.

Perhaps the most tangible sign of the new prosperity was the modern American bathroom. For years, the various functions we associate with the bathroom were separated. There was an outhouse or privy, a portable tin bathtub filled with water heated on the kitchen stove, and a pitcher and washbasin in the bedroom. Hotels and the urban upper class began to install cast-iron bathtubs and primitive flush toilets in the late nineteenth century, but it was not until the early twenties that the enameled tub, toilet, and washbasin became standard. By 1925, American factories turned out 5 million enameled bathroom fixtures annually. The bathroom, with unlimited hot water, privacy, and clean white fixtures, symbolized American affluence.

Electrification

The 1920s marked the climax of the "second industrial revolution." During the first industrial revolution in the nineteenth century, American industry had primarily manufactured goods intended for other producers. In the first quarter of the twentieth century, as some older industries like coal, textiles, and steel stabilized or declined, new manufacturing concerns that produced rubber, synthetic fabrics, chemicals, and petroleum arose. They focused on goods for consumers, such as silk stockings, washing machines, and cars.

Powering the second industrial revolution was electricity—a form of energy that rapidly replaced steam power after 1900. In the previous two decades, inventors such as Thomas A. Edison and George Westinghouse had developed generators for producing electric current and methods for transmitting it and using it to drive machinery. Edison's illuminating company opened the first commercial power station in New York in 1882; by the end of the century, more than 3,000 stations were supplying businesses and homes with electricity. Meanwhile, Edison's most famous invention, the electric light bulb, was rapidly replacing gas lanterns in homes and on streets.

Between 1900 and 1920, the replacement of steam power by electricity worked as profound a change as had the substitution of steam power for water power after the Civil War. In 1902, electricity supplied a mere 2 percent of all industrial power; by 1929, fully 80 percent derived from electrical generators. Less than one of every ten American homes was supplied with electricity in 1907, but more than two-thirds were by 1929. Powered by electricity, American industries reached new heights of productivity. By 1929, the work force was turning out twice as many goods as had a similarly sized work force ten years before.

Electricity brought dozens of gadgets and labor-saving devices into the home. Washing machines and electric irons gradually reduced the drudgery of washday for women, and vacuum cleaners, electric toasters, and sewing machines lightened housework. But the new machines still needed human direction and did not reduce the time the average housewife spent doing housework. For many poor urban and rural women, the traditional female tasks of carrying water, pushing, pulling, and lifting went on as they had for centuries.

Automobility

Automobile manufacturing, like electrification, underwent spectacular growth in the 1920s. The automobile was one major factor in the postwar economic boom. It stimulated and transformed the petroleum, steel, and rubber industries. The auto forced the construction and improvement of streets and highways and caused the spending of millions of dollars on labor and concrete. In 1925, the secretary of agriculture approved the first uniform numbering system for the nation's highways, but it was still an adventure to drive from one city to another. The auto created new suburbs and allowed families to live many miles from their work. The filling station, the diner, and the tourist court became familiar and eventually standardized objects on the American landscape. Traffic lights, stop signs, billboards, and parking lots appeared. Hitching posts and watering troughs became rarer, and gradually the garage replaced the livery stable.

The auto changed American life in a variety of ways. It led to the decline of the small crossroads store as well as many small churches because the rural family could now drive to the larger city or town. The tractor changed methods of farming. Trucks replaced the horse and wagon and altered the way farm products were marketed. Buses began to eliminate the one-room school, because it was now possible to transport students to larger schools. The automobile allowed young people for the first time to escape the chaperoning of parents. It was hardly the "house of prostitution on wheels" that one judge called it, but it did change courting habits in all parts of the country. Gradually, as the decade progressed, the automobile became not just transportation but a status symbol. Advertising helped create the impression that it was the symbol of the good life, of sex, freedom, and speed. The auto in turn transformed advertising and design. It even altered the way products were purchased. By 1926, three-fourths of the cars purchased were bought on some kind of deferred-payment plan. Installment credit, first tried by a group of businessmen in Toledo, Ohio, in 1915 to sell more autos, was soon used to sell sewing machines, refrigerators, and other consumer products. "Buy now, pay later" became the American way.

The United States had a love affair with the auto from the beginning. There were 8,000 motor vehicles registered in the country in 1900, and nearly a million in 1912. Only in the twenties did the auto come within the reach of middle-class consumers. In 1929, 4.5 million cars were sold, and by the end of that year, nearly 27 million were registered. Automobile culture was a mass movement.

The auto industry, like most American businesses, went through a period of consolidation in the 1920s. In 1908, over 250 separate companies were producing automobiles in the United States. By 1929, only 44 remained. In other sectors of business, nearly 6,000 mergers occurred between 1925 and 1931. As a result, the 100 largest companies increased their share of total corporate assets from 35.6 percent to almost 44 percent.

A great many men contributed to the development and production of the auto—William Durant, who organized General Motors; Charles Kettering, an engineering genius who developed the electric self-starter; and Ransom E. Olds, who built the first mass-produced moderately priced light car. But above all the others loomed a name that would become synonymous with the automobile itself—Henry Ford.

Ford had the reputation of being a progressive industrial leader and a champion of the common people. Like all men and women who take on symbolic significance, the truth is less dramatic than the stories. Ford is often credited with inventing the assembly line. In actuality it was the work of a team of engineers. But the Ford Motor Company was the first organization

A major factor in the postwar economic boom was the automobile, which became affordable for middle-class consumers. In the 1920s, Sunday afternoon outings by auto, as here in Louisville, Kentucky, became popular.

Motor Vehicle Registration and Sales, 1900–1930

YEAR	MOTER VECHICLE REGISTRATION	FACTORY SALES
1900	8,000	4,100
1905	78,800	24,200
1910	468,500	181,000
1915	2,490,000	895,900
1920	9,239,100	1,905,500
1925	20,068,500	3,735,100
1930	26,749,800	2,787,400

to perfect the moving assembly line and mass-production technology. Introduced in 1913, the new method reduced the time it took to produce a car from 14 hours to an hour and a half. It was the perfect application of Frederick Taylor's system of breaking down each operation into its components, applying careful timing, and integrating the laborer with the machine. The product of the carefully planned system was the Model T, the prototype of the inexpensive family car.

In 1914, Ford startled the country by announcing that he was increasing the minimum pay of the Ford assembly-line worker to $5 a day (almost twice the national average pay for factory workers). Ford was not a humanitarian. He wanted a dependable work force, and he was one of the first to appreciate that the worker was a consumer as well as a producer and that the workers might buy Model T Fords. But work in the Ford factory had its disadvantages. By 1925, the daily wage at Ford dipped below the average in the industry. When the line closed down, as it did periodically, the workers were released without compensation. Moreover, the work on the assembly line was repetitive and numbing.

Henry Ford was not easy to work for. One newspaper account in 1928 called him "an industrial fascist—the Mussolini of Detroit." He was ruthless at applying pressure on his dealers and used them to bail him out of difficult financial situations. Instead of borrowing money from a bank, he forced dealers to buy extra cars, trucks, and tractors. He used spies on the assembly lines and fired workers and executives at the least provocation. But he did produce a car that transformed America.

The Model T, which cost $600 in 1912, was reduced gradually in price until it sold for only $290 in 1924. The "Tin Lizzie," as it was affectionately called, was light and easily repaired. Some owners claimed all one needed was a pair of pliers and some baling wire to keep it running. If it got stuck on bad roads, as it often did, it could be lifted out by a reasonably healthy man. Replacement parts were standardized and widely available. The Model T did not change from year to year, and it did not deviate from its one color, black. Except for adding a self-starter, offering a closed model, and making a few minor face-lift changes, Ford kept the Model T in 1927 much as he had introduced it in 1913. By that time, its popularity had declined as many people traded up to a sleeker, more colorful, and, they thought, more prestigious autos put out by one of Ford's competitors. The Model A, introduced in 1927, was never as popular or as successful as the Model T. The Chevrolet, rather than the Ford, was America's car by the end of the twenties. In 1929, American manufacturers produced 5.3 million cars, a figure not approached again until the 1950s.

The Exploding Metropolis

The automobile caused American cities to expand into the countryside. In the late nineteenth century, railroads and streetcars had created suburbs near the major cities, but the great expansion of suburban population occurred in the 1920s. Shaker Heights, a Cleveland suburb, was in some ways a typical development. Built on the site of a former Shaker community, the new suburb was planned and developed by two businessmen. They controlled the size and the style of the homes and restricted buyers. No blacks were allowed. Curving roads led off the main auto boulevards, while landscaping and natural areas contributed to a parklike atmosphere. The suburb increased in population from 1,700 in 1919 to over 15,000 in 1929, and the price of lots multiplied by 10 during the decade. Other suburbs grew in an equally spectacular manner. Beverly Hills, near Los Angeles, increased in population by 2,485 percent during the decade. Grosse Pointe Park, near Detroit, grew by 725 percent, and Elmwood Park, near Chicago, by 716 percent. The automobile also allowed industry to move to the suburbs. Employees in manufacturing establishments in the suburbs of the 11 largest cities increased from 365,000 in 1919 to 1.2 million in 1937.

The biggest land boom of all occurred in Florida, where the city of Miami mushroomed from 30,000 in 1920 to 75,000 in 1925. One plot of land in West Palm Beach sold for $800,000 in 1923 and two years later was worth $4 million. A hurricane in 1926 ended the Florida land boom temporarily, but most cities and their suburbs continued to grow during the decade.

The census of 1920 indicated that for the first time, more than half the population of the United States lived in "urban areas" of more than 2,500. The census designation of an urban area was a little misleading because a town of 5,000 could still be more rural than urban. A more significant concept was the metropolitan area of at least 100,000 people. There were only 52 of these areas in 1900, but in 1930 there were 115.

Every city was transformed by the automobile, but the most spectacular growth of all took place in two cities that the car practically created. Detroit grew from 300,000 in 1900 to 1,837,000 in 1930, while Los Angeles expanded from 114,000 in 1900 to 778,000 in 1930. With sprawling subdivisions and shopping centers connected by a growing network of roads, Los Angeles was the city of the future.

While cities expanded horizontally during the 1920s, sprawling into the countryside, city centers grew vertically. A building boom that peaked near the end of the decade created new skylines for most urban centers. Even cities such as Tulsa, Dallas, Kansas City, Memphis, and Syracuse built skyscrapers. By 1929, there were 377 buildings of over 20 stories in American cities. Many were started just before the stock market crash ended the building boom, and the empty offices stood as a stark reminder of the limits of expansion. The most famous skyscraper of all, the Empire State Building in New York, which towered 102 stories in the air, was finished in 1931 but not completely occupied until after World War II.

A Communications Revolution

Changing communications altered the way many Americans lived as well as the way business was conducted. The telephone was first demonstrated in 1876. By 1899, there were already more than a million phones in operation. During the twenties, the number of homes with phones increased from 9 to 13 million. Still, by the end of the decade, more than half of American homes were without phones.

The radio even more than the telephone symbolized the technological and communicational changes of the 1920s. The first station to begin commercial broadcasting was WWJ in Detroit in the summer of 1920. When WWJ and WKDA, in Pittsburgh, broadcast the World Series in the fall of 1921, they began the process that would transform baseball and eventually football and basketball as well. Five hundred stations took to the air waves in 1922 alone, many of them sponsored by department stores and others by newspapers and colleges. In Chicago, KYW began broadcasting with the city's Civic Opera in the fall of 1921.

Much of the early broadcasting was classical music, but soon there was news analysis and coverage of presidential inaugurals and important events. Some stations produced live dramas, but it was the serials such as "Amos 'n' Andy" that more than any other programs made radio a national medium. Millions of people scattered across the country could sit in their living rooms (and after 1927, in their cars) listening to the same program. Radio advertising be-

Ten Largest Cities, 1900–1930

1900	1930
1. New York—4,023,000	1. New York—9,423,000
2. Chicago—1,768,000	2. Chicago—3,870,000
3. Philadelphia—1,458,000	3. Philadelphia—2,399,000
4. Boston—905,000	4. Detroit—1,837,000
5. Pittsburgh—622,000	5. Los Angeles—1,778,000
6. St. Louis—612,000	6. Boston—1,545,000
7. Baltimore—543,000	7. Pittsburgh—1,312,000
8. San Francisco—444,000	8. San Francisco—1,104,000
9. Cincinnati—414,000	9. St. Louis—1,094,000
10. Cleveland—402,000	10. Cleveland—1,048,000

Note: Figures are for the entire metropolitan areas, including suburbs.
Source: U.S. Bureau of the Census.

came an important factor in influencing consumer tastes and in creating demand for products. Sixty thousand households owned radios in 1922; by 1929, the number had increased to 10 million. Actors and announcers became celebrities. The music, voice, and noise of the radio, added to the sound of the automobile, marked the end of silence and, to a certain extent, the end of privacy.

Even more dramatic was the phenomenon of the movies. Forty million viewers a week went to the movies in 1922, and by 1929, that had increased to over 100 million. Men, women, and children flocked to small theaters in the towns and to movie palaces in the cities, where they could dream of romance or adventure and be transported to another world. Charlie Chaplin, Rudolph Valentino, Lillian Gish, and Greta Garbo were more famous and more important to millions of Americans than were most government officials. The motion pictures, which before the war had attracted mostly the working class, now seemed to appeal across class, regional, and generational lines.

The movies had the power to influence attitudes and ideas. Some people had worried that films like *The Birth of a Nation*, the great D. W. Griffith epic on the Civil War and Reconstruction, would influence attitudes toward race and region, but in the twenties many parents worried that the movies would dictate ideas about sex and life. One young college woman remembered, "One day I went to see Viola Dana in *The Five Dollar Baby*. The scenes which showed her as a baby fascinated me so that I stayed to see it over four times. I forgot home, dinner and everything. About eight o'clock mother came after me." She also admitted that the movies taught her how to smoke and in some of the movies "there were some lovely scenes which just got me all hot 'n' bothered."

Not only movie stars became celebrities in the 1920s. Sports figures such as Babe Ruth, Bobby Jones, Jack Dempsey, and Red Grange were just as famous. The great spectator sports of the decade owed much to the increase of leisure time and to the automobile, the radio, and the mass-circulation newspaper. Thousands drove automobiles to college towns to watch football heroes perform.

One writer in 1924 called this era "the age of play." He might better have called it "the age of the spectator." The popularity of sports, like the movies and radio, was in part the product of technology.

The year 1927 seemed to mark the beginning of the new age of mechanization and progress. That was the year Henry Ford produced his fifty-millionth car and introduced the Model A. During that year, radio-telephone service was

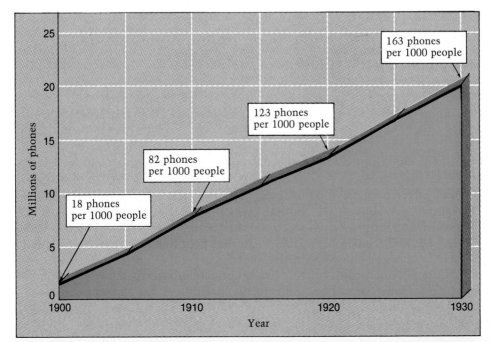

Telephones in Use, 1900–1930

Source: U.S. Bureau of the Census.

Sports figures like Jack Dempsey, depicted here by artist George Bellows in a match against Luis Firpo, became celebrities largely through advances in communication and travel.

Charles Lindbergh carried the mail for the United States government before he became famous for flying alone across the Atlantic.

established between San Francisco and Manila. The first radio network was organized (CBS), and the first talking movie was released *(The Jazz Singer)*. In 1927, the Holland Tunnel, the first underwater vehicular tunnel, was opened between New York and New Jersey. It was also the year that Charles Lindbergh flew from New York to Paris in his single-engine plane in 33½ hours. Lindbergh was not the first to fly the Atlantic, but he was the first to fly it alone, an accomplishment that won him $25,000 in prize money and captured the world's imagination. He was young and handsome, and his feat seemed to represent not only the triumph of an individual but also the triumph of the machine. Lindbergh never talked of his accomplishments in the first person; he always said "we," meaning his airplane as well. He was greeted by 4 million people when he returned to New York for a triumphant ticker-tape parade. When they cheered Lindbergh, Americans were reaffirming their faith in American youth and the American character. Lindbergh symbolized their inventive genius, and his plane signified the progress made through technology.

HOPES RAISED, PROMISES DEFERRED

The 1920s were a time when opportunity seemed to be everywhere. "Don't envy successful salesmen—be one!" one advertisement screamed. Invest in land. Invest in stocks. Buy a car. Build a house. Start a career. Make a fortune. The magazines and newspapers, the radio, business leaders, even the ministers bombarded the nation's citizens with the traditional American message of success. Work hard, save your money, be sober and industrious, believe in God, and you can succeed. "There has never been any necessity in the United States for any healthy human being to remain in a condition of poverty and subordination," wrote Elbert Gary of U.S. Steel. "Families poor in one decade loom leaders in the next."

The benefits of prosperity, however, were no more evenly distributed during that decade than they had been in the past. The income of workers employed in industry increased by only 11 percent from 1923 to 1929, and the real income of farmers declined. On the other hand, corporate profits shot up by 62 percent. The total income of the 12 million American families who made $1,500 a year or less (nearly half of the total) was matched by the income of the 36,000 wealthiest families in the country. Yet there were new benefits for ordinary Americans. Some took advantage of expanding educational opportunities. In 1900, only one in ten young people of high school age remained in school. By 1930, that number had increased to six in ten, and much of the improvement came in the 1920s. In 1900, only one in 33 college-age young people was attending an institution of higher education, but by 1930 the ratio was one in seven. Over a million people were enrolled in the nation's colleges.

In sharp contrast to the nineteenth century, Americans had more leisure time. Persistent efforts by labor unions had gradually reduced the 60-hour workweek of the late nineteenth century to a 45-hour week. Paid vacations, unheard of in the nineteenth century, also became prevalent. In 1916, only 16 of 389 establishments studied had provided paid vacations; by 1926, some 40 percent of 250 companies gave their workers at least one week of vacation with pay.

The American diet also improved during the decade. The consumption of cornmeal and potatoes declined, while the sale of fresh vegetables increased by 45 percent. Health improved and life expectancy increased. But the advantages of better health and more leisure were not equally shared. A white male born in 1900 had a life expectancy of 48 years and a white female of 51 years. By 1930, these figures had increased to 59 and 63 years, respectively. For a black male born in 1900, however, the life expectancy was only 33 years, and for the black female, 35 years. These figures increased to 48 and 47 by 1930, but the discrepancy remained.

Clash of Values

During the 1920s, new inventions and technological and scientific breakthroughs, together with bolshevism, relativism, Freudianism, bibli-

cal criticism, and other new ideas, seemed to threaten old values. A trial over the teaching of evolutionary ideas in a high school in the little town of Dayton, Tennessee, symbolized the clash of the old versus the new, the traditional versus the modern, the city versus the country.

The scientific community and educated people had long accepted the basic concepts of evolution, if not all the details of Darwin's theories. But many Christians, especially those in the rural South, continued to believe the biblical story of creation as the literal truth. In several states, legislators introduced bills forbidding the teaching of evolution. But it was the Tennessee law enacted in 1925 that became famous, for it made it illegal "for any teacher in any of the universities, normal and all other public schools of the state to teach any theory that denies the story of the divine creation of man as taught in the Bible and to teach instead that man has descended from a lower order of animals."

John Scopes, a young biology teacher (who later went to graduate school at the University of Chicago), decided to test the law. For teaching evolutionary theory to his class, he was arrested and brought to trial. Clarence Darrow, perhaps the country's most famous defense lawyer, was hired to defend Scopes, while the World Christian Fundamentalist Association hired William Jennings Bryan, former presidential candidate and secretary of state, to assist the prosecution. Bryan was old and tired (he died only a few days after the trial), but he was still an eloquent and deeply religious man. In cross-examination, Darrow reduced Bryan's statements to intellectual rubble and revealed also that Bryan was at a loss to explain much of the Bible. He could not explain how Eve was created from Adam's rib, nor where Cain got his wife. Nevertheless, Scopes was declared guilty, for he had clearly broken the law. But the press from all over the country covered the trial and upheld science and academic freedom. Journalists like H. L. Mencken had a field day poking fun at Bryan and the fundamentalists. "Heave an egg out a Pullman window," Mencken wrote, "and you will hit a Fundamentalist almost anywhere in the United States today. . . . They are everywhere where learning is too heavy a burden for mortal minds

Have you ever noticed that television commercials can often be more interesting and creative than the programs? One authority has suggested that the best way for a foreign visitor to understand the American character and popular culture is to study TV commercials. Television advertising, the thesis goes, appeals to basic cultural assumptions. The nature of advertising not only reveals for historians the prejudices, fears, values, and aspirations of a people but also makes an impact on historical development itself, influencing patterns of taste and purchasing habits. One modern critic calls advertising a "peculiarly American force that now compares with such long-standing institutions as the school and the church in the magnitude of its social impact."

As long as manufacturing was local and limited, there was no need to advertise. Before the Civil War, for example, the local area could usually absorb all that was produced; therefore, a simple announcement in a local paper was sufficient to let people know that a particular product was available. But when factories began producing more than the local market could ordinarily consume, advertising came into play to create a larger demand.

Although national advertising began with the emergence of "name brands" in the late nineteenth century, it did not achieve the importance it now holds until the 1920s. In 1918, the total gross advertising revenue in magazines was $58.5 million. By 1920, it had more than doubled to $129.5 million, and by 1929, it was nearly $200 million. These figures should not be surprising in a decade that often equated advertising with religion. The biblical Moses was called "the ad-writer for Deity," and in a best-selling book, Bruce Barton, a Madison Avenue advertiser, reinterpreted Jesus, the "man nobody knows," as a master salesman. Wrote Barton: "He would be a national advertiser today."

The designers of ads began to study psychology to determine what motives, conscious or unconscious, influenced consumers. One psychologist concluded that the appeal to the human instinct for "gaining social prestige" would sell the most goods. Another

"... and Jane, dear ... Jack just raved about my teeth."

"I just smiled my prettiest smile... and let him rave. I could have said 'Of course I have beautiful teeth ... I've used Colgate's all my life'. But I didn't want Jack to think I was a living advertisement for Colgate's tooth paste."

* * * * *

Beautiful teeth glisten gloriously. They compel the admiration of all who see them. And there is health as well as beauty in gleaming teeth, for when they are scrupulously kept clean, germs and poisons of decay can't lurk and breed around them.

Remove Those Causes of Decay

Save yourself the embarrassment so often caused by poor teeth. Fight the germs of tooth decay.

Colgate's will keep your teeth scrupulously clean. It reaches all the hard-to-get-at places between the teeth and around the edges of the gums, and so removes causes of tooth decay. It is the dependable tooth paste for you to use.

Washes — Polishes — Protects

The principal ingredients of Colgate's are mild soap and fine chalk, the two

things that dental authorities say a safe dental cream should contain. The combined action of these ingredients washes, polishes and protects the delicate enamel of your teeth.

Use Colgate's Regularly

Just remember that beautiful, healthy teeth are more a matter of good care than of good luck. Use Colgate's after meals and at bedtime. It will keep your teeth clean and gloriously attractive.

And you'll like its taste...even children love to use it regularly.

Priced right too! Large tube 25c.

Colgate's
Established 1806

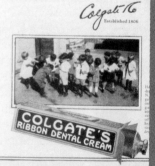

COLGATE'S
RIBBON DENTAL CREAM

By permission of the Colgate-Palmolive Company

Toothpaste advertisement

way to sell products, many learned, was to create anxiety in the mind of the consumer over body odor, bad breath, oily hair, dandruff, pimples, and other embarrassing ailments. In 1921, the Lambert Company used the term *halitosis* for bad breath in an ad for Listerine. Within six years, the sale of Listerine had increased from a little over 100,000 bottles a year to more than 4 million. The appeal to sex also sold products, advertisers soon found, as did the desire for the latest style or invention. But perhaps the most important thing advertisers marketed was youth. "We are going to sell every artificial thing there is," a cosmetic salesman wrote in 1926, "and above all things it is going to be young-young-young! We make women feel young."

Look at the accompanying advertisements carefully. What do they tell you about American culture in the 1920s? What do they suggest about attitudes toward women? Do they reveal any special anxieties? How are they similar to and different from advertising today?

By permission of Leeming Division, Pfizer, Inc.

Shaving cream advertisement

Automobile advertisement (1929)

to carry." Yet religious fundamentalism and people who held to old values and traditional beliefs continued to survive in a world fast becoming urban, modern, and sophisticated.

Immigration and Migration

The flow of immigrants from abroad had been reduced to a trickle during the war, and partly because of the wartime situation, many Americans wondered about the advisability of open borders. A movement to restrict immigration had existed for decades. Many feared that the entry of too many foreigners, especially from Asia and from southern and eastern Europe, would dilute the American racial stock. Some labor leaders had argued for restriction in order to raise wages, and a few liberals and social workers had concluded that some restriction was necessary to care adequately for the immigrants already in the country. An act passed in 1882 prohibited the entry of criminals, paupers, and the insane, and special agreements between 1880 and 1908 restricted both Chinese and Japanese immigration. But it was the fear and intolerance of the war years and the period right after the war that led to the passage of the first major restrictive legislation.

The first strongly restrictive immigration law passed in 1917 over President Wilson's veto. It provided for a literacy test for the first time (an immigrant had to read a passage in one of a number of languages). The bill, which also prohibited the immigration of certain political radicals, was inspired by a growing fear that immigrants would flood to American shores after the war. The literacy test did not stop the more than a million immigrants who poured into the country in 1920 and 1921, however. American diplomats abroad warned that millions more were planning to come. Editorial writers pictured vast hordes of "unassimilable" eastern European Jews and other foreigners arriving to threaten the American way of life. The climate was right for the passage of more restrictive legislation.

The resulting law, which passed Congress in 1921, limited European immigration in any one year to 3 percent of the number of each nationality present in the country in 1910. When even

this did not prove restrictive enough, Congress changed the quota in 1924 to 2 percent of those in the country in 1890, in order to limit immigration from southern and eastern Europe and ban all immigration from Asia. The National Origins Act of 1927 set an overall limit of 150,000 European immigrants a year, with more than 60 percent coming from Great Britain and Germany but less than 4 percent from Italy.

The immigration acts of 1921, 1924, and 1927, in sharply limiting European immigration and virtually banning Asian immigrants, cut off the streams of cheap labor that had provided muscle for an industrializing country since the early nineteenth century. At the same time, by exempting immigrants from the Western Hemisphere from the restrictions, the new laws opened the country to Mexican laborers. Hereafter, this would become the largest immigrant group. The need for farm and mine laborers in California and the Southwest encouraged this immigration, as did widespread poverty in Mexico.

Mexican immigrants came in ever larger numbers in the 1920s, though they never matched the flood of eastern and southern Europeans who entered the country before World War I. Nearly half a million arrived in the 1920s, in contrast to only 31,000 in the first decade of the century. Mexican farm workers often lived in primitive camps, where conditions were unsanitary and health care nonexistent. "When they have finished harvesting my crops I will kick them out on the country road," one employer announced. "My obligation is ended."

Mexicans also migrated to industrial cities such as Detroit, St. Louis, and Kansas City. Often they were recruited, their transportation paid by northern companies. The Bethlehem Steel Corporation brought 1,000 Mexicans into its Pennsylvania plant in 1923, and U.S. Steel imported 1,500 as strikebreakers to Lorain, Ohio, about the same time. During the 1920s, El Paso, Texas, became more than half Mexican, San Antonio a little less than half. The Mexican population in California reached 368,000 in 1929, and Los Angeles was about 20 percent Mexican. Like black Americans, the Mexicans found opportunity by migrating, but they did not escape prejudice or hardship.

Blacks migrated north in great numbers in the period from 1915 to 1920. Reduced European immigration and industrial growth caused many northern companies to recruit southern blacks actively. Trains stopped at the depots in small southern towns, sometimes picking up hundreds of blacks in a single day. Lured by editorials and advertisements placed by industries in northern black newspapers such as the *Chicago Defender* and driven out of the South by an agricultural depression, many blacks eagerly headed north.

One young black man wrote to the *Chicago Defender* from Texas that he would prefer to go to Chicago or Philadelphia, but "I don't care where so long as I go where a man is a man." It was the young who tended to move. "Young folks just aren't satisfied to see so little and stay around on the farm all their lives like old folks did," one older man from South Carolina pointed out. Most black migrants were unskilled. They found work in the huge meat-packing plants of Chicago, East St. Louis, Omaha, and Kansas City and in the shipyards and steel mills. Only 50 blacks worked for the Ford Motor Company in 1916, but there were 2,500 working there in 1920 and 10,000 in 1926. The black population of Chicago increased from 44,000 in 1910 to 234,000 by 1930. Cleveland's black population grew from about 8,500 in 1910 to nearly 68,000 at the end of the 1920s.

Blacks unquestionably improved their lives by moving north. But most were like the Parkers, their dreams only partly fulfilled. In most cases they were crowded into segregated housing, and they faced prejudice and hate. "Black men stay South," the *Chicago Tribune* advised, and offered to pay the transportation for any who would return. In one section of Chicago, a group of white residents, fearing the encroachment of blacks, stretched across the street a banner that read: "They Shall Not Pass." Often the young black men moved first and only later brought their wives and children, putting great pressure on many black families. Some young men, like John Parker, restrained their anger, but others, like Richard Wright's fictional Bigger Thomas, portrayed movingly in *Native Son* (1940), struck out violently against white society. The presence of more blacks in the industrial cities of the North led to the development of black ghettos and increased the racial tension that occasionally flared into violence.

One of the worst race riots took place in Chicago in 1919. The riot began at a beach on a hot July day. A black youth drowned in a white swimming area. Blacks claimed he had been hit by stones, but the police refused to arrest any of the white men. A group of blacks attacked the police, and the riot was on. It lasted four days. Blacks were attacked in all parts of the city by white youths who drove through the black sections shooting from car windows. Blacks returned the fire. Several dozen were killed, and hundreds were wounded. The tension between the races did not die when the riot was over.

Race riots broke out in other places as well. There had been a major riot in East St. Louis, Illinois, in 1917, but in the early 1920s, few cities escaped racial tension and violence. Riots exploded in Knoxville, Tennessee, and Omaha, Nebraska. There was even racial conflict in Tulsa and Elaine, Oklahoma, demonstrating that even the rural Southwest was not immune. In Elaine, a group of black tenant farmers organized to try to end their debt slavery and virtual peonage. A group of local sheriffs broke up one of their meetings and killed several blacks. The blacks retaliated. Before the violence ended, 200 blacks and 40 whites lay dead. Seventy-nine blacks were tried for murder, and 13 were sentenced to death, although their sentences were later commuted. One southerner urged blacks in both North and South to be "real niggers, not fools." But in the 1920s, many blacks were no longer content to be second-class citizens. They wanted to share the American dream.

Marcus Garvey: Black Messiah

A flamboyant black from Jamaica fed a growing sense of black pride in the postwar years. Marcus Garvey arrived in New York at the age of 29. Largely self-taught, he was an admirer of Booker T. Washington. Although he never abandoned Washington's philosophy of self-help, he thoroughly transformed it. Unlike Washington, he had no intention of compromising with white society. In Jamaica, Garvey had founded the United Negro Improvement Associ-

Marcus Garvey, founder of the United Negro Improvement Association, transformed Booker T. Washington's philosophy into one of black pride and separatism.

ation. By 1919, he had established 30 branches in the United States, mostly in northern cities. He also set up the newspaper *The Negro World*, the Universal Black Cross Nurses, and a chain of grocery stores and restaurants. He even started an airline, but his biggest project was the Black Star Line, a steamship company, to be owned and operated by blacks. Advocating the return of blacks to Africa, he declared himself the provisional president of an African empire. He glorified the African past and preached that God and Jesus were black.

Garvey won converts, mostly among lower-class blacks, through the force of his oratory and the power of his personality, but especially through his message that blacks should be proud of being black. "Up you mighty race, you can accomplish what you will," he thundered. Thousands of blacks cheered as his African Legion dressed in blue and red uniforms marched by. They waved the black, green, and red flag and sang "Ethiopia, the Land of Our

Fathers," and thousands invested their money in the Black Star Line. The line collapsed before it got started, however, in part because white entrepreneurs sold Garvey inferior ships and equipment. Garvey was arrested for using the mails to defraud shareholders and was sentenced to five years in prison. President Coolidge commuted the sentence but ordered him deported as an undesirable alien.

Garvey's failures were as spectacular as his successes. He was criticized and attacked for his impractical schemes and for his back-to-Africa movement by other black leaders, especially W. E. B. Du Bois. But despite the exotic and romantic nature of Garvey's crusade, he convinced thousands of American blacks, especially the poor and discouraged, that they could join together and accomplish something and that they should feel pride in their heritage and their future.

Harlem Renaissance and the Lost Generation

A group of black writers, artists, and intellectuals who settled in Harlem after the war led a movement related in some ways to Garvey's black nationalism crusade. It was less flamboyant but in the end more important. They studied anthropology, art, history, and music, and they wrote novels and poetry that explored the ambivalent role of blacks in America. Like Garvey, they expressed their pride in being black and sought their African roots and the folk tradition of blacks in America. But unlike Garvey, they had no desire to go back to Africa. They sought a way to be both black and American.

Alain Locke, a dapper professor of philosophy at Howard University and the first black Rhodes scholar, was in one sense the father of the renaissance. His collection of essays and art, *The New Negro* (1925), announced the movement to the outside world and outlined black contributions to American culture and civilization. Langston Hughes, a poet and novelist born in Missouri, went to high school in Cleveland, lived in Mexico, and traveled in Europe and Africa before settling in Harlem. He wrote bitter but laughing poems, using black vernacular to describe the pathos and the pride of American blacks. In *Weary Blues*, he adapted the rhythm and beat of black jazz and the blues to his poetry. Jazz was an important force in Harlem in the 1920s, and many prosperous whites came from downtown to listen to the music and go to the clubs. The promise of expressing primitive emotions, the erotic atmosphere, the music, and the illegal sex, drugs, and liquor made Harlem an intriguing place for many brought up in a Victorian white America.

The Jamaican Claude McKay, who came to Harlem by way of Tuskegee and Kansas, wrote about the underside of life in Harlem in *Home to Harlem* (1925), one of the most popular of the "new Negro" novels. McKay portrayed two black men, one, Jake, who has deserted the white man's army and finds a life of simple and erotic pleasure in Harlem's cabaret life, the other an intellectual who is unable to make such an easy choice. "My damned white education has robbed me of much of the primitive vitality, the pure stamina, the simple unwaggering strength of the Jakes of the negro race," he laments.

This was the dilemma of many of the Harlem writers: how to be both black and intellectual. They worried that they were dependent on their white patrons, who introduced them to writers and artists in Greenwich Village and made contacts for them at New York publishing houses. Jean Toomer, more self-consciously *avant-garde* than many of the other black writers, came from Washington, D.C., to Harlem, but he moved easily in literary circles in Europe and America. He wrote haunting poems trying to explore the difficulty of black identity, and in a novel, *Cane* (1923), he sketched characters who are maladjusted, almost grotesque figures who shared some of the alienation that many writers felt in the 1920s.

Many of the black writers felt alienated from American society. They tried living in Paris or in Greenwich Village, but most felt drawn to Harlem, which in the 1920s was rapidly becoming the center of black population in New York City. Over 117,000 white people left the neighborhood during the decade, while over 87,000 blacks moved in. Countee Cullen, the only writer in the group actually born in New York, remarked, "In spite of myself I find that I am activated by a strong sense of race consciousness." So was Zora Neale Hurston, born in Florida, who came to New York to study at Barnard College, earned an advanced degree in anthropology from Columbia University, and used her interest in folklore to write stories of robust and passionate blacks. Much of the work of the Harlem writers was read by very small numbers, but they would be rediscovered by another generation of young black intellectuals in the 1960s still struggling with the dilemma of how to be both black and American.

One did not need to be black to be disillusioned with society. Many white intellectuals, writers, and artists also felt alienated from what they perceived as the materialism, comformity, and provincial prejudice that dominated American life. Many writers, including F. Scott Fitzgerald, Ernest Hemingway, E. E. Cummings, and T. S. Eliot, moved to Europe. They wanted to divorce themselves from the country they pretended to detest, but cheap rents and inexpensive food in Paris also influenced their decisions. Many of those who gathered at European cafés, drinking the wine that was illegal in the United States, wrote novels, plays, and poems about America. Like so many American intellectuals in all periods, they had a love-hate relationship with their country.

For many writers, the disillusionment began with the war itself. Hemingway eagerly volunteered to go to Europe as an ambulance driver. But when he was wounded on the Italian front, he reevaluated the purpose of the war and the meaning of all the slaughter. His novel *The Sun Also Rises* (1926) is the story of the purposeless wandering of a group of Americans throughout Europe. But it is also the story of Jake Barnes, made impotent by a war injury. His "unreasonable wound" is a symbol of the futility of life in the postwar period.

F. Scott Fitzgerald, who was married to a beautiful woman and loved to frequent the cafés and the parties in Paris, became a celebrity during the 1920s. He was sometimes confused, even in his own mind, with the dashing heroes he wrote about. He epitomized some of the feelings of despair of his generation, which had "grown up to find all Gods dead, all wars fought, all faiths in man shaken." His best novel, *The Great Gatsby* (1925), was a critique of the American success myth. The book describes the elaborate parties given by a mysterious businessman, who, it turns out, has made his money illegally as a bootlegger. Gatsby hopes to win back a beautiful woman who has forsaken him for another man. But wealth won't buy happiness, and Gatsby's life ends tragically, as so many lives seemed to end in the novels written during the decade.

Paris was the place to which many American writers flocked, but it was not necessary to live in France to be critical of American society. Sherwood Anderson, born in Camden, Ohio, created a fictional midwestern town in *Winesburg, Ohio* (1919) to describe the dull, narrow, warped lives that seemed to provide a metaphor for American culture. Sinclair Lewis, another midwesterner, created scathing parodies of middle-class, small-town life in *Main Street* (1920) and *Babbitt* (1922). The "hero" of the latter novel is a salesman from the town of Zenith. He is a "he-man," a "regular guy" who distrusts "red professors," foreign-born people, and anyone from New York. He lives in a world of gadgets and booster clubs and seems to be the worst product of a standardized civilization. But no one had more fun laughing at the American middle class than H. L. Mencken, who sat in Baltimore, where he edited the *American Mercury* and denounced those he called "the booboisie." He labeled Woodrow Wilson "a self-bamboozled presbyterian" and poked fun at Warren Harding's prose, which he said reminded him of "a string of wet sponges, . . . of stale bean soup, of college yells, of dogs barking idiotically through endless nights. . . ."

Ironically, while intellectuals voiced their despair about the nature of American society and complained that art could not survive in a business-dominated civilization, literature flourished during the decade. The novels of Hemingway, Fitzgerald, Lewis, William Faulkner, and Gertrude Stein, the plays of Eugene O'Neill and Maxwell Anderson, the poetry of T. S. Eliot, Hart Crane, E. E. Cummings, and Marianne Moore, and the work of many black writers marked the 1920s as one of the most creative decades in American literature.

Women Struggle for Equality

Any mention of the role of women in the 1920s brings to mind the image of the flapper—a young woman with a short skirt, bobbed hair, and boyish figure doing the Charleston, smoking, drinking, and being very casual about sex. F. Scott Fitzgerald's heroines in novels like *This Side of Paradise* (1920) and *The Great Gatsby* (1925) provided the role models for young people to imitate, and movie stars such as Clara Bow and Gloria Swanson, who were openly and aggressively seductive on the screen, supplied even more dramatic examples of flirtatious and provocative behavior.

Without question, many young women acquired more sexual freedom in the 1920s. "None of the Victorian mothers had any idea how casually their daughters were accustomed to being kissed," F. Scott Fitzgerald wrote. However, it is difficult, if not impossible, to know how accustomed those daughters (and their mothers) were to kissing and enjoying other sexual activity. Contraceptives, especially the diaphragm, became more readily available during the decade, and Margaret Sanger, who had been indicted for sending birth control information through the mail in 1914, organized the first American birth control conference in 1921. Still, most states made the selling or prescribing of birth control devices illegal, and federal laws prohibited sending literature discussing birth control through the mail.

Family size declined during the decade (from 3.6 births in 1900 to 2.5 in 1930), and young people were apparently more inclined to marry for love than for security. More women expected sexual satisfaction in marriage (nearly 60 percent in one poll) and felt that divorce was the best solution for an unhappy marriage. Nearly 85 percent in another poll approved of sexual intercourse as an expression of love and affection and not simply for procreation. But the polls were hardly scientific and tended to be biased toward the attitudes of the urban middle class. Despite more freedom for women, the double standard still persisted. "When lovely woman stoops to folly, she can always find someone to stoop with her," one male writer announced, "but not always someone to lift her up again to the level where she belongs."

Women's lives were shaped by other innovations of the 1920s. Electricity, running water, washing machines, vacuum cleaners, and other labor-saving devices made housework easier for

Conveniences such as electricity and washing machines remained out of reach for many rural and working-class women.

promoted new dress styles, shorter skirts, no corsets. The young at least adopted them quickly, and they also learned to swim (and to display more of their bodies on the beach), to play tennis (but only if they belonged to a tennis club), and to ride a bicycle.

More women worked outside the home. Whereas in 1890, 17 percent of women were employed in the work force, by 1933, 22 percent were. But their share of manufacturing jobs fell from 19 to 16 percent between 1900 and 1930. The greatest expansion of jobs was in white-collar occupations that were being feminized—secretary, bookkeeper, clerk, telephone operator. In 1930, 96 percent of the stenographers were women. Although more married women had jobs (an increase of 25 percent during the decade), most of them worked at low-paying jobs, and most single women assumed that marriage would terminate their employment. For some working women—secretaries and teachers, for example—marriage often led automatically to dismissal. "A married woman's attitude toward men who come to the office is not the same as that of an unmarried woman," one employment agency decided. Married women are "very unstable in their work; their first claim is to home and children," concluded a businessman. If women could not work after their wedding day (and in one poll of college men, only one in nine said he would *allow* his wife to work after marriage), a job as a secretary could be good preparation for marriage. A business office was a good place to meet eligible men, but more than that, a secretary learned endurance, self-effacement, and obedience, traits that would make her a good wife. Considering these attitudes, it is not surprising that the disparity between male

the middle class. Yet large numbers of rural and urban working-class women were little affected by these developments. Even middle-class women discovered that the new appliances did not reduce the time spent doing housework. Standards of cleanliness rose, and women were urged to make their houses more spotless than any nineteenth-century housekeeper would have felt necessary. At the same time, magazines and newspapers bombarded women with advertising urging them to buy products to make themselves better housekeepers, yet still beautiful. It must have been frustrating for those who could not afford the magic new products or whose hands and teeth and skin failed to look youthful despite all their efforts. The ads also

Women in the Labor Force, 1900–1930

YEAR	WOMEN IN LABOR FORCE	PERCENT OF WOMEN IN TOTAL LABOR FORCE	WOMEN IN LABOR FORCE AS PERCENT OF TOTAL WOMEN OF WORKING AGE	*Percent of Women in Labor Force*		
				SINGLE	MARRIED	WIDOWED OR DIVORCED
1900	4,997,000	18.1	20.6	66.2	15.4	18.4
1910[a]	7,640,000	N.A.	25.4	60.2	24.7	15.0
1920	8,347,000	20.4	23.7	77.0[b]	23.0	—[b]
1930	10,632,000	21.9	24.8	53.9	28.9	17.2

[a] Data not comparable with other censuses due to a difference in the basis of enumeration.
[b] Single includes widowed and divorced.
Source: U.S. Bureau of the Census.

and female wages widened during the decade. By 1930, women earned only 57 percent of what men were paid.

The image of the flapper in the 1920s promised more freedom and equality for women than they actually achieved. The flapper was young, white, slender, and upper-class (Fitzgerald fixed her ideal age at 19), and most women did not fit those categories. The flapper was frivolous and daring, not professional and competent. Although the proportion of women lawyers and bankers increased slightly during the decade, the rate of growth declined, and the number of women doctors and scientists dropped. In the 1920s, women acquired some sexual freedom and a limited amount of opportunity outside the home, but the promise of the prewar feminist movement and the hopes that accompanied the suffrage amendment were left largely unfulfilled.

Winning the vote for women did not assure equality. In most states, a woman's service belonged to her husband. Women could vote, but often they could not serve on juries. In some states, women could not hold office, enter a business, or sign contracts without their husbands' permission. Women were usually held responsible for an illegitimate birth, and divorce laws almost always favored men. Many women leaders were disappointed in the small turnout of women in the presidential election of 1920. To educate women in the reality of politics, they organized the National League of Women Voters to "Finish the Fight." A nonpartisan organization, it became an important educational organization for middle-class women, but it did little to eliminate inequality.

Alice Paul, who had led the militant National Women's Party in 1916, chained herself to the White House fence once again to promote an equal rights amendment to the Constitution. The amendment got support in Wisconsin and several other states, but it was opposed vigorously by progressive women on the grounds that such an amendment would cancel the special legislation that protected women in industry that had taken so long to enact in the two decades before. Feminists disagreed in the 1920s on the proper way to promote equality and rights for women, but the political and social climate was not conducive to feminist causes.

More women began to hold white-collar jobs such as telephone operator, though marriage often resulted in automatic dismissal.

Rural America in the 1920s

Farmers were among those who did not profit from the prosperity of the twenties. Responding to worldwide demands and rising prices for wheat, cotton, and other products, many farmers invested in more land, tractors, and farm equipment during the war. Then prices tumbled. By 1921, the price of wheat had dropped 40 percent, that of corn 32 percent, and hogs 50 percent. Total farm income fell from $10 million to $4 million in the postwar depression. Many farmers could not make payments on their tractors. Because the value of land fell, they often lost both mortgage and land and still owed the bank money. One Iowa farmer remembered, "We gave the land back to the mortgage holder, and then we're sued for the remainder—the deficiency judgment—which we have to pay."

The nature of farming was changing, and that was part of the problem. The use of chemical fertilizers and new hybrid seeds, some developed by government experiment stations and land-grant colleges, increased the yield per acre. By 1930, some 920,000 tractors and 900,000 trucks were in use on American farms. They not only made farming more efficient, but they also released for cash crops land formerly used to raise feed for horses and mules. Production increased at the very time that worldwide demand for American farm products declined. The United States shipped abroad in 1929 only one-third the wheat it had exported in 1919, and only one-ninth the meat.

Not all farmers suffered. During the twenties, the farming class separated into those who were barely getting by or not making it at all and those who earned large profits. Large commercial operations, using mechanized equipment, produced most of the cash crops. At the same time, many small farmers found themselves unable to compete with agribusiness. Some of them, along with many farm laborers, solved the problem of declining rural profitability by leaving the farms. In 1900, fully 40 percent of the labor force worked on farms; by 1930, only 21 percent earned their living from the land.

Farmers received 16 percent of the national income in 1919 but only 9 percent in 1929. While many middle-class urban families were more prosperous than they had ever been, buying new cars, new radios, and new bathrooms, only about one in ten farm families had electricity in the 1920s. The lot of the farm wife was similar to what it had been for centuries. She ran a domestic factory, did all the household chores, and helped on the farm as well. One farm woman on Maryland's Eastern Shore recalled that she heard a neighbor brag about making $1,000 on his cows. "But I saw his wife pumping water for the cows to drink; she always went into the barn to help milk, washed the buckets, helped bottle the milk, and the little boy peddled it before school. The farmer made one thousand dollars, but he had not figured feed or help or interest; that was his 'gross amount.'"

As they had done in the nineteenth century, farmers tried to act collectively in the 1920s through a variety of farm organizations. Congressmen from the farm states began to promote legislation, but they accomplished little during the decade. Most of their effort was spent in supporting the McNary-Haugen Farm Relief Bill, which provided for government support for key agricultural products. The idea was for the government to buy wheat, cotton, and other crops at a "fair exchange value" and then market the excess on the world market at a lower price, thus isolating and protecting the American farmer from the worldwide swing in prices. The bill passed Congress in February 1927, only to be vetoed by President Coolidge. It passed again in revised form the next year, and again the president vetoed it. But farm organizations in all parts of the country learned during the decades how to cooperate and how to influence Congress. That would have important ramifications for the future.

The Workers' Share of Prosperity

Hundreds of thousands of workers improved their standard of living in the 1920s, but inequality grew. The richest 5 percent of the population increased their share of the wealth from a quarter to a third, and the wealthiest one percent controlled a whopping 19 percent of all income. Workers' real wages rose only slightly between 1923 and 1929, and there was also a great disparity among workers. Those employed on the auto assembly lines or in the new factories producing radios saw their wages go up, and many saw their hours decline. Yet the majority of American working-class families did not earn enough to move them much beyond the subsistence level. One study suggested that a family needed $2,000 to $2,400 in 1924 to maintain an "American standard of living." But in that year, 16 million families earned under $2,000. For the chambermaids in New York hotels who worked seven days a week or the itinerant Mexican migrant laborers in the Southwest, labor was so exhausting that at the end of the day, it was impossible to take advantage of new consumer products and modern life styles, even if they had the money.

While some workers prospered in the 1920s, organized labor fell on hard times. Labor union membership fell from about 5 million in 1921 to less than 3.5 million in 1929. Although a majority of American workers had never supported unions, unions now faced competition from employers' new policies. A number of large employers lured workers away from unions with promises that seemed to equal union benefits: profit-sharing plans, pensions, and their own company unions. The National Manufacturing Association and individual businesses carried on a vigorous campaign to restore the open shop. The leadership of the AFL became increasingly conservative during the decade and had little interest in launching movements to organize the large industries.

The more aggressive unions like the United Mine Workers, led by John L. Lewis, also encountered difficulties. The union's attempt to organize the mines in West Virginia had led to violent clashes between union members and imported guards. President Harding called out troops in 1921 to put down an "army organized by the strikers." The next year, Lewis called the greatest coal strike in history, and further violence erupted, especially in Williamson County, Illinois. Internal strife also weakened the union, and Lewis had to accept wage reductions in the negotiations of 1927.

Organized labor, like so many other groups, struggled desperately during the decade to take advantage of the prosperity. It won some victories, and it made some progress. But American affluence was beyond the reach of many groups during the decade. Eventually the inequality would lead to disaster.

THE BUSINESS OF POLITICS

"Among the nations of the earth today America stands for one idea: *Business*," a popular writer announced in 1921. "Through business, properly conceived, managed and conducted, the human race is finally to be redeemed." Bruce Barton, the head of the largest advertising firm in the country, was the author of one of the most popular nonfiction books of the decade. In *The Man Nobody Knows* (1925) he depicted Christ as "the founder of modern business." He took 12 men from the bottom ranks of society and forged them into a successful organization. "All work is worship; all useful service prayer," Barton argued. If the businessman would just copy Christ, he could become a supersalesman.

Business, especially big business, prospered in the twenties, and the image of businessmen, enhanced by their important role in World War I, rose further. The government reduced regulation, lowered taxes, and cooperated to aid business expansion at home and abroad. Business and politics, always intertwined, were especially allied during the decade. Wealthy financiers such as Andrew Mellon and Charles Dawes played important roles in formulating both domestic and foreign policy. Even more significant, a new kind of businessman was elected president in 1928. Herbert Hoover, international engineer and efficiency expert, was the very symbol of the modern techniques and practices that many people confidently expected to transform the United States and the world.

Harding and Coolidge

The Republicans, almost assured of victory in 1920 because of the bitter reaction against Woodrow Wilson, might have preferred to have nominated their old standard-bearer, Theodore Roosevelt, but he had died the year before. Warren G. Harding, a former newspaper editor from Ohio, captured the nomination after meeting late at night with some of the party's most

Warren G. Harding (left) and his successor, Calvin Coolidge, were extremely popular presidents.

powerful men in a hotel room in Chicago. What Harding promised no one ever discovered, but the meeting in the "smoke-filled room" became legendary. To balance the ticket, the Republicans chose as their vice-presidential candidate Calvin Coolidge of Massachusetts, who had gained attention by his firm stand during the Boston police strike. The Democrats seemed equally unimaginative. After 44 roll calls, they finally nominated Governor James Cox of Ohio and picked Franklin D. Roosevelt, a young politician from New York, as vice-president. Roosevelt had been the assistant secretary of the navy but otherwise had not distinguished himself.

Harding won in a landslide. His 61 percent of the vote was the widest margin in a presidential election yet recorded. Perhaps of more significance, barely 50 percent of the eligible voters went to the polls. The newly enfranchised women, especially in working-class neighborhoods, stayed away from the voting booths in large numbers. For many people, it did not seem to matter who was president of the United States.

In contrast to the reform-minded Presidents Roosevelt and Wilson, Harding reflected the conservatism of the 1920s. He was a jovial, fun-loving man who brought many Ohio friends to Washington and placed them in positions of power. A visitor to the White House described Harding and his cohorts discussing the problems of the day, with "the air heavy with tobacco smoke, trays with bottles containing every imaginable brand of whiskey" near at hand. At a little house a few blocks from the White House on K Street, Harry Daugherty, Harding's attorney general and longtime associate, held forth with a group of friends. Amid bootleg liquor and the atmosphere of a brothel, they did a brisk business in selling favors, taking bribes, and organizing illegal schemes. Harding was not personally corrupt, and the nation's leading businessmen approved of his policies of higher tariffs and lower taxes. Nor did he spend all his time drinking with his cronies. He called a conference on disarmament and another to deal with the problems of unemployment, and he pardoned Eugene Debs, who had been in prison since the war. Harding once remarked that he could never be considered one of the great presi-

dents, but he thought perhaps he might be "one of the best loved." He was probably right. When he died suddenly in August 1923, the American people genuinely mourned him.

Only after Calvin Coolidge became president did the full extent of the corruption and scandals of the Harding administration come to light. A Senate committee discovered that the secretary of the interior, Albert Fall, had illegally leased government-owned oil reserves in the Teapot Dome section of Wyoming to private business interests in return for over $300,000 in bribes. Illegal activities were also discovered in the Veterans Administration and elsewhere in government. Harding's attorney general resigned in disgrace, the secretary of the navy barely avoided prison, two of Harding's advisers committed suicide, and the secretary of the interior was sentenced to jail.

Coolidge was somewhat dour and taciturn, but honest. There was no hint of scandal about his administration or his personal life. Born in a little town in Vermont, he was sworn in as president by his father, a justice of the peace, in a ceremony conducted by the light of kerosene lamps at his ancestral home. To many, Coolidge represented old-fashioned rural values, simple religious faith, and personal integrity. In fact, he seemed to represent a world that was fast disappearing in the 1920s. Coolidge, however, was uncomfortable playing the role of rural yokel. He was visibly ill at ease as he posed for photographers holding a pitchfork or sitting on a hay rig; he was much more comfortable around corporate executives.

Coolidge ran for reelection in 1924 with the financier Charles Dawes as his running mate. There was little question that he would win. The Democrats nominated John Davis, an affable, able corporate lawyer with little national following. A group of dissidents, mostly representing the farmers and the laborers dissatisfied with both nominees, formed a new Progressive party. They adopted the name, but little else, from Theodore Roosevelt's party of 1912. Nominating Robert La Follette of Wisconsin for president, they drafted a platform calling for government ownership of railroads and ratification of the child labor amendment. La Follette attacked "the control of government and industry by private monopoly." He managed to get nearly 5 million votes, only 3.5 million short of Davis's total. But Coolidge and prosperity won easily.

Like Harding, Coolidge was a popular president. The symbol of his administration was his secretary of the Treasury, Andrew Mellon, one of the wealthiest men in America. He had served under Harding as well, and he set out to lower individual and corporate taxes. In 1922, Congress, with Mellon's endorsement, had repealed the wartime excess profits tax. Although it raised some taxes slightly, it exempted most families from any tax at all by giving everyone a $2,500 exemption, plus $400 for each dependent. In 1926, the rate was lowered to 5 percent and the maximum surtax to 40 percent. Only families with $3,500 income paid any taxes at all. In 1928, Congress reduced taxes further, removed most excise taxes, and lowered the corporate tax rate. The 200 largest corporations increased their assets during the decade from $43 billion to $81 billion.

"The chief business of the American people is business," Coolidge announced. "The man who builds a factory," he said, "builds a temple. . . . The man who works there worships there." Coolidge's idea of the proper role of the federal government was to have as little as possible to do with the functioning of business and the lives of the people. Not everyone approved of his policies, or his personality. "No other president in my time slept so much," a White House usher remembered. But most Americans approved of his inactivity.

Herbert Hoover

One bright light in the lackluster Harding and Coolidge administrations was Herbert Hoover, who served as secretary of commerce under both presidents. Hoover had made a fortune as an international mining engineer before 1914 and then earned the reputation as a great humanitarian for his work managing the Belgian Relief Committee and directing the Food Administration. His name was mentioned as a candidate for president in 1920, when he had the support of such progressives as Jane Addams, Louis Brandeis, and Walter Lippmann. Even a

young Democrat, Franklin Roosevelt, viewed him as a potential presidential candidate until it was clear that he was a Republican and not a Democrat.

Hoover was a dynamo of energy and efficiency. He expanded his department to control and regulate the airlines, radio, and other new industries. By directing the Bureau of Standards to work with the trade associations and with individual businesses, Hoover managed to standardize the size of almost everything manufactured in the United States, from nuts and bolts and bottles to automobile tires, mattresses, and electric fixtures. He supported zoning codes, the eight-hour day in major industries, better nutrition for children, and the conservation of national resources. He pushed through the Pollution Act of 1924, the first preliminary effort to control oil pollution along the coastline.

While secretary of commerce, Hoover used the force of the federal government to regulate, stimulate, and promote, but he believed first of all in American free enterprise and local volunteer action to solve problems. In 1921, he convinced Harding of the need to do something about the problem of unemployment during the postwar recession. The president's conference on unemployment, convened in September 1921, marked the first time any administration had admitted that the national government had any responsibility to the unemployed. The result of the conference (the first of many on a variety of topics that Hoover was to organize) was a flood of publicity, pamphlets, and advice from experts. Most of all, the conference urged state and local governments and businesses to cooperate on a volunteer basis to solve the problem. The primary responsibility of the federal government, Hoover believed, was to educate and promote. With all his activity and his organizing, Hoover got the reputation during the Harding and Coolidge years as an efficient and progressive administrator and he became one of the most popular figures in government service.

Foreign Policy in the 1920s

The decade of the 1920s is often remembered as a time of isolation, when the United States rejected the League of Nations treaty and turned its back on the rest of the world. It is true that many Americans had little interest in what was going on in Paris, Moscow, or Rio de Janeiro, and it is also true that a bloc of congressmen was determined that the United States would never again enter another European war. But the United States remained involved—indeed, increased its involvement—in international affairs during the decade. Although the United States never joined the League of Nations, and a few dedicated isolationists, led by Senator William Borah, blocked United States membership in the World Court, the United States cooperated with a variety of League agencies and conferences and took the lead in trying to reduce naval armaments and to solve the problems of international finance caused in part by the war.

Indeed, it was business, trade, and finance that marked the decade as one of international expansion. The United States was transformed from a debtor to a creditor nation, and American corporate investments overseas grew sevenfold during the decade. The continued involvement of the United States in the affairs of South American and Central American countries also indicated that the country had little interest in hiding behind its national boundaries. Yet the United States took up its role of international power reluctantly and with a number of contradictory and disastrous results.

"We seek no part in directing the destiny of the world," Harding announced in his inaugural address; but even Harding discovered that international problems would not disappear, and one of those that required immediate attention was the naval arms race. Although there was sentiment among moderates in Japan and Great Britain to restrict the production of battleships, it was the United States, urged on by men like William Borah, that took the lead and called the first international conference to discuss disarmament.

At the Washington Conference on Naval Disarmament, which convened in November 1921, Secretary of State Charles Evans Hughes startled the delegates by proposing a ten-year "holiday" on the construction of warships and by offering to sink or scrap 845,000 tons of American ships, including 30 battleships. He urged Britain and Japan to do the same. Hughes's speech was greeted with enthusiastic cheering and applause, and the delegates set about the task of sinking more ships than the admirals of all their countries had managed to do in a century.

The delegates ultimately reached an agreement fixing the tonnage of capital ships at a ratio of the United States and Great Britain, 5; Japan, 3; and France and Italy, 1.67. Japan agreed only reluctantly, but when the United States promised not to fortify its Pacific island possessions, the Japanese yielded. Retrospectively, in the light of what happened in 1941, the Washington Naval Conference has often been criticized, but in 1921 it was appropriately hailed as the first time in history that the major nations of the world had agreed to disarm. The conference did not cause World War II; neither, as it turned out, did it prevent it. But it was a creative beginning to reducing tensions and to meeting the challenges of the modern arms race. And it was the United States which took the lead by offering to be the first to scrap its battleships.

American foreign policy in the 1920s tried to reduce the risk of international conflict, resist revolution, and make the world safe for trade and investment. Nobody in the Republican administrations of the 1920s even suggested that the United States should remain isolated from Latin America. While American diplomats argued for an open door to trade in China, in Latin America the United States had always assumed a special and distinct role. Throughout the decade, American investment in agriculture, minerals, petroleum, and manufacturing increased in the countries to the south. The United States bought nearly 60 percent of Latin American exports and sold them nearly 50 percent of their imports. "We are seeking to establish a Pax Americana maintained not by arms but by mutual agreement and good will," Hughes maintained. But the United States continued the process of intervention begun earlier. By the end of the decade, the United States controlled the financial affairs of ten Latin American nations. The marines were withdrawn from the Dominican Republic in 1924, but that country remained a virtual protectorate of the United States, until 1941. The marines were ordered from Nicaragua in 1925 but returned the next year when a liberal insurrection threatened the conservative government.

Mexico frightened American businessmen in the mid-1920s by beginning a process of nationalizing foreign holdings in oil and mineral rights. But it was the businessmen and bankers, fearing that further military activity would "injure American interests," who urged Coolidge not to send marines but to negotiate instead. Coolidge appointed Dwight W. Morrow of the J. P. Morgan Company as ambassador, and his conciliatory attitude led to agreements protecting American investments. But it was not until 1928, when Herbert Hoover, as president-elect, made a tour of Latin America, that American policy seemed to change from intervention to cooperation.

The United States' policy of promoting peace, stability, and trade was not always consistent or carefully thought out, and this was especially true in its relationships with Europe. At the end of the war, European countries owed the United States over $10 billion, with Great Britain and France responsible for about three-fourths of that amount. Both countries, caught in the middle of postwar economic problems, suggested that the United States forgive the debts, arguing that they had paid for the war in lives and property destroyed. But the United States, although adjusting the interest and the payment schedule, refused to forget the debt. "They hired the money, didn't they?" Coolidge was supposed to have remarked.

But international debt was not the same as money borrowed at the neighborhood bank; it influenced trade and investment, which the United States wanted to promote. About the only way European nations could repay the United States was by exporting products, but in a series of tariff acts, especially the Fordney-McCumber Tariff of 1922, the United States erected a protective barrier to trade. This act also gave the president power to lower or raise individual rates; both Harding and Coolidge used the power, in almost every case, to raise them. Finally, in 1930, the Hawley-Smoot Tariff raised rates even further, despite the protests of many economists and 35 countries. American policy of high tariffs (a counterproductive policy for a creditor nation) caused retaliation and restrictions on American trade, which American corporations were trying to increase.

The inability of the European countries to export products to the United States and to repay their loans was intertwined with the reparation agreement made with Germany. Germany's economy was in complete disarray in the years after the war, with inflation raging and its industrial plant throttled by the peace treaty. By 1921, Germany was defaulting on its payments. The United States, which believed that a healthy Germany was important to the stability of Europe and of world trade, instituted a plan engineered by Charles Dawes whereby the German debt would be renegotiated and spread over a longer period. In the meantime, American bankers and the American government loaned hundreds of millions of dollars to Germany. In the end, the United States loaned money to Germany so it could make payments to Britain and France so that those countries could continue their payments to the United States.

The United States had replaced Great Britain as the dominant force in international finance, but the nation in the 1920s was a reluctant and inconsistent world leader. The United States had stayed out of the League of Nations and was hesitant to get involved in multinational agreements. However, some agreements seemed proper to sign, and the most idealistic of all was the Kellogg-Briand pact to outlaw war. The French foreign minister, Aristide Briand, suggested a treaty between the United States and France in large part to commemorate long years of friendship between the two countries, but Secretary of State Frank B. Kellogg in 1928 expanded the idea to a multinational treaty to outlaw war. Fourteen nations agreed to sign the treaty, and eventually 62 nations signed, but the only power behind the treaty was moral force rather than economic or military sanctions.

The Survival of Progressivism

The decade of the 1920s was a time of reaction against reform, but progressivism did not simply die with the end of the war. It survived in many forms through the period that Jane Addams called a time of "political and social sag." Progressives who sought efficiency and order were perhaps happier during the 1920s than those who tried to promote social justice, but even the fight against poverty and for better housing and the various campaigns to protect children persisted throughout the decade. In a sense, the reformers went underground, but they did not disappear or give up the fight. Child labor reformers worked through the Women's Trade Union League, the Consumers League, and other organizations to promote a child labor amendment to the Constitution after the 1919 law was declared unconstitutional in 1922.

The greatest success of the social justice movement was the passage in 1921 of the Sheppard-Towner Maternity Act. This was among the first of federal social welfare legislation, and it was passed during the Harding presidency. This bill, which gave limited benefits to protect the health of women and children, was the product of long progressive agitation. A study conducted by the Children's Bureau discovered that more than 3,000 mothers died in childbirth in 1918 and that more than 250,000 infants also died. The United States ranked eighteenth out of 20 countries in maternal mortality and eleventh in infant deaths. Josephine Baker, the pioneer physician and founder of the American Child Health Association, was not being ironic when she remarked, "It's six times safer to be a soldier in the trenches in France than to be born a baby in the United States."

The maternity bill, introduced by Senator Morris Sheppard of Texas and Representative Horace Towner of Iowa, was suggested by the Children's Bureau. It called for a million dollars a year to aid the states in providing medical aid, consultation centers, and visiting nurses to teach expectant mothers how to care for themselves and their babies. The bill was controversial from the beginning. The American Medical Association, which had supported pure food and drug legislation and laws to protect against health quacks and to enforce standards for medical schools, attacked this bill as leading to socialism and interfering with the relationship between doctor and patient and with the "fee for service" system. Others, especially those who had opposed woman suffrage, argued that it was put forward by extreme feminists, that it was

"inspired by foreign experiments in Communism and backed by radical forces in the country," that it "strikes at the heart of American Civilization," and that it would lead to socializing medicine and radicalizing the children.

Despite the opposition, the bill passed Congress and was signed by President Harding in 1921. The appropriation for the bill was only for six years, and the opposition, again raising the specter of a feminist-socialist-Communist plot, succeeded in repealing the law in 1929. Yet the Sheppard-Towner Act, promoted and fought for by a group of progressive women, indicated that concern for social justice was not dead in the age of Harding and Coolidge.

Temperance Triumphant

For one large group of progressives, prohibition, like child labor reform and maternity benefits, was an important effort to conserve human resources. At first they argued for local option whereby states, countries, or cities could decide whether or not to make the sale of alcohol illegal. Then, after 1913, they pressed for an amendment to the Constitution. The modern

People who wanted to drink during the "Noble Experiment" found a way. Here Detroit police raid a basement brewery.

prohibition movement had more success than the earlier movement in translating the reformers' zeal into the passage of laws.

By 1918, over three-fourths of the people in the country lived in dry states or dry counties, but it was the war that allowed the antisaloon advocates to associate prohibition with patriotism. At first the beer manufacturers supported limited prohibition, but in the end the sale of beer and wine was also prohibited in a patriotic fervor. "We have German enemies across the water," one prohibitionist announced. "We have German enemies in this country too. And the worst of all our German enemies, the most treacherous, the most menacing are Pabst, Schlitz, Blatz and Miller." In 1919, Congress passed the Volstead Act banning the brewing and selling of beverages containing more than one half of one percent alcohol. The thirty-sixth state ratified the Eighteenth Amendment in June 1919, but the country had, for all practical purposes, been dry since 1917. One social worker confidently predicted that the Eighteenth Amendment would reduce poverty, nearly wipe out prostitution and crime, improve labor, and "substantially increase our national resources by setting free vast suppressed human potentialities."

The prohibition experiment probably did reduce the total consumption of alcohol in the country, especially in the rural areas and the urban working-class neighborhoods. There were fewer arrests for drunkenness, and deaths from alcoholism declined. But the legislation showed the difficulty of using law to promote moral reform. Most people who wanted to drink during the "noble experiment" found a way. Speakeasies replaced saloons, and people consumed bathtub gin, home brew, and many strange and dangerous concoctions. The cocktail was invented to disguise the poor quality of much of the liquor being served, and women, at least middle- and upper-class women, began to drink in public for the first time. Prohibition also created great bootlegging rings, which were tied to organized crime in many cities. Al Capone of Chicago was the most famous underworld figure whose power and wealth were based on the sale of illegal alcohol. His organization alone is supposed to have grossed over $60 million in 1927;

ironically, most of the profit came from distributing beer. Many of those who had supported prohibition slowly came to favor its repeal, some because it reduced the power of the states, others because it stimulated too much illegal activity and because it did not seem to be worth the social and political costs.

The Election of 1928

On August 2, 1927, President Coolidge announced simply, "I do not choose to run for President in 1928." In the following months, Coolidge refused to say whether he could be persuaded to run, but with the announcement, Hoover immediately became the logical candidate. Hoover and Coolidge were not especially close. Coolidge resented what he considered Hoover's spendthrift ways. "That man has offered me unsolicited advice for six years, all of it bad," Coolidge once remarked. Despite the lack of an enthusiastic endorsement from the president and the opposition of some Republicans who thought him too progressive, Hoover easily won the Republican nomination. In a year when the country was buoyant with optimism and when prosperity seemed as if it would go on forever, few doubted that Hoover would be elected.

The Democrats nominated Alfred Smith, a Catholic Irish-American from New York. With his New York accent, his opposition to prohibition, and his flamboyant style, he stood in contrast to the more sedate Hoover. On one level it was a bitter contest between Protestant "drys" and Catholic "wets," between the urban, ethnic Tammany politician and former governor of New York against the rural-born but sophisticated secretary of commerce. Racial and religious prejudice played a role in the campaign, as it often had on American politics. But looked at more closely, the two candidates differed little. Both were self-made men, both were "progressives." Social workers and social justice reformers campaigned for each candidate. Both candidates made an effort to attract women voters, both were favorable to organized labor, both defended capitalism, and both had millionaires and corporate executives among their advisers.

Presidential Elections, 1920–1928

YEAR	CANDIDATES	PARTY	POPULAR VOTE	ELECTORAL VOTE
1920	WARREN G. HARDING	Republican	16,152,200 (61.0%)	404
	James M. Cox	Democratic	9,147,353 (34.6%)	127
	Eugene V. Debs	Socialist	919,799 (3.5%)	0
1924	CALVIN COOLIDGE	Republican	15,725,016 (54.1%)	382
	John W. Davis	Democratic	8,385,586 (28.8%)	136
	Robert M. La Follette	Progressive	4,822,856 (16.6%)	13
1928	HERBERT C. HOOVER	Republican	21,392,190 (58.2%)	444
	Alfred E. Smith	Democratic	15,016,443 (40.8%)	87

Note: Winners' names appear in capital letters.

Hoover won in a landslide, 444 electoral votes to 87 for Smith, who carried only Massachusetts outside the Deep South. But the 1928 campaign revitalized the Democratic party. Smith polled nearly twice as many votes as the Democratic candidate in 1924, and for the first time the Democrats carried the 12 largest cities.

Stock Market Crash

Hoover, as it turned out, had only six months to apply his progressive and efficient methods to running the country because in the fall of 1929, the prosperity that seemed as if it might go on forever suddenly came to a halt. In 1928 and 1929, speculation had been rampant, and the stock market had boomed. Money could be made everywhere—in real estate and business ventures, but especially in the stock market. "Everybody ought to be Rich," Al Smith's campaign manager argued in an article in the *Ladies' Home Journal* early in 1929. Just save $15 a month and buy good common stock with it, and that money would turn into $80,000 in 20 years (a considerable fortune in 1929). Good common stock seemed to be easy to find in 1929.

Only a small percentage of the American people invested in the stock market, for many had no way of saving even $15 a month. But a large number got into the game in the late 1920s because it seemed a safe and sure way to make money. For many, the stock market came to represent the American economy, and the economy was booming. The New York Times index of 25 industrial stocks reached 100 in 1924, moved up to 181 in 1925, dropped a bit in 1926, and rose again to 245 by the end of 1927.

Then the orgy started. During 1928, the market rose to 331. Many investors and speculators began to buy on margin (borrowing in order to invest). Businessmen and others began to invest money in the market that would ordinarily have gone into houses, cars, and other goods. Yet even at the peak of the boom, probably only about 1.5 million Americans owned stock.

In early September 1929, the New York Times index peaked at 452 and then began to drift downward. On October 23, the market lost 31 points. The next day ("Black Thursday"), it first seemed that everyone was trying to sell, but at the end of the day the panic appeared to be over. It was not. By mid-November, the market had plummeted to 224, about half what it had been two months before. This represented a loss on paper of over $26 billion. Still, a month later, the chairman of the board of Bethlehem Steel could announce, "Never before has American business been as firmly entrenched for prosperity as it is today." Some businessmen even got back into the market, thinking that it had reached its low point. But it continued to go down. Tens of thousands of investors lost everything they owned. Those who had bought on margin had to keep coming up with money to pay off their loans as the value of their holdings declined. There was panic and despair, but the legendary stories of executives jumping out of windows were grossly exaggerated.

CONCLUSION: A New Era of Prosperity and Problems

The stock market crash ended the decade of prosperity. The crash did not cause the Depression, but the stock market debacle revealed the weakness of the economy. The fruits of economic expansion had been unevenly distributed. There were not enough people to buy the autos, refrigerators, and other products pouring from American factories. The prosperity had been built on a shaky foundation. When that foundation crumbled in 1929, the nation slid into a major depression.

Looking back from the vantage point of the 1930s or from the time of World War II, the 1920s seemed like a golden era—an age of flappers, bootleg gin, constant parties, literary masterpieces, sports heroes, and easy wealth. The truth is much more complicated. More than most decades, the 1920s were a time of paradox and contradictions.

The 1920s were a time of prosperity, yet a great many people, including farmers, blacks, and other ordinary Americans, did not prosper. It was a time of modernization, but only about 10 percent of rural families had electricity. It was a time when women achieved more sexual freedom, but the feminist movement declined. It was a time of prohibition, but many Americans increased their consumption of alcohol. It was a time of reaction against reform, yet progressivism survived. It was a time when intellectuals felt disillusioned with America, yet it was one of the most creative and innovative periods for American writers. It was a time of flamboyant heroes, yet the American people elected the lackluster Harding and Coolidge as their presidents. It was a time of progress, when almost every year saw a new technological breakthrough, but it was also a decade of hate and intolerance. The complex and contradictory legacy of the 1920s continues to fascinate and to influence our own time.

Recommended Reading

One place to start reading about the twenties is Frederick Lewis Allen, *Only Yesterday* (1931), written shortly after the decade ended and the book that first defined the period as a golden era. Much more serious and better balanced, however, is William E. Leuchtenburg, *The Perils of Prosperity* (1958).

Robert K. Murray, *Red Scare* (1955) is the best place to begin a study of the hate and intolerance that erupted after the war, but John Higham, *Strangers in the Land* (1955) should also be consulted, especially for the Ku Klux Klan and the immigration restriction movement. Andrew Sinclair, *Prohibition* (1962) describes one of the social justice movements after the war. William H. Chafe, *The American Woman: Her Changing Economic and Political Roles* (1972) should also be consulted for the role of women during the decade. Paula Fass, *The Damned and Beautiful* (1977) describes the lifestyles of college youth during the twenties.

Nathan Huggins, *Harlem Renaissance* (1971) and Frederick Hoffman, *The Twenties* (1955) are indispensable for the study of the literary trends during this innovative decade. Robert Sklar, *Movie-Made America* (1976) is excellent on Hollywood and the film industry. James J. Flink, *The Car Culture* (1975) tells the story of the impact of the auto.

Andrew Sinclair, *The Available Man* (1965); Donald R. McCoy, *Calvin Coolidge* (1967); Oscar Handlin, *Al Smith and His America* (1958); and Joan Hoff Wilson, *Herbert Hoover: The Forgotten Progressive* (1975) chart the lives and activities of some of the political leaders. John Kenneth Galbraith, *The Great Crash, 1929* (1954) explains how the twenties came to a tragic end.

Ernest Hemingway's novel *The Sun Also Rises* (1926) is a classic tale of disillusionment and despair in the 1920s. F. Scott Fitzgerald gives a picture of the life of the rich in *The Great Gatsby* (1925). Claude McKay's novel *Home to Harlem* (1928) is one of the best to come out of the Harlem renaissance.

TIME LINE

1900–1930	Electricity powers the "second industrial revolution"
1917	Race riot in East St. Louis, Illinois
1918	World War I ends
1919	Treaty of Versailles Strikes in Seattle, Boston, and elsewhere Red Scare and Palmer raids Race riots in Chicago and other cities Marcus Garvey's United Negro Improvement Association spreads
1920	Warren Harding elected president Women vote in national elections Sacco and Vanzetti arrested Sinclair Lewis publishes *Main Street*
1921	World Series broadcast on radio Immigration Quota Law Disarmament Conference First birth control conference Sheppard-Towner Maternity Act
1921–1922	Postwar depression
1922	Fordney-McCumber Tariff Sinclair Lewis, *Babbitt*
1923	Harding dies; Coolidge becomes president Teapot Dome scandal
1924	Coolidge reelected president Peak of Ku Klux Klan activity Immigration Quota Law
1925	Scopes trial in Dayton, Tennessee F. Scott Fitzgerald, *The Great Gatsby* Bruce Barton, *The Man Nobody Knows* Alain Locke, *The New Negro* Claude McKay, *Home to Harlem* 5 million enameled bathroom fixtures produced
1926	Ernest Hemingway, *The Sun Also Rises*
1927	National Origins Act McNary-Haugen Farm Relief Bill Execution of Sacco and Vanzetti Lindbergh flies solo, New York to Paris First talking movie, *The Jazz Singer* Henry Ford produces fifty-millionth car
1928	Herbert Hoover elected president Kellogg-Briand Treaty Stock market soars
1929	27 million registered cars in country 10 million households own radios 100 million people attend movies Stock market crashes

CHAPTER 25
THE GREAT DEPRESSION
AND THE NEW DEAL

Diana Morgan grew up in a small North Carolina town, the daughter of a prosperous cotton merchant. She lived the life of a "southern belle," oblivious to the country's social and political problems, but the Depression changed her life. She came home from college for Christmas vacation during her junior year to discover that the telephone had been disconnected. Her world suddenly fell apart. Her father's business had failed, her family didn't have a cook or a cleaning woman anymore, and their house was being sold for back taxes. She was confused and embarrassed. Sometimes it was the little things that were the hardest. Friends would come from out of town, and there would be no ice because her family did not own an electric refrigerator and they could not afford to buy ice. "There were those frantic arrangements of running out to the drug store to get Coca-Cola with crushed ice, and there'd be this embarrassing delay, and I can remember how hot my face was."

Like many Americans, Diana Morgan and her family blamed themselves for what happened during the Depression. Americans had been taught to believe that if they worked hard, saved their money, and lived upright and moral lives, they could succeed. Success was an individual matter for Americans. When so many failed during the Depression, they blamed themselves rather than society or larger forces for their plight. The shame and the guilt affected people at all levels of society. The businessman who lost his business, the farmer who watched his farm being sold at auction, the worker who was suddenly unemployed and felt his manhood stripped away because he could not provide for his family were all devastated by the Depression.

Diana Morgan had never intended to get a job; she expected to get married and let her husband support her. But the failure of her father's business forced her to join the growing number of women who worked outside the home in the 1930s. She finally found a position with the Civil Works Administration, a New Deal agency where at first she had to ask humiliating questions of the people applying for assistance to make sure they were destitute. "Do you own a car?" "Does anyone in the family work?" Diana was appalled at the conditions she saw when she traveled around the county to corroborate their stories. She found dilapidated houses, a dirty, "almost paralyzed-looking mother," and a drunken father, together with malnourished children. She felt helpless that all she could do was write out a food order. One day a woman who had formerly cooked for her family came in to apply for help. Each was embarrassed to see the other in changed circumstances.

She had to defend the New Deal programs to many of her friends, who accused her of being sentimental and told her that the poor, especially the poor blacks, did not know any better than to live in squalor. "If you give them coal, they'd put it in the bathtub," was a charge she often heard. But she knew "they didn't have bathtubs to put coal in. So how did anybody know that's what they'd do with coal if they had it?"

Diana Morgan's experience working for a New Deal agency influenced her life and her attitudes; it made her more of a social activist. Her Depression experience gave her a greater appreciation for the struggles of the country's poor and unlucky. Although she prospered in the years after the Depression, the sense of guilt and the fear that the telephone might again be cut off never left her.

This chapter explores some of the causes and consequences of the Great Depression. We will look at Herbert Hoover and his efforts to combat the Depression and then turn to Franklin Roosevelt, the dominant personality of the 1930s. We examine, the New Deal, Roosevelt's program to bring relief, recovery, and reform to the nation. But this chapter also portrays the other side of the 1930s, for the decade did not consist only of the unemployed and New Deal agencies. It was also a time when the radio, the movies, and the automobile had a large impact on the lives of most Americans.

THE GREAT DEPRESSION

The Great Depression changed Diana Morgan's life as it changed the lives of all Americans who lived through it. The Depression experience also separated her generation from the one that followed. An exaggerated need for security, the fear of failure, a nagging sense of guilt, worry about shattered dreams, and a real sense that it might happen all over again separated the Depression generation from those born after 1940.

Black Thursday

Few people anticipated the stock market crash in the fall of 1929; prosperity seemed to be a permanent American fixture. But even after the collapse of the stock market, few expected the entire economy to go into a tailspin. General Electric stock, selling for 396 in 1929, fell to 34 in 1932; U.S. Steel declined from 261 to 21. By 1932, the median income had plunged to half what it had been in 1929. Construction spending fell to one-sixth of the 1929 level. By 1932, at least one of every four American breadwinners was out of work, and industrial production had almost ground to a halt.

Why did the nation sink deeper and deeper into depression? After all, only about 2 percent of the population owned stock of any kind. The answer is complex, but the prosperity of the 1920s, it appears in retrospect, was a superficial and shallow prosperity. Farmers and coal and textile workers had suffered all through the 1920s from low prices, and the farmers were the first group in the 1930s to plunge into depression. But other aspects of the economy also lurched out of balance. Two percent of the population received about 28 percent of the national income, while the lower 60 percent

only got 24 percent. Businesses increased profits while holding down wages and the prices of raw materials. This pattern had a depressing effect on consumer purchasing power. American workers, like American farmers, did not have the money to buy the goods they helped to produce. There was a relative decline in purchasing power in the late twenties, unemployment was high in some industries, and the housing and automobile industries were already beginning to slacken before the crash.

Well-to-do Americans were speculating a significant portion of their money in the stock market. Their illusion of permanent prosperity helped fire the boom of the 1920s, just as their pessimism and lack of confidence helped exaggerate the depression in 1931 and 1932.

Other factors were also involved. The stock market crash revealed serious structural weaknesses in the financial and banking systems (7,000 banks had failed during the 1920s). Economic relations with Europe contributed to deepening depression. High American tariffs during the 1920s had reduced trade. When American investment in Europe declined in 1928 and 1929, European economies declined. As the European financial situation worsened, the American economy spiraled downward.

The federal government might have prevented the stock market crash and the Depression by more careful regulation of business and the stock market. More central planning might have assured a more equitable distribution of income. But that kind of policy would have taken more foresight than most people had in the 1920s. It certainly would have required different people in power, and it is unlikely that the Democrats, if they had been in control, would have altered the government's policies in fundamental ways.

Hoover and the Depression

The first reaction to the stock market crash on the part of businessmen and those in government was one of optimism. "I see nothing in the present situation that is either menacing or warranting pessimism," Andrew Mellon announced in December 1929. "All the evidence indicates that the worst effects of the crash upon unemployment will have been passed during the next sixty days," Herbert Hoover reported. Hoover, the great planner and progressive efficiency expert, did not sit idly by and watch the country drift toward disorder. His first statements of optimism were calculated to prevent further panic. In his inaugural address, only a few months before, he had promised to eliminate pockets of poverty, reduce special privilege, aid the farmers, and help all Americans who were old or ill or needy. However, his farm bill was

Herbert Hoover, photographed on a visit to Yellowstone National Park, agreed with the many analysts who predicted no serious repercussions from the stock market crash.

the only part of his program enacted by Congress before he had to turn his attention from fine-tuning the economy to trying desperately to save it.

The Agricultural Marketing Act of 1929 set up a $500 million revolving fund to help farmers organize cooperative marketing associations and achieve more efficient production. An amendment tacked on by Congress allowed the Farm Board to attempt to stabilize market fluctuations in the market by establishing minimum prices. The Federal Farm Board was a good example of Hoover's approach to national problems. The Farm Board would loan money to the farmers and help them get organized. Then the government would withdraw, leaving the farmers in control of their life and labor after they had paid the loans back. The Farm Board sought to provide the farmer with equal opportunity through cooperation (a key word for Hoover). As it turned out, the Agricultural Marketing Act of 1929 became the first recovery measure, although it was not intended as such. But as agricultural prices plummeted and banks foreclosed on farm mortgages, the available funds proved inadequate. The Farm Board was helpless to aid the farmer who could not meet his mortgage payments because the price of grain had fallen so rapidly. The Farm Board could not help the Arkansas woman who served lunch to those who came to the auction at her farm and stood weeping in the window as her possessions, including the cows, which all had names, were sold one by one.

Hoover acted aggressively to stem the economic collapse. More than any president before him, he used the power of the federal government and the office of the president to deal with an economic crisis. Nobody called it a depression for the first year at least, for the economic problems seemed very much like other cyclic recessions in the American past. Hoover called conferences of businessmen and labor leaders. He urged cooperation and obtained pledges that businessmen would avoid strikes and keep employment, wages, and production levels from falling. He met with mayors and governors and encouraged them to speed up public works projects. He created agencies and boards, such as the National Credit Corporation and the Emergency

Committee for Employment, to obtain voluntary action to solve the problem.

Hoover even supported a drastic tax cut, which Congress enacted in December 1929. The legislation cut taxes by more than half at the lower end of the scale, to less than one percent for people making less than $5,000. But no laborers made as much as $5,000, and the cuts for most people were so small that the tax reduction did little to stimulate spending. Hoover also went on the radio, though he never felt comfortable with the new medium. He spoke frequently at conferences and launched a massive psychological campaign to convince the American people that the fundamental structure of the economy was sound.

The Collapsing Economy

Voluntary action and psychological campaigns proved inadequate to stop the Depression. The stock market, after appearing to bottom out in the winter of 1930–1931, continued its decline, responding in part to the European economic collapse that threatened international finance and trade. Of course, not everyone lost money in the market. William Danforth, founder of Ralston Purina, and Joseph Kennedy, film magnate, entrepreneur, and the father of a future president, were among those who made millions of dollars by selling short as the market went down.

But more than a collapsing market afflicted the economy. Over 1,300 additional banks failed in 1930. Despite Hoover's pleas, many factories cut back on production, and some simply closed. U.S. Steel announced a 10 percent wage cut in 1931. As the auto industry laid off workers, the unemployment rate rose to over 40 percent in Detroit. Over 4 million Americans were out of work in 1930, and that increased to at least 12 million by 1932. Foreclosures and evictions created thousands of personal tragedies. There were 200,000 evictions in New York City alone in 1930. While the middle class watched in horror as their life savings and their dreams disappeared, the rich were increasingly concerned as the price of government bonds (the symbol of safety and security) dropped. They began to hoard gold and to fear revolution.

There was never any real danger of revolution. Some farmers organized to dump their milk to protest low prices, and when a neighbor's farm was sold, they gathered to hold a penny auction, bidding only a few cents for equipment and returning it to their dispossessed neighbor. But everywhere people despaired as the Depression deepened in 1931 and 1932. For unemployed blacks and for many tenant farmers, the Depression had little immediate effect because their lives were already so depressed. Most Americans (the 98 percent who did not own stock) did not really notice the stock market crash; for them the Depression meant the loss of a job, a bank foreclosure, or another event. For Diana Morgan it was the discovery that the telephone had been cut off; for some farmers it was burning corn rather than coal because the price of corn had fallen so low it was not worth marketing.

For some in the cities, the Depression meant not having enough money to feed the children. "Have you ever heard a hungry child cry?" asked Lillian Wald of the Henry Street Settlement. "Have you seen the uncontrollable trembling of parents who have gone half starved for weeks so that the children may have food?" In Chicago, children fought with men and women over the garbage dumped by the city trucks. "We have

Losing his identity as family breadwinner was sometimes as devastating for a man as the financial crisis of unemployment.

been eating wild greens," a coal miner wrote from Harlan County, Kentucky, "such as Polk salad, violet tops, wild onions . . . and such weeds as cows eat." In Toledo, when municipal and private charity funds were running low, as they did in all cities, those granted assistance were given only 2.14 cents per meal per person. In another city, a social worker noticed that the children were playing a game called "Eviction." "Sometimes they play 'Relief,'" she remarked, "but 'Eviction' has more action and all of them know how to play."

Not everyone went hungry during the Depression or stood in breadlines or lost jobs, but almost everyone was affected in one way or another, and many of the victims tended to blame themselves. A businessman who lost his job and had to stand in a relief line remembered years later how he would bend his head low so nobody would recognize him. A 28-year-old teacher in New Orleans was released because of a cut in funds, and in desperation she took a job as a domestic servant. "If with all the advantages I've had," she remarked, "I can't make a living, I'm just no good, I guess. I've given up ever amounting to anything. It's no use. . . ."

Women's lives were probably disrupted less by the Depression than were those of men. "When hard times hit, it didn't seem to bother mother as much as it did father," one woman remembered. There were many exceptions, of course, but when men lost their jobs, their identity as the family breadwinner was shattered. They wandered around aimlessly with no sense of purpose. Some helped out with family chores, but usually with a sense of bitterness and resentment. For women, however, even when money was short there was still cooking, cleaning, and mending to do, and women were still in command of their homes. Yet many women were forced to do extra work. They took in laundry, found room for a boarder, and made the clothes they formerly would have bought. Women also bore the psychological burden of unemployed husbands, hungry children, and unpaid bills. The Depression altered patterns of family life, and many families were forced to move in with relatives. The marriage rate, the divorce rate, and the birthrate all dropped during the decade. College attendance declined. Many

of these changes created tension and despair that statistics cannot capture.

Hoover reacted to growing despair by urging more voluntary action. "We are going through a period," he announced in February 1931, "when character and courage are on trial, and where the very faith that is within us is under test." He continued to insist on maintaining the gold standard, believing it to be the only responsible currency, and a balanced budget, but so did almost everyone else. Congress was nearly unanimous in supporting those ideals, and Governor Franklin Roosevelt of New York accused Hoover of endangering the country by spending too much. Hoover increasingly blamed the Depression on international economic problems, and he was not entirely mistaken. The world was gripped by depression but, as it deepened, Americans began to blame him for some of the disaster. Hoover became isolated and bitter. The shanties that grew near all the large cities were called "Hoovervilles," and the privies, "Hoover villas." Unable to admit mistakes and to take a new tack, he could not communicate a personal empathy for the poor and the unemployed.

Yet Hoover did try innovative schemes. More public works projects were built during his administration than in the previous 30 years. In the summer of 1931, he attempted to organize a pool of private money to rescue banks and businesses that were near failure. When the private effort failed, he turned reluctantly to Congress, which passed a bill early in 1932 authorizing the Reconstruction Finance Corporation. The RFC was capitalized at $500 million, but a short time later that was increased to $3 billion. It was authorized to make loans to banks, insurance companies, farm mortgage companies, and railroads. Some critics charged that it was simply another trickle-down measure whereby businessmen and bankers would be given aid and the unemployed be ignored. Hoover, however, correctly understood the immense costs to individuals and to communities when a bank or mortgage company failed. The RFC did help shore up a number of shaky financial institutions and remained the major government finance agency until World War II. But it became much more effective under Roosevelt because it loaned directly to industry.

Hoover also asked Congress for a Home Financing Corporation to make mortgages more readily available. The Federal Home Loan Bank Act of 1932 became the basis for the Federal Housing Administration of the New Deal years. He also pushed the passage of the Glass-Steagall Banking Act of 1932, which expanded credit in order to make more loans available to businesses and individuals. Hoover failed to suggest any new farm legislation, even though members of the Farm Board insisted that the only answer to the agricultural crisis was for the federal government to step in and restrict production. Hoover believed that was too much federal intervention. He maintained that the federal government should play an active role, that it should promote cooperation and even create public works. But he firmly believed in loans, not direct subsidies, and he thought it was the responsibility of state and local governments, as well as of private charity, to provide direct relief to the unemployed and the needy.

The Bonus Army

Many World War I veterans lost their jobs during the Depression, and beginning in 1930, they lobbied for the payment of their veterans' bonuses, not due until 1945. A bill passed Congress in 1931, over Hoover's veto, allowing them to borrow up to 50 percent of the bonus due them, but this concession did not satisfy the destitute veterans or their leaders. In May 1932, about 17,000 veterans marched on Washington. Some took up residence in a shantytown, called Bonus City, in the Anacostia flats outside the city.

In mid-June, the Senate defeated the bonus bill, and most of the veterans, disappointed but resigned, accepted a free railroad ticket home. Several thousand remained, however, along with some wives and children, in the unsanitary shacks during the steaming summer heat. Among them were a small group of committed Communists and other radicals. Hoover exaggerated the subversive elements of those still camped out in Washington, refused to talk to the leaders, and finally called out the U.S. Army. However, it was General Douglas Mac-

Arthur, the army chief of staff, who ordered the army to disperse the veterans. He described the Bonus Marchers as "a mob . . . animated by the essence of revolution." With tanks, guns, and tear gas the army routed veterans who 15 years before had worn the same uniform as their attackers. Two Bonus Marchers were killed, and several others were injured. "What a pitiful spectacle is that of the great American Government, mightiest in the world, chasing unarmed men, women and children with Army tanks," commented a Washington newspaper. "If the Army must be called out to make war on unarmed citizens, this is no longer America." The army was not attacking revolutionaries in the streets of Washington but was routing bewildered, confused, unemployed men who had seen their American dream collapse.

The Bonus Army fiasco, bread lines, and Hoovervilles would become the symbols of Hoover's presidency. He deserved better because he tried to use the power of the federal government to solve looming economic problems. But in the end his personality and background limited him. He could not understand why army veterans marched on Washington to ask for a handout when he thought they should all be back home working hard, practicing self-reliance, and cooperating "to avert the terrible situation in which we are today." He believed that the greatest

The Capitol stands serenely in the background as the Bonus Army's shacks burn down, 1932.

problem besetting Americans was a lack of confidence. But he could not communicate with these people or inspire their confidence. Willing to use the federal government to support business, he could not accept federal aid for the unemployed. He feared an unbalanced budget and a large federal bureaucracy that would interfere with "the American way." Ironically, his actions and his inactions led in the next years to a massive increase in federal power and in the federal bureaucracy.

ROOSEVELT AND THE FIRST NEW DEAL

The first New Deal, lasting from 1933 to early 1935, focused mainly on recovery from the Depression and relief for the poor and unemployed. Congress passed legislation to aid business, the farmers, and labor and authorized public works projects and massive spending to put Americans back to work. Some of the programs were borrowed from the Hoover administration, and some had their origin in the progressive period. Others were inspired by the nation's experiences in mobilizing for World War I. No single ideological position united all the programs, for Roosevelt was a pragmatist who was willing to try a variety of programs. More than Hoover, he believed in economic planning and in government spending to help the poor.

Roosevelt's caution and conservatism shaped the first New Deal. He did not promote socialism or suggest nationalizing the banks. He was even careful in authorizing public works projects to stimulate the economy. The New Deal was based on the assumption that it was possible to create a just society by superimposing a welfare state on the capitalistic system, leaving the profit motive undisturbed. During the first New Deal, Roosevelt believed he would achieve his goals through cooperation with the business community. Later he would move more toward reform, but at first his primary concern was simply relief and recovery.

The Republicans nominated Herbert Hoover for a second term, but in the summer of 1932 the Depression and Hoover's unpopularity opened the way for the Democrats. After a shrewd campaign, Franklin D. Roosevelt, governor of New York, emerged from the pack and won the nomination. Walter Lippmann's comment during the campaign that Roosevelt was "a pleasant man, who without any important qualifications for office, would like very much to be President" was exaggerated at the time and seemed absurd later. Yet Roosevelt, despite two reasonably successful terms as governor of the nation's most populous state, was not especially well known by the general public in 1932.

As New York's governor, Roosevelt had promoted cheaper electric power, conservation, and old age pensions. Urged on by social workers Frances Perkins and Harry Hopkins, he became the first governor to support state aid for the

Governor of New York for two terms, Franklin D. Roosevelt was nonetheless a relative stranger to the general public in 1932. As president he inherited the worst national crisis since the Civil War.

unemployed, "not as a matter of charity, but as a matter of social duty." But it was difficult to tell during the presidential campaign exactly what he stood for. He did announce that the government must do something for the "forgotten man at the bottom of the economic pyramid," and he struck out at the small group of men who "make huge profits from lending money and the marketing of securities." Yet he also mentioned the need for balancing the budget and maintaining the gold standard. Ambiguity was probably the best strategy in 1932, but the truth was that Roosevelt did not have a master plan to save the country. Yet he won overwhelmingly, carrying more than 57 percent of the popular vote.

During the campaign, Roosevelt had promised a "new deal for the American people." But after his victory, the New Deal had to wait for four months because the Constitution provided that the new president be inaugurated on March 4 (this was changed to January 20 by the Twentieth Amendment, ratified in 1933). During the long interregnum, the state of the nation deteriorated badly. The banking system seemed near collapse, and the hardship of depression increased. Despite his bitter defeat, Hoover tried to cooperate with the president-elect and with a hostile Congress. But he could accomplish little. Everyone waited for the new president to take office and to act.

In his inaugural address, Roosevelt announced confidently, "The only thing we have to fear is fear itself." This of course was not true, for the country faced the worse crisis since the Civil War, but Roosevelt's confidence and his ability to communicate with ordinary Americans was obvious early in his presidency. He had a group of clever speech writers, a sense of pace and rhythm in his speeches, and an ability, when he spoke on the radio, to convince listeners that he was speaking directly to them. He instituted a series of radio "fireside chats" to explain to the American people what he was doing to solve the nation's problems. When he said "my friends," millions believed that he meant it, and they wrote letters to him in unprecedented numbers to explain their needs.

During the interregnum, Roosevelt surrounded himself with intelligent and innovative advisers. Some, like James A. Farley, a former New York State boxing commissioner with a genius for remembering names, and Louis Howe, Roosevelt's secretary and confidant since 1912, had helped plan his successful campaign. His cabinet was made up of a mixture of people from different backgrounds who often did not agree with one another. Harold Ickes, the secretary of the interior, was a Republican lawyer from Chicago who had been an ardent supporter of Theodore Roosevelt. Another Republican,

The Presidential Election of 1932

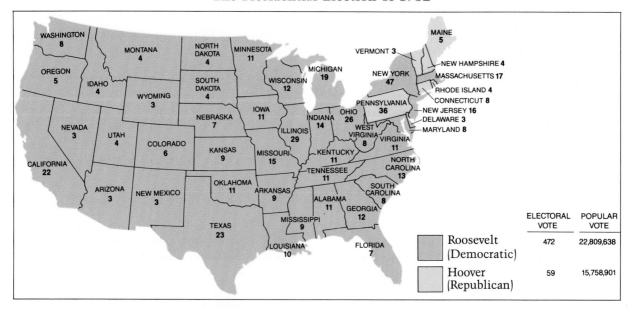

Henry Wallace of Iowa, a plant geneticist and agricultural statistician, became the secretary of agriculture. Frances Perkins, the first woman ever appointed to a cabinet post, had been a New York social worker, secretary of the New York Consumers League, and an adviser to Al Smith.

In addition to the formal cabinet, Roosevelt appointed an informal "Brain Trust," including Adolph Berle, Jr., a young expert on corporation law, and Rexford Tugwell, a Columbia University authority on agricultural economics and a committed national planner. Roosevelt also appointed Raymond Moley, another Columbia professor, who later became one of the president's severest critics, and Harry Hopkins, a nervous, energetic man who loved to bet on horse races and had left Iowa to be a social worker on the Lower East Side of New York. Hopkins's passionate concern for the poor and unemployed would play a large role in formulating New Deal policy.

Then there was Eleanor Roosevelt, the president's wife, who became the most active and controversial first lady. She wrote a newspaper column, made radio broadcasts, traveled widely, and was constantly giving speeches and listening to the concerns of women, minorities, and ordinary Americans all over the country. Attacked by critics who thought she had too much power and mocked for her protruding front teeth, her awkward ways, and her upper-class accent, she courageously took stands on issues of social justice and civil rights. She helped push the president toward social reform.

Roosevelt proved to be an adept politician. He was not particularly well read, especially on economic matters, but he had the ability to learn from his advisers and yet not to be dominated by them. Refusing to work within traditional channels, he continually frustrated subordinates. He took ideas, plans, and suggestions from conflicting sources and somehow combined them. He had "a flypaper mind," one of his advisers decided. There was no overall plan, no master strategy. An improviser and an opportunist who once likened himself to a football quarterback who called one play and if it did not work called a different one, Roosevelt was an optimist by nature. And he believed in action.

ONE HUNDRED DAYS

Roosevelt took office in the middle of a major crisis, and he had a cooperative Congress willing to pass almost any legislation that he put before it. In three months, a bewildering number of bills were rushed through Congress. Some of them were hastily drafted and not well thought out, and some contradicted other legislation. But many of the laws passed during Roosevelt's first hundred days would have far-reaching implications for the relationship of government to society. Roosevelt was an opportunist, but unlike Hoover, he was willing to use direct government action to solve the problems of depression and unemployment. As it turned out, none of the bills passed during the first hundred days cured the Depression, but taken together the legislation constituted one of the most innovative periods in American political history.

The most immediate problem facing Roosevelt was the condition of the banks. Many had closed, and American citizens, no longer trusting the financial institutions, were hoarding money and putting their assets into gold. Using a forgotten provision of a World War I law, Roosevelt immediately declared a four-day bank holiday. He closed all the banks, savings and loan associations, and credit unions. Three days later, an emergency session of Congress approved his action and within a few hours passed the Emergency Banking Relief Act. The bill gave the president broad powers over financial transactions, prohibited the hoarding of gold, and allowed for the reopening of sound banks, sometimes with loans from the Reconstruction Finance Corporation. Within the next few years, Congress passed additional legislation that gave the federal government more regulatory power over the stock market and over the process by which corporations issued stock. It also passed the Banking Act of 1933, which strengthened the Federal Reserve System, established the Federal Deposit Insurance Corporation, and insured individual deposits up to $5,000. Although the American Bankers Association opposed the plan as "unsound, unscientific, unjust and dangerous," banks were soon attracting depositors by advertising that they were protected by government insurance.

The Democratic platform in 1932 called for reduced government spending and an end to prohibition. Roosevelt moved quickly to accomplish both. The Economy Act, which passed Congress easily, called for a 15 percent reduction in government salaries as well as a reorganization of federal agencies in order to save money. The bill also cut veterans' pensions. The Economy Act did save some money, but the small savings were dwarfed by other bills passed the same week, which called for increased spending. The Beer-Wine Revenue Act legalized 3.2 beer and light wines and levied a tax on both. The Twenty-first Amendment, which was ratified December 5, 1933, repealed the Eighteenth Amendment and ended the prohibition experiment. The veterans, who opposed reduced pensions, and the antiliquor forces, two of the strongest lobbying groups in the nation, were both overwhelmed by a Congress that appeared ready to pass any bill that came to it from the president's office.

Congress gave Roosevelt great power to devalue the dollar and to reduce inflation. Senator Burton K. Wheeler of Montana argued for the old Populist solution of free and unlimited coinage of silver, while others called for issuing billions of dollars in paper currency. The bankers and businessmen feared inflation, but farmers and all who were in debt favored an inflationary policy as a way to raise prices and put more money in their pockets. "I have always favored sound money," Roosevelt announced, "and I do now, but it is 'too darned sound' when it takes so much of farm products to buy a dollar." He rejected the more extreme inflationary plans supported by many congressmen from the agricultural states, but he did take the country off the gold standard. No longer would paper currency be redeemable in gold. The action terrified some conservative businessmen, who argued that it would lead to "uncontrolled inflation and

complete chaos." Even Roosevelt's director of the budget announced solemnly that going off the gold standard "meant the end of Western Civilization."

Devaluation did not end Western civilization, but neither did it lead to instant recovery. After experimenting for a time with pushing the price of gold up by buying it in the open market, Roosevelt and his advisers fixed the price at $35.00 an ounce in January 1934 (against the old price of $20.63). This inflated the dollar by about 40 percent. Roosevelt also tried briefly to induce inflation through the purchase of silver, but then the country settled down to a slightly inflated currency and a dollar based on both gold and silver. Some still believed that gold represented fiscal responsibility, even morality, and others still cried for more inflation.

Relief Measures

Roosevelt believed in economy in government and in a balanced budget, but he also wanted to help the unemployed and the homeless. It was estimated in 1933 that 1.5 million Americans were homeless. One man with a wife and six children from Latrobe, Pennsylvania, who was being evicted wrote, "I have 10 days to get another house, no job, no means of paying rent, can you advise me as to which would be the most humane way to dispose of myself and family, as this is about the only thing that I see left to do."

Roosevelt's answer was the Federal Emergency Relief Administration (FERA), which Congress authorized with an appropriation of $500 million in direct grants to cities and states. A few months later, Congress created a Civil Works Administration (CWA) to put more than 4 million people to work on various state, municipal, and federal projects. Hopkins, who ran both agencies, had experimented with work relief programs in New York. Like most social workers, he believed it was much better to pay people for some work done than to give them money for clothes and food. A woman with two daughters from Houston, Texas, wrote and asked, "Why don't they give us materials and let us make our children's clothes . . . you've no idea how children hate wearing relief clothes." An accountant working on a road project said, "I'd rather stay out here in that ditch the rest of my life than take one cent of direct relief."

There were many charges of political favoritism and corruption in the CWA, and it was not until the Works Progress Administration was organized in 1935 that work relief became a major part of the plan to relieve the suffering and restore the morale of the unemployed. But the CWA did hire many who had been unemployed. In just over a year, the agency built or restored a half million miles of roads, constructed 40,000 schools and 1,000 airports. It hired 50,000 teachers to keep rural schools open and others to teach adult education courses in the cities. In many ways the CWA helped millions of people get through the bitterly cold winter of 1933–1934. It also put over a billion dollars of purchasing power into the economy. Roosevelt, who later would be accused of deficit spending, feared that the program was costing too much and might create a permanent class of relief recipients. In the spring of 1934, he ordered the CWA closed down.

The Public Works Administration (PWA), directed by Harold Ickes, in some respects overlapped the work of the CWA, but it lasted longer. Between 1933 and 1939, the PWA built hospitals, courthouses, and school buildings. It helped construct structures as diverse as the port of Brownsville, Texas, a bridge that linked Key West to the Florida mainland, and the library at the University of New Mexico. It built the aircraft carriers *Yorktown* and *Enterprise*, planes for the Army Air Corps, and low-cost housing for slum dwellers. One purpose of the PWA was economic pump priming—the stimulation of the economy and consumer spending through the investment of government funds. In the beginning, Ickes was so afraid that there might be scandals in the agency that he spent money slowly and carefully. There were no scandals, but during the first years, PWA projects did little to stimulate the economy.

Agricultural Adjustment Act

In 1933, farmers were desperate as mounting surpluses and falling prices drastically cut their incomes. Some in the Midwest talked of open rebellion, even of revolution, but many observers saw only hopelessness. Lorena Hickok, a journalist friend of Eleanor Roosevelt who traveled around the country reporting on conditions for Harry Hopkins, described a farmhouse in North Dakota:

> No repairs have been made in years. The kitchen floor was all patched up with pieces of tin, a wash boiler cover, tin can lids, some old automobile

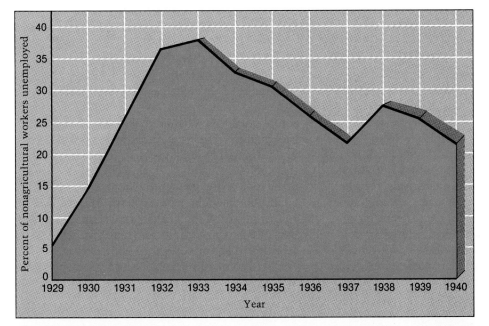

Unemployment Rate, 1929–1940

Source: U.S. Bureau of the Census.

license plates. You could see daylight through the crack under the door. Great patches of plaster had fallen from the walls . . . and in the house two little boys . . . were running about without a stitch on save some ragged overalls.

To deal with the agricultural crisis, Congress passed a number of bills in 1933 and 1934. They included the Emergency Farm Mortgage Act, designed to prevent more farm foreclosures and evictions. But the New Deal's principal solution to the farm problem was the Agricultural Adjustment Act (AAA), which sought to control the overproduction of basic commodities so that farmers might regain the same relative purchasing power they had had before World War I. To guarantee these "parity prices" (the average prices in the years 1909–1914), the production of major agricultural staples—wheat, cotton, corn, hogs, rice, tobacco, and milk— would be controlled by paying the farmers to reduce their acreage under cultivation. The AAA levied a tax at the processing stage to pay for the program.

The act aroused great disagreement among farm leaders and economists, but the controversy was nothing compared to the outcry from the public over the initial action of the AAA in the summer of 1933. To prevent a glut on the cotton and pork markets, the agency ordered 10 million acres of cotton plowed up and 6 million little pigs slaughtered. It seemed strange and unnatural, even immoral, to kill pigs and plow up cotton when millions of people were underfed and in need of clothes. The story circulated that in the South, mules trained for many years to walk between the rows of cotton now refused to walk on the cotton plants. Some suggested that those mules were more intelligent than the government bureaucrats who had ordered the action.

The Agricultural Adjustment Act did raise the prices of some agricultural products. But it helped the larger farmers more than the small operators, and it was often disastrous for the tenant farmers and sharecroppers, whom crop reduction made expendable. There were provisions in the act to help marginal farmers, but little trickled down to them. Many were simply cast out on the road with a few possessions and nowhere to go. As for the large farmers, they

cultivated their fewer acres more intensely, so that the total crop was not altered very much. In the end, the prolonged drought that hit the farm belt in 1934 did more than the AAA to limit production and raise agricultural prices. But the most important long-range significance of the AAA, which was later declared unconstitutional, was the establishment of the idea that the farmer should be subsidized for limiting his production.

Industrial Recovery

The flurry of legislation during the first days of the Roosevelt administration contained something for almost every group. The National Industrial Recovery Act (NIRA) was designed to help business, raise prices, control production, and put people back to work. The act established the National Recovery Administration (NRA) with the power to set fair competition codes in all industries. For a time, everyone forgot about antitrust laws and talked of cooperation and planning rather than competition. To run the NRA, Roosevelt appointed Hugh Johnson, who had helped organize the World War I draft and served on the War Industries Board. Johnson used some of his wartime experiences and the enthusiasm of the bond drives to rally the country around the NRA and, implicitly, around all New Deal measures. There were parades and rallies, even a postage stamp, and industries that cooperated could display a blue eagle, the symbol of the NRA. "We Do Our Part," the posters and banners proclaimed, but the results were somewhat less than the promise.

Section 7a of the NIRA, included at the insistence of organized labor, guaranteed labor's right to organize and to bargain collectively and established the National Labor Board to see that their rights were respected. But the board, usually dominated by businessmen, often interpreted the labor provisions of the contracts loosely. Still, it was the labor provisions that explained business disenchantment with the NIRA. In addition, small businessmen complained that the NIRA was unfair to their interests. Any attempt to set prices led to controversy.

Many consumers suspected that the codes and contracts were raising prices, while others feared the return of monopoly in some industries. One woman wrote the president that she was taking down her blue eagle because she had lost her job; another wrote from Tennessee to denounce the NIRA as a joke because it helped only the chain stores. Johnson's booster campaign backfired in the end because anyone with a complaint about a New Deal agency seemed to take it out on the symbol of the blue eagle. Johnson himself was widely disliked, so when the Supreme Court declared the NIRA unconstitutional in 1935, not too many people were sorry. Still, the NIRA was an ambitious attempt to bring some order into a confused business situation, and the labor provisions of the act were picked up later by the National Labor Relations Act.

Civilian Conservation Corps

One of the most popular and successful of the New Deal programs, the Civilian Conservation Corps (CCC) combined work relief with the preservation of natural resources. It put young unemployed men between the ages of 18 and 25 to work on reforestation, road and park construction, flood control, and other projects. The men lived in work camps (there were over 1,500

in all) and were paid $30 a month, $25 of which had to be sent home to their families. Some complained that the CCC camps, run by the U.S. Army, were unduly military in operation, and one woman wrote from Minnesota to point out that all the best young men were at CCC camps when they ought to be home looking for real jobs and finding brides. Others complained that the CCC did nothing for unemployed young women, so a few special camps were organized for them, but only 8,000 were included in a program that by 1941 had seen 2.5 million men participate. Overall, the CCC was one of the most successful and least controversial of all the New Deal programs.

Tennessee Valley Authority

Roosevelt, like his Republican namesake, believed in conservation. He promoted flood control projects and added many millions of acres to the country's national forests, wildlife refuges, and fish and game sanctuaries. But the most important New Deal conservation project, the Tennessee Valley Authority (TVA), owed more to Republican George Norris, a progressive senator from Nebraska, than to Roosevelt. During World War I, the federal government had

The Tennessee Valley Authority

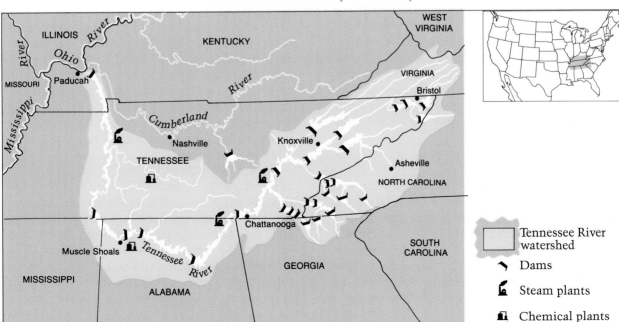

built a hydroelectric plant and two munitions factories at Muscle Shoals, on the Tennessee River in Alabama. The government tried unsuccessfully to sell these facilities to private industry, but all through the 1920s, Norris waged a campaign to have the federal government operate them for the benefit of the people who lived in the valley. Twice Republican presidents vetoed bills that would have allowed federal operation, but Roosevelt endorsed Norris's idea and expanded it to include a regional development plan.

Congress authorized the TVA as an independent public corporation with the power to sell electricity and fertilizer and to promote flood control and land reclamation. Nine major dams and many minor ones were built between 1933 and 1944, and the TVA affected parts of Virginia, North Carolina, Georgia, Alabama, Mississippi, Tennessee, and Kentucky. Some private utility companies claimed that TVA offered unfair competition to private industry, but altogether it was an imaginative experiment in regional planning. It promoted everything from flood control to library bookmobiles. For those who lived in the valley, it meant cheaper electricity. For many, it involved a change in life style. One man from a small town remarked, "I put in an electric hot water heater some time ago, but I have never been about to use it because it cost too much. But now with this new rate I can." For others in the valley, TVA meant radios, electric irons, washing machines, and other appliances for the first time. The largest federal construction project ever launched, it also created jobs for many thousands who helped build the dams. But the regional planning possibilities of TVA were always blunted by government officials and businessmen who feared that the experiment would lead to socialism.

Critics of the New Deal

The furious legislative activity during the first hundred days of the New Deal did something to alleviate the pessimism and despair hanging over the country. Stock market prices rose slightly, and industrial production was up 11 percent at the end of 1933. Still, the country remained locked in depression, and nearly 12 million Americans were without jobs. Yet Roo-

sevelt captured the imagination of ordinary Americans everywhere. Hundreds of thousands of letters poured into the White House, so many that eventually 50 people had to be hired to answer them. "I've always thought of F.D.R. as my personal friend," a man wrote from Georgia. "I feel very grateful to you for all the good you have already done for all of us," another added from Missouri. "If ever there was a saint, he is one," declared a Wisconsin woman.

But conservatives were not so sure that Roosevelt was a savior; in fact, many businessmen, after being impressed with Roosevelt's early economy measures and approving programs such as the NIRA, began to fear that the president was leading the country toward socialism. Appalled by work relief programs, by regional planning such as the TVA, and by the abandonment of the gold standard, many businessmen were also annoyed by the style of the president, whom they called "that man in the White House."

The conservative revolt against Roosevelt surfaced in the summer of 1934 as the congressional elections approached. A group of disgruntled politicians and businessmen formed the Liberty League. Led by Alfred E. Smith and John W. Davis, two unsuccessful Democratic presidential candidates, the league stood for states' rights, free enterprise, and "the American system of the open shop." The league supported conservative or at least anti–New Deal candidates for Congress, but it had little influence. In the election of 1934, the Democrats increased their majority from 310 to 319 in the House and from 60 to 69 in the Senate (only the second time in the twentieth century that the party in power had increased its control of Congress). A few people were learning to hate Roosevelt, but it was obvious that most Americans approved of what he was doing.

Much more disturbing to Roosevelt and his advisers in 1934 and 1935 than people who thought the New Deal too radical were those on the left who maintained that the government had not done enough to help the poor. One threat came from the Communist party. The widespread discontent and talk of the failure of capitalism would seem to have provided great opportunity for the Communists in the United

States. But except for a few college students and a small number of disillusioned intellectuals and writers, the Communist party attracted few converts. The party particularly failed to win many recruits among the working class in America, even during their time of great despair.

Much more important were other movements promising easy solutions to the problems of poverty and unemployment. In Minnesota, Governor Floyd Olson, elected on a Farm-Labor ticket, accused capitalism of causing the Depression and startled some when he thundered, "I hope the present system of government goes right down to hell." In California, Upton Sinclair, the muckraking socialist and author of *The Jungle*, ran for governor on the platform "End Poverty in California." He promised to pay everyone over 60 years of age a pension of $50 a month and to finance the program with higher income and inheritance taxes. He won in the primary but lost the election, and his EPIC program collapsed.

California also produced Dr. Francis E. Townsend, who claimed he had a national following of over 5 million. His supporters backed the Townsend Old Age Revolving Pension Plan, which promised $200 a month to all unemployed citizens over 60 on the condition that they spent it in the same month they received it. Economists laughed at the utopian scheme, but thousands of Townsend Pension Clubs were organized across the country. As one Minnesota woman wrote to Eleanor Roosevelt, "The old folks who have paid taxes all their lives and built this country up will live in comfort." The plan "will banish crime, give the young a chance to work, pay off the national debt which is mounting every day."

More threatening to Roosevelt and the New Deal than Townsend and Sinclair were the protest movements led by Father Charles E. Coughlin and Senator Huey P. Long of Louisiana.

Father Coughlin, a Roman Catholic priest from the Detroit suburb of Royal Oak, attracted an audience of 30 to 45 million to his national radio show. At first he supported Roosevelt's policies, but then he savagely attacked the New Deal as excessively probusiness. Mixing his religious commentary with visions of a society operating without bankers and big businessmen, he roused his audience with blatantly anti-Semitic appeals. The 1930s was a decade in which anti-Semitism peaked in the United States, and Jews, rather than Catholics, bore the brunt of nativist fury. Groups like the Silver Shirts and the German-American Bund lashed out against Jews. To these and to many other Americans, Father Coughlin's attacks made sense. Most often the "evil" bankers he described were Jewish—the Rothschilds, Warburgs, and Kuhn-Loebs. His message was immensely appealing, especially to the urban lower-middle class.

Huey Long, like Coughlin, had a kind of charisma that won him support from the millions still trying to survive in a country where the continuing depression made day-to-day existence a struggle. Elected governor of Louisiana in 1928, he promoted a "Share the Wealth" program. He taxed the oil refineries and built hospitals, schools, and thousands of miles of new highways. By 1934, he was the virtual dictator of his state, personally controlling the police and the state courts. He threatened to run for president in 1936. Long talked about a guaranteed $2,000 to $3,000 income for all American families (18.3 million families earned less than $1,000 per year in 1936) and promised pensions for the elderly and college educations for the young. He would pay for these programs by taxing the rich and liquidating the great fortunes. Had not an assassin's bullet cut Long down in September 1935, he might have mounted a third-party challenge to Roosevelt.

THE SECOND NEW DEAL

Responding in part to the discontent of the lower middle class and to the threat of various utopian schemes, Roosevelt moved his programs in 1935 more toward the goals of social reform and social justice. At the same time, he departed from any attempt to cooperate with the business community. "We find our population suffering from old inequalities," Roosevelt announced in his annual message to Congress in January 1935. "In spite of our efforts and in spite of our talk, we have not weeded out the over-privileged and we have not effectively lifted up the underprivileged."

Work Relief and Social Security

The Works Progress Administration (WPA), authorized by Congress in April 1935, was the first massive attempt to deal with unemployment and its demoralizing effect on millions of Americans. The WPA employed about 3 million people a year on a variety of socially useful projects. The WPA workers, who earned wages lower than private industry paid, built bridges, airports, libraries, roads, and golf courses. Nearly 85 percent of the funds went directly into salaries and wages. A minor but important part of the WPA funding supported writers, artists, actors, and musicians. Richard Wright, Jack Conroy, and Saul Bellow were among the 10,000

Millions of workers participated in the WPA: here a city street is widened and modernized.

writers who were paid less than $100 a month. Experimental theater, innovative and well-written guides to all the states, murals painted on the walls of post offices and other public buildings, and the Historical Records Survey were among the long-lasting results of these projects.

Only one member of a family could qualify for a WPA job, and first choice always went to the man in the family. A woman could qualify only if she was head of the household. But eventually more than 13 percent of the people who worked for the WPA were women, although their most common employment was in the sewing room, where old clothes were made over. "For unskilled men we have the shovel. For unskilled women we have only the needle," one official remarked.

The WPA was controversial from the beginning. There were charges that Communists had been hired to paint murals or work on the state guides. For some, a lazy good-for-nothing leaning on a shovel symbolized the WPA. Others who were employed resented the make-work aspects of many of the projects. The initials WPA, some charged, stood for "We Pay for All" or "We Putter Around." Yet for all the criticism, the WPA did useful work; the program built nearly 6,000 schools, more than 2,500 hospitals, and 13,000 playgrounds. More important, it gave millions of unemployed Americans a sense that

Distribution of Income, 1935–1936

Source: U.S. Bureau of the Census.

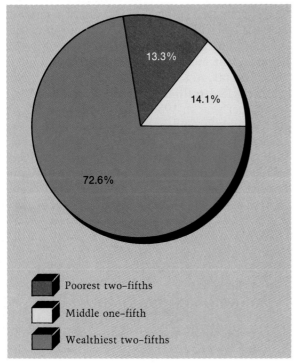

13.3%

14.1%

72.6%

- ■ Poorest two-fifths
- ▫ Middle one-fifth
- ■ Wealthiest two-fifths

they were working and bringing in a paycheck to support their families.

The National Youth Administration (NYA) supplemented the work of the WPA and assisted young men and women between the ages of 16 and 25, many of them students. A young law student named Richard Nixon earned 35 cents an hour working for the NYA while he was at Duke University, and Lyndon Johnson began his political career as director of the Texas NYA.

Since the progressive period, a number of social workers and reformers had been arguing for a national system of health insurance, old age pensions, and unemployment insurance. By the 1930s, the United States remained the only major industrial country without such programs. Within the Roosevelt circle, it was Frances Perkins who argued most strongly for social insurance, but the popularity of the Townsend Plan and other schemes to aid the elderly helped convince Roosevelt of the need to act. The number of people over 65 in the country increased from 5.7 million in 1925 to 7.8 million in 1935, and that group demanded action.

The Social Security Act that Congress finally passed in 1935 was a compromise. The plan for federal health insurance was quickly dropped because of opposition from the medical profession. The best-known provision of the act was old age and survivor insurance to be paid for by a tax of one percent on both employers and employees. The benefits initially ranged from $10 to $85 a month. The act also established a cooperative federal-state system of unemployment compensation. Other provisions authorized federal grants to the states to assist in caring for the crippled and the blind. The Social Security Act also provided some aid to dependent children, which would eventually expand to become the largest federal welfare program.

The National Association of Manufacturers denounced social security as a program that would regiment the people and destroy individual self-reliance. In reality it was a conservative and, in some ways, an inept system. In no other country was social insurance paid for in part by a regressive tax on the workers' wages. "We put those payroll contributions there so as to give the contributors a legal, moral, and political right to collect their pensions and unemploy-

ment benefits," Roosevelt later explained. "With those taxes in there, no damn politician can ever scrap my social security program." But the law also excluded large numbers of people, including those who needed it most, such as farm laborers and domestic servants. It discriminated against married women wage earners, and it failed to protect against sickness. Yet for all its weaknesses, it was one of the most important New Deal measures. A landmark in American social legislation, it signified government's acceptance of some responsibility to care for its citizens.

Aiding the Farmers

The Social Security Act and the Works Progress Administration were the most important, but certainly not the only, signs of Roosevelt's greater concern for social reform. The flurry of legislation in 1935 and early 1936, often called the "second New Deal," also included an effort to help American farmers. Over 1.7 million farm families had incomes of under $500 annually in 1935, and 42 percent of all those who lived on farms were tenants. The Resettlement Administration (RA), motivated in part by a Jeffersonian dream of yeoman farmers working their own land, set out to relocate tenant farmers on land purchased by the government. Lack of funds and

Mexican workers, actively recruited in the 1920s, found themselves excluded from jobs during the Depression and were often deported back to Mexico.

fears that the Roosevelt administration was trying to establish collective farms patterned after those in Russia limited the effectiveness of the Resettlement Administration program.

Much more important in making life easier for farm families was the Rural Electrification Administration (REA), which was authorized in 1935 to loan money to cooperatives to generate and distribute electricity in isolated rural areas not served by private utilities. Only 10 percent of the nation's farms had electricity in 1936. When the REA's lines were finally attached, they dramatically changed the lives of millions of farm families who had only been able to dream about the radios, washing machines, and farm equipment advertised in magazines.

In the hill country west of Austin, Texas, for example, there was no electricity until the end of the 1930s. Life went on in the small towns and on the ranches much as it had for decades. Houses were illuminated by kerosene lamps whose wicks had to be trimmed just right or the lamp smoked or went out, but even with perfect adjustment it was difficult to read by them. There were no bathrooms because bathrooms required running water, and running water depended on an electric pump. "Yes, we had running water," one woman remembered. "I always said we had running water because I grabbed those two buckets up and ran the two hundred yards to the house with them."

Women and children hauled water constantly—for infrequent baths, for continuous canning (because without a refrigerator, fruits and vegetables had to be put up almost immediately or they spoiled), and for washday. Washday, always Monday, meant scrubbing clothes by hand with harsh soap on a washboard; it meant boiling clothes in a large copper vat over a wood stove and stirring them with a wooden fork. It was a hot and backbreaking job, especially in summer. Then the women had to lift the hot, heavy clothes into a rinsing tub. After the clothes were thoroughly mixed with bluing (to make them white), they had to be wrung out by hand, then carried to the lines, where they were hung to dry. Tuesday was for ironing, and even in summer a wood fire was needed to heat the irons. It was a rare ironing day when a woman's hand did not slip and cause an ugly burn. And when irons got dirty on the stove, as could so easily happen, dirt got on a white shirt or blouse, and it had to be washed all over again.

It was memory of life in the hill country and personal knowledge of how hard his mother and grandmother toiled that inspired a young congressman from Texas, Lyndon Johnson, to work hard to bring rural electrification to the area. In November 1939, the lights finally came on in the hill country, connecting the area to the twentieth century.

Controlling Corporate Power and Taxing the Wealthy

In the summer of 1935, Roosevelt also moved to control the large corporations, and he even toyed with radical plans to tax the well-to-do heavily and redistribute wealth in the United States. The Public Utility Holding Company Act, which passed Congress in 1935, was aimed at restricting the power of the giant utility companies, the 12 largest of which controlled more than half the power produced in the country. The act gave various government commissions the authority to regulate and control the power companies and included a "death sentence" clause that gave each company five years to demonstrate that its services were efficient. If it could not demonstrate this, the government could dissolve the company. This was one of the most radical attempts to control corporate power in American history.

In his message to Congress in 1935, Roosevelt also pointed out that the federal revenue laws had "done little to prevent an unjust concentration of wealth and economic power." He suggested steeper income taxes for high-income groups and a much larger inheritance tax. When Congress dropped the stiff inheritance tax provision, however, Roosevelt did not fight to have it restored. Even the weakened bill, increasing estate and gift taxes and raising the income tax rates at the top, angered many in the business community who thought that Roosevelt had sold out to Huey Long's "Share the Wealth" scheme.

The New Deal for Labor

The increasingly prolabor stance of the Roosevelt administration in 1935 fed the fear of the business leaders and other conservatives. Like many reformers of the progressive period, Roosevelt was more interested in improving the lot of the workingman by passing social legislation than by strengthening the bargaining position of organized labor. He had escaped the antilabor bias of most of those of his background and class, but he had no particular understanding or sympathy for organized labor. Yet he saw labor as an important balance to the power of industry, and he listened to his advisers, especially to Frances Perkins and to Senator Robert Wagner of New York, who persistently presented the needs of organized labor to him.

Even before the Supreme Court declared the NIRA, with its strong labor provisions, unconstitutional in 1935, Wagner had been working hard in Congress for a bill that would replace and extend Section 7a. At first Roosevelt was only mildly interested. But a series of strikes in San Francisco, Minneapolis, and Toledo, some bitter and violent, convinced him of the need for action. Belatedly he supported the Wagner Act, officially called the National Labor Relations Act, which outlawed blacklisting and a number of other practices and reasserted labor's right to organize and to bargain collectively. The act also established a Labor Relations Board with the power to certify a properly elected bargaining unit. The act did not require workers to join unions, but it made the federal government a regulator, or at least a neutral force, in management-labor relations. That alone made the National Labor Relations Act one of the most important of the New Deal reform measures.

The Roosevelt administration's friendly attitude toward organized labor helped to increase union membership from under 3 million in 1933 to 4.5 million by 1935. Many groups, however, were left out, including farm laborers, unskilled workers, and women. Approximately 10 million women worked for wages in the 1930s, and the percentage of women in the work force increased slightly during the decade. Yet only about 3 percent of the women who worked belonged to unions, and women were paid only about 60 percent of the wages paid to men for equivalent work. Because women labored at occupations less affected by the economic downturn, fewer women than men lost their jobs during the thirties (there were fewer women employed in heavy industry, for example). Many families survived only because of the woman's paycheck.

Still, many people resented the fact that women were employed at all, and there was a growing assumption, even stronger than in the 1920s, that a woman's place was in the home. The Brotherhood of Railway and Steamship Clerks ruled that no married woman whose husband could support her was eligible for a job. One writer had a perfect solution for the unemployment problem. "There are approximately 10,000,000 people out of work in the United States today," he wrote; "there are also 10,000,000 or more women, married and single, who are jobholders. Simply fire the women, who shouldn't be working anyway, and hire the men. Presto! No unemployment. No relief rolls. No Depression." Women remained underpaid, underunionized, and underrepresented in many "male" occupations. But during a decade when popular culture insisted that women belonged at home, many women had to work for wages.

The American Federation of Labor had little interest in organizing the army of unskilled workers, but a new group of committed and militant labor leaders emerged in the 1930s to take up that task. John L. Lewis, the eloquent head of the United Mine Workers who had won union recognition from the soft coal industry,

Frances Perkins, a former social worker, served as Roosevelt's Secretary of Labor.

was the most aggressive, but he was joined by David Dubinsky of the International Ladies Garment Workers and Sidney Hillman, president of the Amalgamated Clothing Workers. Dubinsky was born in Poland, Hillman in Lithuania. Both were socialists who believed in economic planning, but both had worked closely with social justice progressives. Hillman had even lived for a time at Hull House in Chicago. These new progressive labor leaders formed the Committee of Industrial Organization (CIO) within the AFL and set out to organize workers in the steel, auto, and rubber industries. They organized everyone into an industrywide union much the way the Knights of Labor had done in the 1880s, rather than separating workers by skill or craft as the AFL preferred.

Many young and militant workers, including many blacks, joined the CIO. They were angry at their poor pay and the way management controlled their lives. In 1936, the workers at three rubber plants in Akron, Ohio, went on strike without permission from the leaders. Instead of picketing outside the factory, they occupied the buildings and took them over. The "sit-down strike" became a new protest technique. A strike against a General Motors factory in Atlanta, Georgia, spread to Flint, Michigan. When management tried to cut off the delivery of food to the workers barricaded inside the factories, the workers drove off the police with a barrage of auto door hinges, bolts, stones, bottles, and coffee cups. The police retaliated with tear gas and rifles but were finally driven off by high-powered water hoses that the workers discovered in the factory. Fourteen of the pickets and spectators were wounded, and several policemen were injured by flying objects.

At one point in the struggle, which became known as the "Battle of Running Bulls," a young woman in the crowd grabbed a microphone and urged all the women spectators to join the pickets. Other women organized an emergency brigade to bring food and water to the strikers. "We had not asked for it," Bob Travis, one of the organizers of the strike recalled. "We had been content to allow reason and common sense to rule in our relationship with the company. But when pressed . . . we had to answer blow with blow to convince General Motors of our rights under the law." It took six weeks, but General

Motors finally accepted the United Auto Workers as their employees' bargaining unit.

The General Motors strike was the most important event in a critical period of labor upheaval. A group of workers using disorderly but largely nonviolent tactics (as the civil rights advocates would in the mid-1950s) demanded their rights under the law. They helped to make labor's voice heard in the decision-making process in major industries where labor had long been denied any role. They also helped to raise the status of organized labor in the eyes of many Americans.

"Labor does not seek industrial strife," Lewis announced. "It wants peace, but a peace with justice." As the sit-down tactic spread, justice was often accompanied by violence. Chrysler capitulated without much difficulty. But the Ford Motor Company used hired gunmen to discourage the strikes. A bloody struggle ensued before Ford finally agreed to accept the UAW as the bargaining agent. Even U.S. Steel, which had been militantly antiunion, signed an agreement with the Steel Workers Organizing Committee calling for a 40-hour week and an eight-hour day. But other steel companies refused to go along. In Chicago on Memorial Day in 1937, a confrontation between the police and peaceful pickets at the Republic Steel plant resulted in ten deaths. In the "Memorial Day Massacre," as it came to be called, the police fired without provocation into a crowd of workers and their families, who had gathered near the plant in a holiday mood. All ten of the dead were shot in the back.

Despite the violence and management's use of undercover agents within unions, the CIO gained many members. William Green and the leadership of the AFL were horrified at the aggressive tactics of the new labor leaders. They expelled the CIO leaders from the AFL only to see them form a separate Congress of Industrial Organization (the initials stayed the same). By the end of the decade, the CIO had infused the labor movement with a new spirit. Accepting unskilled workers, blacks, and others who had never belonged to a union before, they won increased pay, better working conditions, and the right to bargain collectively in most of the basic American industries. Jim Cole, a black butcher at one of the meatpacking plants in

Chicago, tried to join the Amalgamated Butchers and Meat Cutters, an AFL union, but they turned him away because he was black. He remembered when the CIO came. "Well, I tell you, we Negroes was glad to see it come. Sometimes the bosses or the company stooges try to keep the white boys from joining the union. They say, 'You don't want to belong to a black man's organization. That's all the CIO is.' Don't fool nobody, but they got to lie, spread lying words around."

America's Minorities in the 1930s

A half million blacks became union members through the CIO during the 1930s, and many blacks were aided by various New Deal agencies. Yet the familiar pattern of discrimination, low-paying jobs, and intimidation through violence persisted. Lynchings in the South actually increased in the New Deal years, rising from 8 in 1932 to 28 in 1933 and 20 in 1935. An NAACP representative investigating the lynching of a young black man in Florida in 1933 decided that the alleged charge of rape was only the surface cause; the more basic reason was economic. "The lynching had two objects; first to intimidate and threaten white employers of Negro labor, and secondly to scare and terrorize Negroes so they would leave the country and their jobs could be taken over by white men."

The migration of blacks to northern cities, which had started during World War I, continued during the 1930s. Lynchings and the threat of violence caused many blacks to migrate. The collapse of cotton prices also forced black farmers and farm laborers to flee north in order to survive. But since most were poorly educated, they discovered that they soon became trapped in northern ghettoes, where they were eligible for only the most menial jobs. The black unemployment rate was triple that of whites, and blacks often received less per person in welfare payments.

Black leaders attacked the Roosevelt administration for supporting or allowing segregation in government-sponsored facilities. The TVA model town of Norris, Tennessee, was off limits for blacks, and AAA policies actually drove blacks off the land in the South. The CCC segregated black and white workers, and the PWA financed segregated housing projects. Some charged that NRA stood for "Negroes Rarely Allowed." Many blacks wrote in broken English to the president or to Eleanor Roosevelt to protest discrimination in New Deal agencies. As one woman from Georgia put it, "I can't sign my name Mr. President they will beat me up and run me away from here and this is my home." Blacks ought to realize, a writer in *The Crisis* warned in 1935, "that the powers-that-be in the Roosevelt administration have nothing for them."

Roosevelt, dependent on the vote of the solid South and fearing that he might antagonize southern congressmen whose backing he needed, refused to support the two major civil rights bills of the era, an antilynching bill and a bill to abolish the poll tax. Yet Harold Ickes and Harry Hopkins worked hard to make sure that blacks were given opportunities in the CCC, the WPA, and other agencies. By 1941, there were 150,000 black federal employees, more than three times the number during the Hoover administration. Although most of them worked in the lower ranks, there were also lawyers, architects, office managers, and engineers.

Partly responsible for the presence of more black employees was the "black cabinet," a group of over 50 young blacks who had appointments in almost every government department and New Deal agency. The group met on many Friday evenings at the home of Mary McLeod Bethune to discuss problems and plan strategy. The daughter of a sharecropper and one of 17 children, Bethune had worked her way through the Moody Bible Institute in Chicago. She had founded a black primary school in Florida and then transformed it into Bethune-Cookman College. In the 1920s, she had organized the National Council of Negro Women. In 1934, Harry Hopkins, following the advice of Eleanor Roosevelt, appointed her to the advisory committee of the National Youth Administration. Mary Bethune had a large impact on New Deal policy and on the black cabinet. She spoke out forcefully, she picketed and protested, and she intervened shrewdly to obtain civil rights and more jobs for black Americans.

Although Roosevelt appointed a number of blacks to government positions, he was never particularly committed to civil rights. That was not true of Eleanor Roosevelt, who was educated in part by Mary McLeod Bethune. In 1939, when the Daughters of the American Revolution refused to allow Marian Anderson, a black concert singer, to use their stage, Mrs. Roosevelt publicly protested and resigned her membership in the DAR. She also arranged for Anderson to sing from the steps of the Lincoln Memorial, where 75,000 people gathered to listen and to support civil rights for all black citizens.

Many Mexicans who had been actively recruited for working American farms and in American businesses in the 1920s discovered that they were not needed in the Depression decade. Hundreds of thousands lost their jobs and drifted from the urban barrios to small towns and farms in the Southwest looking for work. By one estimate, there were 400,000 Mexican migrants in Texas alone. The competition for jobs increased the ethnic prejudice. Signs inscribed "Only White Labor Employed" and "No Niggers, Mexicans, or Dogs Allowed" expressed the hate and fear that the Mexicans faced everywhere.

Some New Deal agencies helped destitute Mexicans. A few worked for the CCC and the WPA, but to be employed, an applicant had to qualify for state relief, and that automatically eliminated most migrants. The primary solution was not to provide aid for the Mexicans but to ship them back to Mexico. The Southern Pacific Railroad offered to return the migrants to Mexico for $14.70 a head. A trainload of repatriates left Los Angeles every month during 1933, and thousands were deported from other cities. One estimate placed the number sent back in 1932 at 200,000.

Not all the Mexicans were repatriated, however, and some who remained became militant in their efforts to obtain fair treatment. Mexican strawberry pickers went on strike in El Monte, California, and 18,000 cotton pickers walked away from their jobs in the San Joaquin Valley in 1933. In Gallup, New Mexico, several thousand Mexican coal miners walked out on strike. They constructed a village of shacks and planned to wait out the strike. Even though the miners were aided by some writers and artists from Santa Fe and Taos, the strikers were evicted from their village. Their leader, Jesus Pallares, was arrested and, like so many other Mexican labor leaders, deported to Mexico.

During the Depression, Native Americans also experienced hunger, disease, and despair, and their plight was compounded by years of exploitation. Since the Dawes Act of 1887 (described in Chapter 18), government policy had sought to make the Indian into a property-owning farmer and to limit tribal rights. Native Americans lost over 60 percent of their original 138 million acres through the sale of land declared surplus or by selling their own land, while

A staunch advocate of equal rights, Eleanor Roosevelt met in 1937, with the National Youth Administration's executive director, Aubrey Williams, and its director of Negro Activities, Mary McLeod Bethume.

another 20 percent had been parceled out in lots of 160 acres to heads of Native American families who "adopted the habits of civilized life." Few Native Americans profited from this system, but many whites did. Just as other progressives sought the quick assimilation of immigrants, the progressive-era Indian commissioners speeded up the allotment process to increase Indian detribalization. But many Native Americans who remained on the reservations were not even citizens. Finally, in 1924, Congress granted citizenship to all Indians born in the United States. The original Americans became United States citizens, but that did not end their suffering.

Franklin Roosevelt brought a new spirit to Indian policy by appointing John Collier as commissioner of Indian affairs. Collier, who had worked with the immigrant poor in New York, discovered among the Pueblo tribe near Taos, New Mexico, the sense of community and culture he missed in urban, industrial America. He had reorganized the American Indian Defense Association in 1923. As commissioner, he was primarily responsible for the passage of the Indian Reorganization Act of 1934, which sought to restore the political independence of the tribes and to end the allotment policy of the Dawes Act. "Even where a tribal group is split into factions, where leadership has broken down, where Indians clamor to distribute the tribal property, even there deep forces of cohesion persist and can be evoked," Collier wrote.

The bill also sought to promote "the study of Indian civilization" and to "preserve and develop the special cultural contributions and achievements of such civilization, including Indian arts, crafts, skills and traditions." Not all Indians agreed with the new policies. Some chose to become members of the dominant culture, and the Navajos voted to reject the Reorganization Act. Some Americans charged that the act was inspired by communism. Others argued that its principal result would be to increase government bureaucracy, while missionaries claimed that the government was promoting paganism by allowing the Indians to practice their native religions. Still, thanks to the Indian Reorganization Act and a more concerned attitude during the New Deal, there was a reversal of land policy, a revival of interest in tribal identity, and a recognition of the importance of Indian culture, language, and ritual.

Women and the New Deal

Women made some gains during the 1930s, and more women were appointed to high government positions than in any previous administration. Besides Frances Perkins, the secretary of labor, there was Molly Dewson, a social worker who had worked for the Massachusetts Girls Parole Department and the National Consumers League before becoming head of the Women's Division of the Democratic Committee and then an adviser to Roosevelt. Working closely with Eleanor Roosevelt to promote women's causes, she helped to achieve a number of firsts: two women appointed ambassadors, a judge on the U.S. Court of Appeals, the director of the mint, and many women in government agencies. Katharine Lenroot, director of the Children's Bureau, and Mary Anderson, head of the Women's Bureau, selected many other women to serve in their agencies. Some of these women had worked together as social workers and now joined government bureaus to continue the fight for social justice. But they were usually located in offices where they did not threaten male prerogatives.

Despite the number of women working for the government, feminism declined in the 1930s. Instead of fighting for the absolute right of women to work, it became necessary to argue for married women's rights to support their families. The older feminists died or retired, and they were not replaced by younger women. Women role models in the 1930s seemed to come from Hollywood rather than from Hull House. One committed feminist who did cause a great stir in the thirties was Amelia Earhart, a former social worker who became fascinated with flying. She was attractive and daring and made good copy. She flew across the Atlantic alone and from Newark to Mexico City, but it was her disappearance somewhere over the Pacific in 1937 that garnered the most attention. Despite some dramatic exceptions, the image of woman's proper role in the 1930s continued to be housewife and mother.

THE END OF THE NEW DEAL

The New Deal was not a consistent or well-organized effort to end the Depression and restructure society. A considerable amount of contradiction riddled the measures passed by Congress. Roosevelt was a politician and a pragmatist, not one who was concerned about ideological consistency. The first New Deal in 1933 and 1934 was basically concerned with relief and recovery, while the legislation passed in 1935 and 1936 was more involved with social reform. In many ways the election of 1936 marked the high point of Roosevelt's power and influence. After 1937, in part because of the growing threat of war but also because of increasing opposition in Congress, the pace of social legislation slowed. Yet several measures passed in 1937 and 1938 had far-reaching significance. Among them were bills that provided for a minimum wage and for housing reform.

The Election of 1936

The Republicans in 1936 nominated Governor Alfred Landon of Kansas, a moderate who had supported Theodore Roosevelt in 1912. Although he attacked the New Deal at every opportunity, charging that new government programs were wasteful and created a dangerous federal bureaucracy, he did not offer to change much. He only promised to do the same thing more cheaply and efficiently. Two-thirds of the newspapers in the country supported Landon, and the *Literary Digest,* on the basis of a "scientific" poll, predicted his victory.

Roosevelt, helped by signs that the economy was recovering and supported by a coalition of the Democratic South, organized labor, the farmers, and urban voters, won easily. A majority of black Americans for the first time deserted the party of Abraham Lincoln, not because of Roosevelt's interest in civil rights for blacks but because New Deal relief programs assisted many blacks, who made up a large part of the country's poor. A viable candidate to the left of the New Deal failed to materialize. In fact, the Socialist party candidate, Norman Thomas, polled less than 200,000 votes. Roosevelt won by over 10 million votes and carried every state except Maine and Vermont. Even the traditionally Republican states of Pennsylvania, Delaware, and Connecticut, which had voted Republican in every election since 1856, went for Roosevelt. "To some generations much is given," Roosevelt announced in his acceptance speech; "of other generations much is expected. This generation has a rendezvous with destiny." Now he had a mandate to continue his New Deal social and economic reforms.

"I see one-third of a nation ill-housed, ill-clad, ill-nourished," Roosevelt declared in his second inaugural address, and he vowed to alter that situation. But the president's first action in 1937 did not call for legislation to alleviate poverty. Instead he announced a plan to reform

FDR's Successful Presidential Campaigns, 1932–1944

YEAR	CANDIDATES	PARTY	POPULAR VOTE	ELECTORAL VOTE
1932	FRANKLIN D. ROOSEVELT	Democratic	22,809,638 (57.3%)	472
	Herbert C. Hoover	Republican	15,758,901 (39.6%)	59
	Norman Thomas	Socialist	881,951 (2.2%)	0
1936	FRANKLIN D. ROOSEVELT	Democratic	27,751,612 (60.7%)	523
	Alfred M. Landon	Republican	16,681,913 (36.4%)	8
	William Lemke	Union	891,858 (1.9%)	0
1940	FRANKLIN D. ROOSEVELT	Democratic	27,243,466 (54.7%)	449
	Wendell L. Willkie	Republican	22,304,755 (44.8%)	82
1944	FRANKLIN D. ROOSEVELT	Democratic	25,602,505 (52.8%)	432
	Thomas E. Dewey	Republican	22,006,278 (44.5%)	99

the Supreme Court and the judicial system. The Court had not only invalidated a number of New Deal measures—including, most importantly, the NIRA and the AAA—but other measures as well. Increasingly angry at the "nine old men" who seemed to be blocking progress, Roosevelt hoped to gain power to appoint an extra justice for each justice over 70 years of age, of whom there were six. His plan also called for modernizing the court system at all levels, but that plan got lost in the public outcry over the "court-packing" scheme.

Roosevelt's plan was aimed at nullifying the influence of some of the older and more reactionary justices, but he miscalculated badly. Republicans accused him of being a dictator and of subverting the Constitution. Many congressmen from his own party refused to support him. After months of controversy, he finally withdrew the legislation and admitted defeat. He had perhaps misunderstood his mandate, and he certainly underestimated the respect, even the reverence, that most Americans felt for the Supreme Court. Even in times of economic catastrophe, Americans proved themselves fundamentally conservative toward their institutions, in stark contrast to Europeans, who experimented radically with their governments.

Ironically, though he lost the battle of the Supreme Court, Roosevelt won the war in the end. By the spring of 1937, the Court began to reverse its position and in a 5–4 decision upheld the National Labor Relations Act. Then on July 1, Justice Willis Van Devanter retired, allowing Roosevelt to make his first Supreme Court appointment. This assured at least a shaky liberal majority on the Court. But Roosevelt triumphed

at great cost. His attempt to reorganize the Court dissipated a lot of energy and caused a loss of momentum in his legislative program. The most unpopular action he took as president, it made him vulnerable to criticism from opponents of one or another aspect of the New Deal.

In late 1936 and early 1937, it appeared that the country was finally recovering from the long depression; employment was up, and even the stock market had recovered some of its losses. But in August, the fragile prosperity collapsed. Unemployment shot back up nearly to the peak levels of 1934, industrial production fell, and the stock market plummeted. Roosevelt had probably helped to cause the recession by assuming that the prosperity of 1936 was permanent. He cut federal spending and reduced outlays for relief. He had always believed in balanced budgets and limited government spending, but now, in the face of an embarrassing economic slump that caused many to charge that the New Deal had been a failure, he gave in to those of his advisers who were followers of John Maynard Keynes, the British economist.

Keynes argued that to get out of a depression, the government must spend massive amounts of money on goods and services. This would increase purchasing power and revive production. For the first time, the administration consciously practiced deficit spending, by increasing the money spent on the WPA and other agencies in order to stimulate the economy. It was not a well-planned or well-coordinated effort, however. The economy responded slowly but never fully recovered until wartime expenditures, beginning in 1941, finally eliminated unemployment and ended the Depression.

Roosevelt's popularity was affirmed with his election to a second term in 1936.

Social Reform Continues

Despite an increasingly hostile Congress, a number of important bills passed during 1937 and 1938 completed the New Deal reform legislation. The Bankhead-Jones Farm Tenancy Act of 1937 created the Farm Security Administration to solve the problem of farm tenants, sharecroppers, and people who had lost their farms. More than a million men, women, and children were drifting aimlessly and hopelessly looking for work. Their plight was worsened by the drought that had created a "dust bowl" in the Southwest. It was these conditions that John Steinbeck captured in *The Grapes of Wrath* (1939) in his description of the Joad family and their desperate condition as they migrated in an ancient Hudson from Oklahoma to California. The Farm Security Administration, which provided loans to grain collectives, also set up camps for migratory workers. Some people saw such policies as the first step toward Communist collectives, but the FSA, in fact, never had enough money to make a real difference.

A new Agricultural Adjustment Act, passed in 1938, attempted to meet the problem of farm surpluses, which still existed even after hundreds of thousands of farmers had lost their farms. The new act replaced the processing tax, which had been declared unconstitutional, with direct payments from the federal Treasury to farmers, added a soil conservation program, and provided for marketing of surplus crops. Like its predecessor, it tried to stabilize farm prices by controlling production. But only the outbreak of World War II would end the problem of farm surplus, and then only temporarily.

One of the dreams of progressive reformers was to provide better housing for the urban poor. They believed that a better home environment would help produce better citizens. They had campaigned for city ordinances and state laws. They had built model tenements, but the first experiment with federal housing occurred during World War I. That brief experience encouraged a number of social reformers, who later became advisers to Roosevelt. They convinced him that federal low-cost housing should be part of New Deal reform.

The Reconstruction Finance Corporation made low-interest loans to housing projects, and a few housing projects were constructed by the Public Works Administration. But it was not until the Wagner-Steagall Housing Act of 1937 that Roosevelt and his advisers tried to develop a comprehensive housing policy for the poor. The act provided federal funds for slum-clearance projects and for the construction of low-cost housing. By 1939, however, only 117,000 units had been built. Many of these housing projects were bleak and boxlike, and many of them soon became problems rather than solutions. Though it made the first effort, the New Deal did not meet the challenge of providing decent housing for millions of American citizens.

In the long run, New Deal housing legislation had a greater impact on middle-class housing policies and patterns. During the first hundred days of the New Deal, Congress passed a bill at Roosevelt's urging creating the Home Owners Loan Corporation (HOLC), which over the next two years made over $3 billion in low-interest loans and helped more than a million people save their homes from foreclosure. The HOLC also had a wide impact on housing policy. It introduced the long-term fixed-rate mortgage for the first time. Formerly, all mortgages were for periods of no more than five years and were subject to frequent renegotiation. The HOLC also introduced a uniform system of real estate appraisal that tended to undervalue urban property, especially in neighborhoods that were old, crowded, and ethnically mixed. The system gave the highest ratings to suburban developments where there had been no "infiltration of Jews" or other undesirable groups. This was the beginning of the practice later called "redlining" that made it difficult if not impossible for prospective homeowners to obtain a mortgage in many urban areas.

The Federal Housing Administration (FHA), created in 1934 by the National Housing Act, expanded and extended many of these HOLC policies. The FHA insured mortgages, many of them for 25 or 30 years, reduced the initial down payment required from 30 percent to under 10 percent, and thus made it possible for over 11 million families to buy homes between 1934 and 1972. The system, however, tended to favor the purchase of new suburban homes rather than the repair of older urban residences. New Deal housing policies helped to make the suburban home with the long FHA mortgage part of the American way of life, but the policies also contributed to the decline of many urban neighborhoods.

Just as important as housing legislation was the Fair Labor Standards Act, which passed Congress in June 1938. Roosevelt's bill proposed for all industries engaged in interstate commerce a minimum wage of 25 cents an hour, to rise in two years to 40 cents an hour, and a maximum workweek of 44 hours, to be reduced to 40 hours. The legislation was much amended by Congress, and many groups, including farm laborers and domestic servants, were exempted from the law. Yet when it went into effect, three-quarters of a million workers immediately

Key New Deal Legislation

YEAR	LEGISLATION	PROVISIONS
1932	Reconstruction Finance Corporation (RFC)	Granted emergency loans to banks, life insurance companies, and railroads. (Passed during Hoover administration.)
1933	Civilian Conservation Corps (CCC)	Employed young men (and a few women) in reforestation, road construction, and flood control projects.
1933	Agricultural Adjustment Act (AAA)	Granted farmers direct payments for reducing production of certain products. Funds for payments provided by a processing tax, which was later declared unconstitutional.
1933	Tennessee Valley Authority (TVA)	Created independent public corporation to construct dams and power projects and to develop the economy of a nine-state area in the Tennessee River valley.
1933	National Industrial Recovery Act (NIRA)	Sought to revive business through a series of fair-competition codes. Section 7a guaranteed labor's right to organize. (Later declared unconstitutional.)
1933	Public Works Administration (PWA)	Sought to increase employment and business activity through construction of roads, buildings, and other projects.
1934	National Housing Act creates Federal Housing Administration (FHA)	Insured loans made by banks for construction of new homes and repair of old homes.
1935	Emergency Relief Appropriation Act creates Works Progress Administration (WPA)	Employed over 8 million people to repair roads, build bridges, and work on other projects; also hired artists and writers.
1935	Social Security Act	Established unemployment compensation and old age and survivors' insurance paid for by a joint tax on employers and employees.
1935	National Labor Relations Act (Wagner-Connery Act)	Recognized the right of employees to join labor unions and to bargain collectively; created a new National Labor Relations Board to supervise elections and to prevent unfair labor practices.
1935	Public Utility Holding Company Act	Outlawed pyramiding of gas and electricity companies through the use of holding companies and restricted these companies to activity in one area; a "death sentence" clause gave companies five years to prove local, useful, and efficient operation or be dissolved.
1937	National Housing Act (Wagner-Steagall Act)	Authorized low-rent public housing projects.
1938	Agricultural Adjustment Act (AAA)	Continued price supports and payments to farmers to limit production, as in 1933 act, but replaced processing tax with direct federal payment.
1938	Fair Labor Standards Act	Established minimum wage of 40 cents an hour and maximum workweek of 40 hours in enterprises engaged in interstate commerce.

received pay raises, and by 1940, some 12 million had had their pay increased. The law also prohibited child labor in interstate commerce, making it the first permanent federal law to prohibit youngsters under 16 from working. And without emphasizing the matter, the law made no distinction between men and women, thus diminishing, if not completely ending, the need for special legislation for women and undercutting the argument of reformers who had opposed an equal-rights amendment to the Constitution.

THE OTHER SIDE OF THE THIRTIES

The Great Depression and the New Deal so dominate the history of the 1930s that it is easy to conclude that nothing else happened, that there were only bread lines and relief agencies. But there is another side of the decade. A communications revolution changed the lives of middle-class Americans. The sale of radios and attendance at movies increased during the thirties, and literature flourished. Americans were fascinated by technology, especially automobiles. Many people traveled during the decade; they stayed in motor courts and looked ahead to a brighter future dominated by streamlined appliances and gadgets that would mean an easier life.

Taking to the Road

"People give up everything in the world but their car," a banker in Muncie, Indiana, remarked during the Depression, and that seems to have been true in all sections of the country. Although automobile production dropped off after 1929 and did not recover until the end of the thirties, the number of motor vehicles registered, which declined from 26.7 million in 1930 to just over 24 million in 1933, increased to over 32 million by 1940. If many people could not afford a new car, they drove a used one. Even the "Okies" fleeing the dust bowl of the Southwest traveled in cars. They were secondhand, run-down cars to be sure, but the fact that even many poor Americans owned cars shocked visitors from Europe, where the automobile was still only for the rich. The American middle class traveled at an increasing rate after the low point of 1932 and 1933. In 1938, the tourist industry was the third largest in the United States, behind only steel and automobile production. Over 4 million Americans traveled every year, and four out of five went by car. Many dragged a trailer to sleep in or stopped at the growing number of tourist courts and overnight cabins. In these predecessors of the motel there were no doormen, no bellhops, no register to sign. At the tourist court, all the owner wanted was the automobile license number.

The Electric Home

If the 1920s were the age of the bathroom, the 1930s were the era of the modern kitchen. The sale of electrical appliances increased throughout the decade, and refrigerators led the way. In 1930, the number of refrigerators produced exceeded the number of iceboxes for the first time. Refrigerator production continued to rise throughout the thirties, reaching a peak of 2.3 million in 1937. At first, the refrigerator was boxy and looked very much like an icebox with a motor sitting awkwardly on top. In 1935, however, the refrigerator, like most other appliances, became streamlined. Sears, Roebuck advertised "The New 1935 Super Six Coldspot . . . Stunning in Its Streamlined Beauty." The Coldspot, which quickly influenced the look of all other models, was designed by Raymond Loewy, one of a group of industrial designers who emphasized sweeping horizontal lines, rounded corners, and a slick modern look. They hoped modern design would stimulate an optimistic attitude and, of course, increase sales.

Replacing an icebox with an electrical refrigerator, as many middle-class families did in the 1930s, altered more than the appearance of the kitchen. It changed habits and life styles, especially for women. An icebox was part of a culture that included icemen, ice wagons (or ice trucks), ice picks, ice tongs, and a pan that had to be emptied continually. The streamlined refrigerator, like the streamlined automobile, became a symbol of progress and modern civilization in the 1930s.

Other appliances signaled changes in life styles. The electric washing machine and electric iron altered the nature of washday. But even with labor-saving machines, most women continued to do their wash on Monday and their ironing on Tuesday, and women spent just as much time at housework. In fact, a great many middle-class families maintained their standard of living during the 1930s only because the women in the family learned to stretch and save and make do. Yet packaged and canned goods became more widely available during the decade. Many women discovered that it was easier, and in some cases cheaper, to serve Kellogg's Corn Flakes or Nabisco Shredded Wheat than to make oatmeal, to serve Van Camp's pork and beans or Heinz spaghetti from a can than to prepare a meal, or to use commercially baked bread than to bake their own.

Household Appliance Production, 1929–1939

Source: U.S. Bureau of the Census.

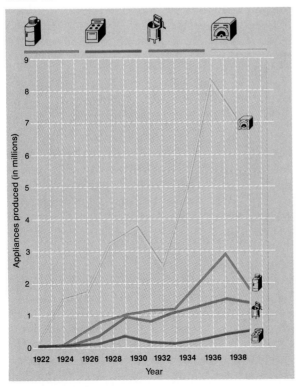

Although most women worked out of dire necessity, some took jobs outside the home to maintain their level of consumption. There was an increase of 50 percent in the number of married women who worked during the decade. At the same time, many rural women, like those in the hill country of Texas and other remote areas, and many wives of the unemployed made do with what was available. Many continued to cook, clean, and sew the way their ancestors had for generations.

The Age of Leisure

It is ironic that the age of the Depression was also a time when many people worried about how to spend leisure time. The 1920s were a time of spectator sports, of football and baseball heroes, of huge crowds that turned out to see boxing matches. Those sports continued during the Depression decade, although attendance suffered. Softball and miniature golf, which were cheap forms of entertainment and did not require expensive travel, also became popular. But the 1930s were a time when leisure became a problem to be analyzed and to be written about by professionals. During the decade, 450 new books on the subject appeared. Leisure was mechanized; millions put their nickels in a slot and listened to a record played on a jukebox. Millions more played a pinball machine, a mechanized device that had no practical use other than entertainment and could end the game with one word: *tilt*. Many of the popular games of the period had elaborate rules and directions. Contract bridge swept the country during the decade, and Monopoly was the most popular game of all. Produced by Parker Brothers, Monopoly was a fantasy of real estate speculation in which chance, luck, and the roll of the dice determined the winner. But one still had to obey the rules: "Go Directly to Jail. Do Not Pass Go. Do Not Collect $200." During a depression brought on in part by frenzied speculation, Americans were fascinated by a game whose purpose was to obtain real estate and utility monopolies and drive one's opponents into bankruptcy.

The 1930s were also a time of fads and of instant celebrities, created by radio, newsreels, and businessmen ready to turn almost anything to commercial advantage. The leading movie box-office attraction between 1935 and 1938 was Shirley Temple, a blond and adorable child movie star. She inspired Shirley Temple dolls, dishes, books, and clothes. Even stranger was the excitement created by the birth of five identical girl babies to a couple in northern Ontario in 1934. The Dionne quintuplets appeared on dozens of magazine covers and endorsed every imaginable product. Millions waited eagerly for the latest news and the latest article about the babies, and over 3 million made the long trek to see their home in Canada. Both Shirley Temple and the Dionne quintuplet craze were products of the new technology, especially radio and the movies.

Literary Reflections of the 1930s

Though much of the serious literature of the 1930s reflected the decade's troubled currents,

More than a source of entertainment, the family radio was a vital link with the world. Here relatives of a crew member on a disabled submarine anxiously await news of the ship's fate.

reading continued to be a popular and cheap form of entertainment. John Steinbeck, whose later novel *The Grapes of Wrath* (1939) followed the fortunes of the Joad family, described the plight of Mexican migrant workers in *Tortilla Flat* (1935). His novels expressed his belief that there was in American life a "crime . . . that goes beyond denunciation." "In the eyes of the hungry there is a growing wrath," he warned his readers.

Other writers questioned the American dream. John Dos Passos's trilogy *U.S.A.* (1930–1936) conveyed a deep pessimism about American capitalism, a pessimism that many other intellectuals shared. Less political were the novels of Thomas Wolfe and William Faulkner, who more sympathetically portrayed Americans caught up in the web of local life and facing the complex problems of the modern era. Faulkner's fictional Yoknapatawpha County, brought to life in *The Sound and the Fury*, *As I Lay Dying*, *Sanctuary*, and *Light in August* (1929–1932), documented the South's racial problems and its poverty as well as its stubborn pride. But the book about the South that became one of the decade's best-sellers was far more optimistic and far less complex than Faulkner's work— Margaret Mitchell's *Gone with the Wind* (1936). Its success suggested that many Americans used reading as an escape, not as an exploration of their problems.

Radio's Finest Hour

The number of radio sets purchased increased steadily during the decade. In 1929, slightly more than 10 million households owned radios; by 1939, fully 27.5 million households had radio sets. The radio was not just something to turn on for music and news but a piece of furniture that dominated the living room. In many homes the top of the radio became the symbolic mantel where family photos were displayed. Families gathered around the radio at night to listen to and laugh at Jack Benny or Edgar Bergen and Charlie McCarthy or to try to solve a murder mystery with Mr. and Mrs. North. "The Lone Ranger," another popular program, had 20 million listeners by 1939.

During the day there were soap operas, which James Thurber described as "a kind of sandwich, whose recipe is simple enough, although it took years to compound. Between thick slices of advertising, spread twelve minutes of dialogue, add predicament, villainy, and female suffering in equal measure, throw in a dash of nobility, sprinkle with tears, season with organ music, cover with a rich announcer sauce and serve five times a week.'' After school, teenagers and younger children argued over whether to listen to ''Jack Armstrong, the All-American Boy'' and ''Captain Midnight'' or ''Stella Dallas'' and ''The Young Widder Brown.''

Most families had only one radio, but everyone could join in the contests or send away for magic rings or secret decoders. The reception was sometimes poor, especially in rural areas and small towns. Voices faded in and out and disappeared completely during storms. But the magic of radio allowed many people to feel connected to distant places and to believe they knew the radio performers personally. Radio was also responsible for one of the biggest hoaxes of all time. On October 31, 1938, Orson Welles broadcast ''The War of the Worlds'' so realistically that thousands of listeners really believed that Martians had landed in New Jersey. If anyone needed proof, that single program demonstrated the power of the radio.

The Silver Screen

The 1930s were the golden years of the movies. Between 60 and 90 million Americans went to the movies every week during the decade. The movies were not entirely depression-proof. But talking films had replaced the silent variety in the late twenties, and this drove attendance up. Though it fell off slightly in the early 1930s, by 1934 attendance was climbing again. For many families, even in the depth of the Depression, movie money was just as important as food money.

In the cities one could go to one of the elaborate movie palaces and live in a fantasy world far removed from the reality of Depression America. In small towns across the country, for 25 cents (10 cents under age 12) one could go to at least four movies during the week. There was a Sunday-Monday feature film (except in communities where the churches had prevented Sunday movies), a different feature of somewhat lesser prominence on Tuesday-Wednesday, and another on Thursday-Friday. On Saturday there was a cowboy movie, or perhaps one featuring a detective. Sometimes a double feature played, and always there were short subjects, a cartoon, and a newsreel. On Saturday there was usually a serial that left the heroine or hero in such a dire predicament that you just had to come back the next week to see how she or he survived.

The movies were a place to take a date, to go with friends, or to go as a family. Movies could be talked about for days. Young women tried to speak like Greta Garbo or to hold a cigarette like Joan Crawford. Jean Harlow and Mae West so

Four movies in one week were commonly billed by small-town theaters during Hollywood's "golden years."

Cultural historians have often looked at recreation—how a people use their leisure time to have fun—as a way to take the pulse of a nation. Fairs and celebrations can help to explain something about a country's spirit and aspirations. The 1876 Centennial Exposition held in Philadelphia attracted millions of Americans, who came to admire the Corless engine, the telephone, and other technological marvels. They looked forward to a time when American industry would make life better for everyone. The World Columbian Exposition, held in Chicago in 1893, featured the Great White City, a planned and ordered array of classical buildings that contrasted sharply with the chaos and unplanned nature of the real Chicago. During the Bicentennial celebration of 1976, there was no giant fair but instead thousands of smaller celebrations. In the aftermath of Vietnam and Watergate, these local affairs tended to idealize the American past rather than celebrate the present and future. The American people have always, in fact, looked both nostalgically back to "better days" as well as optimistically ahead to a glorious future.

Like the combination of Frontierland and Tomorrowland at Walt Disney World, American fairs usually reflect this double vision. County and state fairs, for example, have a rural, agrarian tone, reflecting their nineteenth-century origins as occasions to show off prizewinning heifers, horses, and sows, giant vegetables and melons, and rhubarb pies and other baked delicacies. These fairs also serve to relieve the boredom of rural life by offering country people the amusements, crowds of people, and other attractions of the fair. In addition to livestock exhibits and other contests, country fairs inevitably include carnival rides and games, shooting galleries, candy and ice cream booths, sideshow freaks, dancing girls, trotting races, and other diversions. What would a historian learn about the American people from the study of local fairs? How do they remind us of earlier days, and what do they suggest about enduring values as well as current events?

In 1939, for example, with the country still in the grip of depression and the world on the brink of war, the United States paused to create a world's fair out of Long Island swampland near New York City. The theme of the fair was a glorious streamlined future. The most conspicuous symbols of the fair were the 700-foot Trylon, a three-sided needle representing "the Fair's lofty purpose," and the Perisphere, 200 feet in diameter. One feature of the fair was a giant

Library of Congress, Washington, D.C.

Jack Delano, County Fair

Democracity, a model of "a perfectly integrated, futuristic metropolis." Future citizens would spend their time playing in structured parks and recreation facilities, not wasting their time in "dissipated idleness or carousing." Many visitors to the fair saw a demonstration of television for the first time. They also observed a model of a rocket ship advertised as capable of shooting a projectile from New York to London.

But the most popular building at the fair was the General Motors exhibit, which created the future world of 1960. This world was planned, streamlined, and ordered, and it featured skyscrapers and superhighways. It stood in contrast to the chaotic, terrifying world of 1939. Visitors were given a 15-minute simulated airplane ride over the United States of 1960. There they observed a scientific orchard with

Both photos from the Bel Geddes Collection, University of Texas, Austin; by permission of Edith Lutyens Bel Geddes, executrix

New York World's Fair of 1939–1940. (Above) General Motors building with the Trylon and Perisphere in the background; (right) Armchair Visitors' City of 1960 (Futurama), designed by Norman Bel Geddes

trees under glass, a futuristic amusement park, a superhighway system, and a modern metropolis with widely spaced quarter-mile-high skyscrapers, separated by parks and smaller buildings.

What does the New York World's Fair tell us about the United States at the end of the 1930s? Why do Americans show such faith in technology, inventions, science fiction, and the future, especially during times of crisis? Or are world's fairs more concerned with selling products than with expressing the nation's hopes and fears? Have you ever been to a world's fair, one of the Disney parks, or some other national fair? What did the exhibits, theme areas, and rides tell you about the attitudes, concerns, spirit, and values of the American people? How do they differ from county and state fairs?

popularized blonde hair that the sale of peroxide shot up. Young men tried to emulate Clark Gable or Cary Grant, and one young man admitted that it was "directly through the movies that I learned to kiss a girl on her ears, neck, and cheeks, as well as on the mouth."

Walt Disney, one of the true geniuses of the movie industry, made his animated cartoons so popular that Mickey Mouse was probably more famous and familiar than most real celebrities. In May 1933, right in the middle of Roosevelt's hundred days, Disney released *The Three Little Pigs*, whose theme song "Who's Afraid of the Big Bad Wolf?" became a national hit overnight. Some felt it had as much to do with raising the nation's morale as did the New Deal legislation. One critic suggested that the moral of the story, as retold by Disney, was that the little pig survived because he was conservative, diligent, and hardworking; others felt that it was the pig who used modern tools and planned ahead who won out.

CONCLUSION: The Ambivalent Character of the Great Depression

The New Deal, despite a great variety of legislation, did not end the Depression, nor did it solve the problem of unemployment. For many Americans looking back on the decade, the most vivid memory was the shame and guilt of being unemployed, the despair and fear that came from losing a business or being evicted from a home or an apartment. Parents who lived through the decade urged their children to find a secure job, to get married, and to settle down. "Every time I've encountered the Depression it has been used as a barrier and a club," one daughter of Depression parents remembered; "older people use it to explain to me that I can't understand *anything:* I didn't live through the Depression."

New Deal legislation did not solve all the country's problems, but the New Deal did strengthen the power of the federal government, the presidency, and the executive branch. Federal agencies like the Federal Deposit Insurance Corporation and programs like social security influenced the daily lives of most Americans, and rural electrification, the WPA, and the CCC changed the lives of millions. It also established the principle of federal responsibility for the health of the economy and initiated the concept of the welfare state. Federally subsidized housing, minimum-wage laws, and a policy for paying farmers to limit production, all aspects of these principles, had far-reaching implications.

The New Deal was as important for what it did not do as for what it did. It did not promote socialism or cause the redistribution of income or property. It promoted social justice and social reform, but it provided little for people at the bottom of American society. The New Deal did not prevent business consolidation, and, in the end, it probably strengthened corporate capitalism.

Roosevelt, with his colorful personality and his dramatic response to the nation's crisis, dominated his times in a way few presidents have done. Yet there was another side to the 1930s. For some people who lived through the decade, it was not Roosevelt or bread lines but a new streamlined refrigerator or a Walt Disney movie that symbolized the Depression decade.

Recommended Reading

Lester V. Chandler, *America's Greatest Depression* (1970) discusses the economic impact of the Depression and the government's response to it. Robert S. McElvaine, ed., *Down and Out in the Great Depression* (1983) uses letters written to Eleanor and Franklin Roosevelt to describe the reaction of ordinary Americans. Studs Terkel, *Hard Times* (1970) uses interviews to accomplish the same purpose.

William E. Leuchtenburg, *Franklin Roosevelt and the New Deal* (1963) is a balanced and well-written account. Paul K. Conkin, *The New Deal* (1967) is more critical. Arthur M. Schlesinger, Jr., *The Age of Roosevelt*, 3 vols. (1957–1960) is favorable and fascinating. James MacGregor Burns, *Roosevelt: The Lion and the Fox* (1956) is still the best one-volume biography, but Joseph Lash, *Eleanor and Franklin* (1971) is a lively tale of two lives.

There are a great many specialized studies of the Depression and the New Deal; the following are among the most useful and interesting. Harvard Sitkoff, *A New Deal for Blacks* (1978) discusses the limited attention given to blacks during the decade. Mark Reisler, *By the Sweat of Their Brow* (1976) describes the plight of Mexican-Americans. Lois Scharf, *To Work and to Wed* (1980) and Susan Ware, *Beyond Suffrage* (1981) depict the lot of women during the New Deal era. Irving Bernstein, *Turbulent Years* (1969) discusses the American worker and organized labor. Jerre Mangione, *The Dream and the Deal* (1972) is about the Federal Writer's Project. Richard Pells, *Radical Visions and American Dreams* (1973) describes social thought. Alan Brinkley, *Voices of Protest* (1982) tells the story of Father Coughlin and Huey Long. The other side of the thirties can be followed in Warren Sussman, ed., *Culture and Commitment* (1973) and Siegfreid Giedion, *Mechanization Takes Command* (1948).

John Steinbeck shows Okies trying to escape the dust bowl in his novel, *The Grapes of Wrath* (1939). James Farrell describes growing up in Depression Chicago in *Studs Lonigan* (1932–1935). Richard Wright details the trials of a young black man in *Native Son* (1940).

TIME LINE

1929	Stock market crashes Agricultural Marketing Act
1930	Depression worsens Hawley-Smoot Tariff
1932	Reconstruction Finance Corporation established Federal Home Loan Bank Act Glass-Steagall Banking Act Federal Emergency Relief Act Bonus March on Washington Franklin D. Roosevelt elected president
1933	Emergency Banking Relief Act Home Owners Loan Corporation Twenty-first Amendment repeals Eighteenth, ending prohibition Agricultural Adjustment Act National Industrial Recovery Act Civilian Conservation Corps Tennessee Valley Authority established Public Works Administration established
1934	Unemployment peaks Federal Housing Administration established Indian Reorganization Act
1935	Second New Deal begins Works Progress Administration established Social Security Act Rural Electrification Act Wagner Act Committee for Industrial Organization (CIO) formed
1936	United Auto Workers hold sit-down strikes against General Motors Roosevelt reelected president Economy begins rebound
1937	Attempt to reform the Supreme Court Economic collapse Farm Security Administration established Wagner-Steagall Housing Act
1938	Fair Labor Standards Act Agricultural Adjustment Act

CHAPTER 26
THE AMERICAN PEOPLE
AND WORLD WAR II

N Scott Momaday, a Kiowa Indian born at Lawton, Oklahoma, in 1934, was only 11 when World War II ended, yet the war changed his life. Shortly after the United States entered the war, Momaday's parents moved to Hobbs, New Mexico, where his father got a job with an oil company and his mother worked in the civilian personnel office at an Army Air Force base. Like many couples, they had struggled through the hard times of the Depression. The war meant jobs.

Momaday's best friend was Billy Don Johnson, "a reddish, robust boy of great good humor and intense loyalty." Together they played war, digging trenches and dragging themselves through imaginary mine fields. They hurled grenades and fired endless rounds from their imaginary machine guns, pausing only to drink Kool-Aid from their canteens. At school they were taught history and math, but also how to hate the enemy and be proud of America. They recited the Pledge of Allegiance to the flag and sang "God Bless America," "The Star-Spangled Banner," and "Remember Pearl Harbor."

Momaday's only difficulty was that his Native American face was often mistaken for that of an Asian. Almost every day on the playground, someone would yell, "Hi ya, Jap," and a fight was on. Billy Don always came to his friend's defense, but it was disconcerting, to say the least, to be taken for the enemy. His father read old Kiowa tales to Momaday, who was proud to be an Indian but prouder still to be an American. On Saturday he and his friends would go to the local theater, where they would cheer as they watched a Japanese Zero or a German Me-109 go down in flames. They pretended that they were P-40 pilots. "The whole field of vision shuddered with our fire: the 50-caliber tracers curved out, fixing brilliant arcs upon the span, and struck; then there was a black burst of smoke, and the target went spinning down to death."

Near the end of the war, his family moved again, as so many families did, in order that his father might get a better job. This time they lived right next door to an air force base, and Scott fell in love with the B-17 "Flying Fortress," the bomber that military strategists thought would win the war in the Pacific and in Europe. He felt a real sense of resentment and loss when the B-17 was replaced by the larger but not nearly so glamorous B-29.

Looking back on his early years, Momaday reflected on the importance of the war in his growing up. "I see now that one experiences easily the ordinary things of life," he decided, "the things which cast familiar shadows upon the sheer, transparent panels of time, and he perceives his experience in the only way he can, according to his age." Momaday's life during the war differed from the lives of boys old enough to join the forces, but the war was no less real for him than for those who were older. His youth was influenced by the fact that he was male, but not much by being an Indian or by living in the Southwest. Yet his parents, like all Native Americans in New Mexico and Arizona, could not vote. The Momadays fared better than most Native Americans, who found prejudice against them undiminished and jobs, even in wartime, hard to find. Returning servicemen discovered that they were still treated like "Indians." They were prohibited from buying liquor in many states, and those who returned to the reservations learned that they were ineligible for veterans' benefits.

This chapter traces the gradual involvement of the United States in the international events during the 1930s that finally led to America's participation in the most devastating war the world had seen. We recount the diplomatic and military struggles of the war and the search for a secure peace. We also seek to explain the impact of the war on ordinary people and on American attitudes about the world, as well as its effect on patriotism and the American way of life. The war brought prosperity to some as it brought death to others. It left the American people the most affluent in the world and the United States the most powerful nation.

THE TWISTING ROAD TO WAR

Looking back on the events between 1933 and 1941, which eventually led to American involvement in World War II, it is easy either to be critical of decisions made or actions not taken or to see everything that happened as inevitable. Historical events are never inevitable, and leaders who must make decisions never have the advantage of retrospective vision; they have to deal with the situation as they find it, and they never have all the facts.

Foreign Policy in the 1930s

In March 1933, Roosevelt not only faced an overwhelming domestic crisis but also confronted an international crisis. The worldwide depression had caused near financial disaster in Europe. Germany had defaulted on its reparations installments, and most European countries were unable to keep up the payments on their debts to the United States. Hoover had agreed to a brief moratorium on the war debts in 1931 and had pledged American participation in an international economic conference to be held in London in June 1933.

Roosevelt had no master plan in foreign policy, just as he had none in the domestic sphere. In the first days of his administration, he gave conflicting signals as he groped to find a response to the international situation. At first it seemed that the president would cooperate in some kind of international economic agreement on tariffs and currency. But then he undercut the American delegation in London by refusing to go along with any international agreement. Solving the American domestic economic crisis seemed more important to Roosevelt in 1933 than inter-

national economic cooperation. His actions signaled a decision to go it alone in foreign policy in the 1930s.

Roosevelt did, however, alter some of the foreign policy decisions of previous administrations. For example, he pushed for the recognition of the Soviet government in Russia. There were many reasons why the United States had not recognized the Soviet Union during the 1920s. The new regime had failed to accept the debts of the czar's government, but more important, Americans feared communism and believed that recognition meant approval. In reversing this nonrecognition policy, Roosevelt hoped to gain a market for surplus American grain. Although the expected trade bonanza never materialized, the Soviet Union did agree to pay the old debts and to extend rights to American citizens living in the Soviet Union. Diplomatic recognition opened communications between the two emerging world powers.

Led by Cordell Hull, his secretary of state, Roosevelt's administration also reversed the earlier policy of intervention in South America. The United States continued to support dictators, especially in Central America, because they promised to promote stability and preserve American economic interests. But Roosevelt completed the removal of American military forces from Haiti and Nicaragua in 1934, and, in a series of pan-American conferences, he joined in pledging that no country in the hemisphere would intervene in the "internal or external affairs" of any other. The United States still had economic and trade interests in Latin America, however, and with many of the Latin American economies in disarray because of the Depression, there were pressures to resume the policy of intervention.

The first test case came in Cuba, where a revolution threatened American investments of more than a billion dollars. But the United States did not intervene. Instead Roosevelt sent special envoys to work out a conciliatory agreement with the revolutionary government. A short time later, when a coup led by Fulgencio Batista overthrew the revolutionary government, the United States not only recognized the Batista government but also offered a large loan and agreed to abrogate the Platt Amendment (which made Cuba a virtual protectorate of the United States) in return for the rights to a naval base.

The Trade Agreements Act of 1934 gave the president power to lower tariff rates by up to 50

Elected chancellor in 1933, Adolf Hitler quickly assumed dictatorial powers and implemented a massive rearmament plan.

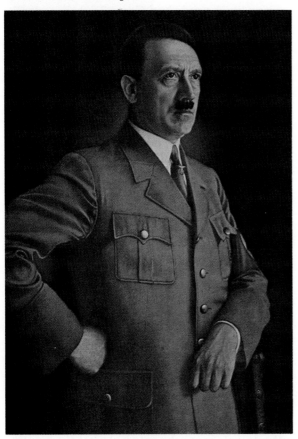

percent and took the tariff away from the pressure of special-interest groups in Congress. Using this act, the Roosevelt administration negotiated a series of agreements that improved trade. By 1935, half of American cotton exports and a good proportion of other products were going to Latin America. So the Good Neighbor policy was also good business for the United States. But increased trade did not solve the economic problems either for the United States or for Latin America.

Another test for Latin American policy came in 1938 when Mexico nationalized the property of a number of American oil companies. Instead of intervening, as many businessmen urged, the State Department patiently worked out an agreement that included some compensation for the companies. The American government might have acted differently, however, if the threat of war in Europe in 1938 had not created a fear that all the Western Hemisphere nations would have to cooperate to resist the growing power of Germany and Italy. At a pan-American conference held in that year, the United States and most Latin American countries agreed to resist all foreign intervention in the hemisphere.

Neutrality in Europe

About the same time that Roosevelt was elected president in the United States, Adolf Hitler came to power in Germany. Hitler, born in Austria in 1889, had served as a corporal in the German army during World War I. Like many other Germans, he was angered by the Treaty of Versailles. But he blamed the Communists and Jews for Germany's defeat. Hitler had a checkered life after the war. He became the leader of a Fascist group, the Brown Shirts, and in 1923, after leading an unsuccessful coup, was sentenced to prison. While in jail he wrote *Mein Kampf* ("My Struggle"), a long, rambling book spelling out his theories of racial purity, his hopes for Germany, and his venomous hatred of the Jews. After his release from prison, Hitler's following grew. He had a charismatic style and a plan. On January 30, 1933, he became chancellor of Germany, and within a few months he made himself the *Führer* (leader) and absolute dictator.

He intended to conquer Europe and to make the Third Reich the center of a new civilization.

In 1934, Hitler announced a program of German rearmament, violating the Versailles Treaty of 1919. Meanwhile, in Italy, a Fascist dictator, Benito Mussolini, was building a powerful military force, and in 1934, he threatened to invade the East African country of Ethiopia. These ominous rumblings in Europe frightened some Americans at the very time they were reexamining American entry into the Great War and vowing that they would never again get involved in a European conflict.

Senator Gerald P. Nye of North Dakota, a conscientious and determined man who had helped expose the Teapot Dome scandal in 1924, turned his attention to investigating the connection between corporate profits and American participation in World War I. His Senate committee held public hearings that revealed that many American businessmen had close relationships with the War Department. Businesses that had produced war materials had made huge profits. Though the committee failed to prove a conspiracy, it was easy to conclude, as many people did, that the United States had been tricked into going to war by the people who profited most from it.

On many college campuses, students demonstrated against war. On April 13, 1934, a day of protest around the country, students at Smith College placed white crosses on the campus as a memorial to the people killed in the Great War and for those who would die in the next one. The next year, even more students went on strike for a day. Students joined organizations like Veterans of Future Wars and Future Gold Star Mothers and protested the presence of the Reserve Office Training Corps on their campuses. One college president, who supported the peace movement, announced. "We will be called cowards . . . [but] I say that war must be banished from civilized society if democratic civilization and culture are to be perpetuated." Not all students supported the peace movement, but in the mid-1930s, a great many young people as well as adults joined peace societies such as the Fellowship of Reconciliation and the Women's International League for Peace and Freedom. They were determined never again to support a

foreign war. But in Europe, Asia, and Africa, there were already rumblings of another great international conflict.

Ethiopia and Spain

In May 1935, Italy invaded Ethiopia after rejecting the League of Nations' offer to mediate the difficulties between the two countries. Italian dive bombers and machine guns made quick work of the small and poorly equipped Ethiopian army. The Ethiopian war, remote as it seemed to most Americans, frightened Congress, which passed a Neutrality Act authorizing the president to prohibit all arms shipments to belligerent nations and to advise all United States citizens not to travel on belligerent ships except at their own risk. Remembering the process that led the United States into World War I, Congress was determined that it would not happen again. Roosevelt used the authority of the Neutrality Act of 1935 to impose an arms embargo. The League of Nations condemned Italy as the aggressor in the war, and Great Britain moved its fleet to the Mediterranean. But neither Britain nor the United States wanted to stop shipments of oil to Italy or to commit its own soldiers to the fight. The embargo on arms had little impact on Italy, but it was disastrous for the poor African nation. Italy quickly defeated Ethiopia, and by 1936, Mussolini had joined forces with Germany to form the Rome-Berlin Axis.

"We shun political commitments which might entangle us in foreign war," Roosevelt announced in 1936. "We are not isolationist except in so far as we seek to isolate ourselves completely from war." But isolation became more difficult when a civil war broke out in Spain in 1936. General Francisco Franco, supported by the Catholic church and large landowners, revolted against the Republican government. Germany and Italy aided Franco, sending planes and other weapons, while the Soviet Union came to the support of the Spanish Republic (the Loyalists).

Great Britain and France, like the United States, tried to remain neutral. But the war split the United States. Most Catholics and many who feared communism sided with Franco. But many American radicals, even those opposed to all war a few months before, found the Loyalist cause worth fighting and dying for. Over 3,000 Americans joined the Abraham Lincoln Brigade, and hundreds were killed fighting against fascism in Spain. "If this were a Spanish matter, I'd let it alone," Sam Levenger, a student at Ohio State, wrote. "But the rebellion would not last a week if it weren't for the Germans and the Italians. And if Hitler and Mussolini can send troops to Spain to attack the government elected by the people, why can't they do so in France? And after France?" Levenger was killed in Spain in 1937 at the age of 20.

Not everyone thought the moral issues in Spain were worth dying for. The United States government tried to stay neutral and to ship arms and equipment to neither side. The Neutrality Act, extended in 1936, technically did not apply to civil wars, but the State Department imposed a moral embargo. However, when an American businessman disregarded it and attempted to send 400 used airplane engines to the Loyalists, Roosevelt asked Congress to extend the arms embargo to Spain. While the United States, along with Britain and France, carefully protected its neutrality, Franco consolidated his dictatorship with the active aid of Germany and Italy. Meanwhile, Congress in 1937 passed another Neutrality Act, this time making it illegal for American citizens to travel on belligerent ships. The act extended the embargo on arms and made even nonmilitary items available to belligerents only on a cash-and-carry basis.

In a variety of ways, the United States tried to make sure that it did not repeat the mistakes that had led it into World War I. Unfortunately, World War II, which moved closer each day, would be a different kind of war, and the lessons of World War I would be of little use.

War in Europe

Roosevelt had no carefully planned strategy to deal with the rising tide of war in Europe in the late 1930s. He was by no means an isolationist, but on the other hand, he wanted to keep the United States out of the European conflagration. When he announced, "I hate war," he was expressing a deep personal belief that wars solve few problems. Unlike his cousin Theodore Roo-

sevelt, he did not view war as dashing and romantic or a place to prove one's manhood. In foreign policy, just as in domestic affairs, he responded to events, but he moved reluctantly (and with agonizing slowness, from the point of view of many of his critics) toward more and more American involvement in the war.

In March 1938, Hitler's Germany annexed Austria and then in September, as a result of the Munich Conference, occupied the Sudetenland, a part of Czechoslovakia. Within six months, Hitler's armies had overrun the rest of Czechoslovakia. There was little protest from the United States. Most Americans sympathized with the victims of Hitler's aggression and were horrified at the reports of the internment and murder of hundreds of thousands of Jews. But they hoped somehow that compromises could be worked out and that Europe could settle its own problems. Then on August 23, 1939, American leaders were shocked by the news of a Nazi-Soviet pact. Fascism and communism were political philosophies supposedly in deadly opposition. Many Americans had secretly hoped that Nazi Germany and Soviet Russia would fight it out, neutralizing each other. Now they were allies. A week later, Hitler's army attacked Poland. The invasion of Poland marked the official beginning of World War II. Britain and France honored their treaties and came to Poland's defense. "This nation will remain a neutral nation," Roosevelt announced, "but I cannot ask that every American remain neutral in thought as well."

Roosevelt asked for a repeal of the embargo section of the Neutrality Act and for the approval of the sale of arms on a cash-and-carry basis to France and Britain. The United States would help the Allies, but not at the risk of entering the war or even at the threat of disrupting the civilian economy. Yet Roosevelt did take some secret risks. In August 1939, Albert Einstein, a Jewish refugee from Nazi Germany, and some other distinguished scientists warned the president that German scientists were at work on an atomic bomb. Fearing the consequences of a powerful new weapon in Hitler's hands, Roosevelt authorized funds for a top-secret project to try to build an American bomb first. Only a few advisers and key members of Congress knew of the project, which was officially organized in 1941 and would ultimately change the course of human history.

The war in Poland ended quickly. With Germany attacking from the west and the Soviet Union from the east, the fighting was over within a month. The fall of Poland in September 1939 brought a lull in the fighting. A number of Americans, including the American ambassador to Great Britain, Joseph Kennedy, who feared Communist Russia more than Fascist Germany, urged the United States to take the lead in negotiating a peace settlement that would recognize the German and Russian occupation of Poland. The British and French, however, were not interested in such a solution, and neither was Roosevelt.

The interlude, sometimes called the "phony war," came to a dramatic end on April 9, 1940, when Germany attacked Norway and Denmark with a furious air and sea assault. A few weeks later, using armed vehicles supported by massive air strikes, the German *Blitzkrieg* swept through Belgium, Luxembourg, and the Netherlands. A week later, the Germans stormed into France. The famed Maginot line, a system of fortifications designed to repulse a German invasion, was useless as German mechanized forces swept around the end of the line and attacked from the rear. The French guns, solidly fixed in concrete and pointing toward Germany, were never fired. The Maginot line, which would have been an effective defensive weapon in World War I, was useless in the new kind of war of the 1940s. France surrendered in June as the British army fled across the English Channel from Dunkirk.

How should the United States respond to the new and desperate situation in Europe? William Allen White, journalist and editor, and other concerned Americans organized the Committee to Defend America by Aiding the Allies, but others, including Robert Wood of Sears, Roebuck and Charles Lindbergh, the hero of the 1920s, supported a group called America First. They argued that the United States should forget about England and concentrate on defending America. Roosevelt steered a cautious course. He approved the shipment to Britain of 50 overage American destroyers. In return, the United States received the right to establish naval and air bases on British territory from Newfoundland to Bermuda and British Guiana.

Winston Churchill, prime minister of Great Britain, asked for much more, but Roosevelt hesitated. In July 1940, he did sign a measure authorizing $4 billion to increase the number of American naval warships. In September, Congress passed the Selective Service Act, which provided for the first peacetime draft in the history of the United States. Over a million men were to serve in the army for one year, but they were authorized to serve only in the Western Hemisphere. As the war in Europe reached a crisis in the fall of 1940, the American people were still undecided about the proper response.

The Election of 1940

Part of Roosevelt's reluctance to aid Great Britain more energetically came from his genuine desire to keep the United States out of the war, but it was also related to the presidential campaign waged during the crisis months of the summer and fall of 1940. Roosevelt, breaking a long tradition by seeking a third term, was opposed by Wendell Willkie of Indiana, a corporation president who won the Republican nomination over more experienced and more isolationist candidates. Despite his big-business ties, Willkie approved most New Deal legislation and supported aid to Great Britain. Energetic and attractive, Willkie was the most persuasive and exciting Republican candidate since Theodore Roosevelt, and he appealed to many who distrusted or disliked Roosevelt. Yet in an atmosphere of international crisis, most voters chose to stay with Roosevelt. He won, 27 million to 22 million, and carried 38 of 48 states.

Lend-Lease

After the election, Roosevelt invented a scheme whereby he could send aid to Britain without demanding payment. He called it "lend-lease." He compared the situation to loaning a garden hose to a neighbor whose house was on fire. Senator Robert Taft of Ohio, however, thought the idea of loaning military equipment and expecting it back was absurd. He decided it was more like loaning chewing gum to a friend: "Once it had been used you did not want it back." Others were even more critical. Senator

Burton K. Wheeler, an extreme isolationist, branded lend-lease "Roosevelt's triple A foreign policy" because it was designed to "plow under every fourth American boy."

The Lend-Lease Act, which passed Congress in March 1941, destroyed the fiction of neutrality. By that time, German submarines were sinking a half million tons of ships each month in the Atlantic. In June, Roosevelt proclaimed a national emergency and ordered the closing of German and Italian consulates in the United States. On June 22, Germany suddenly attacked the Soviet Union. It was one of Hitler's biggest blunders of the war, for now his armies had to fight on two fronts.

The surprise attack, however, created a dilemma for the United States. Suddenly the great Communist "enemy" had become America's friend and ally. When Roosevelt extended lend-lease aid to Russia in November 1941, many Americans were shocked. Charles Lindbergh said he would prefer an alliance with Nazi Germany with all its faults than with the "godlessness and barbarism that exist in the Soviet Union." But most Americans made a quick transition from viewing the Soviet Union as an enemy to treating it like a friend.

By the autumn of 1941, the United States was virtually at war with Germany in the Atlantic. On September 11, Roosevelt issued a "shoot on sight" order for all American ships operating in the Atlantic, and on October 30, a German submarine sank an American destroyer off the coast of Iceland. The war in the Atlantic, however, was undeclared and opposed by many Americans. Eventually the sinking of enough American ships or another crisis would probably have provided the excuse for a formal declaration of war against Germany. It was not Germany, however, but Japan that provided the dramatic incident that catapulted the United States into World War II.

The Path to Pearl Harbor

Japan, controlled by ambitious military leaders, was the aggressor in the Far East as Hitler's Germany was in Europe. Its master plan was to replace the white "imperialist" regimes in China, the Philippines, Malaya, Burma, and all of Southeast Asia. Japan invaded Manchuria in 1931 and launched an all-out assault on China in 1937. The Japanese leaders assumed that at some point the United States would oppose their advance. Certainly the United States would go to war if Japan tried to take the Philippines, but the Japanese attempted to delay that moment as long as possible by diplomatic means. For its part, the United States feared the possibility of a two-front war and was willing to delay the confrontation with Japan until it had dealt with the German threat. Thus between 1938 and 1941, the United States and Japan engaged in a kind of diplomatic shadow boxing.

The United States did exert economic pressure on Japan. In July 1939, the United States gave the required six-months' notice regarding cancellation of the 1911 commercial agreement between the two countries. The next year, the Roosevelt administration forbade the shipment of airplane fuel and scrap metal to Japan, although it permitted the export of some petroleum and other products, hoping that this could avert a crisis. In the spring of 1941, Japan opened negotiations with the United States. But there was little to discuss. Japan would not withdraw from China as the United States demanded. Indeed, Japan, taking advantage of the situation in Europe, occupied French Indochina in 1940 and 1941. In July 1941, Roosevelt froze all Japanese assets in the United States, effectively embargoing trade with Japan.

Japan's surprise attack on Pearl Harbor on December 7, 1941, united the country behind the war effort.

Roosevelt had an advantage in the negotiations with Japan, for the United States had broken the Japanese diplomatic code. The American strategy was to avoid crisis. But after General Hideki Tojo became prime minister in October 1941, the Japanese decided to strike at the United States sometime after November 1941 unless the United States offered real concessions. The strike came at Pearl Harbor, the main American Pacific naval base, in Hawaii.

On the morning of December 7, 1941, Japanese airplanes launched from aircraft carriers attacked the United States fleet at Pearl Harbor. The surprise attack destroyed 19 ships (including 5 battleships) and 150 planes and killed 2,335 soldiers and sailors and 68 civilians. On the same day, the Japanese launched attacks on the Philippines, Guam, and the Midway Islands, as well as on the British colonies of Hong Kong and the Malaya Peninsula. The next day, with only one dissenting vote, Congress declared war on Japan. Jeannette Rankin, a member of Congress from Montana who had voted against the war resolution in 1917, voted no again in 1941. She recalled that in 1917, after a week of tense debate, 50 voted against going to war. "This time I stood alone."

Corporal John J. ("Ted") Kohl, a 25-year-old from Springfield, Ohio, was standing guard that Sunday morning near an ammunition warehouse at Hickam Field, near Pearl Harbor. He had joined the army two years before when his marriage failed and he could not find work. A Japanese bomb hit nearby, and Ted Kohl blew up with the warehouse. It was not until Wednesday evening, December 10, that the telegram arrived in Springfield. "The Secretary of War desires to express his deep regrets that your son Cpl. John J. Kohl was killed in action in defense of his country." Ted's younger brothers cried when they heard the news. There would be hundreds of thousands of telegrams and even more tears before the war was over.

December 7, 1941, was a day that "would live in infamy," in the words of Franklin Roosevelt. But it was a day that would have far-reaching implications for American foreign policy and for American attitudes toward the world. The surprise attack united the country in

a way that nothing else could have done. Even the isolationists and those who argued for "America first" quickly became patriots supporting the war effort.

After the shock and anger subsided, Americans searched for a villain. Someone must have blundered, someone must have betrayed the country to have allowed the "inferior" Japanese to have carried out such a successful and devastating attack. A myth persists to this day that the villain was Roosevelt, who, the story goes, knew the Japanese were going to attack but failed to warn the military commanders so that the American people might unite behind the war effort. But Roosevelt did not know. There was no specific warning that the attack was coming against Pearl Harbor, and the American ability to read the Japanese coded messages was no help because the fleet kept radio silence.

The ironic fact was that the Americans, partly because of racial prejudice against the Japanese, underestimated their ability. They ignored many warning signals because they did not believe that the Japanese were capable of launching an attack on a target as far away as Hawaii. Most of the experts, including Roosevelt, expected the Japanese to attack the Philippines or perhaps the Dutch East Indies. Many people blundered and made mistakes, but there was no conspiracy on the part of Roosevelt and his advisers to get the United States into the war.

Even more important in the long run than the way the attack on Pearl Harbor united the American people was its effect on a generation of military and political leaders. Pearl Harbor became the symbol of unpreparedness. For a generation that experienced the anger and frustration of the attack on Pearl Harbor by an unscrupulous enemy, the lesson was to be prepared and ready to stop an aggressor before it had a chance to strike at the United States. The smoldering remains of the sinking battleships at Pearl Harbor on the morning of December 7, 1941, and the history lesson learned there would influence American policy not only during World War II but also in Korea, Vietnam, and the international confrontations of the 1980s.

THE HOME FRONT DURING THE WAR

Too often wars are described in terms of presidents and generals, emperors and kings, in terms of grand strategy and elaborate campaigns. But wars affect the lives of all people; the soldiers who fight and the women and children and men of all ages who stay home. World War II especially had an impact on all aspects of society—on the economy, on the movies and the radio, even on attitudes toward the proper place for women and blacks. For many people, the war meant opportunity and the end of depression. For others, the excitement of faraway places meant that they could never return home again. For still others, the war left lasting scars.

Mobilizing for War

Converting American industry to war production was a complex task. Many corporate executives refused to admit that there was an emergency. Shortly after Pearl Harbor, Roosevelt created the War Production Board (WPB) and appointed Donald Nelson, the executive vice president of Sears, Roebuck, to mobilize the nation's resources for an all-out war effort. The WPB offered businesses cost-plus contracts,

Full employment was one long-awaited change for the better that the war brought. These workers are changing shifts at an aviation plant in Inglewood, California, 1942.

guaranteeing a fixed and generous profit, and often the government also financed the cost of new plants and equipment. Secretary of War Henry Stimson remarked, "If you . . . go to war . . . in a capitalist country, you have to let business make money out of the process or business won't work." Roosevelt seemed to agree.

The Roosevelt administration leaned over backward to gain the cooperation of businessmen, many of whom had been alienated by New Deal policies. He appointed many business executives to key positions, some of whom, like Nelson, served for a dollar a year. He also abandoned antitrust actions in all industries that were remotely war related. The probusiness policies angered some of the old New Dealers. "The New Dealers are a vanishing tribe," one reformer remarked, "and the moneychangers who were driven from the temple are now quietly established in government offices."•

The policy worked, however. Industrial production increased by 96 percent, and net corporate profits doubled during the war. Large commercial farmers also profited from the war. With many members of Congress supporting their demands, the farmers exacted high support prices for basic commodities. The war years accelerated the mechanization of the farm. A million more tractors joined those already in use in agriculture between 1940 and 1945. At the same time, the farm population declined by 17 percent. But the consolidation of small farms into large ones and the dramatic increase in the use of fertilizer made farms more productive and farming more profitable for the large operators.

In addition to the War Production Board, there were many other government agencies charged with running the war effort efficiently. The Office of Price Administration (OPA), eventually placed under the direction of Chester Bowles, an advertising executive, set prices on thousands of items in an attempt to control inflation. The OPA also rationed scarce products. Because the OPA's decisions affected what people wore and ate and whether they had gasoline, many regarded it as a symbol of unnecessary oppression. The National War Labor Board (NWLB) had the authority to set wages and hours and to monitor working conditions, and it had the right, under the president's wartime emergency powers, to seize industrial plants whose owners refused to cooperate.

Membership in labor unions, despite business opposition, grew rapidly during the war, from a total of 10.5 million in 1941 to 14.7 million in 1945. Labor leaders, however, complained that wage controls coupled with wartime inflation were unfair. The NWLB finally allowed a 15 percent cost-of-living increase on some contracts, but that did not apply to overtime pay, which helped drive up wages in some industries during the war by about 70 percent. Labor leaders were often not content with the raises. In the most famous incident, John L. Lewis broke the no-strike pledge of organized labor by calling a nationwide coal strike in 1943. Lewis sought to raise the average compensation of the mine workers. When Roosevelt ordered the secretary of the interior to take over the mines, Lewis called off the strike. But this bold protest did help raise miners' wages.

In addition to wage and price controls and rationing, the government tried to reduce inflation by selling war bonds and by increasing taxes. The Revenue Act of 1942 raised tax rates, broadened the tax base, increased corporate taxes to 40 percent, and raised the excess-profits tax to 90 percent. In addition, the government initiated a payroll deduction for income taxes. The war made the income tax a reality for most Americans for the first time.

Despite some unfairness and much confusion, the American economy responded to the wartime crisis and turned out the equipment and supplies that eventually won the war. The aviation and auto industries built 300,000 airplanes, 88,140 tanks, and 3,000 merchant ships. In 1944 alone, American factories produced 800,000 tons of synthetic rubber to make up for the supply of natural rubber captured by the Japanese. Although the national debt grew from about $143 billion in 1943 to $260 billion in 1945, the government policy of taxation paid for about 40 percent of the war's cost. In a limited way, the tax policy also helped to redistribute wealth, which the New Deal had failed to do. The top 5 percent income bracket, which controlled 23 percent of the disposable income in 1939, held only 17 percent in 1945. Yet full employment and the increase of two-income families, together with forced savings, would help provide capital for postwar expansion.

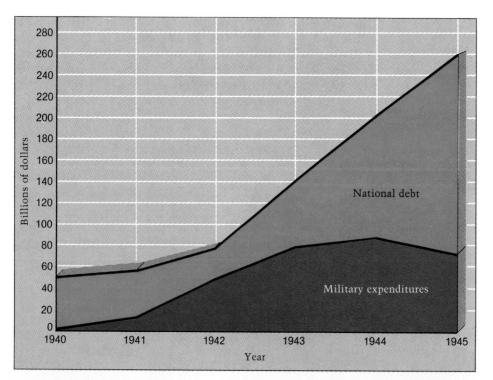

Military Expenditures and the National Debt, 1940–1945

Source: U.S. Bureau of the Census.

The war stimulated the growth of the federal bureaucracy and accelerated the trend, begun during World War I and extended in the 1930s, toward the government's central role in the economy. The war also increased the cooperation between industry and government, creating what would later be called a military-industrial complex. But for most Americans, despite anger at the OPA and the income tax, the war meant the end of the Depression.

Patriotic Fervor

In European and Asian cities, the horror and destruction of war were everywhere. But in the United States, the war was remote. Thousands of American families felt the tragedy of war directly with the arrival of an official telegram telling of a son or husband killed in action. For most Americans, however, the war was a foreign war, far removed from the reality of daily life.

The government tried to keep the war alive in the minds of Americans and to keep the country united behind the war effort. The Office of War Information, staffed by writers and advertising executives, controlled the news the American public received about the war. It promoted patriotism and presented the American war effort in the best possible light.

The government also tried to sell everyone war bonds, not only to help pay for the war and reduce inflation but also to sell the war to the American people. As had been true during World War I, movie stars and other celebrities appeared at war bond rallies. Dorothy Lamour, one of Hollywood's glamorous actresses, was credited with selling $350 million worth of bonds, and the popular Carole Lombard was killed in a plane crash while taking part in a bond tour. Schoolchildren purchased war stamps and faithfully pasted them in an album until they had accumulated stamps worth $18.75, enough to buy a $25 bond (redeemable ten years later). Their bonds, they were told, would purchase bullets or a part for an airplane to kill Japs and Germans and defend the American way of life. "For Freedom's Sake, Buy War Bonds," one poster announced. Working men and women purchased bonds through payroll-deduction plans and looked forward to spending the money on consumer goods after the war. In the end, the government sold over $135 billion in war bonds. While the bond drives did help control inflation, they were most important in making millions of

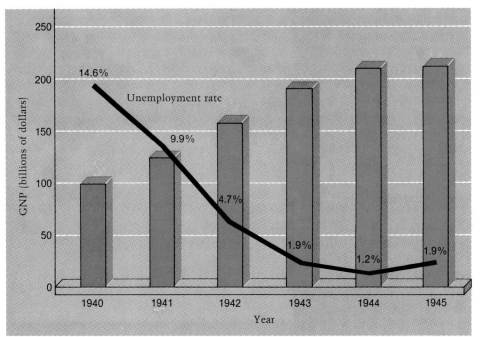

Gross National Product and Unemployment, 1940–1945

Source: U.S. Bureau of the Census.

Americans feel they were contributing to the war effort.

Those too old or too young to join the armed forces served in other ways. Thousands became air-raid wardens or civilian defense and Red Cross volunteers. They raised victory gardens and took part in scrap drives. Even small children could join the war effort by collecting old rubber, waste paper, and kitchen fats. Boys dived into lakes and rivers to recover old tires and even ripped down iron fences to aid their towns and neighborhoods in meeting their scrap quota. Some items, including gasoline, sugar, butter, and meat, were rationed, but few people complained. Even horsemeat hamburgers seemed edible if they helped win the war. Everything, even the most ordinary act, was interpreted by newspaper and magazine advertising as speeding victory or delaying the war effort. "Hoarders are the same as spies," one ad announced. "Everytime you decide *not* to buy something you help win the war."

Internment of Japanese-Americans

Cooperating with the war effort fostered a sense of pride, a feeling of community. But wartime campaigns not only stimulated patriotism; they also promoted hate for the enemy. The Nazis, especially Hitler and his Gestapo, had become synonymous with evil even before 1941. But at the beginning of the war there was little animosity toward the German people. "You and I don't hate the Nazis because they are Germans. We hate the Germans because they are Nazis," announced a character in one of Helen MacInnes's novels. But before long most Americans made few distinctions. All Germans seemed evil, although the anti-German hysteria that had swept the country during World War I never developed.

The Japanese were easier to hate than the Germans. The attack on Pearl Harbor created a special animosity toward the Japanese, but the depiction of the Japanese as warlike and subhuman owed something to a long tradition of fear of the so called "yellow peril" and a distrust of all Asians.

The movies, magazine articles, cartoons, and posters added to the image of the Japanese soldier or pilot with a toothy grin murdering innocent women and children or shooting down helpless Americans. Two weeks after Pearl Harbor, *Time* magazine explained to Americans how they could distinguish our Asian friends the Chinese "from the Japs." "Virtually all Japanese are short, Japanese are seldom fat; they often dry up with age," *Time* declared. "Most Chinese avoid horn-rimmed spectacles. Japanese walk stiffly erect, hard-heeled. Chinese, more relaxed, have an easy gait. The Chinese expression is likely to be more kindly, placid, open; the Japanese more positive, dogmatic, arrogant. Japanese are hesitant, nervous in conversation, laugh loudly at the wrong time."

The racial stereotype of the Japanese played a role in the special treatment of Japanese-Americans during the war. There was some prejudice shown against German- and Italian-Americans, but the Japanese-Americans were

In the greatest abridgement of civil liberties in the nation's history, over 100,000 Japanese-American civilians were forcibly evacuated to "relocation centers" in remote areas of the Southwest.

the only group rounded up and put in concentration camps in the greatest mass abridgment of civil liberties in American history.

At the time of Pearl Harbor, about 127,000 Japanese-Americans lived in the United States, most on the West Coast. About 80,000 were nisei (Japanese born in the United States and holding American citizenship) and sansei (the sons and daughters of nisei); the rest were issei (aliens born in Japan who were ineligible for U.S. citizenship). The Japanese had long suffered from racial discrimination and prejudice in the United States. They were barred from intermarriage with other groups and excluded from many clubs, restaurants, and recreation facilities. Many were employed as tenant farmers, as fishermen, or in small businesses. But there was a small professional class of lawyers, teachers, and doctors and a large number of landowning farmers.

Although many retained cultural and linguistic ties to Japan, they posed no more threat to the country than did the much larger groups of Italian-Americans and German-Americans. But their racial characteristics made them stand out as Italian-Americans and German-Americans did not. After Pearl Harbor, an anti-Japanese panic set in on the West Coast. A Los Angeles newspaper reported that armed Japanese were in Lower California ready to attack. Rumors suggested that Japanese fishermen were preparing to sow mines in the harbor, blow up tunnels, and poison the water supply.

West Coast politicians and ordinary citizens urged the War Department and the president to evacuate the Japanese. The president capitulated and issued Executive Order 9066 authorizing the evacuation in February 1942. "The continued pressure of a largely unassimilated, tightly knit racial group, bound to an enemy nation by strong ties of race, culture, custom and religion, constituted a menace which had to be dealt with," General John De Witt argued, justifying the removal on military grounds. But it was racial fear and animosity, not military necessity, that stood behind the order.

Eventually the government built the "relocation centers" in remote, often arid, sections of the West. "The Japs live like rats, breed like rats and act like rats. We don't want them," the

governor of Idaho announced. The camps were primitive and unattractive. "When I first entered our room, I became sick to my stomach," a Japanese-American woman remembered. "There were seven beds in the room and no furniture nor any partitions to separate the males and the females of the family. I just sat on the bed, staring at the bare wall."

About 110,000 Japanese were evacuated. Those who were forced to leave their homes, farms, and businesses lost almost all their property and possessions. Farmers left their crops to be harvested by their American neighbors. Store owners sold out for a small percentage of what their goods were worth. No personal items or household goods could be transported. The Japanese-Americans lost their worldly possessions, but they lost something more—their pride and respect. One 6-year-old kept asking his mother to "take him back to America." He thought his relocation center was in Japan.

The evacuation of the Japanese-Americans appears in retrospect to have been unjustified. Even in Hawaii, where a much larger Japanese population existed, no evacuation was attempted, and there was no sabotage and little disloyalty. "We believe that the German people bear a common political responsibility for outrages secretly committed by the Gestapo and the SS," one American official wrote in 1945. "What are we to think of our own part in a program which violates every democratic social value, yet has been approved by the Congress, the President and the Supreme Court?"

Black and Hispanic Americans at War

The United States in 1941, even in much of the North, remained a segregated society. Blacks could not live, eat, travel, work, or go to school with the same freedom enjoyed by whites. Blacks profited little from the revival of prosperity and the expansion of jobs early in the war. When blacks joined the military, they were usually assigned to menial jobs as cooks or laborers and were always assigned to segregated units in which the high-ranking officers were white. The myth that black soldiers had failed to perform well in World War I persisted. "Leadership is not imbedded in the negro race yet,"

Secretary of War Henry Stimson wrote, "and to try to make commissioned officers to lead men into battle—colored men—is only to work a disaster to both."

It seemed especially ironic to some black leaders that as the country prepared to fight Hitler and his racist policies, the United States persisted in its own brand of racism. "A jim crow Army cannot fight for a free world," announced *The Crisis,* the journal of the NAACP. But it was A. Philip Randolph who decided to act rather than talk. The son of a Methodist minister, Randolph migrated from Florida to New York at the age of 22. He attended City College and became a socialist for a time, working with the first wave of blacks migrating from the South to the northern cities during and just after World War I. Randolph spent years trying "to carry the gospel of unionism to the colored world." He organized and led the Brotherhood of Sleeping Car Porters, and in 1937, he finally won grudging recognition of the union from the Pullman Company.

Respected and admired by black leaders of all political persuasions, Randolph convinced many of them in 1941 to join him in a march on Washington to demand equal rights. "Dear fellow Negro Americans," Randolph wrote, "be not dismayed in these terrible times. You possess power, great power. Our problem is to harness and hitch it up for action on the broadest, daring and most gigantic scale."

The threat of as many as 100,000 blacks marching in protest in the nation's capital alarmed Roosevelt. At first he sent his assistants, including his wife Eleanor, who was greatly admired in the black community, to dissuade Randolph from such drastic action. But finally he talked to Randolph in person on June 18, 1941. Randolph and Roosevelt struck a bargain. Roosevelt refused to desegregate the armed forces; but in return for Randolph's calling off the march, the president issued Executive Order 8802, which stated that it was the policy of the United States that "there shall be no discrimination in the employment of workers in defense industries or government because of race, creed, color or national origin." He also established the Committee on Fair Employment Practices (FEPC) to enforce the order.

By threatening militant action, the black leaders wrested a major concession from the president. But the executive order did not end prejudice, and the FEPC, which its chairman described as the "most hated agency in Washington," had only limited success in erasing the color line. Many black soldiers were angered and humiliated throughout the war by being made to sit in the back of buses and being barred from hotels and restaurants. Years later, one former black soldier recalled being refused service in a restaurant in Salina, Kansas, while the same restaurant served German prisoners who were in a camp nearby. "We continued to stare," he recalled. "This was really happening. . . . The people of Salina would serve these enemy soldiers and turn away black American G.I.'s."

Many black Americans improved their economic conditions during the war by taking jobs in war industries. Continuing the migration that had begun during World War I, three-quarters of a million blacks moved out of the South into northern and western cities in search of economic opportunity. Some became skilled workers and a few became professionals, but most did the "hard, hot, and heavy" tasks. Those who moved north were often crowded into segregated housing. The racial tension and prejudice were

Blacks and other minorities also benefited from wartime job opportunities. Even before the United States entered the war, black families like this one moved to the North to work in the defense industry.

increased by the presence of many white southerners who had also followed the path of opportunity north.

It was not just southerners who wanted to keep black Americans in their place. In Detroit, where a major race riot broke out in the summer of 1943, Polish-Americans had protested a public housing development that promised to bring blacks into their neighborhood. In one year, more than 50,000 blacks moved into that city, already overcrowded with many others seeking wartime jobs. The new arrivals increased the pressure on housing and on other facilities, and the war accentuated the tension among the various groups.

The riot broke out on a hot, steamy day at a municipal park where a series of incidents led to fights between black and white young people and then to looting in the black community. Before federal and state troops restored order, 34 had been killed (25 blacks and 9 whites) and more than $2 million worth of property had been destroyed. Groups of whites roamed the city attacking blacks, overturning cars, setting fires, and sometimes killing wantonly. A group of young men murdered a 58-year-old black "just for the hell of it." "We didn't know him," one of the boys admitted. "He wasn't bothering us. But other people were fighting and killing and we felt like it too." Other riots broke out in Mobile, Los Angeles, New York, and Beaumont, Texas. In all these cities, and in many others where the tension did not lead to open violence, the legacy of bitterness and hate lasted long after the war.

Mexican-Americans, like most minority groups, profited during the war from the increased job opportunities provided by wartime industry. Many left their villages for the first time. Women broke away from their traditional roles and worked outside the home. Mexican-Americans labored in factories in Texas and California and replaced many of the dust-bowl migrants in the fields. They joined the armed forces in unprecedented numbers and found jobs in the oil fields. On one occasion, the Fair Employment Practice Commission ordered the Shell Oil Company to promote three Mexican-Americans who had been the victims of company discrimination. Although there were other attempts during the war to end unfair treatment, prejudice and discrimination were not easy to eliminate.

In California, and in many parts of the Southwest, Mexicans could not use public swimming pools. Often lumped together with blacks, they were excluded from certain restaurants. Usually they were limited to menial jobs and were constantly harassed by the police, picked up for minor offenses, and jailed on the smallest excuse. It was in Los Angeles that the anti-Mexican prejudice flared into violence. The increased migration of Mexicans into the city and old hatreds created a volatile situation. Most of the hostility and anger focused on Mexican gang members or pachucos, especially those wearing zoot suits. The suits consisted of long, loose coats with padded shoulders, ballooned pants, pegged at the ankles, and a wide-brimmed hat. A watch chain and a ducktail haircut completed the uniform. The zoot suit had originated in the black sections of northern cities and became a national craze during the war. It was a way some teenage males could call attention to themselves and shock conventional society.

The zoot-suiters seemed especially to anger soldiers and sailors who were stationed or on leave in Los Angeles. After a number of provocative incidents, violence broke out between the Mexican-American youths and the servicemen in the spring of 1943. The violence reached a peak on June 7 when gangs of servicemen, often in taxicabs, combed the city, attacking all the young zoot-suiters they could find or anyone who looked Mexican. The servicemen, joined by others, beat up the Mexicans, stripped them of their offensive clothes, and then gave them a haircut. The police, both civilian and military, looked the other way, and when they did move in, they arrested the victims rather than their attackers. The local press and the Chamber of Commerce hotly denied that race was a factor in the riots, but *Time* magazine was probably closer to the truth when it called the riots "the ugliest brand of mob action since the coolie race riots of the 1870s."

SOCIAL IMPACT OF THE WAR

Modern wars have been incredibly destructive of human lives and property, but wars have social results as well. The Civil War ended slavery, ensured the triumph of the industrial North for years to come; it left a legacy of bitterness and transformed the race question from a sectional to a national problem. World War I assured the success of woman suffrage and prohibition, caused a migration of blacks to northern cities, and ushered in a time of intolerance. World War II also had many social results. It altered patterns of work, leisure, education, and family life, caused a massive migration of people, created jobs, and changed life styles. It is difficult to overemphasize the impact of the war on the generation that lived through it.

Wartime Opportunities

More than 15 million American civilians moved during the war. Like the Momadays, many left home to find better jobs. Americans moved off the farms and away from the small towns; they flocked to cities, where defense jobs were readily available. They moved west: California alone gained more than 2 million people during the war. But they also moved out of the South into the northern cities, while others moved from the North to the South. Late in the war, when there was a shortage of farm labor, some reversed the trend and moved back onto the farms. But a great many people moved somewhere. One observer, noticing the heavily packed cars heading west, decided that it was just like *The Grapes of Wrath*, minus the poverty and the hopelessness.

The World War II migrants poured into industrial centers; 200,000 came to the Detroit area, nearly a half million to Los Angeles, and about 100,000 to Mobile, Alabama. They put pressure on the schools, housing, and other services. Often they were forced to live in new Hoovervilles, trailer parks, or temporary housing. In San Pablo, California, a family of four adults and seven children lived in an 8-by-10-foot shack. In Los Angeles, Mrs. Colin Kelley, the widow of a war hero, could find no place to live until a local newspaper publicized her plight. Bill Mauldin, the war cartoonist, showed a young couple with a child buying tickets for a movie with the caption: "Matinee, heck—we want to register for a week."

The overcrowded conditions, the sense of being away from home, the volatile mixture of people from different backgrounds living close together, and the wartime situation often created tension and sometimes open conflict. Some migrants had never lived in a city and were homesick. On one occasion in a Willow Grove, Michigan, school, the children were all instructed to sing "Michigan, My Michigan"; no one knew the words because they all came from other states. One of the most popular country songs of the period, when thousands had left their mountain homes to find work in the city, was "I Wanna Go Back to West Virginia."

For the first time in years, many families had money to spend, but they had nothing to spend it on. The last new car rolled off the assembly line in February 1942. There were no washing machines, refrigerators, or radios in the stores. There was no gasoline and no tires to permit weekend trips. Even when people had time off, they tended to stay at home or in the neighborhood. Some of the new housing developments had the atmosphere of a mining camp, with drinking, prostitution, and barroom brawls a part of the scene.

The war required major adjustments in American family life. With several million men in the service and others far away working at defense jobs, the number of households headed by a woman increased dramatically. The number of marriages also increased. Early in the war, a young man could be deferred if he had a dependent, and a wife qualified as a dependent. Later many servicemen got married, often to women they barely knew, because they wanted a little excitement and perhaps something to come home to. The birthrate also began to rise in 1940, reversing a long decline since the colonial period as young couples started a family as fast as they could. Some of these were "good-bye babies," conceived just before the husband left to join the military or to go overseas. The illegitimacy rate also went up, and from the outset of the war, the divorce rate began to climb sharply. Yet most of the wartime marriages survived, and many of the women left at home looked ahead to a time after the war when they could settle down to a normal life.

Women Workers for Victory

Thousands of women took jobs in heavy industry that formerly would have been considered unladylike. They built tanks, planes, and ships, but they still earned less than men. At first, additional women were rarely employed because as the war in Europe pulled American industry out of the long Depression, unemployed men snapped up the newly available positions. In the face of this male labor pool, one government official remarked that we should "give the women something to do to keep their hands busy as we did in the last war, then maybe they won't bother us."

But by 1943, with many men drafted into the service and male unemployment virtually nonexistent, the government was quick to suggest that it was women's patriotic duty to take their place on the assembly line. A government poster showed a woman worker and her uniformed husband standing in front of an American flag with the caption: "I'm proud . . . my husband *wants* me to do my part." The government tried to convince women that if they could run a vacuum cleaner or a sewing machine or drive a car, they could operate power machinery in a factory. Advertisers in women's magazines joined the campaign by showing fashion models in work clothes. A popular song was "Rosie the Riveter," who was "making history working for victory." She also helped her marine boyfriend by "working overtime on the riveting machine."

There were 19.5 million women in the work force at the end of the war, but three-fourths of that number had been working before the conflict, and some of the additional ones might have sought work in normal times. The new women war workers tended to be older, and they were more often married than single. Some worked for patriotic reasons. "Everytime I test a batch of rubber, I know it's going to help bring my three

sons home quicker," a woman worker in a rubber plant remarked. But others went to work for the money or to have something useful to do. Yet in 1944, women's weekly wages averaged $31.21, compared to $54.65 for men, reflecting women's more menial tasks and their low seniority as well as outright discrimination. Still, many women enjoyed factory work. "Boy have the men been getting away with murder all these years," exclaimed a Pittsburgh housewife. "Why I worked twice as hard selling in a department store and got half the pay."

Black women faced the most difficult situation during the war and often were told when they applied for work such things as "We have not yet installed separate toilet facilities" or "We can't put a Negro in the front office." It was not until 1944 that the telephone company in New York City hired a black telephone operator. Still, some black women moved during the war from domestic jobs to higher-paying factory work. Married women with young children also found it difficult to find work. They found few

Women were encouraged to take jobs in industry as the war progressed.

day-care facilities and were often told that they should be home taking care of their children.

Women workers often had to endure cat-calls, whistles, and more overt sexual harassment on the job. Still, most persisted, and they tried to look feminine despite the heavy work clothes. In one Boston factory, a woman was hooted at for carrying a lunch box. Only men it seemed carried lunch boxes; women brought their lunch in a paper bag.

Many women war workers quickly left their jobs after the war was over. Some left by choice, but dismissals ran twice as high for women as for men. The war had barely shaken the notion that a woman's place was at home. Some women who learned what an extra paycheck meant for the family's standard of living would have preferred to keep working. But most women, and an even larger percentage of men, agreed at the end of the war that women did not deserve "an equal chance with men" for jobs. War work altered individual lives and attitudes, but it did not change dramatically either women's or men's perception of women's proper role. The stereotype of women as weak and dependent persisted in many wartime movies and radio soap operas.

Entertaining the People

According to one survey, Americans listened to the radio an average of 4½ hours a day during the war. The major networks increased their news programs from less than 4 percent to nearly 30 percent of broadcasting time. Americans heard Edward R. Murrow broadcasting from London during the German air blitz with the sound of the air raid sirens in the background. They listened to Eric Sevareid cover the battle of Burma and describe the sensation of jumping out of an airplane. For the first time, news reporters recorded their comments; the recordings were flown to the nearest studio and broadcast back to the United States. There was a delay, but the broadcast had drama and an immediacy never possible before.

Even more than the reporters, the commentators became celebrities on whom the American people depended to explain what was going on around the world. Millions listened to the clipped, authoritative voice of H. V. Kaltenborn or to Gabriel Heatter, whose trademark was "Ah, there's good news tonight." But the war also intruded on almost all other programming. Even the advertising, which took up more and more air time, reminded listeners that there was a war on. Lucky Strike cigarettes, which changed the color of its package from green to white, presumably because there was a shortage of green paint, made "Lucky Strike Green Has Gone to War" almost as famous as "Remember Pearl Harbor."

The serials, the standard fare of daytime radio, also adopted wartime themes. Dick Tracy tracked down spies, while Captain Midnight fought against the enemy on remote jungle islands. Superman outwitted Nazi agents, while Stella Dallas took a job in a defense plant.

Music, which took up a large proportion of radio programming, also conveyed a war theme. There was "Goodby Momma, I'm Off to Yokohama" and "Praise the Lord and Pass the Ammunition." But more numerous were songs of romance and love, songs about separation and hope for a better time after the war. The danceable tunes of Glenn Miller and Tommy Dorsey became just as much a part of wartime memories as ration books and far-off battlefields.

For many Americans, the motion picture was the most important leisure activity and a part of their fantasy life during the war. Attendance at the movies averaged about 100 million individuals a week. There might not be gasoline for weekend trips or Sunday drives, but the whole family could go to the movies; and then, like Scott Momaday, they could replay them in their imaginations. Even those in the military service could watch American movies on board ship or at a remote outpost. "Pinup" photographs of Hollywood stars decorated the barracks and even the tanks and planes wherever American troops were stationed.

Musical comedies, cowboy movies, and historical romances remained popular during the war, but the conflict intruded even on Hollywood. Most movies were preceded by a newsreel that offered a visual synopsis of the war news, always with an upbeat message and a touch of human interest. The theme was that the Americans were winning the war, even if early in the conflict there was little evidence to argue the case. Many feature films also had a wartime theme, picturing the war in the Pacific complete with grinning, vicious Japanese villains (usually played by Chinese or Korean character actors). In the beginning of these films the Japanese were always victorious, but in the end they always got "what they deserved."

The movies set in Europe differed somewhat from those depicting the Far Eastern war. Here British and Americans, sometimes spies, sometimes downed airmen, could dress up like Germans and get away with it. They outwitted the Germans at every turn, sabotaging important installations and finally escaping in a captured plane.

A number of Hollywood actors went into the service, and some even became heroes. But most, like Ronald Reagan, were employed to produce, narrate, or act in government films. The Office of War Information produced short subjects and documentaries, some of them distinguished, like John Huston's *The Battle of San Pietro*, a realistic depiction of war on the Italian front. More typical were propaganda films meant to indoctrinate American soldiers into the reasons why they were fighting the war. *Letter From Bataan*, a short film made in 1942, portrayed a wounded GI who wrote home asking his brother-in-law to save his razor blades because "it takes twelve thousand razor blades to make one two-thousand-pound bomb." The film ended with the announcement that the soldier had died in the hospital.

The GIs' War

GI, an abbreviation that stood for "government issue," became the affectionate designation for the ordinary soldier in World War II. The GIs came from every background and ethnic group. Some served reluctantly, some eagerly. A few became genuine heroes. All were turned into heroes by the press and the public, who seemed to believe that one American could easily defeat at least 20 Japanese or Germans. Ernest Pyle, one of the war correspondents who chronicled the authentic story of the ordinary soldier, wrote:

In the magazines war seemed romantic and exciting, full of heroics and vitality. . . . But when I sat down to write, I saw instead men suffering and wishing they were somewhere else. . . . All of them desperately hungry for somebody to talk to besides themselves, no women to be heroes in front of, damn little wine to drink, precious little song, cold and fairly dirty, just toiling from day to day in a world full of insecurity, discomfort, homesickness and a dulled sense of danger.

Bill Mauldin, another correspondent, told the story of the ordinary soldier in a series of cartoons featuring two tired and resigned infantrymen, Willie and Joe. Joe tries to explain what the war is about, "when they run we try to ketch 'em, when we ketch 'em we try to make 'em run." In another cartoon, Willie says, "Joe, yestiddy ya saved my life an' I swore I'd pay you back. Here's my last pair of dry socks." For the soldier in the front line, the big strategies were irrelevant. The war seemed a constant mix-up; much more important were the little comforts and staying alive.

For those in the middle of a battle, the war was no fun, but only one out of eight who served ever saw combat, and even for many of those the war was a great adventure (just as World War I had been). "When World War II broke out I was delighted," Mario Puzo, author of *The Godfather*, remembered. "There is no other word, terrible as it may sound. My country called. I was delivered from my mother, my family, the girl I was loving passionately but did not love. And delivered *without guilt*. Heroically my country called, ordered me to defend it." World War II catapulted young men and women out of their small towns and urban neighborhoods into exotic places where they met new people and did new things.

The war was important for Mexican-Americans, who were drafted and volunteered in great numbers. A third of a million served in all branches of the military, a larger percentage than for many other ethnic groups. Although they encountered prejudice, they probably found less in the armed forces than they had at home, and many returned to civilian life with new ambitions and a new sense of self-esteem.

World War II was one of those events that in some significant way influenced every family. For those who lost sons, husbands, or fathers, the war was tragic. But for others it meant jobs, travel, adventure, and romance. The Second World War is still the subject of many movies and books, and there are thousands who collect World War II weapons, model planes, and other memorabilia. The generation that lived through the war is inclined to look back nostalgically and to recall the war as a wonderful period in their lives, unlike those who look back at the Vietnam War. In fact, almost as many Americans landed in France in June 1984 to celebrate the fortieth anniversary of D day as invaded Normandy on June 6, 1944. Taking former soldiers and their families back to World War II battlegrounds has become a major tourist industry in Europe.

How did the war influence your family? The study of the family, "humanity's most fundamental and most durable institution," is as important for historians as the study of wars, elections, depressions, and social currents. One's own family, in fact, is a part of these events. By interviewing family members and writing about their lives, which is called oral history, the past is made both more vivid and more personal. Oral history goes beyond names and dates to the rich immediate texture of people's recollections of personal experiences and feelings. Investigating family members is an opportunity not only to "put your own family into history" but also to develop deeper relations and understanding. As such, it is an act requiring a high degree of respect and responsibility.

You can become an oral historian by asking members of your family about their World War II experience, recovering a partial history of both your family and the war. Talk to your father and mother, your grandparents, and other older relatives. Who in your family served in the armed forces? Who went overseas? Did anyone work in a war industry? Was there a "Rosie the Riveter" in your family? Did your family move during the war? For many people the war meant jobs and the end of depression. Was that true

Library of Congress, Washington, D.C.

War effort on the home front

LIFE Magazine, (c) Time Inc.

Alfred Eisenstadt, Soldier's Farewell,
Penn Station, 1944

REMEMBERING THE GOOD WAR

I was nine years old when the war started. It was a typical Chicago working-class neighborhood. It was predominantly Slavic, Polish. There were some Irish, some Germans. When you're a kid, the borders of the world are the few blocks of two-flats, bungalows, cottages, with a lot of little stores in between. My father had a tavern. In those days they put out extras. I remember the night the newsboys came through the neighborhood. Skid-row kind of guys, hawking the papers. Germany had invaded Poland: '39. It was the middle of the night, my mother and father waking. People were going out in the streets in their bathrobes to buy the papers. In our neighborhood with a lot of Poles, it was a tremendous story.

Suddenly you had a flagpole. And a marker. Names went on the marker, guys from the neighborhood who were killed. Our neighborhood was decimated. There were only kids, older guys, and women.

Suddenly I saw something I hadn't seen before. My sister became Rosie the Riveter. She put a bandanna on her head every day and went down to this organ company that had been converted to war work. There was my sister in slacks. It became more than work. There was a sense of mission about it. Her husband was Over There. . . .

There was the constant idea that you had to be doing something to help. It did filter down to the neighborhood: home-front mobilization. We had a block captain. . . .

We'd listen to the radio every night. My father would turn it on to find out what was happening. The way a kid's mind could be shaped by those dulcet voices. The world was very simple. I saw Hitler and Mussolini and Tojo: those were the villains. We were the good guys. And the Russians were the good guys too. The war was always being talked about in the bar. Everybody was a military strategist.

The big event was my brother-in-law coming home, my sister's husband. He had been a combat soldier all the way through. He had all his ribbons and medals on. He was the family hero.

Mike Royko, in Studs Terkel, *"The Good War": An Oral History of World War Two.* Copyright © 1984 by Studs Terkel. Reprinted by permission of Pantheon Books, a Division of Random House, Inc.

for your family? Many young people met their future spouses during the war. Was that true in your family?

Can anyone in your family remember rationing, scrap drives, blackouts, victory gardens? Did anyone eat horsemeat or mix yellow dye with oleomargarine? Can anyone recall the big bands, the movie stars, the newsreels? Although there was widespread support for the war, and patriotism was popular, prejudice and hate still remained. In what ways did your family share in the patriotism or participate in the prejudice? Whether in battles abroad or on the home front, how does the war as recalled by your family differ from the war as described in this chapter?

Look around your home. Are there any surviving memorabilia from the war—old photographs or uniforms, discharge papers, ration books, war stamps, souvenirs, magazines, or other things from the war years? Go to your library and look at a few issues of *Life* or *Look* for the 1940s. What do you notice about the advertisements and the news stories? How do they differ from magazine advertising and reporting today? What happened to the automotive industry and to professional baseball and college football during the war? What do you notice about women's dress styles? What do the two photographs shown here tell you about the American people in World War II?

Did the war mean tragedy or opportunity for your family? "World War II was a holy war and FDR a saint," one writer has remarked. Does your family agree? World War II may have been the last time the country was really united; those who lived through it have inevitably looked at recent events through the perspective of the war years. How did "the Good War," as Studs Terkel called it, influence the political and social views of those in your family old enough to remember it? How do their attitudes about World War II compare with their feelings about more recent American wars?

If the experience of World War II is too distant for the recollections of members of your family, ask them instead about either the Korean War or the Vietnam War. Similar questions are appropriate: ask those who went abroad to describe what the war was like and how they felt about it, and ask those who stayed at home how the war affected or changed their lives.

The accompanying brief excerpt from Studs Terkel's *"The Good War": An Oral History of World War Two* illustrates how the world transformed the family and neighborhood of young Mike Royko, now a Chicago journalist.

Many Native Americans also served. In fact, many Indians were recruited for special service in the Marine Signal Corps. One group of Navajos completely befuddled the Japanese with a code based on their native language. "Were it not for the Navajos, the Marines would never have taken Iwo Jima," one Signal Corps officer declared. But the Navajo code talkers and all other Indians who chose to return to the reservations after the war were ineligible for veterans' loans, hospitalization, and other benefits. They lived on federal land, and that, according to the law, canceled all the advantages that other veterans enjoyed after the war.

For black Americans, who served throughout the war in segregated units and faced prejudice wherever they went, the military experience also had much to teach. Fewer blacks were sent overseas (about 79,000 of 504,000 blacks in the service in 1943), and fewer were in

About 322,000 American servicemen died in the war, but the government tried to protect the public from the real cost of the battles. This photograph published in 1943 was the first to show dead American soldiers.

combat outfits, so the percentage of killed and wounded was low among blacks. Many illiterate blacks, especially from the South, learned to read and write in the service. Blacks who were sent overseas began to realize that not everyone viewed them as inferior. One black army officer said, "What the hell do we want to fight the Japs for anyhow? They couldn't possibly treat us any worse than these 'crackers' right here at home." Most realized the paradox of fighting for freedom when the black had little freedom; they hoped things would improve after the war.

Because the war lasted longer than World War I, its impact was greater. In all, over 16 million men and women served in one branch or another of the military service. About 322,000 were killed in the war, and more than 800,000 were wounded. Some 12,000 listed as missing just disappeared. The war claimed many more lives than World War I, and was the nation's costliest after the Civil War. But because of penicillin, blood plasma, sulfa drugs, and rapid battlefield evacuation, the wounded in World War II were twice as likely to survive as in World War I. Penicillin also minimized the threat of venereal disease, but all men who served saw an anti-VD film, just as their counterparts had in World War I.

Women in Uniform

Women had served in all wars as nurses and cooks and in other support capacities, and during World War II many continued in these traditional roles. A few nurses landed in France just days after the invasion. Nurses served with the army and the marines in the Pacific. They dug their own foxholes and treated men under enemy fire. Sixty-six nurses spent the entire war in the Philippines, most of it as prisoners of the Japanese.

Though nobody objected to women serving as nurses, it was not until April 1943 that women physicians won the right to join the Army and Navy Medical Corps. Some questioned whether it was right for women to serve in other capacities. But Congress authorized full military participation for women (except for combat) because of the military emergency and the argument that women could free men for combat duty. World War II thus became the first war in which women were given regular military status. About 350,000 women joined up, most in the Womens' Army Corps (WACS) and the women's branch of the navy (WAVES). For many of the women who spoke in support of the bill, it was not so much the military situation as the need to assert women's rights to full citizenship, with all its responsibilities, that influenced their support of military service for women.

Many of the recruiting posters suggested that the services needed women "for the precision work at which women are so adept," or to work in hospitals to comfort and attend to the wounded "as only women can do." And most women served in traditional womanly roles, doing office work, cooking, and cleaning. But others were engineers and pilots. Still, men and women were not treated equally. Men were informed about contraceptives and encouraged to use them, but information about birth control was explicitly prohibited for women. Persistent rumors charged many women with drunkenness and sexual promiscuity. On one occasion the secretary of war defended the morality and the loyalty of the women in the service, but the rumors continued. Another delicate problem concerned whether a man should take an order from a woman. The marine corps solved the difficult situation by ruling that a woman officer could command enlisted men if the order originated with a male superior. Despite difficulties, women played important roles during the war, and when they left the service (unlike the women who had served in other wars), they had the same rights and privileges as the male veterans. The women in the service did not permanently alter the military or the public's perception of women's proper role, but they did change a few minds, and many of the women who served had their lives changed and their horizons raised.

A WAR OF DIPLOMATS AND GENERALS

Pearl Harbor catapulted the country into war with Japan, and on December 11, 1941, Hitler declared war on the United States. Why he did so has never been fully explained; he was perhaps impressed by the apparent weakness of America as demonstrated at Pearl Harbor. He was not required by his treaty with Japan to go to war with the United States, and without his declaration the United States might have concentrated on the war against Japan. But with Hitler's declaration the United States was finally at war against the Axis powers in both Europe and Asia.

War Aims

Why was the United States fighting the war? What did it hope to accomplish in a peace settlement once the war was over? Roosevelt and the other American leaders never really decided. In a speech before Congress in January 1941, Roosevelt had mentioned the four freedoms: freedom of speech and expression, freedom of worship, freedom from want, and freedom from fear. For many Americans, especially after Norman Rockwell expressed those freedoms in four sentimental paintings, this was what they were fighting for. Roosevelt, who spoke vaguely of the need to extend democracy and to establish a peacekeeping organization, never spelled out in any detail the political purposes for fighting. The only American policy was to end the war as quickly as possible and to solve the political problems created by it when the time came. That policy, or lack of policy, would have important ramifications.

Roosevelt and his advisers, realizing that it would be impossible to mount an all-out war against both Japan and Germany, decided to fight a holding action in the Pacific at first while concentrating their efforts against Hitler in Europe, where the immediate danger seemed greater. But the United States was not fighting alone. It joined the Soviet Union and Great Britain in what became a difficult, but in the end an effective, alliance to defeat Nazi Germany. Churchill and Roosevelt got along well, although they often disagreed on strategy and tactics. Roosevelt's relationship with Stalin was much more strained, but often he agreed with the Russian leader about the way to fight the war. Stalin, a ruthless leader who had maintained his position of power only after eliminating hundreds of thousands of opponents, distrusted both the British and the Americans, but he needed them, just as they depended on him. Without the tremendous sacrifices of the Russian army and the Russian people in 1941 and 1942, Germany would have won the war before the vast American military and industrial might could be mobilized.

1942: Year of Disaster

Despite the potential of the American-British-Soviet alliance, almost all the war news in the first half of 1942 was disastrous for the Allied cause. In the Pacific, the Japanese captured the Dutch East Indies with its vast riches in rubber, oil, and other resources. They swept into Burma, took Wake Island and Guam, and invaded the Aleutian Islands of Alaska. They pushed the American garrison on the Philippines onto the Bataan peninsula and finally onto the tiny island of Corregidor, where General Jonathan Wainwright surrendered more than 11,000 men to the Japanese. American reporters tried their best to play down the disasters and to concentrate their stories on the few American victories—and to tell the tales of American heroism against overwhelming odds. One of the soldiers on a Pacific island picked up an American broadcast one night. "The news commentators in the States had us all winning the war," he discovered, "their buoyant cheerful voices talking of victory. We were out here where we would see these victories. They were all Japanese."

In Europe, the Germans pushed deep into Russia, threatening to capture all the industrial centers and the valuable oil fields. For a time it appeared that they would even overrun Moscow. In North Africa, General Erwin Rommel and his mechanized divisions, the Afrika Korps, drove the British forces almost to Cairo in Egypt and threatened the Suez Canal. In the Atlantic, German submarines sank British and American ships more rapidly than they could be replaced.

For a few dark months in 1942 it seemed that the Berlin-Tokyo Axis would win the war before the United States got itself ready to fight.

The Allies could not agree on the proper military strategy in Europe. Churchill advocated tightening the ring around Germany, using bombing raids to weaken the enemy and encouraging resistance among the occupied countries but avoiding any direct assault on the continent until success was assured. He remembered the vast loss of British lives during World War I and was determined to avoid similar casualties in this conflict. Stalin, on the other hand, demanded a second front, an invasion of Europe in 1942, to relieve the pressure on the Russian army, which faced 200 German divisions along a 2,000-mile front. Roosevelt agreed to an offensive in 1942. But in the end, the invasion in 1942 came not in France but in North Africa. The decision was probably right from a military point of view, but it created Russian distrust of Britain and the United States. The delay in opening the second front probably contributed indirectly to the Cold War after 1945.

Attacking in North Africa in November 1942, American and British troops tried to link up with a beleaguered British army. The American army, enthusiastic but inexperienced, met little resistance in the beginning, but at Kasserine Pass in Tunisia, the Germans counterattacked and destroyed a large American force, inflicting 5,000 casualties. Roosevelt, who launched the invasion in part to give the American people a victory to relieve the dreary news from the Far East, learned that victories often came with long casualty lists.

He also learned the necessity of political compromise. In order to gain a cease-fire in conquered French territory in North Africa, the United States recognized Admiral Jean Darlan as head of its provisional government. Darlan persecuted the Jews, exploited the Arabs, imprisoned his opponents, and collaborated with the Nazis. He seemed diametrically opposed to the principles the Americans said they were fighting for. Did the Darlan deal mean the United States would negotiate with Mussolini? Or with Hitler? The Darlan compromise reinforced Soviet distrust of the Americans, but it also angered many Americans as well.

Roosevelt never compromised or made a deal with Hitler, but he did aid General Francisco Franco, the Fascist dictator in Spain, in return for safe passage of American shipping into the Mediterranean. But the United States did not aid only right-wing dictators. They also supplied arms to the left-wing resistance in France, to the Communist Tito in Yugoslavia, and to Ho Chi Minh, the anti-French resistance leader in Indochina. Roosevelt also authorized large-scale lend-lease aid to the Soviet Union. Although criticized by liberals for his support of dictators, Roosevelt was willing to do almost anything to win the war. Military expediency often dictated his political decisions.

Even on one of the most sensitive issues of the war, the plight of the Jews in occupied Europe, Roosevelt's solution was to win the war as quickly as possible. By November 1942, confirmed information had reached the United States that the Nazis were systematically exterminating Jews. Yet the Roosevelt administration did nothing for more than a year, and even then did scandalously little to rescue European Jews from the gas chambers. Only 21,000 refugees were allowed to enter the United States over a

World War II: Pacific Theater

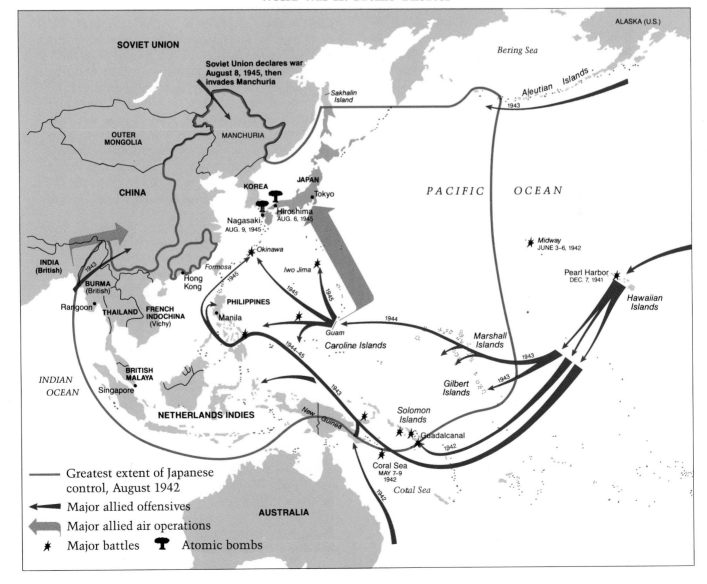

period of 3½ years, just 10 percent of those who could have been admitted under existing immigration quotas. The U.S. War Department rejected suggestions that the Auschwitz gas chambers be bombed, and government officials turned down many rescue schemes. Widespread anti-Semitic feelings in the United States in the 1940s and the fear of massive Jewish immigration help to explain the failure of the Roosevelt administration to act. The fact that the mass media, Christian leaders, and even American Jews failed to mount effective pressure on the government does not excuse the President for his shameful indifference to the systematic murder of millions of people. Roosevelt could not have prevented the Holocaust, but vigorous action on his part could have saved many thousands of lives during the war.

Roosevelt was not always right, nor was he even consistent, but people who assumed he had a master strategy or a fixed ideological position misunderstood the American president.

A Strategy for Ending the War

The commanding general of the Allied armies in the North African campaign emerged as a genuine leader. Born in Texas, Dwight D. Eisenhower spent his boyhood in Abilene, Kansas. His small-town, rural background made it easy for biographers and newspaper reporters to make him into an American hero. Eisenhower, however, had not come to his hero status easily. He saw no action in World War I; he spent that war training soldiers in Texas. Even though he served as assistant to General Douglas MacArthur in the 1930s in the Philippines, he was only a lieutenant colonel when World War II erupted. General George Marshall had discovered Eisenhower's talents even before the war began. He was quickly promoted to general and achieved a reputation as an expert planner and organizer. Gregarious and outgoing, he had a broad smile that made most people instantly like him. He was not a brilliant field commander and made many mistakes in the African campaign. But he had the ability to get diverse people to work together, which was crucial where British and American units had to cooperate.

The American army moved slowly across North Africa, linked up with the British, invaded Sicily in July 1943, and finally stormed ashore in Italy in September. The Italian campaign proved long and bitter. Despite the fact that the Italians overthrew Mussolini and surrendered in September 1943, the Germans occupied the peninsula and gave ground only after bloody fighting. The whole American army seemed to be bogged down for months. One soldier described the "slushy mud that reaches almost up to your knees, . . . making the roads dangerously slippery." The Allies did not reach Rome until June 1944, and they never controlled all of Italy before the war in Europe ended.

Despite the decision to make the war in Europe the first priority, American ships and planes halted the Japanese advance in the spring of 1942. In the Battle of Coral Sea in May 1942, American carrier-based planes inflicted heavy damage on the Japanese fleet and prevented the invasion of the southern tip of New Guinea and probably of Australia as well. It was the first naval battle in history in which no guns were fired from one surface ship against another; all the damage was caused by airplanes. In World War II, the aircraft carrier would be more important than the battleship. A month later, at the

President Roosevelt inspects General Eisenhower's troops on Sicily before returning home from the Cairo-Teheran Conference, 1943.

Battle of Midway, American planes sank four Japanese aircraft carriers and destroyed nearly 300 planes. This was the first major Japanese defeat; it restored some balance of power in the Pacific and ended the threat to Hawaii.

In 1943, the American sea and land forces leapfrogged from island to island, gradually retaking territory from the Japanese and building bases to attack the Philippines and eventually Japan itself. Progress often had terrible costs, however. In November 1943, about 5,000 marines landed on the coral beaches of the tiny island of Tarawa. Despite heavy naval bombardment and the support of hundreds of planes, the

marines met heavy opposition. The four-day battle left more than 1,000 Americans dead and over 3,000 wounded. One marine general thought it was all wasted effort. He thought the island should have been bypassed. Others disagreed. No one asked the marines who stormed the beaches. Less than 50 percent of the first wave survived.

The Invasion of Europe

Operation Overlord, the code name for the largest amphibious invasion in history, the invasion Stalin had wanted in 1942, began only on

World War II: European and North African Theaters

Source: U.S. Bureau of the Census.

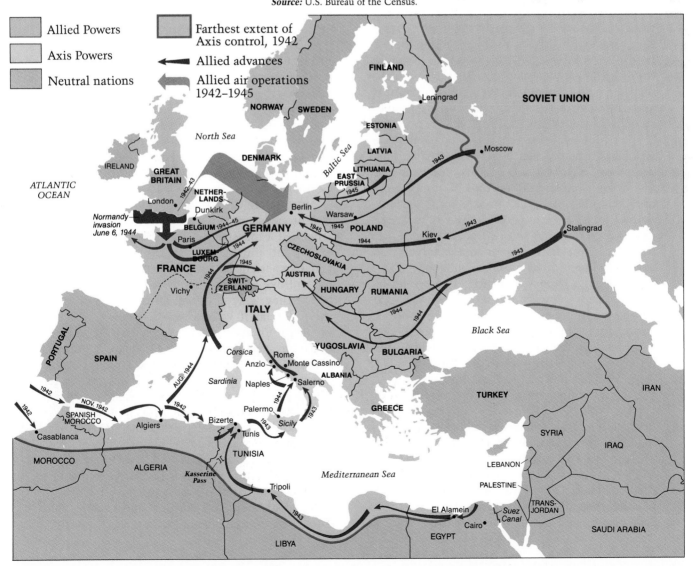

June 6, 1944. It was, according to Churchill, "the most difficult and complicated operation that has ever taken place." The initial assault along a 60-mile stretch of the Normandy coast was conducted with 175,000 men supported by 600 warships and 11,000 planes. Within a month, over a million troops and more than 170,000 vehicles had landed. Such an invasion would have been impossible during World War I.

Eisenhower, now bearing the title Supreme Commander of the Allied Expeditionary Force in Western Europe, coordinated and planned the operation. British and American forces, with some units from other countries, worked together, but Overlord was made possible by American industry, which, by the war's end, was turning out an astonishing 50 percent of all the world's goods. During the first few hours of the invasion, there seemed to be too many supplies. "Everything was confusing," one soldier remembered. It cost 2,245 killed and 1,670 wounded to secure the beachhead. "It was much lighter than anybody expected," one observer remarked. "But if you saw faces instead of numbers on the casualty list, it wasn't light at all."

For months before the invasion, American and British planes had bombed German transportation lines, industrial plants, and even cities. In all, over 1.5 million tons of bombs were dropped on Europe. The massive bombing raids helped make the invasion a success, but evidence gathered after the war suggests that the bombs did not disrupt German war production as seriously as Allied strategists believed at the time. Often a factory or a rail center would be back in operation within a matter of days, sometimes within hours, after an attack. In the end, the bombing of the cities may have strengthened the resolve of the German people to fight to the bitter end rather than destroying their morale.

The most destructive bombing raid of the war, carried out against Dresden on the night of February 13–14, 1945, had no strategic purpose. It was launched by the British and Americans to help demonstrate to Stalin that they were aiding the Russian offensive. Dresden, a city of 630,000, was not an industrial but a communications center. Three waves of planes dropped 650,000 incendiary bombs, creating a firestorm that swept over 8 square miles, destroyed every-thing in its path and killing 135,000 men, women, and children. One of the American pilots remarked, "For the first time I felt sorry for the population below."

With the dashing and eccentric General George Patton and the more staid General Omar Bradley in command, the American army broke out of the Normandy beachhead in July 1944. Led by the tank battalions, it swept across France. It was the American productive capacity and the ability to supply a mobile and motorized army that eventually brought victory. But not all American equipment was superior. The United States was far behind Germany in the development of rockets, but that was not as important in the actual fighting as the inability of the United States, until the end of the war, to develop a tank that could compete in armament or firepower with the German tanks. The American army made up for the deficiency of its tanks in part by having superior artillery. Perhaps even more important, most of the American soldiers had grown up tinkering with cars and radios. Children of the machine age, they managed to make repairs and to keep tanks, trucks, and guns functioning under difficult circumstances. They helped give the American army the superior mobility that eventually led to the defeat of Germany.

Just before Christmas in 1944, when the war in Europe seemed almost over, the Germans launched a massive counterattack along an 80-mile front, much of it held by thinly dispersed and inexperienced American troops. The Germans drove 50 miles inside the American lines before they were checked. During the Battle of the Bulge, as it was called, Eisenhower was so desperate for additional infantry that he offered to pardon any of the military prisoners in Europe if they would take up a rifle and go into battle. Most of the prisoners, who were serving short sentences, declined the opportunity to clear their record. Eisenhower also promised any black soldiers in the service and supply outfits an opportunity to become infantrymen in the white units, though usually with a lower rank. However, Walter Bedell Smith, his chief of staff, pointed out that this was against War Department regulations and was "the most dangerous thing I have seen in regard to race relations."

Eisenhower recanted, not wishing to start a social revolution. Those black soldiers who did volunteer to join the battle fought in segregated platoons with white officers in command.

The Politics of Victory

As the American and British armies raced across France into Germany in the winter and spring of 1945, the political and diplomatic aspects of the war began to overshadow military concerns. It became a matter not only of defeating Germany but also of determining who was going to control Germany and the rest of Europe once Hitler's armies were defeated. The relationship between the Soviet Union and the other Allies had been badly strained during the war; with victory in sight, the tension became even greater. While the American press pictured Stalin as a wise and democratic leader and the

As Allied troops closed in on Berlin, the horror of Nazi concentration camps was revealed to the world.

Russian people as quaint and heroic, a number of high-level American diplomats and presidential advisers distrusted the Russians and looked ahead to a confrontation with Soviet Communism after the war. These men urged Roosevelt to make military decisions with the postwar political situation in mind.

The main issue in the spring of 1945 concerned who would capture Berlin. The British wanted to beat the Russians to the capital city. Eisenhower, however, fearing that the Germans might barricade themselves in the Austrian Alps and hold out indefinitely, ordered the armies south rather than toward Berlin. He also wanted to avoid unnecessary American casualties, and he planned to meet the Russian army at an easily marked spot in order to avoid any unfortunate incidents. The British and American forces could probably not have arrived in Berlin before the Russians in any case, but Eisenhower's decision generated controversy after the war. Russian and American troops met on April 25, 1945, at the Elbe River. On May 2, Berlin fell to the Russians. Hitler committed suicide. The long war in Europe finally came to an end on May 8, 1945. But the political problems remained.

In 1944, the United States continued to tighten the noose on Japan. American long-range B-29 bombers began sustained strikes on the Japanese mainland in June 1944, and by November they were dropping firebombs on Tokyo. In a series of naval and air engagements, especially at the Battle of Leyte Gulf, American planes destroyed most of the remaining Japanese navy. By the end of 1944 an American victory in the Pacific was all but assured. American forces recaptured the Philippines early the next year, yet the American forces had barely touched Japan itself. It might take years to conquer the Japanese on their home islands.

While the military campaigns reached a critical stage in both Europe and the Pacific, Roosevelt took time off to run for an unprecedented fourth term. To appease members of his own party, he agreed to drop Vice-President Henry Wallace from the ticket because some thought him too radical and impetuous. To replace him, the Democratic convention selected a relatively unknown senator from Missouri, Harry S Truman, after passing over several well-known political leaders. Truman, a World War I veteran, had been a judge in Kansas City before being elected to the Senate in 1934. His only fame came when, as chairman of the Senate Committee to Investigate the National Defense Program, he had insisted on honesty and efficiency in war contracts. He got some publicity for saving the taxpayers' dollars. The Republicans nominated Thomas Dewey, the colorless and politically moderate governor of New York, who had a difficult time criticizing Roosevelt without appearing unpatriotic. Roosevelt, who seemed haggard and ill during much of the campaign, still managed to display a sense of humor. Although he won the election easily in 1944, Roosevelt would need more than a sense of humor to deal with the difficult political problems of ending the war and constructing a peace settlement.

The Big Three at Yalta

Roosevelt, Churchill, and Stalin, together with many of their advisers, met at Yalta in the Crimea in February 1945 to discuss the problems of the peace settlements. Most of the agreements reached at Yalta were secret, and in the atmosphere of the subsequent Cold War, many would become controversial. Roosevelt wanted the help of the Soviet Union in ending the war in the Pacific so as to avoid the needless slaughter of American men in an invasion of the Japanese mainland. In return for a promise to enter the war within three months after the war in Europe was over, the Soviet Union was granted the Kurile Islands, the southern half of Sakhalin, and railroads and port facilities in North Korea, Manchuria, and Outer Mongolia. Later that seemed like a heavy price to pay for the promise, but realistically the Soviet Union controlled most of this territory and could not have been dislodged short of going to war.

When the provisions of the secret treaties were revealed much later, many people would accuse Roosevelt of trusting the Russians too much. But Roosevelt wanted to retain a working relationship with the Soviet Union. If the peace was to be preserved, the major powers of the Grand Alliance would have to work together. Moreover, Roosevelt hoped to get the Soviet

Union's agreement to cooperate with a new peace-preserving United Nations organization after the war.

The European section of the Yalta agreement proved even more controversial than its Far Eastern provisions. Here it was decided to partition Germany and to divide the city of Berlin. But it was the Polish agreements that were most difficult for many to swallow, in part because it had been the invasion of Poland in 1939 that had precipitated the war. The Polish government in exile in London was militantly anti-Communist and looked forward to returning to Poland after the war. Stalin, however, demanded that the eastern half of Poland be given to the Soviet Union to protect its western border. Churchill and Roosevelt finally agreed to the Russian demands with the proviso that Poland be compensated with German territory on its western border. Stalin also agreed to include some members of the London-based Polish group in the new Polish government. He also promised to carry out "free and unfettered elections as soon as possible." The Polish settlement would prove divisive after the war, and it became quickly clear that what the British and Americans wanted in eastern Europe contrasted with what the Soviet Union intended. Yet at the time it seemed imperative that Russia enter the war in the Pacific, and the reality was that in 1945 the Soviet army occupied most of eastern Europe.

The most potentially valuable accomplishment at Yalta was agreement on the need to construct a United Nations, an organization for preserving peace and fostering the postwar reconstruction of battered and underdeveloped countries. In 1942, a total of 26 Allied nations had subscribed to the Atlantic Charter, drafted by Churchill and Roosevelt, which laid down several principles for a lasting peace. Discussions among the Allied powers continued during the war, and at Yalta Stalin agreed with Roosevelt and Churchill to call a conference in San Francisco in April 1945 to draft a United Nations charter.

Spirited debate occurred in San Francisco when the representatives of 50 nations gathered for this task. As finally accepted, amid optimism about a quick end to the war, the charter provided for a General Assembly in which every member nation had a seat. However, this General Assembly was designed mainly as a forum for discussing international problems. The responsibility for keeping global peace was lodged in the Security Council, composed of five permanent members (the United States, the Soviet Union, Great Britain, France, and China) and six other nations elected for two-year terms. It was the Security Council's responsibility to suppress international violence by applying economic, diplomatic, or military sanctions against any nation that all permanent members agreed threatened the peace. In addition, the charter established an International Court of Justice and a number of agencies to promote "collaboration among the nations through education, science, and culture." Among these agencies were the International Monetary Fund, the World Health Organization, and the UN Educational, Scientific, and Cultural Organization (UNESCO).

The Atomic Age Begins

Two months after Yalta, on April 12, 1945, as the United Nations charter was being drafted, Roosevelt died suddenly of a massive cerebral hemorrhage. The nation was shocked. When an industrial worker in Springfield, Ohio, heard the news, he remarked that he was glad that "the old son of a bitch was gone"; another worker punched him in the face. Roosevelt, both hated and loved to the end, was replaced by Harry Truman, who was both more difficult to hate and harder to love. In the beginning, Truman seemed tentative and unsure of himself. Yet it fell to the new president to make some of the most difficult decisions of all time. The most momentous of all was the decision to drop the atomic bomb.

The Manhattan Project, first organized in 1941, was one of the best-kept secrets of the war. The task of the distinguished group of scientists whose work on the project was centered at Los Alamos, New Mexico, was to manufacture an atomic bomb before Germany did. But by the time the bomb was successfully tested in the New Mexican desert on July 16, 1945, the war in Europe had ended.

The scientists working on the bomb assumed that they were perfecting a military weapon. Yet when they saw the ghastly power of that first bomb, remembered J. Robert Oppenheimer, a leading scientist on the project, "some wept, a few cheered. Most stood silently." Some opposed the military use of the bomb. They realized its revolutionary power and worried about the future reputation of the United States if it unleashed this new force. But a presidential committee made up of scientists, military leaders, and politicians recommended that it be used on a military target in Japan as soon as possible.

"The final decision of where and when to use the atomic bomb was up to me," Truman later remembered. "Let there be no doubt about it. I regarded the bomb as a military weapon and never had any doubt that it should be used." But the decision had both military and political ramifications. Even though Japan had lost most of its empire by the summer of 1945, it still had a military force of several million men and thousands of kamikaze planes that had already wreaked havoc on the American fleet. The kamikaze pilots gave up their own lives to make sure that their planes, heavily laden with bombs, crashed on an American ship. There was little defense against such fanaticism.

Even with the Russian promise to enter the

The atom bomb's unprecedented destruction is recalled by this 1984 Osaka department store display.

war, it appeared that an amphibious landing on the Japanese mainland would be necessary to end the war. The monthlong battle for Iwo Jima, only 750 miles from Tokyo, had resulted in over 4,000 American dead and 15,000 wounded, and an invasion of Japan would be much more expensive. The bomb, many thought, could end the war without an invasion. But some of those involved in the decision wanted to pay Japan back for Pearl Harbor, and still others needed to justify spending over $2 billion on the project in the first place. The timing of the first bomb, however, indicates that the decision was intended to impress the Russians and ensure that they had little to do with the peace settlement in the Far East. One British scientist later charged that the decision to drop the bomb on Hiroshima was "the first major operation of the cold diplomatic war with Russia."

On August 6, 1945, two days before the Soviet Union had promised to enter the war against Japan, a B-29 bomber dropped a single atomic bomb over Hiroshima. It killed or severely wounded 160,000 civilians and destroyed 4 square miles of the city. One of the men on board the plane saw the thick cloud of smoke and thought that they had missed their target. "It looked like it had landed on a forest. I didn't see any sign of the city." The Soviet Union entered the war on August 8. When Japan failed to surrender immediately, a second bomb was dropped on the city of Nagasaki on August 9. The Japanese surrendered on August 14, 1945. The war was finally over, but the problems of the atomic age and the postwar world were just beginning.

CONCLUSION: Peace, Prosperity, and International Responsibilities

The United States emerged from World War II with an enhanced reputation as the world's most powerful industrial and military nation. The demands of the war had finally ended the Great Depression and brought prosperity to most Americans. The war had also ended American isolationism and made the United States into the dominant international power. Of all the nations that fought in the war, the United States had suffered the least. No bombs were dropped on American factories, and no cities were destroyed. Even though more than 300,000 Americans lost their lives, even this carnage seemed minimal when compared to the more than 20 million Russian soldiers and civilians who died or the 6 million Jews and millions of others systematically exterminated by Hitler.

The American people greeted the end of the war with joy and relief. They looked forward to the peace and prosperity for which they had fought. Yet within two years, the peace would be jeopardized by the Cold War, and the United States would be rearming its former enemies, Japan and Germany, in order to oppose its former friend, the Soviet Union. The irony of that situation reduced some of the joy of celebration and made the American people forever more suspicious of their government and its foreign policy.

Recommended Reading

Many books have been written on the process by which the United States got involved in World War II; the following suggest a variety of approaches. Robert Dallek, *Franklin D. Roosevelt and American Foreign Policy* (1979); Robert A. Divine, *The Reluctant Belligerent* (1979); and Lloyd C. Gardner, *Economic Aspects of New Deal Diplomacy* (1964). For United States policy toward Central America, see Walter La Feber, *Inevitable Revolutions: The United States in Central America* (1983). Gordon W. Prange, *At Dawn We Slept* (1981) is a recent evaluation of the events at Pearl Harbor.

A. Russell Buchanan, *The United States and World War II*, 2 vols. (1965) is a comprehensive account that provides good coverage of the military side of the war. Gaddis Smith, *Diplomacy During the Second World War*, Martin J. Sherwin, *A World Destroyed* (1975), and Gar Alperovitz, *Atomic Diplomacy* (1965) deal with important subjects. Stephen Ambrose, *Eisenhower* (1983) is a well-written account of the most important military commander during the war.

John Morton Blum, *V Was for Victory* (1976), Richard Polenberg, *War and Society* (1972), and Richard R. Lingeman, *Don't You Know There Is a War On?* (1970) are excellent books about the home front. Susan M. Hartmann, *The Home Front and Beyond* (1982) is a fascinating account of women during the war. Richard M. Dalfuime, *Desegregation of the U.S. Armed Forces* (1975) describes segregation in the military during the war. Roger Daniels, *Concentration Camp U.S.A.* (1971) details the depressing story of the relocation of Japanese-Americans during the war.

David S. Wyman, *The Abandonment of the Jews* (1984), tells the story of American policy toward the victims of the Holocaust.

In *The Dollmaker* (1954), Harriette Arnow tells the story of a young woman from Kentucky who finds herself in wartime Detroit. Two other fine novels of the war period are Norman Mailer, *The Naked and the Dead* (1948) and Irwin Shaw, *The Young Lions* (1948).

TIME LINE

1931–1932	Japan seizes Manchuria
1933	Hitler becomes German chancellor United States refuses to join collective sanctions against Germany United States recognizes the Soviet Union Good Neighbor policy announced
1934	Germany begins rearmament
1935	Italy invades Ethiopia First Neutrality Act
1936	Spanish civil war begins Second Neutrality Act
1937	Hitler annexes Austria, occupies Sudetenland Third Neutrality Act
1938	German persecution of Jews heightens
1939	Nazi-Soviet Pact German invasion of Poland; World War II begins
1940	Roosevelt elected for a third term Selective Service Act
1941	"Four Freedoms" speech by FDR Lend-Lease Act Germany attacks Russia Japanese assets in United States frozen Japanese attack Pearl Harbor Proposed black march on Washington
1942	Internment of Japanese-Americans Second Allied front in Africa launched
1943	Invasion of Sicily Italian campaign United Mine Workers strike Race riots in Detroit and many other cities
1944	Operation Overlord G.I. Bill passes Congress Roosevelt elected for a fourth term
1945	Yalta conference Roosevelt dies; Harry Truman becomes president Successful test of atomic bomb Hiroshima and Nagasaki bombed; Japan surrenders

PORTFOLIO FIVE

THE ART OF
A MODERNIZING PEOPLE

1 9 0 0 – 1 9 4 5

Just as the United States gradually became a world power in the period from 1900 to the end of World War II, American art also came of age and emerged as a force to be reckoned with around the world. American architects led by Frank Lloyd Wright had a strong influence in both Europe and Asia, while for many foreign visitors the skyscraper symbolized American vitality and creativity. Two trends dominated American painting during this period: one was the growing popularity of abstract art, the other a continuing concern for documenting the American scene with realistic paintings. Freed by the camera from the need simply to record, a number of European artists, postimpressionists, expressionists, cubists, and others experimented with new forms, and their movements inevitably influenced many artists in America. At the same time, the impulse to paint American subjects in a realistic way remained strong, and this trend was strengthened during the Depression decade as Americans explored the strengths and weaknesses of their civilization through documentaries of all kinds.

In the decade and a half before World War I, a group of young artists who called themselves "the Eight" but whom the critics labeled "the ashcan school" had a large impact on American art. They were called "the ashcan school" not only because they painted ashcans as well as elevated trains, run-down tenements, prostitutes, and other unsavory scenes but also because many of their critics thought their work should be assigned to the ashcan. They painted in different styles and came from many places, but they all eventually settled in New York. Like so many others of the progressive generation, they discovered the city in all its fascinating and appalling details. John Sloan was probably the best known of "the Eight," but George Luks, Maurice Prendergast, and Arthur B. Davies were just as talented. It was Davies who played a large role in organizing the Armory show that opened in New York on February 17, 1913. More than any other single event, this show introduced the American public to modern art and sculpture, both European and American. Many critics were shocked by paintings such as Marcel Duchamp's *Nude Descending a Staircase,* in which the subject was reduced to shapes and lines.

The Armory show marked the acceptance of modern art for sophisticated Americans and inspired Stuart Davis, Georgia O'Keeffe, and many other young artists to join the cubist and abstract movements. Still, the realistic tradition in America remained strong. Edward Hopper, Grant Wood, Thomas Hart Benton, John Curry, and others chose regional subjects and brought vitality to what is sometimes called the "American scene movement." The Depression of the 1930s further stimulated social realism in art, and New Deal programs allowed hundreds of artists to document the look and feel of America.

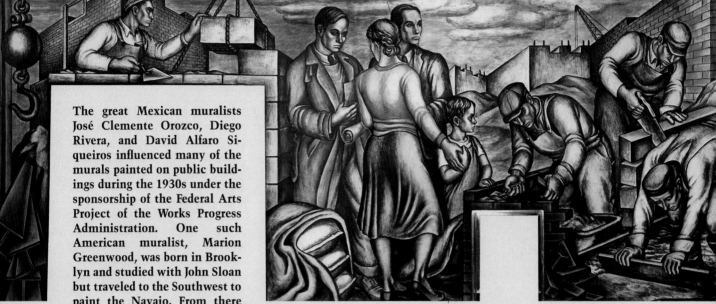

The great Mexican muralists José Clemente Orozco, Diego Rivera, and David Alfaro Siqueiros influenced many of the murals painted on public buildings during the 1930s under the sponsorship of the Federal Arts Project of the Works Progress Administration. One such American muralist, Marion Greenwood, was born in Brooklyn and studied with John Sloan but traveled to the Southwest to paint the Navajo. From there she went to Mexico, where she depicted Indian and Mexican life in several murals. She was strongly influenced by Siqueiros. Later she returned to the United States and did several murals for the Federal Arts Program including this one for a housing project in Brooklyn. It expressed some of the idealism and faith in the future present in the 1930s, but, in a fate met by many of the New Deal murals, a later generation found it ugly and destroyed it.

Marion Greenwood,
Planned Community Life (Blueprint for Living), 1940.
Photograph Vassar College Art Gallery, Poughkeepsie, New York.
Gift of Patricia Ashley.

Frank Lloyd Wright room, 1914.
Metropolitan Museum of Art, New York. Bequest of Emily Crane Chadbourne.
Installation generosity of Saul P. Steinberg and Reliance Group Holdings, Inc.

Frank Lloyd Wright (1867–1959), a native of Wisconsin, was influenced by Louis Sullivan and by the Arts and Crafts Movement, but he was also an innovative genius who became one of the world's leading architects. He began to build his "prairie houses" in the midwest as early as 1894. Rebelling against the boxes with classical decoration that most Americans lived in, he created one-story structures using natural materials and adapting each house to its site. Wright also opened up the interiors of his houses, as shown in this 1914 example. He used a great many windows, allowed one room to flow into another, and built in most of the furniture. He fought against Victorian clutter and gaudy decoration, preferring natural colors and organic materials. His modern architecture had a wide impact even on the modest ranch houses that millions of Americans lived in after World War II.

Edward Hopper, *Early Sunday Morning,* 1930.
Whitney Museum of American Art, New York.

Edward Hopper (1882–1967) grew up in Nyack, New York, on the Hudson River just north of New York City. He studied art in New York and was strongly influenced by some of the "ashcan school" painters. After traveling briefly in Europe, he settled down in the United States and spent his life recording the American scene. Although he painted many seascapes and rural scenes, he is most famous for his stark, almost abstract urban scenes. He was fascinated by light but also by the loneliness and isolation he found everywhere in American life.

John Sloan (1871–1951), one of
the leading members of the
Eight, was born in rural Pennsylvania and studied at the
Academy of Fine Arts in Philadelphia. He moved to New York
in 1905 and, like so many other
artists, made his living drawing
illustrations for magazines. His
paintings, like the scene of
Greenwich Village, do not seem
shocking today, but they startled the viewing public in the
first decades of the twentieth
century. Sloan's rebellion, like
so many of the "ashcan" group,
was not so much in form as in
subject. The ordinary and the
mundane became the subjects
of paintings, and that was as
disturbing as the pop artists of
the 1950s painting soup cans
and comic strips.

Marsden Hartley (1877–
1943) shocked the public in
another way. He took a traditional subject and painted it in
an abstract style. Unlike most
of his contemporaries, he was
influenced by Germany rather
than France, and he was there
when the war broke out. This
painting is one of a series he did
in memory of a friend, a young
German officer who died in the
war.

Thomas Hart Benton, *Boom Town*, 1928. Memorial Art Gallery of the University of Rochester, New York. Marion Stratton Gould Fund.

While some artists discovered their subject in the American city, another group, sometimes called the American scene painters or regionalists, found their inspiration in the great American heartland. The most important of these artists were Thomas Hart Benton (1889–1975), Grant Wood (1891–1941), and John Steuart Curry (1897–1946). Benton, who grew up in Missouri, traveled throughout the country and often focused his paintings on the relationship of the workingman to his environment. *Boom Town* is his interpretation of Borger, Texas, "as it was in 1926 in the middle of its rise from a road crossing to an oil city." Despite the realistic subject, there is an abstract air to the picture. Some critics have compared Benton's work to that of El Greco.

Curry grew up in Kansas, and although he lived in New York for a considerable portion of his life, his subject was always the rural life of the Midwest. Even more than Benton, he seemed intent on recording a way of life that was rapidly disappearing in the 1920s and 1930s.

John Steuart Curry, *Baptism in Kansas*, 1928. Whitney Museum of American Art, New York.

PART SIX
AN ENDURING PEOPLE

1945–1985

The final section of *The American People* traces the development of our country in recent years. Emerging from World War II as the world's most powerful nation, the United States soon became engaged in a so-called Cold War with the Soviet Union, the world's second most powerful nation. Although this international development worried many Americans, most remained confident in the American way of life, which produced such abundant rewards in the postwar years. But in the 1960s, Cold War policies resulted in a hot war in Vietnam, and the American economy weakened. These changes eroded confidence, caused deep social divisions, and highlighted the limits to progress.

Chapters 27 and 28 are paired. In Chapter 27, "Chills and Fever During the Cold War," we see how the United States moved from an uneasy friendship with the Soviet Union to disillusionment and hostility. The Cold War shaped American foreign policy in all parts of the world and had a domestic impact as well, as Americans faced a second Red Scare in the late 1940s and early 1950s. Chapter 28, "The Dreams of Postwar America," explains how, despite the Cold War, many Americans found the postwar years deeply satisfying. Although not all Americans shared the abundance of the 1950s, the general standard of living rose to unprecedented heights. Some of the people for whom the promises of the American dream failed to materialize began to organize. The 1950s marks the beginnings of the modern civil rights movement.

Chapter 29, "From Self-confidence to Self-doubt," traces the course of a new wave of reformism. As Great Society programs tried to eliminate some of the country's social, economic, and racial problems, blacks, Hispanic-Americans, women, and others organized and struggled to improve their situation. Meanwhile, Cold War policies continued. As the nation became entangled in the Vietnam War, conflict and upheaval undermined the nation's self-confidence.

In Chapter 30, "Illusion and Disillusionment," we trace the Vietnam War to its conclusion and see the government's efforts to contain the social turmoil it helped produce. Political scandals contributed to a continuing mood of disillusionment, as did the declining economic position of the nation. The energy and optimism of reform did not disappear altogether, however, and women, blacks, and others made significant gains during these years. Chapter 31, "Austerity and the American Dream: The United States Since 1976," develops the themes established in Chapter 30 and attempts to set our recent past in perspective.

PARALLEL EVENTS

1945 — 1950 — 1955 — 1960 — 19

CULTURAL and TECHNOLOGICAL

1946 Benjamin Spock, *Baby and Child Care*
1947 Jackie Robinson becomes first black to play major-league sports
1948 Kinsey publishes first report on human sexuality
Bell Laboratories develop transistor
1951 J.D. Salinger publishes *The Catcher in the Rye*
1956 Elvis Presley hits No. 1 with "Heartbreak Hotel,"
Allen Ginsberg, "Howl"
1957 First nuclear power plant opened in Shippingport, Pennsylvania
Russians launch *Sputnik*
1960s Electronic calculators in office use
Jet planes used for commercial purposes
1961 Rachel Carson, *Silent Spring*
1962 Bob Dylan gains recognition with "Blowin' in the Wind"
First American orbits the earth
Michael Harrington, *The Other America*
1963 Betty Friedan, *The Feminine Mystique*

SOCIAL and ECONOMIC

1945–1946 Wave of strikes
1947 Report of committee on Civil Rights released
1948 Marshall Plan initiates substantial foreign aid
1952 United States tests first hydrogen bomb
1953 Introduction of "termination" policy to eliminate reservations for Native Americans
1953–1954 Operation Wetback
1955 AFL and CIO merge
Montgomery bus boycott
1957 Baby boom peaks
Little Rock school desegregation crisis
1960 Birth control pills made available
Sit-ins begin
S.D.S. founded
1960s Wave of mergers in American industry
1961 Freedom Rides to the South
1963 Birmingham demonstration
March on Washington
1964 Free Speech movement at Berkeley

POLITICAL

1945 First atomic bombs dropped on Japan; World War II ends
1946 Employment Act
1947 Truman Doctrine
Taft-Hartley Act
Truman establishes Federal Loyalty Program
HUAC probes movie industry
1948 Marshall Plan passed
Berlin Airlift
Truman reelected
1949 NATO established
Truman announces Fair Deal
1950 Alger Hiss convicted
Korean War begins
McCarran Internal Security Act
1951 *Denis v. United States*
1952 Dwight D. Eisenhower elected president
1953 Rosenbergs executed for espionage
1954 Army-McCarthy Hearings
Senate censures Joseph R. McCarthy
Brown v. Board of Education initiates school desegregation
1956 Eisenhower reelected
1957 Civil Rights Act
1960 John F. Kennedy elected
1961 Bay of Pigs invasion
1962 Cuban missile crisis
1963 JFK assassinated; Lyndon B. Johnson becomes president
1964 Civil Rights Act
War on Poverty launched
LBJ reelected

1945–1985

CULTURAL and TECHNOLOGICAL

- 1965 Ralph Nader, *Unsafe at Any Speed*
- 1966 Masters and Johnson, *Human Sexual Response*
- 1969 Woodstock and Altamont
- 1970s Electronics transform traditional industries
- 1972 99.8 percent of American households have television sets
- 1972–1973 Development of minicomputers creates new markets
  Introduction of calculators for home use
- 1973 More than one million photocopiers in use
- 1980s Increasing sales of personal home computers
- 1982 Vietnam Veterans Memorial dedicated
- 1985 17 million VCR's in use; shift of film entertainment into the home
  First space shuttle launched with the sole purpose of gathering military data

SOCIAL and ECONOMIC

- 1965 Teach-ins begin
  Assassination of Malcolm X
- 1966 "Black Power"
- 1967 Antiwar demonstrations
  Urban riots
- 1968 Martin Luther King assassinated
  AIM established
- 1970 Kent State and Jackson State incidents
- 1971–1975 Busing controversies
- 1971 *Pentagon Papers* published
- 1972 *Ms.* magazine founded
  Title 9 of the Educational Amendments provides funding for women's athletics
- 1973 Battle of Wounded Knee
- 1974 OPEC price increase
- 1977 Department of Energy created
  U.S. trade deficit $26.72 billion
- 1979 Three Mile Island accident
- 1984 Antiabortion campaign receives extensive media coverage; continued bombing of family planning clinics
  Strong U.S. dollar abroad contributes to growing trade deficit

POLITICAL

- 1965 Voting Rights Act
  Escalation of U.S. involvement in Vietnam
- 1968 Robert F. Kennedy assassinated
  Richard M. Nixon elected president
- 1969 Nixon Doctrine
- 1970 Environmental Protection Agency created
- 1972 Nixon visits China
  Salt I agreement
  Watergate break-in
  Nixon reelected
- 1973 United States withdraws from Vietnam
  Roe v. Wade strikes down antiabortion laws
- 1974 Nixon resigns as a result of Watergate affair;
  Gerald Ford becomes president;
  Runaway and Homeless Youth Act
- 1976 Jimmy Carter elected president
- 1977 Panama Canal Treaties
- 1978 California passes Proposition 13, cutting property taxes
  Bakke decision upholds affirmative action but prohibits fixed quotas
- 1979 SALT II agreement
- 1979–1981 Iranian hostage crisis
- 1980 Ronald Reagan elected president
- 1981 Sandra Day O'Connor becomes first woman Supreme Court justice
- 1984 Geraldine Ferraro nominated as Democratic vice-presidential candidate
  Reagan reelected
- 1985 Reagan's budget proposes deep cuts in domestic spending
  Tax reform debate

CHAPTER 27
CHILLS AND FEVER
DURING THE COLD WAR

Val Lorwin was in Paris in November 1950 when word of the charges against him arrived. A State Department employee, on leave of absence after 15 years of government service, he was in France working on a book. Now he had to return to the United States to defend himself against the accusation that he was a member of the Communist party and thus a loyalty and security risk.

The accusation surprised Lorwin. It almost seemed like a tasteless joke. Yet it was no joke but a grim consequence of the Cold War. Suspicions of the Soviet Union escalated after 1945, and a wave of paranoia swept through the United States. The threat of communism was no laughing matter at home.

Lorwin was an unlikely candidate to be caught up in the fallout of the Cold War. He began to work for the government in 1935, serving in a number of New Deal agencies, then in the Labor Department and on the War Production Board before he was drafted during World War II. While in the army he was assigned to the Office of Strategic Services, an early intelligence agency, and he was frequently granted security clearances in the United States and abroad.

Lorwin, however, did have a left-wing past as an active Socialist in the 1930s. His social life then had revolved around Socialist party causes, particularly the unionization of southern tenant farmers and the provision of aid to the unemployed. He and his wife Madge drafted statements or stuffed envelopes to support their goals. But that activity was wholly open and legal, and Lorwin had from the start been aggressively anti-Communist in political affairs.

Suddenly, Lorwin, like others in the period, faced the nightmare of secret charges against which the burden of proof was entirely on him and the chance of clearing his name slim. Despite his spotless record, Lorwin was told that an unnamed accuser had identified him as a Communist. He was entitled to a hearing if he chose, or he could resign.

Lorwin requested a hearing, held late in 1950. Still struck by the absurdity of the situation, he refuted all accusations but made little effort to cite his own positive achievements. At the conclusion, he was informed that the government no longer doubted his loyalty but considered him a security risk, still grounds nonetheless for dismissal from his job.

When he appealed the judgment, Lorwin was again denied access to the identity of his accuser. This time, however, he thoroughly prepared his defense. At the hearing, a total of 97 witnesses either spoke under oath on Lorwin's behalf or left sworn written depositions testifying to his good character and meritorious service.

The issues in the hearings might have been considered comic in view of Lorwin's record, had not a man's reputation been at stake. The accuser had once lived with the Lorwins in Washington, D.C. Fifteen years later he claimed that in 1935, Lorwin had revealed that he was holding a Communist party meeting in his home and had even shown him a Party card.

Lorwin proved all the charges were groundless. He also showed that in 1935 the Socialist party card was red, the color the accuser reported seeing, while the Communist party card was black. In March 1952, Lorwin was finally cleared for both loyalty and security.

Though he thought he had weathered the storm, Lorwin's troubles were not yet over. His name appeared on one of the lists waved by Senator Joseph McCarthy of Wisconsin, the most aggressive anti-Communist of the era, and Lorwin was again victimized. The next year, he was indicted for making false statements to the State Department Loyalty-Security Board. The charges this time proved as specious as before. Finally, in May 1954, admitting that its special prosecutor had deliberately lied to the grand jury and had no legitimate case, the Justice Department asked for dismissal of the indictment. Lorwin was cleared at last and went on to a distinguished career as a labor historian.

Lorwin was more fortunate than some victims of the anti-Communist crusade. People rallied around him and gave him valuable support. Despite considerable emotional cost, he survived the witch-hunt of the early 1950s, but his case still reflected vividly the ugly domestic consequences of the breakdown in relations between the Soviet Union and the United States.

The Cold War, which unfolded soon after the end of World War II, powerfully affected all aspects of American life. This chapter describes the worsening relations between the United States and the Soviet Union, the world's two strongest nations, that culminated in a bitter conflict after 1945. It shows how the Cold War, conducted not with bullets but with words and diplomatic maneuvers, colored all foreign policy decisions in the United States. It also reveals its domestic implications, best reflected in the attempt to wipe out all traces of communism at home.

ORIGINS OF THE SOVIET-AMERICAN CONFRONTATION

The Cold War was rooted in longstanding disagreements between the major powers that had been papered over during the Second World War. Though they had different dreams for the shape of the postwar world, the United States and the Soviet Union avoided conflict with each other in the bitter struggle against a common foe. At the war's end, however, their differences became painfully obvious. The Cold War was the unfortunate result.

The American View of the USSR

American policymakers in the Cold War period drew on the hopes that had guided the nation during World War II. They envisioned a world that would be stable and secure after victory. In ideological terms, they hoped to spread the values that provided the underpinning of the American dream—liberty, equality, and democracy—around the globe. At the same time, however, they envisioned a world open to American enterprise. They sought a world characterized by peace and prosperity, free trade, and business expansion.

Government leaders wanted to eliminate trade barriers and economic restraints in order to provide worldwide markets for American farm commodities and industrial products. Recollections of the Depression decade haunted them. "We've got to export three times as much as we exported just before the war if we want to keep our industry running at somewhere near

capacity," Under Secretary of State William L. Clayton told a congressional committee in March 1945.

Policymaking officials also anticipated a world in which the United States played a central role. Their sense of purpose dated back to the first days of settlement, when Americans had been guided by a sense of mission. Postwar planners shared the patriotic fervor that promoted expansion, imperialism, and finally involvement in the First and Second World Wars. Proud of the American system, they hoped to share their principles and ideals and to prevent future wars.

American Leadership in the Cold War

Harry Truman led the nation in the first years of the Cold War. The new president was an unpretentious man who took a straightforward approach to public affairs. He was, however, ill prepared for the office he assumed in the final months of World War II. His three months as vice-president had done little to school him in the complexity of postwar issues. Nor had Franklin Roosevelt confided in Truman. No wonder that the new president felt insecure from the start. The day after he became president, he told reporters, "I don't know whether you fellows ever had a load of hay fall on you, but when they told me yesterday what had happened, I felt like the moon, the stars and all the planets had fallen on me." To a former colleague in the Senate, he groaned, "I'm not big enough. I'm not big enough for this job." Others agreed. Tennessee Valley Authority director David Lilienthal spoke for many who found it hard to accept the fact that Roosevelt was gone. "The country," he complained, "doesn't deserve to be left this way."

Yet Truman matured rapidly. A feisty politician, he responded ably to new challenges. Impulsive and aggressive, he made a virtue out of rapid response. At his first press conference, he answered questions so quickly that reporters could not record his responses. A sign on the president's White House desk read "The Buck Stops Here," and he was willing to make quick decisions on issues, even though associates sometimes wondered if he understood all the implications. Roosevelt had shown a masterful sense of timing during the New Deal and, on complex issues during the war, had been even more willing to delay. Truman was less inclined to wait before acting. His rapid-fire decisions had important consequences for the Cold War.

Truman served virtually all of the term to which Roosevelt had been elected, then won another for himself in 1948. In 1952, war hero Dwight D. Eisenhower, who won the presidency for the Republican party for the first time in 20 years, succeeded him.

Truman's down-to-earth directness was a drawback on formal state occasions, but an asset with the public.

Eisenhower stood in stark contrast to his predecessor. He had a homey, natural manner that made him widely popular. He conveyed a sense of honesty and strength that translated into a captivating appeal. On occasion, in press conferences or other public gatherings, his comments came out convoluted and imprecise. Yet appearances were deceiving, for beneath his casual approach was real shrewdness. At one point, as he prepared for a session with newsmen and his aides briefed him on a delicate matter, he said, "Don't worry. . . . If that question comes up, I'll just confuse them."

Eisenhower had not taken the typical route to the presidency. In fact, he had very little formal political experience. After his World War II success, he served as army chief of staff, president of Columbia University, and then head of the North Atlantic Treaty Organization. Lack of political background notwithstanding, he did have a genuine ability to get people to compromise and to work together. Though he remained aloof from party politics, he may have entertained hopes of holding office after the war. General George Patton commented in 1943 that "Ike wants to be President so badly you can taste it," and his career choices after the war clearly kept him visible and involved in public affairs. Yet he made no move in that direction until he sought the Republican nomination in 1952.

Ike's limited experience with everyday politics conditioned his sense of the presidential role. Whereas Truman was accustomed to political infighting and wanted to take charge, Eisenhower saw things differently. The presidency for him was no "bully pulpit," as it had been for Theodore Roosevelt or even for FDR. "I am not one of those desk-pounding types that likes to stick out his jaw and look like he is bossing the show," he said. "You do not *lead* by hitting people over the head. Any damn fool can do that, but it's usually called 'assault'—not 'leadership.'" Ike's method, Richard Nixon once observed, "was never to take direct action requiring his personal participation where indirect methods would accomplish the same result."

Though the personal styles of Truman and Eisenhower differed, as did their domestic programs (see Chapter 28), they shared a basic view that governed American foreign policy after

World War II. Both subscribed to traditional American attitudes about self-determination and distrusted Soviet ventures during and after the war. Truman's suspicions were obvious even before the United States entered the struggle. He commented in July 1941, "If we see that Germany is winning we ought to help Russia, and if Russia is winning we ought to help Germany." He accepted collaboration as a marriage of necessity, but he became increasingly hostile to Soviet moves as the war drew to an end. It was now time, he said, "to stand up to the Russians."

Like Truman, Eisenhower believed in the notion of a monolithic Communist force struggling for world supremacy, and he thought the Kremlin in Moscow was orchestrating subversive activity around the globe. Like Truman, he viewed the Soviet system as "a tyranny that has brought thousands, millions of people into slave

Indirect action and a low-key public image characterized Eisenhower's handling of the presidency.

camps and is attempting to make all humankind its chattel." For both presidents, the issues could be perceived in such black and white terms. As Eisenhower declared in his 1953 inaugural address, "Forces of good and evil are massed and armed and opposed as rarely before in history. Freedom is pitted against slavery, lightness against dark."

The Soviet View of America

The Soviet Union formulated its own goals after World War II. Devastated by war, the Russians were determined to rebuild and to protect themselves from another such terrible conflict. Unlike the United States, the Soviet Union had seen the destructive struggle unfold on its own soil and had suffered an enormous loss of life.

The Soviets feared they were vulnerable along their western flank. Such anxieties went back at least to the early nineteenth century, when Napoleon had reached the gates of Moscow. Twice in the twentieth century, invasions had come from the west, most recently when Hitler had attacked in 1941. That offensive had finally been repelled, but at a huge cost. Soviet agriculture and industry were in a shambles. Fearful that the Germans would recover quickly after the war to pose a new threat, the Soviets demanded defensible borders and friendly regimes nearby. They insisted on stable, secure governments in eastern Europe receptive to Soviet military and political dictation.

In World War II, the Russians had played down the notion of world revolution and mobilized support for more nationalistic goals. They still feared capitalist encirclement and the penetration of Western ways (as they had since the nineteenth century) but now remained confident that their new system of communism would eventually triumph, just as Marxist-Leninist doctrine had predicted. Yet the message was trumpeted less aggressively than before. As the struggle drew to a close, the Russians talked little of world conquest, emphasizing socialism within the nation itself and in bordering countries. But in those adjoining areas, they intended to prevent any interference in what they viewed as their necessary zone of influence.

Joseph Stalin's highly autocratic approach in both domestic and foreign affairs was an affront to American sensibilities.

Soviet Leadership in the Cold War

The leader of the Soviet Union at the war's end was Joseph Stalin, who had guided his party and state for 20 years. Ruthless and grim in pursuit of both national and personal ends, he had presided over monstrous purges against his opponents in the 1930s. Vain and vindictive, Stalin exercised a power unknown in Western nations. He now spoke in terms that gave the Soviets alone credit for the victory over Hitler and affirmed the superiority of Russian society as he aggressively formulated a set of Soviet demands.

When Stalin died in March 1953, he left a vacuum in Soviet political affairs. His successor, Nikita S. Khrushchev, used his position as party secretary to consolidate his power. Purges of the party bureaucracy took place, and five years after Stalin's death, Khrushchev held the offices of both prime minister and party secretary. A peasant who had risen to the top, Khrushchev was fond of crude jokes and known for rude behavior. On one occasion he pounded a table at the United Nations with his shoe while the British prime minister was speaking. As Khrushchev continued some of Stalin's hard-line policies, he confronted the equally firm stance of the United States. The Cold War was the result.

THE BEGINNING OF THE COLD WAR

The Cold War developed by degrees. Frictions, existing since 1917, had been temporarily eased during the war but now began to resurface as the struggle wound down. With the Fascist threat defeated, disagreements about the shape of the postwar world brought the Soviet Union and the United States into conflict.

Disillusionment with the USSR

During the war, Joseph Goulden, a youngster of about 10, saw the Russians as "brave and skilled partisans." To him, "their heroic stand at Stalingrad was equal to the defense of the Alamo." Soon that comforting image began to fade. In September 1945, fully 54 percent of a national sample trusted the Russians to cooperate with the Americans in the postwar years. Two months later, the figure dropped to 44 percent, and by February 1946, to 35 percent.

Not unlike some of America's most admired presidents, Nikita Khrushchev worked his way from humble beginnings to head the government of a major world power.

In recent years, historians have used a new source of evidence, the public opinion poll. People have always been concerned with what others think, and leaders have often sought to frame their behavior according to the preferences of the populace. As techniques of assessing the mind of the public have become more sophisticated, the poll has emerged as an integral part of the analysis of social and political life. Polls now measure opinion on many questions—social, cultural, intellectual, political, and diplomatic. Because of their increasing importance, it is useful to know how to use the polls in an effort to understand and recover the past.

The principle of polling is not new. Throughout American history efforts have been made to predict electoral results. In 1824, for example, the Harrisburg *Pennsylvanian* sought to predict the winner of that year's presidential race, and in the 1880s the Boston *Globe* sent reporters to selected precincts on election night to forecast final returns. In 1916, *Literary Digest* began conducting postcard polls to predict politi-

cal results. By the 1930s, Elmo Roper and George Gallup had developed further the field of market research and public opinion polling. Despite an embarrassing mistake by *Literary Digest* in predicting a Landon victory over FDR in 1936, polling had by World War II become a scientific enterprise.

According to Gallup, a poll is not magic but "merely an instrument for gauging public opinion," especially the views of those often unheard. As Elmo Roper said, the poll is "one of the few ways through which the so-called common man can be articulate." Polling, therefore, is a valuable way to recover the attitudes, beliefs, and voices of ordinary people.

Yet certain cautions should be observed. Like all instruments of human activity, polls are imperfect and may even be dangerous. Historians using information from polls need to be aware of how large the samples were, when the interviewing was done, and how opinions might have been molded by the form of the poll itself. Questions can be poorly phrased. Some questions hint at the desirable answer or otherwise

FOREIGN POLICY POLLS

DECEMBER 2, 1949—Atom Bomb
Now that Russia has the atom bomb, do you think another war is more likely or less likely?

More likely 45%
Less likely. 28
Will make no difference. 17
No opinion 10
By Education
College
More likely 36%
Less likely. 35
Will make no difference. 23
No opinion 6
High School
More likely 44%
Less likely. 28
Will make no difference. 19
No opinion 9
Grade School
More likely 50%
Less likely. 26
Will make no difference. 12
No opinion 12

May 1, 1950—National Defense
Do you think United States Government spending on national defense should be increased, decreased, or remain about the same?

Increased 63%
Decreased. 7
Same 24
No opinion 6

SEPTEMBER 18, 1953—Indochina
The United States is now sending war materials to help the French fight the Communists in Indochina. Would you approve or disapprove of sending United States soldiers to take part in the fighting there?

Approve. 8%
Disapprove 85
No opinion 7

JANUARY 11, 1950—RUSSIA
As you hear and read about Russia these days, do you believe Russia is trying to build herself up to be the ruling power of the world—or is Russia just building up protection against being attacked in another war?

Rule the world. 70%
Protect herself 18
No opinion 12

By Education
College
Rule the world. 73%
Protect herself 21
No opinion 6
High School
Rule the world. 72%
Protect herself 18
No opinion 10
Grade School
Rule the world. 67%
Protect herself 17
No opinion 16

FEBRUARY 12, 1951—ATOMIC WARFARE
If the United States gets into an all-out war with Russia, do you think we should drop atom bombs on Russia first—or do you think we should use the atom bomb only if it is used on us?

Drop A-bomb first 66%
Only if used on us 19
No opinion 15

The greatest difference was between men and women—72% of the men questioned favored our dropping the bomb first, compared to 61% of the women.

George H. Gallup, *The Gallup Poll: Public Opinion, 1935–1971*, vol. 2 (New York: Random House, 1972) © American Institute of Public Opinion.

influence opinions by planting ideas in the persons interviewed. Polls sometimes provide ambiguous responses that can be interpreted many ways. More serious, some critics worry that human freedom itself is threatened by the pollsters' manipulative and increasingly accurate predictive techniques.

Despite these limitations, polls have become an ever-present part of American life. In the late 1940s and early 1950s, Americans were polled frequently about a variety of topics ranging from foreign aid, the United Nations, and the occupation of Germany and Japan to labor legislation, child punishment, and whether women should wear slacks in public (39 percent of men said no, as did 49 percent of women). Such topics as the first use of nuclear arms, presidential popularity, national defense, and U.S. troop intervention in a troubled area of the world (Indochina) remain as pertinent today as they were then.

The polls included here deal with foreign policy during the Cold War in the early 1950s. How did people respond to the Russian nuclear capability?

Other polls questioned public perceptions of Russian intentions and appropriate American responses. How do you analyze the results of these polls? What do you think is the significance of rating responses by levels of education? In what ways are the questions "loaded"? How might these results influence American foreign policy? What do you think is significant about the Indochina poll? These polls show the challenge and response nature of the Cold War that continues to this day. How do you think Americans would respond today to these questions?

Polls also shed light on domestic issues. Consider the poll on professions for young men and women taken in 1950. What does it tell us about the attitudes of the pollster on appropriate careers for men and women? Why do you think both men and women had nearly identical views on this subject? How do you think people today would answer these qustions? Would they be presented in the same way? Also observe the poll on women in politics. To what extent have attitudes on this issue changed in the 1980s?

DOMESTIC POLICY POLLS

OCTOBER 29, 1949—Women in Politics
If the party whose candidate you most often support nominated a woman for President of the United States, would you vote for her if she seemed qualified for the job?

Yes 48%
No. 48
No opinion 4

By Sex
Men

Yes 45%
No. 50
No opinion 5

Women

Yes 51%
No. 46
No opinion 3

By Political Affiliation
Democrats

Yes 50%
No. 48
No opinion 2

Republicans

Yes 46%
No. 50
No opinion 4

Would you vote for a woman for Vice President of the United States if she seemed qualified for the job?

Yes 53%
No. 43
No opinion 4

MAY 5, 1950—Most Important Problem
What do you think is the most important problem facing the entire country today?

War, threat of war 40%
Economic problems, living costs, inflation, taxes. 15
Unemployment 10
Communism 8
Atomic bomb control 6
Strikes and labor troubles 4
Corruption in Government. 3
Housing 3
Others 11

JULY 12, 1950—Professions
Suppose a young man came to you and asked your advice about taking up a profession. Assuming that he was qualified to enter any of these professions, which one of them would you first recommend to him? (on card)

Doctor of medicine. 29%
Engineer, builder 16
Business executive 8
Clergyman 8
Lawyer. 8
Government worker 6

Professor, teacher. 5
Banker. 4
Dentist. 4
Veterinarian 3
None, don't know 9

JULY 15, 1950—Professions
Suppose a young girl came to you and asked your advice about taking up a profession. Assuming that she was qualified to enter any of these professions, which one of them would you first recommend?

Choice of Women

Nurse. 33%
Teacher 15
Secretary 8
Social service worker 8
Dietician. 7
Dressmaker. 4
Beautician. 4
Airline stewardess 3
Actress. 3
Journalist 2
Musician 2
Model 2
Librarian 2
Medical, dental technician 1
Others 2
Don't know. 4

The views of men on this subject were nearly identical with those of women.

George H. Gallup, *The Gallup Poll: Public Opinion, 1935–1971*, vol. 2 (New York: Random House, 1972). © American Institute of Public Opinion.

Americans became increasingly disillusioned with the Soviet political system. In a series of articles in *Harper's, Life,* and *The New Yorker* in 1946, author-editor John Fischer pointed to the single-minded intensity that characterized the Soviet state. In one story he recalled a conversation with a Soviet official who argued that the United States should cease shortwave broadcasts to the Soviet Union but thought Russia should continue to transmit its messages to the American people. When the perplexed Fischer asked about the apparent contradiction, the Soviet bureaucrat responded that it was "a perfect example of reciprocity." "Your laws," he explained, "provide for free speech, and we observe them. Our laws do *not,* and it would be improper for you to disregard them."

Bill Mauldin, a cartoonist whose work affected millions during the war, published a sketch that captured the repressive nature of the Soviet government. Mauldin depicted two Russian bullies approaching a bedraggled man in a dungeon. One, holding a noose, says, "There's nothing to it, excellency. Comrade Popoff and I have committed hundreds of successful suicides."

As Americans soured on Russia, they began to equate the Nazi and Soviet systems. The hatred of Hitler's Germany was now transferred to Communist Russia. Just as they had in the 1930s, authors, journalists, and public officials began to point to similarities between the regimes, some of them quite legitimate. Both states, they contended, maintained total control over communications and could eliminate political opposition whenever they chose. Both states used terror to silence dissidents. Russian labor camps in Siberia were now compared to the horrible German concentration camps. After the American publication in 1949 of George Orwell's frightening novel *Nineteen Eighty-four, Life* magazine noted in an editorial that the ominous figure Big Brother was but a "mating" of Hitler and Stalin. Truman spoke for many Americans when he said in 1950 that "there isn't any difference between the totalitarian Russian government and the Hitler government. . . . They are all alike. They are police governments—police state governments."

American fears were heightened by the lingering sense that the nation had not been quick enough to resist totalitarian aggression in the 1930s. Had the United States stopped the Germans, Italians, or Japanese, it might have prevented the long, devastating war. The free world had not responded quickly enough before and was determined never to repeat the same mistake.

The Polish Question

The first clash between East and West came, even before the war ended, over Poland. Soviet demands for a sympathetic government there clashed with American hopes for a more representative structure. The Yalta Conference of February 1945 attempted to ensure a representative government for the postwar state (see Chapter 26), but the agreement was loosely worded.

When Truman assumed office, the situation was still unresolved. When his advisers urged a harder line than Roosevelt had been willing to take, Truman determined to stand firm. Averell Harriman, the American ambassador to the Soviet Union, warned that the United States faced a "barbarian invasion of Europe" unless the Soviets could be checked. Truman agreed. "We must stand up to the Russians," he said, "and not be easy with them."

Truman's unbending stance appeared in an April 1945 meeting with Soviet foreign minister Vyacheslav Molotov on the question of Poland. Concerned that the Russians were breaking the Yalta agreements, the president wanted a new, not simply a reorganized, government there. Though Molotov appeared conciliatory, Truman insisted that the Russians keep their word. Truman later recalled that when Molotov protested, "I have never been talked to like that in my life," he himself retorted bluntly, "Carry out your agreements and you won't get talked to like that." Such bluntness contributed to the deterioration of Soviet-American relations.

Truman and Stalin met face to face for the first time at the Potsdam Conference in July 1945, the last of the meetings held by the Big Three during the war. There, as they considered the Russian-Polish boundary, the future fate of Germany, and the American desire to obtain an unconditional surrender from Japan, the two leaders sized each other up. It was Truman's first exposure to international diplomacy at the highest level, and it left him confident of his own abilities. When he was informed, during the meeting, of the first successful atomic bomb test in New Mexico, he became even more determined to stand firm.

Economic Pressure on the USSR

One major source of controversy in the last stage of the Second World War was the question of American aid to its allies. Responding to congressional pressure at home to limit foreign assistance as hostilities ended, Truman acted impulsively. Six days after V-E Day signaled the end of the European war in May 1945, he issued an executive order cutting off lend-lease supplies to the Allies. The struggle against Japan in the Pacific dragged on, and Russia had agreed to assist there, but even so, ship loading in the United States was halted and ships bound for the Soviet Union and elsewhere were ordered to reverse course. Whether the action was a deliberate effort to use economic weapons for diplomatic effect or was simply a bureaucratic blunder, Secretary of State Edward Stettinius felt the action was "particularly untimely" in view of the delicate state of the Grand Alliance. Truman had been warned of the consequences of his actions and later realized that a phased end to shipments would have been preferable. By then it was too late.

The United States hoped to use economic pressure in other ways as well. Russia desperately needed financial assistance to rebuild after the war and, in January 1945, had requested a $6 billion loan. Roosevelt hedged, hoping to win concessions in return. In August, the Russians renewed their application, this time for only $1 billion. The new president dragged his heels. The United States first claimed to have lost the Soviet request, then in March 1946 indicated a willingness to consider the matter—but only if Russia pledged "nondiscrimination in world commerce." In short, the United States tried to use the loan as a lever to gain access to new markets. Stalin refused the offer and launched his own five-year plan instead.

Declaring the Cold War

As Soviet-American disagreements increased, both sides stepped up their rhetorical attacks. Stalin spoke out first, in 1946, asserting his confidence in the triumph of the Russian system. Capitalism and communism were on a collision course, he argued, and a series of cataclysmic disturbances would tear the capitalist world apart. The Soviet Union was prepared to strengthen its military forces, even if that meant forgoing consumer goods, to ensure its own survival in a world no longer pursuing peace. Stalin's speech was a stark and ominous statement that worried the West. Supreme Court Justice William O. Douglas called it "the declaration of World War III."

The response to Stalin's speech came not from an American but from England's former prime minister, Winston Churchill, long suspicious of the Soviet state. Speaking in Fulton, Missouri, in 1946, with Truman on the platform during the address, Churchill declared that "from Stettin in the Baltic to Trieste in the Adriatic, an iron curtain has descended across the Continent." To counter the threat, he urged that a vigilant association of English-speaking peoples work to contain Soviet designs.

CONTAINING THE SOVIET THREAT

Containment became the basis of American policy in the postwar years. Troubled by the rise of a Communist superpower that threatened American interests, both political parties became determined to check Soviet expansion. In an increasingly contentious world, the American government formulated policies to maintain the upper hand.

Containment Defined

George F. Kennan was the man primarily responsible for defining the new policy. Chargé d'affaires at the American embassy in the Soviet Union, he fired off an 8,000-word telegram to the State Department after Stalin's speech in February 1946. Kennan argued that Soviet-American hostility stemmed from "the Kremlin's neurotic view of world affairs," which in turn was rooted in "the traditional and instinctive Russian sense of insecurity." The rigid Soviet stance was not so much a response to American actions as a reflection of the Russian leaders' own efforts to maintain their autocratic rule. Russian fanaticism would not soften, regardless of how accommodating American policy became. Therefore, it had to be opposed at every turn.

When it arrived in Washington, Kennan's analysis struck a resonant chord. It made his diplomatic reputation, led to his assignment to an influential position in the State Department, and encouraged him to publish an important article under the pseudonym "Mr. X" in *Foreign Affairs.* In that essay he extended his former analysis and expressed his reservations about coexistence. The Russians intended to pursue their own ends for as long as they could. "The whole Soviet governmental machine, including the mechanism of diplomacy," he wrote, "moves inexorably along the prescribed path, like a persistent toy automobile wound up and headed in a given direction, stopping only when it meets with some unanswerable force." Many Americans agreed with Kennan that Soviet pressure had to "be contained by the adroit and vigilant application of counter-force at a series of constantly shifting geographical and political points."

The concept of containment provided the philosophical justification for the hard-line stance that Americans, both in and out of government, adopted. During Truman's presidency, containment was viewed as the cornerstone of all diplomatic initiatives in both Europe and Asia. All three secretaries of state—James F. Byrnes, George C. Marshall, and Dean Acheson—firmly supported the concept. Containment created the framework for military and economic assistance around the globe.

Containment in the Mediterranean

The first major application of containment policy came in 1947 with the development of the Truman Doctrine to meet a challenge in the eastern Mediterranean. The Soviet Union was pressuring Turkey for joint control of the Darda-

nelles, between the Black Sea and the Mediterranean. Meanwhile, though Russia was not directly involved, a civil war in Greece pitted Communist elements against the ruling English-aided right-wing monarchy. Revolutionary pressures threatened to topple the government.

In February 1947, the British ambassador to the United States informed the State Department that his country could no longer give Greece and Turkey economic and military aid. Exhausted after massive efforts in two world wars, Britain could not help other countries. Would the United States now move into the void?

The State Department quickly developed a proposal for American aid when Britain pulled out. But the administration needed to persuade reluctant legislators that the national interest was involved. A conservative Congress was concerned with smaller budgets and taxes rather than massive and expensive aid programs. Meeting with congressional leaders, Dean Acheson, at the time under secretary of state, warned that "like apples in a barrel infected by one rotten one, the corruption of Greece would infect Iran and all to the east." Eager to persuade legislators of the importance of the moment, he warned that a Communist victory would "open three continents to Soviet penetration." The major powers were now "met at Armageddon" as the Soviet Union pressed for whatever advantage it could get. Only the United States had the will and power to resist.

Administration leaders knew that bipartisan support was necessary to accomplish such a major policy shift. Senator Arthur Vandenberg of Michigan was one of the key Republicans whose approval was necessary to gain support of other party members. Vandenberg also warned that the administration had to develop public support for an interventionist policy. Quite literally, Vandenberg said, administration officials had to begin "scaring hell out of the country" if they were serious about a bold new course of containment.

Truman followed Vandenberg's advice. On March 12, 1947, he told Congress, in a statement that came to be known as the Truman Doctrine, "I believe that it must be the policy of the United States to support free peoples who are resisting subjugation by armed minorities or by outside pressures." Unless the United States acted, the free world might not survive. "If we falter in our leadership," Truman said, "we may endanger the peace of the world—and we shall surely endanger the welfare of our own Nation." To avert that calamity, he urged Congress to appropriate $400 million for military and economic aid to Turkey and Greece.

Not everyone approved of Truman's request or of the extreme way in which he described the situation. Autocratic regimes controlled Greece and Turkey, some observed. Others warned that the United States could not by itself stop encroachment in all parts of the world. Nonetheless, Congress passed Truman's foreign aid bill.

The Truman Doctrine was a major step in the advent of the Cold War. Truman's address, observed financier Bernard Baruch, "was tantamount to a declaration of . . . an ideological or religious war." Truman had succeeded in persuading many Americans that there would be no accommodation with communism. A crucial test had been passed.

The Marshall Plan, NATO, and NSC-68

The next step involved extensive economic aid for postwar recovery in western Europe. At the war's end, most of Europe was economically and politically unstable, thereby offering opportunities to the Communist movement. In France and Italy, large Communist parties grew stronger and refused to cooperate with established governments. In such circumstances, administration officials believed, Russia might easily intervene. Decisive action was needed, for as the new secretary of state, George Marshall, declared, "The patient is sinking while the doctors deliberate."

Marshall revealed the administration's willingness to assist European recovery in June 1947. He asked all troubled European nations to draw up an aid program that the United States could support, a program "directed not against any country or doctrine but against hunger, poverty, desperation, and chaos." Soviet-bloc countries were welcome to participate, Marshall claimed, although their involvement was un-

likely since they would have to disclose economic records to participate.

The proposed program would assist the ravaged nations while benefiting the United States by providing markets for the booming American economy. And it would advance the nation's ideological aims. American aid, Marshall pointed out, would permit the "emergence of political and social conditions in which free institutions can exist." The Marshall Plan and the Truman Doctrine, Truman noted, were "two halves of the same walnut."

Responding quickly to Marshall's invitation, the western European nations worked out the details of massive requests in the summer of 1947. The Soviets attended the first planning meeting but then withdrew, as American policymakers hoped and expected they would. When the multination request was finally hammered out, American officials pared it down but agreed to provide $17 billion over a period of four years to 16 cooperating nations. This support for European recovery was a unique and unprecedentedly generous act in the nation's history.

Not all Americans supported the Marshall Plan. Henry A. Wallace, former vice-president and secretary of agriculture, who had broken with the administration, called the scheme the "Martial Plan" and argued that it was another step toward war. Some members of Congress feared spreading American resources too thin. But in early 1948, Congress committed the nation to funding European economic recovery, and the containment policy moved forward another step.

Closely related to the Marshall Plan was a concerted Western effort to rebuild Germany and to reintegrate it into a reviving Europe. Germany had been the archenemy during World War II. At Yalta, as the European war drew to an end, Allied leaders had agreed on zonal occupation of Germany and on reparations Germany would pay the victors. Four zones, occupied by the Russians, Americans, British, and French, had been established for postwar administration. A year after the end of the war, however, the balance of power in Europe had shifted. With the Soviet Union threatening to dominate eastern Europe, the West moved to fill the vacuum in central Europe. In late 1946, the Americans and

British merged their zones for economic purposes and began to assign administrative duties to Germans themselves. By the middle of 1947, the process of rebuilding West German industry was under way.

Despite French fears, the United States sought to make Germany strong enough to anchor Europe. Secretary Marshall cautiously laid out the connections for Congress: "The restoration of Europe involves the restoration of Germany. Without a revival of German production there can be no revival of Europe's economy. But we must be very careful to see that a revived Germany cannot again threaten the European community."

In mid-1948, the Soviet refusal to allow land access to West Berlin, located in the Russian zone, put the German issue in bold relief. The blockade was countered by a U.S. and Royal Air Force airlift that flew supplies to the beleaguered Berliners. The fliers named it Operation Vittles, and it worked. It delivered more than 2 million tons of supplies to the city. Operation Little Vittles, so named by Lieutenant Carl S. Halverson, provided bags of candy for the children at the same time. "The difficult we do immediately," a Seabee–Air Force boast proclaimed; "the impossible takes a little longer."

Operation Vittles airlifted badly needed supplies to West Berliners isolated by the Soviet blockade.

The next major link in the containment strategy came with the creation of a military alliance in Europe to complement the economic program. In mid-1947, the Soviets had rigged elections in Hungary and eliminated anti-Communist opposition. The next year, Soviet troops massed on the Czechoslovakian border to keep that nation within the Russian orbit. In response, in 1949, the United States took the lead in establishing NATO, the North Atlantic Treaty Organization. Twelve nations formed the alliance, in which an attack against any one member would be considered an attack against all, to be met by appropriate armed force.

The Senate, resistant to such military pacts in the past, approved this time, and the United States established its first military treaty ties with Europe since the American Revolution. Congress went further than merely authorizing membership by voting to give military aid to its NATO allies. The Cold War had changed traditional American attitudes and softened the longstanding reluctance to become closely involved with European affairs.

Two events in 1949 led the United States to define its aims still more specifically. The first was the Communist triumph in the Chinese civil war. The second was the Russian detonation of an atomic device that ended the short-lived American nuclear monopoly. Truman responded by asking for a full-fledged review of America's foreign and defense policy. The National Security Council, organized in 1947 to

Defense Expenditures, 1945–1960

Source: U.S. Bureau of the Census.

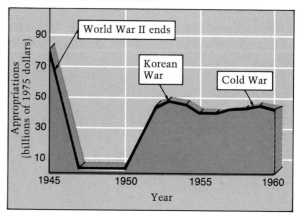

provide policy coordination, undertook the study, with Secretary of State Dean Acheson guiding the effort. The paper that resulted, NSC-68, was an immensely important document that shaped American policy for the next 20 years.

Presented to the National Security Council in 1950, NSC-68 built upon the Cold War rhetoric of the Truman Doctrine, describing America's challenges in cataclysmic terms. "The issues that face us are momentous," the paper said, "involving the fulfillment or destruction not only of this Republic but of civilization itself." Conflict between East and West, the paper assumed, was unavoidable, for amoral Soviet objectives ran totally counter to American aims. Negotiation was useless, for the Soviets could never be trusted to bargain in good faith.

Having eliminated important options, NSC-68 now laid out the remaining alternatives. The nation could continue on its present course, with relatively limited military budgets, but would fail to achieve its objectives. If the United States hoped to meet the Russian challenge, a far more massive effort was necessary. The nation must increase defense spending from the $13 billion set for 1950 to as much as $50 billion per year and increase the percentage of its budget allotted to defense from 5 to 20 percent. The costs were huge, but if the free world were to survive, the document argued, the United States had to move unilaterally to stem the Communist tide.

Cold War Europe in 1950

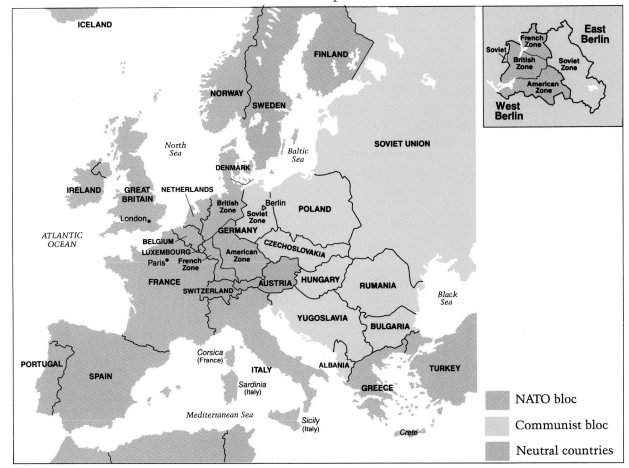

Containment in the 1950s

Containment, the keystone of American policy throughout the Truman years, was the rationale for the Truman Doctrine, the Marshall Plan, NATO, and NSC-68. In the 1950s, however, under Eisenhower's administration, containment came under attack as too cautious to counter the threat of communism.

For most of Eisenhower's two terms, John Foster Dulles was secretary of state. A devout Presbyterian who hated atheistic communism, he sought to take Truman's policy of containment even further. Responsible for the foreign policy plank in the 1952 Republican platform, which condemned containment as a "negative, futile, and immoral" approach that had lost "countless human beings to a despotism and Godless terrorism," Dulles believed a spiritual offensive was necessary. Instead of advocating containment, the United States should make it "publicly known that it wants and expects liberation to occur."

Though the language was extreme, in practice liberation was difficult to implement. Eisenhower, somewhat more conciliatory than Dulles, knew how remote was the possibility of changing the governments of Russia's satellites. The chance to test the policy came in mid-1953, as East Germans mounted anti-Soviet demonstrations. The United States looked on sympa-

Secretary of State John Foster Dulles was an outspoken proponent of active measures against Communism.

thetically but kept its distance. In 1956, when Hungarian "freedom fighters" rose up against Russian domination, the United States again stood back as Soviet forces smashed the rebels. Because Western action could have precipitated a more general conflict, Eisenhower refused to translate rhetoric into action. In the real world of international affairs, liberation was meaningless. Throughout the 1950s, the policy of containment remained in effect.

AMERICAN POLICY IN ASIA, THE MIDDLE EAST, AND LATIN AMERICA

Although containment resulted from the effort to promote European stability, the United States extended the policy to meet challenges around the globe. The Communist victory in the Chinese civil war in 1949 only underscored the growing threat to order Americans wanted in the postwar world. The Korean War that broke out soon after embroiled the United States in another international conflict barely five years after the end of World War II. Elsewhere in Asia and the Middle East, the United States discovered the tremendous appeal of communism as a social and political system and found that even

greater efforts were necessary to advance American aims.

The Chinese Revolution

America's commitment to containment became stronger still with the climax of the Chinese Revolution. China, an ally during World War II, had struggled against the conquering Japanese, even as it fought a bitter civil war. The roots of the civil war lay deep in the Chinese past—in widespread poverty, disease, oppression by the landlord class, and national humiliation

Mao Zedong's effort to reshape China in a Communist mold had begun in the 1920s; in 1949 the People's Republic of China became a reality.

at the hands of foreign powers. Mao Zedong (Mao Tse-tung*), founder of a branch of the Communist party and of a Marxist study group in the early 1920s, gathered followers who wished to reshape China in a Communist mold. Opposing the Communists were the Nationalists, led by Jiang Jieshi (Chiang Kai-shek). Even though the Communists were forced to retreat in the mid-1930s, Mao persevered. By the early 1940s, Jiang Jieshi's regime was exhausted, hopelessly inefficient, and corrupt. Mao's movement, meanwhile, grew stronger during the Second World War as he opposed the Japanese invaders and won the loyalty of the peasant class.

After the war, the United States hoped for a coalition between Nationalists and Communists, but reconciliation proved impossible. Jiang lost city after city and finally fled in 1949 to the island of Taiwan (Formosa). There he nursed the improbable hope that his was still the rightful government of all China and that he would one day return. Mao's Communist revolution had at last succeeded.

---

*Chinese names are rendered in their modern *pinyin* spelling. At first occurrence, the older but perhaps more familiar Wade-Giles spelling is given in parentheses.

The United States failed to understand the long internal conflict in China. Blinded by the fear of communism, Americans could not recognize Mao's immense popular support. As the Communist army moved toward victory, the New York *Times* termed the group a "nauseous force," a "compact little oligarchy dominated by Moscow's nominees." Mao's proclamation of the People's Republic of China on October 1, 1949, underscored fears of Russian domination, for he had already announced that his regime would support the Soviet Union against the "imperialist" United States.

The Chinese question caused near hysteria in America. Staunch anti-Communists argued that the United States was to blame for Jiang's defeat by failing to provide him with more support. Secretary of State Dean Acheson observed that the result was far beyond American control: "Nothing this country did or could have done within the reasonable limits of its capabilities could have changed that result."

Acheson considered granting diplomatic recognition to the new regime but backed off after the Communists seized American property, harassed American citizens, and openly allied themselves with the Russians. Like other Americans, he viewed the Chinese as Soviet puppets. The new government, Acheson remarked, was "not Chinese" and should not receive American support. At the same time, the United States denied aid to the Nationalists on Taiwan, assuming that the Communists on the mainland would soon conquer that island as well. That position, and the entire American stance, infuriated the largely Republican lobby in the United States, which blamed Truman for having "lost" China.

Tension with China increased during the Korean War and then again in 1954 when Mao's government began shelling Nationalist positions on the offshore islands of Quemoy and Matsu. Eisenhower, now president, was by this time committed to defending the Nationalists on Taiwan from a Communist attack, but he was unwilling to respond in the same way to the shelling of Quemoy and Matsu. By resisting recommendations that the United States plunge into the conflict, he demonstrated once again the limits of containment.

The War in Korea

The Korean War marked America's growing intervention in Asian affairs. The concern about China and the determination to contain communism led the United States into involvement in a long and bloody struggle in a faraway land. But American objectives were not always clear and were largely unrealized after three years of war.

The conflict in Korea stemmed from tensions lingering after World War II. Korea, long under Japanese control, hoped for independence after Japan's defeat. But the Allies temporarily divided Korea along the 38th parallel when the rapid end to the Pacific struggle allowed Soviet troops to accept Japanese surrender in the north while American forces did the same in the south. The Soviet-American line, initially intended as a matter of military convenience, rigidified after 1945, and in time the Soviets set up a government in the north and the Americans a government in the south. Though the major powers left Korea, they continued to support the regimes they had created. Each hoped to reunify the country on its own terms.

North Korea moved first. On June 25, 1950, North Korean forces invaded South Korea by crossing the 38th parallel. Following Soviet-built tanks, the North Korean troops steadily advanced against the South Korean soldiers. Was the invasion undertaken at Soviet command? Kim Il Sung, the North Korean leader, had visited Moscow earlier and spoken to Stalin about instability in the south. The Russians may have acquiesced in the idea of an attack, but both the planning and timing came at the initiative of the north.

The United States was taken by surprise. Earlier, America had seemed reluctant to defend Korea, but the Communist victory in China had changed the balance of power in Asia. Certain that Russia had masterminded the North Korean offensive and was testing the American policy of containment, Truman was determined to respond vigorously. "In my generation," he announced,

this was not the first occasion when the strong had attacked the weak. I recalled some earlier

instances: Manchuria, Ethiopia, Austria. . . . Each time that the democracies failed to act it had encouraged the aggressors to keep going ahead. . . . If this was allowed to go unchallenged it would mean a third world war, just as similar incidents had brought on the second world war.

Truman readied American naval and air forces and directed General Douglas MacArthur in Japan to provide supplies to South Korea. The United States also went to the United Nations Security Council. With the Soviet Union absent in protest of the UN's refusal to admit the People's Republic of China, the United States secured a unanimous resolution branding North Korea an aggressor, then another resolution calling on members of the organization to assist the

The Korean War

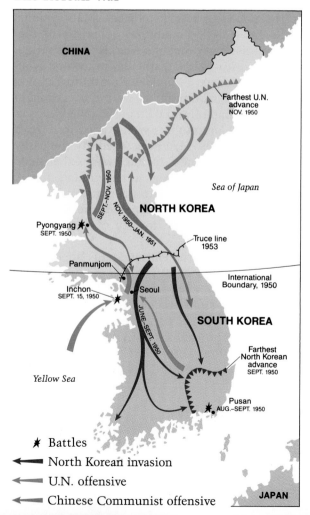

★ Battles

◄— North Korean invasion

◄— U.N. offensive

◄— Chinese Communist offensive

south in repelling aggression and restoring peace.

The president first ordered American air and naval forces into battle south of the 38th parallel, then American ground forces as well. Following a daring amphibious invasion that pushed the North Koreans back to the former boundary line, United Nations troops crossed the 38th parallel, hoping to reunify Korea under an American-backed government. Despite Chinese signals that they regarded this movement toward their border as a threat to their security, the United States pressed on. In October, Chinese troops appeared briefly in battle, then disappeared. The next month, the Chinese mounted a full-fledged counterattack, which pushed the UN forces back below the dividing line again.

Now the war became a brutal stalemate, which provoked a bitter struggle between Douglas MacArthur and his civilian commander in chief. A brilliant but arrogant general, MacArthur called for massive retaliatory air strikes against China. While the administration was most concerned with the containment of communism in Europe, MacArthur argued for

stronger resistance in Asia. Truman was trying to conduct a limited war and to prevent it from becoming a major struggle, but MacArthur wanted to deal the enemy a massive defeat.

MacArthur's public statements, issued from the field, finally went too far. In April 1951, he revealed his views in a letter meant to be made public in the United States. Arguing that the American approach in Korea was wrong, he asserted that "there is no substitute for victory." When the letter appeared, Truman had no choice but to relieve MacArthur for insubordination. The decision outraged many Americans. After the stunning victories of World War II, limited war was frustrating and difficult to understand.

As the furor subsided, Truman pursued more modest goals. After another year of war, the administration was willing to settle for an armistice at the 38th parallel. Peace talks with the North Koreans began while the fighting dragged on. During the campaign of 1952, Eisenhower promised to go to Korea, and three weeks after his election, he did so. When truce talks bogged down again in May 1953, the new administration threatened to use atomic weapons and to launch a massive military campaign. This brought about a resumption of the peace talks.

Although the war was almost over, Anthony Ebron, a marine corporal, noted that "those last

Korean civilians fled south as American troops marched north toward the disputed 38th parallel.

Relieved of his command for insubordination, General Douglas MacArthur returned home to a dignitary's welcome. His wife and son stand next to him in the foreground.

few days were pretty brutal." At the very end, he said, "we shot off so much artillery [that] the ground shook." Finally, on July 27, 1953, an armistice was signed. The Republican administration had managed to do what the preceding Democratic administration could not. After three long years, the unpopular war had ended.

American involvement carried a heavy price. Despite its limited nature, the Korean War led to 54,000 American deaths and many more wounded. But those figures paled beside the numbers of Korean casualties. As many as 2 million may have died in North and South Korea, and countless others were maimed. A BBC journalist's description of napalm, a highly flammable liquid explosive first used in the war, told at least part of the story:

> In front of us a curious figure was standing, a little crouched, legs straddled, arms held out from his sides. He had no eyes, and the whole of his body, nearly all of which was visible through tatters of burnt rags, was covered with a hard black crust speckled with yellow pus. . . . He had to stand because he was no longer covered with a skin, but with a crust-like crackling which broke easily.

The war also brought significant change in American attitudes and institutions. This was the first war in which United States forces fought in integrated units. Blacks were now integral members of the military service. Military expenditures soared from $13 billion in fiscal 1949–1950 to about $60 billion three years later as the United States rearmed. Military retrenchment came to an end as defense spending followed the guidelines proposed in NSC-68. With more money spent for war and defense, less was available for domestic social programs. The Cold War established new priorities and needs. At home, the buildup caused frustrations for many Americans who could not understand the constraints of limited war. Why, they asked, could they not go in with all the force necessary to end the struggle? Why were American objectives not met?

There were important political effects as well. The Korean War led the United States to sign a peace treaty with Japan in September 1951 and to rely on that nation to maintain the balance of power in the Pacific. At the same time, the struggle poisoned relations with China and ensured a diplomatic standoff that lasted more than 20 years.

Civil War in Vietnam

Indochina became another Asian battlefield in the Cold War where the United States became deeply entangled. Since the middle of the nineteenth century, France had controlled Indochina, exploiting its supplies of rubber, tin, tungsten, and rice. During World War II, the Japanese occupied the area but allowed French collaborators to continue to direct internal affairs. The Japanese conquest, however, shattered the image of European invincibility and encouraged an independence movement, led by the tireless Communist organizer and revolutionary Ho Chi Minh. Using the American War for Independence as a model, Ho worked through his political organization, the Viet Minh, to expel the Japanese conquerors. In 1945, the Allied powers were faced with the decision of how to deal with Ho and his revolutionary movement.

Franklin Roosevelt, like Woodrow Wilson, believed in self-determination and wanted to end colonialism. Reluctant to allow France to return after the defeat of the Japanese, Roosevelt favored an international trusteeship scheme as a way of preparing for future Vietnamese independence. But France, believing that the nation could "only be a great power so long as our flag continues to fly in all the overseas territory," was determined to regain its colony, and by the time of his death, Roosevelt had backed down.

Ho Chi Minh and the Vietnamese, however, did not abandon national liberation. Guerrilla warfare had won them most of the countryside, and they had established the Democratic Republic of Vietnam in 1945. Although the new government enjoyed widespread support, the United States refused to recognize it. The head of the American Office of Strategic Services mission predicted that if the French returned, the Vietnamese would fight to the death.

A long, bitter struggle between the French and the forces of Ho Chi Minh did break out and became entangled with the larger Cold War.

President Truman was less concerned about ending colonialism than with checking growing Soviet power in Europe and around the world. France was a nation needed to balance Russian strength in Europe, and that meant cooperating with the French in Vietnam.

While the Vietnamese battled the French, the United States watched with alarm. France had been weakened by World War II, and the United States doubted that it could survive a long colonial war. At the same time, the Truman administration was concerned about Vietnam itself. If France was defeated, the West would lose a foothold in a part of the world where a Communist revolution had already succeeded. Worse still, it would face a regime sympathetic to Moscow and the East, for Ho was a confirmed Marxist-Leninist. Though Ho did not, in fact, have close ties to the Soviet state and was committed to his independent nationalist crusade, Truman and his advisers, who saw communism as a monolithic force, assumed that he took orders from Moscow. Hence in 1950, the United States formally recognized the French puppet government in Vietnam. The Vietnamese viewed the Americans as France's colonialist collaborators. The United States in the Truman years did not provide direct military aid to the French, but American economic assistance freed France to use its own resources in the struggle.

After Eisenhower took office, the situation worsened for France. Some 12,000 French troops prepared for a showdown at the fortress of Dien Bien Phu. With a French defeat looming, Eisenhower reviewed American diplomatic options. He believed in the "domino theory," which held that "you have a row of dominos set up, you knock over the first one, and what will happen to the last one is the certainty that it will go over very quickly." At a press conference in April 1954, he warned that Burma, Thailand, and Indonesia would follow if Vietnam fell, and Japan, Taiwan, the Philippines, Australia, and New Zealand might go next. "So the possible consequences of the loss," he said, "are just incalculable to the free world."

At the same time, a cautious Eisenhower was not ready to bolt into Indochina alone. As the price for United States assistance, the French would have to pledge to grant Vietnamese independence at some point. England would have to cooperate in a joint assistance effort. And Congress would have to authorize the necessary support. Eisenhower believed that "only when there is a sudden, unforeseen emergency should the President put us into war without congressional action." Since, as he suspected, none of the conditions was met, the United States refused to intervene directly. Dien Bien Phu finally fell, and an international conference in Geneva divided Vietnam along the 17th parallel, with elections promised in 1956 to unify the country and determine its political fate.

As a result of that division, two new states emerged. Ho Chi Minh held power in the north, while in the south a separate government was formed under Premier Ngo Dinh Diem, a fierce anti-Communist. Intent on taking France's place in Southeast Asia, the United States supported the anti-Communist government in South Vietnam and refused to sign the Geneva agreement. "We must work with these people," Eisenhower said, "and then they themselves will soon find out that we are their friends and that they cannot live without us." Shortly after this, Eisenhower dispatched a CIA unit to conduct secret missions in Vietnam. In 1956, he supported Diem in refusing to hold the national elections in Vietnam called for in the Geneva agreement. In the next few years, American aid increased and military advisers began to assist the South Vietnamese.

The Middle East

While Cold War attitudes shaped American diplomacy in Southeast Asia, they also influenced responses to events in the Middle East. That part of the world had tremendous strategic importance as the supplier of oil for the industrialized nations. During World War II, the major Allied Powers had occupied Iran, with the provision that they would leave within six months of the war's end. As of early 1946, both Great Britain and the United States had withdrawn, but Russia, which bordered on Iran, remained. Stalin claimed that earlier security agreements had not been honored and, further, demanded oil concessions.

Moving quickly to counter the Soviet threat, the United States took the issue to the newly formed United Nations in March 1946. But the United States was willing to act independently. As Russian tanks neared the Iranian border, Secretary of State Byrnes declared, "Now we'll give it to them with both barrels." The ultimatum threatened vigorous American action and forced the Russians to back down and withdraw.

The Eisenhower administration maintained its interest in Iran. In 1953, the Central Intelligence Agency helped the local army overthrow the government of Mohammed Mossadegh, which had nationalized oil wells formerly under British control, and place the shah of Iran securely on the Peacock Throne. After the coup, British and American companies regained command of the wells, and thereafter the United States government provided military assistance to the shah.

A far more serious episode unfolded west of Iran. In 1948, the United Nations partitioned Palestine into an Arab and a Jewish state. Truman officially recognized the new state of Israel 15 minutes after it was proclaimed. But recognition could not end bitter animosities between Arabs, who felt they had been robbed of their territory, and Jews, who felt they had finally regained their homeland in that region. As Americans looked on, Israel fought its first war against Arab forces from Egypt, Trans-Jordan, Syria, Lebanon, and Iraq.

The United States cultivated close ties with Israel but could not afford to lose the friendship of oil-rich Arab states, nor could it allow them to fall into the Soviet orbit. In Egypt, Arab nationalist General Gamal Abdel Nasser planned a great dam on the Nile River to produce electricity. Nasser proclaimed his country neutral in the Cold War struggle. Dulles offered American financial support for the Aswan project, but Nasser also began discussions with the Soviet Union. The secretary of state furiously withdrew the American offer. Left without funds for the dam, Nasser seized and nationalized the British-controlled Suez Canal in July 1956. At

The Middle East in 1949

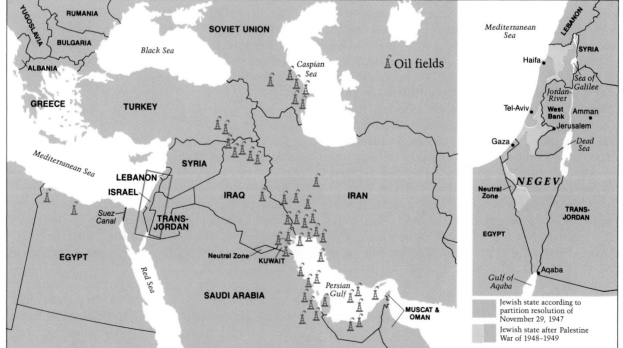

the same time, he closed the canal to Israeli ships. Great Britain, whose citizens owned most of the stock in the canal company, reacted angrily. All of Europe feared that Nasser would disrupt the flow of oil from the Middle East. The United States sought to settle the problem peacefully.

Despite the American stance, Israeli, British, and French military forces invaded Egypt in October and November. Eisenhower, who had not been consulted, was irate. Realizing that the attack might push Nasser into the arms of Moscow, the United States sponsored a UN resolution condemning the attacking nations and cut off oil from England and France. These actions persuaded them to withdraw.

In 1958, the United States again intervened in the Middle East. Concerned about stability there, Eisenhower had declared in the previous year that "the existing vacuum in the Middle East must be filled by the United States before it is filled by Russia." A year later, in line with a congressional resolution that committed the United States to stop Communist aggression, he authorized the landing of 14,000 soldiers in Lebanon to prop up a right-wing government challenged from within.

Restricting Revolt in Latin America

The Cold War also affected relations with Latin America and provided new reasons for intervention in that region. In 1954, Dulles sniffed Communist activity in Guatemala and ordered CIA support for a coup aimed at overthrowing the elected government of reform-minded Colonel Jacobo Arbenz Guzmán. The right-wing takeover succeeded, restored the property of the United Fruit Company that Arbenz had seized, and demonstrated again the American commitment to stability and private investment, whatever the internal effect or ultimate cost.

The effort in Guatemala fed anti-American feeling throughout Latin America. Many abhorred the interference of their northern neighbor that had pledged a Good Neighbor policy under Franklin Roosevelt. Dulles downplayed hostile sentiment, but when Vice-President Richard Nixon traveled to Venezuela in 1958, he found rabid crowds that stoned his car and almost tipped it over.

The next year, when Fidel Castro overthrew the dictatorial regime of Fulgencio Batista in Cuba, the shortsightedness of American policy became even clearer. Nationalism and the thrust for social reform were powerful forces in Latin America, as in the rest of the Third World. As Milton Eisenhower, Ike's brother and adviser, pointed out: "Revolution is inevitable in Latin America. The people are angry. They are shackled to the past with bonds of ignorance, injustice, and poverty. And they no longer accept as universal or inevitable the oppressive prevailing order." But not all officials shared this perspective. When Castro confiscated American property in Cuba, the Eisenhower administration cut off exports and severed diplomatic ties. In response, Cuba turned to Russia for support.

ATOMIC WEAPONS AND THE COLD WAR

Throughout the Cold War period, the atomic bomb was a crucial factor in world affairs. Atomic weapons were destructive enough, but when the United States and the Soviet Union both developed hydrogen bombs, an age of overkill began. Americans spoke casually of "massive retaliation" if the Soviet Union ever went too far, but they feared a similar attack on the United States.

Sharing the Secret of the Bomb

The United States, with British aid, built the first atomic bomb and concealed the project from its wartime ally, the Soviet Union. Soviet spies, however, discovered that the Americans were at work on the bomb. By 1943, a Soviet program to create a Russian atomic bomb was under way.

The question of sharing the atomic secret was pressing in the immediate postwar years. Some felt that Americans should guard their knowledge, arguing that the Russians would take years to duplicate their feat. But nuclear scientists knew that once others saw that the weapon could be made, it would take another nation far less time to do the same thing. Might it not be better to deal with the question of sharing before it was too late? The threat of world destruction was confronted for the first time.

Secretary of War Henry L. Stimson favored cooperating with the Soviet Union. Recognizing the futility of trying to cajole the Russians while "having this weapon ostentatiously on our hip," he suggested that "their suspicions and their distrust of our purposes and motives will increase." International cooperation could be achieved only through mutual accommodation. "The chief lesson I have learned in a long life," Stimson observed, "is the only way you can make a man trustworthy is to trust him, and the surest way you can make a man untrustworthy is to distrust him and to show your distrust."

But the United States never followed Stimson's advice. Truman, increasingly worried about the Soviet presence in eastern Europe, vowed to retain the technological advantage. He resisted a more flexible approach until the creation of a "foolproof method of control" over atomic weapons. Most Americans shared his view.

There was for a time an intent search for a means of international arms control. Realizing by early 1946 that mere possession of the bomb was not making the Russians more malleable, Truman decided to present a plan to the United Nations. Drafted by Dean Acheson and David Lilienthal, the plan proposed an international agency to provide atomic energy control. Bernard Baruch, ambassador to the UN's Atomic Energy Commission, hoping to avoid a Russian veto in the Security Council, modified the plan to establish a system of international inspection and agreement. In fact, as the Russians were quick to point out, this plan allowed American nuclear supremacy until the international agency had gained control of the earth's fissionable material. The Russians called first for destruc-

tion of all atomic weapons, then for a discussion of controls. Negotiations collapsed.

Hence the United States gave up on the process of sharing atomic secrets and moved toward its own internal mechanism of control. The Atomic Energy Act of 1946 established the Atomic Energy Commission to supervise all atomic energy development in the United States and, under the tightest security, to authorize all activity in the nation at large.

Nuclear Proliferation

As the atomic bomb found its way into popular culture, Americans at first showed more excitement than fear. In Los Angeles, the "Atombomb Dancers" appeared at the Burbank Burlesque Theater. In 1946, the Buchanan Brothers recorded "Atomic Power," which soon appeared on the *Billboard* music charts. A Newport, Arkansas, farmer wrote to the atomic research and development center at Oak Ridge, Tennessee, asking, "I have some stumps in my field that I should like to blow out. Have you got any atomic bombs the right size for the job?"

Yet anxiety lurked beneath exuberance, though it did not surface as long as the United States maintained a nuclear monopoly. Then, in September 1949, reporters were called to the White House and handed a mimeographed announcement. President Truman told the stunned reporters, "We have evidence that within recent weeks an atomic explosion occurred in the U.S.S.R."

The Russians had not publicized their achievement. Rather, over the Labor Day weekend, a U.S. Air Force weather reconnaissance plane on a routine mission had picked up air samples showing higher than normal radioactivity counts. Other samples confirmed this, and scientists soon concluded that Russia had conducted a nuclear test.

The American public was shocked. Suddenly the security of being the world's only atomic power vanished. People wondered whether the Soviet test foreshadowed a nuclear attack. At a meeting of the Joint Committee on Atomic Energy, legislators struggled to comprehend the implications of the news. When a thunderclap filled the air, someone in the room said, "My

God, that must be Number Two!" cutting the tension for the moment. Harold C. Urey, a Nobel Prize–winning scientist, summed up the feelings of many Americans: "There is only one thing worse than one nation having the atomic bomb—that's two nations having it." The atomic genie was out of the bottle, and Americans had to accept the fact that their monopoly had disappeared. An entirely new defense strategy now was necessary.

In early 1950, the arms race picked up speed as Truman authorized the development of a new hydrogen superbomb, potentially far more devastating than the atomic bomb. Edward Teller, a physicist on the Manhattan Project, was intrigued with the novelty of the puzzle. During the war, as other scientists struggled with the problem of fission, he contemplated the possibility that fusion might release energy in even greater amounts. Now he had his chance to proceed.

By 1953, both the United States and the Soviet Union had unlocked the secret of the hydrogen bomb. As kilotons gave way to megatons, the stakes rose. The government remained quiet about MIKE, the first test of a hydrogen device in the Pacific Ocean in 1952, but rumors circulated that it had created a hole in the ocean floor 175 feet deep and a mile wide. A year and a

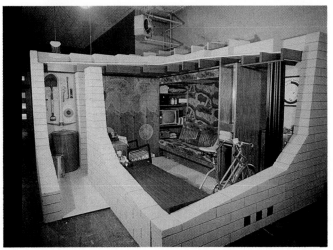

Attractive, homey mock-ups were an effective sales tool in encouraging Americans to build private fallout shelters.

half later, after the 1954 BRAVO test, Lewis Strauss, Atomic Energy Commission chairman, admitted that "an H-bomb can be made . . . large enough to take out a city," even New York. Then, in 1957, Americans learned that the Soviets had fired the first satellite, *Sputnik*, into outer space. The news came shortly after the Soviets had successfully tested their first intercontinental ballistic missile (ICBM). The apparent inferiority of American rocketry and the openness of the country to attack caused great concern.

The discovery of radioactive fallout added another dimension to the nuclear dilemma. Fallout became publicly known after the BRAVO blast, when Japanese fishermen 85 miles away were showered with radioactive dust. They became ill with radiation sickness, and several months later, one of them died. The Japanese, who had earlier seen the effects of atomic weapons at first hand, were outraged and alarmed. Elsewhere people began to realize the terrible impact of the new weapons.

Authors in both the scientific and popular press focused attention on radioactive fallout. Radiation, physicist Ralph Lapp observed, "cannot be felt and possesses all the terror of the unknown. It is something which evokes revulsion and helplessness—like a bubonic plague." Nevil Shute's best-selling 1957 novel *On the Beach*, and the film that followed, also sparked public awareness and fear. The story concerned a war that released so much radioactive waste that all life in the Northern Hemisphere was destroyed, while the Southern Hemisphere was reduced to waiting for the residue to come closer and bring the same deadly end. When *Consumer Reports* warned of the contamination of milk with strontium-90 in 1959, public alarm grew.

One response to growing nuclear stockpiles and the threat of global destruction was the building of bomb shelters. There had been interest in blast shelters in the immediate postwar years, but a national program was prohibitively expensive and never really got under way. With the discovery of fallout, a shelter craze began. Bob Russell, a Michigan sheriff, declared that "to build a new home in this day and age without including such an obvious necessity as a fallout shelter would be like leaving out the bathroom 20 years ago." *Good Housekeeping* magazine carried a full-page editorial in November 1958 that urged the building of family shelters. A cartoon in Pennsylvania's *Harrisburg News* showed the biblical ark, with the caption, "They Laughed at Noah!"

More and more companies advertised ready-made shelters for eager consumers. A firm in Miami reported many inquiries about shelters costing between $1,795 and $3,895, depending on capacity, and planned 900 franchises. *Life* magazine in 1955 featured an "H-Bomb Hideaway" for $3,000. By the end of 1960, the Office of Civil and Defense Mobilization estimated that a million family shelters had been built.

"Massive Retaliation"

As Americans grappled with the consequences of nuclear weapons, government policy came to depend increasingly on an atomic shield. Truman authorized the development of a nuclear arsenal but also stressed conventional forms of defense. After his election in 1952, Eisenhower found the effort fragmented and wasteful. Concerned with controlling the budget and cutting taxes, Eisenhower and the Republicans decided to rely on atomic weapons as the key to American defense.

Drawing on a new breed of nuclear strategists, like Harvard's Henry Kissinger, who believed that atomic weapons might be used in military confrontations, Dulles argued that the new approach allowed for instant response to Communist aggression "by means and at places of our own choosing." Eisenhower liked the "new look," or policy of "massive retaliation," for it left the enemy uncertain about what the United States might do in a given situation. The policy also allowed troop cutbacks and promised to be cost-effective by giving "more bang for the buck."

Massive retaliation provided for an all-or-nothing response, leaving no middle course. It left no real alternatives between nuclear war and passive retreat. Still, it was wholly consonant with the secretary of state's willingness to use extreme threats to assert the American position in the Cold War. The prospect of direct retaliation, properly used, Dulles felt, could deter Soviet challenges around the world. "The ability to get to the verge without getting into war is the necessary art," he declared. "If you cannot master it you inevitably get into war." Critics called the policy "brinkmanship" and wondered what would happen if the line were crossed in the new atomic age.

THE COLD WAR AT HOME

The Cold War affected domestic as well as foreign affairs, and its greatest impact came in the creation of an internal loyalty program that produced serious violations of civil liberties. Americans had feared radical subversion before and after the Russian Revolution (See Chapters 18, 23, and 24), but now their fears intensified. The Soviet Union appeared ever more ominous in confrontations around the world. Maps showed half the world colored red to dramatize the spread of the monolithic Communist system. Now Americans began to suspect Communist infiltration at home. It was not enough to meet the challenge abroad; Americans had to root out any traces of communism inside the United States.

Truman's Loyalty Program

As the Truman administration mobilized support for its containment program in the immediate postwar years, its rhetoric became increasingly shrill. Picturing issues in black and white terms, spokesmen set American virtues against diabolical Russian designs. For Truman, the issue that confronted the world was one of "tyranny or freedom." According to Attorney General J. Howard McGrath, there were "many Communists in America," each bearing "the germ of death for society."

There did seem to be evidence of an internal threat. In February 1945, government agents found some classified government documents in the offices of the allegedly pro-Communist *Amerasia* magazine. A year later, a Canadian commission exposed a number of spy rings and described wartime subversion. Truman responded by appointing a Temporary Commission on Employee Loyalty. Republican gains in the midterm elections of 1946 led him to fear a congressional loyalty probe that could be used for partisan ends, especially since Republicans had accused the Democrats of being "soft on communism." Truman hoped to head off such an investigation by starting his own.

On the basis of the report from his temporary commission, Truman established a new Federal Employee Loyalty Program by executive order in 1947. The FBI was to check its files for evidence of subversive activity, and suspects would then be brought before a new Civil Service Commission Loyalty Review Board. Initially the program included safeguards and assumed that a challenged employee was innocent until guilt had been proved. But those limits did not last long, for as the Loyalty Review Board assumed more and more power, it came to overlook individual rights. Employees about whom there was any doubt, regardless of proof, now found themselves under attack, with little chance to fight back.

The Truman loyalty program examined several million employees and found grounds for dismissing only several hundred. Nonetheless, it bred the largely unwarranted fear of subversion, led to the assumption that absolute loyalty could be achieved, and legitimized investigatory tactics that later became irresponsibly used.

The Congressional Loyalty Program

While Truman's loyalty probe investigated government employees, Congress embarked on its own program. In the early years of the Cold War, the law became increasingly explicit about what was illegal in the United States. The Smith Act of 1940 made it a crime to advocate or teach the forcible overthrow of the U.S. government. In 1949, Eugene Dennis and ten other Communist leaders were found guilty under its terms. In 1951, in *Dennis* v. *United States*, the Supreme Court upheld the Smith Act, declaring that a real danger of subversion existed in America.

That action cleared the way for the prosecution of other Communist leaders. Nearly 100 were indicted in the early 1950s.

The McCarran Internal Security Act of 1950 further circumscribed Communist activity by declaring that it was illegal to conspire to act in a way that would "substantially contribute" to establishing a totalitarian dictatorship in America. Members of Communist organizations had to register with the attorney general and could not obtain passports or work in areas of national defense. Congress passed the measure over Truman's veto and provided further legal backing for the anti-Communist crusade. The American Communist party, which numbered about 80,000 in 1947, declined to 55,000 in 1950 and 25,000 in 1954.

The investigations of the House Committee on Un-American Activities (HUAC) contributed to that decline. Intent on rooting out subversion, HUAC probed the motion picture industry in 1947 to determine the political inclinations of its members.

When hearings were scheduled, many entertainers and movie stars denounced the procedures. "Say your piece. Write your Congressman a letter! Airmail special!" Frank Sinatra warned, "Once they get the movies throttled, how long will it be before we're told what we can say and cannot say into a radio microphone?"

HUAC pressed on. Protesting its scare tactics, some people the committee summoned refused to testify under oath. They were scapegoated for their stand. The so-called Hollywood Ten, a group of writers, were cited for contempt of court and sent to federal prison. At that, Hollywood knuckled under and blacklisted anyone with even a marginally questionable past. No one on these lists could find jobs at the studios anymore.

Congress made a greater splash with the Hiss-Chambers case. Whittaker Chambers, a former Communist who had broken with the Party in 1938 and had become a successful editor of *Time*, charged that Alger Hiss had been a Communist in the 1930s. Hiss was a distinguished New Dealer who had served in the Agriculture Department before becoming assistant secretary of state. Now out of the government, he was president of the Carnegie

Accused of spying for the Soviets, Alger Hiss was convicted of perjury and went to prison.

Endowment for International Peace. He denied Chambers's charge, and the matter might have died there had not freshman congressman Richard Nixon taken up the case. Nixon finally extracted from Hiss an admission that he had once known Chambers. Outside the hearing room, Hiss sued Chambers for libel, whereupon Chambers changed his story and charged that Hiss was a Soviet spy.

With controversial evidence in hand, including several rolls of microfilmed government documents that Chambers contended Hiss had given him to pass to the Russians, HUAC sensed the possibilities of the case. In December 1948, a federal grand jury took the matter a step further. Since the statute of limitations ruled out an espionage indictment, the grand jury indicted Hiss instead for perjury, for lying under oath about his former relationship with Chambers.

The case made front-page news around the nation. Millions of Americans sought to understand what was going on, while also reading about Russia's first atomic explosion and the final victory of the Communist revolution in China. Chambers appeared unstable and changed his story several times. Yet Hiss, too, seemed contradictory in his testimony and never adequately explained how some copies of stolen State Department documents had been typed on a typewriter he had once owned. The first trial ended in a hung jury; the second trial, in January 1950, sent Hiss to prison for almost four years.

For many Americans, the Hiss case proved the Communist threat in the United States. It "forcibly demonstrated to the American people," Richard Nixon declared, "that domestic Communism was a real and present danger to the security of the nation." It also led people to question the Democratic approach to the problem. After Hiss's conviction but before his appeal, Dean Acheson supported his friend. Regardless of what happened, he said, "I do not intend to turn my back on Alger Hiss." Decent though his affirmation was, it caused the secretary of state political trouble. Truman too was broadly attacked for his comments about the case. Earlier he had called it a "red herring," but the courts had decided otherwise. Critics questioned the strength of Truman's commitment to protect the nation from internal subversion. Ironically, his loyalty program, for all its excesses, faced charges of laxity at home. The dramatic Hiss case helped to discredit the Democrats and to justify the even worse witch-hunt that followed.

The Second Red Scare

The key anti-Communist warrior in the 1950s was Joseph R. McCarthy. Coming to the Senate from Wisconsin in 1946, McCarthy had an undistinguished career. As he began to contemplate reelection two years hence, he seized on the Communist issue. Truman had carried Wisconsin in 1948, and McCarthy saw in the Communist question a way of mobilizing Republican support. He first gained national attention with a speech before the Wheeling, West Virginia, Women's Club in February 1950, not long after the conviction of Alger Hiss. In that address, McCarthy claimed he had in his hand a list of 205 known Communists in the State

Department. When pressed for details, McCarthy said first that he would release his list only to the president; then he reduced the number of names to 57.

Early reactions to McCarthy were mixed. A subcommittee of the Senate Foreign Relations Committee, after investigating, called his charge a "fraud and a hoax." Even other Republicans like Robert Taft and Richard Nixon questioned his effectiveness. Yet McCarthy persisted, for he found an anxious public primed by the Hiss Case and international events. As his support grew, Republicans realized his partisan value and egged him on. Senator John Bricker of Ohio allegedly told him, "Joe, you're a dirty s.o.b., but there are times when you've got to have an s.o.b. around, and this is one of them." Taft, also from Ohio, provided similar encouragement when he advised, "If one case doesn't work, try another." McCarthy did.

McCarthy selected assorted targets. In the elections of 1950, he attacked Millard Tydings, the Democrat from Maryland who had chaired the subcommittee that dismissed McCarthy's first accusations. A doctored photograph, showing Tydings with deposed American Communist party head Earl Browder, helped bring about Tydings's defeat. McCarthy called Dean Acheson a "pompous diplomat in striped pants, with a phony British accent" and termed him the "Red Dean of the State Department." He slandered George C. Marshall, the architect of victory in World War II and a powerful figure in formulating Far Eastern policy, as "a man steeped in falsehood . . . who has recourse to the lie whenever it suits his convenience."

A demagogue throughout his career, McCarthy gained visibility through extensive press and television coverage. Playing on his tough reputation, he did not mind appearing disheveled, unshaven, and half sober. He used obscenity and vulgarity freely as he spoke of the "vile and scurrilous" objects of his attacks.

McCarthy's tactics worked because the public was alarmed about the Communist threat. The Korean War, which broke out in mid-1950, showed that the Communists were always ready to attack. That same year, the arrest of Julius and Ethel Rosenberg further aroused fears of subversion from within. The Rosenbergs, a seemingly ordinary American couple with two small children, were charged with stealing and transmitting atomic secrets to the Russians. To many Americans, it was inconceivable that the Soviets could have developed the bomb on their own. Only treachery could explain the Soviet explosion of an atomic device.

The next year, the Rosenbergs were found guilty of espionage and sentenced to death. Judge Irving Kauffman expressed the rage of a nation that felt insecure and menaced by the Soviet Union. "Your conduct in putting into the hands of the Russians the A-bomb," he charged, "has already caused, in my opinion, the Communist aggression in Korea . . . and who knows but that millions more of innocent people may pay the price of your treason."

Although some argued, then and today, that hysteria had victimized the Rosenbergs, efforts to prevent their execution failed. In 1953, they were put to death, but anticommunism continued unabated.

When the Republicans won control of the Senate in 1952, McCarthy's power grew. He became chairman of the Government Operations Committee and head of its Permanent Investigations Subcommittee. He now had a stronger base and two dedicated assistants, Roy Cohn and G. David Schine. Together in early 1953, Cohn and Schine went off to Europe on a whirlwind tour of American information cen-

The Permanent Investigations Subcommittee was headed by Joseph McCarthy (second from left).

ters, where they briefly inspected books and articles and badgered overseas librarians to begin removing items from the shelves.

As McCarthy's anti-Communist witch-hunt continued, Eisenhower became uneasy. He disliked the senator but, recognizing his popularity, was reluctant to challenge him. Once in office, Ike told associates, when it was suggested that he confront McCarthy directly, "I will not get in the gutter with that guy." At the height of his influence, polls showed that McCarthy had half the public behind him, with far fewer people opposed. With the country so inclined, Eisenhower voiced his disapproval quietly and privately.

With the help of Cohn and Schine, McCarthy pushed on, and finally he pushed too hard. In 1953, the army drafted Schine and then refused to allow the preferential treatment that Cohn insisted his colleague deserved. Angered, McCarthy began to investigate army security and even top-level army leaders themselves. When the army charged that McCarthy was going too far, the Senate began to investigate the complaint.

The Army-McCarthy hearings began in April 1954 and lasted 36 days. Televised to a fascinated nationwide audience, they demonstrated the power of TV to shape people's opinions. Americans saw McCarthy's savage tactics on screen. He came across to viewers as irresponsible and destructive, particularly in contrast to Boston lawyer Joseph Welch, who argued the army's case with quiet eloquence.

When the hearings were over, McCarthy's mystical appeal was shattered. He had been challenged, and the challenger survived. In broad daylight, before a national television audience, his ruthless tactics no longer made sense. The Senate finally summoned the courage to condemn him for his conduct. Conservatives there turned against McCarthy because by attacking Eisenhower and the army, he was no longer limiting his venom to Democrats and liberals. Although McCarthy remained in office, his movement was spent. Three years later, at the age of 48, he died, a broken man.

Yet for a time he had exerted a powerful hold in the United States. "To many Americans," radio commentator Fulton Lewis, Jr., said, "Mc-

Carthyism is Americanism." Seizing upon the frustrations and anxieties of the Cold War, McCarthy struck a resonant chord. As his appeal grew, he put together a following that included both lower-class ethnic groups who responded to the charges against established elites and conservative midwestern Republicans. But his real power base was the Senate, where, particularly after 1952, conservative Republicans saw McCarthy as a means of reasserting their own authority. For the most part, his dominance rested on his colleagues' perception of his strength. Some members of both parties spoke out against him, but most did not. His crusade thus encouraged, McCarthy pressed on until he went too far.

The Casualties of Fear

As a result of the anti-Communist crusade, a pervasive sense of suspicion permeated American society. In the late 1940s and early 1950s, it no longer seemed safe to dissent. Civil servants, government workers, academics, and actors all came under attack and found that the right of due process often evaporated as the Cold War Red Scare gained ground. Old China hands lost their positions in the diplomatic services, and social justice legislation faltered.

There were countless examples of the impact of this paranoia on American life. In New York, subway workers were fired when they refused to answer questions about their own political actions and beliefs. In Seattle, a fire department officer who denied current membership in the Communist party but refused to speak of his past was dismissed just 40 days before he reached the 25 years of service that would have given him retirement benefits. Navajos in Arizona and New Mexico, facing starvation in the bitter winter of 1947–1948, were denied government relief because of charges that their communal way of life was communistic and therefore un-American. Black artist Paul Robeson, who along with W. E. B. Du Bois criticized American foreign policy, was accused of Communist leanings, found few opportunities to perform, and eventually, like Du Bois, lost his passport.

Then there was Val Lorwin, introduced at

the beginning of the chapter, who suffered through repeated hearings and trials on the basis of malicious and unsubstantiated accusations that threatened to destroy his career. Lorwin was named on one of McCarthy's famous lists, but like so many others, he was really a victim of the larger anti-Communist crusade. He faced the same hurdles others encountered. Denials under oath made no difference. An adequate

defense was almost impossible to mount. The charges themselves were often enough to smear a person, regardless of whether they were true or false. Lorwin weathered the storm and was finally vindicated, but others were less lucky. They were the unfortunate victims as the United States became consumed by the passions of the Cold War.

Major Events of the Cold War

YEAR	EVENT	EFFECT
1946	Winston Churchill's "Iron Curtain" speech	First Western "declaration" of the Cold War.
	George F. Kennan's long telegram	Spoke of Russian insecurity and the need for containment.
1947	George F. Kennan's article signed "Mr. X"	Elaborated on arguments in the telegram.
	Truman Doctrine	Provided economic and military aid to Greece and Turkey.
	Federal Employee Loyalty Program	Sought to root out subversion in the U.S. government.
	HUAC investigation of the motion picture industry	Sought to expose Communist influences in the movies.
1948	Marshall Plan	Provided massive American economic aid in rebuilding postwar Europe.
	Berlin airlift	Brought in supplies when Russia closed off land access to the divided city.
1949	NATO formed	Created a military alliance to withstand a possible Russian attack.
	First Russian atomic bomb	Ended the American nuclear monopoly.
	Communist victory in China	Made American's fearful of the worldwide spread of communism.
1950	Alger Hiss convicted	Seemed to bear out Communist danger at home.
	Joseph McCarthy makes first charges	Launched aggressive anti-Communist campaign in the United States.
	NSC-68	Called for vigilance and increased military spending to counter the Communist threat.
	Outbreak of Korean War	North Korean invasion of South Korea viewed as part of a Russian conspiracy.
1953	Armistice in Korea	Brought little change after years of bitter fighting.
1954	Vietnamese victory over French at Dien Bien Phu	Early triumph for nationalism in Southeast Asia.
	Army-McCarthy hearings	Brought downfall of Joseph McCarthy.

CONCLUSION: The Cold War in Perspective

The Cold War was the greatest single force affecting American society in the decade and a half after World War II. Tensions grew throughout the postwar years as a bitter standoff between the United States and the Soviet Union emerged. What caused the Cold War? Historians have long differed over the question of where responsibility should be placed. In the early years after the Second World War, policymakers and other commentators justified the American stance as a bold and courageous effort to meet the Communist threat. Later, particularly in the 1960s, as the public started to have doubts about the course of American foreign policy, revisionist historians began to argue that American policy was misguided, insensitive to Soviet needs, and at least a contributing factor to the worsening frictions. As with most historical questions, there are no easy answers, but both sides need to be weighed.

The Cold War stemmed in part from an American vision of the way the world should be. That vision involved peace and prosperity for all, with the United States leading the way. The American view, so eager and hopeful, helped to put the nation on a collision course with nations having a different vision of what the postwar world should be like and with anticolonial movements in Third World countries around the globe. When challenged, Americans proved ready, even eager, to contain communism, just as George Kennan had demanded, to preserve their version of a safe and stable order. The Cold War, with its profound effects at home and abroad, was the unfortunate result.

Recommended Reading

A number of outstanding books deal with the background and development of the Cold War. Walter La Feber, *America, Russia, and the Cold War, 1945–1980* (4th ed., 1980) is the best brief account of the Cold War from beginning to end. John Lewis Gaddis, *The United States and the Origins of the Cold War, 1941–1947* (1972) is a well-argued and readable examination of the tension that culminated in the breakdown of relations between the United States and the Soviet Union. Thomas G. Patterson, *On Every Front: The Making of the Cold War* (1979) is a perceptive essay on foreign policy in the Cold War years. Thomas H. Etzold and John Lewis Gaddis, *Containment: Documents on American Policy and Strategy, 1945–1950* (1978) is an outstanding collection of the major documents of the early Cold War years.

For foreign policy in the Eisenhower period, the best books are Townsend Hoopes, *The Devil and John Foster Dulles* (1973), a searching examination of the secretary of state, and Robert A. Divine, *Eisenhower and the Cold War* (1981), a brief but sympathetic account of the president's efforts.

On the Korean War, David Rees, *Korea: The Limited War* (1964) gives a good assessment of the major foreign conflict in the 1950s. James A. Michener, *The Bridges at Toko-Ri* (1953) is a contemporary novel that provides a sense of the frustrations during the war.

On the anti-Communist crusade, Richard H. Rovere, *Senator Joe McCarthy* (1960) is a short and readable account of McCarthy and his methods. Robert Griffith, *The Politics of Fear: Joseph R. McCarthy and the Senate* (1970) is a perceptive analysis of McCarthy's position of power in the Senate and the forces that brought him down. Thomas C. Reeves, *The Life and Times of Joe McCarthy: A Biography* (1982) is a full-scale treatment of the anti-Communist leader. David M. Oshinsky, *A Conspiracy So Immense: The World of Joe McCarthy* (1983) is a vivid examination of McCarthy and his times. See also Allen Weinstein, *Perjury: The Hiss-Chambers Case* (1978) and Ronald Radash and Joyce Milton, *The Rosenberg File: A Search For Truth* (1984).

TIME LINE

1945	Yalta Conference Roosevelt dies; Harry Truman becomes president Potsdam Conference	1950	*(continued)* McCarran Internal Security Act
1946	American Plan for control of atomic energy fails Atomic Energy Act Iran crisis Churchill's "iron curtain" speech	1950–1953	Korean War
		1951	Japanese-American Treaty *Dennis* v. *United States*
1947	Truman Doctrine Marshall Plan launched Federal Employee Loyalty Program House Un-American Activities Committee (HUAC) investigates the movie industry	1952	Dwight D. Eisenhower elected president McCarthy heads Senate Permanent Investigations Subcommittee
		1953	Stalin dies; Krushchev consolidates power East Germans stage anti-Soviet demonstrations Shah of Iran returns to power in CIA-supported coup
1948	Berlin airlift Israel created by UN Hiss-Chambers case Truman reelected president	1954	Fall of Dien Bien Phu ends French control of Indochina Geneva Conference Guatemalan government overthrown with CIA help Mao's forces shell Quemoy and Matsu Army-McCarthy hearings
1949	Soviet Union tests atomic bomb North Atlantic Treaty Organization (NATO) established George Orwell publishes *Nineteen Eighty-four* Mao Zedong's forces win Chinese civil war; Jiang Jieshi flees to Taiwan		
		1956	Suez incident Hungarian "freedom fighters" suppressed Eisenhower reelected
1950	Truman authorizes development of the hydrogen bomb Alger Hiss convicted Joseph McCarthy's Wheeling speech on subversion	1957	Russians launch *Sputnik* satellite
		1958	U.S. troops sent to support Lebanese government
		1959	Castro deposes Batista in Cuba

CHAPTER 28
THE DREAMS OF POSTWAR AMERICA

Ray Kroc, an ambitious salesman, headed toward San Bernardino, California, on a business trip in 1954. For more than a decade he had been selling "multimixers"—stainless steel machines that could make six milkshakes at once—to restaurants and other eating establishments around the United States. On this trip he was particularly interested in checking out a hamburger stand run by Richard and Maurice McDonald, who had bought eight of his "contraptions" and could therefore make 48 shakes at the same time.

Always eager to increase sales, Kroc wanted to see the McDonalds' operation for himself. The 52-year-old son of Slavic parents had sold everything from real estate to radio time to paper cups before peddling the multimixers but had enjoyed no stunning success. Yet he was still on the alert for the key to the fortune that was part of the American dream. As he watched the lines of people at the San Bernardino McDonald's, the answer seemed at hand.

The McDonald brothers sold only standard hamburgers and french fries, but they had developed a system that worked exceedingly well. It was fast, efficient, and clean. It drew on the automobile traffic that moved along Route 66. And it was profitable indeed. Sensing the possibilities, Kroc proposed that the two owners open other establishments as well. When they balked, he negotiated a 99-year contract that allowed him to sell the fast-food idea and the name—and their golden arches design—wherever he could.

On April 15, 1955, Kroc opened his first McDonald's in Des Plaines, a suburb of Chicago. Three months later, he sold his first franchise in Fresno, California, and others soon followed. Kroc scouted out new locations, almost always on highway "strips," persuaded people to put up the capital, and provided them with specifications guaranteed to ensure future success. For his efforts, he received a percentage of the gross take.

From the start, Kroc insisted on rigid standardization. Every McDonald's was the same—from the two functional arches supporting the glass enclosure that housed the kitchen and take-out window to the single arch near the road bearing a sign indicating how many 15-cent hamburgers had already been sold. All menus and prices were exactly the same, and Kroc demanded that everything from hamburger size to cooking time be constant. He insisted, too, that the establishments be clean. No pinball games or cigarette machines were permitted; the premium was on a good hamburger, quickly served, at a nice place.

Kroc had tremendous drive. He was fond of Calvin Coolidge's dictum—"Press on. Nothing in the world can take the place of persistence"—and it soon appeared in McDonald's offices everywhere. Kroc was interested in expanding rapidly. He believed that "when you're green, you're growing; when you're ripe, you rot." As far as he was concerned, he had only just begun.

McDonald's, of course, was an enormous success. In 1962, total sales exceeded $76 million. In 1964, before the company had been in operation ten years, it had sold over 400 million hamburgers and 120 million pounds of french fries. By the end of the next year, there were 710 McDonald's stands in 44 states. In 1974, only 20 years after Kroc's vision of the hamburger's future, McDonald's did $2 billion worth of business. When Kroc died in 1984, 45 billion burgers had been sold at 7,500 outlets in 32 countries. Ronald McDonald, the clown who came to represent the company, became known to children around the globe after his Washington, D.C., debut in November 1963. When McDonald's began to advertise, it became the country's first restaurant to buy TV time. Musical slogans like "You deserve a break today" and "We do it all for you" became better known than some popular songs.

The tale of McDonald's is more than the simple success story of one firm. It provides an example of the development of new trends in the 1950s in the United States. Kroc capitalized on the changes of the automobile age. He understood that a restaurant, not in the city but along the highways, where it could draw on heavier traffic, had a better chance of success. The drive-in design, catering to a new and ever-growing clientele, soon became a common pattern.

He understood, too, how the franchise notion provided the key to rapid growth. He was not prepared to open up thousands of stands himself. Instead he sold the idea to eager entrepreneurs who stood to make sizable profits themselves as long as they remained a part of the larger whole. Not simply in the hamburger business but in numerous other industries as well, the franchise method helped create a nationwide web of firms.

Finally, Kroc sensed the importance of standardization and uniformity. He understood the mood of the time, the quiet conformity of Americans searching for success. The McDonald's image may have been monotonous, but that was part of its appeal. Customers always knew just what they would get wherever they found the golden arches. If the atmosphere was "bland", that too was deliberate. As Kroc said, "Our theme is kind of synonymous with Sunday school, the Girl Scouts, and the YMCA. McDonald's is clean and wholesome." It was a symbol of the age.

This chapter describes the changes in American society in the decade and a half after World War II. It shows how, for most Americans, this was a period of material comfort at home. After years of depression and war, they were ready to settle into new homes and cars and jobs, to enjoy all the trappings of the good life. Yet the chapter also shows that while millions of Americans led lives as sunny as McDonald's, the lives of others—blacks, Indians, and Hispanic-Americans—were still defined by the struggle for social justice and economic viability. Their experience suggested the limits of the postwar American dream.

Americans knew just what they would get wherever the McDonald's golden arches were found.

DEMOBILIZATION AND ECONOMIC BOOM

In spite of Cold War anxieties, most Americans found security and stability after 1945. As servicemen came home and resumed their lives, the population grew and the economy boomed. Large corporations increasingly dominated the business world. New products flooded the market. There were affordable gadgets galore. For the growing middle class, the revival of prosperity conveyed the sense that all was well in the United States.

Returning GIs

When World War II ended, American servicemen wanted to come home as quickly as possible. After peace was declared, politicians were deluged with messages. Families at home applied additional pressure. One serviceman's wife communicated her appeal through the Wyoming *State Tribune:* "He's fat, sway-backed, has several teeth missing and hobbles into age thirty-eight this month. . . . But he has a nice smile —with what teeth he has left—and I love him. So why don't you send him home?" A senator received more than 200 pairs of baby booties carrying notes that said, "I miss my daddy."

With that kind of pressure, the GIs did come home rapidly. The number of servicemen on active duty dropped from 12 million in 1945 to 3 million in mid-1946 to 1.6 million in mid-1947. The influx of ex-servicemen caused competition in the housing and employment markets and complicated the transition to civilian life.

The GI Bill of 1944 eased the process of reentering American society. The package of benefits it provided was far superior to that awarded veterans of any previous war. It gave returning GIs priority for many jobs and allowances while they looked for work. It promised loans so that they could establish small businesses and low-interest mortgages to purchase homes. Most important, it provided education benefits, up to $500 a year for college or trade school tuition and $75 a month for expenses.

Millions of Americans took advantage of the GI benefits. Almost half of 16 million eligible GIs went to school, and this caused the greatest

wave of college building in American history. At the same time, the proportion of Americans owning their own homes soared, from 45 percent in 1940 to 65 percent in 1960. The postwar boom was partly a result of the provisions of the GI Bill, and it helped millions of families move into the middle class.

The Peacetime Economy

Americans in the aftermath of war, realizing that only wartime spending had ended the Depression, feared a postwar collapse. When *Fortune* magazine took a poll of businessmen, it discovered that 58 percent of them anticipated the return of hard times.

Inflation soon caused concern. While Americans wanted to keep prices under control, they also wished to end wartime restrictions. Rationing, imposed by the Office of Price Administration (OPA) during the war, kept price levels stable but was often frustrating. As Sidney W. May, a New York businessman, protested, "My Dear President: With so many automobiles around, how did they gather so many horses asses and put them in the OPA?" With consumer goods initially in short supply, the administration feared that if controls were abandoned too quickly, prices would soar.

In 1946, an increasingly conservative Congress extended the OPA's authority for another year but stripped it of enforcement powers. Truman vetoed the bill and left the country without any control mechanism. Almost immediately, prices rose. Within a month, the cost-of-living index was up 6 points, and consumers began to demand action.

In Princeton, New Jersey, housewives calling themselves the Militant Marketers boycotted stores charging inflated prices. In Detroit, auto workers shut down production lines for a day and congregated in Cadillac Square to protest. Eventually Congress passed a weak bill to stem the tide, but the damage had already been done. A year and a half after the end of the war, the consumer price index was up almost 25 percent. One critic tartly observed that the OPA name and acronym should be changed to the Office for Cessation of Rationing and Priorities, or OCRAP.

Working-class Americans found the transition to a peacetime economy as difficult as they had in the past (see Chapter 23). Massive layoffs left 2.7 million workers without jobs by March 1946. Wage issues were also unresolved. After the wartime years of restraint, workers wanted pay increases they regarded as long overdue. Furthermore, many more of them belonged to unions. The percentage of nonagricultural workers who were union members rose from 13 percent in 1935 to 27 percent in 1940 and to 35 percent by 1945. When wage demands were refused, millions of workers walked out. In 1946, some 4.6 million workers marched on picket lines, more than had turned out ever before in the history of the United States. They struck in the automobile, steel, and electrical industries. The most serious trouble came with the railroads and soft-coal mines.

The railroad problem came to a head in the spring of 1946. When union leaders rejected an arbitrated settlement and set a strike date, Truman told them, "If you think I'm going to sit here and let you tie up this whole country, you're crazy as hell." When that blunt approach failed to work, the president asked Congress for the power to draft strikers into the armed forces if their actions caused a national emergency. Questioned about the constitutionality of his proposal, he said, "We'll draft 'em first and think about the law later." Although a settlement was reached, Truman still pushed for his retaliatory draft. Though the House of Representatives went along, cooler heads in the Senate allowed the plan to die.

The coal miners, led by John L. Lewis, the United Mine Workers' arrogant and defiant head, went out on strike in April 1946, accepted a settlement, then backed out of it. Determined to break the strike, Truman obtained a court injunction, which Lewis defied. Both leader and union were cited for contempt of court. Eventually Lewis was fined $10,000 and the union $3.5 million. The disgruntled workers returned to the mines, but Truman's bold actions alienated many working-class Americans. Labor had been a major segment of the Democratic coalition under Roosevelt in the 1930s. Now that loyalty began to wane.

The strikers had problems enough of their own. Steve Hutchinson, a semiskilled operator working for U.S. Steel in Pittsburgh, was anxious about giving up a sure wage in the hope of getting a larger paycheck. But he went out in 1946 with the rest of the union. Food was sometimes scarce. His wife would "buy a big old soup bone, something with just a small bit of meat on it, and boil it in a pot of white beans. That was lunch and dinner and maybe lunch the next day. Day-old bread, no sugar in the coffee, hamburger when we had meat, which wasn't often. I even gave up cigarettes, and me a two-pack-a-day man." But it turned out to be worth it when the union won a favorable settlement.

For all the early postwar difficulties, it was a time of hope and high expectations for most Americans. Charles Lehman, a veteran from Missouri, later recalled, "I was a twenty-one-year-old lieutenant with a high school education, and my only prewar experience was as a stock boy in a grocery store. But on V-J day, I *knew* it was only a matter of time before I was rich—or well-off, anyway." In the postwar years, hopes triumphed over fears as the economy boomed.

The statistical evidence of economic success was impressive. The gross national product (GNP) jumped from just over $200 billion in 1940 to around $300 billion in 1950 and by 1960 had climbed above $500 billion. Per capita income rose from $2,100 in 1950 to $2,435 in 1960. Almost 60 percent of all families in the country were now part of the middle class, a dramatic change from the class structure of nineteenth- and early twentieth-century America. With real purchasing power rising by 22 percent between 1946 and 1960, families had far more discretionary income—money to satisfy wants as well as needs—than before. At the end of the Great Depression, fewer than one-quarter of all households had any discretionary income; in 1960, three of every five did.

The United States, which produced half the world's goods, was providing new products that average Americans, unlike their parents, could afford. Higher real wages allowed people across social classes to buy consumer goods, and that consumer power, in contrast to the underconsumption of the 1920s and 1930s, spurred the economy. In the words of one government official, Adolf A. Berle, Jr., Americans were caught up in a spirit of "galloping capitalism."

The automobile industry was a key part of the economic boom. Just as cars and roads transformed America in the 1920s when mass production came of age, so they contributed to the transformation three decades later. Limited to the production of military vehicles during World War II, the auto industry expanded dramatically in the postwar period. Two million cars were made in 1946, four times as many in 1955. Customers now chose from a wide variety of engines, colors, and optional accessories. Fancy grills and tail fins distinguished each year's models.

Weekly Earnings of Manufacturing Workers

YEAR	INDEX OF AVERAGE WEEKLY EARNINGS OF WORKERS IN MANUFACTURING	INDEX OF REAL AVERAGE WEEKLY EARNINGS OF WORKERS IN MANUFACTURING
1940	21.9	53.1
1941	25.8	59.3
1942	31.9	66.3
1943	37.6	73.5
1944	40.1	77.3
1945	38.6	72.8
1946	38.2	66.2
1947	43.5	66.0
1948	47.1	66.4
1949	47.8	68.0
1950	51.6	72.8
1951	56.3	73.5
1952	59.2	75.5
1953	62.4	79.0
1954	62.6	78.9
1955	66.4	84.3
1956	69.6	86.8
1957	71.7	86.4
1958	72.7	85.2
1959	76.8	89.3
1960	78.1	89.5

Note: 1967 = 100
Source: U.S. Bureau of Labor Statistics.

The development of a massive interstate highway system also stimulated auto production. Rather than encourage the growth of a mass transit system, the Eisenhower administration underscored the American commitment to the car. Through the Interstate Highway Act of 1956 it provided $26 billion, the largest public works expenditure in American history, to build over 40,000 miles of federal highways, linking all parts of the United States.

Though highways added to the problem of pollution and triggered urban flight, the interstate complex was hailed as a key to the country's material development. Justified in part on the grounds that it would make evacuation quicker in the event of nuclear attack, the highway system made its proponents proud. In his memoirs, Eisenhower wrote:

> The total pavement of the system would make a parking lot big enough to hold two-thirds of all the automobiles in the United States. The amount of concrete poured to form these roadways would build . . . six sidewalks to the moon. . . . More than any single action by the

Widening and improvement of existing routes was a small part of the massive interstate highway program funded by Congress in 1956.

government since the end of the war, this one would change the face of America.

The Baby Boom

Population growth was one clear indication of prosperity's return. During the Great Depression, the birthrate had dropped to an all-time low of 19 births per 1,000 population as hard times obliged people to delay marriage and parenthood. As the Second World War boosted the economy, the birthrate began to rise again. Some experts questioned whether the trend was a long-term one, and the Census Bureau cautiously claimed that it was at least partly due to "occasional furloughs," but in fact a real shift was under way.

The birthrate soared in the postwar years as millions of Americans began families. The "baby boom" peaked in 1957, with a rate of more than 25 births per 1,000. In that year, 4.3 million babies were born, one every seven seconds. While the population growth of 19 million in the 1940s was double the rise of the decade before, that increase paled against the increase in the 1950s, which totaled 29 million.

The effects of the baby boom were visible everywhere. There was Monroe Park, a community of 95 house trailers for veterans and their families at the University of Wisconsin. It was called the "state's most fertile five acres." In one week alone in 1947, five families had babies.

Birth and Population Rates, 1900–1960

Source: U.S. Bureau of the Census.

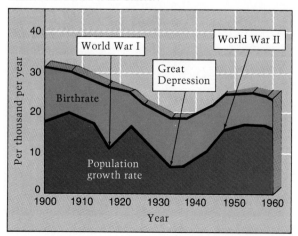

Similar fertility was evident in communities throughout the United States.

The rising birthrate was the dominant factor affecting population growth, but the death rate was also declining. Miracle drugs, such as streptomycin and aureomycin, played a large part in curing illnesses attacking all ages, especially the young. Life expectancy rose: midway through the 1950s, the average was 70 years for whites and 64 for blacks, compared to 55 for whites and 45 for blacks in 1920.

The baby boom had a powerful impact on family patterns and material needs. With the two-child family no longer the norm, growing numbers of youngsters had to be cared for by their parents and by society as a whole. Many women who had taken jobs during the war now left the work force to raise their children and care for their homes. The demand grew for diaper services and baby foods. When they entered school, the members of the baby boom generation strained the educational system. Between 1946 and 1956, enrollment in grades 1 through 8 soared from 20 million to 30 million. Since school construction had slowed during the Depression and had virtually halted during the Second World War, classrooms were needed. Teachers, too, were in short supply.

Population Shifts and the New Suburbs

As Americans became more populous, they also became more mobile. For many generations, lower-class Americans had been the most likely to move; now geographic mobility spread to the middle class. Each year in the 1950s, over a million farmers left their farms in search of new employment. Other Americans picked up stakes and headed on as well. Some moved to look for better jobs. Others, like Bob Moses of Baltimore, simply wandered a while after returning home from the war and then settled down. Moses, traveling in a 1937 Chevrolet with some high school friends, was going "nowhere in particular, just roaming. We'd see a kink in a river on the map, and head there." After regimented military life, it was good to be free.

The war had produced increasing movement, most of it westward, as people gravitated toward the cities where shipyards, airplane factories, and other industrial plants were located.

After the war, that migration pattern persisted, as the West and the Southwest continued to grow. Sun Belt cities like Houston, Albuquerque, Tucson, and Phoenix underwent phenomenal expansion. The population of Phoenix soared from 65,000 in 1940 to 439,000 in 1960. In the 1950s, Los Angeles pulled ahead of Philadelphia as the third largest city in the United States. One-fifth of all the growth in the period took place in California's promised land. By 1963, California had passed New York as the nation's most populous state.

After the war, another form of movement became even more important in the United States. Although the proportion of Americans defined as residents of metropolitan areas increased from 51 to 63 percent between 1940 and 1960, this disguised another shift. Millions of white Americans fled from the inner city to suburban fringes, intensifying a movement that had begun before the war. Fourteen of the nation's largest cities actually lost population in that decade, including New York, Boston, Chicago, Philadelphia, and Detroit. As central cities became places where poor nonwhites clustered, new urban and racial problems emerged.

For people of means, cities were places to work and then to leave at five o'clock. In Man-

METROPOLITAN AREAS	YEAR 1920	1940	1960	1980
Los Angeles	879	2,916	6,039	7,478
San Diego	74	289	1,033	1,862
Phoenix	29	186	664	1,509
Tucson	20	37	266	531
Dallas	185	527	1,084	2,430
Houston	168	529	1,418	2,905
San Antonio	191	338	716	1,072
New Orleans	398	552	907	1,256
Atlanta	249	559	1,017	2,030
Miami	30	268	935	1,626

POPULATION (in thousands)

0–250	250–1,000	1,000–3,000	Over 3,000

Growth of Sun Belt Cities, 1920–1980
Source: U.S. Bureau of the Census.

Population Shifts, 1940 to 1950

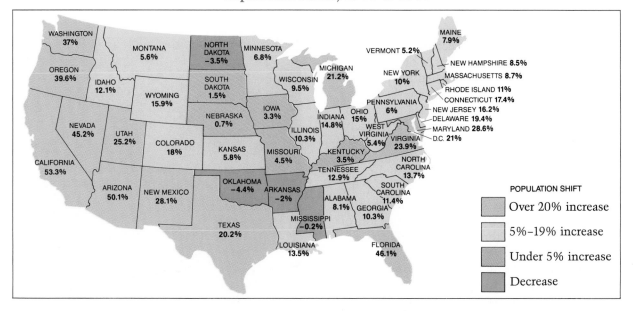

| POPULATION SHIFT |
| Over 20% increase |
| 5%–19% increase |
| Under 5% increase |
| Decrease |

hattan, south of City Hall, the noontime population of 1.5 million dropped to 2,000 during the night. The outlying regions, writer John Brooks argued, were "draining downtown of its nighttime population, except for night watchmen and derelicts; it was becoming a part-time city, tidally swamped with bustling humanity every weekday morning when the cars and commuter trains arrived, and abandoned again at nightfall when the wave sucked back—left pretty much to thieves, policemen, and rats."

As the cities declined, the suburbs blossomed. If the decade after World War I had witnessed a rural-to-urban shift, the decades after World War II saw a reverse shift to the regions outside the central cities, usually accessible only by car. By the end of the 1950s, a third of all Americans resided in suburbs.

Americans moved to the suburbs to buy homes that would accommodate their larger families. The number of owner-occupied houses rose from 15.2 million in 1940 to 23.5 million ten years later. Often rapidly constructed and overpriced, suburban tract houses provided the appearance of comfort and space and the chance to have at least one part of the American dream, a place of one's own. Set in developments with names like Scarborough Manor, Peppermill Village, and Woodbury Knoll, they seemed safe from the growing troubles of the cities, insulated from the difficulties of the world outside.

A key figure in the suburbanization movement was William J. Levitt, a builder eager to take a gamble and reap the rewards of a growing demand. Levitt, who had erected custom-built homes before, saw the advantages of mass production during World War II, when his firm put up dwellings for war workers. Aware that mortgage money was readily available as a result of the GI Bill, he felt that suburban development was a sure bet. But to cash in, Levitt knew he had to use new methods of construction.

Mass production was the key. Individually designed houses were a thing of the past, he believed. "The reason we have it so good in this country," he said, "is that we can produce lots of things at low prices through mass production." Houses were among them. Working on a careful schedule, Levitt's team brought precut and preassembled materials to each site, put them together, and then moved on to the next location.

As on an assembly line, tasks were broken down into individual steps. Groups of workers performed but a single job, moving from one tract to another.

Levitt proved that his system worked. Construction costs at Levittown, New York, a new community of 17,000 homes built in the late 1940s, were only $10 per square foot, compared to the $12 to $15 that was common elsewhere. The next Levittown appeared in Bucks County, Pennsylvania, several years after the first, and another went up in Willingboro, New Jersey, at the end of the 1950s. Having guessed right, Levitt provided a model for other developers.

Suburbanization changed the landscape of the United States. Huge tracts of land now contained acres of standardized squares, each with a house with a two-car garage and a manicured lawn. Woods disappeared, for it was cheaper to cut down all trees than to work around them. Folksinger Malvina Reynolds described the new developments she saw:

> Little boxes on the hillside
> Little boxes made of ticky tacky
> Little boxes on the hillside
> Little boxes all the same.
> There's a green one and a pink one
> And a blue one and a yellow one

The step-by-step mass production of Levitt's housing can be seen in this 1957 view of the partially completed Bucks County tract.

And they're all made out of ticky tacky
And they all look just the same.

As suburbs flourished, businesses followed their customers out of the cities. Shopping centers led the way. At the end of World War II, there were eight, but the number multiplied rapidly in the 1950s. In a single three-month period in 1957, 17 new centers opened; by 1960, there were 3,840 in the United States. Developers like Don M. Casto, who built the Miracle Mile near Columbus, Ohio, understood the importance of location as Americans moved out of the cities. "People have path-habits," he said, "like ants."

Shopping centers catered to the suburban clientele and transformed consumer patterns. They offered easy parking and convenient late-evening hours. Suburban dwellers could remain entirely insulated from the cities if they wished, but their new shopping patterns undermined the downtown department stores.

Corporate Change

In the years after 1945, the major corporations increased their hold on the American economy. World War II had encouraged the growth of big business. Antitrust activity was suspended in the interest of wartime production, while government contracts encouraged expansion. During the war, two-thirds of all military contracts were awarded to 100 firms, and half of all contracts went to three dozen giants. Tremendous industrial concentration occurred during the war. In 1940, some 100 companies accounted for 30 percent of all manufacturing output in the United States. Three years later, that figure had risen to 70 percent.

Concentration continued after the war. There had been several waves of mergers in the twentieth century. Another wave took place in the 1950s, making oligopoly—domination of a given industry by a few firms—a dominant feature of American capitalism. At the same time, the economy saw the development of conglomerates—firms that diversified with holdings in a variety of industries. That process began in the 1950s and continued thereafter.

Expansion took other forms as well. Even as the major corporations expanded, so too did smaller franchise operations like McDonald's, Kentucky Fried Chicken, and Burger King. Other firms, providing services rather than products, changed the shape of the American work force. Fewer Americans worked in manufacturing jobs, a reversal of a 150-year trend, and the growth of jobs in the service sector also reduced the number of Americans engaged in farming. Offices, hospitals, restaurants, computer companies, and a variety of other firms employed people who performed services increasingly in demand in a highly sophisticated economy.

Huge corporations became even more impersonal than before. In many firms, the bureaucratic style predominated, with white-collar employees seemingly dressing, thinking, and

Shifts in Population Distribution, 1940–1960

Source: U.S. Bureau of the Census.

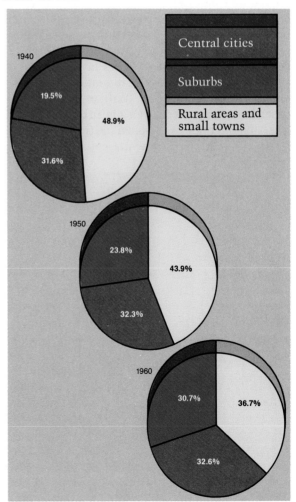

acting the same (as depicted in a popular novel and film of the 1950s, *The Man in the Gray Flannel Suit*). Money and material well-being were the prizes of corporate life. Corporations provided a secure working atmosphere and a comfortable leisure environment. The country clubs built by IBM or the model homes constructed by Richfield Oil were perquisites that kept employees loyal to their firms.

White-collar employees paid a price for the comfort. Corporations, preaching that teamwork was far more important than individuality, indoctrinated employees and conveyed the appropriate standards of conduct. RCA issued company neckties. IBM had training programs to teach employees the company line. Some large firms even set up training programs to show wives how their own behavior could help their husbands' careers. Just as product standardization became increasingly important, individual acceptance of company norms became necessary. "Personal views can cause a lot of trouble," an oil company recruiting pamphlet noted, suggesting that business favored moderate or conservative ideas that would not threaten the system. Author William H. Whyte described young executives whose ultimate goal was "belongingness." Social critic C. Wright Mills observed, "When white-collar people get

jobs, they sell not only their time and energy but their personalities as well."

Technology Supreme

Rapid technological change occurred in the postwar years. Some of the developments—the use of atomic energy, for example—flowed directly from war research. Others emerged from the research and development activities sponsored by big business.

Computers led the way. A German engineer, Konrad Zuse, had devised an electromagnetic computer before the war. Supported by IBM, Howard H. Aiken, a young professor of mathematics at Harvard, was not far behind. The Mark I computer was switched on in 1943. It stood 8 feet high and 55 feet long and contained about a million components.

Other computational machines soon followed. In 1946, the Electronic Numerical Integrator and Calculator, called ENIAC, was built at the University of Pennsylvania. It contained 18,000 electronic tubes and required tremendous amounts of electricity and special cooling. But the machine worked. In an advertised test, it set out to multiply 97,367 by itself 5,000 times. A reporter pushed the necessary button, and the task was completed in less than half a second.

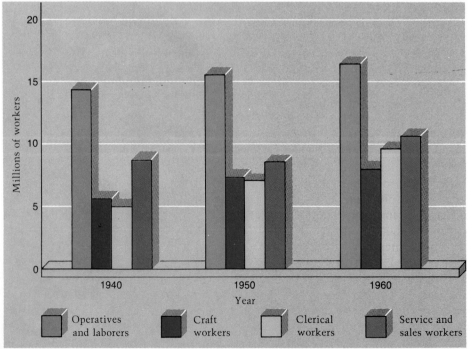

Occupational Distribution, 1940–1960

Source: U.S. Department of Labor.

Yet even that machine was limited. Its tubes occasionally failed, it had a small memory, and it could perform only one task at a time. Mathematician John Von Neumann's system for storing instructions within the computer itself was the next step. As research continued, IBM, Bell Telephone, and Sperry-Rand all developed computers for business uses. But costs were high and components often unreliable. The computer seemed to be a specialized piece of equipment, intended only for companies with massive needs. The breakthrough came with the development of the transistor. In 1948, three scientists at Bell Laboratories created minuscule solid-state components that ended reliance on electronic tubes. Faster and more reliable, transistors became indispensable in the decade that followed.

The computer transformed American society as surely as industrialization had changed it a century before. It allowed for sophisticated forms of space exploration. Airlines, hotels, and other businesses computerized their reservation systems. Business accounting, inventory control, and even decision making began to rely on computers. Computer programmers and operators were in increasing demand. Computer technology also opened the way for change in other fields. Tiny transistors could power not only radios but miniature hearing aids that could be incorporated into the frame of a pair of eyeglasses. Stereophonic hi-fi sets, using new transistor components, could provide a better sound.

Americans continued their love affair with appliances and gadgets. By the end of the 1950s, most families had at least one automobile, as well as the staple appliances they had begun to purchase before—a refrigerator, a washing machine, a television, and a vacuum cleaner. Dozens of less essential items also became popular. There were electric can openers, electric pencil sharpeners, and electric toothbrushes. There were push-button phones and aerosol bombs, and automatic transmissions to take care of shifting car gears.

Tempting the Consumer

Americans hungered for the new goods, but if and when demand faltered, a revitalized advertising industry was ready to persuade consumers that their needs were greater than they knew. Advertising had come of age in the 1920s, as businesses persuaded customers that only by buying new products could they attain status and satisfaction. Advertising faltered when the economy collapsed in the 1930s but began to revive during the war as firms sought to keep the public aware of consumer goods, even those in short supply. With the postwar boom, advertisers again began to hawk their wares.

Although marketing staffs of major firms maintained that the customer was supreme and made up his or her own mind, subtle manipulation was involved. Acquisitive desires were encouraged, with the means of gratification spelled out. One researcher for the J. Walter Thompson agency even quoted Benjamin Franklin, that apostle of thrift, to justify purchasing whenever possible: "Is not the hope of being one day able to purchase and enjoy luxuries a great spur to labor and industry? . . . May not luxury therefore produce more than it consumes, if, without such a spur, people would be, as they are naturally enough inclined to be, lazy and indolent?"

Motivational research became more sophisticated, uncovering new ways of persuading people to buy. Taking the place of radio, television played an important part in conveying the spirit of consumption to millions of Americans. Unlike radio, which could only describe new commodities, television could show them to consumers. Shows like "The Price Is Right" stressed consumption in direct ways: Contestants were awarded goods for quoting their correct retail price. Drawing on a talent that was sharpened in the shopping centers and department stores, the show encouraged the acquisition of ever more material goods.

If the appeal often seemed overdone, advertisers had their defenders too. Vance Packard argued in 1957 in his best-selling book *The Hidden Persuaders* that advertisers "fill an important and constructive role in our society. Advertising, for example, not only plays a vital role in promoting our economic growth but is a colorful, diverting aspect of American life; and many of the creations of ad men are tasteful, honest works of artistry." That may have been true of some ads, but others were garish and conveyed a sense of material wealth run amok.

With its emphasis on the benefits of consuming, the United States became, in economist John Kenneth Galbraith's phrase, "the affluent society." Americans had weathered the poverty and unemployment of the 1930s, made sacrifices during a long war, and now intended to enjoy their newfound abundance and leisure time. By 1950, most wage laborers worked a 40-hour week, and 60 percent of nonagricultural workers enjoyed paid vacations, whereas few had in 1930. Most Americans regarded all this as their due, sometimes neglecting to look beyond the immediate objects of their desire. The decade, journalist William Shannon wrote, was one of "self-satisfaction and gross materialism . . . . The loudest sound in the land has been the oink and grunt of private hoggishness . . . . It has been the age of the slob."

Supermarkets burgeoning with convenience foods were an everyday manifestation of the 1950's consumer revolution.

CONSENSUS AND CONFORMITY

As the economy grew, an increasing sense of sameness pervaded middle-class society. This was the great age of conformity, when Americans of all social groups learned to emulate those around them rather than strike out on their own. Even children could not escape the homogenizing tendencies. Sociologist David Riesman pointed out that in the classic nursery rhyme "This Little Pig Went to Market," each pig went his own way. "Today, however, all little pigs go to market; none stay home; all have roast beef, if any do; and all say 'we-we.'"

The Impact of Television

If stories helped indoctrinate children into society's basic norms, television played an even more important part. Developed commercially in the 1930s, television became a major influence on American life after World War II. In 1946, there were fewer than 17,000 sets; by 1949, some 250,000 a month were being bought; and by 1960, three-quarters of all American families owned at least one set. In 1955, the average American family had the set on four to five hours each day. Some studies predicted that an American student, on graduating from high school, would have spent 11,000 hours in class

and 15,000 hours before the "tube." Viewers were bombarded by the advertising images exposing them to the luxury items needed for the good life, even as they watched the often insipid shows that dominated the medium in its early days.

Young Americans grew up to the strains of "Winky Dink and You," "The Mickey Mouse Club," and "Howdy Doody Time" in the 1950s. Older viewers attended to situation comedies

Households Owning Radios and Televisions, 1940–1960

Source: U.S. Bureau of the Census.

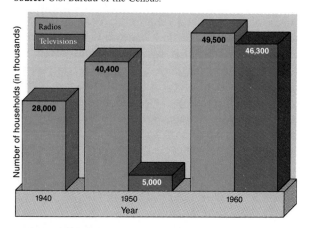

like "I Love Lucy" and "Father Knows Best" and live dramas such as "Playhouse 90." They watched Elvis Presley play his guitar and sing, and they danced to the rock and roll music played on "American Bandstand." Many of the programs aimed at children depicted violence and crime. Hopalong Cassidy was one of America's defenders who became a cult hero in his time. The gunslinging cowboy provided a role model that hundreds of American manufacturing firms capitalized on by making toy guns.

The youth of the 1950s grew up with a common, shared experience that others in the past had not known. Television, far more seductive with its visual imagery than radio, helped shape societal norms. Louis Kronenberger, a cultural critic, pointed out that whereas the automobile in the 1920s had taken Americans away from the home, the television set was bringing them back, but changing the very nature of the home in the process. In the past, he wrote, "where Mother and Father, Jane and John on their treks and travels exchanged pleasantries and ideas, they sit now for hours, side by side, often shoulder to shoulder, scarcely exchanging a glance. Or if they do address one another, they do so crossly, campaigning for this program or that."

Conformity in School and Religious Life

The willingness to conform to group norms spread to colleges and universities, where students were cautious and sought security. They joined fraternities and sororities and engaged in panty raids and other pranks but took little interest in world affairs. "I observe," Yale President A. Whitney Griswold told a graduating class in 1950, "that you share the prevailing mood of the hour, which in your case consists of bargains privately struck with fate—on fate's terms."

Americans in the postwar years returned to their churches in record numbers. Church membership doubled between 1945 and 1970. In part, church attendance reflected a desire to challenge "godless communism" at the height of the Cold War (see Chapter 29); in part, it resulted from the power of suggestion that led Americans to do

Billy Graham offered an appealingly traditional philosophy for those who questioned the morality of society's changes.

what others did. Religion also seemed to reinforce the importance of family life. As one slogan put it, "The family that prays together stays together." Moreover, religion became increasingly appealing. Evangelist Billy Graham, often introduced as "a man with God's message for these crisis days," preached to millions at his revivals. He capitalized on the media, using radio, television, and film to spread his message. By the end of the 1950s, fully 95 percent of all Americans identified with some religious denomination.

Dwight D. Eisenhower reflected the national mood when he observed that "our government makes no sense unless it is founded in a deeply felt religious faith—and I don't care what it is." In 1954, Congress added the words "under God" to the pledge to the flag, and the next year voted to require the phrase "In God We Trust" on all American currency. Yet religion was often devoid of piety and doctrinal understanding. In one public opinion poll, 80 percent of the respondents indicated that the Bible was God's revealed word, but only 35 percent were able to name the four Gospels and over half were unable to name even one.

Back to the Kitchen

World War II had interrupted traditional patterns of behavior for both men and women. As servicemen went overseas, women left their homes to work. After 1945, there was a period of adjustment as the men returned. In the 1950s, traditional gender roles were reaffirmed although, paradoxically, more women entered the work force than ever before.

Men, of course, were expected to go to school and then find jobs to support their families. Viewing themselves as the primary breadwinners, they expected their jobs to be waiting for them after the war. For women, the situation was more difficult. Many had enjoyed working during the war and were reluctant to retreat to the home, although they were persistently encouraged by the government and their employers to do so. In 1947, *Life* magazine ran a long photo essay called "The American Woman's Dilemma." It argued that women were caught in a conflict between the traditional expectation to stay home and the desire to have a paid job. A 1946 *Fortune* poll also captured the discontent of some women. Asked whether they would prefer to be born again as men or women, 25 percent of the women asked said they would prefer to be men. That dissatisfaction was strongest among white, well-educated, middle-class women, which was understandable since black and lower-class white women were usually required by their families' economic circumstances to continue working outside the home.

By the 1950s, doubts and questions had been mostly suppressed. The baby boom increased average family size and made the decision to remain home easier. The flight to the suburbs gave women more to do, and they settled into the routines of redecorating their homes and gardens and transporting children to and from activities and schools.

In 1956, when *Life* produced a special issue on women, the message differed strikingly from that of nine years earlier. Profiling Marjorie Sutton, the magazine spoke of the "Busy Wife's Achievements" as "Home Manager, Mother, Hostess, and Useful Civic Worker." Married at 16, Marjorie was now busy with the PTA, Campfire Girls, and charity causes. She cooked and sewed for her family, which included four children, supported her husband by entertaining 1,500 guests a year, and worked out on the trampoline "to keep her size 12 figure."

Marjorie Sutton reflected the widespread social emphasis on marriage and home. Many women who went to college did so to find husbands; if this succeeded, they dropped out. Almost two-thirds of the women in college stopped before completing a degree, compared to less than half of the men. Women were expected to marry young, have children early, and support their husbands' careers. "Modern man needs an old-fashioned woman around the house," novelist Sloan Wilson asserted.

Despite the reaffirmation of the old ideology that a woman's place was in the home, the 1950s was a period of unnoticed but important change. Because the supply of single women workers was diminished by the low birthrate of the Depression years and by increased schooling and early marriage, older married women began entering the labor force in large numbers for the first time. In 1940, only 15 percent of American wives had jobs. By 1950, 21 percent were employed, and ten years later, the figure had risen to 30 percent. Moreover, married women now composed over half of all working women, a dramatic reversal of earlier patterns.

Although many working women were poor, divorced, or widowed, many came from the middle class. Their income helped their families acquire the desirable new products that were badges of middle-class status. They stepped into the new jobs created by economic expansion. Women clustered in office, sales, and service positions, occupations already defined as female. They and their employers considered their work subordinate to their primary role as wives and mothers. Comparatively few entered professions where they would have challenged traditional notions of woman's place. As *Life* magazine pointed out in 1956, "Household skills take her into the garment trades; neat and personable, she becomes office worker and sales lady; patient and dextrous, she does well on competitive, detailed factory work; compassionate, she becomes teacher and nurse."

Black women worked as always, but after the war they often lost the jobs they had won during the conflict. As the total percentage of women in the Detroit automobile industry dropped from 25 to 7.5, for example, jobs for black women nearly disappeared. Their median income at the end of the 1940s was less than half that of white women. Nor did they obtain white-collar work so easily as white women. But during the 1950s, they succeeded both in moving into white-collar positions and improving their income. By 1960, more than a third of all black women had clerical, sales, service, or professional jobs, and their paychecks were 70 percent of those of white women.

Despite the mixed character of women's experience, society at large continued to view women in traditional ways. The belief that women's main role was still at home justified paying them low wages and denying them promotions. Adlai Stevenson, Democratic presidential candidate in 1952 and 1956, defined their role in politics by telling a group of women that "the assignment for you, as wives and mothers, you can do in the living room with a baby in your lap or in the kitchen with a can opener in your hand." As in much of the nineteenth century, a woman was "to influence man and boy" in her "humble role of housewife."

Pediatrician Benjamin Spock agreed. In his enormously popular *Baby and Child Care* (1946), responsible more than any other book for the child-rearing patterns of the postwar generation, he advised mothers to stay at home with their children and not to work if they wanted to raise stable and secure youngsters.

Movies seized on popular stereotypes and dramatized them. Doris Day, with her charm and clean appearance, was a favorite heroine. In movie after movie, she showed how an attractive woman who played her cards right could land her man—the assumed goal of every woman.

Sexuality was a troublesome if compelling topic in the postwar years. In 1948, Alfred C. Kinsey's *Sexual Behavior in the Human Male* was published. Kinsey was an Indiana University zoologist who had previously studied the gall wasp. When asked to teach a course on marriage problems, he found little published material about human sexual activity and decided to collect his own. He compiled case histories of 5,300 white males, analyzed their personal backgrounds, and recorded patterns of sexual behavior.

Kinsey shocked the country with his statistics on premarital, extramarital, and otherwise illicit sexual activity. Sixty-seven percent of all males who went to college, he concluded, had engaged in sexual intercourse before marriage; 84 percent of those who went to high school but not beyond had done the same. Thirty-seven percent of the total male population had experienced some kind of overt homosexual activity. One out of every six farm boys in America had copulated with animals. Kinsey published a companion volume, *Sexual Behavior in the Human Female* (1953), that detailed many of the same sexual patterns. Although many denounced the books, both sold widely, for they opened the door to a subject that had previously been considered taboo.

Such interest in sexuality appeared in the fascination with sex goddesses like Marilyn Monroe. With her blonde hair, breathy voice, and raw sexuality, she seemed to personify the

Sex goddesses of the screen—such as Marilyn Monroe, shown here in Gentlemen Prefer Blondes—*represented the fantasies of American males in the family-oriented 1950s.*

forbidden side of the good life and became one of Hollywood's most popular stars. The images such film goddesses presented corresponded to male fantasies of women. As for these men's wives, they were expected to manage their suburban homes and to be cheerful and willing objects of their husbands' desire.

Cultural Rebels

Not all Americans fit the stereotypes of the 1950s. Some were alienated from the culture and rebelled against its values. Even as young people struggled to meet the standards and expectations of their peers, they were intrigued by Holden Caulfield, the main figure in J. D. Salinger's popular novel, *Catcher in the Rye* (1951). Holden, a sensitive student at boarding school, felt surrounded by "phonies" who threatened individuality and independence. Holden's sad and ill-fated effort to preserve his own integrity in the face of pressures to conform aroused readers' sympathy and struck a resonant chord in them.

A group of writers, often called the "beat generation," espoused unconventional values in their stories, poems, and "happenings." Confronting apathy and conformity, they insisted there were alternatives. Stressing spontaneity and spirituality, they claimed that intuition was more important than reason, Eastern mysticism more valuable than Western faith. The "beats" went out of their way to challenge the norms of respectability. They rejected materialism, engaged in overt sexual activity designed to shock, and helped popularize marijuana.

Their literary work reflected their approach to life. Finding conventional academic forms confining, they rejected them. Jack Kerouac typed his best-selling novel *On the Road* (1957), describing freewheeling trips across country, on a 250-foot roll of paper. Lacking conventional punctuation and paragraph structure, the book was a paean to the free life the beats espoused.

Poet Allen Ginsberg, like Kerouac a Columbia University dropout, became equally well known for his poem "Howl." Written during one wild weekend in 1955 while Ginsberg was under the influence of drugs, the poem was a scathing critique of the modern, mechanized culture and its effects.

Reading the poem to a group of poets in San Francisco, Ginsberg bobbed and weaved as he communicated the electric rhythm of his verse. He became a celebrity when "Howl" appeared in print in 1956. The poem developed into a cult piece, particularly after the police seized it on the grounds that it was obscene. When the work survived a court test, national acclaim followed for Ginsberg. He and the other beats would furnish a model for rebellion in the 1960s.

The popularity of Salinger, Kerouac, and Ginsberg owed much to a revolution in book publishing and to the democratization of education that accompanied the program of GI educational benefits. More Americans than ever before acquired a taste for literature, and they found huge numbers of inexpensive books available because of the "paperback revolution." The paperback had been introduced in 1939, but it was not until after World War II that it began to dominate the book market. By 1965, readers could choose among some 25,000 titles, available not only in bookstores but in supermarkets, drugstores, and airplane terminals, and they purchased these cheap volumes at the rate of nearly 7 million copies per week.

The signs of cultural rebellion also appeared in popular music. Parents recoiled as their children flocked to hear a young Tennessee singer named Elvis Presley belt out "rock and roll" songs. Presley's black leather jacket and ducktail haircut became standard dress for rebellious male teenagers.

American painters, shucking off European influences that had shaped American artists for two centuries, also became a part of the cultural rebellion. They were led by Jackson Pollock and his "New York school." This group of artists discarded the easel, laid gigantic canvases on the floor, and then used trowels, putty knives, and sticks to lay on paint, glass shards, sand, and other materials in wild explosions of color. Known as abstract expressionists, these painters regarded the unconscious as the source of their artistic creations. "I am not aware of what is taking place [as I paint]," Pollock explained; "it is only after that I see what I have done." Like much of the literature of rebellion, abstract expressionism reflected the artist's alienation from a world becoming filled with nuclear threats, computerization, and materialism.

DOMESTIC POLICY UNDER TRUMAN AND EISENHOWER

In the prosperous postwar era, two very different men exercised presidential leadership. Harry S Truman took the same aggressive stance at home as he adopted in foreign affairs. A conservative Congress, however, blocked him at every turn. His successor, Dwight D. Eisenhower, created a very different imprint. Genial and calm, the war hero conveyed to Americans the feeling that everything was all right.

Postwar Public Policy

Even as he grappled with the immediate problems of postwar reconversion, Truman addressed broader questions. Like his predecessor, Franklin Roosevelt, he believed that the federal government should move toward defined economic and social goals. To that end, less than a week after the end of World War II, Truman called on Congress to pass legislation guaranteeing all Americans jobs, decent housing, educational opportunities, and a variety of other rights. His 21-point program, he contended, would produce stability and security in the postwar era. He wanted full-employment legislation, a higher minimum wage, greater unemployment compensation, and housing assistance. During the next ten weeks, Truman sent blueprints of further proposals to Congress, including health insurance and atomic energy legislation. This liberal program soon ran into fierce political opposition.

The debate surrounding the Employment Act of 1946 hinted at the fate of Truman's proposals. The Employment Act was a deliberate effort to apply the theory of English economist John Maynard Keynes to maintain economic equilibrium and prevent depression. The initial bill committed the government to maintaining full employment by monitoring the economy and taking remedial actions in case of decline. Those actions included tax cuts and spending programs to stimulate the economy and reduce unemployment.

Liberals hailed the measure, but business groups like the National Association of Manufacturers claimed that such government intervention would undermine free enterprise and move the United States one step closer to socialism. Congress cut the proposal to bits. As finally passed, the act created a Council of Economic Advisers to make recommendations to the president, who was to report annually on the state of the economy. But it stopped short of committing the government to using fiscal tools to maintain full employment when economic indicators turned downward. The act was only a modest continuation of New Deal attempts at economic planning.

Truman Battles a Conservative Congress

As the midterm elections of 1946 approached, Truman and his supporters knew they were vulnerable. Many Democrats still pined for FDR, and when they questioned what Roosevelt would have done had he been alive, the standard retort was, "I wonder what Truman would do if he were alive." Often seeming like a petty, bungling administrator, Truman became the butt of countless political jokes. Support for Truman dropped from 87 percent of those polled after he assumed the presidency to 32 percent in November 1946. Gleeful Republicans asked the voters, "Had enough?"

The voters answered that they had. Republicans won majorities in both houses of Congress for the first time since the 1928 elections, and a majority of the governorships as well. In Atlantic City, New Jersey, a Republican candidate for justice of the peace who had died a week before the election was victorious in the sweep.

After the 1946 election, Truman faced an unsympathetic 80th Congress. Republicans and conservative Democrats, dominating both houses, sought to reverse the liberal policies of the Roosevelt years. Hoping to reestablish congressional authority and cut the power of the executive branch, they insisted on less government intervention in the business world and in private life. Their goals included tax reduction and curtailment of the privileged position they felt labor had come to enjoy.

When the new Congress met, it moved to cut federal spending and reduce taxes. Robert A.

RECOVERING THE PAST

One way to recover the past is through music. Popular songs not only provide insight into attitudes and beliefs but also quickly convey the mood and feelings of an era. Through their lyrics, songwriters express the hopes and fears of a people and the emotional tone of an age. Consider, for example, the powerful message conveyed in the Democratic party adoption of "Happy Days Are Here Again" as a campaign theme during the Great Depression. The decline of pop music and the rise of rock and roll in the 1950s tells historians a great deal about social moods and changes in that decade.

The pop music style of romantic ballads and novelty numbers with smooth singing and a quiet beat dominated the early 1950s. Popular songs such as "I Believe," "Young at Heart," and "Tennessee Waltz," sung by Frankie Laine, Frank Sinatra, and Patti Page, respectively, typified the musical tastes of young adults eager to establish a secure suburban family life in the aftermath of the upheavals of the Depression and World War II. The lyrics in these songs are bland, homey, and overly sentimental.

Contrasting with these syrupy ballads was the rhythm and blues performed by black artists for black audiences. A strong beat and mournful tone were the distinguishing marks of this music. The two styles not only had different beats and rhythms but also treated common themes, like love, in different ways. Pop artists sang of sentimental love, while rhythm and blues singers expressed emotional and physical love.

In the 1950s, the first baby-boom teenagers emerged with a distinctive musical taste and enough discretionary income to influence the growth of the popular music industry. No longer children and not yet adults, these affluent teenagers struggled to define themselves in the Eisenhower age of suburban conformity. At first they were drawn to the beat of rhythm and blues as a rebellion against the mellow pop music of their parents. As the teenage market grew, white groups began to imitate black rhythm-and-blues songs, as in the 1954 song "Sh-Boom," done originally by the Chords and remade by the Crew Cuts.

But teenage listeners became increasingly dissatisfied with these imitations and looked for a livelier type of music. They found it in rock and roll (the name referred to descriptions of sex in black music). One of the first rock hits was "Rock Around the Clock" by Bill Haley and the Comets, from the controversial movie about an urban high school, *Blackboard Jungle* (1955). Parents worried about the

Paul Schutzer, **Little Anthony,** *1958*

Robert Kelley, **Elvis Presley,** *1956*

899a

influence this music would have on their children. Some thought rock music caused juvenile delinquency, while others worried about its origins in "race music" and its sexual suggestiveness.

It took a truck driver from Memphis, Elvis Presley, to turn rock and roll into virtually a teenage religion, giving it a preeminence in teenage culture it has yet to relinquish. Presley's sexy voice, gyrating hips, and other techniques borrowed from black singers helped make him the undisputed "king of rock." A multimedia blitz of movies, television, and radio helped to make songs like "Heartbreak Hotel," "Don't Be Cruel," and "Hound Dog" smash singles. Eighteen Presley hits sold more than a million copies in the last four years of the 1950s. Almost alone, Presley mobilized a whole new teenage record market, making himself a millionaire in the process. In 1956, teenagers bought 50 percent of all records, and in two years that figure had risen to 70 percent. The popularity of Elvis Presley helped bring black singers like Fats Domino and Chuck Berry into the mainstream of rock music.

Pop music died a rapid death as rock and roll swept the nation. "Your Hit Parade," a popular television show featuring top pop hits in the early 1950s, was canceled in 1957 because its singers looked ridiculous singing rock songs. In that same year, "American Bandstand" attracted teenage viewers with 90 minutes of dancing and rock music every day after school. The clean-looking young host, Dick Clark, gave rock and roll a better image with parents. In addition, many black artists toned down the sexual references and softened the hard beat of their songs in hopes of appealing to the larger white audience.

As rock and roll developed in the late 1950s, it focused on topics that appealed to the teenage market. Favorite themes were dances ("At the Hop"), love ("Why Must I Be a Teenager in Love?"), and the fear of parental punishment for teenage romance ("Wake Up, Little Susie"). Adults, then as now, were slow to understand the appeal of such music, reflecting a wider gap in generational perspective, as the lyrics of the song "Teen-Age Crush" suggest.

The 1950s saw a revolution in music that reflected a larger demographic shift and changing social values in the United States. How did popular music reflect the changes that occurred in the 1960s and 1970s, decades featuring the Beatles, Bob Dylan, the Rolling Stones, Simon and Garfunkel, the Doors, Stevie Wonder, the Eagles, Elton John, Neil Young, Michael Jackson, and others? What changes in the younger generation might account for these continuing musical shifts? What historical forces brought about changes in rock music? What music is popular today, and what does it say about the beliefs, values, and concerns of contemporary American youth?

LIFE Magazine, (c) Time Inc.

Paul Schutzer, Dick Clark and Dancers, *1958*

TEEN-AGE CRUSH

They call it a Teen-Age Crush,
They don't know how I feel,
They call it a Teen-Age Crush
They can't believe this is real.

They've forgotten when they were young,
And the way they tried to be free.
All they say is this young generation
Is not just the way it used to be.

I know my own heart,
But you say I'm trying to rush.
Please don't try to keep us apart,
Don't call it a Teen-Age Crush.

Words and music by Joe and Audrey Allison. © 1956 Central Songs, a Division of Beechwood Music Corporation.

Taft, Senate Republican leader, believed that cuts of $5 to $6 billion could be made to bring the budget down to $30 billion. In 1947, Congress twice passed tax-cut measures. Both times Truman vetoed them, but in 1948, another election year, Congress overrode the veto.

Congress also struck at Democratic labor policies. Republicans wanted to keep labor unions in check and were particularly concerned with limiting their right to engage in disruptive strikes as had occurred immediately after the war. Early in Truman's presidency, Congress passed a bill requiring notice for strikes as well as a cooling-off period if a strike occurred. Truman had vetoed that measure. But in 1947, commanding more votes, the Republicans passed the Taft-Hartley Act, which was intended to limit the power of unions by restricting the weapons they could employ. Revising the Wagner Act of 1935, the legislation spelled out unfair labor practices (such as preventing workers from working if they wished) and ruled illegal the closed shop whereby an employee had to join a union before getting a job. States were allowed by the legislation to outlaw the union shop, which forced workers to join the union after they had been hired. The act also allowed the president to call for an 80-day cooling-off period in strikes affecting national security and required union officials to sign non-Communist oaths in order to use governmental machinery designed to protect their rights.

Understandably, union leaders and members were furious. As he vetoed the measure, Truman claimed that it was unworkable and unfair, then went on nationwide radio to seek public approval. He regained some of the support he had earlier lost by his aggressive antistrike position; however, Congress passed the Taft-Hartley measure over the president's veto.

The Fair Deal and Its Critics

As 1948 approached, Truman determined to win election in his own right. Some Democrats wanted to nominate Eisenhower or William O. Douglas, but that effort failed, leaving Truman with what most people thought was a worthless nomination. Not only was his own popularity waning; the Democratic Party itself seemed to be falling apart.

The civil rights issue—aimed at securing rights for black Americans—led to a Democratic split. Truman hoped to straddle the issue, at least until after the election, to avoid alienating the South. When liberals defeated a moderate platform proposal and pressed for a stronger stand on black civil rights, angry delegates from Mississippi and Alabama stormed out of the convention. They later formed a States' Rights, or Dixiecrat, party. At their own convention, delegates from 13 states nominated Governor J. Strom Thurmond of South Carolina as their candidate for president. They stood for continued racial segregation and wanted no interference with existing customs and practices.

Meanwhile, Henry A. Wallace, for seven years secretary of agriculture, then vice-president during Roosevelt's third term and secretary of commerce after that, was mounting his own challenge. Truman had fired Wallace from his cabinet for supporting a more temperate stand on Soviet relations. Now Wallace became the presidential candidate of the Progressive party. Initially he attracted widespread liberal interest because of his moderate position on Soviet-American affairs, his promotion of desegregation, and his promise to nationalize the railroads and major industries. But as Communists and "fellow travelers" appeared active in his organization, other support dropped off.

In that fragmented state, against the first real third-party challenges since 1912, the Democrats faced the Republicans, who coveted the White House after 16 years out of power. Once again they nominated Thomas E. Dewey, the governor of New York. Egocentric and stiff, Dewey was hardly a charismatic figure. Still, the polls uniformly picked the Republicans to win. Dewey saw little value in brawling with his opponent and conducted his campaign, in the words of one commentator, "with the humorless calculation of a Certified Public Accountant in pursuit of the Holy Grail."

Truman, as the underdog, conducted a vigorous campaign. He sought to appeal to ordinary Americans as an unpretentious man engaged in an uphill fight. Believing that everyone was against him but the people, he addressed the people in terms they could understand. He called the Republicans "a bunch of old mossbacks" out to destroy the New Deal. He attacked the "do nothing" 80th Congress, which he had called into special session in 1948 with instructions to live up to the planks of the Republican platform. Predictably, the legislators failed, providing Truman with handy ammunition. Speaking without a prepared text in his choppy, aggressive style, he warmed to crowds, and they warmed to him. "Give 'em hell, Harry," they yelled. "Pour it on." He did.

All the polls predicted a Republican win. But the pollsters were wrong. On election day, despite the bold headline "Dewey Defeats Truman" in the Chicago *Daily Tribune*, the incumbent president scored one of the most unexpected political upsets in American history, winning a 303–189 margin in the electoral college. Democrats also swept both houses of Congress.

Truman won primarily because he was able to revive the major elements of the Democratic coalition that Franklin Roosevelt had constructed more than a decade before. Despite the rocky days of 1946, Truman managed to hold on to labor, farm, and black votes. The fragmentation of the Democratic party, which had threatened to hurt him severely, helped instead. The splinter parties drew off some votes but allowed Truman to make a more aggressive, direct appeal to the center, and that ultimately accounted for his success.

With the election behind him, Truman pursued his liberal program. In his 1949 State of the Union message, he declared, "Every segment of our population and every individual has a right to expect from our Government a fair deal." Fair Deal became the name for his domestic program, which included the measures he had proposed since 1945.

Some parts of Truman's Fair Deal worked; others did not. The minimum wage was raised, and social security programs were expanded. A housing program brought modest gains but did not really meet housing needs. A farm program, aimed at providing income support to farmers if prices fell, never made it through Congress. Most of his civil rights program failed to win congressional support. The American Medical Association undermined the effort to provide national health insurance, and Congress rejected a measure to provide federal aid to education.

In domestic affairs, Truman often seemed

In one of America's most remarkable political upsets, Democrats astonished pollsters by winning a sweeping victory in 1948.

unpragmatic and too ambitious in his confrontations with a conservative and unsympathetic Congress. He frequently appeared most concerned with foreign policy as he strove to secure bipartisan support for his efforts in the Cold War (see Chapter 27). Committed to checking the perceived Soviet threat, he allowed his domestic program to suffer. As defense expenditures mounted, correspondingly less money was available for projects at home.

The Election of Eisenhower

In 1952, Truman had the support of only 23 percent of the American people, and all indicators pointed to a political shift. The Democrats nominated Adlai Stevenson, Illinois's able and articulate, moderately liberal governor. The Republicans turned to Dwight D. Eisenhower, the World War II hero Americans knew as Ike.

Stevenson approached political issues in intellectual terms. "Let's talk sense to the American people," he said. "Let's tell them the truth." While liberals loved his approach, Stevenson himself anticipated the probable outcome. How, he wondered, could a man named Adlai beat a soldier called Ike?

The Republicans focused on communism, corruption, and Korea as major issues and called the Democrats "soft on communism." They criticized assorted scandals surrounding Truman's cronies and friends. The president himself was blameless, but some of the people near him were not. The Republicans also promised to end the unpopular Korean War.

Throughout the campaign, Eisenhower himself struck a grandfatherly pose, unified the various wings of his party, and went on to win a massive victory at the polls. He received 55 percent of the vote and carried 41 states. The new president took office with a Republican Congress as well and had little difficulty gaining a second term four years later.

"Modern Republicanism"

Eisenhower believed firmly in limiting the presidential role. Like the Republicans in Congress with whom Truman tangled, he wanted to restore balance in government and to reduce the growth of the federal government. In the process, however, he hoped to preserve gains of the last 20 years that even Republicans accepted. Eisenhower sometimes termed his approach "dynamic conservatism." More often it carried the name "modern Republicanism," which, he explained, meant "conservative when it comes to money, liberal when it comes to human beings."

Above all, economic concerns dominated the Eisenhower years. The president and his chief aides wanted desperately to preserve the value of the dollar, pare down levels of funding, cut taxes, and balance the budget after years of deficit spending.

To achieve those aims, the president appointed George Humphrey, a fiscal conserva-tive, as secretary of the Treasury. Humphrey placed a picture of Andrew Mellon, Calvin Coolidge's ultraconservative Treasury head, in his office and declared, "We have to cut one-third out of the budget and you can't do that just by eliminating waste. This means, whenever necessary, using a meat axe." His words reflected the administration's approach to economic affairs. In times of economic decline, Republican leaders were willing to risk unemployment to keep inflation under control. The business orientation became obvious when Defense Secretary Charles E. Wilson, former president of General Motors, stated his position at confirmation hearings. "What was good for our country was good for General Motors," he declared, "and vice versa."

Eisenhower fulfilled his promise to reduce government's economic role. After support from oil interests in the campaign, the Republican Congress, with a strong endorsement from the president, passed the Submerged Lands Act in 1953. That measure transferred control of about $40 billion worth of oil lands from the federal government to the states. *The New York Times* called it "one of the greatest and surely the most unjustified give-away programs in all the history of the United States."

The administration also sought to reduce federal activity in the electric-power field. Eisenhower favored private rather than public development of power. That sentiment came out clearly in a private comment about the Tennessee Valley Authority, the extensive public power and development project begun during the New Deal. "I'd like to see us *sell* the whole thing," he

Presidential Elections, 1948–1956

YEAR	CANDIDATES	PARTY	POPULAR VOTE	ELECTORAL VOTE
1948	HARRY S. TRUMAN	Democratic	24,105,812 (49.5%)	303
	Thomas E. Dewey	Republican	21,970,065 (45.1%)	189
	J. Strom Thurmond	States' Rights	1,169,063 (2.4%)	39
	Henry A. Wallace	Progressive	1,157,172 (2.4%)	0
1952	DWIGHT D. EISENHOWER	Republican	33,936,234 (55.2%)	442
	Adlai E. Stevenson	Democratic	27,314,992 (44.5%)	89
1956	DWIGHT D. EISENHOWER	Republican	35,590,472 (57.4%)	457
	Adlai E. Stevenson	Democratic	26,022,752 (42.0%)	73

Note: Winners' names appears in capital letters.

said, "but I suppose we can't go that far." Still, he opposed a TVA proposal for expansion to provide power to the Atomic Energy Commission and instead authorized a private group, the Dixon-Yates syndicate, to build a plant in Arkansas to meet the need. Later, when charges of scandal arose, the administration canceled the agreement, but the basic preference for private development remained.

Committed to supporting business interests, the administration sometimes saw its program backfire. As a result of its reluctance to stimulate the economy too much, the annual rate of economic growth declined from 4.3 percent between 1947 and 1952 to 2.5 percent between 1953 and 1960. The country suffered three recessions in Eisenhower's eight years. During the slumps, the deficits that Eisenhower so wanted to avoid increased.

Eisenhower's understated approach led to a legislative stalemate, particularly when the Democrats regained control of Congress in 1954. Opponents of the president jibed at Ike's restrained stance and laughed about limited White House leadership. One observed that Eisenhower proved that the country did not "need" a president. Another spoke of the Eisenhower doll —you wound it up and it did nothing at all. Those jokes notwithstanding, Eisenhower remained popular with the voters, who approved of his efforts to cut back on government's role. He left office as highly regarded as he entered it. He was what Americans wanted in prosperous times.

THE OTHER AMERICA

In the years after World War II, not all Americans enjoyed the prosperity of the growing middle class. While most Americans were unconscious of poverty, it existed in inner cities and rural areas. Nor did all Americans enjoy the same privileges, as became evident when minorities began to press for equal treatment and equal rights. Black Americans and Jews, in the forefront of the civil rights struggle, were joined by Hispanics and Native Americans, who built their protest movements on the model of black protest but moved more slowly than blacks.

Poverty Amid Affluence

Many people in the "affluent society" lived in poverty. Economic growth favored the upper- and middle classes. Although the popular "trickle-down" theory argued that economic expansion brought benefits to all classes, little, in fact, reached the citizens at the bottom of the ladder. In 1960, according to the Federal Bureau of Labor Statistics, a yearly subsistence-level income for a family of four was $3,000, and for a family of six, $4,000. The Bureau reported that 40 million people (almost a quarter of the population) lived below those levels, and nearly the same number only marginally above the line.

Two million migrant workers labored long hours for a subsistence wage. Many less mobile people were hardly better off. According to the 1960 census, 27 percent of the residential units in the United States were substandard, and even acceptable dwellings were often hopelessly overcrowded in some slums.

Michael Harrington, Socialist author and critic, exposed those conditions in *The Other America*, a devastating account that shocked the country when it appeared in 1962. The poor were everywhere. Harrington described the "economic underworld" in New York City, where "Puerto Ricans and Negroes, alcoholics, drifters, and disturbed people" sought daily positions as "dishwashers and day workers, the fly-by-night jobs" at employment agencies. In the afternoon, "the jobs have all been handed out, yet the people still mill around. Some of them sit on benches in the larger offices. There is no real point to their waiting, yet they have nothing else to do."

Harrington also pictured the rural poor living in what songwriter Woody Guthrie called the "pastures of plenty." The mountain folk of Appalachia, the tenant farmers of Mississippi, and the migrant farmers of Florida, Texas, and California were all caught in the relentless cycle.

Advent of the Civil Rights Revolution

Between 1945 and 1960, American blacks carried on an energetic campaign to win civil rights. The postwar civil rights movement had many roots. Black leaders had pressed for concessions during World War II and had won some, but not enough to satisfy rising black aspirations; moreover, as the war drew to a close, wars of national liberation inspired American black leaders. The desire for black equality appeared as part of a wider struggle. Adam Clayton Powell, a Harlem preacher (and later congressman), warned that the black man "is ready to throw himself into the struggle to make the dream of America become flesh and blood, bread and butter, freedom and equality. He walks conscious of the fact that he is no longer alone—no longer a minority." Changes in the South also contributed to the new activism. New Deal farm legislation, the popularity of synthetic fabrics, and foreign competition robbed "King Cotton" of his world markets. As cotton farmers turned to less labor-intensive crops like soybeans and peanuts, they ousted their tenants. Between 1930 and 1960, the southern agricultural population declined from 16 million to 6 million. Millions of blacks moved to southern cities, where they found better jobs, better schooling, and freedom from landlord control. Some achieved middle-class status. Still not entirely free, these southern blacks were now ready to attack Jim Crow.

Millions of blacks also headed for northern cities between 1940 and 1960. In the 1950s, Detroit's black population increased from 16 to 29 percent, Chicago's from 14 to 23 percent. Since northern blacks could vote, and usually voted for the Democrats, civil rights became an issue that northern Democratic leaders could not avoid.

During the Truman administration, the racial question was dramatized in 1947 when Jackie Robinson broke the color line and began playing major-league baseball. After four years of preparation by Branch Rickey, general manager of the Brooklyn Dodgers, Robinson was ready to break into white baseball. Sometimes teammates were hostile, sometimes opponents crashed into him with spikes flying high, but Robinson kept his frustrations to himself. A splendid first season helped ease the way, and after Robinson's trailblazing effort, other blacks, formerly confined to the old Negro leagues, started to move into the major leagues, then into professional football and basketball.

The United States found its racial problems caught up with Cold War politics. As leader of the "free world," America appealed for support in Africa and Asia. Discrimination in the United States was an obvious drawback in the struggle to gain new friends. Now there was another compelling reason for whites to confront racial problems at home.

Truman supported the civil rights movement. A moderate on questions of race, he responded to political realities, understanding the growing strength of the black vote. He saw that black interests needed protection and realized that, in urban areas in particular, black support could make the difference between victory and defeat.

Truman first moved in 1946 when the National Emergency Committee Against Mob Violence told him of lynchings and other brutalities still taking place in the South. Disturbed by the account and determined to end such terror, he appointed a Committee on Civil Rights to investigate the problem and make recommendations. Released in October 1947, the report showed that blacks remained second-class citizens in every area of American life. The first such report, it demonstrated unequal treatment in education, housing, and medical care. It was time, the committee vehemently asserted, for the federal government to secure the rights of all Americans, and it set a civil rights agenda for the next two decades.

Though Truman hedged at first, the changing political situation and his own notion of what was just prompted him to action. In February 1948, he sent a ten-point civil rights program to Congress—the first presidential civil rights program since Reconstruction. When the southern wing of the Democratic party bolted later that year, he moved forward even more aggressively. First he issued an executive order barring discrimination in the federal establishment. Then he ordered equality of treatment in the military services. A committee appointed in 1948 oversaw the implementation of the policy and ended military segregation. Equal opportunities for all Americans in the navy, air force, and marine corps were now promised, and, after some resistance, in the army as well. Manpower needs in the Korean War led to the elimination of the last restrictions, particularly when the army found that blacks fought better in integrated than in segregated units.

Elsewhere the administration made small gains. The Justice Department, not previously supportive of NAACP litigation on behalf of equal rights for blacks, entered the battle against segregation and filed briefs challenging the constitutionality of restrictions in housing, education, and interstate transportation. Those helped build the pressure for change that influenced the Supreme Court. Congress, however, did little. Though Truman called for civil rights laws guaranteeing equal rights, southern Democrats like Mississippi senators John Stennis and James Eastland headed subcommittees responsible for considering such legislation. In such circumstances, liberal measures hardly had a chance.

Integrating the Schools

In the 1950s, as the civil rights struggle gained momentum, the judicial system played a crucial role. The NAACP was determined to overturn the doctrine established in *Plessy* v. *Ferguson* in 1896. In that decision, the Supreme Court had declared that segregation of the black and white races was constitutional if the facilities used by each were "separate but equal." The decree had been used for generations to sanction rigid segregation, primarily in the South, even though separate facilities were seldom, if ever, equal. In attempting to remove this judicial roadblock to black equality, the NAACP had fought many cases over the previous decades.

A direct challenge came in 1951 when Oliver Brown, the father of 8-year-old Linda Brown, sued the school board of Topeka, Kansas, to allow his daughter to attend a school for white children that she passed as she walked to the bus that carried her to a black school farther away. Rebuffed in the local federal court (even though the Kansas judge disagreed with segregation), the plaintiffs appealed, and the case reached the Supreme Court. Justices there were fully aware

of the importance of the case. Schools in 21 states and the District of Columbia were segregated at the time, and the Court's ruling would affect them all. Adding other school segregation cases to the one before it, the Court confronted the legal questions.

On May 17, 1954, the Supreme Court released its bombshell ruling in *Brown* v. *Board of Education*. For more than a decade, Supreme Court decisions had gradually expanded black civil rights, and now the Court unanimously decreed that "separate facilities are inherently unequal" and concluded that the "separate but equal" doctrine had no place in public education. A year later, the Court turned to the question of implementation and declared that local school boards, acting with the guidance of lower courts, should move "with all deliberate speed" to desegregate their facilities.

Charged with the ultimate responsibility for executing the law was Dwight D. Eisenhower. Doubting that simple changes in the law could improve race relations, he once observed, "I don't believe you can change the hearts of men with laws or decisions." Privately commenting on the *Brown* ruling, he said, "I personally think the decision was wrong." But he understood that "it makes no difference whether or not I endorse it." Though reluctant to act aggressively, the president knew that according to the Constitution it was his duty to see that the law was carried out.

Eisenhower moved quickly. Even while urging sympathy for the South in its period of transition, he acted immediately to desegregate the Washington, D.C., schools as a model for the rest of the country. He sought to end continuing discrimination in other areas too, mandating desegregation in navy yards and veterans' hospitals.

Even so, the South resisted. In district after district, vicious scenes occurred. White children often echoed the feelings of their parents. One Tennessee teacher heard such taunts as "If you come back to school, I'll cut your guts out." Blacks endured eggs splattered on their books, ink spread on their clothes, and worse.

The crucial confrontation came in Little Rock, Arkansas, in 1957. A desegregation plan, to begin with the token admission of a few black students to Central High School, was ready to go into effect. Then, just before the school year was to begin, Governor Orval Faubus declared on television that it would not be possible to maintain order if integration took place. National Guardsmen, posted by the governor to keep the peace and armed with bayonets, turned away nine black students as they tried to enter the school. After three weeks, a federal court ordered the troops to leave. When the black children entered, the white students, spurred on by the example of their elders, belligerently opposed them, chanting such slogans as "Two, four, six, eight, we ain't gonna integrate." In the face of hostile mobs, the black children left the school.

With the lines drawn, attention focused on the moderate man in the White House. While the Guardsmen were still at the school, the president had met with the Arkansas governor and had taken a cautious stand in the hope that the crisis would dissolve of its own accord. Now, however, he faced a situation in which Little Rock whites were clearly defying the law. As a former military officer, Ike knew that such resistance could not be tolerated. He denounced the "disgraceful occurrence," urged those obstructing the law to "cease and desist," and finally took the one action he had earlier called unthinkable.

For the first time since the end of Reconstruction, an American president called out federal troops to protect the rights of black citizens. Paratroopers converged on Little Rock, and National Guardsmen were placed under federal command. The black children entered the school and attended classes with the military protecting their rights. Under those circumstances, desegregation began.

Black Gains on Other Fronts

Meanwhile, blacks themselves began to organize in ways that profoundly advanced the civil rights movement. The crucial event occurred in Montgomery, Alabama, in December 1955. Rosa Parks, a 42-year-old black seamstress who was also secretary of the state NAACP, sat down in the front of a bus in a section reserved by custom for whites. Tired from a hard day's work, she refused when ordered to move back. Told she would be arrested, she quietly held her ground. The police were called at the next stop, and Parks was arrested and ordered to stand trial for violating the segregation laws. She had not intended to challenge the law or cause a scene. Modestly, she recalled, "I felt it was just something I had to do."

Black civil rights officials seized the issue.

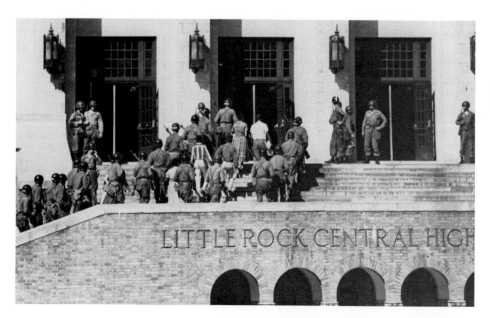

National Guardsmen and federal troops escorted Little Rock, Arkansas black students to class in 1957 as Eisenhower's desegregation program was enforced.

Baptist minister Martin Luther King, Jr., emerged as the spokesman for blacks protesting transit discrimination in Montgomery, Alabama.

E. D. Nixon, state NAACP president, told Parks, "This is the case we've been looking for. We can break this situation on the bus with your case." Though Parks knew she would lose her job, she agreed to cooperate. The next evening, resistance began. Fifty black leaders met to discuss the case and decided to organize a massive boycott of the bus system. Martin Luther King, Jr., the 27-year-old minister of the Baptist church in which the meeting was held, soon emerged as the most prominent spokesman of the protest. King held a Ph.D. in philosophy in addition to religious credentials. He was an impressive figure and an inspiring speaker. In his moving speeches, he conveyed his concern at the economic and social discrimination suffered by blacks. "There comes a time when people get tired . . . of being kicked about by the brutal feet of oppression," he declared. It was time to be more assertive, to cease being "patient with anything less than freedom and justice." The black clergy was to play a vital role in mobilizing civil rights protesters in the next two decades.

King was arrested, as he was to be many times, but 50,000 blacks in Montgomery walked or formed car pools to avoid the transit system. Their actions cut gross revenue by 65 percent on city buses. Almost a year later, the Supreme Court ruled that bus segregation, like school segregation, violated the Constitution, and the boycott ended. But the mood it fostered continued, and peaceful protest became a way of life for many blacks.

Meanwhile, a concerted effort developed to guarantee black voting rights. The provisions of the Fifteenth Amendment notwithstanding, many states had circumvented the law for decades (see Chapter 19). Some required a poll tax or a literacy test or an examination of constitutional understanding. Blacks often found themselves excluded from the polls.

Eisenhower believed in the right to vote, yet even there he had reservations. To a press conference he declared, "I personally believe if you try to go too far too fast in this delicate field that has involved the emotions of so many millions of Americans, you are making a mistake." As a bill worked its way through Congress, Ike was not much help. He seemed unsure about specific provisions and took a characteristically restrained stance toward congressional actions.

Due largely to the legislative genius of Senate majority leader Lyndon B. Johnson of Texas, the civil rights bill, the first since Reconstruction, moved toward passage. With his eye on the presidency, Johnson wanted to establish his credentials as a man who could look beyond narrow southern interests. Paring the bill down to the provisions he felt would pass, Johnson pushed the measure through.

The Civil Rights Act of 1957 created a Civil Rights Commission and empowered the Justice Department to go to court in cases where blacks were denied the right to vote. The bill was a compromise measure, yet it was the first successful effort to protect civil rights in 82 years.

To plug loopholes and add enforcement mechanisms to the 1957 act, civil rights activists worked for another measure. Johnson again took the lead, and after breaking a filibuster, he helped secure the Civil Rights Act of 1960. It set stiffer punishments for people who interfered with the right to vote, but again stopped short of authorizing federal registrars to register blacks to vote and so was generally ineffective.

The civil rights movement made important

strides during the Eisenhower years, though little of the progress resulted from the president's leadership. Rather, the efforts of blacks themselves and the rulings of the Supreme Court brought significant change. The period of civil rights activities, now launched, would continue in the next decade.

Mexican Migrant Laborers

In the years after World War II, Spanish-speaking groups in the United States suffered from many of the same problems blacks faced. They came from Cuba, Puerto Rico, Mexico, and Central America. Often unskilled and illiterate, they gravitated to the cities like other less fortunate Americans. Chicanos, or Mexican-Americans, were the most numerous newcomers. Like black Americans, they sought to better their lives, but they were less successful in their quest.

Chicanos faced peculiar difficulties and widespread discrimination. During World War II, as the country faced a labor shortage at home, American farmers sought Mexican braceros (helping hands) to harvest their crops. A program to encourage the seasonal immigration of farm workers continued after the war when the government signed a Migratory Labor Agreement with Mexico. Between 1948 and 1964, some 4.5 million Mexicans were brought to the United States for temporary work. Braceros were expected to return to Mexico at the end of their labor contract, but often they stayed, hoping to better their lives in America. Joining them were millions more who entered the country illegally.

Conditions were harsh for the braceros in the best of times. In periods of economic difficulty, they worsened. During the 1953–1954 recession, the government mounted Operation Wetback to deport illegal entrants and braceros who had illegally remained in the country. Deportations numbered 1.1 million. As immigration officials searched out illegal workers, all Chicanos found themselves vulnerable. They bitterly protested the violations of their rights, to little effect.

Operation Wetback did not end the reliance on Mexican farm laborers. A coalition of south-

ern Democrats and conservative Republicans, mostly representing farm states, extended the Migratory Labor Agreement with Mexico. Two years after the massive deportations of 1954, a record 445,000 braceros crossed the border to work on American farms.

The political attacks in the heated days of the Red Scare also brought persecution to Chicanos active in radical causes. Agapito Gómez had lived in the United States for 25 years. He had an American-born wife. Nonetheless, he found himself questioned for past union activities. In the 1930s, he had been part of a Depression-relief organization and had joined the CIO. When he refused to divulge the names of people with whom he had worked, immigration officials took away his alien card. José Noriega found himself in the same position. He had been in the United States for more than 40 years. He too had a union past, as a member of a longshoremen's association. When questioned in 1952, like Gómez, he refused to cooperate. The government initiated deportation proceedings.

In addition to economic oppression, Chicanos in all walks of life faced discrimination in the schools, uncertain access to public facilities, and occasional exclusion from the governing

Exclusion from public swimming pools was one form of discrimination faced by Chicanos. These children swam in an irrigation ditch.

process, which they did not always understand. They protested such restrictions and occasionally met with success. In mid-1946, the Tempe, Arizona, Chamber of Commerce allowed Chicanos entrance to the city's swimming pool as a result of pressure from a Chicano veterans' group. A concerted effort to register new voters in Los Angeles led to the election of Edward Roybal to the Los Angeles City Council in 1949. He was the first person of Mexican descent to serve there since 1881 and later was elected to Congress.

The advances, however, were limited. In the late 1940s, many Chicanos sought official classification as Caucasian in the hope that the change would lead to better treatment. But even when the designation changed, their status did not. They still faced discrimination and police brutality, particularly in the cities with the largest Chicano populations.

Los Angeles, with its large number of Chicanos, was the scene of numerous unsavory racial episodes. In mid-1951, on receiving a complaint about a loud record player, police officers raided a baptismal gathering at the home of Simon Fuentes. Breaking into the house without a warrant, they assaulted the members of the party. At the end of the year, in the "Bloody Christmas" case, officers removed seven Mexican-Americans from jail cells and beat them severely. Chicanos protested such episodes, often through the *Asociación Nacional México-Americana*, an organization founded the year before in New Mexico to protect the human rights of those facing discrimination. Sometimes they achieved recourse; more often they did not.

Yet in the 1950s, Chicano activism was fragmented. Many Mexican-Americans considered their situation hopeless. More effective mobilization had to wait for another day.

Native Americans

American Indians also acted to defend their own interests, but with even greater difficulties. Not only did they have to fight the forces of cultural change that were eroding tribal tradition, but they also had to resist the federal government's reversal of New Deal Indian policy.

In the postwar years, Indians faced the same technological developments affecting other Americans. As power lines reached the reservations, Indians purchased televisions, refrigerators, washing machines, and automobiles. This inevitably changed old ways of life. Those Indians who gravitated to the cities often had difficulty adjusting to urban life and faced discrimination much like that experienced by Mexican-Americans and blacks.

Just after the end of World War II, Native Americans achieved an important victory when Congress established the Indian Claims Commission. The commission was mandated to review tribal cases pleading that ancestral lands had been illegally taken from them through violation of federal treaties. Hundreds of tribal suits against the government in federal courts were now possible. Many of them would lead to large settlements of cash—a form of reparation for past injustices—and sometimes the return of long-lost lands.

The Eisenhower administration, determined to cut back on federal activity wherever possible, dramatically turned away from the New Deal policy of government support for tribal autonomy. In the Indian Reorganization Act of 1934, the government had stepped in to restore lands to tribal ownership and end their loss or sale to outsiders. In 1953, instead of trying to encourage Native American self-government, the administration adopted a new approach, known as the "termination" policy. The government proposed settling all outstanding claims and eliminating reservations as legitimate political entities. To encourage their assimilation into mainstream society, the government offered small subsidies to families who would leave the reservations and relocate in the cities.

The new policy victimized the Indians. With their lands no longer federally protected and their members deprived of treaty rights, many tribes became unwitting victims of people who wanted to seize their land, just as they had been throughout the nineteenth century. Though promising more freedom, the new policy caused undue disruption and was discontinued in 1961.

Almost all tribes resisted termination, and as they did they began to articulate a new sense of identity to the outside world. A Seminole petition to the president in 1954 summed up a general view. "We do not say that we are superior or inferior to the White Man and we do not say that the White Man is superior or inferior to us," the document said. "We do say that we are not White Men but Indians, do not wish to become White Men but wish to remain Indians, and have an outlook on all things different from the outlook of the White Man."

CONCLUSION: Qualms Amid Affluence

In general, the United States in the decade and a half after World War II was stable and secure. Recessions occurred periodically, but the economy righted itself after short downturns. For the most part, business boomed. Millions of middle-class Americans joined the ranks of suburban property owners, enjoying the benefits of shopping centers and fast-food establishments and other material manifestations of what they considered the good life.

Some Americans, however, never shared in the prosperity, but they were not visible from the suburbs. Black Americans and other minority groups were beginning to mobilize, yet their protest remained peaceful. Many still believed they could share in the American dream and remained confident that deeply rooted patterns of discrimination could be changed.

Toward the end of the period, after the Soviet Union became the first nation to place a satellite in orbit, a wave of anxiety swept the nation. Some Americans began to criticize the materialism that apparently had caused the nation to fall behind. Critics began to explore questions of national purpose. Raising these questions made them more willing to criticize other shortcomings in American life. It also legitimated challenges by other groups.

Criticisms and anxieties notwithstanding, the United States continued to develop according to Ray Kroc's dreams as he first envisioned McDonald's establishments across the land. The standard of living remained high for many of the nation's citizens. Healthy and comfortable, upper- and middle-class Americans assumed that their society would continue to prosper. But the "other Americans" had begun to make their voices heard, and the echoes would reverberate even more loudly in future years.

Recommended Reading

A number of good books describe domestic developments in the years between 1945 and 1960. Richard Polenberg, *One Nation Divisible: Class, Race, and Ethnicity in the United States Since 1938* (1980) is a useful survey of recent America that includes a description of the growth of suburbia. William Leuchtenburg, *A Troubled Feast* (1979) is a perceptive assessment of the entire post-1945 period that focuses on the consumer culture that came into prominence after World War II.

Robert J. Donovan, *Conflict and Crisis: The Presidency of Harry S Truman, 1945–1948* (1977) is a detailed overview of Truman's first term. *Tumultuous Years: The Presidency of Harry S Truman* (1982), by the same author, carries the story through the second term. Barton J. Bernstein and Allen J. Matusow, *The Truman Administration: A Documentary History* (1966) is an excellent collection of documents on various facets of policy in Truman's two terms. Harry S Truman, *Memoirs* (2 vols., 1955, 1956) is Truman's own account of his years at the top.

For the Eisenhower period, Charles C. Alexander, *Holding the Line: The Eisenhower Era, 1952–1961* (1975) provides a good general introduction to the American mood and government policy during Ike's years as president. Dwight D. Eisenhower, *Mandate for Change, 1953–1956* (1963) is the first volume of Ike's memoirs of his years in office; *Waging Peace* (1965) is the concluding volume.

Fiction can often give a good sense of period. Sloan Wilson, *The Man in the Gray Flannel Suit* (1955) is a novel that conveys a good sense of the materialism of the affluent 1950s.

On women, William H. Chafe, *The American Woman: Her Changing Social, Economic, and Political Roles, 1920–1970* (1972) is an outstanding survey of women's struggle in the past 50 years, with some particularly pertinent observations on the postwar years. Betty Friedan, *The Feminine Mystique* (1963) is a polemical book describing the stereotypical role of women in the 1950s as they focused on being housewives and mothers.

For further details on civil rights, see Harvard Sitkoff, *The Struggle for Black Equality, 1954–1980* (1981), a readable survey of the movement since the early 1950s. Richard Kluger, *Simple Justice* (1975) tells the full story of the *Brown* v. *Board of Education* decision and its implications.

Several recent books provide useful background on the equality efforts of other minorities in the United States. Rodolfo Acuña, *Occupied America: A History of Chicanos* (1981) gives insight into the Chicanos' struggle in the years after World War II. Alvin M. Josephy, Jr., *Now That the Buffalo's Gone* (1982) details Indian struggles over the past several decades.

TIME LINE

1943	Mark I computer developed
1944	GI Bill passed
1945	World War II ends Wave of strikes in heavy industries
1946	Truman vetoes bill extending Office of Price Administration Prices rise by 25 percent in 18 months Union strikes in the auto, coal, steel, and electrical industries Employment Act Dr. Spock's *Baby and Child Care*
1947	Taft-Hartley Act Jackie Robinson breaks the color line in major-league baseball
1948	Executive order bars discrimination in federal government Armed forces begin to desegregate "Dixiecrat" party formed Truman defeats Dewey Kinsey Report on human sexuality Transistor developed at Bell Lab
1949	Truman launches Fair Deal
1950	Asociación Nacional México-Americana formed
1951	J. D. Salinger's *Catcher in the Rye*
1952	Dwight D. Eisenhower elected president
1953	Submerged Lands Act Rosenbergs executed for espionage
1954	*Brown* v. *Board of Education*
1955	Montgomery bus boycott begins First McDonald's opens in Illinois
1956	Eisenhower reelected Interstate Highway Act Allen Ginsberg's "Howl"
1957	Little Rock school integration crisis Civil Rights Act "Baby boom" peaks with 4.3 million births *Sputnik* launched by Soviet Union
1959	One-third of all Americans reside in suburbs
1960	Three-fourths of all families own a TV Civil Rights Act GNP hits $500 billion John F. Kennedy elected president

CHAPTER 29

FROM SELF-CONFIDENCE
TO SELF-DOUBT

R on Kovic was a typical all-American boy. Born in 1946, he grew up on Long Island. Life was secure in the comfortable post–World War II years, as Kovic shared the dreams of millions of others his age.

"I loved baseball more than anything else in the world." Later he recalled "playing catch-a-fly-you're-up for hours with a beat-up old baseball. We played all day long out there, running across that big open field with all our might, diving and sliding face-first into the grass, making one-handed, spectacular catches."

When baseball did not occupy him, television did. "The whole block grew up watching television," he observed. "There was Howdy Doody and Rootie Kazootie, Cisco Kid and Gabby Hayes, Roy Rogers and Dale Evans. The Lone Ranger was on Channel 7. We watched cartoons for hours on Saturdays".

Anxious moments occasionally intervened. Kovic, like others, wondered how the Russians had managed to put a satellite into space before the United States. He grew up fearing "the Communist threat" and even became persuaded that Communists "were infiltrating our schools, trying to take over our classes and control our minds."

Yet that fear was but a reflection of the patriotism of his day. Like most Americans, Kovic had an unquestioning confidence in the "American way." Moreover, he had been born on the Fourth of July and could take the words of "I'm a Yankee Doodle Dandy" to heart as holiday fireworks went off.

Caught up in the spirit of the New Frontier, Kovic was stunned when President John F. Kennedy was shot. "I truly felt I had lost a dear friend," he wrote. "I was deeply hurt. . . . The pain stuck with me for a long time after he died."

Still, life went on, and Kovic remained intent on doing something for his nation. After graduating from high school, Kovic enlisted in the marines. The desire to be a hero drove him on, carried him through basic training, and stayed with him through a first tour of duty in the war in Vietnam. Proud of what he was doing, he signed up for a second tour. Only then did the conflict begin to tear him apart.

Kovic wanted to win medals, to be brave, but instead was increasingly haunted by his conduct in the war. He accidently shot and killed an American corporal and, as if to atone for his deed, plunged on even more aggressively, certain that he was "serving America in this its most critical hour, just like President Kennedy had talked about." Yet that effort, too, ended in disaster when his unit shot at shadowy figures moving in a village hut, only to learn that the wounded and dead were innocent children.

For Kovic the final blow came later. First hit in the foot, he then took a 30-caliber sniper bullet in the spine. The pain in his foot vanished, but so did all sensation below his chest. Suddenly, all he could feel was "the worthlessness of dying right here in this place at this moment for nothing."

Ron Kovic returned from the war paralyzed from the chest down. As he went from hospital to hospital, feeling the muscle tone of his legs disappear, he became overwhelmed by despair, heightened by the growing opposition to the war in the United States. Kovic grew to believe that he had been trapped in a meaningless crusade and then left to dangle on his own. He became one of the many protesters who finally helped bring the war to an end.

Yet he could never forget the price he had paid. "I feel like a big clumsy puppet with all his strings cut," he wrote. Even more poignantly he observed:

> I am the living death
> the memorial day on wheels
> I am your yankee doodle dandy
> your john wayne come home
> your fourth of july firecracker
> exploding in the grave

Ron Kovic's passage through the 1960s reflected that of American society as a whole. Millions of Americans shared his views as the decade began, feeling sure of their nation's destiny. Mostly comfortable and confident, they were nonetheless ready to embrace John Kennedy's New Frontier. They agreed that social reform was necessary at home, a vigilant anti-Communist course needed abroad. Though people were shocked when Kennedy was assassinated in November 1963, they rallied behind Vice-President Lyndon Johnson, who pressed ahead to complete Kennedy's reform program. But when the Johnson administration deepened American involvement in the civil war in faraway Vietnam, the middle-class consensus in the United States began to come apart. The reform movement fell victim to the turbulence of the war and the opposition it raised. And the values of the nation, particularly of its young, began to change. Not all Americans suffered what Ron Kovic went through. But they did experience many of the same transitions, and they too came to question their own actions and those of their nation in troubled times.

This chapter describes the transitions that occurred in the 1960s. It explores the shift from optimistic hope that the nation could solve all problems to pessimistic doubt that it could deal with crises anywhere. And it examines the groups who raised doubts about American values and policies as the decade came to an end.

THE PRESIDENCY IN THE SIXTIES

As the new decade dawned, fresh political leadership emerged, as men much younger than Dwight Eisenhower vied for the presidency. John Kennedy in particular sought to reaffirm a sense of national purpose, yet both candidates, Kennedy and Richard Nixon, still clung to many of the assumptions that had guided America in the past. Both saw incremental reform and a vigilant foreign policy as the keys to keeping the nation safe and strong.

The Election of 1960

In 1960, Richard Nixon, vice-president for eight years under Eisenhower, set his sights on the presidency. Incumbency should have served as an advantage, but an economic recession hurt the Republicans, and Eisenhower's own lukewarm support proved damaging. Never close to Nixon, Eisenhower made matters worse when asked what decisions his vice-president had helped make. "If you give me a week, I might think of one," he responded.

In the Democratic party, John Kennedy, an ambitious young senator from Massachusetts who had eyed the presidency for some time, now made his bid. First, however, he had to overcome the Catholic hurdle, for no Roman Catholic had ever been elected president, and conventional wisdom held that none could win in the aftermath of Al Smith's defeat in 1928. Pointed stories injected a hostile note into the campaign. One critic advised voters to join the church of their choice—while there was still time. Despite such attacks, Kennedy managed to defuse the religious issue in the primary campaign. His primary victory in Protestant West Virginia, where opponent Hubert Humphrey had long been friendly with organized labor, showed that religion did not harm his chances for election.

Kennedy and Nixon squared off against each other in the first televised debates ever held between presidential candidates. Television changed the course of the campaign. Both men were articulate, but by projecting a more energetic and dynamic image, Kennedy gained the upper hand. While Nixon challenged points his opponent made, Kennedy looked beyond Nixon and seemed to be addressing the American people at large. Television, increasingly important in shaping American attitudes, had now become a significant part of the political process.

Kennedy's victory was a narrow one. The electoral margin of 303 to 219 concealed the close popular tally, in which he triumphed by less than 120,000 of 68 million votes. Given the curious nature of the electoral college, the actual result was even closer. If but a few thousand people had voted differently in Illinois and Texas, the election would have gone to Nixon.

Kennedy won in 1960 because he carried traditionally Democratic areas and did well in the cities among black and ethnic voters. The debates, too, had an important impact on the outcome. In a survey for CBS, pollster Elmo Roper estimated that 57 percent of the people voting felt that the debates had influenced their choice. Another 6 percent indicated that their final decision resulted from the debates alone. As Kennedy himself concluded after his narrow victory, "It was TV more than anything else that turned the tide."

JFK and LBJ

Kennedy's style gave a new stamp to the office. At 43, he was the youngest man ever elected to the presidency. Son of a former ambassador to England and grandson of an Irish-American mayor of Boston, he appeared energetic, able, and articulate. He had the capacity to voice his aims in language the average American could understand. During the campaign he had noted "uncharted areas of science and space, unsolved problems of peace and war, unconquered pockets of ignorance and prejudice, unanswered questions of poverty and surplus" that must be confronted, for "the New Frontier is here whether we seek it or not." He made the same point even more eloquently in his inaugural address: "The torch has been passed to a new generation of Americans—born in this century, tempered by war, disciplined by a hard and bitter peace, proud of our ancient heritage." Noting the need to reaffirm American values and to move ahead together, he concluded, "And so, my fellow Americans: Ask not what your country can do for you—ask what you can do for your country."

Kennedy generated confidence, viewing himself as "tough-minded" and "hard-nosed." Unlike Ike, Kennedy believed in strong leadership. He admired the political figures he described in his Pulitzer Prize–winning book *Profiles in Courage*. The president, he believed, "must serve as a catalyst, an energizer," who

The Confusing 1960 Presidential Election

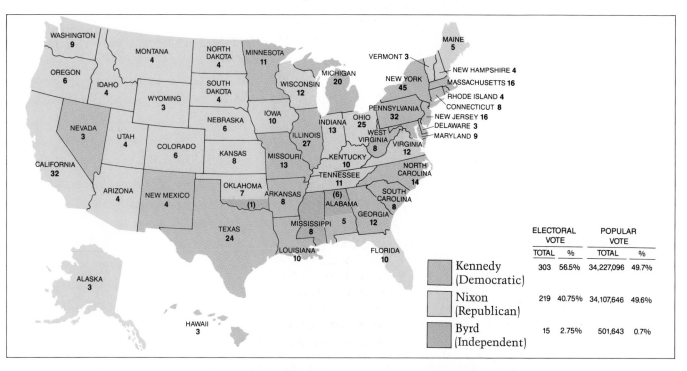

	ELECTORAL VOTE		POPULAR VOTE	
	TOTAL	%	TOTAL	%
Kennedy (Democratic)	303	56.5%	34,227,096	49.7%
Nixon (Republican)	219	40.75%	34,107,646	49.6%
Byrd (Independent)	15	2.75%	501,643	0.7%

would perform "in the very thick of the fight." Widely read, especially in history, Kennedy sought to follow Franklin Roosevelt's example of keeping power in his own hands and working through problems himself.

Kennedy surrounded himself with talented assistants. On his staff were 15 Rhodes scholars and several famous authors. The secretary of state was Dean Rusk, a former member of the State Department who had then served as president of the Rockefeller Foundation. The secretary of defense was Robert S. McNamara, the president of the Ford Motor Company, who had proved creative in using computer analysis.

Also contributing to the Kennedy style was his glamorous, charming, and graceful wife Jacqueline. Nobel Prize winners came to a special White House dinner; artists and musicians performed before invited guests. The Kennedys and their friends played touch football on the grass and promoted 50-mile hikes. Energy and exuberance filled the air. The administration seemed like the Camelot of King Arthur's day.

When the president was tragically cut down in his prime by an assassin's bullet, his vice-president tried to carry on the dream in his own way. Johnson was a less charismatic figure than Kennedy but a more effective politician. He used his considerable political talents to construct an impressive legislative program.

Schooled in Congress and influenced by FDR, Johnson was the most able legislative leader of the postwar years. As Senate majority leader, he became famous for his ability to get things done. He was an enormously egotistical man and a fountain of energy and force. Ceaseless in his search for information, tireless in his attention to detail, he knew the strengths and weaknesses of everyone he faced. He could flatter and cajole and was famous for the "Johnson treatment": he would confront someone in the hall and bear down until he got his way.

In the 1960s, Kennedy and Johnson, each in turn, sought to remobilize the nation after the placid Eisenhower years. Both used the presidency more aggressively to shape public opinion. Like Theodore Roosevelt, they saw the office as a "bully pulpit," yet with added possibilities, for radio and television had become enormously influential. Kennedy sparked the public imagination and generated a sense of hope; Johnson produced the legislative results that made

Glamour and grace characterized the Kennedy style. The president and first lady were photographed at a reception in Vienna while on a state visit to Europe.

change possible. Both shared the vision of a society in which the comforts of life would be more widely shared and poverty eliminated. By the middle of the decade, they had made progress toward these goals. Both had a vision of the nation so dominant and strong in the world that it could impose its will in all parts of the globe. That misperception finally turned their dream into a nightmare at home and abroad.

THE NEW FRONTIER AND SOCIAL REFORM

In the early 1960s, the Democratic administration addressed questions of domestic reform. While the 1950s had been prosperous for most Americans, segments of the society remained caught in the web of poverty, and minority groups continued to face discrimination. Confident of America's destiny and design, Kennedy and his associates began to consider how to alleviate these problems without challenging the system as a whole.

The Kennedy Approach

As his presidency progressed, Kennedy realized not only the necessity of maintaining a healthy economic system but also the need to provide welfare programs that went beyond the liberal offerings of the past. In late 1962, Kennedy told one of his advisers, "I want to go beyond the things that have already been accomplished. Give me facts and figures on things we still have to do." As for civil rights, Kennedy knew that blacks were an important part of the Democratic coalition. He had made promises to them during the campaign and now would have to make good. Yet while Kennedy espoused liberal goals and social justice, in reality his policies and programs were limited and restrained. The president spoke out eloquently on occasion, but his close electoral victory limited his mandate to embark on major reform programs. Furthermore, his party lost two seats in the Senate and 22 in the House in 1960. Though they retained majorities in both chambers, the Democrats included many conservative southerners who were often unsympathetic to liberal goals and opposed any changes in race relations.

One of Kennedy's major aims was to end the lingering recession by working with the business community. At the same time, he was determined to keep inflation under control. These two goals conflicted when, in the spring of 1962, steel companies sought what the administration regarded as excessive price increases. Democratic leaders were especially disturbed because the administration had proved its friendship for business by persuading steelworkers to accept a modest contract, assuming that management would show similar restraint in controlling prices. The angry president termed the price increases unreasonable and unjustifiable and went on television, charging that the firms showed "utter contempt" for the interests of 185 million Americans. Determined to force the steel companies to their knees, Kennedy pressed for a congressional investigation. The Justice Department and the Federal Trade Commission moved to examine the possibility that the steel firms were working too closely with one another in making price agreements. The Defense Department threatened to deny contracts to the offending companies.

The large companies backed down and reinstituted the earlier price levels. Although Kennedy won, he paid a price for his victory. Business leaders disliked the heavy-handed approach and decided that this Democratic administration, like all the others, was hostile to business. In late May, six weeks after the steel crisis, the stock market plunged in the greatest drop since the Great Crash of 1929. Kennedy received the blame. "When Eisenhower had a heart attack," Wall Street analysts joked, "the market broke . . . if Kennedy would have a heart attack, the market would go up."

It now seemed doubly pressing to end the economic slump. Earlier a proponent of a balanced budget, Kennedy adopted a Keynesian approach to economic growth. Budget deficits had promoted prosperity during the Second

World War and might work in the same way in peacetime too. In June 1962, the president announced that deficits, properly used, might help the economy. In early 1963, he called for a $13.5 billion cut in corporate taxes over the next three years. While that cut would cause a large deficit, it would also provide capital that could stimulate the economy and ultimately bring added tax revenues.

Opposition mounted on all sides. Conservatives refused to accept the basic premise that deficits would stimulate economic growth and argued, as Eisenhower declared, that "no family, no business, no nation can spend itself into prosperity." In Congress, opponents pigeonholed the proposal in committee, and there it remained.

On other issues Kennedy also encountered resistance. Though he proposed legislation increasing the minimum wage and providing for federal aid for education, medical care for the elderly, housing subsidies, and urban renewal, the legislative results were disappointing. His new minimum-wage measure passed Congress, in pared-down form, but Kennedy did not have the votes in Congress to achieve most of his legislative program.

That became even more evident in the struggle to aid public education. Soon after taking office, Kennedy proposed a $2.3 billion program of grants to the states over a three-year period to help build schools and raise teachers' salaries. Immediately, a series of prickly questions emerged. Was it appropriate to spend large sums of money for social goals? Would federal aid bring federal control of school policies and curriculum? Should assistance go to segregated schools? Should it go to parochial schools? The administration proved willing to allow assistance to segregated schools, thereby easing white southern minds. On the Catholic question, however, it stumbled to a halt. Kennedy at first insisted that he would not allow his religion to influence his actions and opposed aid for parochial schools. As Catholic pressure mounted and the administration realized that Catholic votes were necessary for passage, Kennedy began to reconsider. But in the end, the school aid measure died in the House Rules Committee.

Black Activism and the Fight for Civil Rights

In the volatile area of civil rights, the administration's efforts also faltered. The movement that had begun to grow in the 1950s became more intense in the next decade, forcing political leaders of all persuasions, including Kennedy, to scramble to keep abreast of events.

The Montgomery bus boycott marked the advent of a mass civil rights movement in the South. While the National Association for the Advancement of Colored People (NAACP) continued to challenge segregation in the courts, activists continued to urge civil disobedience and nonviolent direct action. Sit-in demonstrations began in North Carolina in 1960 when black college students took their places at a segregated Woolworth's lunch counter and deliberately violated southern segregation laws by refusing to leave. The sit-ins captured media attention, and soon thousands of blacks were involved in the campaign. The following year, the sit-ins gave rise to freedom rides, aimed at testing southern transportation facilities, recently desegregated by a Supreme Court decision. Organized initially by the Congress of Racial Equality (CORE) and aided by the Student Nonviolent Coordinating Committee (SNCC), the program sent groups of blacks and whites together on buses heading south and stopping at terminals along the way. The riders, peaceful themselves, anticipated confrontations that would publicize their cause and generate political support.

In North and South alike, consciousness of the need to combat racial discrimination grew. Young people in particular, most of them students, enlisted in the effort to change restrictive patterns deeply rooted in American life. White clergy of all denominations became socially active in ways not seen since the Social Gospel movement of the late ninteenth century (when civil rights was not one of their concerns). The civil rights movement became the most powerful moral campaign since the abolitionist crusade before the Civil War. Often working together, blacks and whites vowed to eliminate racial barriers.

Participants in the movement came from every direction. Anne Moody, who grew up in a small town in Mississippi, personified the awakening of black consciousness that led to action. As a child, she had watched the passivity of blacks in the face of discrimination and struggled to understand just what "the white folks' secret" really was. She saw the murder of friends and acquaintances who had somehow transgressed the limits set for blacks. And she became frustrated at members of her own race for not doing anything about the injustices she saw. "I began to look upon Negro men as cowards," she later wrote. "I could not respect them for smiling in a white man's face, addressing him as Mr. So-and-So, saying yessuh and nossuh when after they were home behind closed doors that same white man was a son of a bitch, a bastard, or any other name more suitable than mister."

Through her own efforts, Moody became the first of her family to go to college. Once there, she found her own place in the civil rights movement. At Tougaloo College in Jackson, Mississippi, she joined the NAACP and also became involved in the activities of SNCC and CORE. Slowly, she noted, "I could feel myself beginning to change. For the first time I began to think something would be done about whites killing, beating, and misusing Negroes. I knew I was going to be a part of whatever happened." She participated in sit-ins where she was thrashed and jailed for her role, but she remained deeply involved. She learned how to protect herself when threatened by angry whites. Though often exhausted and discouraged, she knew that she was part of something important.

Many whites also joined the struggle in the South. Mimi Feingold, a white student at Swarthmore College in Pennsylvania, had been active in northern civil rights protests and antinuclear efforts in the late 1950s, but when the sit-in movement began, she became much more deeply involved. She helped picket Woolworth's in Chester, Pennsylvania, and sought to unionize Swarthmore's black dining hall workers. But she wanted to do still more. In 1961, after her sophomore year, she headed south to join the freedom rides sponsored by CORE.

The civil rights workers she met often got the confrontations they expected. On the freedom rides, they frequently stepped off the buses to face derogatory shouts and brutal assault. Injuries were common as southern whites attacked them with rocks and chains. One bus was pelted with stones, then burned. Feingold's group had a bomb scare in Montgomery, Alabama, and knew that the last such bus to enter the state had been blown up. Like many others, Mimi went to jail as an act of conscience. In Jackson, Mississippi, where she spent a month behind bars, she heard other women screaming in response to the humiliating searches local police conducted. Background made no difference to officials in the South. Yale University chaplain William Sloane Coffin, Jr., was one of many arrested for trying to use facilities in a Montgomery terminal with an integrated group of clergymen.

In 1962, the civil rights movement gained further momentum. James Meredith, a black air force veteran and student at Jackson State College, sought to enter the all-white University of Mississippi, only to be rejected on racial grounds. Suing to gain admission, he carried his case to the Supreme Court, where Justice Hugo Black affirmed his claim. But then Governor Ross Barnett, an adamant racist, asserted that Meredith would not be admitted, whatever the Court decision, and on one occasion personally blocked the way. "We never have trouble with our people," he told Attorney General Robert F. Kennedy, who was supporting Meredith's claim, "but the NAACP, they want to stir up trouble down here." With the issue joined, a major riot began. One angry white southerner's effort to drive a bulldozer into the administration building failed only when the vehicle stalled. Tear gas covered the university grounds, and by the end of the riot, two men were dead and hundreds hurt.

An even more violent confrontation began in April 1963, in Birmingham, Alabama, where Martin Luther King, Jr., decided to launch another attack on southern segregation. Forty percent black, the city was rigidly segregated along racial and class lines. King later explained, "We believed that while a campaign in Birmingham would surely be the toughest fight of our civil rights careers, it could, if successful, break the back of segregation all over the nation."

Though the protests were nonviolent, the responses were not. City officials declared that protest marches violated city regulations against parading without a license, and, over a five-week period, they arrested 2,200 blacks, some of them young school children. Police Commissioner Eugene "Bull" Connor used high-pressure fire hoses, electric cattle prods, and trained police dogs to force the protesters back. Newspaper photographers and television camera operators recorded the events for people around the world to see, and many who saw them were aghast. As newsman Eric Sevareid observed, "A newspaper or television picture of a snarling police dog set upon a human being is recorded in the permanent photo-electric file of every human brain."

Kennedy's Response

When Kennedy ran for office, he was well aware of the importance of the black vote. During the campaign, he announced that "if the President does not himself wage the struggle for equal rights—if he stands above the battle—then the battle will inevitably be lost." He asserted too that a "stroke of the pen" could end racial segregation in federally funded housing. That approach succeeded in bringing him 70 percent of the black vote, and in some states where the tally had been close, particularly Michigan and Illinois, black support made a crucial difference.

Once in office, however, Kennedy dragged his heels. Reluctant to press white southerners on civil rights when he needed their votes on other issues, Kennedy failed to sponsor any civil rights legislation. Nor did he fulfill his campaign promise to end housing discrimination by presidential order, despite gifts of numerous bottles of ink. Not until November 1962, after the midterm elections, did he take a modest action —an executive order ending segregation in federally financed housing. Under Robert Kennedy the Justice Department worked to end discrimination in interstate transportation and to guarantee blacks the right to register and vote in the South. But to Martin Luther King, Jr., this was hardly enough: "If tokenism were our goal, this

Administration has moved us adroitly towards its accomplishment."

Events finally forced Kennedy to take actions he had hoped to avoid. When James Meredith was refused admission to the University of Mississippi because of his color in 1962, the president, like his predecessor in the Little Rock crisis, had to send federal troops to restore control and to guarantee Meredith's right to attend. The administration also forced the desegregation of the University of Alabama and helped arrange a compromise providing for desegregation of Birmingham's municipal facilities, implementation of more equitable hiring practices, and formation of a biracial committee. And when violence erupted in Birmingham and thousands of blacks abandoned nonviolence and rampaged through the streets, Kennedy readied federal troops to intervene.

The events in Birmingham raised the horrifying possibility of black revolution and helped to push Kennedy toward a bold stance. In a nationally televised address, he called the quest for equal rights "a moral issue" and asserted, "We preach freedom around the world, and we mean it . . . ; but are we to say to the world, and much more importantly, to each other that this is a land of the free except for the Negroes . . . ?" He sent Congress a new civil rights bill, far stronger than the moderate one proposed earlier in the year. The legislation prohibited segregation in public places, banned discrimination wherever federal money was involved, and advanced the process of school integration. Polls showed that 63 percent of the nation supported his stand.

To lobby for passage of that measure, civil rights leaders, pressed from below by black activists, arranged a massive march on Washington in August 1963. Kennedy did not favor the demonstration, for he feared it would alienate Congress and provoke violence in the capital city. After his efforts failed to get the organizers to call it off, however, Kennedy supported the march, which proved to be an almost festive affair. More than 200,000 people gathered from across the country and demonstrated enthusiastically. Celebrities were present: Ralph Bunche, James Baldwin, Sammy Davis, Jr., Harry Belafonte, Jackie Robinson, Lena Horne. The folk-

Martin Luther King's famous "I have a dream" speech was delivered to the assembled crowd during the 1963 march on Washington.

music artists of the early 1960s were there as well. Joan Baez, Bob Dylan, and Peter, Paul, and Mary sang songs associated with the movement such as "Blowin' in the Wind" and "We Shall Overcome."

But the high point of the day was the address by Martin Luther King, Jr., who had become the nation's preeminent spokesman for civil rights. For many blacks and whites, he seemed to represent the struggle itself. Long interested in Gandhi's theory of nonviolent protest, he had become committed to nonviolent resistance. Working through his own Southern Christian Leadership Conference, he pressed vigorously for racial change. At the March on Washington, in a powerful address, he proclaimed his faith in the decency of his fellow citizens. With all the power of a southern preacher, he implored his audience to share his faith.

The Struggle for Equal Rights

YEAR	EVENT	EFFECT
1947	Report of Truman's Committee on Civil Rights	Showed that blacks remained second-class citizens in America.
1948	Truman issues executive order integrating the armed forces	Opened the way for equal opportunities in the armed forces.
1954	*Brown* v. *Board of Education* decision	Supreme Court ruled that local school boards should move "with all deliberate speed" to desegregate facilities.
1955	Montgomery bus boycott	Black solidarity tested local petty segregation laws and customs.
1957	Little Rock school integration crisis	White resistance to integration of Little Rock's Central High School resulted in Eisenhower's calling in federal troops.
	Civil Rights Act	Created Civil Rights Commission and empowered Justice Department to go to court to guarantee blacks the right to vote.
1960	Civil Rights Act	Plugged loopholes in Civil Rights Act of 1957.
	Sit-in demonstrations begin	Gained support for desegregation of public facilities.
1961	Freedom rides begin	Dramatized struggle to desegregate transportation facilities.
1962	James Meredith attempts to attend University of Mississippi	Required federal intervention to uphold blacks' rights to attend public institutions.
1963	Effort to desegregate Birmingham, Alabama	Brutal response of police televised, sensitizing entire nation to plight of blacks.
	March on Washington	Gathered support and inspiration for the civil rights movement; scene of Martin Luther King's "I Have a Dream" speech
1964	Civil Rights Act	Outlawed racial discrimination in public accommodations.
1965	Voting Rights Act	Allowed federal examiners to register black voters where necessary.
1971	Busing decision	Supreme Court ruled that court-ordered desegration was constitutional, even if it employed busing.
1978	*Bakke* decision	Supreme Court declared that affirmative action was constitutional but that firm racial quotas were not.

"I have a dream," King declared, "that one day this nation will rise up and live out the true meaning of its creed: 'We hold these truths to be self-evident, that all men are created equal.' I have a dream that one day on the red hills of Georgia, the sons of former slaves and the sons of former slave-owners will be able to sit together at the table of brotherhood." It was a fervent appeal, and one to which the crowd responded. Each time King used the refrain "I have a dream," thousands of blacks and whites roared together. King concluded by quoting from an old hymn: "Free at last! Free at last! Thank God almighty, we are free at last!"

Despite the power of the rhetoric, not all listeners were moved. Anne Moody, who had come up from her activist work in Mississippi to attend the event, sat on the grass by the Lincoln Memorial as the speaker's words rang out. "Martin Luther King went on and on talking about his dream," she said. "I sat there thinking that . . . we never had time to sleep, much less dream." Nor was the Congress prompted to do much. Despite large Democratic majorities, strong southern resistance to the cause of civil rights remained, and as of November 1963, Kennedy's bill was still bottled up in committee. Not even the March on Washington had moved it along.

THE GREAT SOCIETY

Kennedy found that too often he had to bow to political realities. Real movement toward social goals came only when large congressional majorities allowed his successor, Lyndon Johnson, to use his considerable talents to pass programs intended to realize the "Great Society."

Assassination and Change in Command

Facing reelection in 1964, Kennedy hoped not only to win the presidency for a second term but also to increase Democratic strength in Congress. In November 1963, he traveled to Texas, where he hoped to unite the state's Democratic party for the upcoming election. Dallas, one of the stops on the trip, had a reputation as being less than cordial to the administration. Four weeks before, Adlai Stevenson, ambassador to the United Nations, had been abused there by a conservative mob. Now, on November 22, Kennedy had a chance to see for himself. Arriving at the airport, Henry González, a congressman accompanying the president in Texas, remarked jokingly, "Well, I'm taking my risks. I haven't got my steel vest yet." As the party entered the city in an open car, the president encountered friendly crowds. Suddenly shots rang out, and Kennedy slumped forward. Desperately wounded, he died a short time later at a Dallas hospital. Lee Harvey Oswald, the assassin, was himself shot and killed a few days later in the jail where he was being held.

Without warning, Lyndon Johnson was president of the United States. As vice-president, he had never been comfortable with the Kennedy crowd and had felt stifled in his subordinate role. He was, he knew, a far better legislative leader than JFK, but he was out of Congress in a position where he seemed to have no power.

Despite his own ambivalence about Kenne-

The assassination of Kennedy thrust Lyndon Johnson into the presidency amid an atmosphere of shocked grief and loss.

dy, Johnson understood the profound shock gripping the nation. Well aware that millions of Americans regarded him as a pretender to the throne, he embraced Kennedy's goals. Four days after he assumed office, he made his first public address. He began, in a measured tone, with the words, "All I have, I would have given gladly not to be standing here today." He asked members of Congress to work with him, and he underscored the theme "Let us continue" throughout his speech.

Johnson was determined to secure the measures that Kennedy sought but had been unable to extract from Congress. He took the bills to reduce taxes and ensure civil rights as his first and most pressing priorities, but he was interested too in aiding public education, providing medical care for the aged, and eliminating poverty. By the spring of 1964, the outlines of his own expansive vision were taking shape, and he had begun to use the phrase "Great Society" to describe his reform program. After a landslide victory over conservative Republican challenger Barry Goldwater in 1964, in which LBJ received 61 percent of the popular vote and an electoral margin of 486 to 52, he had a far more impressive mandate than Kennedy had ever enjoyed.

Civil Rights Under Johnson

Civil rights reform was LBJ's first legislative priority, although his own earlier record on the issue was mixed. A southerner from Texas, he first voted against a series of civil rights measures in his years in the House of Representatives, then became more sympathetic as his own career advanced and he recognized a larger constituency. By 1955, when he became Senate majority leader and eyed the White House, he was ready to play a much more active role. He broke with the South when he guided the Civil Rights Acts of 1957 through Congress. His commitment to racial justice was far stronger than Kennedy's. Indeed, Johnson had urged Kennedy to visit the South and to tell whites that segregation was evil and un-Christian.

In 1963, Johnson revived Kennedy's civil rights proposal, which had been sidetracked in Congress. Seizing the opportunity provided by Kennedy's assassination, Johnson told Congress, "No memorial oration or eulogy could more eloquently honor President Kennedy's memory than the earliest possible passage of the civil rights bill." Soon after he took office, he assured black leaders that he would push for the civil rights bill.

Johnson indicated that he would accept no compromise on civil rights. After the House of Representatives passed the bill, the Senate became bogged down in a lengthy filibuster. Johnson responded by persuading his old colleague, minority leader Everett Dirksen, to work for cloture—a two-thirds vote to cut off debate. In June 1964, the Senate for the first time imposed cloture to advance a civil rights measure, and passage soon followed. "No army can withstand the strength of an idea whose time has come," Dirksen commented.

The Civil Rights Act of 1964 outlawed racial discrimination in all public accommodations and authorized the Justice Department to act with greater authority in school and voting matters. In addition, an equal-opportunity provision prohibited discriminatory hiring on grounds of race, gender, religion, or national origin in firms with more than 25 employees. The legislation was one of the great achievements of the 1960s. The system of segregation put in place in the South in the late nineteenth century lost its legal sanctions. Blacks now were promised legal equality as they had been 100 years before.

Johnson realized that the Civil Rights Act of 1964 was a starting point, not the stopping point. Patent discrimination still existed in American society. Despite the voting rights measures of 1957 and 1960, blacks still found it difficult to vote in large areas of the South. Freedom Summer, sponsored by SNCC and other civil rights groups in Mississippi in 1964, focused attention on the problem by sending black and white students south to work for black rights. Early in the summer, two whites, Michael Schwerner and Andrew Goodman, and one black, James Chaney, were murdered. By the end of the summer, 80 workers had been beaten, 1,000 arrests had been made, and 37 churches had been bombed. The following year, Martin Luther King, Jr., proposed another march, this one from Selma to Montgomery, Alabama, to dramatize the situation.

Just a few days before the Selma march,

President Johnson addressed a joint session of Congress, with television cameras carrying the speech nationwide. Pleading for a voting bill that would close the loopholes of the previous two acts, he began by saying, "I speak tonight for the dignity of man and the destiny of democracy. . . . It is wrong . . . to deny any of your fellow Americans the right to vote." Stopping at one point and raising his arms, he slowly repeated the words from the old hymn that had become the marching song of the movement: "And . . . we . . . shall . . . overcome." The members of Congress responded with thunderous applause. Once again using all the pressure he could muster, he helped break a filibuster and signed a second civil rights measure into law.

The Voting Rights Act of 1965, perhaps the most important law of the decade, singled out the South for its restrictive practices and authorized the U.S. attorney general to appoint federal examiners to register voters where local officials were obstructing the registration of blacks. In the year after passage of the act, 400,000 blacks registered to vote in the Deep South; by 1968, the number reached a million.

The Great Society in Action

Had Johnson achieved nothing more than the two civil rights acts, his administration would have been notable. In fact, he accomplished much more. Under his prodding, Congress responded with the strongest legislative program since the New Deal. The president directed much of the activity. He appointed task forces that included legislators to study problems and suggest solutions, worked with them to draft bills, and maintained close contact with congressional leaders through a sophisticated liaison staff. Not since the Roosevelt years had there been such a coordinated effort to promote legislation.

Action followed in many areas. Following Kennedy's lead, Johnson pressed for a tax cut to stimulate the economy. To gain conservative support, he agreed to hold down spending; the tax bill passed. With the tax cut in hand, the president pressed for the poverty program that Kennedy had begun to plan. For the first time in

American history, the government developed a program specifically directed at ending poverty. As Johnson declared in his 1964 State of the Union message, "This administration today, here and now, declares unconditional war on poverty in America." The center of the effort to eradicate poverty was the Economic Opportunity Act of 1964. It created an Office of Economic Opportunity to provide education and training for unskilled young people trapped in the poverty cycle, VISTA (Volunteers in Service to America) to assist the poor at home, and assorted community-action programs to give the poor themselves a voice in improving housing, health, and education in their own neighborhoods.

The election of 1964 gave Johnson the mandate he needed to enact the rest of his program. Receiving 61 percent of the popular vote, he scored a clear victory over Republican Barry Goldwater with 486 electoral votes. With congressional majorities of 68–32 in the Senate and 295–140 in the House, Johnson broke the conservative Republican–Southern Democratic alignment that had hobbled reform programs in the past.

Aware of the escalating costs of medical care, Johnson proposed a medical assistance plan. Truman had proposed such a measure almost two decades before but had failed to win congressional approval. Nor had Kennedy accomplished anything in this area. Johnson, however, provided the necessary leadership. To head off conservative attacks, the administration tied the Medicare measure to the established social security system and limited the program to the elderly. Medicaid met the needs of the poor below the age of 65 who could not afford private insurance. The Medicare-Medicaid program was the most important extension of federally directed social benefits since the Social Security Act of 1935.

Johnson was similarly successful in his effort to provide aid for elementary and secondary schools. Kennedy had met defeat when Catholics had insisted on assistance to parochial schools. Johnson, a Protestant, was able to deal with that ticklish question without charges of favoritism. He endorsed a measure to give money to the states based on the numbers of children from low-income families. Those funds would then be distributed to public as well as private schools to benefit all needy children.

In LBJ's expansive vision, the federal government would ensure that all shared in the promise of American life. As a result of his prodding, Congress passed a new housing act to provide rent supplements to the poor and created a Department of Housing and Urban Development. It reformed the restrictive immigration policy, which for decades had rested on racial and national quotas, although immigration was still restricted in terms of numbers. It provided legal assistance for the poor. It moved further in funding education, including colleges and universities in its financial grants. Finally, Congress provided artists and scholars with assistance through new National Endowments for the Arts and Humanities. Not since the Works Progress Administration in the New Deal had such groups been granted government aid.

A Sympathetic Supreme Court

The Supreme Court also supported and promoted social change in the 1960s. Under the leadership of Chief Justice Earl Warren, the Court followed the lead it had taken in 1954 in *Brown* v. *Board of Education.* Several decisions reaffirmed the Court's support of black rights. Having disposed of the issue of school segregation, the Court moved against Jim Crow practices in other public establishments. Providing quick support for the Civil Rights Act of 1964 and the Voting Rights Act of 1965, the justices gave notice that the Court would no longer uphold discriminatory customs.

The Court also supported civil liberties. Where earlier judicial decisions had affirmed restrictions on members of the Communist party and radical groups, now the Court began to protect the rights of individuals who held radical political views. Similarly, the Court sought to protect accused suspects from police harassment. In *Gideon* v. *Wainwright* (1963) the justices decided that poor suspects had the right to free legal counsel. In *Escobedo* v. *Illinois* (1964) they ruled that an offender had to be given access to an attorney during questioning, while in *Miranda* v. *Arizona* (1966) they argued that

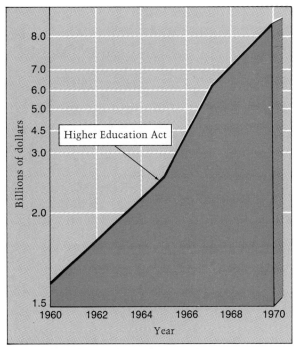

Federal Aid to Education in the 1960s
Source: U.S. Bureau of the Census.

offenders had to be warned that statements extracted by the police could be used against them and that they could remain silent.

Other decisions also broke new ground. *Baker* v. *Carr* (1962) opened the way to reapportionment of state legislative bodies, according to the standard, in Justice William O. Douglas's words, of "one person, one vote." Meanwhile, the Court ruled that prayer in the public schools was unconstitutional and decided that obscenity laws could no longer restrict allegedly pornographic material that might have some "redeeming social value."

The Great Society Under Attack

For a few years, the Great Society worked as Johnson had hoped. The tax cut proved effective. After its passage, GNP rose steadily, 7.1 percent in 1964, 8.1 percent in 1965, and 9.5 percent in 1966. At the same time, the budget deficit dropped. Unemployment fell, and inflation remained under control. Medical programs provided a measure of security for the old and the poor. Education flourished as schools were built,

Major Great Society Programs

DATE OF PASSAGE	PROGRAM	EFFECT
January 23, 1964 (ratified)	Twenty-fourth Amendment	Banned poll tax as prerequisite in federal elections.
February 26, 1964	Tax Reduction Act	Lowered federal personal tax rates.
July 2, 1964	Civil Rights Act	Banned discrimination in public accommodations; gave attorney general right to file suit to desegregate schools or other facilities; banned discrimination in employment on basis of race, color, religion, sex, or national origin.
July 9, 1964	Urban Mass Transportation Act	Provided $375 million in financial aid to urban-transit systems.
August 30, 1964	Economic Opportunity Act	Authorized ten separate programs to be conducted by the Office of Economic Opportunity, including Job Corps and VISTA.
September 3, 1964	Wilderness Preservation Act	Designate 9.1 million acres of national forest lands to be safeguarded permanently against commercial use and construction of permanent roads and buildings.
April 11, 1965	Elementary and Secondary Education Act	Provided $1.3 billion in aid to elementary and secondary schools.
July 30, 1965	Medicare	Provided medical care for the aged through the social security system.
August 6, 1965	Voting Rights Act	Suspended literacy tests and other voter tests; authorized federal supervision of registration in states and districts where few voting-age residents had voted earlier.
August 10, 1965	Omnibus Housing Act	Provided rent supplements to low-income families and federal aid to place low-income persons in private housing.
September 9, 1965	Department of Housing and Urban Development	Provided special programs concerned with housing needs, fair-housing opportunities, and the improvement and development of communities.
September 9, 1965	National Foundation of the Arts and Humanities	Provided financial assistance for painters, actors, dancers, musicians, and others in the arts.
October 2, 1965	Water Quality Act	Required states to establish and enforce water quality standards for all interstate waters within their boundaries.
October 3, 1965	Immigration laws	Revision set new quotas.
October 20, 1965	Air Quality Act	Amended earlier laws.
October 20, 1965	Higher Education Act	Provided federal scholarships to undergraduates and others.
September 9, 1966	National Traffic and Motor Vehicle Safety Act	Set federal safety standards.
September 9, 1966	Highway Safety Act	Required states to set up federally approved safety programs.
September 23, 1966	Minimum wage	Raised minimum wage from $1.25 to $1.40 per hour; extended coverage.
October 15, 1966	Department of Transportation	Provided federal agencies to administer policies, in conjuction with state and local officials, regarding highway planning, development, and construction; urban mass transit; railroads; aviation; and safety of waterways, ports, highways; and oil and gas pipelines.
November 3, 1966	Model Cities	Encouraged rehabilitation of slums.

and salaries increased in response to the influx of federal aid.

Yet the gains proved short-lived. Some programs promised too much, and disillusionment followed when they failed to meet expectations. Often the criticisms that surfaced had been heard from the start. Conservatives were uneasy about centralization of authority as they saw government take over more of the responsibility for defining the national welfare. They also worried about involving the poor themselves, for they argued that recipients of aid often lacked a broad vision of the nation's needs.

More incisive were the criticisms from the left. Radicals claimed that the Great Society was a warmed-over version of the New Deal three decades before. The same middle-class liberal orientation remained, with the real intent of programs to provide the poor with middle-class values. "The welfare state is more machinery than substance," young critic Tom Hayden charged. No real effort had been made to redistribute income. Great Society programs rested on the belief that the American system was basically sound and that economic growth, not the redistribution of wealth, would secure the benefits of the American dream for all. Nor was enough money allocated to the new social programs. Though several billion dollars were spent before the Vietnam War drew off resources and disrupted the economy, even that was not enough to meet the needs of 30 or 40 million disadvantaged people. As Michael Harrington concluded, "What was supposed to be a social war turned out to be a skirmish and, in any case, poverty won."

Black Power Challenges Liberal Reform

Nowhere were criticisms more pronounced than in the area of civil rights. There as elsewhere, expectations had been raised, but many blacks still saw fundamental inequalities in American life and vociferously declared their unwillingness to wait any longer for reform. The civil rights movement initially had been an integrated, nonviolent campaign with Martin Luther King, Jr., as its acknowledged leader. But now black-white tensions began to appear within organizations, and the dominance of King's nonviolent approach ended. More militant spokesmen articulated a long-suppressed rage in language that often shocked white liberals.

Anne Moody, the stalwart activist in Mississippi, voiced some of the doubts so many blacks felt about the possibility of real change. Tired and discouraged after months of struggle, on one occasion she boarded a bus taking civil rights workers north to testify about the abuses that still remained. As she listened to the others singing the movement's songs, she could only think of the suffering she had so often seen. "We Shall Overcome" reverberated around her, but all she could think was, "I WONDER. I really WONDER."

One episode that contributed to a black sense of betrayal by white liberals occurred at the Democratic National Convention of 1964 in Atlantic City. SNCC, active in the Freedom Summer project in Mississippi, had founded a Freedom Democratic party as an alternative to the all-white delegation that was to represent the state. Before the credentials committee, black activist Fannie Lou Hamer testified that she had been beaten, jailed, and denied the right to vote. Yet the committee's final compromise was that the white delegation would still be seated, with two members of the protest organization offered seats at large. That response hardly satisfied those who had risked their lives and families to try to vote in Mississippi. As civil rights leader James Forman observed, "Atlantic City was a powerful lesson, not only for the black people from Mississippi, but for all of SNCC. . . . No longer was there any hope . . . that the federal government would change the situation in the Deep South." SNCC, once a religious, integrated organization, began to change into an all-black cadre that could mobilize poor blacks for militant action.

Increasingly, angry blacks argued that something was going to have to give. In *The Fire Next Time* (1962), James Baldwin, a prominent black author, wrote of the "rope, fire, torture, castration, infanticide, rape; death and humiliation; fear by day and night, fear as deep as the marrow of the bone" that were part of the black past. "For the horrors of the American Negro's life," he declared, "there has been almost no language." Unless change came soon, the worst could be expected: "If we do not now dare everything, the fulfillment of that prophecy, recreated from the Bible in song by a slave, is upon us: *God gave Noah the rainbow sign, No more water, the fire next time!"*

Even more responsible for focusing aggressive black sentiment was Malcolm X. Born Malcolm Little and raised in ghettos from Detroit to New York, he became intimately familiar with the sordid side of black urban life. In his preconversion days, he wore a zoot suit, conked his hair, and hustled numbers and prostitutes in the big cities. Only when he was arrested did he begin to question his past. In prison, he became a convert to the Nation of Islam and a disciple of black leader Elijah Muhammad. He began to preach that the white man was responsible for the black man's condition and that blacks had to help themselves.

Malcolm had little use for the moderate civil rights movement represented by SNCC and Martin Luther King. He grew tired of hearing "all of this nonviolent, begging-the-white-man kind of dying . . . all of this sitting-in, sliding-in, wading-in, eating-in, diving-in, and all the rest." The March on Washington he termed the "Farce on Washington." Arguing in favor of black sepa-

"The day of nonviolence is over," proclaimed Malcolm X; many poor blacks listened enthusiastically.

ration from the white race for most of his public career, he urged blacks to take care of themselves. He appealed to blacks to fight racism "by any means necessary" and insisted that the "day of nonviolent resistance is over."

Malcolm's articulate affirmation of blackness and his justification of self-defense struck a resonant chord. With widespread media attention, he became the most dynamic spokesman for poor blacks since Marcus Garvey in the 1920s. Though he was assassinated by a black antagonist in 1965, his perspective helped shape the ongoing struggle against racism.

One man influenced by Malcolm's message was Stokely Carmichael. Born in Trinidad, he came to the United States at the age of 11 and became an American. Because his family remained involved in the black nationalist independence movement in the Caribbean, Carmichael grew up with an interest in political affairs. At the Bronx High School of Science he read voraciously, attended left-wing meetings, became interested in socialism, and gravitated into black protest. Aware of civil rights activity at predominantly black Howard University in Washington, D.C., he went there for college. Soon after arriving at Howard, he and other students took over the Washington chapter of SNCC. He participated in pickets and demonstrations and was beaten and jailed. Frustrated with the strategy of civil disobedience, he urged fieldworkers to carry weapons for self-defense. It was time for blacks to cease depending on whites, he argued, and to make SNCC into a black organization. His election as head of SNCC in 1966 reflected the movement's shifting course.

The split in the black movement became clear in June 1966 when Carmichael's followers challenged those of Martin Luther King at a demonstration. King still adhered to nonviolence and to interracial cooperation. Their movement's song, "We Shall Overcome," was drowned out by Carmichael's followers' song, "We Shall Overrun." The turning point came when Carmichael, just out of jail, jumped onto a flatbed truck to address the group. "This is the twenty-seventh time I have been arrested—and I ain't going to jail no more!" he shouted. "The only way we gonna stop them white men from whippin' us is to take over. We been saying freedom for six years and we ain't got nothing. What we gonna start saying now is Black Power!'' Carmichael had the audience in his hand. As he repeated, ''We . . . want . . . Black . . . Power!'' the crowd roared back the same words.

Meanwhile, other blacks proposed more drastic action. Huey Newton of the Black Panthers, another militant organization that vowed to eradicate not only racial discrimination but capitalism as well, proclaimed that ''political power comes through the barrel of a gun.'' H. Rap Brown, who followed Carmichael as head of SNCC, became known for his statement that ''violence is as American as cherry pie.''

Violence accompanied the more militant calls for reform and showed that racial injustice was not a southern problem but an American one. In the North, blacks faced informal segregation, poverty, and inferior housing and schools.

Many were unwilling to wait quietly for their lives to improve. Riots erupted in Rochester, New York City, and several New Jersey cities in 1964. In 1965, in the Watts neighborhood of Los Angeles, a massive uprising lasting five days left 34 dead, more than 1,000 injured, and hundreds of structures burned to the ground. Violence broke out again in other cities in 1966 and again in 1967. Now cries of ''Get Whitey'' and ''Burn, baby, burn'' replaced the nonviolence of the earlier civil rights movement. Martin Luther King, Jr., fell before a white assassin's bullet in April 1968. Angry blacks reacted by demonstrating once more in cities around the country. As the National Advisory Commission on Civil Disobedience noted in the Kerner Report of 1968, ''The nation is rapidly moving toward two increasingly separate Americas.'' Black protest highlighted inequities and dramatized the inadequacy of white liberal reform.

THE RISING CALL FOR REFORM

Blacks were not the only Americans to demand justice and to decry racism. Native Americans and Hispanic-Americans also pressed for change, while women became increasingly militant and better organized in their efforts to eliminate sexism in America.

Tribal Voices

Native Americans continued to suffer second-class status as the 1960s began. They had endured the termination policy of the Eisenhower years, when the federal government embarked on a program of urban relocation aimed at forcing them to assimilate into mainstream American life. That effort had worked poorly, as thousands of Native Americans traded reservation poverty for urban poverty. In 1961, the United States Commission on Civil Rights observed that for Indians, ''poverty and deprivation are common. Social acceptance is not the rule. In addition, Indians seem to suffer more than occasional mistreatment by the instruments of law and order on and off the reservations.'' Indians, in short, faced obstacles much like those blacks encountered.

As the Indian population grew from 550,000 in 1960 to 790,000 in 1970, Democratic administrations abandoned Eisenhower's termination policy and tried to give Native Americans a greater voice in their own affairs. Many tribes,

Poverty and discrimination marked the daily lives of most Native Americans, both on reservations and in mainstream urban communities.

however, still protested what they called the federal government's "colonial rule."

Led by a new generation of leaders, Native Americans tried to protect what was left of their tribal lands. Elders reminded young people, "Once we owned all the land." For generations, federal and state governments had steadily encroached on Native American territory. "Everything is tied to our homeland," D'Arcy McNickle, a Flathead anthropologist, told other Indians in 1961 as they started to organize.

The new activism was apparent on the Seneca Nation's Allegany reservation in New York State. Although the Seneca's right to the land was established by a treaty made in 1794, the federal government had planned since 1928 to build the Kinzua Dam there as part of a flood-control project. Surveys were taken, but for years little was done. In 1956, after hearings to which the Indians were not invited and about which they were not informed, Congress appropriated funds for the project. When court appeals failed to block the scheme, the Seneca turned to President Kennedy in 1961. Kennedy, however, supported the government's right to take the land it had promised not to take in 1794. The dam was eventually built, and although the government belatedly passed a $15 million reparations bill, money did not compensate for the loss of 10,000 acres of land that contained sacred sites, hunting and fishing grounds, and homes.

Native American leaders then brought a wave of lawsuits charging violations of treaty rights. In 1967, in the first of many decisions upholding the Indian side, the U.S. Court of Claims ruled that the government had forced the Seminole in Florida to cede their land in 1823 for an unreasonably low price. The court directed the government to pay additional funds 144 years later. That decision was a source of some satisfaction to the Seminole population, although the compensation had not yet been paid by 1982.

The most dramatic displays of the new Native American militancy began with the founding of the American Indian Movement (AIM) in 1968. Organized by George Mitchell and Dennis Banks, Chippewa living in Minneapolis, AIM sought to help neglected Indians in the city. It managed to get Office of Economic Opportunity funds channeled to Indian-controlled organiza-tions. It also established patrols to protect drunken Indians from harassment by the police. As its successes became known, chapters formed in other cities.

César Chávez and the United Farm Workers

Hispanic-Americans also became actively involved in efforts to gain their share of the American dream. Some were Puerto Ricans living in the Northeast; others were Cubans settling mainly in Florida. Many more were Mexican-Americans, who lived in the Southwest and called themselves Chicanos in California and Tejanos in Texas. In these names they expressed more ardently a sense of solidarity and group pride. In 1960, just under 3.5 million people with Spanish surnames lived in the Southwest. Their per capita income was half that of Anglos, and their social and cultural separation was reinforced by inferior education and political weakness.

With Johnson's poverty program, Mexican-Americans hoped for improved opportunities. But they soon found that most efforts were oriented toward black Americans and that bureaucrats were often less sensitive to the problems of equally exploited but less vocal groups. From this they learned the value of pressure politics in a pluralistic society. In the election of 1960, Mexican-Americans supported Kennedy, helping him win Texas. In 1961, Henry B. González was elected to Congress from San Antonio. Three years later, Elizo ("Kika") de la Garza of Texas won election to the House and Joseph Montoya of New Mexico went to the Senate. Chicanos were gaining a political voice and began to anticipate the day when it could help them improve their lives.

More important than political representation, which came only slowly, was direct action. César Chávez, founder of the United Farm Workers, proved what could be done by organizing one of the most exploited and ignored groups of laboring people in the country, the migrant farm workers of the West. Born in Yuma, Arizona, Chávez went to California in the 1940s. There he acquired organizational skills. Two decades later, he established his own union, the United Farm Workers. Concentrating on migrant Mexican fieldhands who worked long hours in the fields for meager pay, he chose a loyal cadre to conduct a door-to-door and field-to-field campaign. By 1965, his organization had recruited 1,700 members and was beginning to attract volunteer help. His intent was to present the farm workers' struggle as part of the larger national struggle for civil rights.

Chávez first took on the grape growers of California. Calling the grape workers out on strike, the union demanded better pay and working conditions as well as the recognition of the union. When the growers did not concede, Chávez launched a nationwide consumer boycott of their products. Although the Schenley Corporation and several wine companies came to terms, others held out. In 1966, the DiGiorgio Corporation agreed to permit a union election but then rigged the results. When California governor Edmund G. Brown launched an investigation that resulted in another election, he became the first major political figure to support the long

Migrant Mexican field hands were organized by César Chávez who led their fight for better pay and working conditions.

powerless Chicano fieldhands. This time the United Farm Workers won.

Chávez himself became a national figure. Stories about him ran in the *Wall Street Journal,* *Life,* and *Time.* Robert Kennedy befriended him and helped rally support by visiting him and his strikers in the fields. When Kennedy was assassinated in 1968, Chicanos believed they had lost their best ally. But Chávez continued to inspire other Mexican-Americans. Soon, militant groups like the Young Citizens for Community Action and the Brown Berets were operating in numerous cities.

Attacking the Feminine Mystique

The women's movement, like the Mexican-American and Native American movements, had roots in the civil rights activity of the 1950s and 1960s. Women involved in civil rights agitation discovered that men, black and white, held the policy positions, while women were relegated to menial chores when not actually involved in demonstrations or voter drives. Many women also felt sexually exploited by the men with whom they worked. Stokely Carmichael's comment only underscored their point. "The only position for women in SNCC," he said, "is prone." Despite growing dissatisfaction and their awareness of sexual exploitation, the women recognized the importance of militant, well-publicized pressure groups in bringing about change.

Although the civil rights movement supplied some of the impetus behind the women's movement, broad social changes provided the preconditions. During the 1950s and 1960s, increasing numbers of married women entered the labor force, and half of all women worked. Cries for fair treatment arose from some of them. In 1963, the average working woman earned only 63 percent of what a man could expect, in 1973, only 57 percent. Just as important, many more young women were attending college. By 1970, women earned 41 percent of all B.A.'s awarded, in comparison to only 25 percent in 1950. These educated young women held high hopes for themselves. Many found that sexual liberation failed to bring equality. They would find feminism compelling both in its analysis of women's problems and in the solutions it offered.

Just as in the civil rights movement, reform legislation led the effort to end sexual discrimination. Title 7 of the 1964 Civil Rights bill, as originally drafted, prohibited discrimination on the grounds of race. During legislative debate, conservatives opposed to black civil rights proposed an amendment to include discrimination on the basis of gender. In this way, they hoped to defeat the entire bill. But the amendment passed, giving women a legal tool for attacking discrimination. They discovered, however, that the Equal Employment Opportunities Commission regarded women's complaints of discrimination as far less important than those of blacks.

When a small group of women failed to win support from existing women's groups to pressure the commission to change its policies, they decided to form their own civil rights organization. In 1966, 28 professional women, including Betty Friedan, established the National Organization for Women (NOW) "to take action to bring American women into full participation in the mainstream of American society *now.*" By full participation the founders not only meant fair pay and equal opportunity but a new, more egalitarian form of marriage. NOW also attacked "the false image of women now prevalent in the media." By 1967, some 1,000 women had joined the organization, and four years later, its membership reached 15,000.

NOW was a political pressure group and did not seem radical enough to some young women. The radical feminists, who had come up through the civil rights movement, felt that NOW's

Women Working Outside the Home, 1890–1970

Source: U.S. Bureau of the Census.

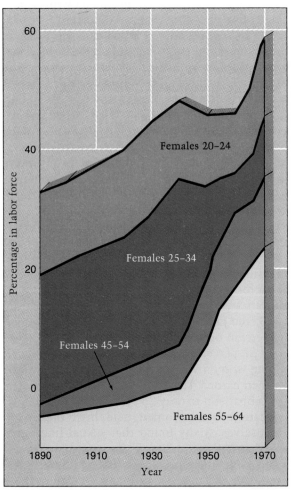

Awareness of racial discrimination led to women's speaking out against unequal opportunity based on sex, as in this advertisement sponsored by the National Organization for Women.

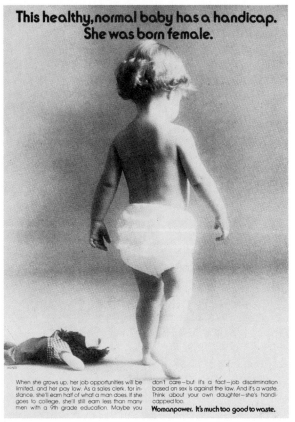

agenda did not adequately confront the problem of gender discrimination. They sought to make women understand the extent of their oppression through the technique of consciousness raising. Soon used by other radical groups, con-sciousness raising encouraged women to analyze "a women's experience at the hands of men as a *political* phenomenon," as writer Susan Brownmiller explained.

INTENSIFICATION OF THE COLD WAR

While activists challenged inequities and contradictions in American life, the nation remained locked in confrontation abroad. Kennedy and Johnson both saw the world in Cold War terms, just as their predecessors had, and perceived threats by Communists in near and far corners of the globe. Their responses to overseas Communist actions increased America's web of foreign entanglements and led to war in Vietnam. The opposition to that war helped to shatter the Cold War consensus at home.

John Kennedy entered office interested above all in foreign policy and determined to stand firm in the face of the Russian threat. Despite all the talk about a New Frontier, most of his foreign policy ideas were old. During the campaign, Kennedy declared: "The enemy is the communist system itself—implacable, insatiable, unceasing in its drive for world domination." In his inaugural address, he dramatically described the dangers and challenges the United States faced. "In the long history of the world," he cried out, "only a few generations have been granted the role of defending freedom in its hour of maximum danger." The United States would "Pay any price, bear any burden, meet any hardship, support any friend, oppose any foe, to assure the survival and success of liberty." Under Kennedy, the space program was expanded in an effort to meet Russian challenges in space. In 1962, the first American, John Glenn, orbited the earth. Kennedy promised that within ten years an American would land on the moon. His promise was realized a mere seven years later.

Kennedy's most imaginative approach to the Cold War involved the promotion of "peaceful revolution" in unaligned Third World countries. By providing nonmilitary assistance programs that increased agricultural productivity and built modern transportation and communica-tions systems, Kennedy hoped to promote stable and pro-Western governments throughout Latin America, Africa, and Asia. The Peace Corps, established in 1961, was a part of this approach. Under its auspices, thousands of idealistic volunteers spent two-year terms as teachers, health workers, sanitation engineers, and agricultural advisers in dozens of developing nations.

Such attempts at "nation building" often brought medical care, schools, and sanitation to isolated villages in Third World countries. Much of the economic aid, however, disappeared in administration costs or ended up in the hands of local elites. Moreover, acceptance of American values and forms of enterprise rarely took hold simply because of the presence of Peace Corps volunteers.

Confrontations in Cuba and Berlin

While attempts to promote social progress and pro-American governments in developing nations went forward, Kennedy faced direct challenges from the Soviet Union almost from the beginning of his presidency. The first came at the Bay of Pigs in the spring of 1961. Cuban-American relations had been strained since Fidel Castro's revolutionary army had overthrown the dictatorial Fulgencio Batista, a longtime American ally, in 1959. As Castro expropriated private property of major American corporations, which for decades had dominated the Cuban economy, the United States became increasingly concerned. More than simply economic issues were involved. American officials were convinced that a radical regime in Cuba that was leaning toward the Soviet Union provided a model for upheaval elsewhere in Latin America and threatened the venerable Monroe Doctrine.

Just before Kennedy assumed office, the United States broke diplomatic relations with

Cuba. The CIA, meanwhile, was covertly training anti-Castro exiles to storm the Cuban coast at the Bay of Pigs. The American planners assumed the invasion would lead to an uprising of the Cuban people against Castro. When Kennedy learned of the plan, he approved it. The plan was bold and offered the kind of challenge that Kennedy thought would prove his toughness. He overruled the opposition of Senator J. William Fullbright, chairman of the Foreign Relations Committee, who argued that "the Castro regime is a thorn in the flesh; but it is not a dagger in the heart." Nor did he listen to the objection of marine commandant David Shoup, who claimed that Cuba could not be taken easily.

The invasion, on April 17, 1961, was an unmitigated disaster. Castro was able to keep troops from coming ashore, and there was no popular uprising to greet the invaders. The United States stood exposed in the eyes of the world for attempting to overthrow a sovereign government. It had broken agreements not to interfere in the internal affairs of hemispheric neighbors and had intervened clumsily and unsuccessfully.

Although chastened by the debacle at the Bay of Pigs, Kennedy remained determined to deal sternly with the perceived Communist threat. On meeting Soviet leader Nikita Khrushchev in Vienna, in June 1961, he felt cornered on the question of Berlin. The Russians were pressing for a settlement that would reflect the reality of the city's division into eastern and western zones in the aftermath of World War II and prevent the flight of East Germans to the West. Fearful that the Soviet effort signaled designs on the Continent as a whole, Kennedy sought $3 billion more in defense appropriations, more men for the armed forces, and funds for a civil defense fallout shelter program, as if to warn of the possibility of nuclear war. After the Russians erected a wall in Berlin to seal off their section, the crisis eased. But Kennedy felt he had overreacted. Sensitive to his image as world leader, he believed he had come off second-best in the struggle.

The Cuban Missile Crisis

The next year, Kennedy had a chance to recoup some of his lost prestige, though again at the risk of war. Fearful of American designs on Cuba, Castro had secured Russian assistance. According to American aerial photographs of October 1962, the Soviet Union had begun to place offensive missiles on Cuban soil. The missiles did not change the strategic balance significantly, for the Soviets could still wreak untold damage on American targets from bases farther away, and American missiles stood on the borders of the Soviet Union in Turkey. But with Russian weapons installed just 90 miles from American shores, appearance was more important than strategic balance. Kennedy was determined to confront the Russians (not the Cubans) and win.

Meeting with top staff members, the president went over the alternatives, ruling out an air strike to knock out the missile sites. He moved nonetheless to a position of full alert. Bombers and missiles were fueled, armed with nuclear weapons, and readied to go. The fleet prepared to move, and troops stood set to invade. Kennedy himself went on nationwide TV to tell the American people about the missiles and to demand their removal. He declared that the United States would not shrink from the risk of nuclear war and announced a naval blockade around Cuba to prevent Soviet ships from bringing in additional missiles. He called the move a quarantine, for a blockade was an act of war.

As the Soviet ships steamed toward the blockade, and the nations stood "eyeball to eyeball" at the brink, the American and Russian people held their breath. Americans, on the one hand, applauded the president and accepted the situation in the terms he had defined. On the other hand, they feared a cataclysmic confrontation that could bring the world to an end.

After several days, the tension broke, but only because Khrushchev called the Russian ships back and then sent a long letter to Kennedy pledging to remove the missiles if the United States ended the blockade and promising to stay out of Cuba altogether. A second letter demanded that America remove its missiles from Turkey as well. The United States responded affirmatively to the first letter, ignored the second, and said nothing about its intention, already voiced, of removing its own missiles from Turkey. With that the crisis ended.

The Cuban missile crisis was the most terrifying confrontation of the Cold War. Kennedy had led the world closer to nuclear war than it had ever been. The president emerged from the crisis as a hero who had stood firm. His reputation was enhanced, as was the image of his party in the coming congressional elections. Yet as the relief of the moment began to fade, critics charged that what Kennedy saw as his finest hour was in fact an unnecessary crisis. Though Kennedy had shown some restraint in not authorizing an air attack, he had neglected normal channels of diplomacy and had moved precariously close to the brink. He had avoided disaster only, as Dean Acheson observed, by "plain dumb luck," when the Russians showed restraint. One consequence of the affair was the establishment of a Soviet-American hot line to avoid similar episodes in the future. Another was Russia's determination to increase its nuclear arsenal so that it would never again be exposed as inferior to the United States.

The Vietnam Quagmire

In another part of the world, neither Kennedy nor his successor proved as fortunate in avoiding armed conflict. In Southeast Asia, the United States almost entered Laos in the spring of 1961 to head off Communist influence. In Vietnam, however, America refused to maintain such neutrality. There, Vietnamese leader Ho Chi Minh continued his struggle to liberate his land in what had become a bitter civil war (see Chapter 27).

Unsympathetic to Ho's regime in North Vietnam, the United States steadily increased its support to South Vietnam. By the time Eisenhower left the presidency in 1961, some 675 American military advisers were assisting the South Vietnamese. After the Bay of Pigs, Kennedy decided to increase that level of assistance. Not only advisers, however, went to South Vietnam. American troops began to be sent there, and by the end of 1963, over 16,000 Americans were engaged in the war.

Despite American backing, South Vietnamese leader Ngo Dinh Diem was rapidly losing support within his own country. Buddhist priests burned themselves alive in the capital of Saigon to dramatize Diem's unpopularity. American officials began to realize that Diem would never reform. After receiving assurances that the United States would not object to an internal coup, South Vietnamese military leaders assassinated Diem and seized the government.

As he considered the situation in Vietnam, Kennedy faced a dilemma. He understood the importance of popular support for the South Vietnamese government if that country were to maintain its independence. But he was reluctant to withdraw and let the Vietnamese solve their own problems. When Kennedy met with a violent death shortly after Diem's assassination, Lyndon Johnson faced a situation in flux in Vietnam.

Johnson shared many of Kennedy's assumptions about the threat of communism. His understanding of the past led him to believe that aggressors had to be stopped or their actions would lead to world war, as had been true in World War II. Like Kennedy, Johnson believed in the domino theory, which held that if one country in a region fell, others were bound to follow.

In office, Johnson was determined to defend American interests from communism. Often

In an extreme demonstration of disapproval, a Buddhist monk burns himself alive to protest the American-backed Diem government.

frustrated by what he called those "piddly little pissant" countries, he involved himself in a small crisis in Panama over the question of which flag—the American or the Panamanian—should fly in the Canal Zone. In the Dominican Republic, the issue was more serious. In 1965, he sent 20,000 troops to help buttress a military junta. His flimsy claims about the threat of communism and the importance of protecting American tourists created a wedge between his administration and liberals.

That wedge would widen over the question of Vietnam. Though Kennedy had expanded the American commitment there, Johnson took the Vietnam War and made it his own. Soon after assuming office, he reached a fundamental decision that guided policy for the next four years. South Vietnam was more unstable than ever after the assassination of Diem. Guerrillas, known as Viet Cong, challenged the regime, sometimes covertly, sometimes through the National Liberation Front, their political arm. Aided by Ho Chi Minh and the North Vietnamese, the insurgent Viet Cong slowly gained ground. Henry Cabot Lodge, the American ambassador to South Vietnam, told Johnson that if he wanted to save that country, and indeed the whole region, he had to stand firm. "I am not going to lose Vietnam," Johnson replied. "I am not going to be the President who saw Southeast Asia go the way China went."

In the election campaign of 1964, Johnson posed as a man of peace. "We don't want our American boys to do the fighting for Asian boys," he declared. "We are not going to send American boys nine or ten thousand miles away from home to do what Asian boys ought to be doing for themselves." He criticized those who suggested moving in with American bombs. All the while, however, he was planning to increase American involvement in the war.

In August 1964, Johnson cleverly obtained congressional authorization for the war. North Vietnamese torpedo boats, he announced, had, without provocation, attacked American destroyers in the international waters of the Gulf of Tonkin, 30 miles from North Vietnam. Only later did it become clear that the American ships had violated the territorial waters of North Vietnam by assisting South Vietnamese commando

raids in offshore combat zones. With the details of the attack still unclear, Johnson used the episode to obtain from Congress a resolution giving him authority to "take all necessary measures to repel any armed attack against the forces of the United States and to prevent further aggression." Not aware that the president had been carrying the resolution around for some time, Congress passed it by a vote of 416 to

The Vietnam War

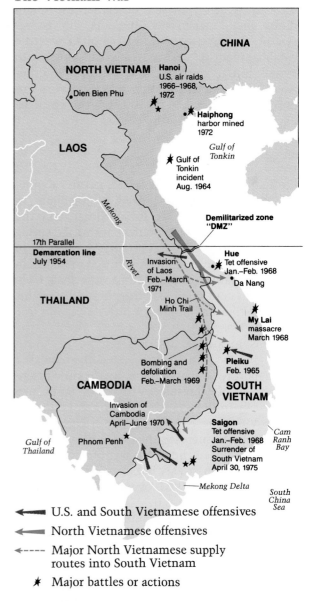

◀━━ U.S. and South Vietnamese offensives

◀━━ North Vietnamese offensives

◀---- Major North Vietnamese supply routes into South Vietnam

✹ Major battles or actions

0 in the House and 88 to 2 in the Senate. It gave Johnson the leverage he sought. As he noted, it was "like grandma's nightshirt—it covered everything."

Military escalation began in earnest in February 1965, after Viet Cong forces killed 7 Americans and wounded 109 in an attack on an American base at Pleiku. Johnson responded by authorizing retaliatory bombing of North Vietnam to cut off the flow of supplies and to ease pressure on South Vietnam. At the same time, the president sent American ground troops into action. Only 25,000 American soldiers were in Vietnam at the start of 1965. By the end of the year, there were 184,000, and the number swelled to 385,000 in 1966, 485,000 in 1967, 500,000 in 1968. "Remember, escalation begets escalation," Senator Mike Mansfield futilely warned the president in mid-1965.

Massive amounts of American supplies and personnel changed the character of the conflict. No longer simply military advisers in Southeast Asia, American forces became direct participants in the fight to prop up a dictatorial regime in faraway South Vietnam. Although a more effective government headed by Nguyen Van Thieu and Nguyen Cao Ky was finally established, the level of violence increased. Saturation bombing of North Vietnam continued. Fragmentation bombs, killing and maiming countless civilians, and napalm, which seared

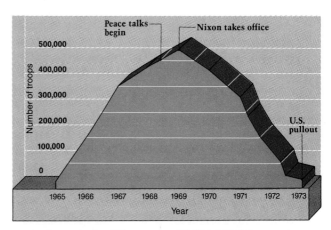

U.S. Troops in Vietnam, 1965–1973
Source: U.S. Department of Defense.

off human flesh, were used extensively. Similar destruction wracked South Vietnam. Yet the North Vietnamese and their revolutionary allies in South Vietnam pressed on. Like LBJ, they sought not compromise but victory.

In early 1968, the North Vietnamese mounted the massive Tet offensive, attacking provincial capitals and district towns in South Vietnam. In Saigon, they struck the American embassy, Tan Son Nhut air base, and the presidential palace. Though beaten back, they won a psychological victory. American audiences, tuned to the television for nightly reports, came to realize that the war perhaps could not be won.

UPHEAVAL AT HOME

As the American people became more deeply involved in revolutionary struggles abroad that never brought the promised victories, they also experienced the disruption of their own society. Different groups clamored for greater access to the American dream. Rejecting the stable patterns of affluent life that their parents had forged in the decade before, some young middle-class Americans embraced radical political activity; many more adopted new standards of music and dress. A sexual revolution accompanied a drug revolution, leading some Americans to believe that society itself was collapsing.

The Roots of Change

The demographic patterns of the post–World War II years lay behind youthful activism and helped explain the generation gap. Members of the baby boom generation came of age in the 1960s, and many more of them, especially from the large middle class, moved on to some form of higher education than in any previous generation. Between 1950 and 1964, the number of students in college more than doubled. By the end of the 1960s, college enrollment was more than four times what it had been in the 1940s.

In the last 30 years, television has played an increasingly important part in American life, providing historians with another source of evidence about American culture and society in the recent past.

Television's popularity by the 1950s was the result of decades of experimentation dating back to the nineteenth century. In the 1930s, NBC installed a television station in the new Empire State Building in New York. With green makeup and purple lipstick to provide better visual contrast, actors began to perform before live cameras in studios. At the end of the decade, "Amos 'n' Andy," a popular radio show, was telecast, and as the 1940s began, Franklin D. Roosevelt became the first president to appear on television. World War II interrupted the development of television as Americans relied on radio to bring them news from abroad. In the aftermath of the war, however, the commercial development of television quickly resumed. Assembly lines that had made electronic implements of war were now converted to consumer production, and thousands of new sets appeared on the market. The opening of Congress could be seen live in 1947; baseball coverage improved that same year due to the adaptation of the zoom lens; children's shows like "Howdy Doody" and "Kukla, Fran, and Ollie" made their debut; and "Meet the Press," a radio interview program, made the transition to television.

Although sports programs, variety shows hosted by Ed Sullivan and Milton Berle, TV dramas, and episodic series ("I Love Lucy" and "Gunsmoke," for example) dominated TV broadcasting in the 1950s, television soon became entwined with politics and public affairs. Americans saw Senator Joseph McCarthy for themselves in the televised Army-McCarthy hearings in 1954; his malevolent behavior on camera contributed to his downfall. The 1948 presidential nominating conventions were the first to be televised, but the use of TV to enhance the public image of politicians was most thoroughly developed by the fatherly Dwight D. Eisenhower and the charismatic John F. Kennedy. Some argue that the televised debate in 1960 between the tanned, handsome Kennedy and a pasty white Richard Nixon helped elect Kennedy.

In 1963, a horrified public watched as officials used snarling police dogs and thunderous fire hoses on peaceful marchers in the Birmingham civil rights demonstrations, thus arousing public opinion against southern resistance. And people throughout the United States shared the tragedy of John Kennedy's assassination in November 1963, sitting stunned before their sets trying to understand the events of his fateful Texas trip. The shock and sorrow of the American people was repeated in the spring of 1968 as they watched the funerals of Martin Luther King and Robert Kennedy. A year later, a quarter of the world's population watched as Neil Armstrong became the first man to set foot on the moon. Whether depicting tragedies or triumphs, few Americans complained when these television news spectaculars pushed popular series such as "Bonanza," "The Beverly Hillbillies," "I Spy," and "Dr. Kildare" off the screen.

TELEVISION TONIGHT

6:30—WTTV **4**: Leave It to Beaver. Beaver tries to help a friend who has run away from home. Repeat.

6:30—WLW-I **13**: Cheyenne has a Laramie adventure in which Slim, Jess and Jonesy work on a cattle drive. Repeat.

7:30—WTTV **4**: The Untouchables. Eliot Ness tries to deal with a late gangster's niece who has a record of the murdered hood's career. Repeat.

7:30—WLW-I **13**: Voyage to the Bottom of the Sea presents "Mutiny," in which Admiral Nelson shows signs of a mental breakdown during the search for a giant jellyfish which supposedly consumed a submarine.

7:30—WFBM-TV **6**: Members of the Indianapolis Rotary Club discuss the 1965 business outlook with former U.S. Sen. Homer Capehart.

8:00—WFBM-TV **6**: The Man From UNCLE is in at a new time and night. Thrush agents try to recapture one of their leaders before Napoleon Solo can deliver him to the Central Intelligence Agency. Ralph Taeger is guest star.

8:00—WISH-TV **8**: I've Got a Secret welcomes the panel from To Tell the Truth: Tom Poston, Peggy Cass, Kitty Carlisle and Orson Bean.

8:30—WLW-I **13**: Basketball, I.U. vs. Iowa.

8:30—WISH-TV **8**: Andy Griffith's comedy involves Goober's attempts to fill in at the sheriff's office.

9:00—WFBM-TV **6**: Andy Williams is visited by composer Henry Mancini, Bobby Darin and Vic Damone. Musical selections include "Charade," "Hello Dolly" and "Moon River."

9:00—WTTV **4**: Lloyd Thaxton welcomes vocal group, Herman's Hermits.

9:00—WISH-TV **8**: Lucille Ball is driven to distraction by a secret package she has been instructed not to open.

9:30—WISH-TV **8**: Many Happy Returns. Walter's plan for currying favor with the store's boss hits a snag.

10:00—WFBM-TV **6**: Alfred Hitchcock presents Margaret Leighton as a spinster who goes mad when she cannot cope with the strain of rearing an orphaned niece in "Where the Woodbine Twineth."

10:00—WLW-I **13**: Ben Casey gets help in diagnosing a boy's illness from an Australian veterinarian with terminal leukemia. The vet's knowledge of bats provides the key.

10:00—WISH-TV **8**: "Viet Nam: How We Got In—Can We Get Out?" is the topic of CBS Reports.

Indianapolis *News,* January 11, 1965.

This combination of visual entertainment and enlightenment made owning a television set virtually a necessity. By 1970, fully 95 percent of American households owned a TV set, a staggering increase from the 9 percent only 20 years earlier. Fewer families owned refrigerators or indoor toilets.

The implications of the impact of television on American society are of obvious interest to historians. How has television affected other communications and entertainment industries, such as radio, newspapers, and movies? What does the content of TV programming tell us about the values, interests, and tastes of the American people?

Perhaps most significant, what impact has TV had on the course of historical events like presidential campaigns, human relations, and wars? In the late 1960s, for example, television played an important part in shaping impressions of the war in Vietnam. More and more Americans began to understand the nature and impact of the war as TV newscasters brought visual images of burning huts and wounded soldiers into American living rooms every evening. As the combined Viet Cong–North Vietnamese forces attacked Saigon during the Tet offensive of 1968, American TV networks showed scenes of a kind never screened before. One such clip, on NBC News, showed the chief of the South Vietnamese National Police, General Loan, looking at a Viet Cong prisoner, lifting his gun, and calmly blowing out the captive's brains.

The picture you see here is a still snapshot of the execution that appeared on television and later won the Pulitzer Prize for the photographer. The picture makes a powerful impression on its own, but the impact was even stronger when the film clip on TV replayed the actual event for 20 million people.

Examine the image closely. What feelings do you see on the face of the prisoner? What is the mood of General Loan? Now try to imagine seeing this action unfold on the television screen. Following a brief introduction by Chet Huntley, an NBC News correspondent reported on the battle for Saigon. After some background on the struggle, he said that government forces had captured the commander of the Viet Cong commando unit. "He was roughed up badly but refused to talk," the narrator continued, and declared that General Loan "was waiting for him." After that he said no more. On screen, Loan moved to the prisoner's side and shot him in the side of the head. Viewers watched the corpse drop to the ground.

How do you respond to such an image? Knowing that this drama involved real people, how do you think the television audience might have reacted to this segment of the evening news? How vivid does violence need to be to make a strong impression? How might such a scene have helped focus the growing frustration with the war and aid efforts to end it? Reflect on more recent incidents you have seen "live" on TV, and ponder how they have affected the history of events in your lifetime.

General Loan, Southeast Vietnam's police chief executing a Vietcong suspect in Saigon, a news photo by Eddie Adams, from LIFE Magazine, March 1, 1968

Wide World Photos

There were far more students than there were farmers, coal miners, or railroad workers. College had become a training ground for industry and corporate life; more important, it gave students time to experiment and grow before they went out into the world to make a living.

In college, some students joined the struggle for civil rights. Hopeful at first, they gradually became discouraged by the limitations of the government's commitment, despite the rhetoric of Kennedy and the New Frontier.

The Student Movement

Out of that disillusionment arose the radical spirit of the New Left. Civil rights activists were among those who in 1960 organized Students for a Democratic Society (SDS) from the older Student League for Industrial Democracy. In 1962, SDS issued a manifesto, the Port Huron Statement, written largely by Tom Hayden of the University of Michigan. "We are people of this generation, bred in at least modest comfort, housed now in universities, looking uncomfortably at the world we inherit," it began. It went on to deplore the vast social and economic distances separating people from each other and to condemn the isolation and estrangement of modern life. The document called for a better system, one rooted in "self-cultivation, self-direction, self-understanding and creativity." Seeking "a democracy of individual participation," the Port Huron Statement pledged SDS to the creation of a "New Left."

Folksinger Bob Dylan, politically active himself, captured something of the new, more radical mood with a song in 1963:

Come mothers and fathers
Throughout the land
And don't criticize
What you can't understand
Your sons and daughters
Are beyond your command
There's a battle
Outside and it's ragin'
It'll soon shake your windows
And rattle your walls . . .
For the times they are a-changin'.

The first blow of the growing student rebellion came at the University of California in Berkeley. There civil rights activists became involved in a confrontation that quickly became known as the free-speech movement. It began in

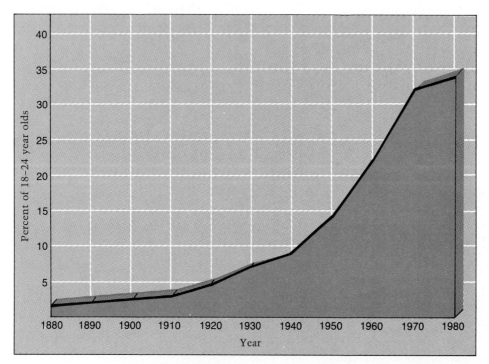

College Enrollment, 1940–1980

Source: U.S. Department of Commerce.

September 1964 when the university refused to allow students to distribute protest material outside the main campus gate. The students, many of whom had worked in the movement in the South, argued that their tables were off campus and therefore not subject to university restrictions on political activity. Defiantly, they resolved to fight back. When police arrested one of the leaders, students surrounded the police car and kept it from moving all night.

Although the administration eventually sought a compromise, the university regents chose to take disciplinary action against the student leaders. Mario Savio, one who found himself in the spotlight, was charged with biting a policeman on the thigh, and other accusations followed. When the regents refused to drop the charges, the students occupied the administration building. Savio called the university an impersonal machine: "It becomes odious, so we must put our bodies against the gears, against the wheels . . . and make the machine stop until we're free." Joan Baez sang "We Shall Overcome," the marching song of the civil rights movement, and something of the mood of that struggle prevailed. Then, as in the South, police stormed in and arrested the students in the building. A student strike, with faculty aid, mobilized wider support for the right to free speech.

"Stop the war now!" was a familiar chant as students across America rallied for peace. In 1968 Columbia University protestors barricaded themselves inside the school's main library.

Though the free-speech movement at Berkeley was the opening blow of the student revolt, it was still basically a plea for traditional liberal reform. Students sought only the reaffirmation of a longstanding right, the right to express themselves as they chose, and they aimed their attacks at the university, not at society as a whole. Later, in other institutions, the attack broadened.

As in the civil rights movement, student protest, once launched, developed and swelled. The ferment at Berkeley spread to other campuses in the spring of 1965 as students questioned methods of college discipline, attacked conservative drinking and visitation rules, sought student involvement in university affairs, argued for curricular reform, and demanded admission of more minority students. Their success in gaining their demands changed the shape of American higher education.

The New Left Struggles Against the War

The mounting protest against the escalation of the Vietnam War fueled the youth movement and gave it a new focus. Initially the critics were few. As the troop buildup began, 82 percent of the public felt that American forces should stay in Vietnam until the Communist elements withdrew. Then students began to question assumptions about the need to battle communism in every corner of the globe. The first antiwar teach-in took place in March 1965 at the University of Michigan. Other teach-ins followed across the country. Initially both supporters and opponents of the war appeared at the teach-ins, but soon the sessions became more like antiwar rallies than instructional affairs.

SDS seized upon the growing antiwar sentiment. Earlier, the radical student organization had been more interested in the struggle for civil rights and the organization of working-class elements in the cities. But as the antiwar movement grew, SDS recognized the possibilities for increasing its influence and plunged in, campaigning against the draft, attacking ROTC units on campus, and seeking to discredit firms that produced the destructive tools of war. "Make love, not war," slogans proclaimed as more and more students became involved in political demonstrations at dozens of colleges. "Hey, hey, LBJ. How many kids did you kill today?" opponents of the war chanted. In 1967, some 300,000 people marched in New York City. In Washington, D.C., 100,000 tried to close down the Pentagon. By 1968, protest had become almost a way of life. Between January 1 and June 15, hundreds of thousands of students staged 221 major demonstrations at more than 100 educational institutions.

Confrontation became the new tactic of radical students. The most dramatic episode came in April 1968 at Columbia University, where the issues of civil rights and war were tightly interwoven. A strong SDS chapter urged the university to break ties with the Institute of Defense Analysis, which specialized in military research. The Students' Afro-American Society tried to stop the building of a new gymnasium, which it claimed encroached on the Harlem community and disrupted life there. Together the two groups marched on Low Memorial Library. Then the alliance split, as whites occupied one building, blacks another. Finally, the president of the university called in the police, and the uprising was quelled. Hundreds of students were arrested; many were hurt. A student sympathy strike followed, and Columbia closed its doors early that spring.

The New Left became a powerful force in the 1960s. Although activists were never in the majority, radicals did succeed in attracting more and more students to their cause as the decade drew to an end. Together they focused opposition to the Vietnam War, even as they issued new challenges to American society. The impatience and frustration evident in the student protest movement could also be seen in other areas of American life as political upheaval was accompanied by cultural change.

Challenging Cultural Norms

In the 1960s, many Americans, particularly young people, lost faith in the sanctity of the American system. "There was," observed Joseph Heller, the irreverent author of *Catch-22* (1955), "a general feeling that the platitudes of Americanism were horseshit." The protests exposed the emptiness of some of the old patterns, and many Americans, some politically active, some not, found new ways to assert their individuality and independence. As in the political sphere, the young led the way. Often drawing on the example of the beats of the 1950s, the literary figures who had rejected conventional canons of respectability, they sought new means of expressing themselves.

Surface appearances were most visible and, to older Americans, most troubling. The "hippies" of the 1960s carried themselves in different ways. Men let their hair grow and sprouted beards; men and women both donned jeans, muslin shirts, and other simple garments. Stressing spontaneity above all else, some rejected traditional marital customs and gravitated to communal living groups. Their example, shocking to some, soon found its way into the culture at large. More men grew long hair and discarded ties and jackets. Women threw off confining clothing like girdles and embraced new fashions—miniskirts, longer dresses, slacks and jeans for casual wear.

Sexual norms underwent a revolution as more people separated sex from its traditional ties to family life. A generation of young women came of age with access to "the pill"—an oral contraceptive that was effortless to use and rid sexual experimentation from the threat of pregnancy. Americans of all social classes became more open to exploring, and enjoying, their sexuality. Scholarly findings supported natural inclinations. In 1966, William H. Masters and Virginia E. Johnson published *Human Sexual Response*, based on intensive laboratory observation of couples engaged in sexual activities. Describing the kinds of response that women, as well as men, could experience, they destroyed the myth of the sexually passive woman.

Nora Ephron, author and editor, summed up the sexual changes of the 1960s as she reflected on her own experiences. In 1962, after graduating from Wellesley College, she had moved to New York to work. Wanting a method of regular birth control, she visited the Margaret Sanger Clinic and began taking the pill. Initially she had "a hangover from the whole Fifties virgin thing," she recalled. "The first man I went to bed with, I was in love with and wanted to marry. The second one I was in love with, but I didn't have to marry him. With the third one, I thought I *might* fall in love." For a time she stopped taking the pill whenever she broke up with someone, but that proved inconvenient. As her doctor asked, "Who knows what's coming around the corner?" For many Americans in the 1960s, someone new was rounding the corner all the time.

The arts reflected the sexual revolution. Federal courts ruled that books like D. H. Lawrence's *Lady Chatterley's Lover* were not obscene, as had earlier been determined. Many suppressed works, long available in Europe, now began to appear. Nudity became more common on stage and screen. In *Hair*, a rock musical, one scene featured the disrobing of performers of both sexes in the course of an erotic celebration. What had been unthinkable a decade before now became commonplace in the arts.

Paintings reflected both the mood of dissent and the urge to innovate that were apparent in the larger society. "Op" artists painted sharply defined squares, circles, stripes, and other geometric figures in clear, vibrant colors, starkly different from the flowing, chaotic work of the abstract expressionists. "Pop" artists like Andy Warhol, Roy Lichtenstein, and Jasper Johns made ironic comments on American materialism and taste with the representations of everyday objects like soup cans, comic strips, or pictures of Marilyn Monroe. Their paintings broke with formal artistic conventions. Some used spray guns and fluorescent paints to gain effect. Others even tried to make their pictures look like giant newspaper photographs.

Hallucinogenic drugs also became a part of the counterculture. The beats had experimented with drugs, as had others, but now their use became common. One prophet of "the drug scene" was Timothy Leary, who, with Richard Alpert, was doing scientific research at Harvard University on LSD. Fired from their research posts for violating a pledge to the University Health Service not to experiment with undergraduates, the two men promoted the cause of LSD nationally. As Alpert drifted into a commune in New Mexico, Leary aggressively asserted that drugs were necessary to free the mind. Working through his group, the League for

Spiritual Discovery, he dressed in long robes and preached his message, "tune in, turn on, drop out."

Another apostle of life with drugs was Ken Kesey. Born and raised in Oregon, he had finished college in 1958 and entered Stanford for graduate work. There he wrote his first novel, *One Flew Over the Cuckoo's Nest,* and began participating in medical experiments at a hospital where he was introduced to LSD. With the profits from his novel, Kesey established a commune of "Merry Pranksters" near Palo Alto, California. In 1964, the group headed east in a converted school bus painted in psychedelic Day-Glo colors, wired for sound, and stocked with enough orange juice and acid to sustain the Pranksters across the continent. After a series of outlandish adventures, they returned to California, where many of them were arrested. That only enhanced Kesey's standing in the drug culture.

Drug use was no longer confined to an urban subculture of musicians, artists, and the streetwise. Young professionals began experimenting with cocaine as a stimulant. Taking a "tab" of LSD became part of the coming-of-age ritual for many middle-class college students. But it was marijuana that became phenomenally popular in the 1960s. "Joints" of "grass" were passed around at high school, neighborhood, and college parties as readily as were cans of beer in the previous generation.

Music became intimately connected with these cultural changes. The rock and roll of the 1950s and the gentle strains of folk music gave way to a new kind of rock that swept the country—and the world. The Beatles were the major influence, as they took first England, then the United States, by storm. Other groups enjoyed enormous commercial success while attacking materialism and other bourgeois values. Mick Jagger of the Rolling Stones was an aggressive, sometimes violent showman on stage whose androgynous style showed his contempt for conventional sexual norms. Jim Morrison of the Doors conveyed a raw sexuality in his dialogue with the audience. Janis Joplin, a hard-driving, hard-drinking woman with roots in the blues, reflected the intensity of the new rock world until her early death by drugs.

Though spontaneous and exuberant, the counterculture had a dismal underside. Young people gathered where they could, many in the Haight-Ashbury section of San Francisco, where runaway "flower children" mingled with "burned-out" drug users and radical activists. Many of its heroes, like Jimmy Hendrix, died of drug overdoses. Joan Didion, a perceptive essayist, wrote of American society in 1967: "Adolescents drifted from city to torn city, sloughing off both the past and the future as snakes shed their skins, children who were never taught and would never now learn the games that had held the society together."

CONCLUSION: The Unraveling of the Affluent Society

The people of the United States had been severely buffeted in the eight years after electing John Kennedy to the presidency. In 1960, there was confidence that the nation, though not without problems, was healthy and strong, able to withstand challenges around the world and protect the American way of life. The New Frontier and the Great Society pushed forward liberal reforms. Yet they had not taken the measure of deep-running cultural shifts that had occurred. Idealistic Americans who joined organizations like the Peace Corps found, as one of them observed, that their experience "forever altered our view of our own country, and more significantly, it altered our perception of ourselves and our responsibilities." Political leaders seemed out of touch with their constituents, particularly the young.

The nation was drifting. The consensus that had bound together successful Americans—and those still hopeful of success—had vanished. Serious problems, at home and abroad, seemed almost beyond solution.

Recommended Reading

For a good introduction to the basic foreign and domestic policies of the period, see Jim F. Heath, *Decade of Disillusionment: The Kennedy-Johnson Years* (1975). On John Kennedy, Herbert S. Parmet, *JFK: The Presidency of John F. Kennedy* (1983) is a comprehensive account of the White House years. Henry Fairlie, *The Kennedy Promise* (1972) is a scathing assessment of the actual record of the Kennedy administration. Doris Kearns, *Lyndon Johnson and the American Dream* (1976) is a readable analysis of the Johnson presidency by a political scientist and former White House fellow. Allen J. Matusow provides a brilliant analysis of the 1960s in *The Unraveling of America: A History of Liberalism in the 1960s* (1984).

A great deal has been written about the Vietnam War. George C. Herring, *America's Longest War: The United States and Vietnam, 1950–1975* (1979) is the best brief account of American policy in that conflict, particularly in the 1960s and thereafter.

The civil rights movement has also been extensively described. Harvard Sitkoff, *The Struggle for Black Equality, 1954–1980* (1981) is a short but stimulating overview of the civil rights struggle. Clayborne Carson, *In Struggle: SNCC and the Black Awakening of the 1960s* (1981) provides a good treatment of one phase of the movement. Anne Moody, *Coming of Age in Mississippi* (1968) is the eloquent autobiography of a young southern black woman who became involved in the civil rights movement.

On the women's movement, Sara Evans, *Personal Politics: The Roots of Women's Liberation in the Civil Rights Movement and the New Left* (1979) offers a penetrating examination of the links between various reform movements in the 1960s. Sara Davidson, *Loose Change* (1977) is a novel describing the lives of women in the 1960s.

For a good treatment of recent Indian struggles see Alvin M. Josephy, Jr., *Now That the Buffalo's Gone* (1982).

Rodolfo Acuña, *Occupied America: A History of Chicanos* (1981) provides a useful overview of Chicano affairs.

For the growth of the counterculture, see William L. O'Neill, *Coming Apart* (1971). Tom Wolfe, *The Electric Kool-Aid Acid Test* (1968) is a vivid account of Ken Kesey and the drug culture of the 1960s.

TIME LINE

1960	John F. Kennedy elected president Sit-ins begin Students for a Democratic Society (SDS) founded

1961	Freedom rides
	Bay of Pigs invasion fails
	Khrushchev and Kennedy meet in
	    Vienna
	Berlin Wall constructed
	Michael Harrington publishes *The
	    Other America*; Joseph Heller,
	    Catch-22; Ken Kesey, *One Flew Over
	    the Cuckoo's Nest*

1962	JFK confronts steel companies Meredith crisis at the University of Mississippi Cuban missile crisis SDS's Port Huron Statement
1963	Birmingham demonstration Civil rights march on Washington Kennedy assassinated; Lyndon B. Johnson becomes president Buddhist demonstrations in Vietnam President Diem assassinated in Vietnam Betty Friedan, *The Feminine Mystique*

1964	Freedom Democratic party attempts to
	    gain recognition at the Democratic
	    national convention
	Gulf of Tonkin Resolution
	Civil Rights Act
	Economic Opportunity Act initiates
	    War on Poverty
	Race riots in New York City
	Free-speech movement, Berkeley
	Johnson reelected president

1965	Vietnam conflict escalates
	Marines sent to Dominican Republic
	Martin Luther King leads march from
	    Selma to Montgomery
	Voting Rights Act
	United Farm Workers grape strike
	Teach-ins begin
	Department of Housing and Urban
	    Development established
	Elementary and Secondary Education
	    Act
	Assassination of Malcolm X
	Watts riot in Los Angeles

1966	Stokely Carmichael becomes head of
	    SNCC and calls for "black power"
	Black Panthers founded
	NOW founded
	Masters and Johnson, *Human Sexual
	    Response*

1967	Antiwar demonstrations Urban riots in 22 cities

1968	Kerner Commission report on urban
	    disorders
	Martin Luther King, Jr., assassinated
	Robert F. Kennedy assassinated
	Antiwar demonstrations increase
	Tet offensive
	Student demonstrations at Columbia
	    and elsewhere
	Chicago Democratic convention riots
	Richard Nixon elected president

CHAPTER 30
ILLUSION AND DISILLUSIONMENT

Ann Clarke—as she chooses to call herself now—always wanted to go to college. But girls from Italian families rarely did when she was growing up. Her mother, a Sicilian immigrant and widow, asked her brother for advice: "Should Antonina go to college?" "What's the point?" he said. "She's just going to get married."

Life had not been easy for Antonina Rose Rumore. As a child in the 1920s, her Italian-speaking grandmother cared for her while her mother worked to support the family, first in the sweatshops, then as a seamstress. Even as she dreamed, Ann accommodated her culture's demands for dutiful daughters.

Responsive to family needs, Ann finished the high school Commercial Course in three years. She struggled with ethnic prejudice as a legal secretary on Wall Street, but still believed in the American dream and the Puritan work ethic. She was proud of her ability to bring money home to her family.

When World War II began, Ann wanted to join the WACS. "Better you should be a prostitute," her mother said. Ann went off to California instead, where she worked at resorts. When she left California, she vowed to return to this land of freedom and opportunity.

After the war, Ann married Gerard Clarke, a college man with an English background. Her children would grow up accepted with Anglo names. Over the next 15 years, Ann devoted herself to her family. She was a mother above all, and that took all her time. But she waited for her own chance: "I had this hunger to learn, this curiosity."

By the early 1960s, her three children were all in school. Promising her husband to have dinner on the table at six, she enrolled at Pasadena City College. It was not easy. Family still came first. A simple problem was finding time to study. When doing dishes or cleaning house, she memorized lists of dates, historical events, and other material for school.

Holiday time was difficult. Ann occasionally felt compelled to give everything up "to make Christmas." Terminating a whole semester's work two weeks before finals, she sewed nightgowns instead of writing her art history paper.

Her conflict over her studies was intensified by her position as one of the first older women to go back to college. "Sometimes I felt like I wanted to hide in the woodwork," she admitted. Often her teachers were younger than she. It took four years to complete the two-year program. But she was not yet done. She wanted a bachelor's degree. Back she went, this time to California State College at Los Angeles.

As the years passed and the credits piled up, Ann became an honors student. Her children, now in college themselves, were proud and supportive; dinners became arguments over Faulkner and foreign policy. Even so, Ann still felt caught between her worlds at home and outside. Since she was at the top of her class, graduation should have been a special occasion. But she was only embarrassed when a letter from the school invited her parents to attend the final ceremonies. Ann could not bring herself to go.

With a college degree in hand, Ann returned to school for teaching credentials. Receiving her certificate at age 50, she faced the irony of social change. Once denied opportunities, Italians had assimilated into American society. Now she was just another Anglo in Los Angeles, caught in a changing immigration wave; the city now sought Hispanics and other minorities to teach in the schools. Jobs in education were tightening, and she was close to "retirement age," so she became a substitute in Mexican-American areas for the next ten years, specializing in bilingual education.

Meanwhile, Ann was troubled by the Vietnam War. "For every boy that died, one of us should lie down," she told fellow workers. She was not an activist, rather one of the millions of quieter Americans who ultimately helped bring change.

The social adjustments caused by the war affected her. Her son grew long hair and a beard and attended protest rallies. He would antagonize the ladies in Pasadena, she worried. Her daughter came home from college in boots and a leather miniskirt designed to shock. Ann accepted her children's changes as relatively superficial, confident in their fundamental values; "they were good kids." She trusted them, even as she worried.

Ann Clarke's experience paralleled that of millions of women in the 1960s and 1970s. Caught up for years in traditional patterns of family life, these women began to recognize their need for something more. Even as their lives changed, society changed too. New social and political issues compelled some to speak out. And their involvement helped change the political and social dialogue in the United States.

This chapter describes the trials the nation endured between 1968 and 1976. It deals with the changes Ann Rumore Clarke and others experienced as they struggled with their own problems, only to see their communities polarize. It shows how the country responded to war, injustice, and political scandal. And it portrays the efforts of concerned Americans to promote reform on all fronts, even in troubled times.

REPUBLICAN LEADERSHIP

After eight years of Democratic rule, the ferment sparked by the Vietnam War led to a change in command. Elected president in 1968, Richard Nixon faced deep divisions in the country as he sought to end the war and restore tranquility at home. But his efforts produced a backlash, and his own quest for political power eventually brought him disgrace. He was succeeded by Gerald Ford, a more modest man whose major achievement was to restore some confidence in the United States.

The Election of 1968

Nixon had long dreamed of the nation's highest office. In 1968, his chances seemed good. The Democratic party, like the country itself, was split by the Vietnam War. Senator Eugene McCarthy of Minnesota opposed further American involvement in the struggle, challenged incumbent Lyndon Johnson in the New Hampshire primary, and almost won. Americans were tired of the drawn-out, expensive war and ready to express their frustration at the polls. His popularity waning, Johnson dramatically announced that he would not seek another term. As McCarthy promoted his candidacy, Robert F. Kennedy, the charismatic brother of the slain president, launched his own bid for the nomination. It ended in his assassination, which shook the country. Inheriting the role of leading contender was Vice-President Hubert H. Humphrey, a longtime advocate of civil rights and social justice but also a firm supporter of the anti-

Communist doctrine of containment that had provided the rationale for involvement in Vietnam.

When the Democratic party convened in Chicago in August 1968, it was severely fragmented. Party regulars wanted to close ranks, while insurgents demanded recognition of their position on the draft and the war. On the radical fringe, some groups adopted confrontation tactics to dramatize their militancy. The National Mobilization to End the War in Vietnam was one such group. More important was the Yippie organization, led by Jerry Rubin and Abbie Hoffman. The Youth International Party sought to merge hippies and radicals and provided guerrilla theater. The group envisioned a "festival of life" to compete with the "convention of death" the Democrats were holding. They spoke of putting LSD into the Chicago water supply, having thousands of people run naked through the streets, and disarming the police. As they anticipated, they came up squarely against the longtime boss of Chicago, Mayor Richard Daley, who determined to use his police force to keep order.

The Chicago police swept demonstrators out of the parks at night. The first confrontations took place soon after the convention began, but the major incident came on the climactic evening when the convention nominated Hubert Humphrey. As thousands of demonstrating Yippies and others massed outside the hotel where the convention was being held, the police, seeking to push them back, lost

control. What occurred was, quite simply, a police riot, in which the forces of order went wild, clubbing not only demonstrators but also newsmen, bystanders, men and women both, all in front of the television cameras recording the incident for the country to see. Inside the hall, Senator Abraham Ribicoff of Connecticut denounced the "Gestapo tactics on the streets of Chicago" as delegate polling took place. Humphrey won the nomination, but by then the prize was badly tarnished.

Complicating the general election was the third-party campaign of Governor George C. Wallace of Alabama, a southern demagogue who exploited racial tensions for his own ends. Broadening his appeal to include northern working-class voters as well as southern whites, Wallace criticized the "left-wing theoreticians, briefcase-totin' bureaucrats, ivory-tower guideline writers, bearded anarchists, smart-aleck editorial writers and pointy-headed professors." Wallace hoped to ride the considerable blue-collar resentment of the radical forces causing upheaval in America into office.

Nixon's nomination by the Republicans was a triumph in a turbulent career. Running for vice-president in 1952, Nixon had almost been dropped from the ticket when charges of a slush fund surfaced. Only his maudlin televised appeal to the American public saved him then. After his loss to Kennedy in 1960 and his defeat in a race for governor of California in 1962, his political career appeared over. He told the press on that latter occasion, "You won't have Nixon to kick around any more because, gentleman, this is my last press conference." But after the Goldwater disaster in 1964, Nixon began to campaign for Republican candidates and reestablished a base of support.

Delighting in the Democratic convention debacle, Nixon worked to add the same constituency Wallace sought to his political base. He demanded law and order in America, claimed he had a plan to end the Vietnam War, and ran a

The presence of left-wing demonstrators in confrontation with the Chicago police started as a nonviolent protest but turned ugly during the course of the 1968 Democratic Convention.

Speaking to the "silent majority," Nixon promised to reinstitute traditional values and restore law and order.

carefully orchestrated campaign. No longer bitter or shrill, he adopted a stable, even aloof, stance and let his vice-presidential running mate, Governor Spiro Agnew of Maryland, lead the attack. Agnew, much like the Nixon of old, called Hubert Humphrey "squishy soft on Communism" and declared that "if you've seen one city slum, you've seen them all."

Even those comments, however, failed to slow the Republican momentum. As the campaign closed, Johnson halted all bombing of North Vietnam, but that gesture did not help Humphrey. Nixon received 43.4 percent of the popular vote, not quite one percent more than Humphrey, with Wallace capturing the rest, but it was enough to give Nixon a majority in the electoral college. The Democrats won both houses of Congress.

The Nixon Administration

In and out of office, Nixon was a remote man, lacking humor and grace. As one of his speech writers said, there was "a mean side to his nature" that he strove to conceal. Earlier in his career he was labeled "Tricky Dick." Later he tried to bury that image. But he appeared to be a mechanical man, always calculating his next step.

Nixon embraced political life, but never with the exuberance of Lyndon Johnson. He was most comfortable alone or with a few wealthy friends. Even at work, he insulated himself, preferred written contacts to personal ones, and often retreated to a small room in the executive office building to be alone.

In Nixon's cabinet sat only white, male Republicans. Yet for the most part, Nixon worked around his cabinet, relying on other White House staff appointees. In domestic affairs, Arthur Burns, a former chairman of the Council of Economic Advisers, and Daniel Patrick Moynihan, a Harvard professor of government (and a Democrat) were the most important. In foreign affairs, the major figure was Henry A. Kissinger, another Harvard government professor, even more talented and ambitious, who directed the National Security Council staff and later became secretary of state.

Still another tier of White House officials insulated the president from the outside world and carried out his commands. None had public policy experience, but all shared an intense loyalty to their leader, a quality that Nixon prized. Advertising executive H. R. Haldeman, a tireless Nixon campaigner, became chief of staff. Of his relationships with the president, Haldeman remarked, "I get done what he wants done and I take the heat instead of him."

Working with Haldeman was lawyer John Ehrlichman. Starting as a legal counselor, Ehrlichman rose to the post of chief domestic adviser. Haldeman and Ehrlichman framed issues and narrowed options for Nixon. They came to be known as the "Berlin Wall" for the way they guarded the president's privacy. Finally there was John Mitchell, known as "El Supremo" by the staff, as the "Big Enchilada" by Ehrlichman. A tough, successful bond lawyer from Nixon's New York law office, he became a fast friend and managed the 1968 campaign. In the new administration he assumed the post of attorney general and gave the president daily advice.

Gerald Ford

Gerald Ford succeeded to the presidency when Richard Nixon and his closest counselors became embroiled in a political scandal following the 1972 reelection campaign. Ford proved to be a very different leader.

From the start, Ford was a reassuring presence, for he was a decent, popular man. In a long congressional career that began after World War II, he became House minority leader and was well liked by his colleagues on Capitol Hill. He was an unassuming, unpretentious man who believed in traditional virtues. Republicans felt a burst of relief when Nixon chose him as vice-president in 1973, after Spiro Agnew resigned in disgrace for accepting bribes. Yet some critics questioned his capacity. Ford himself acknowledged his limitations when he declared, "I am a Ford, not a Lincoln." Those limitations soon became evident. Yet his genial personality quieted some of the fears Americans harbored about their country.

REPUBLICAN FOREIGN POLICY

When Nixon assumed office in 1969, the nation was deeply divided by the Vietnam War. He understood that he must end the conflict, either by victory or withdrawal. Long fascinated by international relations, he hoped to play a major diplomatic role. "I've always thought this country could run itself domestically without a President," he once observed, implying that such was not the case with foreign affairs.

The Agony of the Vietnam War

Nixon gave top priority to extricating the country from Vietnam while still finding a way to win the war. For the first time in American history, a president faced huge numbers of people opposed to their government's war policy. In mid-1969, the president announced the Nixon Doctrine, which asserted that the United States would give aid to friends and allies but would not undertake the full burden of troop defense. He thereupon embarked on the policy of Vietnamization, which entailed removing American forces and replacing them with Vietnamese ones. At the same time, Americans launched ferocious air attacks on North Vietnam. "Let's blow the hell out of them," Nixon instructed the Joint Chiefs of Staff. Between 1968 and 1972, American troop strength dropped from 543,000 to 39,000, and the reduction won political support for Nixon at home. Yet as the transition occurred, the South Vietnamese steadily lost ground to the Viet Cong.

War protests multiplied in 1969 and 1970. In November 1969, as a massive protest demonstration took place in Washington, D.C., the first stories surfaced about the massacre of civilians in Vietnam the year before. Journalist Seymour M. Hersh had heard rumors about the My Lai episode and had begun to piece together an account of what had occurred. His efforts provided the American people with horrifying evidence of the war's brutality.

My Lai, a small village in Vietnam, was allegedly harboring 250 members of the enemy Viet Cong. An American infantry company was helicoptered in to clear out the village. C Company had already had heavy combat losses, but instead of soldiers, this time it found women, children, and old men. Perhaps inured to the random destruction already wrought by the American military, perhaps concerned with the sometimes fuzzy distinction between combatants and civilians in a guerrilla war, the American forces lost control.

Lieutenant William L. Calley, Jr., a mild-mannered officer, first ordered, "Round everybody up," and then said, "Take care of 'em." When Paul Meadlo, a private from a small Indiana farm town, simply guarded the people he had collected, Calley said, "Hey, Meadlo, I said take care of 'em." At that the Americans began mowing down the civilians in cold blood. Later Meadlo recalled:

> We huddled them up. We made them squat down. . . . I poured about four clips into the group. . . . The mothers was hugging their children. . . . Well, we kept right on firing. They was waving their arms and begging. . . . I still dream about it. About the women and children in my sleep. Some days . . . some nights, I can't even sleep.

Americans at home were shocked at stories of the civilian slaughter. Yet once the initial revulsion began to subside, they proved less willing to condemn. Some sympathized with Calley, who, they argued, was simply responding to the demands of war. When Calley was court-martialed, convicted for at "least twenty-two murders" and sentenced to life imprisonment, Nixon realized that many Americans thought the sentence too harsh. He ordered Calley released from prison while the case was under appeal and announced that he would personally review it before any sentence was carried out. As the furor died down, the military reduced his sentence to ten years. Eligible for parole in six months, Calley was soon free.

While the My Lai episode led many to wonder about American conduct of the war, incidents on several college campuses made them question the use of troops at home. A disaster at Kent State University was set in motion by a series of presidential decisions in April 1970. Much as Nixon wanted to defuse opposition to the Vietnam War, like LBJ he was determined not to lose it either. Therefore, as he publicized his Vietnamization policy, he looked for other ways to achieve victory. Realizing that the Vietnamese relied on supplies funneled through Cambodia, Nixon announced that American and Vietnamese troops were invading that country to clear out the Communist enclaves there. The United States, he said, would not stand by as "a pitiful helpless giant" when there were actions it could take to stem the Communist advance.

Nixon's invasion of Cambodia brought renewed demonstrations on college campuses, some with tragic results. At Kent State, in Ohio, the response was fierce. The day after the president announced his moves, disgruntled students gathered downtown. Worried about the crowd, the local police called in sheriff's deputies to disperse the students. The next evening, groups of students collected on college grounds. Assembling around the ROTC building, they began throwing firecrackers and rocks at the structure, which had become a hated symbol of the war. Then they set it on fire and watched it burn to the ground.

The governor of Ohio ordered the National Guard to the university. Tension grew as they set up tents on campus and took over the gym. Finally, it exploded. Loading their guns and donning gas masks, the Guardsmen prepared to disperse the gathering mob. As the students fell back, some threw rocks or empty canisters of gas. Most, however, were so far away that they could not have reached the troops. At midday, the soldiers knelt down and aimed their rifles at the students as if to warn them to stop. Then they rose together, huddled with one another, and finally began to retreat to a different position. At the top of a hill they turned and suddenly began firing in unison at the students below.

When the firing ceased, four students lay dead, nine wounded. Two of the dead had been demonstrators, who were more than 250 feet away when shot. The other two were innocent bystanders, almost 400 feet from the troops.

Students around the country, as well as other Americans, were outraged by the attack. Many were equally disturbed about a similar attack at Jackson State University in Mississippi. Policemen and highway patrolmen poured automatic weapon fire into a women's dormitory without warning. When the shooting stopped, two people were dead, more wounded. The dead there, however, were black students at a black institution, and white America paid less attention to that attack.

In 1971, the Vietnam War made major headlines once more when the New York *Times* began publishing a secret Department of Defense account of American involvement in the war. The so called Pentagon Papers, leaked by Daniel Ellsberg, a defense analyst, gave Americans a firsthand look at the fabrications and faulty assumptions that had guided the steady expansion of the struggle. Even though the study stopped with the Johnson years, the Nixon administration was furious and sought a Supreme Court injunction to halt publication of the series. By a split vote the Court ruled against the government, and readers continued to learn more about the nightmarish war.

Vietnam remained a political football as Nixon ran for reelection in 1972. Negotiations aimed at a settlement were under way, and just before election day, Henry Kissinger announced, "Peace is at hand." When South Vietnam seemed to balk at the proposed settlement, however, the administration responded with the most intensive bombing campaign of the war.

When Ohio National Guardsmen fired on a crowd of antiwar demonstrators, killing four students, even prowar Americans were shocked.

Hanoi, the capital of North Vietnam, was hit hard; then the North Vietnamese harbors were mined. Only in the new year was a cease-fire finally signed. Kissinger shared the 1973 Nobel Peace Prize with his North Vietnamese counterpart Le Duc Tho. Tho rejected his part of the prize with the observation that the war between North and South Vietnam was not yet over, even though the American troops were finally going home. Kissinger had no such compunctions and accepted his share of the award.

After Nixon left office, the conflict in Vietnam lingered on into the spring of 1975, yet by that time American troops had been evacuated. When at last the North Vietnamese consolidated their control over the entire country, Gerald Ford called for another $1 billion in aid, even as the South Vietnamese were abandoning arms and supplies in chaotic retreat. Congress refused, leaving the crumbling government of South Vietnam to fend for itself. Republicans hailed Kissinger for having finally freed the United States from the Southeast Asian quagmire. Antiwar critics, on the other hand, condemned him for continuing involvement in the war for so long. *New Republic* wryly observed that Kissinger brought peace to Vietnam in the same way Napoleon brought peace to Europe: by losing.

The conflict was finally over, but the costs were immense. In the longest war in its history, the United States lost almost 58,000 men, with far more wounded or maimed. Blacks and Chicanos suffered more than whites since they were disproportionately represented in the armed forces. Financially, the nation spent over $150 billion in an ultimately unsuccessful war. Domestic reform had slowed, then stopped. American society had been deeply divided. Only time would heal the wounds.

Détente

If the Republicans' Vietnam policy was a questionable success, in other areas Nixon's accomplishments were impressive. The Red-baiter of the past was able to deal imaginatively and successfully with the Communist powers. In so doing he reversed the direction of American policy since the Second World War. Bypassing Congress, often bypassing his own

Department of State, the president depended most heavily on Kissinger, his national security adviser. Kissinger grasped the complexity of the world situation, understood the tensions within the Communist realm, and exploited them to restore better American relations with both the Soviet Union and China.

Nixon's most dramatic step was opening formal relations with the People's Republic of China. In the two decades since Mao Zedong's victory on the Chinese mainland in 1949, the American position had been that Jiang Jieshi's rump government on Taiwan was the rightful government of the Chinese people; consequently, there had been no diplomatic relations with the Communist regime. In 1971, with an eye on the forthcoming political campaign, the administration began softening its rigid stand. After the Chinese invited an American table-tennis team to visit the mainland, the United States eased some of the trading restrictions in force. Then in August 1971, Nixon announced that he intended to visit China the following year, the first American president ever to do so.

That bold step signified Nixon's understanding that the People's Republic was an established force representing the Chinese people. The president knew that the rest of the world had for years recognized the People's Republic and wanted to seat it in the United Nations.

Secretary of State Henry Kissinger was instrumental in arranging Nixon's visit to China, which opened the way to American recognition of the Communist state.

Moreover, he suspected that he could use Chinese friendship as a bargaining chip when he dealt with the Soviet Union. Finally, American leaders officially acknowledged what most nations already knew: Communism was not monolithic. At home, Nixon believed that he could open a dialogue with the Chinese Communists without political harm, for he had long been a vocal critic of communism and could hardly be accused of being "soft" on it. He knew also that the coverage of a dramatic trip could give him a real boost in the press.

Nixon went to China in February 1972. He met with Chinese leaders Mao Zedong and Zou Enlai (Chou En-lai), talked about international problems, exchanged toasts, and saw some of the major sights. Wherever he went, American television cameras followed, helping to introduce the American public to a nation about which they knew little. Though formal relations were not yet restored, détente between the two countries had begun.

Nixon also used his new China policy to seek better ties with the Soviet Union. He and Kissinger hoped to be able to play one Communist state against the other, and by and large, they accomplished their aim. Several months after his trip to China, Nixon visited Russia, where he was also warmly welcomed. After several cordial meetings, the president and Soviet premier Leonid Brezhnev agreed to limit missile stockpiles, work together in space, and ease the longstanding restrictions on trade. Businessmen applauded the new approach, and most Americans approved of détente.

Nixon dealt with the Communist governments with tact and skill. Using his Chinese and Russian initiatives to neutralize opposition to the phased withdrawal of troops in Vietnam, he bought time to pursue Vietnamization on his own terms.

When Gerald Ford assumed office, he followed the policies begun under Nixon. Kissinger remained secretary of state and continued to play an influential role in foreign affairs. In May 1975, an episode in another part of Southeast Asia reflected the difficulties of new policies. Cambodian forces captured the *Mayaguez*, an American merchant ship cruising inside the territorial waters of that country. When American protests went unanswered, the United States sent 350 marines to attack an island where the crew was thought to be held. The operation's cost was 41 American lives. Since the Cambodians were evidently preparing to return both ship and crew, the bloodshed proved unnecessary. Yet in the aftermath of the Vietnamese defeat, Kissinger and Ford were anxious to respond vigorously and to avoid the impression that the United States had been weakened by the war. Their opponents, however, called the raid a case of overkill.

Ford continued the Strategic Arms Limitation Talks (SALT) that provided hope for eventual nuclear disarmament. He also accepted the Helsinki Accords, which defined European security arrangements and underscored basic human rights. He pursued friendly relations with China and elsewhere maintained the spirit of détente, even while rejecting the term. In the mid-1970s, American foreign policy tended to be reactive, yet the country remained at peace, avoided major confrontations, and continued to define a less aggressive role for itself abroad.

Improved relations with the Soviet Union resulted from Nixon's shrewd foreign policy. In 1972 Brezhnev joined him in a toast on signing the Strategic Arms Limitation Pact.

SEARCHING FOR STABILITY

As the Republicans struggled with Vietnam and détente, they faced serious problems as home. The economy suffered a series of shocks. Social fragmentation and polarization were more pronounced than they had ever been in the twentieth century. Nixon hoped that his victory and strong presidential leadership could defuse antiwar protest. But forces were smoldering that even he could not control. And eventually political scandal compounded his difficulties and brought him down.

The Oil Embargo and the Economy Under Nixon

Nixon inherited an already faltering economy. President Johnson had escalated the war in Vietnam but had been unwilling to raise taxes from 1965 to 1967 to pay for it. As demand generated by war needs rose, so too did prices and the wages employers had to pay their workers. Inflation slowly crept up, from 2.2 percent in 1965 to 4.5 percent in 1968.

Nixon tried to restrain inflation by tightening monetary and fiscal policy. Although parts of the plan worked, a mild recession occurred in 1969–1970, and inflation did not abate. Realizing the political dangers of pursuing his policy further, Nixon imposed wage and price controls to stop inflation and used monetary and fiscal policies to stimulate the economy. After his reelection, however, he lifted wage and price controls, and inflation began to rise.

Other factors contributed to the spiral of rising prices. Eager to court the farm vote, the administration made a large wheat sale to Russia in 1972. But government officials had miscalculated. With insufficient wheat left for the American market, grain prices shot up. Twenty-five years of grain surpluses suddenly disappeared, and shortages occurred. Other agricultural setbacks like corn blight compounded the problem. Between 1971 and 1974, farm prices rose 66 percent as agricultural inflation accompanied industrial inflation.

The most critical factor in disrupting the economy, however, was the Arab oil embargo. American economic expansion had rested on cheap energy just as American patterns of life had depended on inexpensive gasoline. Although OPEC (the Organization of Petroleum Exporting Countries) had slowly raised oil prices in the early 1970s, the 1973 war between Israel, Egypt, and Syria led Saudi Arabia to impose an embargo on oil shipped to Israel's ally, the United States. Other OPEC nations quadrupled

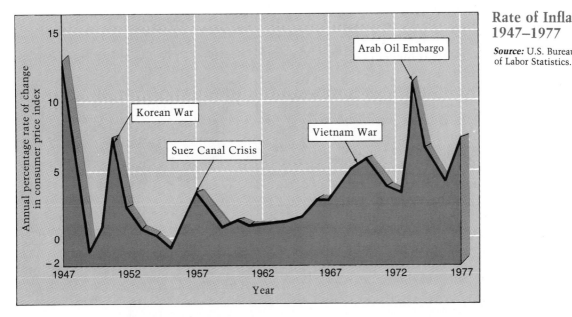

Rate of Inflation, 1947–1977

Source: U.S. Bureau of Labor Statistics.

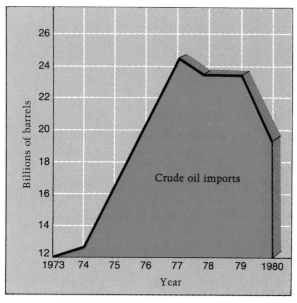 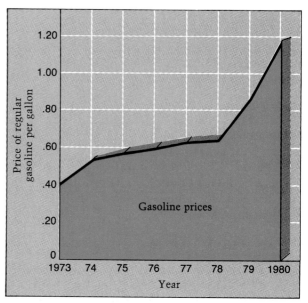

Oil Imports and Gasoline Prices, 1973–1980
Source: U.S. Energy Information Administration.

their prices. Dependent on imports for one-third of their energy needs, Americans faced shortages and skyrocketing prices. When the embargo ended in 1974, prices remained high.

The oil crisis affected all aspects of American economic life. Manufacturers, farmers, homeowners—all were touched by high energy prices. A loaf of bread that had cost 28 cents in the early 1970s jumped to 89 cents, and automobiles cost 72 percent more in 1978 than they had in 1973. Accustomed to filling up their cars' tanks for only a few dollars, Americans were shocked at paying 65 cents a gallon. In 1974, inflation reached 11 percent. But as higher energy prices encouraged consumers to cut back on their purchases, the nation also entered a recession. Unemployment climbed to 9 percent, the highest level since the 1930s. Inflation and high unemployment were worrisome bedfellows.

As economic growth and stability eluded him, Nixon also tried to reorganize the rapidly expanding welfare programs. As a result of the Great Society programs, the government was spending more, in an effort that critics claimed was inefficient and unnecessary since it discouraged people from seeking work. Nixon faced a dilemma. He recognized the conservative tide growing in the Sun Belt regions of the country

from Florida to Texas to California, where many voters wanted cutbacks in what they viewed as excessive government programs. At the same time, he wanted to win traditionally Democratic blue-collar workers over to his side by reassuring them that the Republicans would not dismantle the parts of the welfare state on which they relied. At the urging of domestic adviser Daniel

Unemployment Rate, 1940–1982
Source: U.S. Bureau of Labor Statistics.

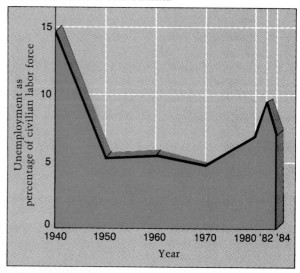

Moynihan, Nixon endorsed an expensive but feasible work-incentive program. The Family Assistance Plan would have guaranteed a minimum yearly stipend of $1,600 to a family of four, with food stamps providing about $800 more. The program, aiming to cut "welfare cheaters" who took unfair advantage of the system, required all participants to register for job training and to accept employment when found. Proponents, who probably exaggerated the number of "welfare cheaters," wanted to make it more profitable to work than to subsist on the public rolls. Though promising, the program died in the Senate, but it indicated what the administration hoped to do.

Social Polarization

While dealing with economic questions, Nixon also had to confront the deep social divisions engendered by the Vietnam War and the "generation gap" that divided Americans on moral and social issues. In his election victory statement, Nixon declared that his overriding objective was "to bring the American people together. We want to bridge the generation gap. We want to bridge the gap between the races." But the fragmentation continued to grow.

Large numbers of young people, embracing the ethos of the counterculture and profoundly apolitical, were not moved by election campaigns and victory statements. Seven months after Nixon's inauguration, on the weekend of August 15–16, 1969, some 400,000 gathered in a large pasture in upstate New York for the Woodstock rock festival. There, despite intense heat and torrential rain, despite inadequate supplies of water and food, the festival unfolded in a spirit of affection. Some people took off their clothes and paraded in the nude, some engaged in public lovemaking, and most shared whatever they had, particularly the marijuana that seemed endlessly available, while major rock groups provided ear-splitting, around-the-clock entertainment for the assembled throng.

The weekend went off without a hitch. The police chose not to enforce the drug laws and thereby avoided confrontations. The promoters had chartered helicopters to whisk away anyone suffering a drug overdose. For the most part, the gigantic crowd remained under control. Supporters hailed the festival as an example of the new and better world to come.

Other Americans, however, viewed the antics of the young with distaste. They deplored the uninhibited drug use, nudity, and sexuality, all brought into their living rooms on nightly television news shows. No matter how much the proponents hailed the "Woodstock Nation," much of America was appalled. The festival only underscored the generational polarization.

Other aspects of the counterculture became more visible at another festival four months later in Altamont, California. There 300,000 people gathered at a stock-car raceway to attend a rock concert climaxing an American tour by the immensely popular Rolling Stones. Woodstock had been well planned; the Altamont affair was not. In the absence of adequate security, the Stones hired a band of Hell's Angels to maintain control. Those tough motorcyclists, fond of terrorizing the open road, prepared to keep order in their own way.

The spirit at Altamont was different from the start. The peace and joy of Woodstock were replaced by a lurking fear of what could go wrong. "It was a gray day, and the California hills were bare, cold and dead," wrote Greil Marcus, a music critic. The crowd was "ugly, selfish, territorialist, throughout the day." One

The 1969 rock festival at Woodstock represented the "dawning of the age of Aquarius" for some; for others it was an orgy of illicit and disreputable behavior.

naked woman made a game of selecting a male, approaching him, and rubbing her body against his. When he began to respond, she screamed and ran away. A fat man bounded onto the stage to dance naked to the music of one of the preliminary groups but clumsily trampled those around him and finally aroused the Hell's Angels, who charged him with weighted pool cues and beat him to the ground. An undercurrent of violence simmered, Marcus observed, as "all day long people . . . speculated on who would be killed, on when the killing would take place. There were few doubts that the Angels would do the job."

With the Stones on stage, the fears were realized. As star Mick Jagger looked on, the Hell's Angels beat a young black man to death. A musician who tried to intervene was knocked senseless. Other beatings occurred, accidents claimed several more lives, and drug-overdosed revelers found no adequate medical support.

Altamont revealed the underside of the counterculture and exposed the worst fears of less sympathetic Americans. *Rolling Stone*, the rock world's journal, deplored the commercial, promotional greed that had inspired the concert. Greil Marcus summed up the contradictions of both the concert and the movement: "A young black man murdered in the midst of a white crowd by white thugs as white men played their version of black music—it was too much to kiss off as a mere unpleasantness." But Altamont represented more than continuing racial tension; it also showed the dark side of the counterculture, its self-indulgent, anarchic nature.

Another episode in Nixon's first year reflected the political, as opposed to cultural, split in the United States. The Weathermen, a militant fringe group of the Students for a Democratic Society (SDS), sought in October 1969 to show that the revolution had arrived with a frontal attack on Chicago, scene of the violent Democratic convention of 1968.

The New Left had been increasingly active in the late 1960s, and as it seized upon the issue of the Vietnam War and broadened its critique of American society, the SDS became a significant force. After a series of factional disputes, the Weathermen (who took their name from a line in a Bob Dylan song, "You don't need a weather-man to know which way the wind blows") emerged as one of the most radical groups.

Starting on October 8, Weathermen from all over the country converged on Chicago, mobilized themselves, and prepared to attack. In the evening, dressed in hard hats and jackboots, wearing work gloves and other forms of padding, they rampaged through the streets with clubs and pipes, chains and rocks. They ran into the police, as they had expected and hoped, and continued the attack. Some were arrested, others were shot, and the rest withdrew to regroup. For the next two days, they plotted strategy, engaged in minor skirmishes, and prepared for the final thrust. It came on the fourth day, once again pitting aggressive Weathermen against hostile police.

Why had the Weathermen launched their attack? "The status quo meant to us war, poverty, inequality, ignorance, famine and disease in most of the world," Bo Burlingham, a participant from Ohio, reflected. "To accept it was to condone and help perpetuate it. We felt like miners trapped in a terrible poisonous shaft with no light to guide us out. We resolved to destroy the tunnel even if we risked destroying ourselves in the process."

The rationale of the Chicago "national action" may have been clear to the participants, but it convinced few other Americans. There and elsewhere, citizens were infuriated at what they saw. In New York City, when students demonstrated in the Wall Street area in the aftermath of the Kent State affair, angry construction workers on their lunch break attacked them. Carrying signs reading "Don't worry, they don't draft faggots," and "Get the hippie! Get the traitor!" they rushed at the demonstrators with lead pipes and fists. As was so often the case, middle-class and working-class Americans found themselves on different sides.

Law and Order

Underlying Nixon's hopes of bringing America together was the conviction that this process must begin by restoring law and order. He hoped to exploit the growing backlash as most working-class and many middle-class Americans became increasingly hostile to the protest movements of the 1960s. Crime rates seemed to be rising as drug use spread. Permissive attitudes toward sex flouted old codes. Racial and political disruptions threatened the pursuit of the middle-class American dream. At home, by promising to restore the old values they shared, Nixon intended to cultivate the groups who felt change had gone too far.

One part of the administration's campaign involved denouncing disruptive elements. Nixon lashed out at demonstrators—he called the students "bums" at one point. More and more, however, he relied on his vice-president to play the part of hatchet man, just as Nixon had done for Eisenhower as his vice-president. Spiro Agnew had a gift for jugular attack. In one campaign speech he told students sympathetic to the SDS, "I know you'd like to overthrow the government, but on November fifth, we'll put a man in office who'll take this country forward without you." In office he was no less vituperative. "Ideological eunuchs" he called students, "parasites of passion." Opposition elements made up an "effete corps of impudent snobs," who did untold damage in the United States, he stated.

Another part of Nixon's effort to promote stability involved attacking the communications industry, which he believed undermined consensus in America. The media, he felt, not only represented the views of the "Eastern establishment" but showed a personal hostility toward him as well. Nixon had long grumbled about his treatment in the press, considering "the influential majority of the news media to be part of my political opposition." Early in his term, he decided to take on the television networks for what he considered biased and distorted coverage of his policies. Again Agnew was directed to spearhead the attack, and he did so with relish.

Most important, however, was the effort of Attorney General John Mitchell to demonstrate that the administration supported the values of citizens upset by domestic upheavals. Mitchell sought enhanced powers for a campaign on crime, sometimes at the expense of individuals' constitutional rights. With little respect for the right of dissent, he intended to send a message to the entire country that the new team in the

White House would not tolerate the excesses that had led to violence in the streets.

One part of Mitchell's plan involved reshaping the Supreme Court, which had rendered increasingly liberal decisions on the rights of defendants in the past decade and a half. That shift, Republican leaders argued, had led to moral and ethical looseness in the United States and had encouraged the recent disruptions. In his first term, Nixon had the extraordinary opportunity to name four judges to the Court, and he nominated men who shared his views. His first choice was Warren E. Burger as Chief Justice to replace the liberal Earl Warren, who was retiring. Burger, a moderate, was confirmed quickly. Other appointments, however, were more partisan and reflected Nixon's aggressively conservative approach. Intent on appealing to white southerners, he first selected Clement Haynesworth of South Carolina, then G. Harrold Carswell of Florida. Both men on examination showed such racial biases or limitations that the Senate refused to confirm them. Nixon then appointed Harry Blackmun, Lewis F. Powell, Jr., and William Rehnquist, all able and qualified, and all inclined to tilt the Court in a more conservative way.

Over the next few years, the Court shifted to the right. It narrowed defendants' rights in an attempt to ease the burden of the prosecution in its cases and slowed the process of liberalization by upholding pornography laws if they mirrored community standards. On other questions, however, the Court did not always move as the president had hoped. In the 1973 *Roe* v. *Wade* decision, the Court legalized abortion, stating that women's rights included the right to control their own bodies. This decision was one that the feminists, a group hardly supported by the president, had ardently sought.

"Southern Strategy" and Showdown on Civil Rights

Nixon's intent was to underscore his allegiance to conservative groups in order to solidify a firm political base. Nowhere was that approach more evident than in the area of civil rights. Nixon felt that he had little to gain by courting blacks, for in 1968 the Republicans had won barely 5 percent of the black vote. Further-more, an effort to woo the black electorate could endanger the attempt to obtain white southern support. Both the president and the attorney general felt that the civil rights movement had run its course. It was now in their interest to shape government policy to secure the votes of southern whites.

From the start, the administration sought to dampen the federal commitment to civil rights. Nixon himself once declared that "there are those who want instant integration and those who want segregation forever. I believe that we need to have a middle course between those two extremes." Given the continued resistance to racial change in some parts of the country, such a middle course involved very little action at all.

In line with political priorities, the administration moved, at the start of Nixon's first term,

Busing was mandated to end de facto school segregation in the North, drawing violent opposition from whites in some cities and requiring police protection for those bused.

to reduce the appropriation for fair-housing enforcement. Then the Department of Justice tried to prevent extension of the Voting Rights Act of 1965, which had added a million blacks to the voting rolls and led to the election of thousands of black officials, especially in northern cities. Congress approved the extension, but the administration had made clear its position on racial issues. When South Carolina senator Strom Thurmond and others tried to suspend federal school desegregation guidelines, the Justice Department urged a delay in meeting desegregation deadlines in 33 of Mississippi's school districts. The NAACP appealed, and the Supreme Court ruled unanimously that "the obligation of every school system is to terminate dual school systems at once." Publicly disagreeing with the decision, Nixon showed his sympathy with white southern sentiment while at the same time avoiding blame for the integration of Mississippi's schools.

Nixon also faced the growing controversy over busing as a means of desegregation, a highly charged issue in the 1970s. Transporting students from one area to another to attend school was nothing new. A century before, in 1869, Massachusetts had set aside money to send children to and from school in carriages and wagons, and over the next 50 years, public funding for student transport became lawful in all states. Busing, in fact, had usually been viewed by parents as an educational advantage, for their children could be moved from a one-room schoolhouse to a consolidated school. By 1970, over 18 million students, almost 40 percent of those in the United States, rode buses to school. Yet when busing became tangled with the question of integration, it inflamed passions.

The busing question first surfaced in the South. There, in the years before the Supreme Court endorsed integration, busing had long been used to maintain segregated schools. Some black students in Selma, Alabama, for example, traveled 50 miles by bus to an entirely black trade school in Montgomery, even though a similar school for whites stood nearby. Now, however, busing had become a means of breaking down racial barriers.

The issue came to a head in North Carolina, in the Charlotte-Mecklenburg school system.

The 550-square-mile district had over 84,000 students in more than 100 schools. Twenty-nine percent of the pupils were black, and they were concentrated primarily in one section of the region. A desegregation plan involving voluntary transfer was in effect, but there, as elsewhere, many blacks still attended largely segregated schools. A federal judge ruled that the district was not in compliance with the latest Supreme Court decisions, and in 1971, the Supreme Court ruled that district courts had broad authority to order the desegregation of school systems—by busing, if necessary.

Earlier, Nixon had opposed such busing, and the Court decision did not affect his position. The fact that George Wallace had spoken out against busing and won Florida's Democratic primary in March 1972 was not lost on Nixon. The president approached Congress for a moratorium or even a restriction on busing and went on television to denounce it. Although Congress did not accede to his request, southerners knew where the president stood. As more and more southern cities were obliged to establish transportation plans to integrate their schools, however, resistance grew.

As the busing mandate spread to the North, resistance spilled out of the South. In the North, in many of the nation's largest cities, schools were as rigidly segregated as in the South, largely due to residential patterns. This segregation was called *de facto* to differentiate it from the *de jure* or legal segregation that had existed in the South. Mississippi senator John C. Stennis, a bitter foe of busing, hoped to stir up the North by making it subject to the same standards as the South. "Parents," he said, "are not going to permit their children to be boxed up and crated and hauled around the city and the country like common animals." And, he informed Northern colleagues, "if you have to [integrate] in your area, you will see what it means to us." His proposal, adopted in the Senate, required that federal desegregation guidelines be enforced uniformly throughout the nation or not used at all. Court decisions subsequently ordered many northern cities to desegregate their schools.

In Boston, the effort to integrate proved rockier than anywhere else in the North. In 1973, despite a state measure eight years earlier requiring districts to desegregate any schools more than half black, 85 percent of the blacks in Boston attended schools that had a black majority. More than half the black students were in schools that were 90 percent black. In June 1974, a federal judge ordered that busing begin. The first phase, involving 17,000 pupils, was to start in the fall of that year.

Watching the process unfold, Thomas J. Cottle, of the Children's Defense Fund of the Washington Research Project in Boston, closely followed two families, one white, one black. Though he changed their names in a report he presented in the popular press, he captured their sentiments and their words.

Clarence Charles McDonough III, a white parent, was irate when he learned that his son Cassie was to be transferred by bus from the white school he attended to a black school farther away. "They did it to me," he screamed as Cottle visited one day.

> They went and did it to me. . . . I told you they would. I told you there'd be no running from 'em. You lead your life perfect as a pane of glass, go to church, work 40 hours a week at the same job—year in, year out—keep your complaints to yourself, and they still do it to you. They're forcing that boy to go to school miles from here in a dangerous area to a school no one knows a damn thing about, just so they can bring these other kids in, kids who don't belong here.

Black father Ronald Dearborn also had anxieties of his own about what his son Claudell might face in a white area. "It's a long way," he said, "even by car. Let's hope they keep those buses running fine. I'd hate to think what would happen if they broke down some night over there. If white folks don't look kindly at having black folks attending their schools, they sure won't like to see a bunch of black youngsters parked outside their home all night." Unlike Clarence McDonough, however, he supported school desegregation. As Francine, Claudell's mother, pointed out, such steps were necessary, even if bruises were involved, for "when you're black, you know all about falling—and what you don't know this country teaches you mighty fast, even when you go to schools where everyone is black, like we did."

For both Cassie and Claudell, attendance at different elementary schools went smoothly. Reassigned high school students were less fortunate. A white boycott at South Boston High cut attendance from the anticipated 1,500 to less than 100 on the first day. Buses bringing in black students were stoned and some children cut. White working-class South Bostonians felt that they were being asked to carry the burden of middle-class liberals' racial views. Similar resentments and anger triggered racial episodes elsewhere. In many cases, white families either enrolled their children in private schools or fled the city altogether.

Busing became a bitter issue, one that reflected the still volatile nature of the quest for equal rights. Given his own private views and political ends, Nixon hoped to slow down the civil rights movement, and to a degree, he did. Yet he never viewed himself as a racial bigot. Rather he saw himself as a man who would do whatever was practical to assist in racial relations. "I care," he once insisted to James Farmer, a black leader appointed to the post of assistant secretary of health, education, and welfare. "I just hope people will believe that I *do* care." But actions spoke louder than words, and only pressures from others kept the civil rights movement alive.

Watergate and the 1972 Reelection Campaign

Shortly after taking office, the Nixon administration found itself at a standoff with the legislative branch: Both houses of Congress were solidly Democratic. Nixon was determined to end the legislative stalemate by winning a second term and sweeping Republican majorities into both houses of Congress in 1972.

Nixon's reelection campaign was even better organized than the effort four years before. Sparing no expense, the president relied on aides who were fiercely loyal and prepared to do anything to win. Special counsel Charles W. Colson described himself as a "flag-waving, . . . anti-press, anti-liberal Nixon fanatic." He had earlier played an important part in developing an "enemies list" of prominent figures judged to be unsympathetic to the administration. White House counsel John Dean defined his task as finding a way to "use the available federal machinery to screw our political enemies." Active in carrying out commands were E. Howard Hunt, a former CIA agent and a specialist in "dirty tricks," and G. Gordon Liddy, a one-time member of the FBI, who prided himself on his willingness to do anything without flinching. Hunt and Liddy had earlier been members of the "Plumbers," who tried to plug government leaks after the Pentagon Papers affair.

The Committee to Re-elect the President (CREEP), headed by John Mitchell, who resigned as attorney general to do so, launched a massive fund-raising drive, aimed at collecting as much money as it could before the reporting of contributions became necessary under a new campaign-finance law. That money could be used for any purpose, including payments for the performance of dirty tricks aimed at disrupting the opposition's campaign. Other funds financed an intelligence branch within CREEP that had Liddy at its head and included Hunt.

Early in 1972, Liddy and his lieutenants proposed an elaborate scheme to wiretap the phones of various Democrats and to disrupt their nominating convention. Twice Mitchell refused to go along, arguing that the plan was too risky and expensive. Finally he approved a modified version of the plan to tap the phones of the Democratic National Committee at its headquarters in the Watergate apartment complex in Washington, D.C. Mitchell, formerly the top justice official in the land, had authorized breaking the law.

The wiretapping attempt took place on the evening of June 16 and ended with the arrest of those involved. They carried with them money and documents that could be traced to CREEP and incriminate the reelection campaign. Top officials of the Nixon reelection team had to decide quickly what response to make.

Cover-up and Catastrophe

Reelection remained the most pressing priority, so Nixon's aides played the matter down and used federal resources to head off the investigation. When the FBI traced the money carried by the burglars to CREEP, the president authorized the CIA to call off the FBI on the grounds that national security was at stake. Though not involved in the planning of the break-in, the president was now party to the cover-up. In the succeeding months, he authorized payment of hush money to silence Hunt and others. Top members of the administration, including Mitchell, perjured themselves in court to shield the higher officials who were involved.

Nixon won the election of 1972 in a landslide, receiving 60.7 percent of the popular vote and trouncing his opponent, George McGovern, a liberal senator from South Dakota, even more soundly in the electoral college. He failed, however, to gain the congressional majorities necessary to support his programs.

Even worse, he had to watch the trial of the Watergate burglars. While the matter seemed closed when the defendants pleaded guilty and were sentenced to jail, it refused to die. Judge John Sirica was not satisfied that justice had been done, asserting that the evidence indicated that others had played a part. Meanwhile, two zealous reporters, Bob Woodward and Carl Bernstein of the Washington *Post*, were following a trail of leads on their own. Slowly they recognized who else was involved. On one occasion, when they reached Mitchell and asked him about a story tying him to Watergate, he turned on them in fury. "All that crap, you're putting in the paper?" he said. "It's all been denied."

Mitchell's irritation notwithstanding, the unraveling of Watergate continued. The Senate Select Committee on Presidential Campaign Activities undertook an investigation, and one of the convicted burglars testified that the White House had been involved in the episode. Newspaper stories provided further leads, and the Senate hearings in turn provided new material for the press. Faced with rumors that the White House was actively involved, Nixon decided that he had to release Haldeman and Ehrlichman, his two closest aides, in an effort to save his own neck. On nationwide TV he declared that he would take the ultimate responsibility for the mistakes of others, for "there can be no whitewash at the White House."

In May 1973, the Senate committee began televised public hearings, reminiscent of the earlier McCarthy hearings of the 1950s. As millions of Americans watched, the drama built. John Dean, seeking to save himself, testified that Nixon knew about the cover-up, and other staffers revealed a host of illegal activities undertaken at the White House: Money had been paid to the burglars to silence them; State Department documents had been forged to smear a previous administration; wiretaps had been used to prevent top-level leaks. The most electrifying moment was the disclosure that the president had in his office a secret taping system that recorded all conversations. Tapes could verify or disprove the growing rumors that Nixon had in fact been party to the cover-up all along.

In an effort to demonstrate his own honesty, Nixon agreed to the appointment of Harvard law professor Archibald Cox as a special prosecutor in the Department of Justice. But when Cox tried to gain access to the tapes, Nixon resisted and finally fired him. Nixon's own popularity had begun to drop, and even the appointment of another special prosecutor, Leon Jaworski, did

Presidential Elections, 1968 and 1972

YEAR	CANDIDATES	PARTY	POPULAR VOTE	ELECTORAL VOTES
1968	RICHARD M. NIXON	Republican	31,783,783 (43.4%)	301
	Hubert H. Humphrey	Democratic	31,271,839 (42.7%)	191
	George C. Wallace	Amer. Independent	9,899,557 (13.5%)	46
1972	RICHARD M. NIXON	Republican	45,767,218 (60.6%)	520
	George S. McGovern	Democratic	28,357,668 (37.5%)	17

Note: Winners' names appears in capital letters.

In an earlier chapter we looked at political cartoons of Theodore Roosevelt to gain insight into the past through the cartoons found on the editorial pages of newspapers. We saw how cartoonists depend on caricature in distorting the features of a subject, thus making their point at a moment's glance. With sometimes biting humor, they make us laugh in recognition of a political predicament or larger social truth. Some galvanize our emotions to action. The best cartoons hold up a mirror to help us see ourselves as we are, full of human frailties yet touched with nobility.

Editorial cartoons are not the only kind of graphic technique to stir such reactions. Many other forms of humorous cartoons, from Saturday morning television films to comic books and newspaper "funny pages," suggest the issues and moral questions that concern the people of a particular era. Historians, therefore, can sometimes recover the deepest truths about the past by noticing what makes people laugh. We laugh at those aspects of our personalities and culture that matter the most to us.

From 1972 to 1975, no issue mattered more to the American people than the truth about the events associated with "Watergate" and how much President Nixon knew about those affairs. Nixon's combative relationship with the press, coupled with his easily identified features (heavy jowls, pointed nose), made

Herbert Block, "Tape Job," August 28, 1973

Tony Auth, "I cannot tell the truth . . . ," August 8, 1974, from Behind the Lines by Tony Auth

961a

Garry Trudeau, "Doonesbury," September 17, 1973

him a ready target of cartoonists. The mysteriously missing 18½ minutes from the White House tapes and other examples of a presidential cover-up of the truth about Watergate provided clever cartoonists with irresistible opportunities to poke fun. At stake, however, was not just some petty criminal actions, or even the fate of the Nixon presidency, but rather deeper, troublesome questions about justice, liberty, truth, and the nation's faith in the American constitutional system.

The accompanying cartoons, drawn by four of the most incisive cartoonists of recent times, all originated in the Watergate crisis of the 1970s. Tony Auth and Herbert Block (known as Herblock) were then editorial political cartoonists for the Philadelphia *Inquirer* and the Washington *Post*, respectively. Jules Feiffer, like Garry Trudeau ("Doonesbury"), creates comic strips not only on political subjects but on every conceivable aspect of modern culture. Each is syndicated nationally and has published several volumes of his collected cartoons. Each provided wit and insight to help the American people interpret the events of Watergate. Historians, too, can understand some of the emotional power and anguish all Americans, including the president himself, went through during this era by looking at cartoon humor. Like all great cartoons, they speak for themselves.

Jules Feiffer, "King Kong," from Jules Feiffer's America from Eisenhower to Reagan, 1982

not help. More and more Americans now believed that the president had had at least some part in the cover-up and should take responsibility for his acts. *Time* magazine ran an editorial headlined "The President Should Resign," and Congress considered impeachment. The first steps, in accordance with constitutional mandate, began in the House of Representatives.

In late July 1974, the House Judiciary Committee, made up of 21 Democrats and 17 Republicans, debated the impeachment case. By sizable tallies, it voted to impeach the president on the grounds of obstruction of justice, abuse of power, and refusal to obey a congressional subpoena to turn over his tapes. A full House of Representatives vote still had to occur, and the Senate would have to preside over a trial before removal could take place. But for Nixon the handwriting was on the wall.

After a brief delay, on August 5 Nixon obeyed a Supreme Court ruling and released the tapes. They contained clear evidence of his complicity in the cover-up. His ultimate resignation became but a matter of time. Four days later, on August 9, 1974, the extraordinary episode came to an end as Nixon became the first American president ever to resign.

The Ford Interlude

In the aftermath of the Watergate affair, Washington was in a state of turmoil. Americans wondered whether any politician could be trusted to guide public affairs. The new president, Gerald Ford, suddenly found himself thrust into an office he had never planned to hold. As the economy spiraled downward, Ford faced the task of trying to restore national confidence.

Ford worked quickly to restore trust in the government. He emphasized conciliation and compromise, and he promised to cooperate both with Congress and with American citizens. The nation responded gratefully. *Time* magazine pointed to "a mood of good feeling and even exhilaration in Washington that the city had not experienced for many years."

The new president weakened that base of support, however, by pardoning Richard Nixon barely a month after his resignation. Haldeman,

Ehrlichman, Mitchell, Dean, and other Nixon administration officials faced indictment, trial, and imprisonment for their part in the Watergate affair, but their former leader, even before a hearing, was to go free of prosecution for any crimes committed while president of the United States. Ford hoped that his magnanimous gesture would help heal the nation's wounds, but in fact it only raised doubts about his judgment. Now Ford was booed and jeered, just as Johnson and Nixon before him had been, and he too had to leave speaking engagements through back doors to avoid demonstrators angry over the pardon.

On policy questions, Ford followed the direction established during the Nixon years. Staying on as secretary of state, Kissinger maintained continuity in the field of foreign affairs. On the domestic front, the president's decidedly conservative bent often threw him into confrontation with a Democratic Congress. Economic problems proved most pressing in 1974 as inflation, fueled by oil-price increases, rose to 11 percent a year, unemployment stood at 5.3 percent, and gross national product declined. Home construction slackened and interest rates rose, while stock prices fell. Nixon, preoccupied with the Watergate crisis, had been unable to curb

Gerald Ford's genial, unpretentious personality made him a reassuring presence after the Nixon administration; here he seeks the White House photographer's advice on the use of a camera.

rising inflation and unemployment. Not since Franklin Roosevelt took office in the depths of the Great Depression had a new president faced economic difficulties so severe.

Like Herbert Hoover 45 years before him, Ford hoped to restore confidence and persuade the public that conditions would improve. His WIN campaign called on Americans to "Whip Inflation Now" and urged them to wear red and white WIN lapel buttons, save rather than spend a part of their income, and plant their own vegetable gardens to challenge rising prices in the stores. The plan had no substantive machinery to back it up, ignored the root causes of the problem, and soon disappeared.

The administration introduced a tight-money policy as a means of curbing inflation. It led to the most severe recession since the Depression, with unemployment peaking at 12 percent in 1975. Congress pushed for an antirecession spending program. Recognizing political reality, Ford endorsed a multibillion-dollar tax cut coupled with higher unemployment benefits. The economy made a modest recovery, although inflation and unemployment remained high, and federal budget deficits soared.

Ford proved unable to develop a successful response to the energy crisis, which played such a crucial role in disrupting the economy. In the civil rights arena, Ford asked his own attorney general, Edward H. Levi, to consider supporting antibusing advocates in a Boston court case, then accepted the advice that the idea be dropped. In the aftermath of the Vietnam War, he proposed an amnesty program for those who had fled the draft. It seemed excessively harsh to those concerned and consequently failed to work; in a six-month period, of 126,900 eligible, only 22,500 applied. The others remained abroad or in hiding, still unable or unwilling to come home.

Throughout his short tenure as president, Ford was often embroiled in conflict with Congress. He vetoed numerous bills, including those creating a consumer-protection agency and expanding programs in education, housing, and health. In response, Congress overrode a higher percentage of vetoes than at any time since the presidency of Franklin Pierce more than a century before. Rather than reviving the country after Watergate, Ford frequently found himself powerless to affect it.

THE CLIMAX OF SOCIAL REFORM

The turbulent 1960s had spawned an assortment of movements and groups. In the troubled 1970s, they continued to grow, although they were often affected by the uncertain economy.

Feminism at High Tide

In 1971, Helen Reddy expressed the energy of the woman's movement in a song called "I Am Woman":

I am woman, hear me roar
In numbers too big to ignore
And I know too much to go back and pretend
'Cause I've heard it all before
And I've been down there on the floor,
No one's ever gonna keep me down again.
Oh, yes, I am wise
But it's wisdom born of pain.
Yes, I've paid the price

But look how much I gained.
If I have to
I can do anything.
I am strong,
I am invincible,
I am woman.

Only a few years before, in 1962, a Gallup poll revealed that a majority of women did not believe that American women suffered discrimination. The facts, however, told a different story, for even though more women were working, they did not receive equal pay for equal work. In 1977, the working woman earned 57 percent of what her male counterpart did; in 1939, she had earned 61 percent. Moreover, employers systematically excluded women from many positions. Most still held "female" jobs in the clerical, sales, and service sectors.

The confrontations of the 1960s began to alter that state of affairs as well as the perception of women's role. In the early 1970s, a survey noted that in a two-year period, the number of college students who felt that women were oppressed had doubled, and the numbers continued to rise. Whereas in 1970 a survey of first-year college students showed that men interested in such fields as business, medicine, engineering, and law outnumbered women eight to one, in 1975 the ratio had dropped to three to one. The proportion of women beginning law school quadrupled between 1969 and 1973.

Several publications helped to spread the ideas of the women's movement. Gloria Steinem, author of a regular political column in *New York* magazine, first thought of herself as a professional journalist with no particular interest in women's affairs. "I certainly didn't understand that women were an 'out' group," she noted, "and I would even insist that I wasn't discriminated against as a woman." While working on a story about abortion, however, she began to realize that discrimination took many forms. She realized she "had been unable to get an apartment because, the reasoning was, a single woman wasn't financially responsible— and if she *was* responsible, she was probably a prostitute." Steinem began writing more about

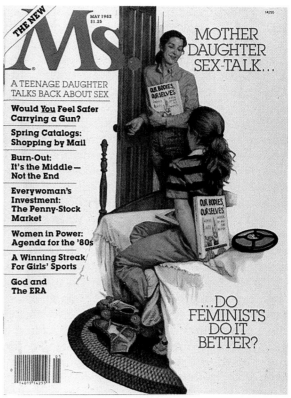

Our Bodies, Ourselves *and* Ms. *magazine were among the publications spawned by the women's movement to give women greater control over various aspects of their lives.*

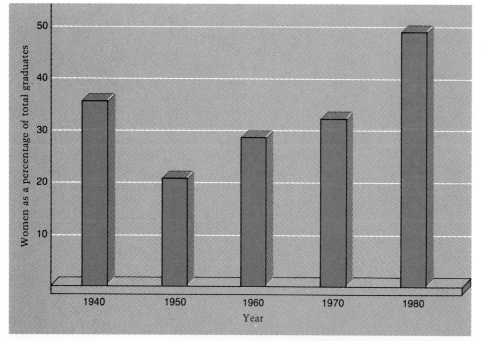

Women College Graduates, 1940–1980

Source: U.S. Department of Commerce.

women, and in 1971 she banded together with several other women to found a new magazine. *Ms.* succeeded beyond their wildest dreams and reached a wide audience of women who were not members of feminist organizations. In the first eight days, the 300,000 copies of the preview issue sold out. By 1973, there were almost 200,000 subscribers. Most of them were under 35, had graduated from college, and were working in professional, managerial, or technical jobs.

Other publications also publicized the issues and concerns of the women's movement. *The New Woman's Survival Catalogue* provided useful advice to women readers. *Our Bodies, Ourselves,* a handbook published by a woman's health collective, encouraged women to understand and control their bodies; it sold 850,000 copies between 1971 and 1976.

These new books and magazines differed radically from older women's magazines like *Good Housekeeping* and *Ladies' Home Journal.* Those publications aimed at women at home and focused on their domestic interests, needs, and sometimes fantasies. *Ms.*, on the other hand, dealt with abortion, and provided a forum for the discussion of important feminist issues.

Despite certain shared interests, women's struggle for equality was decentralized, diffuse, and often internally divided. As *Time* magazine pointed out in 1972, "The aims of the movement range from the modest, sensible amelioration of the female condition to extreme and revolutionary visions." Groups like NOW pressed for equal employment opportunities, child-care centers, and abortion reform. Women both in and out of NOW who were concerned with legal reforms worked for congressional passage, then ratification, of the Equal Rights Amendment (ERA) to the Constitution. Passed by Congress in 1972, it stated simply, "Equality of rights under the law shall not be denied or abridged by the United States or by any State on account of sex." Thirty of the required 38 states quickly ratified it, a few others followed, and for a time final approval seemed imminent.

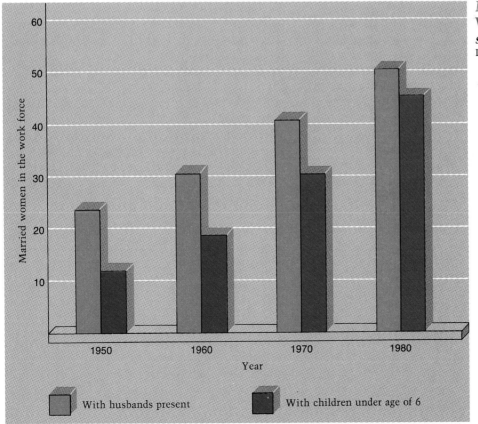

Married Women in the Work Force, 1950–1980

Source: U.S. Bureau of Labor Statistics.

With husbands present   With children under age of 6

Other feminist groups adopted more radical positions. Legal changes were not enough, they argued. Fundamental changes in sexual identity were needed to end male domination and social exploitation. Shulamith Firestone, a former member of the New Left, explained in *The Dialectic of Sex* (1970) the necessity of a new society in which women were freed "from the tyranny of their reproductive biology by every means available." Moreover, traditional gender and family roles must be discarded and "the childbearing and childrearing role [diffused] to the society as a whole, men as well as women." Other socialist feminists claimed that it was not enough to strike out at male domination, for capitalist society itself was responsible for women's plight. Only through the process of revolution could women be free.

Moderates and radicals alike generated opposition. Gloria Steinem was often ridiculed. One man, she recalled, approached her on the street and said, "I have ten women employees and I pay them a third of what I pay men, and if I had to pay them more, I'd fire them. What do you think of *that*?" Nixon himself sided with the traditionalists when in 1971 he vetoed an appropriation for day-care centers with the argument that they undermined the sanctity of the family. He insisted that "the vast moral authority of national government . . . must be . . . consciously designed to cement the family in its rightful position as the keystone of our civilization."

Women themselves resisted feminism for many reasons. Many felt the women's movement was contemptuous of women who stayed at home to perform all the tasks that had traditionally been expected of them. Marabel Morgan was one who still insisted that the woman had a place at home by her husband's side. The wife of a Florida attorney, she argued that "it is only when a woman surrenders her life to her husband, reveres and worships him, and is willing to serve him, that she becomes really beautiful to him." In her book *The Total Woman* (1973) she counseled others to follow the 4A approach: accept, admire, adapt, appreciate. She suggested ways of meeting a husband at the door and cited approvingly the case of one woman who "welcomed her husband home in black mesh stockings, high heels, and an apron. That's all." Everything was designed to move from "fizzle to sizzle," and substantial numbers of women wanted to hear the message. As of 1975, some 500,000 copies of the hardcover volume had been sold before a paperback version appeared.

In the realm of politics, Phyllis Schlafly headed a nationwide campaign to block ratification of the ERA. Author of several books, including one strongly supporting the conservative presidential candidate Barry Goldwater a decade before, she was both vigorous and articulate. On the ERA she was adamant: "It won't do anything to help women, and it will take away from women the rights they already have, such as the right of a wife to be supported by her husband, the right of a woman to be exempted from military combat, and the right, if you wanted it, to go to a single-sex college." The ERA, she predicted, would lead to the establishment of coed bathrooms, the elimination of alimony, and the legalization of homosexual marriage. Women, she argued, already had legal backing enough for their rights.

Despite the counterattacks, the women's movement flourished in the 1970s. But like other earlier attempts to change the status of women, it was fueled largely by the grievances of middle-class women. Focusing on issues of interest to them, the movement often ignored the special problems of black and white working-class women. As one black woman told Betty Friedan, "We don't want anything to do with that feminist bag." Most black women found race a far more compelling problem than gender. Black women, Friedan was told, wanted "black men to get ahead." Nor did the feminists' emphasis on the satisfaction of working outside the home make much sense to white working-class women who could only expect dull, monotonous, and poorly paid jobs if they went to work. They preferred to stay at home if they could.

Hispanics and Native Americans

As women pressed for reform, Native Americans remained intent on voicing their grievances and publicizing their demands. The American Indian Movement (AIM), founded in

1968, gave them a platform and a focus for gaining rights and regaining lost lands.

The new militancy was dramatized in November 1969, when a landing party of 78 Indians seized Alcatraz Island in San Francisco Bay. It was the site of a defunct federal prison, declared surplus property five years before. Pointing to the Fort Laramie Treaty of 1868, which permitted male Indians to file homestead claims on federal lands, the occupiers took over the island to protest symbolically the inability of the Bureau of Indian Affairs to "deal practically" with questions of Indian welfare. They converted the island into a cultural and educational center but in 1971 were removed by federal officials.

In 1972, militants launched the Broken Treaties Caravan to Washington. For six days, insurgents occupied the Bureau of Indian Affairs. In 1973, AIM took over the South Dakota village of Wounded Knee, where in 1890 the U.S. 7th Calvary had massacred the Sioux. The reservation surrounding the town was mired in poverty. Half the families were on welfare, alcoholism was widespread, and 81 percent of the student population had dropped out of school. The occupation was meant to dramatize these conditions and to draw attention to the 371 treaties AIM leaders claimed the government had broken. Federal officials responded by encircling the

The American Indian Movement's 1973 occupation of Wounded Knee dramatized unfair government treatment of Native Americans.

area, and, when AIM tried to bring in supplies, killed one Indian and wounded another. The confrontation ended with a government agreement to reexamine the treaty rights of the Indians, although little of substance was subsequently done.

Hispanics in America also adopted more militant tactics. Their population, approximately 9 million in 1970, increased by a third during the decade as a result of growing immigration and a high birthrate. Hispanics constituted the nation's largest minority group after black Americans; Spanish, rather than Italian, became the most commonly spoken foreign language. The Mexican-American population in particular soared, as did a consciousness of its rights.

In the West and Southwest, Mexican-American studies programs flourished. By 1969, at least 50 existed in California alone. They offered degrees, built library collections, and provided Chicanos access to their own past. The campuses also provided a network linking students together and mobilizing them for political action.

Beginning in 1968, Mexican-American students began to protest conditions in the secondary schools. They pointed bitterly to overcrowded and run-down institutions and to the 50 percent dropout rate that came from expulsion, transfer, or failure because students had never been taught to read. In March 1968, some 10,000 Chicano students walked out of five high schools in Los Angeles. Their actions inspired other walkouts in Colorado, Texas, and other parts of California and led to demands for Mexican teachers, counselors, and courses and better facilities.

At the same time, new organizations sprang up. A few years before, teenager David Sánchez and four Chicanos in East Los Angeles had formed a group called Young Citizens for Community Action. Gradually the organization evolved from a service club to a defensive patrol. Now known as Young Chicanos for Community Action, the group adopted a paramilitary stance. Its members became identified as the Brown Berets and formed chapters throughout the Midwest and Southwest.

Other Hispanics began to organize politically. José Angel Gutiérrez was one of those in

Texas who recognized the need for political activism to change conditions that had existed for generations. On one occasion, at a press conference, he gained national attention by exploding, "Kill the *gringo!*" Anglo-Americans were afraid that he meant it literally. Gutiérrez attended a rally in March 1969 at San Félipe del Río to protest the cancellation of a government-funded neighborhood project. Three months later, he and a few others went to his hometown of Crystal City, Texas, to begin organizing Hispanics at the grass-roots level. When students began to protest conditions at the local high school, a citizens' organization led by Gutiérrez stepped in to develop a spirit of solidarity. From that group emerged the La Raza Unida political party, which began to play a major role in the area and successfully promoted Mexican-American candidates for political offices. Throughout the 1970s, it gained strength in the West and Southwest.

Hispanic-Americans also participated in the more general protest against the Vietnam War. Because the draft drew most heavily from the poorer segments of society, the Hispanic casualty rate was far higher than that of the population at large. In 1969, the Brown Berets organized the National Chicano Moratorium Committee and staged antiwar demonstrations. They argued that this was a racial war, with black and brown Americans being used against their Third World compatriots. Some of the rallies ended in confrontations with the police and brought charges of police brutality.

Aware of the growing numbers and growing demands of Hispanic-Americans, the Nixon adminstration sought to defuse their anger and win their support. Recognizing that with 5 percent more of the Mexican-American vote in Texas in 1968, Nixon would have carried the state, political analysts advised an effort to lure Mexican-Americans into the Republican camp. By dangling political positions, government jobs, and promises of better programs for Mexican-Americans they attempted to secure their support. The effort paid off; Nixon received 31 percent of the Hispanic vote in 1972. Rather than reward his Hispanic followers, however, the president moved to cut back the poverty program that had begun under Johnson.

Chicano pride showed itself in thousands of urban murals, a by-product of the grass-roots Hispanic rights movement of the early 1970s.

Although disillusioned and discouraged in the mid-1970s, Mexican-Americans could take some comfort from a Supreme Court decision in 1974 that declared that schools had to meet the needs of children with a limited grasp of English. That decision led to federal funding of bilingual education.

They could also take pride in their achievements in the fields. A nationwide consumer boycott of grapes, lettuce, and other products harvested by exploited labor finally ended in success. In 1975, César Chávez's long struggle for farmworkers ended in the successful passage in California of a measure that required growers to bargain collectively with the elected representatives of the workers. Farmworkers had never been covered by the National Labor Relations Board. Now they were guaranteed legitimate elections and the representation they had long sought. This soon brought higher wages and improved working conditions—proof that strenuous organizing could bring results.

Environmental and Consumer Movements

While women and ethnic minorities pursued their own demands, other groups mobilized for action. The environmental movement, which emerged in the mid-1960s, grew rapidly.

A Gallup poll revealed that while only 17 percent of the public considered air and water pollution to be one of the three major governmental problems in 1965, that figure had risen to 53 percent by 1970.

The modern environmental movement, which revived issues raised during the progressive era, gathered momentum after the publication in 1962 of Rachel Carson's *Silent Spring*. She took aim at chemical pesticides, particularly DDT, which had increased crop yields yet had disastrous side effects. As Americans learned of the pollutants surrounding them, they became increasingly worried about pesticides, the automobile, and industrial wastes that filled the air with smog. Lyndon Johnson, whose vision of the Great Society included "an environment that is pleasing to the senses and healthy to live in," pressed for and won basic legislation to halt the destruction of the country's natural resources.

Public concern mounted further in 1969 when it was discovered that thermal pollution from nuclear power plants was killing fish in both eastern and western rivers. DDT was threatening the very existence of the bald eagle, the nation's emblem. A massive oil spill off the coast of southern California turned white beaches black and wiped out much of the marine life in the immediate area.

Some environmentalists pressed for preservation of unspoiled areas, but far more pressured legislative and administrative bodies to regulate polluters. During Nixon's presidency, Congress passed a Clean Air Act, a Water Quality Improvement Act, and a Resource Recovery Act, and mandated a new Environmental Protection Agency to spearhead the effort to control abuses. Conservation and environmental protection were predominately middle-class concerns and often conflicted with the need of working-class Americans for economic growth and the greater employment opportunities it promised.

Related to the environmental movement was a growing consumer movement dating from the 1960s. Americans throughout the twentieth century, particularly in the 1950s, had become attracted to fashionable clothes, house furnishings, and electrical and electronic gadgets, their appetites whetted by mass advertising. Congress had established a variety of regulatory efforts to protect citizens from unscrupulous sellers. In the 1970s, a strong consumer movement grew, aimed at protecting the interests of the purchasing public and making business more responsible to consumers.

Leading the movement was Ralph Nader. He had become interested in the issue of automobile safety while studying law at Harvard and had pursued that interest as a consultant to the Department of Labor. His book, *Unsafe at Any Speed: The Designed-in Dangers of the American Automobile* (1965), argued that many cars were coffins on wheels. Head-on collisions, even at low speeds, could easily kill, for cosmetic bumpers could not withstand modest shocks. He termed the Corvair "one of the nastiest-handling cars ever built" because of its tendency to roll over in certain situations. His efforts paved the way for the National Traffic and Motor Vehicle Safety Act of 1966.

Nader's efforts attracted scores of volunteers, called "Nader's Raiders." They turned out critiques and reports and, more important, inspired consumer activists at all levels of government—city, state, and national. Consumer-protection offices began to monitor a flood of complaints as ordinary citizens became more aware of their rights.

Countercurrents of Self

While some Americans worked to change the system through political action, others rejected the idealism of the 1960s and followed their own bent, "doing their own thing," as a popular phrase put it. Social commentator Tom Wolfe termed the 1970s the "Me Decade." Millions of Americans began to look inward rather than outward. Books like Eric Berne's *Games People Play* (1969) popularized transactional analysis, a therapeutic approach focusing on interpersonal relationships. The Esalen Institute in Big Sur, California, offered encounter sessions to those who could afford to come to the center for a week. Participants were encouraged to face their feelings as honestly as they could, and screams and sobs, moans and groans filled the air.

That entire approach, whether through Esalen or a similar group, aimed, in Wolfe's words, at "changing one's personality—remaking, remodeling, elevating, and polishing one's very *self* . . . and observing, studying, and doting on it." People were encouraged to strip away the excess baggage tied on by society or self "in order to find the Real Me." Broken marriages became the norm as more and more couples chose to acknowledge that husband and wife had to go their own way.

While some Americans sought salvation in narcissistic quests, increasing numbers became involved in mystical religious movements that promised internal peace of a different sort. Some embraced transcendental meditation. Others became involved with Zen. Cults proliferated, as the Hare Krishnas, the Unification Church of the Reverend Sun Myung Moon, the Children of God, and a host of other groups drew people, mostly young, into their midst.

Barbara Garson, author of a New Left drama about Lyndon Johnson in the 1960s, observed the personal consequences of the new age. Her husband had assisted her earlier. Now "my husband Marvin forsook everything (me included) to find peace. For three years he wandered without shoes or money or glasses. Now he is in Israel with some glasses and possibly some peace." Like Marvin, many former members of the radical fringe were set adrift. "Some follow a guru," wrote Garson, "some are into Primal Scream, some seek a rest from the diaspora—a home in Zion."

CONCLUSION: The Struggle for Stability

By 1976, political upheaval had subsided, and the nation, often in private ways, embarked on the struggle for stability. America had finally extricated itself from Vietnam, only to fall into a domestic quagmire—Watergate.

Many Americans tried to escape the shocks by withdrawing to their personal world, but this could not undo the changes that had occurred. Civil rights pressures remained intense. Women like Ann Clarke, met at the start of the chapter, were going back to school in ever-increasing numbers and finding jobs after years of hearing that they should stay at home. Though Richard Nixon had declared that he wanted to draw the nation together, his actions had only split it further apart. The nation was again in pursuit of tranquility and economic health.

Recommended Reading

A number of books provide good introductions to the 1960s. Milton Viorst, *Fire in the Streets: America in the 1960's* (1979) is a vivid account of the turbulence of the decade that gives a real sense of the participants involved. William L. O'Neill, *Coming Apart: An Informal History of America in the 1960s* (1971) deals largely with the earlier part of the decade but has a good assessment of the latter period as well.

On the Nixon presidency, Rowland Evans, Jr., and Robert D. Novak, *Nixon in the White House* (1972) offers the best assessment of public policy and politics in the first term. Richard Nixon, *RN: The Memoirs of Richard Nixon* (1978) is his own account of his life and achievements.

On Gerald Ford, John Hersey, *The President* (1975) is a perceptive treatment of how Nixon's successor operated in the White House by one of America's best-known authors. Richard Reeves, *A Ford, Not a Lincoln* (1975) is an even more penetrating account of how Ford functioned as president.

For the Watergate affair, J. Anthony Lukas, *Nightmare: The Underside of the Nixon Years* (1976) provides the background necessary to understand the scandal and places that crisis in the proper perspective. Carl Bernstein and Bob Woodward, *All the President's Men* (1974) is the vivid story by two journalists of how they helped unravel the Watergate scandal and implicate the White House in the crisis.

On women's issues, Sara Evans, *Personal Politics: The Roots of Women's Liberation in the Civil Rights Movements and the New Left* (1979) contains some perceptive observations about the state of the women's movement in the 1970s. Peter Gabriel Filene, *Him/Her/Self: Sex Roles in Modern America* (1975) begins with the nineteenth century and has a useful section on the changes and developments of recent years. For more detail on Ann Clarke, see Barbara Clarke Mossberg, *Backstage of the American Dream* (1986).

Rodolfo Acuña, *Occupied America: A History of Chicanos* (1981) is a good account of Chicanos in America, particularly in the modern period.

TIME LINE

1966	National Traffic and Motor Vehicle Act
1968	Police and protesters clash at Democratic national convention Chicano student walkouts Richard Nixon elected president My Lai massacre American Indian Movement (AIM) founded
1969	Nixon Doctrine announced Moratorium against the Vietnam War SALT talks begin Woodstock and Altamont rock festivals Weathermen's "Days of Rage" in Chicago Native Americans seize Alcatraz La Raza Unida founded
1970	U.S. invasion of Cambodia Kent State and Jackson State shootings
1971	New York *Times* publishes Pentagon Papers *Ms.* magazine founded
1971–1975	School busing controversies in North and South
1972	Nixon visits China and the Soviet Union Watergate break-in Nixon reelected president SALT I treaty on nuclear arms Congress passes Equal Rights Amendment Broken Treaties Caravan to Washington
1973	Vietnam cease-fire agreement Arab oil embargo Watergate hearings in Congress *Roe* v. *Wade* Agnew resigns as vice-president AIM occupies Wounded Knee
1974	OPEC price increases Inflation hits 11 percent Unemployment reaches 7.1 percent Nixon resigns; Gerald Ford becomes president Ford pardons Nixon
1975	*Mayaguez* incident South Vietnam falls to the Communists Farmworkers grape boycott Unemployment reaches 12 percent

CHAPTER 31

AUSTERITY AND
THE AMERICAN DREAM:
THE UNITED STATES SINCE 1976

After 11 years as a baggage handler, Andy Hjelmeland of Maple Plain, Minnesota, found himself out of work in December 1980. Hjelmeland was not immediately concerned, however, for he had never before had trouble finding employment. Like Hjelmeland, Jerry Espinoza of Los Angeles also lost his job in the early 1980s. He had been with the Bethlehem Steel plant in California for 23 years. Now it closed its doors, and he too was faced with finding a new job.

Both Hjelmeland and Espinoza, in their mid-forties, discovered that conditions had changed since they had last sought work. The unemployment rate, which stood at 3.5 percent in 1969, was now almost three times as high. Old industries suffered serious difficulties and could not compete with more vital firms abroad. As they declined, they laid off their employees.

Millions of unemployed Americans pursued every lead for the few jobs available in the early 1980s. Hjelmeland found himself up against 300 applicants when he responded to a local newspaper advertisement calling for a "handyman." Espinoza, facing similar competition, discovered that his search for work was complicated by his Hispanic background.

Although Hjelmeland had a happy marriage and two healthy sons, he found the strains difficult to bear. He continued to fill out applications and to answer ads, but the repeated rejections filled him with dismay. "It was a new experience for me to confront an impenetrable wall," he observed. "I began to feel like a person on a blacklist." After years of paying bills on time, he now faced a growing stack of unpaid bills. A parking ticket lost in the pile was followed by an arrest warrant that added insult to injury.

Espinoza faced similar strains. He had five children to support and mortgage payments due. Unemployment benefits and his wife's paychecks kept the family going. Like Hjelmeland, his problems mounted. After his two decades at Bethlehem, he was worn out. He had hearing problems, a result of running noisy machines without ear protection. His left hand was scarred, and two fingers were numb from an accident on the job. A back injury from work still troubled him. "When I go looking for a job, no one is hiring," Espinoza said. "Or maybe they are hiring but they look at me and maybe I'm too old or maybe it's my nationality, because they still discriminate."

The discrimination rankled most of all. Hispanics had an annual jobless rate of 13.8 percent in 1982, far higher than the Anglo unemployment rate of 8.6 percent. Latinos with jobs worked vigorously for their part of *el sueño americano*, the American dream. But often the doors were closed.

For both Hjelmeland and Espinoza, old attitudes gave way as the months of unemployment grew. Hjelmeland had previously viewed food stamp and welfare recipients as "freeloaders," but now he had to apply for food stamps himself. "My wavering self-esteem plummeted," he confessed. "By my own lights I had officially become a loser." Espinoza was similarly glum. "One day you're OK, the next day you're depressed," he said. "We're just lost souls now, that's what we are, lost souls."

Both Hjelmeland and Espinoza found the administration in Washington insensitive to their fate. When President Ronald Reagan, who took office in early 1981, lashed out at television officials for harping on the continuing economic troubles across the country and asked, "Is it news that some fellow out in South Succotash someplace has just been laid off . . . should be interviewed nationwide?" Hjelmeland was irate. "I wish," he said, "the President could be that unemployed guy in South Succotash for just one month." The administration had an economic recovery program, but to the unemployed it often seemed far too slow or unworkable.

The difficulties of Hjelmeland and Espinoza mirrored those of countless Americans who could not understand what had gone wrong. At a time when people were recovering from the shocks of the Vietnam War and the disillusionment of the Watergate affair, they found their nation mired in the worst economic recession since the dismal days of the Great Depression half a century before. The years of post–World War II abundance had ended. Earlier, in the midst of plenty, some observers had pointed to the pockets of poverty that still existed, but the poor were easily ignored. Now even middle-class citizens found themselves unemployed.

Americans understood that their nation was less competitive in the international arena, but they felt powerless to remedy this. Policymakers discovered that the old economic formulas did not work. Some people, particularly the hardest hit, began to worry about the durability of the capitalist economic system itself.

This chapter describes America's efforts to regain its economic health after 1976. It deals with the program of a Democratic president who never managed to promote the stability he promised in his campaign. It describes the approach of his conservative Republican successor, who sought to roll back the welfare programs of the past and deregulate the economy while embarking on the greatest arms buildup in United States history. This chapter also shows the struggles of ordinary Americans to cope with hard times. Old and new groups, defined by gender, race, and class, sought to advance their own interests. Women continued to press for reform. Ethnic and racial groups likewise remained committed to the goals they had pursued in the past. But they faced more resistance now, particularly as new groups defined goals of their own. American society changed in the late 1970s and early 1980s, but not as much as some Americans demanded. This chapter charts their continuing quest for the American dream.

THE DISORDERED ECONOMY

From the early 1970s on, the economy reeled under the impact of declining productivity, galloping inflation, oil shortages, and high unemployment. Some people in the middle and higher ranks suffered, but the recession most seriously affected working-class Americans while the middle and upper classes improved their standard of living. Economists disagreed about the reasons for the economic slump and recommended contradictory remedies. None of their remedies succeeded in restoring the growth rate or confidence that the American economy would resume its steady expansion.

Economic Stagnation

The United States had been the world's technological leader since the late nineteenth century, but by the 1970s it seemed to be losing that position. After 1973, productivity slowed in virtually all American industries; in the early 1970s, economic growth averaged 2.3 percent annually in contrast to its average of 3.2 percent in the 1950s. Thereafter, it dropped to 1.3 percent annually.

The causes of this decline were complex. The oil crisis and rising oil prices (see Chapter 30) played a part, as did government policies aimed at curbing inflation by keeping machines idle and environmental regulations intended to make industries change their methods of operation. The war in Vietnam diverted federal funds from support for research and development at the same time that Japan, Germany, and the Soviet Union were increasing their R&D expenditures.

While American industry became less productive, other industrial nations moved forward. German and Japanese industries, rebuilt after World War II with American aid and aggressively modernized thereafter, reached new heights of efficiency. As a result, the United States began to lose its share of the world market for industrial goods. In 1946, the country had provided the world with 60 percent of its iron and steel. In 1978, it provided a mere 16 percent. Some of this decline was inevitable as other nations rebuilt their economies after World War II. But so efficient and cost-effective were foreign steel producers that the United States found itself importing a fifth of its iron and steel. By 1980, Japanese car manufacturers had also captured nearly a quarter of the American automobile market. The auto industry, which had been a mainstay of economic growth for much of the twentieth century, suffered plant shutdowns and massive layoffs.

Unemployment emerged as the most visible sign of the country's economic problems. In 1975, during the administration of Gerald Ford, it reached a high of 9 percent and then declined to 7.5 percent after Jimmy Carter took office in early 1976. Under Carter the rate hovered between 5.6 and 7.8 percent. During Reagan's first year, the job situation deteriorated badly. By the end of 1982, the unemployment rate had climbed to 10.8 percent, with black unemployment over 20 percent. Nearly a third of America's industrial capacity lay idle, and 12 million Americans were out of work.

Blue-collar workers, now a declining percentage of the work force, were the first to feel

Share of Total Manufacturing Output of Four Industrial Countries, 1950–1977

Source: U.S. Bureau of Labor Statistics.

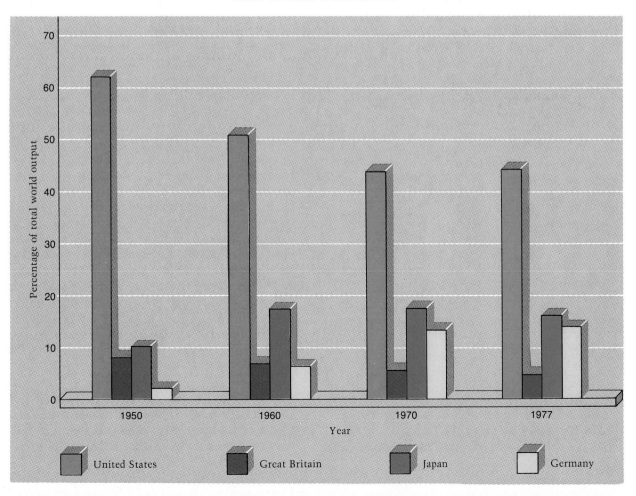

the effects. After World War II, American workers had enjoyed both a rise in real income and a reduction in hours of work. In the disordered economy, wages failed to keep pace with inflation, however, and many industrial workers were laid off.

The ability of blue-collar workers to protect themselves against adversity was hampered by the economic problems of the nation at large and by the faltering position of the trade union movement as a whole. Although unions had emerged from World War II claiming 35 percent of American nonagricultural workers as members, this percentage began to decrease steadily in the mid-1950s. Union membership rose in the public sector, but this increase did not reverse the general decline in membership. In 1956, some 26 percent of nonagricultural workers had belonged to unions. By 1984, only 21 percent did.

This contraction stemmed from several factors—the shift from blue-collar to white-collar work, the growing numbers of women and young people in the work force (groups that have historically been difficult to organize), and the more forceful opposition to unions by managers applying the provisions of the Taft-Hartley Act of 1947. This erosion of membership made un-

For millions of unemployed, Christmas dinner 1982 was eaten at charity soup kitchens.

ions less effective in dealing with employers. For example, in Groton, Connecticut, an affiliate of the United Auto Workers called a strike of ship workers in 1983. But after 15 months, workers accepted a "very bad" contract, leaving 43 percent of the strikers unemployed. As union leaders admitted, "No one will attempt . . . to defend the package." This pattern was repeated elsewhere.

White-collar workers were not immune to economic difficulties. Unemployment rose among all groups, and many professionals in their forties who had lost their jobs found it as difficult to find work as Andy Hjelmeland and Jerry Espinoza. Middle-class college graduates who expected professional positions were often "underemployed."

Inflation accompanied widespread unemployment and undermined the purchasing power of people already in difficulty. The rate, which had reached about 12 percent early in Ford's presidency, dropped to 4.8 precent when Carter took office. Soon, however, it spiraled upward again, reaching 12.4 percent in 1980. Under Reagan that rate began to fall, to 8.9 percent in his first year and to about 5 percent during the remainder of his first term.

The Farmer's Paradox of Plenty

After the mid-1970s, American farmers suffered too. Continuing a trend that began in the early twentieth century, the number of farmers

Union Membership, 1950–1980

Source: U.S. Bureau of Labor Statistics.

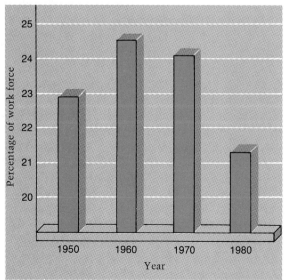

declined steadily. When Franklin Roosevelt took office in 1933, some 6.7 million farms covered the American landscape. Fifty years later, farm families numbered only 2.4 million. Overall, the lot of American farmers improved during this half century, much of the earlier pervasive rural poverty having given way to a decent existence and sometimes considerable wealth. Part of this improvement stemmed from the huge strides that were made in agricultural productivity through the use of chemical fertilizers, irrigation, pesticides, and scientific agricultural management. Equally important were the government's price-support programs, initiated during the New Deal to shield struggling farmers from unstable prices.

Yet, paradoxically, family farms continued to disappear, and farming income became more concentrated in the hands of the largest operators. In 1983, the largest one percent of the nation's farmers produced 30 percent of all farm products; the top 12 percent generated 90 percent of all farm income. The top one percent of America's growers had average annual incomes of $572,000, but most small and medium-size farmers had incomes below the official government poverty line.

The extraordinary productivity of American farmers led to unexpected setbacks in the 1980s.

Farm Indebtedness, 1950–1982

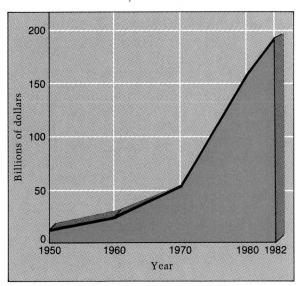

In the 1970s, as food shortages developed in many countries, the United States became the "breadbasket of the world." Farmers increased their output to meet multibillion-bushel grain orders from India, China, Russia, and other countries and profited handsomely from high grain prices caused by global shortages. Often they borrowed heavily to increase production, sometimes at interest rates up to 18 percent. However, the fourfold increase in oil prices beginning in 1973 drove up the cost of running the modern mechanized farm. When a world-wide economic slump began in 1980, overseas demand for American farm products declined sharply, and farm prices fell. Farmers who had borrowed money at high interest rates, when corn sold at $3 to $4 per bushel, now found themselves trying to meet payments on these loans with corn that brought only $2 per bushel.

Thousands of farmers, caught in the cycle of overproduction, heavy indebtedness, and falling prices, watched helplessly as banks and federal agencies foreclosed on their mortgages and drove them out of business. For example, Dale Christensen, an Iowa corn grower, faced foreclosure in 1983 when the Farmers Home Administration called in his overdue payments on debts totaling $300,000. "I am 58 years old," he said. "My whole life has gone into this farm." He was one of many struggling farmers, who, in spite of government crop-support programs that cost more in 1982 than all welfare programs for the poor, had to face leaving behind a livelihood that went back generations in his family.

Business Failures

The recession of 1980–1983 afflicted every region of the country. Business failures proliferated as large and small businessmen closed their doors and fired their employees. In 1982, business bankruptcies rose 50 percent from the previous year. In one week in June 1982, a total of 548 businesses failed, close to the 1932 weekly record of 612.

No area was immune from the recession. Louisville, Kentucky, had considered itself safe from the threats other areas faced but found it was mistaken in 1982. Despite the hope that people would continue drinking and smoking in bad times as well as good, the Brown & Williamson Tobacco Corporation, manufacturer of Kool, Raleigh, and Viceroy cigarettes, closed down its Louisville branch. Then Joseph E. Seagram & Sons shut its bottling plant. General Electric released almost 10,000 of its 23,000 workers, and International Harvester closed a plant employing 6,500 people.

Detroit was one of the hardest-hit areas in the United States. An industrial city revolving around automobile manufacturing, it suffered from the high interest rates that made car sales plummet. Thousands of workers were left to fend for themselves as assembly lines slowed or stopped altogether. The unemployment rate rose to more than 19 percent. The entire city suffered from the decline. The $357 million Renaissance Center, which included a large hotel surrounded by four modern office buildings, had been expected to revitalize downtown Detroit when it opened in 1977. Instead it wallowed in red ink, and in early 1983 its owners defaulted on a huge mortgage.

The closing of Hudson's department store symbolized Detroit's severe depression. That magnificent block-square centerpiece of the J. L. Hudson Company had served downtown Detroit for 91 years and had become a local institution. With its wood-paneled elevators and brass water fountains, it was Detroit's symbol of elegance. Hudson's replaced women's stockings torn in the store. It provided clerks who spoke 14 languages to assist the immigrant population. Everyone had a favorite memory of the store, which had seemed to represent the vitality of the city. Larry Hanlin remembered shopping excursions with his ten brothers and sisters: "My mother would get all of us dressed in our best, line us up and give us all a spanking, just in case we had any remote thoughts about misbehaving in the store." When he was older, he occasionally skipped school to spend a day there. "It was our big adventure—" he said, "our Disneyland." But then Hudson's, like so many other places, fell upon hard times. It had earned $153 million in 1953, but by 1981 profits had declined to $43 million, with 1982 expected to be even lower. With that, the management decided to maintain the suburban branches but to close the downtown store that had spawned all the rest.

Some areas initially seemed "recession-proof." The Sun Belt—the vast southern region stretching from coast to coast—prospered far more than other parts of the country. Economic growth there was fostered by the availability of cheap, nonunion labor, tax advantages that state governments offered corporations willing to locate plants there, and its favorable climate. Journalist Kirkpatrick Sale described the economic boom there in 1975 in his book *Power Shift: The Rise of the Southern Rim and Its Challenge to the Eastern Establishment.* Newspapers and magazines picked up the theme and ran stories showing how the area was outstripping other parts of the country in winning government grants, attracting modern industries, and enjoying new wealth. To some observers, the Sun Belt, once a relatively backward region, had become the new promised land.

By the early 1980s, however, the Sun Belt also suffered economic problems. Despite an enviable record of growth and prosperity in parts of the region, large areas began to stagnate. The unemployment rate in California in mid-1982 reached the national average of 9.5 percent, while in Texas it was 7 percent, higher than it had been for ten years. There was more joblessness in Greenlee County, Arizona, than anywhere in the country. In Jefferson County,

Even such prosperous sun-belt states as Texas felt the effects of the recession.

Mississippi, 67 percent of the population lived below the poverty line.

Millions of Americans, like Andy Hjelmeland and Jerry Espinoza, had to deal with the sudden loss of material comfort and the security they earned through hard work. Struggle became their way of life. Michael Wilk, a 31-year-old auto technician from Hamtramck, Michigan, lost his $18,000-a-year job in 1981. His wife Nydia continued to earn $240 a week as an inspector at the same factory, but that was the family's only income. When Nydia tried to make ends meet by working two full-time jobs, she lost 27 pounds and developed ulcers. Michael initially went out looking for work, but in depressed Detroit few jobs were available, and gasoline became too expensive to waste. Finally he resorted to reading want ads and watching TV. "I go from feeling depressed to not caring about anything and then back again," he said. "Sometimes I'm so paralyzed by it all that I just sit and stare out the window."

Not all Americans suffered, however. With 10 percent of the population unemployed, 90 percent remained at work, and many improved their standard of living. But virtually everyone felt the recession in some way. Everyone had a jobless friend or relative. Nobody could avoid the numerous For Sale signs on the lawns of houses where residents, unable to meet their mortgage payments, had moved out, their faith in the American dream of home ownership badly shaken because losing a home was an attack on the status they had struggled to achieve. Everyone watched tax revenues, and then public services, decline as hard-hit Americans paid fewer taxes than before.

THE DEMOGRAPHIC TRANSFORMATION

As Americans confronted extraordinary economic problems, basic population patterns continued to develop in unspectacular but significant ways. Urban growth tailed off. The population became older. The number of nontraditional households increased. New immigrants streamed into the country. Such changing demographic contours often brought changes that challenged local, state, and federal governments charged with meeting the needs of their constituents.

American Society in 1980

The 1980 census revealed that in the previous decade the population of the United States had increased from 203 million to 227 million. That rise of 11.5 percent was the second-lowest rate of growth in the nation's history. In the baby boom decade between 1950 and 1960, population had grown by 19 percent; between 1960 and 1970, it had increased 13.3 percent. Only the growth rate in the Depression decade of 1930–1940 had been lower.

The census highlighted important structural changes that had been occurring. The urban rate of growth, which had been slowing since 1950, leveled off entirely. In 19 states, the rural part of the population actually increased. The age distribution of the population shifted toward the elderly. Between 1960 and 1980, the part of the population under the age of 5 decreased by one fifth, while the part over the age of 65 increased by about 53 percent.

Household composition also changed. Gone was the traditional household headed by a male wage earner with his wife at home. Less than a quarter of all American households fit that description. Another quarter of all households were classified as "nonfamily households," while the proportion of families headed by women who had children under 18 grew from 10 percent to 18 percent in the decade of the 1970s. Among whites, the proportion of families headed by women rose from 8 percent to 13 percent; among blacks it grew from 31 percent to 47 percent.

The New Pilgrims

Another shift occurred as the United States admitted new immigrants from a variety of foreign nations. A fifth of the decade's population growth stemmed from this immigration,

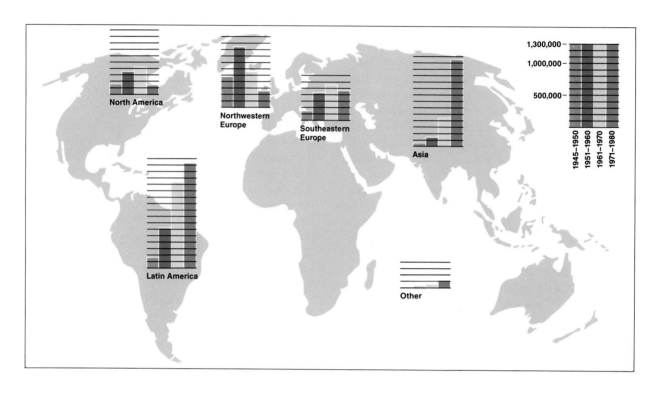

Immigration: Volume and Sources, 1941–1980

Source: U.S. Bureau of the Census.

Population Shifts, 1970 to 1980

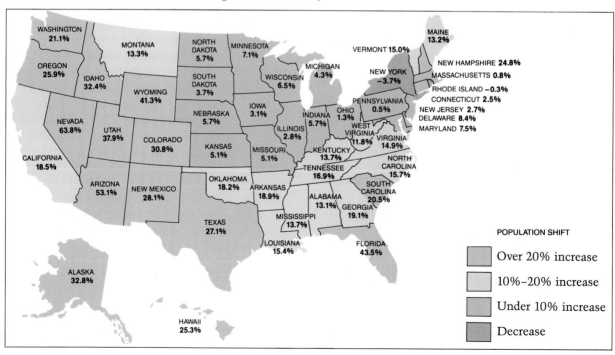

WASHINGTON 21.1%
MONTANA 13.3%
NORTH DAKOTA 5.7%
MINNESOTA 7.1%
MAINE 13.2%
VERMONT 15.0%
OREGON 25.9%
IDAHO 32.4%
SOUTH DAKOTA 3.7%
WISCONSIN 6.5%
MICHIGAN 4.3%
NEW YORK −3.7%
NEW HAMPSHIRE 24.8%
MASSACHUSETTS 0.8%
RHODE ISLAND −0.3%
CONNECTICUT 2.5%
NEW JERSEY 2.7%
DELAWARE 8.4%
MARYLAND 7.5%
WYOMING 41.3%
NEBRASKA 5.7%
IOWA 3.1%
INDIANA 5.7%
OHIO 1.3%
PENNSYLVANIA 0.5%
NEVADA 63.8%
UTAH 37.9%
COLORADO 30.8%
KANSAS 5.1%
ILLINOIS 2.8%
WEST VIRGINIA 11.8%
VIRGINIA 14.9%
CALIFORNIA 18.5%
MISSOURI 5.1%
KENTUCKY 13.7%
NORTH CAROLINA 15.7%
ARIZONA 53.1%
NEW MEXICO 28.1%
OKLAHOMA 18.2%
ARKANSAS 18.9%
TENNESSEE 16.9%
SOUTH CAROLINA 20.5%
ALABAMA 13.1%
GEORGIA 19.1%
TEXAS 27.1%
MISSISSIPPI 13.7%
LOUISIANA 15.4%
FLORIDA 43.5%
ALASKA 32.8%
HAWAII 25.3%

POPULATION SHIFT

Over 20% increase
10%–20% increase
Under 10% increase
Decrease

which was spurred by the Immigration and Nationality Act of 1965. Part of Lyndon Johnson's Great Society program, this act authorized the acceptance of immigrants impartially from all parts of the world. Because the national-origins system of the 1920s had favored western Europeans and was therefore frankly racist, most immigrants between 1930 and 1960 had come from Europe or Canada. Between 1977 and 1979, however, only 16 percent came from these areas, while 40 percent came from Asia and another 40 percent from Latin America. Always a nation of immigrants, the United States was once again receiving new ethnic infusions.

As had long been true, the desire for jobs fostered immigration. But foreign crises also fueled the influx. After 1975, the United States accepted more than a half million Vietnam refugees. In 1980, more than 160,000 arrived. That same year, the nation admitted 125,000 Cubans and Haitians to southern Florida. The official total of all immigrants in 1980 was 808,000, the highest in 60 years.

Millions more arrived illegally. As the popu-

Cuban "boat people," classified as refugees from Castro's Communist regime, were permitted to register for resident status.

lations of Latin American nations soared and as economic conditions deteriorated, more and more people looked to the United States for relief. In the mid-1970s, Leonard Chapman, commissioner of the Immigration and Naturalization Service, estimated that there might be 12 million foreigners in the nation illegally. While official estimates were lower, Attorney General William French Smith declared in 1983, "Simply put, we've lost control of our own borders."

The United States had once again become a melting pot of people from very different parts of the world. In Los Angeles, Samoans, Taiwanese, Koreans, Vietnamese, and Cambodians competed for jobs and apartments with Mexicans, blacks, and Anglos, just as newcomers from different countries had contended with one another in New York City a hundred years earlier. Throughout the country, in Miami, in Houston, in Brooklyn, the languages heard in the schools and on the streets changed, as did the very complexion of the society.

Each group, each family, had its own story. Nguyen Ninh and Nguyen Viet, two brothers who remained in Vietnam after the victory of the North Vietnamese in 1975, were among the many who finally fled their war-torn country by boat. The boat sank, but they were rescued, only to be shuttled to Kuwait, then Greece, and finally to the United States, where another brother had arrived a few years before. Though they spoke no English, they immediately began to look for work. One became a carpenter's helper; the other, an attendant at a valet-parking firm. With the money they earned, they helped other members of their family emigrate. Slowly they learned English, obtained better jobs, and saved enough money to purchase a home.

Growing Up

In the mid-1970s, the birthrate began to rise after 18 years of decline. Demographers viewed the increase as part of a long-term trend. The Census Bureau estimated that there would be 4 million births in 1983, compared to 3.1 million in 1975.

In an era of economic austerity, new children sometimes posed problems for their families. An extra mouth to feed could make a difference to a family on the fringe. The arrival

As we reach our own time, the historical past most worth recovering, perhaps, is our own. Our own story is as valid a part of the story of American history as Revolutionary War soldiers, frontier women, reform politicians, and immigrant grandparents. In this increasingly computerized and depersonalized age, the person we need to recover and know is ourself, a self that has been formed, at least in part, by the entire American experience we have been studying.

Autobiography is the form of writing in which people tell their own life's history. Although written autobiographies are at least as old as the literature of the early Christians, such as *The Confessions of St. Augustine,* the word itself dates from 1808, shortly after the French and American revolutions. That is no accident. These momentous events represented the triumph of individual liberty and the sovereignty of the self. *The Autobiography of Benjamin Franklin,* written between 1771 and his death in 1790, is a classic celebration of the American success story. Franklin's work set the standard for one autobiographical form, the memoir of one's public achievements and success. The other brief autobiographical excerpt also reflects the tone and range of this tradition.

Not all autobiographies are written late in life to celebrate one's accomplishments. The confessional autobiography, unlike most memoirs explores the author's interior life, acknowledging flaws and failures as well as successes; it may be written at any age. The purpose of this type of autobiography is not just to reconstruct one's past to preserve it for posterity, but rather to find from one's past an identity in order to know better how to live one's future. The story of religious confessions and conversions is an obvious example. This form also includes secular self-examinations such as those by Maxine Hong Kingston in *The Woman Warrior* (1976), Piri Thomas in

AUTOBIOGRAPHICAL MEMOIRS

BENJAMIN FRANKLIN

DEAR SON,
I have ever had a pleasure in obtaining any little anecdotes of my ancestors. You may remember the enquiries I made among the remains of my relations when you were with me in England and the journey I undertook for that purpose. Imagining it may be equally agreeable to you to know the circumstances of *my* life—many of which you are yet unacquainted with—and expecting a week's uninterrupted leisure in my present country retirement, I sit down to write them for you. Besides, there are some other inducements that excite me to this undertaking. From the poverty and obscurity in which I was born and in which I passed my earliest years, I have raised myself to a state of affluence and some degree of celebrity in the world. As constant good fortune has accompanied me even to an advanced period of life, my posterity will perhaps be desirous of learning the means, which I employed, and which, thanks to Providence, so well succeeded with me. They may also deem them fit to be imitated, should any of them find themselves in similar circumstances.

The Autobiography of Benjamin Franklin (1771)

ELIZABETH CADY STANTON

It was 'mid such exhilarating scenes that Miss Anthony and I wrote addresses for temperance, anti-slavery, educational and woman's rights conventions. Here we forged resolutions, protests, appeals, petitions, agricultural reports, and constitutional arguments; for we made it a matter of conscience to accept every invitation to speak on every question, in order to maintain woman's right to do so. To this end we took turns on the domestic watchtowers, directing amusements, settling disputes, protecting the weak against the strong, and trying to secure equal rights to all in the home as well as the nation.

It is often said, by those who know Miss Anthony best, that she has been my good angel, always pushing and goading me to work, and that but for her pertinacity I should never have accomplished the little I have. On the other hand it has been said that I forged the thunderbolts and she fired them. Perhaps all this is, in a measure, true. With the cares of a large family I might, in time, like too many women, have become wholly absorbed in a narrow family selfishness, had not my friend been continually exploring new fields for missionary labors. Her description of a body of men on any platform, complacently deciding questions in which woman had an equal interest, without an equal voice, readily aroused me to a determination to throw a firebrand into the midst of their assembly.

Elizabeth Cady Stanton, *Eighty Years and More: Reminiscences, 1815–1897* (1898)

AUTOBIOGRAPHY

Down These Mean Streets (1967), or by Maya Angelou in a series of five autobiographical sketches beginning with *I Know Why the Caged Bird Sings* (1969). The remaining excerpts are two of the finest examples of confessional autobiography and suggest its variety.

These examples hardly suggest the full range of the autobiographical form or how available to all people is the opportunity to tell the story of one's life. In 1909, William Dean Howells called autobiography the "most democratic province in the republic of letters." A recent critic agrees, pointing out that "to this genre have been drawn public and private figures: poets, philosophers, prizefighters; actresses, artists, political activists; statesmen and penitentiary prisoners; financiers and football players; Quakers and Black Muslims; immigrants and Indians. The range of personality, experience, and profession reflected in the forms of American autobiography is as varied as American life itself."

Your story, too, is a legitimate part of American history. But writing an autobiography, while open to all, is deceptively difficult. Like historians, autobiographers face problems of sources, selection, interpretation, and style. As in the writing of any history, the account of one's past must be objective, not only in the verifiable accuracy of details but also in the honest selection of representative events to be described. Moreover, as in the writing of fiction as well as history, the autobiographer must provide a structured form, an organizing principle, literary merit, and thematic coherence to the story. Many other challenges face the would-be autobiographer, such as finding an appropriate balance between one's external, public life and the internal, private self, or how to handle problems of memory, ego (should one, for example, use the first or third person?), and death.

To get an idea of the difficulties of writing an autobiography, try writing your own. Limit yourself to 1,000 words. Good luck.

CONFESSIONAL AUTOBIOGRAPHIES

MALCOLM X

I want to say before I go on that I have never previously told anyone my sordid past in detail. I haven't done it now to sound as though I might be proud of how bad, how evil, I was.

But people are always speculating—why am I as I am? To understand that of any person, his whole life, from birth, must be reviewed. All of our experiences fuse into our personality. Everything that ever happened to us is an ingredient.

Today, when everything that I do has an urgency, I would not spend one hour in the preparation of a book which has the ambition to perhaps titillate some readers. But I am spending many hours because the full story is the best way that I know to have it seen, and understood, that I had sunk to the very bottom of the American white man's society when—soon now, in prison—I found Allah and the religion of Islam and it completely transformed my life.

The Autobiography of Malcolm X, with the assistance of Alex Haley (1964)

BLACK ELK

And so it was all over.

I did not know then how much was ended. When I look back now from this high hill of my old age, I can still see the butchered women and children lying heaped and scattered all along the crooked gulch as plain as when I saw them with eyes still young. And I can see that something else died there in the bloody mud, and was buried in the blizzard. A people's dream died there. It was a beautiful dream.

And I, to whom so great a vision was given in my youth,—you see me now a pitiful old man who has done nothing, for the nation's hoop is broken and scattered. There is no center any longer, and the sacred tree is dead.

Black Elk Speaks, as told through John G. Neihardt (1932)

of children often required new decisions about the relationship between family and career. Women entering the work force with long-range employment commitments had to juggle work and home schedules and find adequate child-care facilities.

The rising divorce rate also affected children. By 1980, the divorce rate had reached a historic peak. In that year, the courts granted nearly 1.2 million divorces, the highest total in the nation's history. For each 1,000 marriages, 490 divorces occurred, up from 328 per 1,000 in 1970 and 258 per 1,000 in 1960. Many splits involved fights over the young.

In the past, divorced mothers had almost always gained custody over the children, but now husbands increasingly asserted their parental rights. Sometimes the struggles became angry and intense. In 1977, Diane and James Tilden fought over their 10-year-old son Jimmy. A New York judge gave James custody, except in the summer. When he handed over his son to his ex-wife, James was concerned, and with good reason, for she promptly disappeared. He found her in Florida, but a judge there gave her custody of the boy. James then smuggled his son back to New York and successfully appealed the Florida case. Finally he had complete custody—and $34,000 in legal fees. Jimmy had become a pawn in a larger game.

Runaways also became a problem. According to some estimates, more than a million children between the ages of 10 and 17 were on the run. They left home for various reasons. Some were driven out. Others were victims of physical abuse. Still others fled violent arguments or other recession-induced strains in family life. Many returned home within a few days. Some, however, remained on city streets. In 1974, Congress passed a Runaway and Homeless Youth Act, which established telephone hot lines and temporary shelters. But the shelters served only 45,000 youths a year, leaving countless others without help.

Even more ominous was the rising death rate among the young. The Public Health Service reported in 1982 that the death rate for most Americans had dropped significantly over a 30-year period, but the rate for those between 15 and 24 rose steadily after 1976. Automobile accidents, murders, and suicides caused three out of four deaths for that group.

Growing Old

As concern with the problems of the young increased, awareness of the plight of the old also grew. Elderly people made up the fastest-growing age group in modern America. Between 1900 and 1980, when the population of the country tripled, the number of people over 65 rose eightfold. In the 1970s alone, Americans over 75 grew by more than 37 percent. Underlying the rapid increase was the steady advance in medical care, which in the twentieth century had increased life expectancy from 47 to 73 years. Americans watched Bob Hope celebrate his eightieth birthday, George Burns, approaching 90, continue to act, and Ronald Reagan, over 70, govern the country. They became aware of what columnist Max Lerner called "the aging revolution," which promised to become the most lasting of all of the twentieth-century social changes.

The elderly raised new issues in a nation suffering economic stagnation. Many wanted to continue working and resented mandatory retirement rules that drove them from their jobs. Pleading their cause was Representative Claude Pepper of Florida, the octogenarian head of the House Select Committee on Aging, who declared, "I am like an old hickory tree. The older I get, the tougher I get." Legislation in 1978 raised the mandatory retirement age from 65 to 70. That helped older workers but decreased employment opportunities for younger workers seeking jobs.

Generational resentment over jobs was compounded by the knotty problems faced by the social security system established a half century before. As more and more Americans retired, the system could not generate sufficient revenue to make the payments due without assistance from the general governmental fund. In the early 1980s, it appeared that the entire system might collapse. A temporary solution, in part involving higher taxes for those still employed and a later age for qualifying for benefits, rescued the fund, but other hard decisions for the future were postponed.

At an intensely personal level, American families faced difficult decisions about how to care for older parents who could no longer care for themselves. In the past, the elderly might naturally have come into their children's homes, but attitudes and family patterns had changed. Children were fewer than in earlier generations, and as women gravitated to jobs outside, they were less able to assist in the home care of an elderly parent. Retirement villages and nursing homes provided two alternatives, but the decision to place a parent under institutional care was often excruciating.

Margaret Stump, an occupational therapist from Tenafly, New Jersey, agonized over such a decision. For six years she flew to Lima, Ohio, every three months to see her mother, who was over 90 years old. Finally she decided to bring her to a New Jersey nursing home. "I felt that she'd be better once she got to a home," Margaret recalled. "But I knew she wanted to be in her own house. It was a very difficult decision. I had to wait until I thought she wouldn't know where she was."

The New Students

Another group of Americans faced the future more aggressively. College students were more numerous than ever before. After World War II, partly as a result of GI education benefits, higher education became broadly accessible for the first time in American history. College enrollment, which had never exceeded 1.5 million before 1945, rose to nearly 3 million in the early 1960s and reached 12 million in 1981. Women and minority students entered college in unprecedented numbers.

Students in the late 1970s and 1980s became more conservative. Gone was the sense of outrage that had mobilized thousands in the social struggles of the 1960s. Now students were more willing to work within the system. Howard Shapiro, a Yale senior, noted in 1983, "If you want to change things, you have to work with those in power. I see a whole new cycle, with people aiming at the same good goals but in different ways. Instead of having a sit-down strike, students will meet with the administration and try to compromise."

Some students, not sure of themselves or their goals, gravitated toward the various cults that grew up and recruited on campus. The Unification Church of the Reverend Sun Myung Moon grew rapidly, as did The Way International and the International Society for Krishna Consciousness. "I didn't know anything about cults when I got involved," said Heidi Feiwel, a Cornell University student who became part of The Way International. But in her freshman year, "I didn't have that many friends, and this was a source of community." By the end of her second year, her family had become concerned, and her father arranged for "deprogramming" to try to make her understand why she had become so committed to the religious group.

Most students coped with uncertain times by preparing for careers. Large numbers of them chose business or economics courses, while enrollment in the liberal arts dropped sharply. Conscious of the need to repay the loans that often provided their major source of support and of the difficulty of finding good jobs, students made choices reflecting concern for a career in a particular field rather than concern for a broad general education.

THE CONTINUING STRUGGLE FOR EQUALITY

In the 1970s and 1980s, women, blacks, Hispanic-Americans, and Native Americans continued their struggle for equal opportunity and treatment. But the pace of change slowed as the economic climate made many Americans, convinced that enough had been done already for these groups, less sympathetic to reform.

Consolidating Feminist Gains

In general, liberals applauded the accomplishments of the women's movement. Betty Friedan, whose book *The Feminine Mystique* (1963) had helped mobilize a pervasive discontent two decades before, admitted in 1983:

I am still awed by the revolution that book helped spark. . . . I keep being surprised, as the changes the women's movement set in motion continue to play themselves out in our lives—the enormous and mundane, subtle and not so subtle, delightful, painful, immediate, far-reaching, paradoxical, inexorable and probably irreversible changes in womens's lives—and in men's.

Changes had indeed occurred. Affirmative action had made jobs for women more accessible. Women made tremendous gains in such diverse fields as coal mining, where the percentage of women rose from 0.001 to 11.4 between 1973 and 1979, and banking, where the percentage increased from 18 to 34 in the ten years after 1970. According to the U.S. Census Bureau, 45 percent of mothers with preschool children held jobs away from home in 1980. That figure was four times greater than it had been 30 years before. More day-care centers existed, although not nearly enough to meet the need; they allowed women greater flexibility in finding work. At the same time, fathers were playing a greater role in their children's lives.

Legal changes brought women more benefits and opportunities. Title 9 of the Education Amendments of 1972, which barred gender bias in federally assisted education activities and programs, stimulated colleges to admit far more women to law, medical, dental, and business schools and to drop nepotism restrictions that kept husbands and wives from teaching at the same schools. The same measure changed the nature of intercollegiate athletics. Big Ten schools, which spent millions of dollars on men's programs, in 1974 spent an average of $3,500 a year on women's sports. That was no longer legal, and while complete equity remained a distant goal, women's athletics benefited. By 1980, 30 percent of the participants in intercollegiate athletics were women, compared to 15 percent before Title 9 had become law.

In politics women also made important strides forward. Jane Byrne succeeded Richard Daley as Chicago's mayor, and women also won mayoral races in Houston, Honolulu, and San Francisco. In 1981, President Ronald Reagan appointed Sandra Day O'Connor as the first woman Supreme Court justice, and in 1984, Geraldine Ferraro, a Democratic member of Congress, became the first woman vice-presidential candidate for a major party. Far more women were elected to state legislatures and to Congress. As women began to win elective office, political analysts noted that women voters began to show distinctive voting behavior. In the election of 1980, analysts observed a "gender gap": For the first time, women were voting significantly differently from men. Men supported Ronald Reagan by a margin of 56 to 36. Women, alarmed by his hard-line foreign policy and opposition to the Equal Rights Amendment, voted for him by a much smaller margin of 46 to 45.

In 1982, a film about a man who dressed as a woman to get a job became one of the major hits

Changes in Female Employment, 1940–1980
Percent of all employed women

	1940	1950	1960	1970	1980
Professional and technical	13.2%	10.8%	12.4%	15.3%	16.7%
Managers and administrators	3.8	5.5	5.7	3.6	6.9
Sales	7.0	8.8	7.7	7.4	6.8
Clerical	21.2	26.4	30.3	34.5	35.1
Craft workers	0.9	1.1	1.6	1.8	1.8
Operatives	18.4	18.7	15.2	15.1	10.7
Laborers	0.8	0.4	0.4	1.0	1.3
Service workers	28.9	22.9	23.7	20.5	19.5
Farm workers	5.8	5.4	4.4	0.8	1.2

Source: Oppenheimer, *The Female Labor Force in the United States,* 1976.

of the season. *Tootsie*, starring Dustin Hoffman, was a funny film with a serious side. Posing as Dorothy Michaels, Michael Dorsey, a rather unpleasant man, challenged sexual harassment, argued with the male chauvinists at work, and became a real battler for women's rights. In the process, Dorothy came across as a much nicer person than Michael had ever been. When he finally reverted to being himself, Betty Friedan noted, "the sensitivity he acquired, sharing woman's experience, made him a much better, stronger, more tender man."

In the tenth anniversary issue of *Ms.* magazine, in 1982, founding editor Gloria Steinem noted the differences a decade had made. "Now, we have words like 'sexual harassment' and 'battered women,'" she wrote. "Ten years ago, it was just called 'life.'" Other examples followed: "Now, rape is defined as a crime of violence—and victims are less likely to be raped again by the law." Perhaps best of all: "Now, we are becoming the men we wanted to marry. Ten years ago, we were trained to marry a doctor, not be one."

Yet old problems persisted. Perhaps the most troubling involved continuing wage differentials between women and men. In 1982, full-time working women earned an average of 62 cents for every dollar earned by men. Though new

Disappointment and frustration cloud the faces of Chicago mayor Jane Byrne and NOW president Eleanor Smeal as the Illinois state legislature, despite a massive rally, fails to ratify the ERA in 1982.

opportunities were opening up, most women remained in waitressing, nursing, secretarial, or light industry jobs—the so-called pink-collar positions that paid poorly. Arguments that women should receive equal pay for equal work now led to demands for equal pay for different jobs of similar value. Comparable-worth cases began to work their way through the courts. The issue surfaced, too, in the campaign of 1984, though without any agreement on the question.

The women's rights movement, in its long history, had never been unified, and in the decade 1974 to 1984 women continued to debate their roles and rights. Despite changes in their portrayal by the media, a subtle sex-appeal image remained. Ellen Goodman took exception to an advertisement showing the Maidenform woman as a doctor. "There she was," Goodman wrote, "hair tied back primly, medical chart in her left hand, pen in her right hand, long white jacket over her shoulders, exposing her lacy magenta bra and panties." There she was, according to the caption, "making the rounds in her elegant Delectables." Goodman was disgusted, for, she observed, "I always thought she was a candidate for a cold, not a medical degree." More troubling was the implication that the doctor "is revealed in the flesh, to be—yes, indeed—just another woman insecure about her femininity, just another woman in search of sex appeal, just another woman who needs 'silky satin tricot with antique lace scalloping.'"

Women who applauded when the Supreme Court legalized abortion in 1973 discovered that the question of abortion remained very much alive. The number of abortions increased dramatically in the decade after the decision. By some estimates there were 10 million lawful abortions, or one for every three births. In response, "pro-life" forces mobilized as never before. Nellie Gray organized a march on Washington every January 22 to call attention to the anniversary of the *Roe* v. *Wade* decision. "It's murder, pure and simple," she said. "Abortion means killing babies." Opponents lobbied to cut off federal funds that allowed the poor to obtain the abortions the better off could pay for themselves; they insisted that abortions should be performed in hospitals and not in less expensive clinics; and they worked to reverse the original decision itself. Though the Supreme Court, which included the first woman in its history, reaffirmed its judgment in 1983, the pro-life movement was not deterred.

Agitation over the ERA also became more intense. Ratification of the Equal Rights Amendment had been taken for granted after its favorable vote in Congress in 1972, so much so that no ratification strategy was thought necessary. Within a few years, 35 states had agreed to the measure, but then the momentum disappeared. Even with an extension in the deadline granted in 1979, the amendment could not win the necessary 38-state support. Phyllis Schlafly and others continued their highly effective opposition campaign, gaining the assistance of women who felt threatened by the changes occurring and men, particularly in state legislatures, who had long been uncomfortable with the women's movement. By mid-1982, the ERA was dead.

Although women could savor their gains, some worried that complacency was setting in. Many young women who enjoyed the fruits of the movement avoided the feminist label and shunned involvement in militant campaigns. Others remained active, convinced that only with continued pressure would women achieve full equality.

The Continuing Significance of Race

Like the women's movement, the black and Hispanic movements found that progress came at a slower pace than in the decade before. Some gains were made, but racial inequality persisted in many areas of American life.

Significant change occurred in politics and education. Black political candidates won mayoral elections in major cities, including Detroit, Los Angeles, Cleveland, and Chicago. In the election of 1982, the number of black representatives in Congress increased from 18 to 21, and in state and local elective offices some 6,000 blacks served their constituents. Federal affirmative-action guidelines brought more blacks into colleges and universities. In 1950, only 83,000 black students were enrolled in college. A decade later, more than one million were working for college degrees. But black enrollment in colleges peaked at 9.3 percent of the population in 1976 and by 1980 dropped to 9.1 percent, just what it had been in 1973.

As many blacks moved into the middle class, they left far behind a much larger and deeply impoverished black lower class, most of it living in urban ghettos. By 1981, fully 34 percent of black families were classified as poor, in contrast to 11 percent of white families. Black poverty was intimately tied to the worsening state of the economy, a changing job market, and remnants of racism. The automobile, steel, rubber, and coal industries, which had traditionally employed many unskilled and semiskilled laborers and had given immigrants their start in America, were shrinking. The new need was for highly trained workers who knew how to operate computers or could qualify for jobs in banks and offices. Many urban blacks lacked the education and training for these jobs. By 1981, the black unemployment rate was twice that of whites, and in almost every major city, the unemployment rate of black teenagers exceeded 40 percent. A troubling phenomenon that con-

Black Occupational Progress, 1940–1980

	1940	1950	1960	1970	1980
Black males as percentage of white males employed as professional, technical, managerial, or administrative workers	18%	21%	22%	32%	63%
Ratio of median black to white family income	.37	.54	.55	.61	.58

Source: U.S. Department of Labor.

tributed to black poverty was the dramatic rise in female-headed families. In 1940, only 18 percent of black families had a female head. By 1980, 49 percent did. (By contrast, the figures were 10 and 13 percent for whites.)

Some whites protested that black progress came at their expense and hence was the product of "reverse discrimination." In 1973 and 1974, for example, Allan Bakke, a white, applied to the medical school at the University of California at Davis. Twice rejected, he sued on the grounds that a racial quota reserving 16 of 100 places for minority-group applicants was a form of reverse discrimination that violated the Civil Rights Act of 1964. In 1978, the Supreme Court ordered Bakke's admission to the medical school, but in a complex ruling involving six separate opinions, the Court upheld the consideration of race in admissions policies, even while arguing that quotas could no longer be imposed. The decision received widespread attention and caused many people to fear a white backlash.

Hispanics in the United States, their numbers continuing to grow, began to play an increasingly important role in American affairs. According to the 1980 census, there were 14.6 million Hispanics, up 61 percent from the 9 million a decade before (the figures did not include the millions in the country illegally). Hispanics made up the fastest-growing minority group and promised soon to overtake the blacks as the country's largest minority. A government official pointed out that this means: "Not too far in the future, many areas will have Spanish-speaking majorities, and Latin American culture will make a very deep impression on the mainstream of U.S. society."

Despite population gains, economic conditions remained grim for many Hispanics. While the median family income for white families reached $17,900 in 1978, for Hispanic-Americans it was, though higher than for blacks, only $12,800. And in rural areas, many Mexican-Americans, living in shanties that had no electricity or plumbing, survived on about $4,000 a year.

Language difficulties and other problems of adjustment plagued Hispanic children in the schools. Richard Rodriguez, an articulate Chicano who did graduate work in English at Yale, recalled the boyhood shock of coming to school and coping with a new language. His experience paralleled that of newcomers from virtually all immigrant groups throughout the history of the United States, but that did not make the experience any smoother. "All my classmates certainly must have been uneasy on that first day of school," he wrote. "But I was astonished." For the first time he heard his name in English.

Eventually Rodriguez acquired fluency in English and became caught up in school and Anglo culture. Like other immigrant children, he found himself growing away from his family, using one form of expression with his parents and relatives and another with the world outside. In time he came to understand how "I had been educated away from the culture of my mother and father." Rodriguez's prizewinning book *Hunger of Memory* (1982) poignantly described the experience of Mexican-American youths in this era.

A movement to implement bilingual education in the schools made some progress but was not necessarily helpful for those who wished to move into the English-speaking mainstream. Most Hispanics failed to receive the education necessary for upward mobility in modern America. Only 30 percent of Hispanic high school students graduated, and less than 7 percent completed college.

Bilingual classrooms in public schools made learning easier for Hispanic students; some argued that such classes slowed assimilation.

But affirmative-action efforts helped Hispanics as well as blacks, and a growing network of Hispanic educators and programs promised to ease the way for future students. "Ten years ago, there was no national Chicano academic community," declared Arturo Madrid, president of the National Chicano Council on Higher Education, in 1982. "Now we have a professional presence in higher education." A colleague estimated that there were 5,000 Chicano faculty members in 1980, compared to 2,000 a decade before. Chicanos found themselves, like members of other minority groups, moving from the ranks of the "missing persons" to positions as "the onlys," where, Madrid noted, they served as "the only Chicano dean of this or the only Chicano professor of that."

Hispanics slowly extended the political gains they had made in the early 1970s. In San Antonio, Rudy Ortiz was appointed mayor pro tem in 1978, and Henry Cisneros was elected mayor in 1982. In the following year, Colorado state legislator Federico Peña was elected mayor of Denver. In New Mexico, Governor Toney Anaya called himself the nation's highest elected Hispanic and moved to create a national "Hispanic force." In the 1984 election, recognition grew that large concentrations of Hispanics in states like California, Texas, Florida, and New York could make a major difference in the final result. That gave them a political influence they had not enjoyed earlier.

The First Americans Still Last

In the decade after 1970, the Native American population increased by 72 percent. Although roughly half continued to live on reservations, an educated elite emerged. From the few hundred Indians in college in the early 1960s, the number reached tens of thousands by 1980. That created a network of educated Native Americans in industries and professions and contributed to a determination to press harder for tribal goals.

One major struggle involved the longstanding effort to hold on to a land base. In the 1970s, when New York State tried to condemn a section of Seneca land for a superhighway running through part of the Allegany reservation, the Seneca went to court. In 1981, the state finally agreed to an exchange: state land elsewhere in addition to a cash settlement in return for an easement through the reservation. That decision encouraged tribal efforts in Montana, Wyoming, Utah, New Mexico, and Arizona to resist similar incursions on reservation lands.

Native Americans also vigorously protested a new assault on their long-abused water rights. On the northern plains, large conglomerates, responding to the international oil shortage, vastly extended their coal strip-mining operations. Fierce legal struggles over possession of limited water resources resulted. Litigating tribes had some legal ammunition because a federal court had ruled in 1973 in a landmark case, involving the water rights of the Paiute on the Nevada-California border, that the government must carry out its obligation as trustee to protect Indian property.

Another effort involved the reassertion of fishing rights. In the Northwest, as in other parts of the nation, the Nisquallie, Puyallup, Muckleshoot, Chippewa, and other Indian tribes argued that they had treaty rights to fish where they chose, without worrying about the intrusive regulatory efforts of the states. Despite pressure from other fishermen, a series of court cases provided the tribes with some of the protection they claimed on the basis of old treaty rights and once again showed that aggressive litigation could make a difference.

THE NEW REFORMERS

Encouraged by the example of the traditional minorities, other groups began to demand equal opportunity and respect. Homosexuals sought the same freedom from discrimination that women and racial minorities claimed. Consumer advocates insisted that the government curb rampant abuses by advertisers and manufacturers of food, cars, and other products. Vietnam veterans asserted their need for material and emotional support after their wartime sacrifices. These new groups cut across gender, race, and class lines and testified to the continuing ferment for reform in the United States.

Gay Liberation

Homosexuals of both sexes worked openly to end discrimination. There had always been people who accepted the "gay" life style, but American society as a whole was unsympathetic, and many homosexuals kept their preferences to themselves. The climate of the 1970s encouraged gays to become more open. A nightlong riot in response to a police raid on the Stonewall Inn, a homosexual bar in Greenwich Village in New York, in 1969 helped spark a new consciousness and a movement for gay rights.

Throughout the decade, homosexuals made important gains. In 1973, the American Psychiatric Association ruled that homosexuality should no longer be classified as a mental illness, and that decision was overwhelmingly supported in a vote by the membership the next year. In 1975, the U.S. Civil Service Commission lifted its ban on employment of homosexuals.

In the new climate of acceptance, many gays

"Round up and quarantine AIDS carriers," urges the placard of one marcher in a KKK anti-gay demonstration in Houston, 1985.

who had hidden or suppressed their sexuality came "out of the closet." In early 1982, Dan Bradley, head of the national Legal Services Corporation, announced his own homosexuality and described the tensions of a life of concealment. "I subscribed to *Playboy* magazine—I must be the only man who subscribed to it but never read it—just to make sure that when people came to my house there was evidence of my straightness," he said. "I'd make up names of women and told people I had a lot of 'dates'—all sheer fabrication, all lies." Though he was single, he wore a wedding ring for seven years. Far more comfortable after his revelation, Bradley left his former job and worked to promote the passage of a gay civil rights bill.

Women also became more open about their sexual preferences and insisted on freedom from discrimination. A lesbian movement developed, sometimes involving women active in the more radical wing of the women's movement.

Many Americans were unsympathetic to anyone who challenged traditional sexual norms. Churches and some religious groups often lashed out against gays. In 1982, James Tinney, a Pentecostal preacher who had announced his homosexuality three years before, was excommunicated from the Church of God in Christ as he prepared a revival meeting for gays in Washington. In Atlanta, the Metropolitan Community Church, part of a gay domination, was burned after a series of attacks by vandals. Throughout the country, Americans, even those unsympathetic to gay rights, became concerned about AIDS (acquired immune deficiency syndrome), a new disease that struck homosexuals with numerous partners more often than any other group.

Regulating Corporate America

The consumer movement, sparked by Ralph Nader in the 1960s, continued its efforts despite Republican attempts to dismantle the regulatory apparatus. In 1982, Congress rejected a relatively weak Federal Trade Commission rule that would have required used-car dealers to tell prospective buyers of known problems with the automobiles for sale. Opponents of the FTC measure contended that it would raise the price of a used car. But consumer criticism forced Congress slowly to shift course. The Consumer Federation of America proved willing to play politics and endorse candidates, and 77 of the 94 congressional candidates it backed won. In early 1983, pollster Louis Harris announced that the public rejected, by a 55 to 36 percent margin, "the notion that the consumer movement has run out of steam." Indeed, four of every five Americans felt that "unless they keep fighting, consumer groups may begin to lose what they have achieved."

Concern about the deterioration of the environment increased as people learned more about substances they had once taken for granted. In 1978, the public became alarmed about the lethal effects of toxic chemicals dumped in the Love Canal neighborhood of Niagara Falls, New York. A few years later, attention focused on dioxin, one of the poisons permeating from the Love Canal, which now surfaced in other areas in even more concentrated form. Dioxin, a by-product of the manufacture of herbicides, plastics, and wood preservatives, remained active upon being released in the environment and seemed almost to defy control. Thousands of times more potent than cyanide, it was one of the most deadly substances ever made.

Dioxin made national headlines as a result of problems in Times Beach, Missouri. In the early 1970s, this suburb of St. Louis had sprayed its unpaved streets with waste oil to control dust. The oil later proved to be contaminated, and, after floods in 1982, the contamination spread throughout the town. Finally, the Environmental Protection Agency ordered a $33 million buy-out of all homes and businesses in the area. Other sites in Missouri, New Jersey, and California also revealed the presence of dioxin.

Acid rain also threatened the environment. In the eastern United States and southeastern Canada, industrial and automobile emissions had contaminated the atmosphere enough to kill fish, corrode building surfaces, and damage plants and trees. After extensive monitoring of ecological disruptions, the National Academy of Sciences attributed the damage to polluted rain. Only later, in mid-1983, did the Reagan administration acknowledge the problem, but it proposed no solutions.

Environmental activists also campaigned against nuclear power. Once hailed as the solution to America's energy needs, nuclear plants fell on hard times, particularly after an accident at one of the reactors at Three Mile Island, Pennsylvania, in 1979. There a faulty pressure relief valve led to a loss of coolant that was initially undetected by plant operators, who refused to believe indicators showing a serious malfunction. Part of the nuclear core became uncovered, part began to disintegrate, and the surrounding steam and water became highly radioactive. An explosion releasing radioactivity into the atmosphere appeared possible, and thousands of residents of the area fled. The scenario of nuclear disaster depicted in the film *The China Syndrome* (1979) seemed frighteningly real. The worst never occurred, and the period of maximum danger passed, but the plant remained shut down, filled with radioactive debris, a monument to a form of energy now deemed more potentially destructive than any ever known.

The Three Mile Island episode eroded public confidence in nuclear energy. Nuclear power proved both expensive and dangerous. After 1972, a total of 102 projected plants were canceled, and no new plants were ordered after 1978. In 1983, the nuclear industry suffered another jolt. The Washington Public Power Sup-

Closed down from 1979 to 1985 because of defective operation, Three Mile Island's nuclear plant is a reminder of the hazards of nuclear power.

ply System, which had sold $2.25 billion in bonds to finance two new reactors as part of a five-reactor complex, found that huge cost overruns made further construction unfeasible. After extensive efforts to maintain financing, the system succumbed in the largest municipal-bond default in history. Two of the plants were mothballed when analysts concluded that the energy to be produced was not needed. Existing nuclear facilities around the country continued to operate, but antinuclear activists had won a major round in their struggle to make society safer in the atomic age.

Vietnam Veterans

Another group that became more vocal than before was Vietnam veterans. America abandoned the Vietnam War in 1973, but the aftereffects lingered. Increasing numbers of veterans called attention to Agent Orange, a chemical used widely to defoliate trees in Southeast Asia. It contained dioxin, among other substances, and caused contamination that lasted indefinitely. Former soldiers with a variety of medical ailments now demanded compensation and care for the debilitating results of their service.

Other veterans suffered psychological problems. Delayed stress syndrome, a slow-fuse emotional reaction to the trauma of combat,

Nearly as controversial as the war it commemorates, the Vietnam Memorial was designed and built in the early 1980s, about a decade after the war ended.

afflicted many. In late 1982, in Ocala, Florida, Stanley Moody, a former Green Beret, dressed in his combat fatigues, armed himself with an assortment of guns, and rushed from his house. He was going to stop the Viet Cong. An hour or so later, after a one-man gun battle with himself, he lay dead, shot in the head. "Stanley wasn't shooting at anything in particular," said the sheriff's investigator. "He was just having his own war." Most veterans were not as severely disturbed, but many suffered continuing traumas.

Veterans complained particularly about having done their duty only to return to a society that seemed to have little but contempt for the struggle and those who had fought in it. Not until almost a decade after the United States had extricated itself from the war did the nation erect a memorial in Washington to the war dead. But even that gesture generated controversy.

Calls for some kind of monument had resulted in a nationwide design competition. Maya Ying Lin, a 22-year-old Yale University student, triumphed over thousands of other entrants. Her design showed two large black granite walls, inscribed with the names of the 57,939 American dead, forming a V. The memorial was simple and stark, so much so that some veterans argued that it was more of a political statement about the conflict than an honor for the dead soldiers. The government's Fine Arts Commission agreed to add a 50-foot flagpole and a larger-than-life statue of three soldiers.

With the monument complete, the Vietnam Veterans Memorial Fund sponsored a five-day tribute in the capital. It began with the reading of the names of the Americans who died in Vietnam, included a parade down Constitution Avenue, and culminated with the dedication of the monument. The parade was a festive affair. Men appeared with beards and ponytails, looking very much like their antiwar contemporaries 15 years before. "Worst-looking bunch I ever saw," said Colonel Max Sullivan, "and I loved every one of them." Some brought their wives, children, and dogs. People wandered in and out of line, embracing old friends. Marching in the nation's capital before vast crowds, they sensed they had finally gained long-overdue recognition.

For Infantry Captain William Harris of Knoxville, Tennessee, the parade satisfied a deep need. He had run a mortar crew abroad, come home wounded, and had trouble piecing his life together again. When he found he could not talk to anyone but other veterans, he dropped out of the University of Tennessee, got divorced, lived in communes, and only later, after entering law school, managed to settle down. For Harris, the parade ended years of emotional difficulty. "It's catharsis for me," he said. "It washes it out, closes the chapter."

The Moral Majority

Another group seeking to refashion society was the so-called Moral Majority. Convinced that the country was in the midst of a moral decline, members sought to return religion to a central place in their lives and to revive the values they believed had traditionally made the country strong.

The Moral Majority was deeply concerned about social change. Its members pointed particularly to an increase in crime and immorality. Between 1970 and 1980, the murder rate rose 31 percent, the robbery rate 42 percent, the burglary rate 56 percent, the assault rate 79 percent, and the rape rate 99 percent. The use of drugs spread. Marijuana was not simply a fad but an institution for a broad segment of society. Cocaine use also appeared common. In 1982, Don Reese, a football player, confessed in a cover story in *Sports Illustrated* that "cocaine arrived in my life with my first-round draft into the National Football League in 1974. It has dominated my life ever since." He went on to declare that "cocaine can be found in quantity throughout the NFL," and subsequent disclosures substantiated his charge.

Moral Majority members were also dis-

The Reverend Jerry Falwell, leader of the Moral Majority, stood up for religious fundamentalism and political conservatism.

turbed by the vocal efforts of other groups to foster their own interests. They feared the increased openness of homosexuality, objected to abortion, and argued that it was time to respond. Led by the Reverend Jerry Falwell of Virginia, the Moral Majority reflected the revival of fundamental Protestantism in the United States. The movement was part of the growing strength of conservatism in American politics. The right had momentarily seized control of the Republican party in 1964. Now the well-organized religious right determined to enter the political arena. Using modern communication and fund-raising techniques, its proponents attacked liberals and their programs. In 1980, the movement helped Ronald Reagan and other politicians who shared his views to gain office. Members hoped that the Republican victory would enable them to translate their vision of America into the law of the land.

THE CARTER AND REAGAN PRESIDENCIES

As Americans put scandal behind them in the mid-1970s, they elected national leaders who seemed to represent traditional American values. Jimmy Carter, a relative unknown from Georgia when he ran for the presidency, tried to take a fresh approach to the office but soon became bogged down in partisan squabbles. He was followed by former actor Ronald Reagan, who shifted America's course in both foreign and domestic affairs.

The Election of 1976

In the nation's bicentennial year, incumbent Gerald Ford hoped to win for himself the office he had inherited from Richard Nixon. He faced Jimmy Carter, former governor of Georgia, who stressed that he was not from Washington and that, unlike many of those mired in past scandal, he was not a lawyer. Although Carter's initial lead faltered, most elements of the old Democratic coalition held. Carter won a 50 to 48 percent majority of the popular vote and a 297 to 240 margin in the electoral college. He did well with the working class, blacks, and Catholics. He won most of the South, heartening to the Democrats after Nixon's gains there.

Human Rights Diplomacy

Carter enjoyed his greatest success in foreign policy, though he had had little diplomatic experience when he took office. Trained as a manager and an engineer at the U.S. Naval Academy and an avowed "born-again" Christian, Carter sought to conduct American foreign policy according to the standards that were part of his personal life.

Carter's major achievement came in the

Surrounded by aides, secret service, and newsmen, President Carter gives Prime Minister Begin of Israel and President Sadat of Egypt a walking tour of the battlefield at Gettysburg during a recess from the peace talks at Camp David.

Middle East, where Israel and the Arab nations had fought a series of bitter wars. When Anwar el-Sadat of Egypt and Menachem Begin of Israel began to negotiate a peace settlement in 1978, Carter invited the two adversaries to come to Camp David, in the Maryland hills. There his personal diplomacy helped bring about a peace treaty, signed in March 1979. Israel withdrew from the occupied Sinai peninsula in return for Egyptian recognition and normalized relations. After 30 years of hostilities, Israel and Egypt were at peace.

At home, Carter fought for Senate acceptance of two treaties returning the Panama Canal to Panama by the year 2000. The United States had built the canal and long controlled it, but resentment had grown in Panama over the presence of a foreign power and the way in which the United States had acquired the right to build it. In the agreements, accepted by the margin of a single vote, the United States retained certain rights in the event of crisis but otherwise yielded to Panamanian demands.

In Asia, Carter successfully followed Nixon's initiatives by extending diplomatic recognition to the People's Republic of China. Attempting to modernize their economy, the Chinese sought technical assistance from the United States. American wheat farmers and businessmen eyed the Chinese market of nearly a billion people with enthusiasm, and American diplomats were eager to keep China and Russia at odds.

With the Soviet Union, Carter was less successful. Russian-American relations, the major U.S. diplomatic concern since World War II, fluctuated in the Carter years. Taking over with détente at high tide, the new president declared that the United States had finally escaped its "inordinate fear of Communism" and should forge closer ties with the Soviet state. But then American actions and Russian ventures left the conciliatory policy in shreds.

Like Woodrow Wilson, Carter believed morality should guide foreign policy. But his dedication to a policy of human rights complicated his diplomacy and exposed the difficulties of using morality as "the soul of . . . foreign policy." Carter's position that "our commitment to human rights must be absolute" antagonized the Soviets. They charged the American president with meddling in their internal affairs when he verbally supported Russian dissidents. Consequently, Russian leaders resisted working with Carter on concrete disputes between the two superpowers.

One prickly issue was arms control. Negotiations for a more comprehensive strategic arms limitation treaty than the agreement of 1972 threatened to break down. Misjudging the Russians, the president offered new weapon-reduction proposals that went much farther than the Soviet Union was prepared to accept. When this threw matters into confusion, Carter backed off, patient negotiation succeeded, and the SALT II agreement was reached in June 1979.

The Soviet Invasion of Afghanistan in December 1979 complicated ratification, however. The Russians considered internal agitation there a threat to their security and invaded the country. After a year and a half of watching the bloody involvement, Carter responded by calling the Soviet move the most serious blow to world peace since World War II. He postponed presenting SALT II to the Senate and imposed an American boycott of the 1980 Olympic Games in Moscow. Détente was effectively dead.

Carter also stumbled in his effort to defuse a major crisis with Iran. Americans had long supported the shah of Iran. Overlooking the corruption and abuse in his regime, they viewed him as a reliable supplier of oil and defender of stability in the Persian Gulf region. In January 1979, revolutionary groups drove the shah from power. In his place sat the Ayatollah Ruholla Khomeini, an Islamic priest who returned from exile in Paris to lead a new fundamentalist Islamic regime.

When Carter admitted the shah to the United States for medical treatment in October 1979, angry Iranian students seized the American embassy in Tehran and held 53 Americans hostage. Their capture became a national cause in the United States. Carter broke diplomatic relations and froze Iranian assets, but this did not bring a release of the hostages. Faced with mounting public criticism, Carter finally authorized a commando raid. Its failure cost Carter the frustration and anger of a large part of the public, which blamed the president for the stalemate. An agreement to free the hostages was finally reached in 1981, but not until the very day Carter left office were the Americans finally released.

Carter's Domestic Program

On the economic front, Carter pursued a policy of deficit spending. When the Federal Reserve Board increased the money supply to help meet mounting deficits, which reached peacetime records under Carter, inflation rose to about 10 percent a year. Seeking to reduce inflation in 1979, Carter slowed down the economy and cut the deficit slightly. Budget cuts fell largely on social programs and distanced Carter from reform-minded Democrats who had supported him three years before. Yet even that effort to arrest growing deficits was not enough. When the budget released in early 1980 still showed high spending levels, the financial community reacted strongly. Bond prices fell, and interest rates rose dramatically.

Carter failed to construct an effective energy policy. OPEC had been increasing oil prices rapidly since 1973 and would not promise restraint in the future. Americans began to resent their dependence on foreign oil—over 40 percent was imported by the end of the decade—and clamored for energy self-sufficiency. Carter responded in April 1977 with a comprehensive energy program, which he called the "moral equivalent of war." Critics seized on the acronym of that expression, MEOW, to describe the plan and had a field day criticizing the president. Never an effective leader in working with the legislative branch, Carter watched his proposals bog down in Congress for 26 months. Eventually the program committed the nation to move from oil dependence to reliance on coal, possibly even on sun and wind, and established a new synthetic-fuel corporation. Nuclear power, another alternative, seemed less attractive as costs rose and accidents, like the one at Three Mile Island, occurred.

Parts of Carter's domestic program worked, but he often provided ineffective leadership. He frequently reversed course and failed to develop consistent policies. His critics charged that he had no legislative strategy at all, no priorities to communicate to Congress. As columnist Tom

Wicker noted at the end of four years, "He never established a politically coherent administration." That was largely because Carter was less comfortable as a politician, more comfortable as a problem solver and engineer. Like Herbert Hoover, he was a technocrat in the White House. As they had in 1932, Americans wanted a president who promised to lead them out of economic hard times.

The Election of 1980

Although Carter had wanted to reestablish Democratic control of the country, by the end of his term, his disapproval rating reached 77 percent. With Watergate behind them, the Republicans regrouped and called for a return to conservative principles of government.

Carter faced Ronald Reagan, an actor turned politician. Reagan had served as California's governor for eight years and had sought the presidency in 1976. As heir to Barry Goldwater's conservative mantle, he could count on the support of the growing right. Reagan had a pleasing manner and in the campaign proved his skill as a media communicator. Charging the Carter administration with "a litany of broken

Governor of California for two terms, Ronald Reagan drew on his earlier experience in the movies to project an appealing, if old-fashioned, image to the public.

promises," he provided a soothing contrast to the incumbent. He showed real wit as he quibbled with Carter over economic definitions. "I'm talking in human terms and he is hiding behind a dictionary," Reagan said. "If he wants a definition, I'll give him one. A recession is when your neighbor loses his job. A depression is when you lose yours. A recovery is when Jimmy Carter loses his."

Reagan started with an enormous lead in the campaign and held it to the end. He scored a landslide victory, gaining a popular margin of 51 to 41 percent and a 489 to 49 electoral college advantage. He also led the Republican party to control of the Senate. Reagan's strength showed in all areas of the country. He split the traditionally Democratic Jewish vote and working-class vote, though blacks supported Carter as before.

Reviving the Cold War

In foreign affairs, Reagan asserted American interests far more aggressively than Carter. Rooted in the Cold War tradition, he believed in high defense budgets and a militant approach toward the Soviet Union. To assist him in the formulation and conduct of foreign policy, Reagan appointed as secretary of state General Alexander Haig, former chief of staff in the Watergate White House. When Haig proved both contentious and ambitious, George Shultz, secretary of the Treasury under Nixon, took over.

Reagan moved decisively in a number of areas. Though he spoke of economy in government, he proposed unprecedented defense spending for a massive arms buildup. Over a five-year period, the administration sought a military budget of $1.5 trillion dollars. Arguing that the nation was otherwise vulnerable, the president insisted that spending for weapons, both nuclear and conventional, had to increase.

Reagan also argued that a nuclear war could be fought and won. Discounting scientists' studies that showed cataclysmic destruction in the event of nuclear war, he claimed that the nation would survive. T. K. Jones, deputy undersecretary of defense for strategic and theater nuclear forces, even revived the dormant notion of civil defense. "Dig a hole, cover it with a couple of doors, and then throw three feet of dirt on top . . . ," he advised. "It's the dirt that does it . . . if there are enough shovels to go around, everybody's going to make it."

While promoting defense spending and nuclear superiority, the administration abandoned Senate ratification of SALT II, the arms-reduction plan negotiated under Carter, although it observed its restrictions. Instead the administration proposed that Russia destroy certain missiles in return for an American pledge not to deploy new weapons in Europe. The Soviet Union balked at that idea, so different from the careful negotiation accompanying previous arms talks. The arms race escalated, new U.S. missiles were deployed in western Europe, and in both countries military budgets soared.

Seeing Central America as a Cold War battlefield, the administration intervened there frequently in Reagan's first term. The administration openly opposed the left-wing guerrillas of El Salvador who fought against a repressive right-wing regime. Fearful that another nation might follow the Marxist examples of Cuba and Nicaragua, the United States increased its aid to the antirevolutionary El Salvador government, heedless of a similar course followed years before in Vietnam. It also channeled support to exiled Nicaraguans attempting to overthrow the Socialist government in that country.

In foreign affairs, Reagan proved more rigidly ideological than any president since the end of World War II. He took stands that invited confrontation with Russia and often echoed approaches taken in the early Cold War years. Détente, though initiated under Republican leadership a decade before, collapsed.

Dismantling the Welfare State

Rooted in Middle America, Reagan fervently believed in the American dream. He looked back nostalgically at a world of heroes and heroic deeds, where a person could make a mark through individual effort. He had played by the rules of the system himself and had won. Others should do the same.

Faced with a stagnating economy and a growing federal establishment, Reagan sought to reverse the twentieth-century movement toward what conservatives saw as government management of every aspect of American life. Upon taking office he announced that he in-

tended to reduce government spending by eliminating "waste, fraud, and abuse." Concerned about the federal deficit, he committed himself to a balanced budget before the end of his term. To accomplish this he demanded cuts, particularly in social programs he viewed as unnecessary.

At the heart of his economic recovery program was the theory of supply-side economics, which held that the reduction of taxes would encourage business expansion, which in turn would lead to a larger supply of goods to help stimulate the system as a whole. "Reaganomics," promoted during the campaign, promised a revitalized economy.

To allow for tax reduction and military expansion, the administration proposed huge cuts in social programs. Public service jobs, mandated under the Comprehensive Employment and Training Act, were eliminated. Unemployment compensation was cut back. Medicare patients were required to pay more for treatment. Welfare benefits were lowered, and food stamp allocations were reduced.

While cutting social programs, the administration also pushed through regressive tax reductions. As finally passed, a 5 percent cut went into effect on October 1, 1981, followed by 10 percent cuts in 1982 and 1983. Although all taxpayers enjoyed some savings, the rich benefited far more than middle- and lower-income Americans. As a result of tax cuts and huge defense expenditures, the budget deficit grew even larger—approaching $200 billion in 1983 and 1984. Deficit spending had long been associated with the Democratic party and balanced budgets with the Republicans, but under Reagan the annual deficit reached historic heights.

As a political conservative distrustful of central government, Reagan also yearned to place power in the hands of state and local government and to reduce the ways in which the federal government touched people's lives. He was determined to cut back the federal regulatory apparatus, for he believed government regulations were partially responsible for the weakening performance of the American economy. Safety regulations were deemed "paternalistic." States, he argued, should not have social goals imposed on them by the national government.

The "New Federalism" was Reagan's attempt to shift responsibilities from the federal to the state level. The program never really got off the ground, as critics charged that the proposal was merely a backhanded way of moving programs from one place to another and then eliminating the funds.

Reagan also took a decidedly conservative approach to social issues. He willingly accepted the support of the New Right and spoke out for public prayer in the schools. The first nongovernmental group to receive an audience at the White House was an antiabortion March for Life contingent.

The president was less supportive of minority groups than his recent predecessors. He opposed busing to achieve racial balance, and his attorney general worked to dismantle affirmative-action programs. Initially reluctant to support extension of the enormously successful Voting Rights Acts of 1965, Reagan relented only under severe criticism from Republicans as well as Democrats. He directed the Internal Revenue Service to cease banning tax exemptions for private schools that discriminated against blacks, only to see that move overturned by the Supreme Court in 1983. Blacks were understandably critical of Reagan, as were Native Americans, who charged that his stance toward government affairs in general and Indian problems in particular was undoing the progress of the preceding ten years.

The Election of 1984

In 1984, Ronald Reagan sought reelection. After a bitter primary campaign that included black activist Jesse Jackson and Colorado senator Gary Hart, the Democrats nominated Walter Mondale, who had served as Jimmy Carter's vice-president. For his running mate, the Democrats selected Geraldine Ferraro, a congresswoman from New York, the first woman ever to receive a major party's nomination on the presidential ticket.

Reagan ran a bouyant, upbeat campaign with a patriotic theme. His appearance sometimes featured fireworks and swarms of tiny parachutes holding miniature American flags. His unofficial campaign song was "I'm Proud to Be an American." To his audiences he declared, "You ain't seen nothing yet."

Mondale hammered away at the huge and growing budget deficit and criticized the president's foreign policy, especially Reagan's seeming disinterest in halting the massive nuclear arms buildup, while contending that he could be every bit as tough toward the Soviet Union. But he appeared colorless and unexciting, and by mid-September, Mondale trailed Reagan in the polls by 18 percentage points.

His campaign enjoyed its only success in early October, in the aftermath of a televised debate. Invoking the image of John F. Kennedy, Mondale appeared more articulate and aggressive. Reagan seemed unsure of himself, tired at the end. Many Americans questioned whether the 73-year-old president was fit for another term. Reagan regained command in the next TV debate, defusing the age issue when he declared with a grin, "I am not going to exploit my opponent's youth and experience, not at all."

On election day, Reagan scored a second landslide victory. He received 59 percent of the popular vote and swamped Mondale in the electoral college, where he lost only Minnesota, his opponent's home state, and the District of Columbia. Though disappointed, the Democrats netted two additional seats in the Senate and

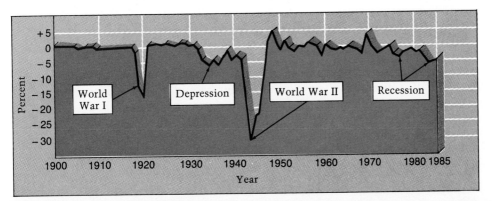

Federal Budget Surplus or Deficit as Percentage of GNP

Sources: U.S. Bureau of the Census; and Office of Management and Budget.

Presidential Elections, 1976–1984

YEAR	CANDIDATES	PARTY	POPULAR VOTE	ELECTORAL VOTE
1976	JIMMY CARTER	Democratic	40,828,657 (50.6%)	297
	Gerald R. Ford	Republican	39,145,520 (48.4%)	240
1980	RONALD REAGAN	Republican	43,899,248 (51%)	489
	Jimmy Carter	Democrat	36,481,435 (41%)	49
	John B. Anderson	Independent	5,719,437 (6%)	0
1984	RONALD REAGAN	Republican	53,428,357 (59%)	525
	Walter F. Mondale	Democrat	36,930,923 (41%)	13

Note: Winners' names appear in capital letters.

managed to maintain superiority in the House of Representatives.

Reagan's impressive electoral success symbolized not only a personal victory but also an endorsement of the new vision of government that he espoused. Since the New Deal, both Democrats and Republicans had agreed that the national government should monitor the economy and assist the least fortunate. Reagan's 1980 campaign and the efforts of his first administration challenged this vision. By 1984, even the Democrats were hesitant to question the claim that the federal government must curtail its activities. Liberal ideals were in retreat.

The election itself dramatized the collapse of the popular coalition that had sustained the Democratic party since the 1930s. Eighty-five percent of black voters supported Mondale, but only 35 percent of white voters cast their ballot for the national Democratic ticket. Contrary to Democratic party expectations, the nomination of Geraldine Ferraro did not rescue Mondale. The "gender gap" never materialized, and Ferraro's ethnic background failed to win back white ethnic voters.

Analysts offered varying explanations for the apparent collapse of the Democratic coalition and the racial polarization of the voters. Some suggested that whites abandoned the Democrats when blacks pressed for increasing government assistance in the 1960s and 1970s because many of the whites had already profited from government programs. Others pointed out that the economic slowdown of the 1970s had forced Democrats to choose between defense and social programs. Each choice offended some part of the old coalition. Many proclaimed that the election proved that New Deal liberalism was dead, but in 1984 no one could know whether its decline was permanent or temporary. Only time could reveal the full meaning of the election of 1984.

By the time Reagan embarked on his second term, the economy had made a strong recovery. With interest rates and unemployment dropping and economic growth partially restored, the country emerged from the deep recession of the early 1980s. Yet the hardening of the nation's economic arteries had not been completely cured. With unemployment still above 7 percent, millions of disillusioned Americans, like Andy Hjelmeland and Jerry Espinoza, introduced at the beginning of the chapter, wondered if they would ever recapture security and dignity in their lives.

CONCLUSION: The Recent Past in Perspective

Reagan's second term began with a mixture of hope and fear. His supporters foresaw a new era of conservative government that would foster a less regulated economy, restore older moral codes, continue the steel-ribbed posture toward the Soviet Union, and squelch any Socialist challenges to Western Hemisphere governments aligned with the United States. Reagan's detractors feared that the attacks on the welfare state, which by the beginning of the second term included proposals to cut such programs as Amtrak, subsidies to urban mass-transit systems, legal assistance to the poor, farm-support programs, and student loans, would once again divide the nation into a society of haves and have-nots. Not since the 1930s, when Franklin Roosevelt began his second term, had such wholesale change in government policies centered on the presidency.

Although the assault on the welfare state became dubbed the "Reagan revolution," such programs as social security and Medicare remained securely in place, accepted by all but the most implacable splinter groups. Even the most conservative president in the last half century could not return to a romanticized past of unbridled individualism and puny federal government. The domestic and international challenges facing a modern nation of multiple interest groups—a nation that was incorporated into a worldwide economic and diplomatic system—were far too complex for a government structure on nineteenth-century lines. So, as during many eras of the past, Americans in the 1980s listened to new formulas for facing the future, continued to consult the past for guidance in contemporary problems, argued among themselves on issues ranging from abortion to deficit spending, and for the most part retained a bedrock faith in a national two-party system and their local instruments of government.

Recommended Reading

There is understandably less published material available for the most recent period than for earlier years. Historians have not yet had a chance to deal in detail with the developments of the immediate past, and fuller descriptions must be found in other sources. The best writing about the years in this chapter appears in the newspapers and magazines of the popular press. But there are a number of useful treatments about selected topics that provide good starting points in various areas.

Andrew Hacker, ed., *U/S: A Statistical Portrait of the American People* (1983) is a helpful compilation of demographic trends based on the 1980 census. Richard Rodriguez, *Hunger of Memory: The Education of Richard Rodriguez* (1982) is a penetrating autobiographical account of a Hispanic boy growing up in the United States. Alvin M. Josephy, Jr., *Now That the Buffalo's Gone* (1982) is a comprehensive survey of recent American Indian struggles. Jimmy Carter, *Keeping Faith: Memories of a President* (1982) is Carter's own story of the White House years. Lou Cannon, *Reagan* (1982) is a veteran reporter's assessment of Reagan's background and early years as president.

TIME LINE	
1976	Jimmy Carter elected president
1977	Carter energy program, human rights policy Panama Canal Treaties
1978	Israeli-Egyptian peace accords at Camp David *Bakke* v. *University of California*
1979	Three Mile Island nuclear power plant accident Russians invade Afghanistan Iranian revolution overthrows shah SALT II agreement on nuclear arms
1979–1981	Iranian hostage crisis
1980	Ronald Reagan elected president
1981	Sandra Day O'Connor became first woman Supreme Court justice
1981–1983	Tax cuts; deficit spending increases
1982	Vietnam Veterans Memorial dedicated Equal Rights Amendment fails
1984	Geraldine Ferraro nominated for vice-president Reagan reelected

PORTFOLIO SIX

THE ART OF
AN ENDURING PEOPLE

1945 – 1985

The United States emerged from World War II as the most powerful nation in the world. Other countries looked to the United States for help in adjusting to the problems of the postwar world. At the same time, the rest of the world depended on America as a source for vital artistic expression and innovation. New York, not Paris or London, became the artistic capital of the world in the years immediately following the war. Although the 1930s had witnessed an increased migration of artists to New York, other factors also contributed to making the city a vital center for artistic expression. A large group of working artists, the presence of many collectors and galleries, the Museum of Modern Art, and other institutions helped to make New York a stimulating place to work. The New York school of abstract expressionism, as it came to be called, drew strength from many other places in the country, however.

Abstract expressionism included many different styles, each as shocking to the general public as it was exciting to the avant-garde. Jackson Pollock (1912–1956) painted pictures with no apparent focal point, no edge, the paint apparently poured on. Willem de Kooning (1904–) created giant splashes, Mark Rothko (1903–1970) constructed great swaths of color on huge canvases, and others abandoned the square canvas entirely. No sooner had the abstract expressionists reached what seemed the last possible extreme of abstraction, with paintings of a single line or a canvas with only shades of black, when a new group emerged on the scene. Pop art, op art, superrealism, flags, and comic strips all had their day. Artists painted soup cans, geometric designs, and ordinary street scenes, and the critics, if not always the general public, were impressed.

American art remained vital and diverse in the last decades of the twentieth century, and there was not just one center of innovation. Artists from Maine to California, from Texas to Minnesota, in the cities and the towns, took inspiration from their environment. If the ordinary citizens had difficulty understanding the abstract expressionists or appreciating pop art, they could find meaning in the paintings of Andrew Wyeth, who recalled a simpler age and painted in a style that reminded some of Winslow Homer. Folk art and ethnic art took on a new meaning in a postindustrial age when a search for community and family heritage extended to an appreciation of a colorful mural on a city building, a handmade quilt, and simple paintings created by untrained artists.

Willem de Kooning, *Woman*, 1949–1950.
Weatherspoon Art Gallery,
University of North Carolina at Greensboro.
Lena Kernodle McDuffie Memorial Gift.

Both these paintings are of women. The de Kooning has a kind of restless energy about it, as well as a sense of being incomplete. It puts a greater burden on the viewer than does the Wyeth. But Andrew Wyeth has great technical skill and works in a tradition that is familiar and perhaps nonthreatening. Both styles represented in these two paintings existed side by side in the decades after World War II.

Andrew Wyeth, *Christina's World*, 1948.
Museum of Modern Art, New York.

Jasper Johns, *Three Flags*, 1958.
Whitney Museum of American Art,
New York. Fiftieth anniversary gift
of the Gilman Foundation, Inc.,
the Lauder Foundation, A. Alfred
Taubman, an anonymous donor,
and purchase.

The movement called "pop art" burst onto the scene in the late 1950s and early 1960s. Although the name originated in England, the movement itself was very American. A group of talented artists took ordinary objects and symbols from advertising, the newspaper, and everyday life and forced the viewer to look at them in a different way. Jasper Johns (1930–) did a series on the American flag, a symbol so familiar that most people had never really looked at it. In a similar way, Andy Warhol (1928–) isolated commercial products such as Campbell's soup cans, while other artists created sculpture out of ordinary objects.

Andy Warhol, *Campbell's Soup Can
with Peeling Label*, 1962.
Leo Castelli Gallery, New York.

"Joe" chair, 1970.
Designers: De Pas, D'Urbino, and Lonazzi. Manufacturer: Poltronova.
Distributor: Stendig International. Photo courtesy of Stendig
International.

American pop art and other postwar movements had
an enormous influence in Europe and around the
world. One example is the "Joe" chair, a large version
of a baseball glove, created by three Italian designers
in 1970 and named after Yankee star Joe DiMaggio.

The paintings of Robert Bechtle (1932–), based on
photographs of familiar scenes, are startling for their
detailed photographic realism.

Robert Bechtle, '61 Pontiac, 1968–1969.
Whitney Museum of American Art, New York.
Richard and Dorothy Rodgers Fund.

Jackson Pollock, *Number 27*, 1950.
Whitney Museum of American Art, New York.

Jackson Pollock was influenced by the work of Thomas Hart Benton and the murals of José Orozco, but he eliminated the subject matter and simply used color and form. His paintings are sometimes called action paintings. He literally stood in the middle of his paintings when he created them, and he forced his viewer to recapture the creative experience to make any meaning out of his art.

Mark Rothko worked in bright colors and softly edged shapes. "Pictures must be miraculous," he said at one point. After a painting was completed, he maintained, "the intimacy between the creation and the creator is ended. He is an outsider. The picture must be for him, as for anyone experiencing it later, a revelation, an unexpected and unprecedented resolution of an eternally familiar need."

Mark Rothko, *Number 22*, 1949.
Museum of Modern Art, New York.
Gift of the artist.

Oscar Howe,
Sioux Seed Player, 1974.
University Art Galleries, University of
South Dakota, Vermillion.

These two paintings exemplify another kind of art that exploded in the years after World War II. Mural art took on new meaning, and a great many young artists sought subjects related to their ethnic and racial heritage as they tried to define their place in America. Oscar Howe (1915–) is a full-blooded Sioux, and in his art, which has been a major influence in the contemporary Indian art movement, he seeks themes from the legends, ceremonies, and traditions of the Sioux people. John Biggers (1924–) was born in North Carolina but in recent years has lived in Houston, Texas, where he has been one of the leaders in a renaissance of black art. His murals are influenced by a long tradition of mural painting, but his subject is the struggle of ordinary black people.

John Biggers,
The Quilting Party, 1981.
Music Hall, Houston Civic
Center. Photo Earlie Hudnall
for Artcetera, Houston.

APPENDIX

Declaration of Independence in Congress, July 4, 1776

THE UNANIMOUS DECLARATION OF THE THIRTEEN UNITED STATES OF AMERICA

When, in the course of human events, it becomes necessary for one people to dissolve the political bonds which have connected them with another, and to assume, among the powers of the earth, the separate and equal station to which the laws of nature and of nature's God entitle them, a decent respect to the opinions of mankind requires that they should declare the causes which impel them to the separation.

We hold these truths to be self-evident: That all men are created equal; that they are endowed by their Creator with certain unalienable rights; that among these are life, liberty, and the pursuit of happiness; that, to secure these rights, governments are instituted among men, deriving their just powers from the consent of the governed; that whenever any form of government becomes destructive of these ends, it is the right of the people to alter or to abolish it, and to institute new government, laying its foundation on such principles, and organizing its powers in such form, as to them shall seem most likely to effect their safety and happiness. Prudence, indeed, will dictate that governments long established should not be changed for light and transient causes; and accordingly all experience hath shown that mankind are more disposed to suffer, which evils are sufferable, than to right themselves by abolishing the forms to which they are accustomed. But when a long train of abuses and usurpations, pursuing invariably the same object, evinces a design to reduce them under absolute despotism, it is their right, it is their duty, to throw off such government, and to provide new guards for their future security. Such has been the patient sufferance of these colonies; and such is now the necessity which constrains them to alter their former systems of government. The history of the present King of Great Britain is a history of repeated injuries and usurpations, all having in direct object the establishment of an absolute tyranny over these states. To prove this, let facts be submitted to a candid world.

He has refused his assent to laws, the most wholesome and necessary for the public good.

He has forbidden his governors to pass laws of immediate and pressing importance, unless suspended in their operation till his assent should be obtained; and, when so suspended, he has utterly neglected to attend to them.

He has refused to pass other laws for the accommodation of large districts of people, unless those people would relinquish the right of representation in the legislature, a right inestimable to them, and formidable to tyrants only.

He has called together legislative bodies at places unusual, uncomfortable, and distant from the depository of their public records, for the sole purpose of fatiguing them into compliance with his measures.

He has dissolved representative houses repeatedly, for opposing, with manly firmness, his invasions on the rights of the people.

He has refused for a long time, after such dissolutions, to cause others to be elected; whereby the legislative powers, incapable of annihilation, have returned to the people at large for their exercise; the state remaining, in the mean time, exposed to all the dangers of invasions from without and convulsions within.

He has endeavored to prevent the population of these states; for that purpose obstructing the laws for naturalization of foreigners; refusing to pass others to encourage their migration hither, and raising the conditions of new appropriations of lands.

He has obstructed the administration of justice, by refusing his assent to laws for establishing judiciary powers.

He has made judges dependent on his will alone, for the tenure of their offices, and the amount and payment of their salaries.

He has erected a multitude of new offices, and sent hither swarms of officers to harass our people and eat out their substance.

He has kept among us, in times of peace, standing armies, without the consent of our legislatures.

He has affected to render the military independent of, and superior to, the civil power.

He has combined with others to subject us to a jurisdiction foreign to our constitution, and unacknowledged by our laws, giving his assent to their acts of pretended legislation:

For quartering large bodies of armed troops among us;

For protecting them, by a mock trial, from punishment for any murders which they should commit on the inhabitants of these states;

For cutting off our trade with all parts of the world;

For imposing taxes on us without our consent;

For depriving us, in many cases, of the benefits of trial by jury;

For transporting us beyond seas, to be tried for pretended offenses;

For abolishing the free system of English laws in a neighboring province, establishing therein an arbitrary government, and enlarging its boundaries, so as to render it at once an example and fit instrument for introducing the same absolute rule into these colonies;

For taking away our charters, abolishing our most

valuable laws, and altering fundamentally the forms of our governments.

For suspending our own legislatures, and declaring themselves invested with power to legislate for us in all cases whatsoever.

He has abdicated government here, by declaring us out of his protection and waging war against us.

He has plundered our seas, ravaged our coasts, burned our towns, and destroyed the lives of our people.

He is at this time transporting large armies of foreign mercenaries to complete the works of death, desolation, and tyranny already begun with circumstances of cruelty and perfidy scarcely paralleled in the most barbarous ages, and totally unworthy the head of a civilized nation.

He has constrained our fellow-citizens, taken captive on the high seas, to bear arms against their country, to become the executioners of their friends and brethren, or to fall themselves by their hands.

He has excited domestic insurrection among us, and has endeavored to bring on the inhabitants of our frontiers the merciless Indian savages, whose known rule of warfare is an undistinguished destruction of all ages, sexes, and conditions.

In every stage of these oppressions we have petitioned for redress in the most humble terms; our repeated petitions have been answered only by repeated injury. A prince, whose character is thus marked by every act which may define a tyrant, is unfit to be the ruler of a free people.

Nor have we been wanting in our attentions to our British brethren. We have warned them, from time to time, of attempts by their legislature to extend an unwarrantable jurisdiction over us. We have reminded them of the circumstances of our emigration and settlement here. We have appealed to their native justice and magnanimity; and we have conjured them, by the ties of our common kindred, to disavow these usurpations, which would inevitably interrupt our connections and correspondence. They, too, have been deaf to the voice of justice and of consanguinity. We must, therefore, acquiesce in the necessity which denounces our separation, and hold them, as we hold the rest of mankind, enemies in war, in peace friends.

We, therefore, the representatives of the United States of America, in General Congress assembled, appealing to the Supreme Judge of the world for the rectitude of our intentions, do, in the name and by the authority of the good people of these colonies, solemnly publish and declare, that these United Colonies are, and of right ought to be, FREE AND INDEPENDENT STATES; that they are absolved from all allegiance to the British crown, and that all political connection between them and the state of Great Britain is, and ought to be, totally dissolved; and that, as free and independent states, they have full power to levy war, conclude peace, contract alliances, establish commerce, and do all other acts and things which independent states may of right do. And for the support of this declaration, with a firm reliance on the protection of Divine Providence, we mutually pledge to each other our lives, our fortunes, and our sacred honor.

Constitution of the United States of America*

PREAMBLE

We the people of the United States, in order to form a more perfect union, establish justice, insure domestic tranquillity, provide for the common defense, promote the general welfare, and secure the blessings of liberty to ourselves and our posterity, do ordain and establish this Constitution for the United States of America.

ARTICLE I

Section 1 All legislative powers herein granted shall be vested in a Congress of the United States, which shall consist of a Senate and a House of Representatives.

Section 2 The House of Representatives shall be composed of members chosen every second year by the people of the several States, and the electors in each State shall have the qualifications requisite for electors of the most numerous branch of the State Legislature.

No person shall be a Representative who shall not have attained to the age of twenty-five years, and been seven years a citizen of the United States, and who shall not, when elected, be an inhabitant of that State in which he shall be chosen.

Representatives and direct taxes shall be apportioned among the several States which may be included within this Union, according to their respective numbers, *which shall be determined by adding to the whole number of free persons, including those bound to service for a term of years and excluding Indians not taxed, three-fifths of all other persons.* The actual enumeration shall be made within three years after the first meeting of the Congress of the United States, and within every subsequent term of ten years, in such manner as they shall by law direct. The number of Representatives shall not exceed one for every thirty thousand, but each State shall have at least one Representative; *and until such enumeration shall be made, the State of New Hampshire shall be entitled to choose three, Massachusetts eight, Rhode Island and Providence Plantations one, Connecticut five, New York six, New Jersey four, Pennsylvania eight, Delaware one, Maryland six, Virginia ten, North Carolina five, South Carolina five, and Georgia three.*

When vacancies happen in the representation from any State, the Executive authority thereof shall issue writs of election to fill such vacancies.

The House of Representatives shall choose their Speaker and other officers; and shall have the sole power of impeachment.

Section 3 The Senate of the United States shall be composed of two Senators from each State, *chosen by the legislature thereof,* for six years; and each Senator shall have one vote.

Immediately after they shall be assembled in consequence of the first election, they shall be divided as equally as may be into three classes. The seats of the Senators of the first class shall be vacated at the expiration of the second year, of the second class at the expiration of the fourth year, and of the third class at the expiration of the sixth year, so that one-third may be chosen every second year; *and if vacancies happen by resignation or otherwise, during the recess of the legislature of any State, the Executive thereof may make temporary appointments until the next meeting of the legislature, which shall then fill such vacancies.*

No person shall be a Senator who shall not have attained to the age of thirty years, and been nine years a citizen of the United States, and who shall not, when elected, be an inhabitant of that State for which he shall be chosen.

The Vice-President of the United States shall be President of the Senate, but shall have no vote, unless they be equally divided.

The Senate shall choose their other officers, and also a President *pro tempore,* in the absence of the Vice-President, or when he shall exercise the office of President of the United States.

The Senate shall have the sole power to try all impeachments. When sitting for that purpose, they shall be on oath or affirmation. When the President of the United States is tried, the Chief Justice shall preside; and no person shall be convicted without the concurrence of two-thirds of the members present.

Judgment in cases of impeachment shall not extend further than to removal from the office, and disqualification to hold and enjoy any office of honor, trust or profit under the United States: but the party convicted shall nevertheless be liable and subject to indictment, trial, judgment and punishment, according to law.

Section 4 The times, places and manner of holding elections for Senators and Representatives shall be prescribed in each State by the legislature thereof; but the Congress may at any time by law make or alter such regulations, except as to the places of choosing Senators.

The Congress shall assemble at least once in every year, and such meeting *shall be on the first Monday in December, unless they shall by law appoint a different day.*

---

* The Constitution became effective March 4, 1789.

Section 5   Each house shall be the judge of the elections, returns and qualifications of its own members, and a majority of each shall constitute a quorum to do business; but a smaller number may adjourn from day to day, and may be authorized to compel the attendance of absent members, in such manner, and under such penalties, as each house may provide.

Each house may determine the rules of its proceedings, punish its members for disorderly behavior, and with the concurrence of two-thirds, expel a member.

Each house shall keep a journal of its proceedings, and from time to time publish the same, excepting such parts as may in their judgment require secrecy; and the yeas and nays of the members of either house on any question shall, at the desire of one-fifth of those present, be entered on the journal.

Neither house, during the session of Congress, shall, without the consent of the other, adjourn for more than three days, nor to any other place than that in which the two houses shall be sitting.

Section 6   The Senators and Representatives shall receive a compensation for their services, to be ascertained by law and paid out of the treasury of the United States. They shall in all cases except treason, felony and breach of the peace be privileged from arrest during their attendance at the session of their respective houses, and in going to and returning from the same; and for any speech or debate in either house, they shall not be questioned in any other place.

No Senator or Representative shall, during the time for which he was elected, be appointed to any civil office under the authority of the United States, which shall have been created, or the emoluments whereof shall have been increased, during such time; and no person holding any office under the United States shall be a member of either house during his continuance in office.

Section 7   All bills for raising revenue shall originate in the House of Representatives; but the Senate may propose or concur with amendments as on other bills.

Every bill which shall have passed the House of Representatives and the Senate, shall, before it becomes a law, be presented to the President of the United States; if he approve he shall sign it, but if not he shall return it with objections to that house in which it originated, who shall enter the objections at large on their journal, and proceed to reconsider it. If after such reconsideration two-thirds of that house shall agree to pass the bill, it shall be sent, together with the objections, to the other house, by which it shall likewise be reconsidered, and, if approved by two-thirds of that house, it shall become a law. But in all such cases the votes of both houses shall be determined by yeas and nays, and the names of the persons voting for and against the bill shall be entered on the journal of each house respectively. If any bill shall not be returned by the President within ten days (Sundays excepted) after it shall have been presented to him, the same shall be a law, in like manner as if he had signed it, unless the Congress by their adjournment prevent its return, in which case it shall not be a law.

Every order, resolution, or vote to which the concurrence of the Senate and House of Representatives may be necessary (except on a question of adjournment) shall be presented to the President of the United States; and before the same shall take effect, shall be approved by him, or being disapproved by him, shall be repassed by two-thirds of the Senate and House of Representatives, according to the rules and limitations prescribed in the case of a bill.

Section 8   The Congress shall have power:

To lay and collect taxes, duties, imposts, and excises, to pay the debts and provide for the common defense and general welfare of the United States; but all duties, imposts and excises shall be uniform throughout the United States;

To borrow money on the credit of the United States;

To regulate commerce with foreign nations, and among the several States, and with the Indian tribes;

To establish an uniform rule of naturalization, and uniform laws on the subject of bankruptcies throughout the United States;

To coin money, regulate the value thereof, and of foreign coin, and fix the standard of weights and measures;

To provide for the punishment of counterfeiting the securities and current coin of the United States;

To establish post offices and post roads;

To promote the progress of science and useful arts by securing for limited times to authors and inventors the exclusive right to their respective writings and discoveries;

To constitute tribunals inferior to the Supreme Court;

To define and punish piracies and felonies committed on the high seas and offenses against the law of nations;

To declare war, grant letters of marque and reprisal, and make rules concerning captures on land and water;

To raise and support armies, but no appropriation of money to that use shall be for a longer term than two years;

To provide and maintain a navy;

To make rules for the government and regulation of the land and naval forces;

To provide for calling forth the militia to execute the laws of the Union, suppress insurrections, and repel invasions;

To provide for organizing, arming, and disciplining the militia, and for governing such part of them as may be employed in the service of the United States, reserving to the States respectively the appointment of the officers, and the authority of training the militia according to the discipline prescribed by Congress;

To exercise exclusive legislation in all cases whatsoever, over such district (not exceeding ten miles square) as may, by cession of particular States, and the acceptance of Congress, become the seat of government of the United States, and to exercise like authority over all places purchased by the consent of the legislature of the State, in which the same shall be, for erection of forts, magazines, arsenals, dockyards, and other needful buildings;—and

To make all laws which shall be necessary and proper for carrying into execution the foregoing powers, and all other powers vested by this Constitution in the government of the United States, or in any department or officer thereof.

Section 9 *The migration or importation of such persons as any of the States now existing shall think proper to admit shall not be prohibited by the Congress prior to the year 1808; but a tax or duty may be imposed on such importation, not exceeding $10 for each person.*

The privilege of the writ of habeas corpus shall not be suspended, unless when in cases of rebellion or invasion the public safety may require it.

No bill of attainder or ex post facto law shall be passed.

No capitation or other direct tax shall be laid, unless in proportion to the census or enumeration herein before directed to be taken.

No tax or duty shall be laid on articles exported from any State.

No preference shall be given by any regulation of commerce or revenue to the ports of one State over those of another; nor shall vessels bound to, or from, one State be obliged to enter, clear, or pay duties in another.

No money shall be drawn from the treasury, but in consequence of appropriations made by law; and a regular statement and account of the receipts and expenditures of all public money shall be published from time to time.

No title of nobility shall be granted by the United States: and no person holding any office of profit or trust under them, shall, without the consent of the Congress, accept of any present, emolument, office, or title, of any kind whatever, from any king, prince, or foreign state.

Section 10 No State shall enter into any treaty, alliance, or confederation; grant letters of marque and reprisal; coin money; emit bills of credit; make anything but gold and silver coin a tender in payment of debts; pass any bill of attainder, ex post facto law, or law impairing the obligation of contracts, or grant any title of nobility.

No States shall, without the consent of Congress, lay any imposts or duties on imports or exports, except what may be absolutely necessary for executing its inspection laws: and the net produce of all duties and imposts, laid by any State on imports or exports, shall be for the use of the treasury of the United States; and all such laws shall be subject to the revision and control of the Congress.

No State shall, without the consent of Congress, lay any duty of tonnage, keep troops or ships of war in time of peace, enter into any agreement or compact with another State, or with a foreign power, or engage in war, unless actually invaded, or in such imminent danger as will not admit of delay.

ARTICLE II

Section 1 The executive power shall be vested in a President of the United States of America. He shall hold his office during the term of four years, and, together with the Vice-President, chosen for the same term, be elected as follows:

Each State shall appoint, in such manner as the legislature thereof may direct, a number of electors, equal to the whole number of Senators and Representatives to which the State may be entitled in the Congress; but no Senator or Representative, or person holding an office of trust or profit under the United States, shall be appointed an elector.

The electors shall meet in their respective States, and vote by ballot for two persons, of whom one at least shall not be an inhabitant of the same State with themselves. And they shall make a list of all the persons voted for, and of the number of votes for each; which list they shall sign and certify, and transmit sealed to the seat of government of the United States, directed to the President of the Senate. The President of the Senate shall, in the presence of the Senate and House of Representatives, open all the certificates, and the votes shall then be counted. The person having the greatest number of votes shall be the President, if such number be a majority of the whole number of electors appointed; and if there be more than one who have such majority, and have an equal number of votes, then the House of Representatives shall immediately choose by ballot one of them for President; and if no person have a majority, then from the five highest on the list said house shall in like manner choose the President. But in choosing the President the votes shall be taken by States, the representation from each State having one vote; a quorum for this purpose shall consist of a member or members from two-thirds of the States, and a majority of all the States shall be necessary to a choice. In every case, after the choice of the President, the person having the greatest number of votes of the electors shall be the Vice-President. But if there should remain two or more who have equal votes, the Senate shall choose from them by ballot the Vice-President.

The Congress may determine the time of choosing the electors and the day on which they shall give their votes; which day shall be the same throughout the United States.

No person except a natural-born citizen, *or a citizen of the United States at the time of the adoption of this Constitution,* shall be eligible to the office of President; neither shall any person be eligible to that office who shall not have attained to the age of thirty-five years, and been fourteen years a resident within the United States.

In case of the removal of the President from office or of his death, resignation, or inability to discharge the powers and duties of the said office, the same shall devolve on the Vice-President, and the Congress may by law provide for the case of removal, death, resignation, or inability, both of the President and Vice-President, declaring what officer shall then act as President, and such officer shall act accordingly, until the disability be removed, or a President shall be elected.

The President shall, at stated times, receive for his services a compensation, which shall neither be increased nor diminished during the period for which he shall have been elected, and he shall not receive within that period any other emolument from the United States, or any of them.

Before he enter on the execution of his office, he shall take the following oath or affirmation:—"I do solemnly swear (or affirm) that I will faithfully execute the office of the President of the United States, and will to the best of my ability preserve, protect and defend the Constitution of the United States."

Section 2   The President shall be commander in chief of the army and navy of the United States, and of the militia of the several States, when called into the actual service of the United States; he may require

the opinion, in writing, of the principal officer in each of the executive departments, upon any subject relating to the duties of their respective offices, and he shall have power to grant reprieves and pardons for offenses against the United States, except in cases of impeachment.

He shall have power, by and with the advice and consent of the Senate, to make treaties, provided two-thirds of the Senators present concur; and he shall nominate, and by and with the advice and consent of the Senate, shall appoint ambassadors, other public ministers and consuls, judges of the Supreme Court, and all other officers of the United States, whose appointments are not herein otherwise provided for, and which shall be established by law: but Congress may by law vest the appointment of such inferior officers, as they think proper, in the President alone, in the courts of law, or in the heads of departments.

The President shall have power to fill up all vacancies that may happen during the recess of the Senate, by granting commissions which shall expire at the end of their next session.

Section 3   He shall from time to time give to the Congress information of the state of the Union, and recommend to their consideration such measures as he shall judge necessary and expedient; he may, on extraordinary occasions, convene both houses, or either of them, and in case of disagreement between them, with respect to the time of adjournment, he may adjourn them to such time as he shall think proper; he shall receive ambassadors and other public ministers; he shall take care that the laws be faithfully executed, and shall commission all the officers of the United States.

Section 4   The President, Vice-President and all civil officers of the United States shall be removed from office on impeachment for, and on conviction of, treason, bribery, or other high crimes and misdemeanors.

ARTICLE III

Section 1   The judicial power of the United States shall be vested in one Supreme Court, and in such inferior courts as the Congress may from time to time ordain and establish. The judges, both of the Supreme and inferior courts, shall hold their offices during good behavior, and shall, at stated times, receive for their services a compensation which shall not be diminished during their continuance in office.

Section 2   The judicial power shall extend to all cases, in law and equity, arising under this Constitution, the laws of the United States, and treaties made, or which shall be made, under their authority—to all cases affecting ambassadors, other public ministers and consuls;—to all cases of admiralty and maritime jurisdiction;—to controversies to which the United States shall be a party;—to controversies between two or more States;—*between a State and citizens of another State;*—between citizens of different States;—between citizens of the same State claiming lands under grants of different States, and between a State, or the citizens thereof, and foreign states, citizens or subjects.

In all cases affecting ambassadors, other public ministers and consuls, and those in which a State shall be party, the Supreme Court shall have original jurisdiction. In all the other cases before mentioned, the Supreme Court shall have appellate jurisdiction, both as to law and fact, with such exceptions, and under such regulations, as the Congress shall make.

The trial of all crimes, except in cases of impeachment, shall be by jury; and such trial shall be held in the State where said crimes shall have been committed; but when not committed within any State, the trial shall be at such place or places as the Congress may by law have directed.

Section 3   Treason against the United States shall consist only in levying war against them, or in adhering to their enemies, giving them aid and comfort. No person shall be convicted of treason unless on the testimony of two witnesses to the same overt act, or on confession in open court.

The Congress shall have power to declare the punishment of treason, but no attainder of treason shall work corruption of blood, or forfeiture except during the life of the person attainted.

ARTICLE IV

Section 1   Full faith and credit shall be given in each State to the public acts, records, and judicial proceedings of every other State. And the Congress may by general laws prescribe the manner in which such acts, records, and proceedings shall be proved, and the effect thereof.

Section 2   The citizens of each State shall be entitled to all privileges and immunities of citizens in the several States.

A person charged in any State with treason, felony, or other crime, who shall flee from justice, and be found in another State, shall on demand of the executive authority of the State from which he fled, be delivered up, to be removed to the State having jurisdiction of the crime.

No person held to service or labor in one State, under the laws thereof, escaping into another, shall, *in consequence of any law or regulation therein, be discharged from such service or labor, but shall be delivered up on claim of the party to whom such service or labor may be due.*

Section 3   New States may be admitted by the Congress into this Union; but no new State shall be formed or erected within the jurisdiction of any other State; nor any State be formed by the junction of two or more States, or parts of States, without the consent of the legislatures of the States concerned as well as of the Congress.

The Congress shall have power to dispose of and make all needful rules and regulations respecting the territory or other property belonging to the United States; and nothing in this Constitution shall be so construed as to prejudice any claims of the United States, or of any particular State.

Section 4   The United States shall guarantee to every State in this Union a republican form of government, and shall protect each of them against invasion; and on application of the legislature, or of the executive (when the legislature cannot be convened), against domestic violence.

ARTICLE V

The Congress, whenever two-thirds of both houses shall deem it necessary, shall propose amendments to this Constitution, or, on the application of the legislatures of two-thirds of the several States, shall call a convention for proposing amendments, which, in either case, shall be valid to all intents and purposes, as part of this Constitution, when ratified by the legislatures of three-fourths of the several States, or by conventions in three-fourths thereof, as the one or the other mode of ratification may be proposed by the Congress; provided *that no amendments which may be made prior to the year one thousand eight hundred and eight shall in any manner affect the first and fourth classes in the ninth section of the first article; and* that no State, without its consent, shall be deprived of its equal suffrage in the Senate.

ARTICLE VI

All debts contracted and engagements entered into, before the adoption of this Constitution, shall be as valid against the United States under this Constitution, as under the Confederation.

This Constitution, and the laws of the United States which shall be made in pursuance thereof; and all treaties made, or which shall be made, under the authority of the United States, shall be the supreme law of the land; and the judges in every State shall be bound thereby, anything in the Constitution or laws of any State to the contrary notwithstanding.

The Senators and Representatives before mentioned, and the members of the several State legislatures, and all executive and judicial officers, both of the United States and of the several States, shall be bound by oath or affirmation to support this Constitution; but no religious test shall ever be required as a qualification to any office or public trust under the United States.

ARTICLE VII

The ratification of the conventions of nine States shall be sufficient for the establishment of this Constitution between the States so ratifying the same.

Done in Convention by the unanimous consent of the States present, the seventeenth day of September in the year of our Lord one thousand seven hundred and eighty-seven and of the Independence of the United States of America the twelfth. In witness whereof we have hereunto subscribed our names.

AMENDMENTS TO THE CONSTITUTION*

AMENDMENT I [1791]

Congress shall make no law respecting an establishment of religion, or prohibiting the free exercise thereof; or abridging the freedom of speech, or of the press; or the right of the people peaceably to assemble, and to petition the government for a redress of grievances.

AMENDMENT II [1791]

A well-regulated militia being necessary to the security of a free State, the right of the people to keep and bear arms shall not be infringed.

AMENDMENT III [1791]

No soldier shall, in time of peace, be quartered in any house without the consent of the owner, nor in time of war, but in a manner to be prescribed by law.

AMENDMENT IV [1791]

The right of the people to be secure in their persons, houses, papers, and effects, against unreasonable searches and seizures, shall not be violated, and no warrants shall issue but upon probable cause, supported by oath or affirmation, and particularly describing the place to be searched, and the persons or things to be seized.

AMENDMENT V [1791]

No person shall be held to answer for a capital or otherwise infamous crime, unless on a presentment or indictment of a grand jury, except in cases arising in the land or naval forces, or in the militia, when in actual service in time of war or public danger; nor shall any person be subject for the same offense to be twice put in jeopardy of life or limb; nor shall be compelled in any criminal case to be a witness against himself, nor be deprived of life, liberty, or property, without due process of law; nor shall private property be taken for public use without just compensation.

AMENDMENT VI [1791]

In all criminal prosecutions, the accused shall enjoy the right to a speedy and public trial, by an impartial jury of the State and district wherein the crime shall have been committed, which district shall have been previously ascertained by law, and to be informed of the nature and cause of the accusation; to be confronted with the witnesses against him; to have compulsory process for obtaining witnesses in his favor, and to have the assistance of counsel for his defense.

AMENDMENT VII [1791]

In suits at common law, where the value in controversy shall exceed twenty dollars, the right of trial by jury shall be preserved, and no fact tried by a jury shall be otherwise reexamined in any court of the United States, than according to the rules of the common law.

AMENDMENT VIII [1791]

Excessive bail shall not be required, nor excessive fines imposed, nor cruel and unusual punishments inflicted.

---

* The first ten Amendments are known as the Bill of Rights.

AMENDMENT IX [1791]

The enumeration in the Constitution, of certain rights, shall not be construed to deny or disparage others retained by the people.

AMENDMENT X [1791]

The powers not delegated to the United States by the Constitution, nor prohibited by it to the States, are reserved to the States respectively, or to the people.

AMENDMENT XI [1798]

The judicial power of the United States shall not be construed to extend to any suit in law or equity, commenced or prosecuted against one of the United States by citizens of another State, or by citizens or subjects of any foreign state.

AMENDMENT XII [1804]

The electors shall meet in their respective States, and vote by ballot for President and Vice-President, one of whom, at least, shall not be an inhabitant of the same State with themselves; they shall name in their ballots the person voted for as President, and in distinct ballots the person voted for as Vice-President, and they shall make distinct lists of all persons voted for as President, and of all persons voted for as Vice-President, and of the number of votes for each, which lists they shall sign and certify, and transmit sealed to the seat of government of the United States, directed to the President of the Senate;—the President of the Senate shall, in the presence of the Senate and House of Representatives, open all the certificates and the votes shall then be counted;—the person having the greatest number of votes for President shall be the President, if such number be a majority of the whole number of electors appointed; and if no person have such majority, then from the persons having the highest numbers not exceeding three on the list of those voted for as President, the House of Representatives shall choose immediately, by ballot, the President. But in choosing the President, the votes shall be taken by States, the representation from each State having one vote; a quorum for this purpose shall consist of a member or members from two-thirds of the States, and a majority of all the States shall be necessary to a choice. And if the House of Representatives shall not choose a President whenever the right of choice shall devolve upon them, before *the fourth day of March* next following, then the Vice-President shall act as President, as in the case of the death or other constitutional disability of the President.

The person having the greatest number of votes as Vice-President shall be the Vice-President, if such number be a majority of the whole number of electors appointed; and if no person have a majority, then from the two highest numbers on the list the Senate shall choose the Vice-President; a quorum for the purpose shall consist of two-thirds of the whole number of Senators, and a majority of the whole number shall be necessary to a choice. But no person constitutionally ineligible to the office of President shall be eligible to that of Vice-President of the United States.

AMENDMENT XIII [1865]

Section 1   Neither slavery nor involuntary servitude, except as a punishment for crime whereof the party shall have been duly convicted, shall exist within the United States, or any place subject to their jurisdiction.

Section 2   Congress shall have power to enforce this article by appropriate legislation.

AMENDMENT XIV [1868]

Section 1   All persons born or naturalized in the United States, and subject to the jurisdiction thereof, are citizens of the United States and of the State wherein they reside. No State shall make or enforce any law which shall abridge the privileges or immunities of citizens of the United States; nor shall any State deprive any person of life, liberty, or property, wihtout due process of law; nor deny to any person within its jurisdiction the equal protection of the laws.

Section 2   Representatives shall be apportioned among the several States according to their respective numbers, counting the whole number of persons in each State, excluding Indians not taxed. But when the right to vote at any election for the choice of Electors for President and Vice-President of the United States, Representatives in Congress, the executive and judicial officers of a State, or the members of the legislature thereof, is denied to any of the male inhabitants of such State, being twenty-one years of age and citizens of the United States, or in any way abridged, except for participation in rebellion, or other crime, the basis of representation therein shall be reduced in the proportion which the number of such male citizens shall bear to the whole number of male citizens twenty-one years of age in such State.

Section 3   No person shall be a Senator or Representative in Congress, or Elector of President and Vice-President, or hold any office, civil or military, under the United States, or under any State, who, having previously taken an oath, as a member of Congress, or as an officer of the United States, or as a member of any State legislature, or as an executive or judicial officer of any State, to support the Constitution of the United States, shall have engaged in insurrection or rebellion against the same, or given aid or comfort to the enemies thereof. Congress may, by a vote of two-thirds of each house, remove such disability.

Section 4   The validity of the public debt of the United States, authorized by law, including debts incurred for payment of pensions and bounties for services in suppressing insurrection or rebellion, shall not be questioned. But neither the United States nor any State shall assume or pay any debt or obligation incurred in aid of insurrection or rebellion against the United States, or any claim for the loss of emancipation of any slave; but all such debts, obligations, and claims shall be held illegal and void.

Section 5   The Congress shall have power to enforce, by appropriate legislation, the provisions of this article.

AMENDMENT XV [1870]

Section 1   The right of citizens of the United States to vote shall not be denied or abridged by the United States or by any State on account of race, color, or previous condition of servitude.

Section 2   The Congress shall have power to enforce this article by appropriate legislation.

AMENDMENT XVI [1913]

The Congress shall have power to lay and collect taxes on incomes, from whatever source derived, without apportionment among the several States, and without regard to any census or enumeration.

AMENDMENT XVII [1913]

Section 1   The Senate of the United States shall be composed of two Senators from each State, elected by the people thereof, for six years; and each Senator shall have one vote. The electors in each State shall have the qualifications requisite for electors of [voters for] the most numerous branch of the State legislatures.

Section 2   When vacancies happen in the representation of any State in the Senate, the executive authority of such State shall issue writs of election to fill such vacancies: Provided that the legislature of any State may empower the executive thereof to make temporary appointments until the people fill

the vacancies by election as the legislature may direct.

Section 3   This amendment shall not be so construed as to affect the election or term of any Senator chosen before it becomes valid as part of the Constitution.

AMENDMENT XVIII [1919]

Section 1   After one year from the ratification of this article the manufacture, sale, or transportation of intoxicating liquors within, the importation thereof into, or the exportation thereof from the United States and all territory subject to the jurisdiction thereof, for beverage purposes, is hereby prohibited.

Section 2   The Congress and the several States shall have concurrent power to enforce this article by appropriate legislation.

Section 3   This article shall be inoperative unless it shall have been ratified as an amendment to the Constitution by the legislatures of the several States, as provided by the Constitution, within seven years from the date of the submission thereof to the States by the Congress.

AMENDMENT XIX [1920]

Section 1   The right of citizens of the United States to vote shall not be denied or abridged by the United States or by any State on account of sex.

Section 2   The Congress shall have power to enforce this article by appropriate legislation.

AMENDMENT XX [1933]

Section 1   The terms of the President and Vice-President shall end at noon on the 20th day of January, and the terms of Senators and Representatives at noon on the 3d day of January, of the years in which such terms would have ended if this article had not been ratified; and the terms of their successors shall then begin.

Section 2   The Congress shall assemble at least once in every year, and such meeting shall begin at noon on the 3d day of January, unless they shall by law appoint a different day.

Section 3   If, at the time fixed for the beginning of the term of the President, the President-elect shall have died, the Vice-President-elect shall become President. If a President shall not have been chosen before the time fixed for the beginning of his term, or if the President-elect shall have failed to qualify, then the Vice-President-elect shall act as President until a President shall have qualified; and the Congress may by law provide for the case wherein neither a President-elect nor a Vice-President-elect shall have qualified, declaring who shall then act as President, or the manner in which one who is to act shall be selected, and such persons shall act accordingly until a President or Vice-President shall have qualified.

Section 4   The Congress may by law provide for the case of the death of any of the persons from whom the House of Representatives may choose a President whenever the right of choice shall have devolved upon them, and for the case of the death of any of the persons from whom the Senate may choose a Vice-President whenever the right of choice shall have devolved upon them.

Section 5   Sections 1 and 2 shall take effect on the 15th day of October following the ratification of this article.

Section 6   This article shall be inoperative unless it shall have been ratified as an amendment to the Constitution by the legislatures of three-fourths of the several States within seven years from the date of its submission.

AMENDMENT XXI [1933]

Section 1   The eighteenth article of amendment to the Constitution of the United States is hereby repealed.

Section 2   The transportation or importation into any State, Territory, or Possession of the United States for delivery or use therein of intoxicating liquors, in violation of the laws thereof, is hereby prohibited.

Section 3   This article shall be inoperative unless it shall have been ratified as an amendment to the Constitution by conventions in the several States, as provided in the Constitution, within seven years from the date of submission thereof to the States by the Congress.

AMENDMENT XXII [1951]

Section 1   No person shall be elected to the office of President more than twice, and no person who has held the office of President, or acted as President, for more than two years of a term to which some other person was elected President shall be elected to the office of President more than once. But this article shall not apply to any person holding the office of President when this article was proposed by the Congress, and shall not prevent any person who may be holding the office of President, or acting as President, during the term within which this article becomes operative from holding the office of Presi-

dent or acting as President during the remainder of such term.

Section 2   This article shall be inoperative unless it shall have been ratified as an amendment to the Constitution by the legislatures of three-fourths of the several States within seven years from the date of its submission to the States by the Congress.

AMENDMENT XXIII [1961]

Section 1   The District constituting the seat of Government of the United States shall appoint in such manner as the Congress may direct:

A number of electors of President and Vice-President equal to the whole number of Senators and Representatives in Congress to which the District would be entitled if it were a State, but in no event more than the least populous State; they shall be in addition to those appointed by the States, but they shall be considered for the purposes of the election of President and Vice-President, to be electors appointed by a State; and they shall meet in the District and perform such duties as provided by the twelfth article of amendment.

Section 2   The Congress shall have the power to enforce this article by appropriate legislation.

AMENDMENT XXIV [1964]

Section 1   The right of citizens of the United States to vote in any primary or other election for President or Vice-President, for electors for President or Vice-President, or for Senator or Representative in Congress, shall not be denied or abridged by the United States or any State by reason of failure to pay any poll tax or other tax.

Section 2   The Congress shall have the power to enforce this article by appropriate legislation.

AMENDMENT XXV [1967]

Section 1   In case of the removal of the President from office or of his death or resignation, the Vice-President shall become President.

Section 2   Whenever there is a vacancy in the office of the Vice-President, the President shall nominate a Vice-President who shall take office upon confirmation by a majority vote of both houses of Congress.

Section 3   Whenever the President transmits to the President pro tempore of the Senate and the Speaker of the House of Representatives his written declaration that he is unable to discharge the powers and duties of his office, and until he transmits to them a written declaration to the contrary, such powers and duties shall be discharged by the Vice-President as Acting President.

Section 4 Whenever the Vice-President and a majority of either the principal officers of the executive departments or of such other body as Congress may by law provide, transmit to the President pro tempore of the Senate and the Speaker of the House of Representatives their written declaration that the President is unable to discharge the powers and duties of his office, the Vice-President shall immediately assume the powers and duties of the office as Acting President.

Thereafer, when the President transmits to the President pro tempore of the Senate and the Speaker of the House of Representatives his written declaration that no inability exists, he shall resume the powers and duties of his office unless the Vice-President and a majority of either the principal officers of the executive department[s] or of such other body as Congress may by law provide, transmit within four days to the President pro tempore of the Senate and the Speaker of the House of Representatives their written declaration that the President is unable to discharge the powers and duties of his office. Thereupon Congress shall decide the issue, assembling within forty-eight hours for that purpose if not in session. If the Congress, within twenty-one days after receipt of the latter written declaration, or, if Congress is not in session, within twenty-one days after Congress is required to assemble, determines by two-thirds vote of both Houses that the President is unable to discharge the powers and duties of his office, the Vice-President shall continue to discharge the same as Acting President; otherwise, the President shall resume the powers and duties of his office.

AMENDMENT XXVI [1971]

Section 1 The right of citizens of the United States, who are eighteen years of age or older, to vote shall not be denied or abridged by the United States or by any State on account of age.

Section 2 The Congress shall have power to enforce this article by appropriate legislation.

States of the United States

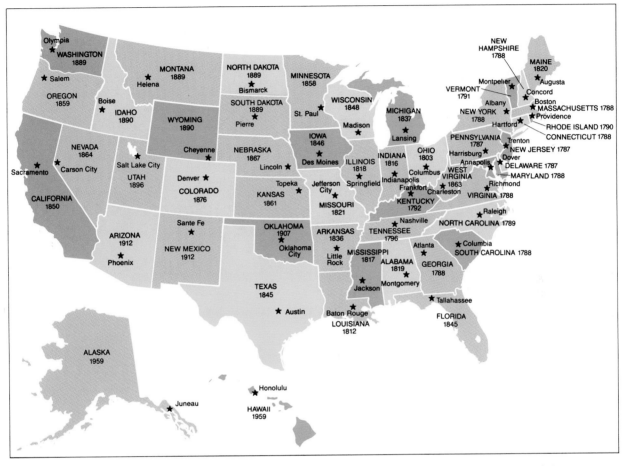

STATE	DATE OF ADMISSION	STATE	DATE OF ADMISSION
Delaware	December 7, 1787	Michigan	January 16, 1837
Pennsylvania	December 12, 1787	Florida	March 3, 1845
New Jersey	December 18, 1787	Texas	December 29, 1845
Georgia	January 2, 1788	Iowa	December 28, 1846
Connecticut	January 9, 1788	Wisconsin	May 29, 1848
Massachusetts	February 6, 1788	California	September 9, 1850
Maryland	April 28, 1788	Minnesota	May 11, 1858
South Carolina	May 23, 1788	Oregon	February 14, 1859
New Hampshire	June 21, 1788	Kansas	January 29, 1861
Virginia	June 25, 1788	West Virginia	June 19, 1863
New York	July 26, 1788	Nevada	October 31, 1864
North Carolina	November 21, 1789	Nebraska	March 1, 1867
Rhode Island	May 29, 1790	Colorado	August 1, 1876
Vermont	March 4, 1791	North Dakota	November 2, 1889
Kentucky	June 1, 1792	South Dakota	November 2, 1889
Tennessee	June 1, 1796	Montana	November 8, 1889
Ohio	March 1, 1803	Washington	November 11, 1889
Louisiana	April 30, 1812	Idaho	July 3, 1890
Indiana	December 11, 1816	Wyoming	July 10, 1890
Mississippi	December 10, 1817	Utah	January 4, 1896
Illinois	December 3, 1818	Oklahoma	November 16, 1907
Alabama	December 14, 1819	New Mexico	January 6, 1912
Maine	March 15, 1820	Arizona	February 14, 1912
Missouri	August 10, 1821	Alaska	January 3, 1959
Arkansas	June 15, 1836	Hawaii	August 21, 1959

Territorial Expansion of the United States

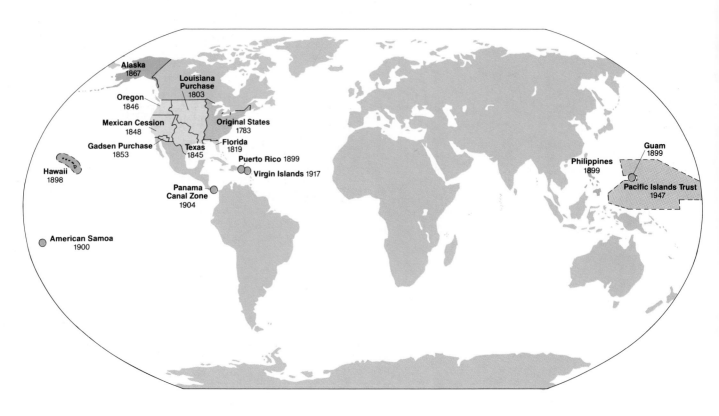

DATE	TERRITORY	AREA (sq. mi.)	CUMULATIVE TOTAL (sq. mi.)
1793	Original States	888,685	888,685
1803	Louisiana Purchase	827,192	1,715,877
1819	Florida	72,003	1,787,880
1845	Texas	390,143	2,178,023
1846	Oregon	285,580	2,463,603
1848	Mexican cession	529,017	2,992,620
1853	Gadsden Purchase	29,640	3,022,260
1867	Alaska	589,757	3,612,017
1898	Hawaii	6,450	3,618,467
1899	Philippines	115,600	3,734,067
1899	Puerto Rico	3,435	3,737,502
1899	Guam	212	3,737,714
1900	American Samoa	76	3,737,790
1904	Panama Canal Zone	553	3,738,343
1917	Virgin Islands	133	3,738,476
1947	Pacific Islands Trust	8,489	3,746,965
	All Others	46	3,747,011

Presidential Elections

YEAR	CANDIDATES	PARTIES	% OF POPULAR VOTE*†	ELECTORAL VOTE‡	% VOTER PARTICIPATION†
1789	GEORGE WASHINGTON	No party designations		69	
	John Adams			34	
	Other candidates			35	
1792	GEORGE WASHINGTON	No party designations		132	
	John Adams			77	
	George Clinton			50	
	Other candidates			5	
1796	JOHN ADAMS	Federalist		71	
	Thomas Jefferson	Democratic-Republican		68	
	Thomas Pinckney	Federalist		59	
	Aaron Burr	Democratic-Republican		30	
	Other candidates			48	
1800	THOMAS JEFFERSON	Democratic-Republican		73	
	Aaron Burr	Democratic-Republican		73	
	John Adams	Federalist		65	
	Charles C. Pinckney	Federalist		64	
	John Jay	Federalist		1	
1804	THOMAS JEFFERSON	Democratic-Republican		162	
	Charles C. Pinckney	Federalist		14	
1808	JAMES MADISON	Democratic-Republican		122	
	Charles C. Pinckney	Federalist		47	
	George Clinton	Democratic-Republican		6	
1812	JAMES MADISON	Democratic-Republican		128	
	DeWitt Clinton	Federalist		89	
1816	JAMES MONROE	Democratic-Republican		183	
	Rufus King	Federalist		34	
1820	JAMES MONROE	Democratic-Republican		231	
	John Quincy Adams	Independent Republican		1	
1824	JOHN QUINCY ADAMS	Democratic-Republican	30.5	84	26.9
	Andrew Jackson	Democratic-Republican	43.1	99	
	Henry Clay	Democratic-Republican	13.2	37	
	William H. Crawford	Democratic-Republican	13.1	41	
1828	ANDREW JACKSON	Democratic	56.0	178	57.6
	John Quincy Adams	National Republican	44.0	83	
1832	ANDREW JACKSON	Democratic	54.5	219	55.4
	Henry Clay	National Republican	37.5	49	
	William Wirt	Anti-Masonic	8.0	7	
	John Floyd	Democratic		11	
1836	MARTIN VAN BUREN	Democratic	50.9	170	57.8
	William H. Harrison	Whig		73	
	Hugh L. White	Whig	49.1	26	
	Daniel Webster	Whig		14	
	W. P. Mangum	Whig		11	
1840	WILLIAM H. HARRISON	Whig	53.1	234	80.2
	Martin Van Buren	Democratic	46.9	60	
1844	JAMES K. POLK	Democratic	49.6	170	78.9
	Henry Clay	Whig	48.1	105	
	James G. Birney	Liberty	2.3		
1848	ZACHARY TAYLOR	Whig	47.4	163	72.7
	Lewis Cass	Democratic	42.5	127	
	Martin Van Buren	Free Soil	10.1		
1852	FRANKLIN PIERCE	Democratic	50.9	254	69.6
	Winfield Scott	Whig	44.1	42	
	John P. Hale	Free Soil	5.0		
1856	JAMES BUCHANAN	Democratic	45.3	174	78.9
	John C. Frémont	Republican	33.1	114	
	Millard Fillmore	American	21.6	8	

YEAR	CANDIDATES	PARTIES	% OF POPULAR VOTE*†	ELECTORAL VOTE‡	% VOTER PARTICIPATION†
1860	ABRAHAM LINCOLN	Republican	39.8	180	81.2
	Stephen A. Douglas	Democratic	29.5	12	
	John C. Breckinridge	Democratic	18.1	72	
	John Bell	Constitutional Union	12.6	39	
1864	ABRAHAM LINCOLN	Republican	55.0	212	73.8
	George B. McClellan	Democratic	45.0	21	
1868	ULYSSES S. GRANT	Republican	52.7	214	78.1
	Horatio Seymour	Democratic	47.3	80	
1872	ULYSSES S. GRANT	Republican	55.6	286	71.3
	Horace Greeley	Democratic	43.9		
1876	RUTHERFORD B. HAYES	Republican	48.0	185	81.8
	Samuel J. Tilden	Democratic	51.0	184	
1880	JAMES A. GARFIELD	Republican	48.5	214	79.4
	Winfield S. Hancock	Democratic	48.1	155	
	James B. Weaver	Greenback-Labor	3.4		
1884	GROVER CLEVELAND	Democratic	48.5	219	77.5
	James G. Blaine	Republican	48.2	182	
1888	BENJAMIN HARRISON	Republican	47.9	233	79.3
	Grover Cleveland	Democratic	48.6	168	
1892	GROVER CLEVELAND	Democratic	46.1	277	74.7
	Benjamin Harrison	Republican	43.0	145	
	James B. Weaver	People's	8.5	22	
1896	WILLIAM McKINLEY	Republican	51.1	271	79.3
	William J. Bryan	Democratic	47.7	176	
1900	WILLIAM McKINLEY	Republican	51.7	292	73.2
	William J. Bryan	Democratic; Populist	45.5	155	
1904	THEODORE ROOSEVELT	Republican	57.4	336	65.2
	Alton B. Parker	Democratic	37.6	140	
	Eugene V. Debs	Socialist	3.0		
1908	WILLIAM H. TAFT	Republican	51.6	321	65.4
	William J. Bryan	Democratic	43.1	162	
	Eugene V. Debs	Socialist	2.8		
1912	WOODROW WILSON	Democratic	41.9	435	58.8
	Theodore Roosevelt	Progressive	27.4	88	
	William H. Taft	Republican	23.2	8	
	Eugene V. Debs	Socialist	6.0		
1916	WOODROW WILSON	Democratic	49.4	277	61.6
	Charles E. Hughes	Republican	46.2	254	
	A. L. Benson	Socialist	3.2		
1920	WARREN G. HARDING	Republican	60.4	404	49.2
	James M. Cox	Democratic	34.2	127	
	Eugene V. Debs	Socialist	3.4		
1924	CALVIN COOLIDGE	Republican	54.0	382	48.9
	John W. Davis	Democratic	28.8	136	
	Robert M. La Follette	Progressive	16.6	13	
1928	HERBERT C. HOOVER	Republican	58.2	444	56.9
	Alfred E. Smith	Democratic	40.9	87	
1932	FRANKLIN D. ROOSEVELT	Democratic	57.4	472	56.9
	Herbert C. Hoover	Republican	39.7	59	
1936	FRANKLIN D. ROOSEVELT	Democratic	60.8	523	61.0
	Alfred M. Landon	Republican	36.5	8	
1940	FRANKLIN D. ROOSEVELT	Democratic	54.8	449	62.5
	Wendell L. Willkie	Republican	44.8	82	
1944	FRANKLIN D. ROOSEVELT	Democratic	53.5	432	55.9
	Thomas E. Dewey	Republican	46.0	99	
1948	HARRY S TRUMAN	Democratic	49.6	303	53.0
	Thomas E. Dewey	Republican	45.1	189	

YEAR	CANDIDATES	PARTIES	% OF POPULAR VOTE*†	ELECTORAL VOTE‡	% VOTER PARTICIPATION†
1952	DWIGHT D. EISENHOWER	Republican	55.1	442	63.3
	Adlai E. Stevenson	Democratic	44.4	89	
1956	DWIGHT D. EISENHOWER	Republican	57.6	457	60.6
	Adlai E. Stevenson	Democratic	42.1	73	
1960	JOHN F. KENNEDY	Democratic	49.7	303	64.0
	Richard M. Nixon	Republican	49.5	219	
1964	LYNDON B. JOHNSON	Democratic	61.1	486	61.7
	Barry M. Goldwater	Republican	38.5	52	
1968	RICHARD M. NIXON	Republican	43.4	301	60.6
	Hubert H. Humphrey	Democratic	42.7	191	
	George C. Wallace	American Independent	13.5	46	
1972	RICHARD M. NIXON	Republican	60.7	520	55.5
	George S. McGovern	Democratic	37.5	17	
1976	JIMMY CARTER	Democratic	50.1	297	54.3
	Gerald R. Ford	Republican	48.0	240	
1980	RONALD REAGAN	Republican	50.7	489	53.0
	Jimmy Carter	Democratic	41.0	49	
	John B. Anderson	Independent	6.6	0	
1984	RONALD REAGAN	Republican	58.4	525	52.9
	Walter F. Mondale	Democratic	41.6	13	

*Candidates receiving less than 2.5 percent of the popular vote have been omitted. Hence the percentage of popular vote may not total 100 percent.

†Prior to 1824, most presidential electors were chosen by state legislators rather than by popular vote.

‡Before the Twelfth Amendment was passed in 1804, the electoral college voted for two presidential candidates; the runner-up became the vice-president.

Voter Participation

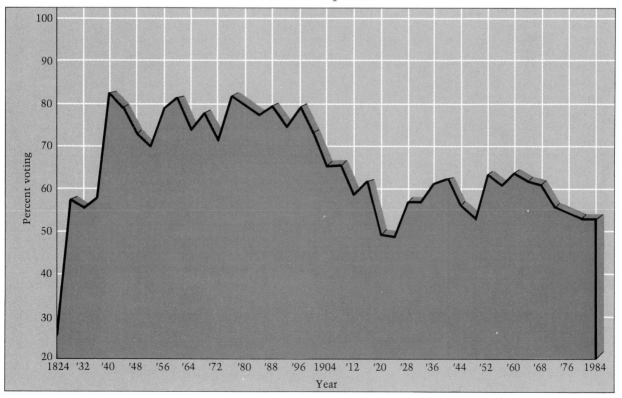

Vice-Presidents, Cabinet Members, and Justices of the Supreme Court

VICE-PRESIDENT

John Adams	1789–1797	Adlai E. Stevenson	1893–1897
Thomas Jefferson	1797–1801	Garret A. Hobart	1897–1899
Aaron Burr	1801–1805	Theodore Roosevelt	1901
George Clinton	1805–1812	Charles W. Fairbanks	1905–1909
Elbridge Gerry	1813–1817	James S. Sherman	1909–1913
Daniel D. Tompkins	1817–1825	Thomas R. Marshall	1913–1921
John C. Calhoun	1825–1833	Calvin Coolidge	1921–1923
Martin Van Buren	1833–1837	Charles G. Dawes	1925–1929
Richard M. Johnson	1837–1841	Charles Curtis	1929–1933
John Tyler	1841	John Nance Garner	1933–1941
George M. Dallas	1845–1849	Henry A. Wallace	1941–1945
Millard Fillmore	1849–1850	Harry S Truman	1945
William R. King	1853	Alben W. Barkley	1949–1953
John C. Breckinridge	1857–1861	Richard M. Nixon	1953–1961
Hannibal Hamlin	1861–1865	Lyndon B. Johnson	1961–1963
Andrew Johnson	1865	Hubert H. Humphrey	1965–1969
Schuyler Colfax	1869–1873	Spiro T. Agnew	1969–1973
Henry Wilson	1873–1877	Gerald R. Ford	1973–1974
William A. Wheeler	1877–1881	Nelson Rockefeller	1974–1977
Chester A. Arthur	1881	Walter F. Mondale	1977–1981
Thomas A. Hendricks	1885	George Bush	1981–
Levi P. Morton	1889–1893		

SECRETARY OF STATE (1790–)

Thomas Jefferson	1790	Elihu B. Washburne	1869
Edmund Randolph	1794	Hamilton Fish	1869
Timothy Pickering	1795	William M. Evarts	1877
John Marshall	1800	James G. Blaine	1881
James Madison	1801	Frederick T. Frelinghuysen	1881
Robert Smith	1809	Thomas F. Bayard	1885
James Monroe	1811	James G. Blaine	1889
Richard Rush	1817	John W. Foster	1892
John Q. Adams	1817	Walter Q. Gresham	1893
Henry Clay	1825	Richard Olney	1895
Martin Van Buren	1829	John Sherman	1897
Edward Livingston	1831	William R. Day	1897
Louis McLane	1833	John M. Hay	1898
John Forsyth	1834	Elihu Root	1905
Daniel Webster	1841	Robert Bacon	1909
Hugh S. Legaré	1843	Philander C. Knox	1909
Abel P. Upshur	1843	William Jennings Bryan	1913
John C. Calhoun	1844	Robert Lansing	1915
James Buchanan	1845	Bainbridge Colby	1920
John M. Clayton	1849	Charles E. Hughes	1921
Daniel Webster	1850	Frank B. Kellogg	1925
Edward Everett	1852	Henry L. Stimson	1929
William L. Marcy	1853	Cordell Hull	1933
Lewis Cass	1857	Edward R. Stettinius, Jr.	1944
Jeremiah S. Black	1860	James F. Byrnes	1945
William H. Seward	1861	George C. Marshall	1947

SECRETARY OF STATE *(continued)*

Dean G. Acheson	1949	Henry A. Kissinger	1973
John Foster Dulles	1953	Cyrus R. Vance	1977
Christian A. Herter	1959	Edmund S. Muskie	1980
Dean Rusk	1961	Alexander M. Haig, Jr.	1981
William P. Rogers	1969	George P. Shultz	1982

SECRETARY OF THE TREASURY (1789–)

Alexander Hamilton	1789	Walter Q. Gresham	1884
Oliver Wolcott	1795	Hugh McCulloch	1884
Samuel Dexter	1801	Daniel Manning	1885
Albert Gallatin	1801	Charles S. Fairchild	1887
George W. Campbell	1814	William Windom	1889
Alexander J. Dallas	1814	Charles Foster	1891
William H. Crawford	1816	John G. Carlisle	1893
Richard Rush	1825	Lyman J. Gage	1897
Samuel D. Ingham	1829	Leslie M. Shaw	1902
Louis McLane	1831	George B. Cortelyou	1907
William J. Duane	1833	Franklin MacVeagh	1909
Roger B. Taney	1833	William G. McAdoo	1913
Levi Woodbury	1834	Carter Glass	1919
Thomas Ewing	1841	David F. Houston	1919
Walter Forward	1841	Andrew W. Mellon	1921
John C. Spencer	1843	Ogden L. Mills	1932
George M. Bibb	1844	William H. Woodin	1933
Robert J. Walker	1845	Henry Morgenthau, Jr.	1934
William M. Meredith	1849	Fred M. Vinson	1945
Thomas Corwin	1850	John W. Snyder	1946
James Guthrie	1853	George M. Humphrey	1953
Howell Cobb	1857	Robert B. Anderson	1957
Philip F. Thomas	1860	C. Douglas Dillon	1961
John A. Dix	1861	Henry H. Fowler	1965
Salmon P. Chase	1861	Joseph W. Barr	1968
William P. Fessenden	1864	David M. Kennedy	1969
Hugh McCulloch	1865	John B. Connally	1970
George S. Boutwell	1869	George P. Shultz	1972
William A. Richardson	1873	William E. Simon	1974
Benjamin H. Bristow	1874	W. Michael Blumenthal	1977
Lot M. Morrill	1876	G. William Miller	1979
John Sherman	1877	Donald T. Regan	1981
William Windom	1881	James A. Baker	1985
Charles J. Folger	1881		

SECRETARY OF WAR (1789–1947)

Henry Knox	1789	John Armstrong	1813
Timothy Pickering	1795	James Monroe	1814
James McHenry	1796	William H. Crawford	1815
John Marshall	1800	Isaac Shelby	1817
Samuel Dexter	1800	George Graham	1817
Roger Griswold	1801	John C. Calhoun	1817
Henry Dearborn	1801	James Barbour	1825
William Eustis	1809	Peter B. Porter	1828

SECRETARY OF WAR *(continued)*

John H. Eaton	1829	George W. McCrary	1877
Lewis Cass	1831	Alexander Ramsey	1879
Benjamin F. Butler	1837	Robert T. Lincoln	1881
Joel R. Poinsett	1837	William C. Endicott	1885
John Bell	1841	Redfield Proctor	1889
John McLean	1841	Stephen B. Elkins	1891
John C. Spencer	1841	Daniel S. Lamont	1893
James M. Porter	1843	Russell A. Alger	1897
William Wilkins	1844	Elihu Root	1899
William L. Marcy	1845	William H. Taft	1904
George W. Crawford	1849	Luke E. Wright	1908
Charles M. Conrad	1850	Jacob M. Dickinson	1909
Jefferson Davis	1853	Henry L. Stimson	1911
John B. Floyd	1857	Lindley M. Garrison	1913
Joseph Holt	1861	Newton D. Baker	1916
Simon Cameron	1861	John W. Weeks	1921
Edwin M. Stanton	1862	Dwight F. Davis	1925
Ulysses S. Grant	1867	James W. Good	1929
Lorenzo Thomas	1868	Patrick J. Hurley	1929
John M. Schofield	1868	George H. Dern	1933
John A. Rawlins	1869	Harry A. Woodring	1936
William T. Sherman	1869	Henry L. Stimson	1940
William W. Belknap	1869	Robert P. Patterson	1945
Alphonso Taft	1876	Kenneth C. Royall	1947
James D. Cameron	1876		

SECRETARY OF THE NAVY (1798–1947)

Benjamin Stoddert	1798	Adolph E. Borie	1869
Robert Smith	1801	George M. Robeson	1869
Paul Hamilton	1809	Richard W. Thompson	1877
William Jones	1813	Nathan Goff, Jr.	1881
Benjamin Williams Crowninshield	1814	William H. Hunt	1881
Smith Thompson	1818	William E. Chandler	1881
Samuel L. Southard	1823	William C. Whitney	1885
John Branch	1829	Benjamin F. Tracy	1889
Levi Woodbury	1831	Hilary A. Herbert	1893
Mahlon Dickerson	1834	John D. Long	1897
James K. Paulding	1838	William H. Moody	1902
George E. Badger	1841	Paul Morton	1904
Abel P. Upshur	1841	Charles J. Bonaparte	1905
David Henshaw	1843	Victor H. Metcalf	1907
Thomas W. Gilmer	1844	Truman H. Newberry	1908
John Y. Mason	1844	George von L. Meyer	1909
George Bancroft	1845	Josephus Daniels	1913
John Y. Mason	1846	Edwin Denby	1921
William B. Preston	1849	Curtis D. Wilbur	1924
William A. Graham	1850	Charles Francis Adams	1929
John P. Kennedy	1852	Claude A. Swanson	1933
James C. Dobbin	1853	Charles Edison	1940
Isaac Toucey	1857	Frank Knox	1940
Gideon Welles	1861	James V. Forrestal	1945

SECRETARY OF DEFENSE (1947–　)

James V. Forrestal	1947	Clark M. Clifford	1968
Louis A. Johnson	1949	Melvin R. Laird	1969
George C. Marshall	1950	Elliot L. Richardson	1973
Robert A. Lovett	1951	James R. Schlesinger	1973
Charles E. Wilson	1953	Donald H. Rumsfeld	1975
Neil H. McElroy	1957	Harold Brown	1977
Thomas S. Gates, Jr.	1959	Caspar W. Weinberger	1981
Robert S. McNamara	1961		

POSTMASTER GENERAL (1789–1971)

Samuel Osgood	1789	Walter Q. Gresham	1883
Timothy Pickering	1791	Frank Hatton	1884
Joseph Habersham	1795	William F. Vilas	1885
Gideon Granger	1801	Don M. Dickinson	1888
Return J. Meigs, Jr.	1814	John Wanamaker	1889
John McLean	1823	Wilson S. Bissel	1893
William T. Barry	1829	William L. Wilson	1895
Amos Kendall	1835	James A. Gary	1897
John M. Niles	1840	Charles E. Smith	1898
Francis Granger	1841	Henry C. Payne	1902
Charles A. Wickliff	1841	Robert J. Wynne	1904
Cave Johnson	1845	George B. Cortelyou	1905
Jacob Collamer	1849	George von L. Meyer	1907
Nathan K. Hall	1850	Frank H. Hitchcock	1909
Samuel D. Hubbard	1852	Albert S. Burleson	1913
James Campbell	1853	Will H. Hays	1921
Aaron V. Brown	1857	Hubert Work	1922
Joseph Holt	1859	Harary S. New	1923
Horatio King	1861	Walter F. Brown	1929
Montgomery Blair	1861	James A. Farley	1933
William Dennison	1864	Frank C. Walker	1940
Alexander W. Randall	1866	Robert E. Hannegan	1945
John A. J. Creswell	1869	Jesse M. Donaldson	1947
James W. Marshall	1874	A. E. Summerfield	1953
Marshall Jewell	1874	J. Edward Day	1961
James N. Tyner	1876	John A. Gronouski	1963
David M. Key	1877	Lawrence F. O'Brien	1965
Horace Maynard	1880	W. Marvin Watson	1968
Thomas L. James	1881	Winston M. Blount	1969
Timothy O. Howe	1881		

ATTORNEY GENERAL (1789–　)

Edmund Randolph	1789	William Wirt	1817
William Bradford	1794	John M. Berrien	1829
Charles Lee	1795	Roger B. Taney	1831
Theophilus Parsons	1801	Benjamin F. Butler	1833
Levi Lincoln	1801	Felix Grundy	1838
Robert Smith	1805	Henry D. Gilpin	1840
John Breckenridge	1805	John J. Crittenden	1841
Caesar A. Rodney	1807	Hugh S. Legaré	1841
William Pinkney	1811	John Nelson	1843
Richard Rush	1814	John Y. Mason	1845

ATTORNEY GENERAL (continued)

Nathan Clifford	1846	George W. Wickersham	1909
Isaac Toucey	1848	J. C. McReynolds	1913
Reverdy Johnson	1849	Thomas W. Gregory	1914
John J. Crittenden	1850	A. Mitchell Palmer	1919
Caleb Cushing	1853	Harry M. Daugherty	1921
Jeremiah S. Black	1857	Harlan F. Stone	1924
Edwin M. Stanton	1860	John G. Sargent	1925
Edward Bates	1861	William D. Mitchell	1929
Titian J. Coffey	1863	Homer S. Cummings	1933
James Speed	1864	Frank Murphy	1939
Henry Stanbery	1866	Robert H. Jackson	1940
William M. Evarts	1868	Francis Biddle	1941
Ebenezer R. Hoar	1869	Tom C. Clark	1945
Amos T. Akerman	1870	J. Howard McGrath	1949
George H. Williams	1871	J. P. McGranery	1952
Edwards Pierrepont	1875	Herbert Brownell, Jr.	1953
Alphonso Taft	1876	William P. Rogers	1957
Charles Devens	1877	Robert F. Kennedy	1961
Wayne MacVeagh	1881	Nicholas de B. Katzenbach	1964
Benjamin H. Brewster	1881	Ramsey Clark	1967
Augustus H. Garland	1885	John N. Mitchell	1969
William H. H. Miller	1889	Richard G. Kleindienst	1972
Richard Olney	1893	Elliot L. Richardson	1973
Judson Harmon	1895	William B. Saxbe	1974
Joseph McKenna	1897	Edward H. Levi	1975
John W. Griggs	1897	Griffin B. Bell	1977
Philander C. Knox	1901	Benjamin R. Civiletti	1979
William H. Moody	1904	William French Smith	1981
Charles J. Bonaparte	1907	Edwin Meese	1985

SECRETARY OF THE INTERIOR (1849–)

Thomas Ewing	1849	Richard A. Ballinger	1909
Thomas M. T. McKennan	1850	Walter L. Fisher	1911
Alexander H. H. Stuart	1850	Franklin K. Lane	1913
Robert McClelland	1853	John B. Payne	1920
Jacob Thompson	1857	Albert B. Fall	1921
Caleb B. Smith	1861	Hubert Work	1923
John P. Usher	1863	Roy O. West	1928
James Harlan	1865	Ray L. Wilbur	1929
Orville H. Browning	1866	Harold L. Ickes	1933
Jacob D. Cox	1869	Julius A. Krug	1946
Columbus Delano	1870	Oscar L. Chapman	1949
Zachariah Chandler	1875	Douglas McKay	1953
Carl Schurz	1877	Fred A. Seaton	1956
Samuel J. Kirkwood	1881	Stewart L. Udall	1961
Henry M. Teller	1881	Walter J. Hickel	1969
Lucius Q. C. Lamar	1885	Rogers C. B. Morton	1971
William F. Vilas	1888	Stanley K. Hathaway	1975
John W. Noble	1889	Thomas S. Kleppe	1975
Hoke Smith	1893	Cecil D. Andrus	1977
David R. Francis	1896	James G. Watt	1981
Cornelius N. Bliss	1897	William C. Clark	1984
Ethan A. Hitchcock	1899	Donald Hodel	1985
James R. Garfield	1907		

SECRETARY OF AGRICULTURE (1889–   )

Norman J. Colman	1889	Claude R. Wickard	1940
Jeremiah M. Rusk	1889	Clinton P. Anderson	1945
J. Sterling Morton	1893	Charles F. Brannon	1948
James Wilson	1897	Ezra Taft Benson	1953
David F. Houston	1913	Orville L. Freeman	1961
Edwin T. Meredith	1920	Clifford M. Hardin	1969
Henry C. Wallace	1921	Earl L. Butz	1971
Howard M. Gore	1924	John A. Knebel	1976
William M. Jardine	1925	Bob S. Bergland	1977
Arthur M. Hyde	1929	John R. Block	1981
Henry A. Wallace	1933		

SECRETARY OF COMMERCE AND LABOR (1903–1913)

George B. Cortelyou	1903	Oscar S. Straus	1906
Victor H. Metcalf	1904	Charles Nagel	1909

SECRETARY OF COMMERCE (1913–   )

William C. Redfield	1913	Frederick H. Mueller	1959
Joshua W. Alexander	1919	Luther H. Hodges	1961
Herbert C. Hoover	1921	John T. Connor	1965
William F. Whiting	1928	Alex B. Trowbridge	1967
Robert P. Lamont	1929	Cyrus R. Smith	1968
Roy D. Chapin	1932	Maurice H. Stans	1969
Daniel C. Roper	1933	Peter G. Peterson	1972
Harry L. Hopkins	1939	Frederick B. Dent	1973
Jesse Jones	1940	Rogers C. B. Morton	1975
Henry A. Wallace	1945	Elliot L. Richardson	1976
W. Averell Harriman	1946	Juanita M. Kreps	1977
Charles Sawyer	1948	Philip M. Klutznick	1979
Sinclair Weeks	1953	Malcolm Baldrige	1981
Lewis L. Strauss	1958		

SECRETARY OF LABOR (1913–   )

William B. Wilson	1913	W. Willard Wirtz	1962
James J. Davis	1921	George P. Shultz	1969
William N. Doak	1930	James D. Hodgson	1970
Frances Perkins	1933	Peter J. Brennan	1973
L. B. Schwellenbach	1945	John T. Dunlop	1975
Maurice J. Tobin	1948	William J. Usery, Jr.	1976
Martin P. Durkin	1953	F. Ray Marshall	1977
James P. Mitchell	1953	Raymond J. Donovan	1981
Arthur J. Goldberg	1961	William Brock	1985

SECRETARY OF HEALTH, EDUCATION AND WELFARE (1953–1979)

Oveta Culp Hobby	1953	Robert H. Finch	1969
Marion B. Folsom	1955	Elliot L. Richardson	1970
Arthur S. Flemming	1958	Caspar W. Weinberger	1973
Abraham A. Ribicoff	1961	Forrest David Matthews	1975
Anthony J. Celebrezze	1962	Joseph A. Califano, Jr.	1977
John W. Gardner	1965	Patricia Roberts Harris	1979
Wilbur J. Cohen	1968		

SECRETARY OF HEALTH AND HUMAN SERVICES (1979–   )

Patricia Roberts Harris	1979	Margaret Heckler	1983
Richard S. Schweiker	1981		

SECRETARY OF EDUCATION (1979–   )

Shirley Mount Hufstedler	1979	William Bennett	1985
Terrell H. Bell	1981		

SECRETARY OF HOUSING AND URBAN DEVELOPMENT (1966–1981)

Robert C. Weaver	1966	Carla Anderson Hills	1975
Robert C. Wood	1969	Patricia Roberts Harris	1977
George W. Romney	1969	Moon Landrieu	1979
James T. Lynn	1973	Samuel R. Pierce, Jr.	1981

SECRETARY OF TRANSPORTATION (1966–   )

Alan S. Boyd	1966	Brock Adams	1977
John A. Volpe	1969	Neil E. Goldschmidt	1979
Claude S. Brinegar	1973	Andrew L. Lewis, Jr.	1981
William T. Coleman, Jr.	1975	Elizabeth Dole	1983

SECRETARY OF ENERGY (1977–   )

James R. Schlesinger	1977	Donald Hodel	1982
Robert W. Duncan, Jr.	1979	John Herrington	1985
James B. Edwards	1981		

JUSTICES OF THE UNITED STATES SUPREME COURT

Chief Justices

John Jay	1789–1795	Edward D. White	1910–1921
John Rutledge	1795	William H. Taft	1921–1930
Oliver Ellsworth	1796–1799	Charles E. Hughes	1930–1941
John Marshall	1801–1835	Harlan F. Stone	1941–1946
Roger B. Taney	1836–1864	Frederick M. Vinson	1946–1953
Salmon P. Chase	1864–1873	Earl Warren	1953–1969
Morrison R. Waite	1874–1888	Warren E. Burger	1969–
Melville W. Fuller	1888–1910		

Associate Justices

John Rutledge	789–1791	William Johnson	1804–1834
William Cushing	1789–1810	Henry B. Livingston	1806–1823
James Wilson	1789–1798	Thomas Todd	1807–1826
John Blair	1789–1796	Joseph Story	1811–1845
James Iredell	1790–1799	Gabriel Duval	1811–1836
Thomas Johnson	1791–1793	Smith Thompson	1823–1843
William Paterson	1793–1806	Robert Trimble	1826–1828
Samuel Chase	1796–1811	John McLean	1829–1861
Bushrod Washington	1798–1829	Henry Baldwin	1830–1844
Alfred Moore	1799–1804	James M. Wayne	1835–1867

ASSOCIATE JUSTICES *(continued)*

Philip P. Barbour	1836–1841	Joseph R. Lamar	1911–1916
John Catron	1837–1865	Mahlon Pitney	1912–1922
John McKinley	1837–1852	James C. McReynolds	1914–1941
Peter V. Daniel	1841–1860	Louis D. Brandeis	1916–1939
Samuel Nelson	1845–1872	John H. Clarke	1916–1922
Levi Woodbury	1845–1851	George Sutherland	1922–1938
Robert C. Grier	1846–1870	Pierce Butler	1923–1939
Benjamin R. Curtis	1851–1857	Edward T. Sanford	1923–1930
John A. Campbell	1853–1861	Harlan F. Stone	1925–1941
Nathan Clifford	1858–1881	Owen J. Roberts	1930–1945
Noah H. Swayne	1862–1881	Benjamin N. Cardozo	1932–1938
Samuel F. Miller	1862–1890	Hugo L. Black	1937–1971
David Davis	1862–1877	Stanley F. Reed	1938–1957
Stephen J. Field	1863–1897	Felix Frankfurter	1939–1962
William Strong	1870–1880	William O. Douglas	1939–1975
Joseph P. Bradley	1870–1892	Frank Murphy	1940–1949
Ward Hunt	1873–1882	Robert H. Jackson	1941–1954
John M. Harlan	1877–1911	James F. Byrnes	1941–1942
William B. Woods	1880–1887	Wiley B. Rutledge	1943–1949
Stanley Matthews	1881–1889	Harold H. Burton	1945–1958
Horace Gray	1882–1902	Tom C. Clark	1949–1967
Samuel Blatchford	1882–1893	Sherman Minton	1949–1956
Lucius Q. C. Lamar	1888–1893	John Marshall Harlan	1955–1971
David J. Brewer	1889–1910	William J. Brennan, Jr.	1956–
Henry B. Brown	1890–1906	Charles E. Whittaker	1957–1962
George Shiras	1892–1903	Potter Stewart	1958–1981
Howell E. Jackson	1893–1895	Byron R. White	1962–
Edward D. White	1894–1910	Arthur J. Goldberg	1962–1965
Rufus W. Peckham	1896–1909	Abe Fortas	1965–1969
Joseph McKenna	1898–1925	Thurgood Marshall	1967–
Oliver W. Holmes	1902–1932	Harry A. Blackmun	1970–
William R. Day	1903–1922	Lewis F. Powell, Jr.	1972–
William H. Moody	1906–1910	William H. Rehnquist	1972–
Horace H. Lurton	1910–1914	John Paul Stevens	1975–
Charles E. Hughes	1910–1916	Sandra Day O'Connor	1981–
Willis Van Devanter	1910–1937		

Population of the United States

YEAR	NUMBER OF STATES	POPULATION	PERCENT INCREASE	POPULATION PER SQUARE MILE
1790	13	3,929,214		4.5
1800	16	5,308,483	35.1	6.1
1810	17	7,239,881	36.4	4.3
1820	23	9,638,453	33.1	5.5
1830	24	12,866,020	33.5	7.4
1840	26	17,069,453	32.7	9.8
1850	31	23,191,876	35.9	7.9
1860	33	31,443,321	35.6	10.6
1870	37	39,818,449	26.6	13.4
1880	38	50,155,783	26.0	16.9
1890	44	62,947,714	25.5	21.2
1900	45	75,994,575	20.7	25.6
1910	46	91,972,266	21.0	31.0
1920	48	105,710,620	14.9	35.6
1930	48	122,775,046	16.1	41.2
1940	48	131,669,275	7.2	44.2
1950	48	150,697,361	14.5	50.7
1960	50	179,323,175	19.0	50.6
1970	50	203,235,298	13.3	57.5
1980	50	226,545,805	11.5	64.1
1985	50	237,839,000	—	67.2

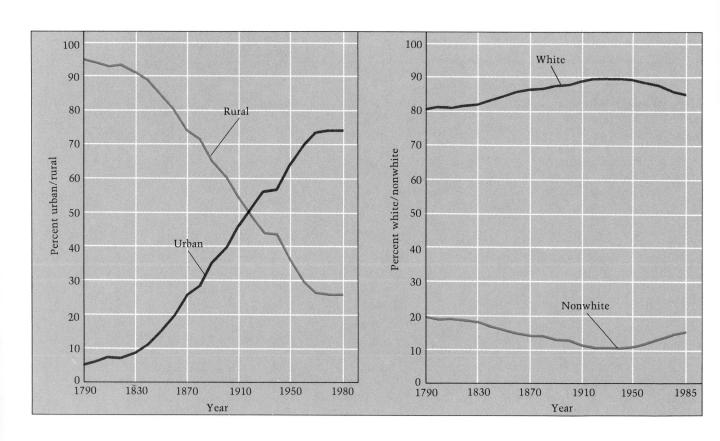

Demographic Contours of the American People

YEAR	LIFE EXPECTANCY FROM BIRTH		AGE AT FIRST MARRIAGE (YEARS)		NUMBER OF CHILDREN UNDER 5 PER 1000 WOMEN AGE 20–44	AGE DISTRIBUTION %		
	WHITE	BLACK	MALE	FEMALE		UNDER 15	15–59	OVER 59
1800					1,342			
1810					1,358			
1820					1,295			
1830					1,145			
1840					1,085			
1850					923	41.5	54.3	4.1
1860					929	40.5	55.1	4.3
1870					839	39.2	55.8	5.0
1880					822	38.1	56.3	5.6
1890			26.1	22.0	716	35.5	58.0	6.2
1900	47.6	33.0	25.9	21.9	688	34.4	59.0	6.4
1910	50.3	35.6	25.1	21.6	643	32.1	61.0	6.8
1920	54.9	45.3	24.6	21.2	604	31.8	60.6	7.5
1930	61.4	48.1	24.3	21.3	511	29.4	62.1	8.5
1940	64.2	53.1	24.3	21.5	429	25.0	64.5	10.4
1950	69.1	60.8	22.8	20.3	589	26.9	61.0	12.2
1960	70.6	63.6	22.8	20.3	737	31.1	55.7	13.2
1970	71.7	65.3	22.5	20.6	530	28.5	57.4	14.1
1980	74.4	69.8	23.6	21.8	440	22.6	61.6	15.7

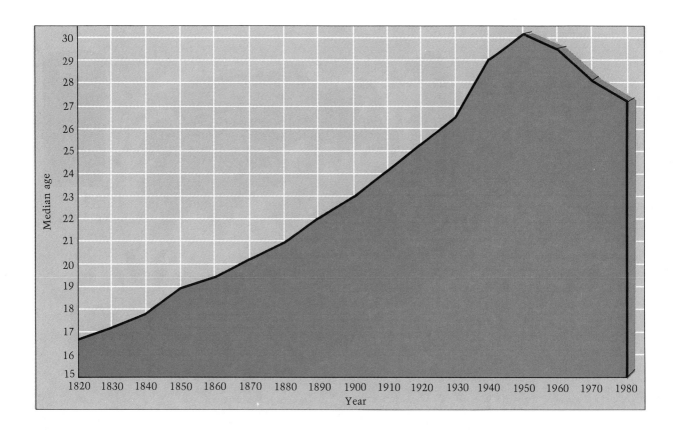

National Origins of U.S. Immigrants, 1821–1980

YEAR	TOTAL IMMIGRANTS	TOTAL EUROPE No. %	EUROPE NORTH AND WEST No. %	EUROPE EAST AND CENTRAL No. %	EUROPE SOUTH AND OTHER No. %	WESTERN HEMI-SPHERE No. %	ASIA No. %	OTHER No. %
1821–1830	144	99 (69.2)	96 (67.1)	——	3 (2.1)	12 (8.4)	——	32 (22.4)
1831–1840	599	496 (82.8)	490 (81.8)	——	1 (1.0)	33 (5.5)	——	70 (11.7)
1841–1850	1,713	1,599 (93.3)	1,592 (92.9)	2 (0.1)	5 (0.3)	62 (3.6)	——	53 (3.1)
1851–1860	2,598	2,453 (94.4)	2,432 (93.6)	3 (0.1)	21 (0.8)	75 (2.9)	42 (1.6)	29 (1.1)
1861–1870	2,315	2,065 (89.2)	2,032 (87.8)	12 (0.5)	21 (0.9)	167 (7.2)	65 (2.8)	19 (0.8)
1871–1880	2,812	2,272 (80.8)	2,070 (73.6)	127 (4.5)	76 (2.7)	405 (14.4)	124 (4.4)	11 (0.4)
1881–1890	5,247	4,738 (90.3)	3,778 (72.0)	624 (11.9)	331 (6.3)	425 (8.1)	68 (1.3)	16 (0.3)
1891–1900	3,688	3,559 (96.5)	1,641 (44.5)	1,210 (32.8)	704 (19.1)	41 (1.1)	70 (1.9)	18 (0.5)
1901–1910	8,795	8,136 (92.5)	1,909 (21.7)	3,914 (44.5)	2,313 (26.3)	361 (4.1)	246 (2.8)	53 (0.6)
1911–1920	5,736	4,376 (76.3)	998 (17.4)	1,916 (33.4)	1,463 (25.5)	1,141 (19.9)	195 (3.4)	23 (0.4)
1921–1930	4,107	2,477 (60.3)	1,302 (31.7)	591 (14.4)	587 (14.3)	1,516 (36.9)	99 (2.4)	16 (0.4)
1931–1940	528	348 (65.9)	205 (38.8)	58 (11.0)	85 (16.1)	160 (30.3)	15 (2.8)	5 (0.9)
1941–1950	1,035	622 (60.1)	492 (47.5)	48 (4.6)	82 (7.9)	355 (34.3)	32 (3.1)	26 (2.5)
1951–1960	2,516	1,328 (52.8)	445 (17.7)	611 (24.3)	272 (10.8)	996 (39.6)	151 (6.0)	40 (1.6)
1961–1970	3,322	1,239 (37.3)	394 (11.9)	419 (12.6)	426 (12.8)	1,579 (47.6)	445 (13.4)	58 (1.9)
1971–1980	4,384	801 (18.3)	188 (4.3)	246 (5.6)	368 (8.4)	1,929 (44.0)	1,634 (37.3)	19 (0.4)

Note: Numbers are given in thousands.

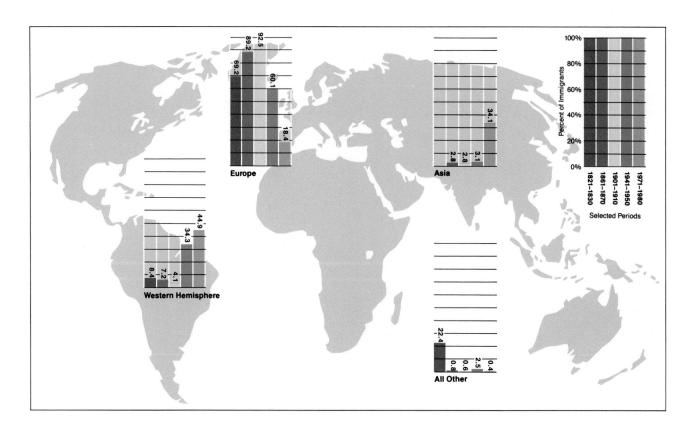

Characteristics of the American Work Force

YEAR	TOTAL NUMBER OF WORKERS* (THOUSANDS)	MALE (%)	FEMALE (%)	LABOR UNION MEMBERS (%)
1820	3,135			—
1830	4,200			—
1840	5,660			—
1850	8,250			—
1860	11,110			—
1870	12,930	85	15	—
1880	17,390	85	15	—
1890	23,320	83	17	—
1900	29,070	82	18	3
1910	37,480	79	21	6
1920	41,610	79	21	12
1930	48,830	78	22	7
1940	56,290	76	24	17
1950	65,470	72	28	22
1960	74,060	67	33	24
1970	82,715	62	38	23
1980	104,400	58	42	20
1984	114,464	55	45	18

*From 1870 to 1930, military employees are included.

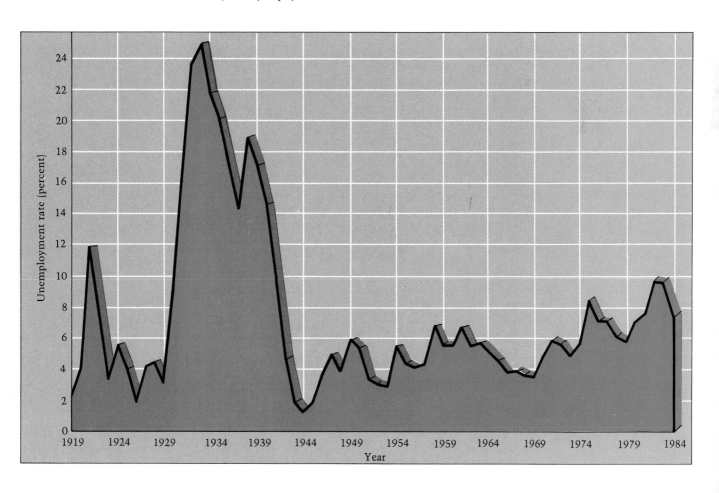

CREDITS

PART- AND CHAPTER-OPENING ILLUSTRATIONS

Chapter 17 *A Black Polling Official Aiding Voters*, engraving, c. 1865–1875. The Granger Collection, New York.
Part Four John Ferguson Wier, *Forging the Shaft: A Welding Heat*, 1877. Metropolitan Museum of Art, New York, gift of Lyman G. Bloomingdale. **Chapter 18** George Inness, *Peace and Plenty*, 1865. Metropolitan Museum of Art, New York, gift of George A. Hearn. **Chapter 19** Anonymous trade sign, Oswego Starch Factory, after 1848. Museum of American Folk Art, New York. **Chapter 20** Eastman Johnson, *The Funding Bill*, 1881. Metropolitan Museum of Art, New York, gift of Robert Gordon. **Chapter 21** T. de Thulstrup, *General Shafter and Admiral Sampson Landing on the Beach at Aserradero, June 20, to Confer with General Garcia*, c. 1898. Brown University Library, Providence, R.I., Anne S. K. Brown Military Collection.
Part Five John Sloan, *Gloucester Trolley*, 1917. Canajoharie Library and Art Museum, Canajoharie, N.Y. **Chapter 22** George Bellows, *Cliff Dwellers*, 1913. Los Angeles County Museum of Art, Los Angeles County Funds. **Chapter 23** Hayley Lever, *Armistice Celebration Parade, Fifth Avenue*, 1919. Sotheby's, New York. **Chapter 24** Kenneth Hayes Miller, *The Shopper*, 1928. Whitney Museum of American Art, New York. **Chapter 25** Isaac Soyer, *Employment Agency*, 1937. Whitney Museum of American Art, New York. **Chapter 26** Jacob Lawrence, *War Series: Beachhead*, 1947. Whitney Museum of American Art, New York.
Part Six Jack Beal, *Harvest*, 1979–1980. Galerie Claude Bernard, Paris. **Chapter 27** Nuclear test, Las Vegas, Nevada, 1953. J. R. Eyerman, Life Magazine, © Time Inc. **Chapter 28** Charles Sheeler, *Architectural Cadences*, 1954. Whitney Museum of American Art, New York. **Chapter 29** Robert Rauschenberg, *Retroactive I*, 1964. Wadsworth Atheneum, Hartford, Conn., gift of Susan Morse Hilles. **Chapter 30** Mural, *The Mall, Venice, Calif.*, n.d. © Craig Aurness 1980, Woodfin Camp & Associates. **Chapter 31** Mural, New York City, *Impact of Federal Budget Cuts on the Poor*, n.d. © Michael Heron, Woodfin Camp & Associates.

TEXT ILLUSTRATIONS (*listed by page numbers*)

535 Despairing Southern Family, *Frank Leslie's Illustrated Newspaper*, February 23, 1867. Library of Congress. **536** Freedmen, Richmond, Virginia. Library of Congress. **540** Slavery is Dead? *Harper's Weekly*, January 12, 1867. Library Company of Philadelphia. **541** Burning a Freedmen's School-House, *Harper's Weekly*, May 26, 1866. Library Company of Philadelphia. **545** Waiting for Aid, Freedmen's Bureau, Memphis, *Harper's Weekly*, June 2, 1866. Library of Congress. **548** Negro Home in the South: Sharecroppers. Brown Brothers. **551** Black Schoolchildren. Valentine Museum, Richmond, Va. **552** J. Karst, ''I shall discharge every Nigger who votes to adopt this Radical Yankee constitution,'' from Trowbridge, *A Picture of the Desolated States*, 1868. Library of Congress. **555** *A Visit from the Ku Klux Klan*, 1878. The Granger Collection, New York. **556** Currier & Ives, ''Middle Age,'' from *The Four Seasons of Life*, 1868. Museum of the City of New York.
566 Currier & Ives: *Winter Morning in the Country*, 1873. Metropolitan Museum of Art, New York, bequest of Adele S. Colgate. *The Pioneer's Home on the Western Frontier*, 1867, The Granger Collection, New York. *The Route to California*, 1871. Metropolitan Museum of Art, New York, gift of George S. Amory. **567** W. A. Raymond, *Oregon Wheat Harvest*, c. 1880. The Bettman Archive. **571** Solomon D. Butcher, *Settlers in Custer County, Nebraska, 1886.* Nebraska State Historical Society, Lincoln, Solomon D. Butcher Collection. **572** Frederic Remington, *In a Stampede*, 1888. The Granger Collection, New York. **574** Country Store, c. 1890–1900. Vermont Historical Society, Montpelier. **575** Will Soule, *Asa-to-yet, Comanche Chief*, c. 1870. National Archives, Bureau of Indian Affairs. **576** Anonymous, *Custer's Last Fight.* National Museum of American History, Smithsonian Institution, Washington, D.C. **581** Loading Bales of Cotton. Library of Congress **583** Currier & Ives, *The Darktown Fire Brigade*, 1887. Museum of the City of New York. **587** Strobridge & Co., *The Purposes of the Grange: Gift for the Granger*, 1873. Library of Congress. **597** Albertype Co., *New York and the Brooklyn Bridge*, 1889. Library of Congress. **599** Strobridge & Co., *Interior of Dining Cars on the Cincinnati, Hamilton & Dayton R. R.* The Granger Collection, New York. **602** Randolph Street West from the Wabash Elevated Station,

1896. Chicago Historical Society. **604** Burt G. Phillips, *Women and a Child at the Battery*, c. 1907. Museum of the City of New York. **605** Street Car, Washington, D.C., c. 1895. Library of Congress. **607** Home of Mrs. James L. Morgan, Jr., 7 Pierrepont St., Brooklyn, dining room, photographed 1888 by Butler. Museum of the City of New York. **608** Laying Bricks. Temple University Urban Archives, Philadelphia. **610** Stetson Factory, Fur-Cutting Room. Pennsylvania Historical and Museum Commission, Division of Archives and Manuscripts, Harrisburg. **613** Domestic Servants. State Historical Society of Wisconsin, Madison. **614** Home Washing Machine and Wringer, 1869. The Granger Collection, New York. **619** Surrender of Pinkerton Detectives, *Harper's Weekly*, July 16, 1892. New York Public Library: Astor, Lenox and Tilden Foundations. **628** Edward Bellamy. The Granger Collection, New York. **630** Campaign poster, Harrison and Morton, 1888. Library of Congress. **634** *Victoria Claflin Woodhull reading her argument . . .* The Granger Collection, New York. **638** *Sunshine and Shadow in New York.* The Bettmann Archive. C. P. Arnold, *World Columbian Exposition, Chicago*, 1893. Chicago Historical Society. **639** *Happy Home, Oro Grande, New Mexico*. Frances Benjamin Johnston, *Family Dining, Hampton, Virginia, 1899*. Both, Library of Congress. **640** Women Bicyclists, Crawfordsville, Indiana. Crawfordsville District Public Library. **643** Armour's Army and Navy Calendar, April 1899. The Granger Collection, New York. *Jane Addams*. University of Illinois at Chicago Circle, Jane Addams Memorial Collection. **646** Seymour J. Guy, *The William H. Vanderbilt Family in 1873*. Biltmore House and Gardens, Asheville, N.C. **648** Detroit Photographic Co., *End of an Era*, c. 1900. Library of Congress. **649** Denison House Public Health Clinic, Dorchester, Boston, 1900. Schlesinger Library, Radcliffe College, Cambridge, Mass. **651** Thomas Nast, The Spirit of Tweed is Mighty Still, *Harper's Weekly*, December 18, 1886. Library of Congress. **653** William Jennings Bryan, 1896. Library of Congress. **660** U.S. Troops in a Trench, Philippines. Library of Congress. **664** Annexation Ceremony, Iolani Palace, August 13, 1898, Pan Pacific Press photo. Library of Congress. **668** Some Ships of the U.S. Fleet, *Harper's Weekly*, January 30, 1892. New York Public Library: Astor, Lenox and Tilden Foundations. **670** Charles Henry Currier, *Ladies and Officers of the Massachusetts State Militia at Summer Encampment*, c. 1890–1900. Library of Congress. **671** *The Mast of the USS Maine*, 1900. The Granger Collection, New York. **672** Frances Benjamin Johnston, *William McKinley*, 1898. Library of Congress. **674** W. G. Read, *Teddy's Rough Riders*. The Granger Collection, New York. Underwood & Underwood, *Troop A, Ninth U.S. Cavalry*, 1898. Library of Congress. **676** Filipino Guerrillas Captured at Pasay and Paranaque, 1899. Library of Congress. **679** Cartoon of T. Roosevelt and Big Stick, *Judge*, January 14, 1905. Library of Congress. **681** John Barrett, *Panama Canal Construction Scene*. Library of Congress. **692** Count Waldersee Arriving at Sacred Gate, Peking, August 1900. Library of Congress.
693 Lewis Hine, *Breaker Boys Working in Ewen Breaker, Pittston, Pennsylvania*, January 1911. National Archives, Records for the Children's Bureau. **696** Two Officials of the New York City Tenement House Department Inspecting an Apartment, c. 1900. National Archives. **698** Poster for *Tess of the Storm Country*, starring Mary Pickford, 1914. The Memory Shop, New York. **700** Jewish Immigrants, Galveston, c. 1909. Eugene C. Barker Texas History Center, University of Texas, Austin. **703** Triangle Shirtwaist Company Fire, 1911. Brown Brothers. **706** Alfred Stieglitz, *The Steerage*, 1907. Museum of Modern Art, New York, gift of Alfred Stieglitz. **707** Dearborn Street, Looking South from Randolph Street, 1909. Chicago Historical Society. **710** Theodore Roosevelt Speaking in New York City, 1910. Brown Brothers. **712** Cover, *Collier's*, May 11, 1912. The Granger Collection, New York. **714** History Class, Tuskegee Institute, c. 1910. Library of Congress. **719** Suffrage Parade, May 1913. Library of Congress, G. G. Bain Collection.
727 Saying Goodbye, 1917. National Archives, Records of the War Dept. **730** Front page, *New York Times*, Saturday, May 8, 1915. New York Public Library: Astor, Lenox and Tilden Foundations. **732** *Woodrow on Toast*, 1913. Library of Congress. **736** Howard Chandler Christie, *Gee! I wish I were a man*. The Granger Collection, New York. **740** Black Women Open a Club to Entertain Their Men in the Service, Newark, N.J., 1917–1918. National Archives, War Dept. General and Special Staffs. Salvation Army Women in a Field Kitchen, 1918. National Archives, U. S. Signal Corps. **741** Stretcher

INDEX

Abortion, 957, 965, 985–986

Abstract expressionism, 898

Acheson, Dean, 860, 863, 865, 872, 876, 877

Acid rain, 990

Adams, Brooks, 647

Adams, Dudley, 586

Adams, Henry, 556–558, 628–629, 632, 656

Adamson Act, 734

Addams, Jane, 642–643, 644, 648–649, 695, 698, 716, 727, 728, 759, 780
- Hull House and, 641, 643, 649, 691, 697, 698, 708, 714
- in the Women's International League for Peace and Freedom, 751

Advertising industry, 893–894, 969

Affirmative action
- for blacks, 986
- for Hispanic Americans, 988
- for women, 984

Afghanistan, 994

Africa, 679
- return of blacks to, 770
- in World War II, 842, 844

African Methodist Episcopal (AME) church, 550, 606–607

Afro-American culture
- Harlem Renaissance, 770–771
- music in, 771
- religion in, 550, 606–607

Afro-American League, 584–585

Agent Orange, 991

Aging persons, 982–983

Agnew, Spiro, 948, 957

Agricultural Adjustment Act of 1933, 797–798, 807

Agricultural Adjustment Act of 1938, 812

Agricultural Marketing Act of 1929, 789

Agriculture
- foreign trade and, 566, 977
- migrant workers in, 768, 808, 908–909, 930–931
- modernization of, 564–574, 774–775
  - in California, 572–574
  - cattle and, 571–572
  - equipment in, 569, 573
  - falling prices in, 568, 581–582, 588

- farmer protests in, 586–592
- Great Plains, 569–572
- large-scale farms, 567, 573
- myth versus reality in, 564–567
- Southern, 578–579, 581–582, 588–592
- New Deal programs, 797–798, 803–804, 812
- in the 1920s, 774–775
- price supports, 775, 798
- setbacks in the 1970s, 976–977

Aguinaldo, Emilio, 659, 660, 674

AIDS (acquired immune deficiency syndrome), 989

Aiken, Howard H., 892

Airplanes
- Lindbergh flight, 766
- in World War I, 741, 744
- in World War II, 844–845

Alabama, 579, 919–920
- civil rights movement in, 906–907
- Reconstruction era, 554

Alaska
- gold in, 655
- purchase from Russia, 663

Alcohol
- repeal of prohibition, 796
- temperance movements
  - nineteenth-century, 632, 633–634, 697
  - post–World War I, 781–782
  - progressivism and, 697–698, 781–782
- Whiskey Ring affair, 557
- World War I and, 748

Alger, Horatio, Jr., 645

Allston, Adele, 531, 547

Allston, Elizabeth, 531

Allston, Robert Francis Withers, 531

Alpert, Richard, 941

Altamont, California, rock festival, 955–956

Amalgamated Association of Iron, Steel, and Tin Workers, 619

American Communist Party, 757

American Federation of Labor (AFL), 618, 746
- New Deal era, 805–807
- in the 1920s, 775–776
- scientific management and, 701–702

American Indian Movement (AIM), 930, 966–967

American Protective League, 737–738

American Railway Union (ARU), 619–620

American Union Against Militarism, 731

Anaya, Toney, 988

Anderson, Marian, 808

Anderson, Mary, 809

Anderson, Sherwood, 772

Andrews, Eliza, 538

Anthony, Susan B., 544, 545, 556, 643, 644, 749

Anti-imperialism, 675–676

Anti-Imperialist League, 675

Anti-Saloon League, 697

Anti-Semitism
- Nazi, 843–844
- New Deal era, 801

Antitrust legislation, 634–635, 710–711, 720

Appliances
- in the 1930s, 814–815
- post–World War II use of, 893

Architecture. See also Housing
- skyscrapers, 764

Armed forces, 731. See also Navy; specific wars
- blacks in
  - Filipino-American War, 676
  - Korean War, 868, 905
  - Spanish-American War, 673
  - World War I, 736, 737, 740–741, 742, 743
  - World War II, 833–834, 840, 846–847
- Brownsville, Texas, riot of 1906, 714
- Cuba and, 934
- Houston, Texas, riot of 1917, 740–741
- National Guard in. See National Guard
- Native Americans in, 840
- nineteenth-century, 665, 671–676, 684
- women in, 739, 840–841

Arms control, 994

Arms race
- nuclear proliferation in, 872–874, 995–996
- Reagan and, 995–996

Army Reorganization Bill of 1916, 731

Harper & Row
STUDY-AID

The American People:
Creating a Nation and a Society

by Nash / Jeffrey / Howe / Frederick / Davis / Winkler
Study Guide by Julie Roy Jeffrey
and Peter Frederick

An easier way to study.

For only $12.95, STUDY-AID, a
computer software guide, gives you
an easier way to master your course.

(Cut along dotted lines and mail card below.)

**HARPER
&
ROW**

Harper & Row
STUDY-AID

School is tough enough.
Get an edge on studying this semester with STUDY-AID.

STUDY-AID is a new computer program for the Apple, the Macintosh, and the IBM PC (and most IBM PC compatible) computers keyed directly to your text.

After reading each chapter in the text, you can use STUDY-AID to review how much you have learned with various types of exercises and self-tests. Automatic scoring enables you to check your progress as you learn.

To purchase a copy, check with your local college bookstore. To order by mail or telephone, complete the card or call Soft Productions, Inc. at (219) 255-3911. Be sure to indicate the type of computer disk you want and to include your method of payment. If the order card has been removed, mail your order to Soft Productions, Inc., P.O. Box 1003, Notre Dame, IN 46556. Be sure to indicate the title and author of the text and the type of computer disk you want (Apple, Macintosh, or IBM) and to include your method of payment.

(Cut along dotted lines and mail card below.)